Technology Use and Research Approaches for Community Education and Professional Development

Valerie Carson Bryan
Florida Atlantic University, USA

Victor C.X. Wang
Florida Atlantic University, USA

Information Science
REFERENCE

Managing Director: Lindsay Johnston
Editorial Director: Joel Gamon
Book Production Manager: Jennifer Yoder
Publishing Systems Analyst: Adrienne Freeland
Development Editor: Christine Smith
Assistant Acquisitions Editor: Kayla Wolfe
Typesetter: Christy Fic
Cover Design: Jason Mull

Published in the United States of America by
Information Science Reference (an imprint of IGI Global)
701 E. Chocolate Avenue
Hershey PA 17033
Tel: 717-533-8845
Fax: 717-533-8661
E-mail: cust@igi-global.com
Web site: http://www.igi-global.com

Library of Congress Cataloging-in-Publication Data

Technology use and research approaches for community education and professional development / Valerie Carson Bryan and Victor C.X. Wang, editors.
p. cm.
Includes bibliographical references and index.
Summary: "This book investigates how the role of information technology is impacting the academic and workplace environments, exploring areas such as unique learning styles, various methods of disseminating information, and technology's role and impact within these settings"--Provided by publisher.
ISBN 978-1-4666-2955-4 (hardcover) -- ISBN 978-1-4666-2956-1 (ebook) -- ISBN 978-1-4666-2957-8 (print & perpetual access) 1. Educational technology. 2. Information technology. 3. Career development. I. Bryan, Valerie C., editor of compilation. II. Wang, Victor C. X., editor of compilation. III. Bryan, Valerie C. Power, peril and promise of information technology to community education.
LB1028.26.T43 2013
371.33--dc23
2012037379

British Cataloguing in Publication Data
A Cataloguing in Publication record for this book is available from the British Library.

Editorial Advisory Board

Table of Contents

Foreword xiii

Preface xvi

Acknowledgment xxiii

Chapter 1
The Power, Peril, and Promise of Information Technology to Community Education 1
Valerie Carson Bryan, Florida Atlantic University, USA

Chapter 2
Use of Information Technology in Organizational Learning: Effective Practices of Award-Winning Organizations 24
Lila Holt, University of Tennessee, USA
Jeffrey Beard, University of Tennessee, USA
Debra S. Lee, Vanderbilt University, USA

Chapter 3
The Impact of New Technologies on Professional Development 40
Sarah T. Meltzer, Western Carolina University, USA

Chapter 4
Examining Adult Learning Assumptions and Theories in Technology-Infused Communities and Professions 53
Judith E. Parker, Columbia University, USA

Chapter 5
Preferred Learning Tools in Online Mathematics Classes: Digital College Learners 66
Ana M. Porro, Palm Beach State College, USA

Chapter 6
Informatization and Digital Citizenship 85
Lesley S. J. Farmer, California State University – Long Beach, USA

Chapter 7
Emergency Management Professional Development: Linking Information Communication Technology and Social Communication Skills to Enhance a Sense of Community and Social Justice in the 21st Century 102
Marianne Robin Russo, Florida Atlantic University, USA

Chapter 8
Social Networking, Cyber Bullying, and the Role of Community Education 117
Michelle Sofo, University of Canberra, Australia
Francesco Sofo, University of Canberra, Australia

Chapter 9
Technology Use and Its Changing Role in Community Education 134
Lesley Farmer, California State University – Long Beach, USA

Chapter 10
Developing an Autonomous Language Learning Framework in a Blended Learning Environment: A Hong Kong Case Study 150
Helen W. M. Yeh, Hong Kong Polytechnic University (HKCC), China

Chapter 11
Online Professional Development for Adults: Utilizing Andragogical Methods in Research and Practice 171
J. Bernard Bradley, American Council on Grant Writing, USA
John Rachal, The University of Southern Mississippi, USA
Lin Harper, The University of Southern Mississippi, USA

Chapter 12
Technology Use and Research Approaches for Community Education and Professional Development: Diffusion of Innovation from Medical Schools to Phlebotomy Certificate Programs 194
Grace L. Reynolds, California State University – Long Beach, USA

Chapter 13
Using Information and Communication Technology to Maximize Workforce Readiness 209
Merideth Dee, Florida Atlantic University, USA

Chapter 14
Using Educational Technology to Guide Literacy Teaching Candidates in the Delivery of Adjusted Practices for Speakers of Urban AAVE 225
Michelle McAnuff-Gumbs, The College of Saint Rose, USA

Chapter 15
E-Learning Quality through Second Life: Exploiting, Investigating, and Evaluating the Efficiency Parameters of Collaborative Activities in Higher Education 250
Pellas Nikolaos, University of the Aegean, Greece
Kazanidis Ioannis, Kavala Institute of Technology, Greece

Chapter 16
Technological Advancements Usage: Demographic Variations 274
Sujana Adapa, University of New England, Australia

Compilation of References 294

About the Contributors 328

Index 335

Detailed Table of Contents

Foreword xiii

Preface xvi

Acknowledgment xxiii

Chapter 1
The Power, Peril, and Promise of Information Technology to Community Education 1
Valerie Carson Bryan, Florida Atlantic University, USA

The democratization of information serves as a powerful force for change in both our lives and our global world. The paradigm shift from the providers of information to the users of the information has in many cases been brought about through the use of information technologies and the creation of more diverse and accessible Web-enabled devices. Educational equity helps to provide democratic and accessible educational opportunities for all citizenry and supports the tenets of community education. The question arises whether the proliferation of information brings power, peril, or promise for the communities of the world and the people it serves. This chapter investigates the changing rate of information, how it is distributed through online communities of practice and social networks, and what impact some of this information may have on areas of interest for training, research, and online development in fields of education, law enforcement, medicine, and sociology.

Chapter 2
Use of Information Technology in Organizational Learning: Effective Practices of Award-Winning Organizations 24
Lila Holt, University of Tennessee, USA
Jeffrey Beard, University of Tennessee, USA
Debra S. Lee, Vanderbilt University, USA

Education and development in the workplace that promotes continual improvement is vital for sustainability and performance excellence for 21st century organizations. Likewise, organizational learning has become a focal point for organizations to quickly adapt to global markets and dynamic economies. Using two theoretical frameworks, the 2010 and 2011 National Baldrige Award Winners' applications and websites are examined to better understand how technology can support organizational learning. Information technologies are classified through the use of Huber's (1991) constructs, while Argyris and Schön's (1978) double-loop learning theory becomes a foundation for examining continuous improvement within organizations. Results indicate technology is an integral part of the Baldrige Award Winners' day-to-day processes and the improvement thereof is a focal point for these organizations.

While technology itself does not create a winning organization, appropriate use of technology enables an organization to track the processes that lead to customer satisfaction, thus enabling the organization to be both innovative and agile in the global workplace.

Chapter 3
The Impact of New Technologies on Professional Development 40
Sarah T. Meltzer, Western Carolina University, USA

Professional development in schools is not a new concept; however, the impact of new technologies in the past two decades has shown it is important to incorporate research-based strategies in order to be effective. While strategies for curriculum-focused trainings may have been effective in the past, technology-focused training must take a different approach in the 21st century. Effective professional development will positively impact student achievement and is critical for sustainable school reform. This chapter addresses the importance of developing a new learning environment conducive to supporting professional development in technology. Key strategies necessary to support students' needs in the 21st century are explained. Without an emphasis on specific activities and opportunities throughout the phases of planning and implementation, professional development will not be sustainable and student achievement will not be impacted.

Chapter 4
Examining Adult Learning Assumptions and Theories in Technology-Infused Communities and Professions 53
Judith E. Parker, Columbia University, USA

Adult learning in today's society is primarily focused on the needs of adults as they function in their communities and professions. Adult learning principles and theories have been the foundation of adult education practice for over a century. However, a review of the historical context reveals that this new technology-infused learning landscape is dramatically different from its predecessor. This makes a reexamination of these ideas important for their future application. This chapter will reexamine the adult-learning principles of transformative learning, andragogy, and critical reflection in this technology-infused world and propose a new paradigm and corresponding practices for the new learning landscape in communities and professions.

Chapter 5
Preferred Learning Tools in Online Mathematics Classes: Digital College Learners 66
Ana M. Porro, Palm Beach State College, USA

The review of the literature on the role of instructional strategies in online mathematics learning addresses the following major areas and their related subsets: motivation and academic success; online learning and andragogy; and instructional design and learning strategies. It is noted that the hypothesis that motivational strategies promote achievement and success in online mathematics courses is supported by recent investigators who suggested the need to research the effectiveness of incorporating motivational strategies in the implementation of online instructional designs (Bellon & Oates, 2002; Kelsey & D'Souza, 2004; Patall, et al., 2008; Sanacore, 2008; Skinner, 2005). Additionally, the limited role documented on motivation in online mathematics courses by both mathematicians and educators is included. Next, discussions of online learning, andragogy and learning theories, learners' characteristics and heuristics in interpersonal and cognitive tools are addressed. Lastly, laying the foundation of theory into practice, considerations for instructional designs are included along with suggestions for design and implementation of learning strategies.

Chapter 6
Informatization and Digital Citizenship 85
Lesley S. J. Farmer, California State University – Long Beach, USA

This chapter examines the bases for informatization and describes the conditions for meaningful and responsible participation in the informatized society, both in the workplace and in the civic world in general. Where eighty percent of U.S. labor is concentrated in the service sector, and technology permeates workplace functions, society is becoming informatized: driven by information. Information and digital literacy are required worker skills. Additionally, workers need to use information and technology ethically. Governments and workplaces need to set the conditions for knowledgeable, responsible, and participatory citizens and workers so that institutions and society as a whole can improve. Because informatization intersects with globalization, responsible cross-cultural interaction also needs to be addressed.

Chapter 7
Emergency Management Professional Development: Linking Information Communication Technology and Social Communication Skills to Enhance a Sense of Community and Social Justice in the 21st Century 102
Marianne Robin Russo, Florida Atlantic University, USA

Although there is current research describing technology efforts utilized in the 21st century as it relates to emergency management, there are adult educational factors to examine regarding Information Communication Technology (ICT) and the Social Communication Skills (SCS) of emergency personnel. Technology is quickly evolving and the the population is becoming increasingly more diverse, driving the efforts of emergency personnel to harness more technological emergency advances and navigate the culture of each community to assure effective emergency measures are taken. Within the ICT and SCS framework, emergency management must concern itself with: (a) the basic tenets of emergency management; (b) the changing and new nature of global threats in the 21st century; (c) evolving emergency management technologies; (d) social considerations when interfacing with the communities served; and (e) recommendations for those who are involved in emergency management mitigation, preparation, response, and recovery emergency efforts. All of these factors revolve around the education and re-education of adults; therefore, the focus of this chapter explores subsequent educational implications for the emergency personnel workforce as well as positive results for affected communities. This chapter proposes a larger implication, one of emergency personnel professional development within technology-based response systems as well as the cultivation of social communication in an effort to build a Sense of Community (SOC) with the diverse citizenry they serve. Emergency first responders, as well as other emergency personnel, must be educated in technology and social skills to better serve the community and to become a part of a holistic community. It is in this way that safety, and ultimately social justice, efforts for specific groups who may be marginalized and disenfranchised during an emergency are enhanced.

Chapter 8
Social Networking, Cyber Bullying, and the Role of Community Education 117
Michelle Sofo, University of Canberra, Australia
Francesco Sofo, University of Canberra, Australia

This chapter explores the link between social capital, the bullying that can occur via social networking sites, and community education. It becomes evident that social networking sites are influential sources of informal learning despite the published literature being somewhat divided on the sociological, psychological, and emotional benefits of social networking. Through the presentation of Australian statistics and case studies, the chapter demonstrates how social capital can be eroded through the misuse of social networking sites particularly in the form of cyber bullying. The Australian government has responded to the social impacts of cyber bullying by funding an extensive community education program. Through examining this program, it is possible to see how important it is to have effective and accessible community education regarding safe and responsible social networking.

Chapter 9
Technology Use and Its Changing Role in Community Education 134
Lesley Farmer, California State University – Long Beach, USA

Technology, particularly as it supports interactive learning communities, now plays a central role in community education. While technology affords access to information more efficiently than ever before, it also requires additional skills. For technology to play out its role effectively, community educators need to design instruction, curriculum, and programs that offer customizable learning and socially rich learning environments. Every effort needs to be made to make sure that learners have opportunities to access and learn with technology. Successful community efforts to incorporate technology tend to include these factors: local needs, local resources, local broad-based planning, partnerships among organizations, accessible and appropriate technologies, opportunities for community building and socializing, and locally meaningful content and outcomes.

Chapter 10
Developing an Autonomous Language Learning Framework in a Blended Learning Environment: A Hong Kong Case Study 150
Helen W. M. Yeh, Hong Kong Polytechnic University (HKCC), China

Educational technologies in language learning has undergone a shift from learner's interaction with computers to interaction with other humans via the computer, and now moves towards the blended learning where traditional classroom teaching methods and computer-mediated activities are combined. However, the effectiveness of the blended learning is still inconclusive. The present chapter examines the effectiveness of autonomous language learning programmes in a blended learning environment and presents a framework that was derived from the programme. The framework describes the roles of teacher, the learning construction, and the learning process for autonomous language learning, and suggests a number of techniques that teachers can use to formulate their teaching plans for the blended learning. Findings revealed that students had favorable attitudes towards the autonomous language learning, the blended learning, and the programme, which could not only motivate them to continue autonomous learning but also improve their English competence.

Chapter 11
Online Professional Development for Adults: Utilizing Andragogical Methods in Research and Practice 171
J. Bernard Bradley, American Council on Grant Writing, USA
John Rachal, The University of Southern Mississippi, USA
Lin Harper, The University of Southern Mississippi, USA

Online professional development programs for adults are increasing in frequency. Numerous scholarly articles have been written that offer polemical or anecdotal evidence supporting the effectiveness of andragogically facilitated non-formal professional development courses, including those conducted online. However, few empirical studies have been conducted to validate their usefulness, especially those offered via the Internet. Such non-formal educational programming may be most conducive to both implementing and empirically testing a more purist definition of andragogy (Pratt, 1988; Rachal, 2002; Bradley, 2011). This chapter explores the theoretical frameworks of andragogy, as well as existing experimental or quasi-experimental research studies, with a view toward creating more learner-centered non-formal educational transactions that meet the unique needs of adult learners. Lastly, suggestions for both practitioners and researchers alike are offered to help build the body of evidence-based research and extend practical advice to educators when designing and facilitating virtual learning programs for adults that emphasize professional development.

Chapter 12
Technology Use and Research Approaches for Community Education and Professional Development: Diffusion of Innovation from Medical Schools to Phlebotomy Certificate Programs........................ 194
Grace L. Reynolds, California State University – Long Beach, USA

This chapter describes the use of technology in the education of health care providers. Advances in technology have led to consistent use of on-line course content such as posting of syllabi, course materials, videos, and other training materials, and deployment of on-line quizzes, tests, and certification exams that take advantage of the high availability of Internet access in most educational institutions. The diffusion of other more advanced technology, such as virtual patients, and virtual worlds, such as Second Life, is much less available across training programs for health care providers. This chapter explores differences across training programs for health care providers ranging from medical education of surgeons through the education of lower-level technicians such as phlebotomists. Consistent with the theory of diffusion of innovations, early adopters of advanced technology for student training are those with the resources who recognize the relative advantages in the technology, such as medical schools. Community education also plays a role in the diffusion of innovation in the training of lower-level technicians and clinicians as community education recognizes that processes of empowerment and social justice are important components of community capacity building. The community education philosophy is consistent with the institutions, such as community colleges, that have the largest role in training health care providers and technicians. Despite advances in the use of technology for the delivery of didactic materials, there are still challenges in the acquisition of clinical skills.

Chapter 13
Using Information and Communication Technology to Maximize Workforce Readiness 209
Merideth Dee, Florida Atlantic University, USA

The following chapter will provide a general discussion regarding the use of Information and Communication Technology (ICT) and how ICT can be used to help prepare students for the demands of the workforce. Additionally, the chapter will explore why ICT fluency is an important factor in preparing students for the demands of the workforce. Furthermore, the chapter will review the literature and empirical research concerned with: attitudes toward the use of ICT, the value of using ICT with regards to workforce readiness and professional development, how different learning environments, such as blended-learning, e-learning, m-learning, virtual learning communities, and social interaction impact workforce readiness, and the theories to consider when designing multimedia and why multimedia can help to prepare students for the workforce.

Chapter 14
Using Educational Technology to Guide Literacy Teaching Candidates in the Delivery of Adjusted Practices for Speakers of Urban AAVE 225
Michelle McAnuff-Gumbs, The College of Saint Rose, USA

The chapter discusses ways in which educational technology facilitated a strengthening of literacy leadership candidates' awareness of adjusted practices suitable for application in culturally complex classrooms. It shows how the instructor in a specific course was able to infuse critical content and tasks into what would have otherwise been a generic course in literacy theories and instruction, and ensure that candidates were trained in customizing literacy practices for culturally and linguistically diverse students. Multiple online readings, lecture captures using Camtasia, WIKIs, blogs, and Elluminate virtual classroom sessions allowed for an enrichment of course content and for communication of content in powerful ways. Additionally, the tools facilitated engagement of candidates in guided reflection and case problem solving that facilitated a transfer of information on adjusted practices to a specific case. Through the use of tools, the instructor was also able to monitor candidates' uptake of practices. The difference in quality and level of candidate exposure, given use of the tools, is demonstrated primarily through content analysis of their online postings. The chapter and the research it describes qualifies as what Robleyer (2005) refers to as research "address[ing] a significant educational problem" while spotlighting "a proposed technology solution" (p. 19).

Chapter 15
E-Learning Quality through Second Life: Exploiting, Investigating, and Evaluating the Efficiency Parameters of Collaborative Activities in Higher Education 250
Pellas Nikolaos, University of the Aegean, Greece
Kazanidis Ioannis, Kavala Institute of Technology, Greece

The systematic utilization and dissemination of e-learning, in juxtaposition with the expansion needs for collaborative knowledge, has led to a new generation system, Virtual Worlds (VWs). The quintessence and assistance of VWs allows adult users to immerse themselves in a common 3D multimedia environment, emphasizing co-creation and co-construction of their "knowledge field." The corollary of interactivity and social form of modeling, allows the design of e-learning activities in accordance with contemporary pedagogical approaches. This chapter focuses both on how using the most advanced 3D Web-emulator of the real world, Second Life (SL), will increase users' learning ability and vehemently consecrate the common multi-user environment as an incubator of knowledge and action. The methodology is to evaluate SL with the assistance of 70 trainee users, according to four different parameters that postulate the learning progression in a virtual system. The main contribution of this research will be to highlight the suitability of SL for organizing and conducting collaborative scenarios in higher education.

Chapter 16
Technological Advancements Usage: Demographic Variations 274
Sujana Adapa, University of New England, Australia

Technological advancements have provided many advantages to individuals, businesses, and communities throughout the world. However, technological advancements have also caused challenges. This chapter focuses on one particular banking service innovation that is being used by many individuals and businesses throughout the world on a day-to-day basis. This study relates to the Australian context and explores the variations in the demographic variables in determining the key factors responsible for the adoption or non-adoption of Internet banking. The data presented in this chapter relates to a part of a large survey carried out in a busy shopping mall. Results obtained are discussed and possible solutions and recommendations that are critical from the retail banking management's perspective have been provided.

Compilation of References 294

About the Contributors 328

Index 335

Foreword

Drs. Bryan and Wang are presenting much of the latest thinking and practices that are in use or have the potential for use by the cohort of educators that refer to themselves as "community educators," which is a distinctive title that sets them apart from their school-oriented colleagues. The distinctiveness of community education is underpinned by several core beliefs, values, and foundational principles.

Briefly:

- Each community is unique, as each individual is unique.
- One has to understand the wants and needs of each community before you can address their needs.
- Decisions are made at the operational level. No big one size fits all bureaucracy is needed or practiced.

These foundational practices are enough to mobilize authoritarian bureaucratic mindsets to set off alarms and spark resistance to turning decision-making to the uninitiated. At the same time as those resistances to the principles of community education were in vogue, the idea caught the imagination and attention of the individuals who have become icons to those who embrace the concept of community education.

In the 1930s, Frank J. Manley, a physical education director, championed providing physical education and recreation for teenagers in depression-mired Flint, Michigan, USA. At the same time, Charles Stewart Mott was looking for ways to "give back to a community in need." Juvenile crime was rampant in depression-riddled Flint, Michigan, as was unemployment with a 26-30% unemployment rate, and both men were looking for creative solutions.

Charles Stewart Mott was considering funding several boys clubs, when he heard Frank Manley's idea to open the potential boys clubs in often vacant school buildings. The schools were closed in the afternoons, evenings, weekends, and summers, so given proper resources, the schools could become boys clubs. The Mott Foundation as funded by Charles Stewart Mott in several schools in Flint later became the Foundation's hallmark nationally.

Opening the first Flint community schools became Frank Manley's responsibility. Manley handpicked a "team" of community educators. These community directors carried forth Charles Stewart Mott's humanitarianism and philanthropy, and Manley's charisma and understanding of people. Both Mott and Manley were people- and community-oriented, and the new cadre of community school directors carried those ideas to the community.

Today's news is replete with the Emmer Gantry stories of takers, not givers, who enrich themselves at the expense of their followers. In life, it is important to know with whom you are dealing, and C. S. Mott and Frank Manley were the real thing.

One of several illustrations follows the "Mott" approach. Mr. Mott and Charles "Boss" Kettering were friends and associates. They both had large foundations dedicated to serving humanity and the community. While both men were alive, the word on the street was that Kettering had all of the staff "read bureaucracy." Kettering maintained large staffs, with few working programs, while Charles Mott had a small staff, with many working, successful programs.

Up until Mott's retirement, a grant from the Mott Foundation was drawn on Charles Mott's personal checking account, and was written by his own hand. What is equally illustrative is that Frank Manley delivered these checks himself, in person.

A great deal of technological water has passed under the bridge since the passing of both men. In fact, the water has become a torrent that few could have predicted, and continues sweeping away old ideas and institutions.

Both Mott and Manley had core values and beliefs that would withstand the onrush of the technological tsunami. They were both people-oriented, rather than object-oriented. Both saw good in people, not gold. The Mott Foundation funded hospitals at Wayne State, the University of Michigan, and the child health service in Flint. For both men, people came first. Neither one was a Luddite, but neither one would welcome money-saving notions that reduced the "quality of life" to enhance bottom line profits. They both promoted high tech, as well as high touch. An example, customer answering services that push out employees as well as customers were seen as false economies. Automatic tellers and unemployed business majors would not make sense in their scheme of things.

Specializations that divide us, not unite us, is not progress. Technologies that reduce the quality of life and make some individuals redundant again did not make sense. Redundant, in Great Britain, describes a lifetime of unemployment and being unemployable.

When you look at the people Mr. Mott and Mr. Manley surrounded themselves with, you find individuals that grow people, not reduce them. Both men brought women on-board long before it became fashionable or required.

In too many cases, some with high tech skills have become "smart-alecs," who have little respect for those who bake bread or fix the plumbing. A person can have dignity, even if they do not have a Facebook, Twitter, or YouTube. Charles and Frank did not like the word "boss" and would not have championed technocrats that would become the "new bosses."

The quality of life for individuals, in groups or communities, is the first and major priority. Community educators, as individuals and in groups, must not let the machine become the end-all. For it makes no matter how fast, small, or impressive it becomes, it is still a tool. Mankind should never become a tool of its own tools. Change at its best is creative construction, and/or destruction. The creative aspects should always protect the sanctity of the individual.

The air of caution in the humanitarianism of Mott and Manley should not detract from the fact that if they were alive today, they would double down on the best practices and promises of technology, as a management and leadership tool. As an example of a specific, Manley's bulletin board of activities would be replaced by a grid of demographics from the latest census on that center's community.

Vasil M. Kerensky
Florida Atlantic University, USA

Vasil M. Kerensky *passed away unexpectantly on Wednesday, November 21, 2012. Dr. Vasil M. Kerensky was a former Charles Stewart Mott Eminent Scholar of Community Education and Professor of Educational Leadership (1982-2003) and more recently Professor Emeritus in Educational Leadership. He was a member of the faculty for over 35 years. He was a leader in Florida and the nation in community education and gave tirelessly to the field. Dr. Kerensky published: The Sovereign: New Perspectives on People, Power, and Public Education (Kendall Hunt Publishing Company, 1989), Education II: The Social Imperative (Pendell Publishing Company, 1971), A New Foundation: Perspectives on Community Education (Pendell Publishing Company, 1979), Education II: Revisited – A Social Imperative (Pendell Publishing Company, 1975). Prior to moving to Florida, Kerensky was the principal at Haslett High School in Michigan. Prior to retirement, he traveled around the world promoting and speaking on behalf of Community Education. He was very active in the community and served on the board of the Greater Boca Raton Beach Tax District for 10 years.*

Preface

INTRODUCTION

The book, *Technology Use and Research Approaches for Community Education and Professional Development,* investigates how technology is impacting community education and professional development in a host of academic and workplace settings. The role of information technology is also being explored and its significance in reshaping learning organizations and workplaces across the globe. As stated by Bryan and Musgrove (2003):

Educators are faced with challenging times filled with dwindling resources, proliferation of information, complex systems of legalities and infrastructures, and an even more complex and diverse customer base. Today's educator is part of a global learning community that fluctuates at exponential rates. No one person in this educational arena can afford to operate in a vacuum, nor can any one person be expected to have all the answers to all the learning or management-related problems or issues. To be informed and knowledgeable the educator of tomorrow must serve as a knowledge broker and operate as a part of a larger consortium of learners to cope with the amount of information that will be available. The ability to locate information at a moment's notice that is relevant to the immediate educational climate and to work with groups separated by both time and space has become a necessity (p. 1).

Chapters will address research regarding the advantages and disadvantages of using online learning, blended learning, and enhanced face-to-face learning through the technologies, on the learners and the learners' environments. Questions will be asked as to the impact of varied learning styles, modes of communication, and information overload with the technologies themselves in our ever-changing environment. Authors will explore how our need to select, summarize, sort, and assess information may be evolving based on the devices or methodology applied and how the bombardment of information may require a new management system and possibly new learning systems that are not tied to the agrarian calendar or the traditional twenty-four hour clock to work, play, learn, and rest.

Select chapters will address readiness principles, ethics, accessibility, and social justice as it relates to the use of technology. Questions will be raised: Are the needs of the disenfranchised, non-exposed-to-technology individual across the continents being addressed in the learning environments or in the professional arenas? Are differences in race, gender, access, age, literacy levels, being multiplied as the technology usage increases? Does the device one uses, or does not use, to be technologically "with-it" presuppose one to a digital class stratum? Is social isolation becoming a reality as the technology usage increases or is the reverse occurring? Are the various social media tools, such as Facebook, Twitter, and

YouTube, moving us all to a more level playing field where we can impact not only our own lives but those across the globe? Is technology causing a power paradigm shift from providers to users? Are the technocrats becoming our "new bosses"?

Select chapters will showcase research findings regarding best practices principles in online instruction and technology-rich environments. Research will be included that reflects what strategies to use and how those strategies differ from one setting to another (e.g., emergency preparedness vs. a non-profit organization vs. a school setting), the specific tools or devices to use, and when these should be introduced. The methodology, both qualitative and quantitative, that has been used in the varied community education and professional development settings will be shared as well.

Chapters also explore: a) what new careers may be evolving based on the technology use that have not even been imagined; b) what perils we may expect or predict from the technology usage (e.g., information overload that can bring stress and require higher and higher copying skills, proliferations of high skilled positions with accompanying job losses for individuals with minimal technical skills, changes in formal language, crimes such as identify theft that have become more and more sophisticated); and c) what promise the technology may offer to offset the perils.

The various authors in this book present how their use of the information technologies and the research related to those tools enhance community education or professional development, and even community development. Please note that authors are not limited to one continent, one viewpoint, or one field of study. The authors, in varied ways and through various lenses, support the tenets of community education. In this book, community education:

. . . is a philosophical concept that promotes lifelong learning and community building activities while emphasizing an expanded role for public education and other human service organizations in meeting the needs of communities and improving the quality of life for all. Community Education is a way for people to enhance their lives and communities through learning and collaboration. Community Education emphasizes increased involvement of parents, businesses, and community members with the local public (or even private) school system and lifelong learning while providing opportunities for local (and international) community members, schools, and other organizations to become partners in addressing educational and community concerns (Missouri Department of Elementary and Secondary Education, p. 1).

The relationship between the concept of community education and information technologies are illustrated through the chapters.

OBJECTIVE OF THE BOOK

The book, *Technology Use and Research Approaches for Community Education and Professional Development*, is authored by leading experts and offers an in-depth description of empirical research and findings related to community education and professional development worldwide. Additionally, this volume discusses how technology impacts community education and professional development in a host of disciplines.

Topics in this book address: a) the role of information communication technologies and community education, professional development, learning organizations, and workplaces across the globe; b) the nuances of online learning, blended learning, and face-to-face learning via technologies; c) various modes of communication and their impact on information and cognitive overload; d) how new management and learning systems are needed to support the new technologies; e) discussions about race, gender, access, age, literacy levels in relation to the use of technology; f) how social media tools and social isolation can impact research needed in varied disciplines (Martin, 2012); g) views of the new power paradigm shift through the technologies in a host of career areas and how these shifts can impact workplace ethics, social capital, and social justice; and h) the new career paths that have not even been imagined in emergency preparedness, medical advances, gaming, artificial intelligence, and lifelong learning.

The various authors in this book present how their use of the information technologies and the research related to those tools enhance community education, professional development, and community development. The authors are not limited to one continent in sharing these views or limited to one discipline. The authors are from a host of disciplines including health care, online mathematics, organizational learning, public schools, community and civic organizations, emergency management settings, medical schools, internet banking, literacy and workforce readiness programs, and higher education. The authors are also not confined to geographic boundaries and do represent movement to a global perspective for community education:

We live in a global community, where events that shape our lives are as likely to occur in the Mideast as they are next door. Continued dependence on an obsolete model does not give us the resources to meet the challenges of living in a global community. The need for community educators to raise issues, promote partnerships, and meet challenges is greater now than ever, but we must have new and creative ways to deal with the complexity of our world.

The goal is to redefine "community" so that it can address the multitude of needs people confront daily. This redefinition must include a willingness to form communities based on interest, need, and commonality that is not bounded by location, distance, or time. This goal is achievable through technology.

Technology continues to transform every aspect of our lives, so it is not surprising that it can change the meaning of "community" . . . . Community becomes the choices we make in connecting with other human beings, no longer limited by geographic or temporal boundaries (Turner, 1991, p. 60).

THE INTEGRATION OF COMMUNITY EDUCATION

In 1991, Larry Horyna and Larry Decker, a Charles Stewart Mott Eminent Scholar, envisioned a set of community education principles for the National Coalition for Community Education. The principles, cited at http://dpi.wi.gov/fscp/ceprin.html, were: a) self-determination; b) self-help; c) leadership development; d) localization; e) integrated delivery of services; f) maximum use of resources; g) inclusiveness; h) responsiveness; and i) lifelong learning (Horyna & Decker, 1991). The principles apply to the needs of programs and processes in today's world and suggest we all need to partner to address community concerns. Each of the principles presented can be directly supported using the various technologies that are present today.

Even though the principles are still significant in today's world, the way in which the principles may have to be employed have morphed considerably. Our "connected" world now evolves at exponential speeds. Not only is the information exploding, but how the information is being exchanged has drastically changed and will continue to do so. Today's population is simultaneously using their phones while surfing the Internet, answering emails, visiting websites while also watching television and playing games on various digital devices (Smith & Boyles, 2012). You only have to sit for a few minutes in any crowded space and see a proliferation of tools and techniques that are being used to be "connected."

With our Twitter accounts and Hoot Suite, we can each tell thousands of individuals in the click of 140 characters where we are, what we are doing, and why they should be interested. The "community" that can exist through these exchanges has not been refined or researched and offers rich opportunities for a new form of education directed at a new kind of learner.

Imagine how Charles Stewart Mott, Frank Manley, and other early community educators could have used the technology tools to marshal the communities around educational and community development. Can you see them using their Facebook accounts or LinkedIn as global tools for communication, as means to solve problems, to market services and create sense of community, to alter employment trends or alter lives?

ROLE OF THE INFORMATION TECHNOLOGIES

Information technologies provide service and program functions, including communication, and information retrieval useful in the administration of organizations worldwide and increasingly in the management of our everyday lives. Through information technologies, individuals stay connected to their families, communities, and cultures. Corporations remain connected to their constituencies to stay ahead of their competitors. Governments are able to function in a global economy.

Information technologies are being used by people of all walks of life to formulate solutions to problem scenarios. Virtual learning teams across the globe operate on intranets in all types of hierarchical and matrix organizations. These learning communities are made possible through Virtual Learning Teams (VLTs) using a metamorphosis of group calendars, listservs, group discussion boards, and a host of social media tools—Twitter, blogs, Facebook, and the lists goes on and on.

Information technologies are also being used by individuals of all ages to seek education, often in virtual settings. Ultimately, the same skills used in seeking one's education at any level may translate into skills needed to: a) conduct research and/or find employment; b) to pursue avocations, maximize everyday living, and function as a productive citizen; or c) to assist others in their life as parents, friends, or caregivers. As individuals gain the skills to secure the latest information through public documents, electronic libraries and journals, and the Internet, they become empowered as citizens in their world.

Information technology can also serve as an aid for us to become more human and more humane. We can create careers, find our soul mates, pursue leisure pursuits, and become humanitarians on a grand scale. Through the various tools, we can market ourselves, our talents, our organizations, and our platform of beliefs. However, with all the potential that information technologies bring there are cautions throughout the publication as to how we must remain vigilant in the use of the technologies and the role access can play.

As learners, educators, business owners, and governmental entities, the information technologies are invaluable as we unearth the various layers of data found in public documents and electronic libraries and journals. With electronic surveys, we can capture data, analyze and report using more and more engaging tools that combine databases, spreadsheets, and statistical modeling tools with voice, animation, Second Life formats, and avatars.

We can extend our education to a 24/7 format through listservs, email, group discussion boards, online newsletters, blogs, vlogs, wikis, and the list goes on and on—and most of the information is readily accessible on our phones. Lifelong learning has become a survival skill for not only traditional school-aged youth but for pre-school, young adults, and seniors (Thornburg, 1991, p. 106). Our day-to-day lives require access to the Internet to get permission to drive, to hunt or fish, to vote, to secure governmental services, or to obtain legal information.

However, this education, enhanced through information technologies, can also have a greater impact on the vibrancy of communities. We know from our research:

1. Communities are better served by a literate citizenry (Talking Page Literacy Organization, 2007).
2. Education is a direct predictor of individuals electing to pursue more or continued education (Kasworm, Rose, & Ross-Gordon, 2010).
3. The less schooling one has generally impacts the income the person will earn in a lifetime (Snyder, Dillow, & Hoffman, 2009; Kirsch, Jungeblut, Jenkins, & Kolstad, 2002).
4. Individuals with lower levels of education reportedly experience more negative consequences of a life, victims of crime, more health-related problems, higher levels of homelessness, or poor standards of housing (Brown, 2012).
5. Wife and child abuse issues, health maladies due to lack of nutrition or other related problems, poorer diets are generally more evident in homes with high levels of illiteracy (Brown, 2012).

Worldwide there has been a shift to a knowledge-based economy where earnings are associated with one's ability to search and retrieve information. People in our communities are being asked to think, find information, and use that information rather than produce goods and services. The proliferation of information will continue to drive the need for knowledge brokers in all our communities worldwide. As we move more and more into Second Life domains, augmented lives, and virtual worlds, the communities we serve will require more advanced education to meet the needs of the citizenry we serve (Mancuso, Chlup, & McWhorter, 2010).

The educators that serve the various communities must be users of the technology to guide the citizens of tomorrow. Community educators must assume the role of knowledge brokers. They must become avid researchers to identify what works and does not work for a myriad of learners. For this to occur, learning communities need to be created where the focus is on the relationships, the shared ideals, and the strong culture (Senge, 1990; Dufour & Eaker, 1998). We need to turn our communities into professional learning communities. As stated by Eaker (2002), we need to:

1. Acknowledge collaboration,
2. Know the professional learning community concepts,
3. Create a shared mission, vision, and values,
4. Focus and communicate a mission of student learning,
5. Visualize the school as a school of excellence,
6. Implement the vision statement,
7. Value the vision statement,
8. Develop the short-term and long-term processes,
9. Use research-based and data-driven plans, and
10. Remember that a professional learning community is a cyclical process.

As you visit the chapters of this book, you will see that each of the authors in his or her own way has addressed many of the elements needed for a professional learning community and comprehends the need to use all the resources available, including the information technologies, to accomplish that end.

REFERENCES

Brown, B. K. (2012). The impact of illiteracy. *Literacy Council of West Alabama*. Retrieved from http://literacywa.org/the-impact-of-illiteracy/

Bryan, V. C., & Musgrove, A. (2003). Creating virtual teams with blackboard. In *Proceedings of the Society for Information Technology & Teacher Education International Conference*. Albuquerque, NM: Society for Information Technology & Teacher Education. Retrieved from http://www.coe.fau.edu/faculty/bryan/documents/resume.pdf

Dufour, R., & Eaker, R. (1998). *Professional learning communities at work: Best practices for enhancing student achievement*. Bloomington, IN: National Educational Service.

Eaker, R., Dufour, R., & DuFour, R. (2002). *Getting started: Reculturing schools to become professional learning communities*. Bloomington, IN: Solution Tree.

Hornya, L., & Decker, L. (1991). *Community education principles*. Retrieved from http://dpi.wi.gov/fscp/ceprin.html

Kasworm, C. E., Rose, A. R., & Ross-Gordon, J. (Eds.). (2010). *Handbook of adult and continuing education*. Thousand Oaks, CA: Sage.

Kirsch, I. S., Jungeblut, A., Jenkins, L., & Kolstad, A. (2002). *Adult literacy in America: A first look at findings of the national adult literacy survey* (3rd ed.). Washington, DC: National Center for Education Statistics Government Printing Office.

Mancuso, D., Chlup, D. T., & McWhorter, R. R. (2010). A study of adult learning in a virtual world. *Advances in Developing Resources, 12*(6), 681-699. Retrieved from http://intl-adh.sagepub.com/content/12/6/681.full.pdf+html

Martin, G. Z. (2010). *30 days to social media success*. Pompton Plains, NY: Career Press, Inc.

Missouri Department of Elementary and Secondary Education. (2012). What is community education? *Extended Learning*. Retrieved from http://dese.mo.gov/eel/exl/eel-exl-community-ed.htm

Rawls, J. A. (2003). *Community educators' perceptions regarding the status and role of community education*. (Ph.D. Dissertation). Southern Illinois University. Carbondale, IL.

Senge, P. (1978). *The fifth discipline: The art and practice of the learning organization*. New York, NY: Currency Doubleday. doi:10.1002/pfi.4170300510

Smith, A., & Boyles, J. L. (2012, July 17). *The rise of the "connected viewer"*. Washington, DC: Pew Research Center's Internet & American Life Project. Retrieved from http://pewinternet.org/Reports/2012/Connected-vieweres.aspx

Snyder, T. D., Dillow, S. A., & Hoffman, C. M. (2009). *Digest of education statistics: 2008 (NCES No. 2009-20)*. Washington, DC: National Center for Education Statistics, U.S. Department of Education.

Talking Page Literacy Organization. (2007). *The national adult illiteracy action project, 2007-2012*. Retrieved from http://www.talkingpage.org/NIAP2007.pdf

Turner, T. (1991). Why community education must embrace technology now: From "community education journal". *Education Digest*, *57*(4), 60.

US Bureau of Labor Statistics. (2009). *Employment projections: 2008-2018 summary*. Washington, DC: US Department of Labor. Retrieved from http://www.bls.gov/opub/mlr/2009/11/art1full.pdf

Acknowledgment

We express our heart-felt thanks to the editorial advisory board members who have graciously and generously reviewed all the chapters during the blind review process in spite of their busy administrative and teaching schedules. Some have contributed innovative chapter(s) to this book. Their friendship and hard work are deeply appreciated. We express our gratitude to IGI Global, whose editorial/production team has never stopped publishing our research projects in the field. To the users of this book and university libraries, please accept a hug thank you for adopting this book as a textbook or reference book.

Chapter 1
The Power, Peril, and Promise of Information Technology to Community Education

Valerie Carson Bryan
Florida Atlantic University, USA

ABSTRACT

The democratization of information serves as a powerful force for change in both our lives and our global world. The paradigm shift from the providers of information to the users of the information has in many cases been brought about through the use of information technologies and the creation of more diverse and accessible Web-enabled devices. Educational equity helps to provide democratic and accessible educational opportunities for all citizenry and supports the tenets of community education. The question arises whether the proliferation of information brings power, peril, or promise for the communities of the world and the people it serves. This chapter investigates the changing rate of information, how it is distributed through online communities of practice and social networks, and what impact some of this information may have on areas of interest for training, research, and online development in fields of education, law enforcement, medicine, and sociology.

INTRODUCTION

In our current world, having access to information and knowing how to use that information has become an integral part of being an educated citizen. Today's information is a dynamic, living thing that is being changed drastically and at warp speed by technology. As we all know, information overload is occurring at exponential rates and we are being asked to change or to move out of the way.

For our communities to remain vibrant, we must have a citizenry that possesses the skills necessary to perform in this constantly changing environment, but the citizenry must also be able to morph into the needs of the next stage of this information evolution. As stated in the values expressed by the Charles Stewart Mott Foundation (2012), we need to nurture

DOI: 10.4018/978-1-4666-2955-4.ch001

strong, self-reliant individuals with expanded capacity for accomplishment . . . (that can) create a sense of community, whether at the neighborhood level or as a global society . . . ; (we need to build) . . . strong communities through collaboration to provide a basis for positive change; (encourage) responsible citizen participation to help foster social cohesion; (promote) the social, economic and political empowerment of all individuals and communities to preserve fundamental democratic principles and rights; (develop) leadership to build upon the needs and values of people and to inspire the aspirations and potential of others; and (respect) the diversity of life to maintain a sustainable human and physical environment (Charles Stewart Mott Foundation, 2012, p. 1).

BACKGROUND/THEORETICAL FRAMEWORK

Five centuries ago, a new technology swamped the world with data. This new technology, the Gutenberg's invention of the printing press, changed the way information was processed. Prior to Gutenberg's press, it took a scribe one year to prepare a book (Blair, 2012). Today, the number of text messages sent and received every day exceeds the population of the planet. The popular podcast, *Shifthappens 6.0,* that went viral following the 4.0 version, provides us a summary of factoids that helps to paint the picture of the exponential nature of the information explosion (see Table 1).

As reported in video clip "Did you know 4.0" video (Dachus Group/XPLANE, The Economist, McLeod, Fisch, & Berstler, 2009), Americans have access to over 1,000, 000,000,000 Web-pages, 65,000 iPhone apps, 10,500 radio stations, 5500 magazines, and 200+ cable TV network programs, and the number of each of these statistics continues to multiply.

Is there value in all this new information? Will all these increases in information serve a greater good for the individuals or for society they serve? In 2001, Wikipedia was launched featuring over 13 million articles in over 200 languages-a major increase in the amount of information available in Gutenberg's day (Fisch, McLeod, & Bestler, 2011).

Yes, there is new information, but who are the individuals creating and interpreting this

Table 1. Exponential nature of information explosion

Quotes from *Shifthappens 6.0*	Slides
Currently there are "540,000 words in the year English language or about five times as many words as was during Shakespeare's time"	37-38
On a daily basis "more than 4000 new books are published"	39
It is also estimated that a "week's worth of the *New York Times* contains more information than a person was likely to come across in a lifetime in the 18th century."	40
With "40 exabytes (4.0x 10^{19}) of unique and new information will be generated worldwide this year. That estimation is more than in any previous 5000 years."	41-42
Years it took to market information to reach a target "audience of 50 million" people via: • Radio 38 years • TV 13 years • Internet 4 years • iPod 3 years • Facebook 2 years • Google+ 1 year	36
Courtesy of Creative Commons Attribution Non-Commercial Share-Alike license, http://creativecommons.org/licenses/by-nc-sa/3.0/. Retrieved from http://www.youtube.com/watch?v=XVQ1ULfQawk	
(Rose, Brenman, XPLANE, Sony/BMG, the Economist, McLeod, Bestler, & Fisch, 2012)	

new information? Is this new information valid, reliable, and generalizable or is it pitted with inaccuracies, misinterpretations, or even attempts to mislead and persuade? What impact can the quality and credibility of this information have on our community learners and leaders? What strategies or deciphering processes do we, as community educators, need to develop to enable our community learners and leaders to:

1. Evaluate the vast sums of information for its credibility, relevance, and accuracy?
2. Assure that the information is current, objective, and has a real purpose?
3. Verify that the information has been created by individuals that have some level of expertise?
4. Assure the information is disseminated, examined, and adopted by other researchers worldwide to further expand the knowledge base (Mohawk College Library, 2012)?

By the end of 2012, information is expected to double every 72 hours. For students starting a four-year technical or college degree this means that half of what the students have learned in their first year of study may be outdated by their third year of study (Rose, et al., 2012, slide 44 and 45). This fact alone speaks to the need to educate learners and leaders to deal with change and the information explosion within our communities and beyond. As community educators we need to not react to what is, but to help our communities, its learners and its leaders, identify what information is available to move our civilization forward. It is also essential that community educators lead the charge as Charles Stewart Mott envisioned:

We recognize that our obligation to fellow men does not stop at the boundaries of the community. In an even larger sense, every man is in partnership with the rest of the human race in the eternal conquest which we call civilization (Quote from Charles Stewart Mott, 1973 (As cited by Charles Stewart Mott Foundation, 2010, p. 2).

So what does this mean to our community learners and leaders? Does this mean that we are being afforded more *power* within our community education settings using all the information technologies that are available? Does this mean that we are being placed in greater *peril* as a result of this proliferation of information? Or does this mean that the communities of the world and the people served find *promise* in this expansion of information via the various technologies?

Let's take a look at our current use of some of the technologies. Based on current information today's 21-year-olds have played 10,000 hours of video games received or sent 250,000 e-mails or instant messages and 50% of these individuals have created content for the Web format. Do these figures represent increased *power* for the individuals, possible *peril* for those same individuals, or possibilities of *promise* for this new generation?

The experts also suggest that the 21-year-olds will soon be outpaced by their younger counterparts in this information shift. At this moment, 70% of the four-year-olds have used a computer. Could these individuals, even prior to the age of 21, become our next information brokers using the Internet and social media of their generation?

This chapter will investigate some of the tools that will be needed as the information continues to expand. There will also be an opportunity to take a brief view of what *power* the new technologies may bring to our communities. We will also look briefly at what *perils* are being reported and see if this can be changed into opportunities by leveraging intellectual capital. The chapter will finally reflect on the *promise* that information technologies may bring for the current generations and those that are to follow.

GROUP COLLABORATION TOOLS: COMMUNITIES OF PRACTICE AND SOCIAL NETWORKS

The rise of Web 2.0 increased the proliferation of group collaboration tools such as the social networks, Facebook, LinkedIn, Twitter, and production tools such as YouTube and Flickr. The Web 2.0 phenomenon is described as "a social and behavioral sea change" (El-Ghareeb & Riad, 2011, p. 374).

Instead of serving up static fixed content to Web surfers, the Web has become an interactive place for people to congregate and do things virtually. Web 2.0 refers to the social use of the Web which allows people to collaborate, to get actively involved in creating content, to generate knowledge and to share information online (Grosseck, 2009; El-Ghareeb & Riad, 2011, p. 374).

Web 2.0 has drawn attention to online social communities and collaboration tools. These new technologies have expanded the Communities of Practice (CoP) in many cases to Online Communities of Practice (OCoP).

Community of Practice (CoP) and Online Community of Practice (OCoP)

A community of practice (CoP) is composed of members sharing a common profession for a type of work beyond an institutional affiliation. Generally, the CoP does not share a workplace, but through informal alliances does: a) share goals, b) share common interests, c) share ownership of an ideal or a concept, or d) are located in similar area or space.

Members of the CoP generally share:

a common language or set of terms related to their profession, practice or interest; a common set of problems; common training or experience; a common way of working or doing things; a common set of tools or technologies; a common tacit understanding of the topic. And, CoPs also contribute to learning and to building knowledge, whether this goal is implicit where explicitly stated.... Generally a high level of cohesion and intentionality, ... Most CoPs reflect a mixture of problem-solving and socializing discourse. COPs that specifically and intentionally commit to building the field of knowledge are most typically associated with scholarship, research, science, new technologies, new forms of artistic and cultural expression or social activism (Harasim, 2012, p. 146).

The Online Community of Practice (OCoP) offers certain strengths and limitations. Using the Web 2.0 format expanded the learning communities and enabled far greater scope and scale of interaction and discourse then face-to-face meetings for the community members; the OCoPs were not place bound, time bound, bound to one individual, or just text-based. These factors allow the OCoPs to function like an informal knowledge community that builds knowledge related to practice. For the OCoPs to be successful the community has to be sustained over time and the participants must remain engaged as with any community format. As the OCoPs expand, the advantages of the format may information overload for its users due to the number of participants or the number of postings and other cyber-related disadvantages and place the OCoP in peril.

Table 2 describes some of the social and collaboration technology tools that offer new opportunities. These tools offer opportunities for "academic collaboration and innovation" (Lomas, Burke, & Page, 2008, p. 5).

Social Media

Social media sites offer opportunities to meet potential learners and collaborators in your community. Social media helps you to share information without geographic boundaries and often with

Table 2. Role of social and collaboration tools in today's world

Activities	Opportunities	Sample Tools
Immediacy	Synchronous collaboration anywhere in the world	Instant Messages (IM), text chat, audio and/or video chat, file transfer or exchange, desktop sharing
Enhanced voice communications	One-to-many voice and video conferencing, recording conversations and chat	Skype and other VoIP applications
Ambient communications	Ability to ask a question of experts, friends, or acquaintances at any time and to share and communication. Possible sharing of links, resources, and notes. Place for community dialogue.	Twitter (micro-interactions or tweets of 140 characters; synchronous and/or asynchronously) Can be paired with other tools to share URLs, pictures, videos, etc.
Image sharing	Image-sharing and possible online collaboration centered around images and visuals for "analysis, comparisons, annotations, publishing, and remixing"	Flickr (allows uploading of photos with enhancement software, addition of tags or annotations)
Document construction	Synchronous collaboration on a single document to enhance co-writing, editing, brainstorming, creation of ideas and concepts	Google Docs (allows authors to work on same document in real time)
Social interaction	Developing common links and interests "to build shared networks and affinity groups"	Facebook (individual or group pages)-offers promise for large group collaboration
Geographic richness	Geographic and mapping tools to "create spatial connections between users" to support geo-spatial learning for visual learners	Google Earth (provides" rich, visual, and geographic data") for users to share conversations of common interests
Table information summarized from Lomas, Burke, and Page (2008). Collaboration tools. EDUCAUSE Learning Initiative, ELI Paper 2, 2008. Retrieved from http://net.educause.edu/ir/library/pdf/ELI3020.pdf		

less cost than traditional marketing techniques. You can provide links to videos, podcasts, YouTubes, or Webpages, on your Facebook account, or through your Twitter site, which allows you far more opportunities to touch the lives of those you wish to impact.

You can raise the visibility of your issues, your program, or your services to your consumers and to the media. You can even reach a worldwide audience to share research or to collaborate on projects that impact people across the globe. You can also use the information and the technologies to change the state of affairs for the field, for your consumers, and for the communities you serve. Social media is a great way to expand your horizons, to find others that share your views, to gain support for specific agendas, or to help to prioritize where you need to place your efforts.

Not all social media falls under the umbrella of an Online Community of Practice (OCoP). For community educators it is important to look at these social media sites to determine the advantages and disadvantages of using these tools as possible online communities of practice to serve their communities.

Facebook

Let's take a look at some of the social media that may impact our new generations and the communities they are part of. For a few moments, let's visit the world of Facebook, Twitter, and YouTube. In February 2004, Mark Zuckerberg, Dustin Moskovitz, and Chris Hughes launched a new way of sharing information from their dorm room at Harvard. These entrepreneurs created a way of sharing information that we now know as Facebook. Facebook was designed as a social networking website, which allowed users to join geographic or interest-based networks, to add friends, to create personal profiles, and to send messages across the globe.

As of December, 2011, Facebook has over 800 million users (Rose, Brenman, McLeod, Bestler,

& Fisch, 2012) and over 1 million websites are integrated with Facebook (http://www.youtube.com/watch?v=XKTfCjMsUNc) indicating that the initial design was successful. Halsey (2011) made the following statement from 2010 data on Facebook: "Facebook's 500 Million users, a massive 41% log in every single day and that 12%, that's 60 million people, update their status every day" (Halsey, 2011, p. 1).

Fifty-four percent of Facebook users in 2010 were men and 46% women; in 2012, 43% users are male and 57% are female and the females are posting more on their walls, earning between $26k and $75k (Halsey, 2011) indicating that the medium is used by both sexes, but other data suggests that certain economic or racial groups are more likely to be active in this medium.

More than 3.5 billion minutes are spent on Facebook worldwide each day. Facebook is the fourth most visited website in the world behind Google, Yahoo, and YouTube. The site showcases in print, visuals, video, and audio, the lives and times of families, groups, and organizations. One billion pieces of content (photos, news stories, video, and Web links) are shared daily (YouTube, 2012). Eight hundred and fifty million photos are uploaded to the Facebook site each month; 70% of those photos are loaded by users out of the United States. Facebook was "born in the USA," but now is definitely a global entity (see Figure 1).

Twitter

Another popular social medium, Twitter, is a combination of a "microblogging tool and a social networking site" with the users utilizing 140 characters of information to connect to other users who may share their interests or who may wish to hear what they have to say (Duxbury, 2012). Twitter currently has 106 million registered users with 27% logging in every day. New users sign up at the rate of 300,000 per day. Twitter users tweet an average of 55 million tweets a day with 60% of the users being from outside the USA; 37% of those twittering use their phone to tweet (Halsey, 2011).

Figure 1. Facebook vs. Twitter: a breakdown of 2010 social demographics. Retrieved from http://www.digitalsurgeons.com/Facebook-vs-twitter-infographic/ (Permission granted for use of figure by Digitalsurgeons)

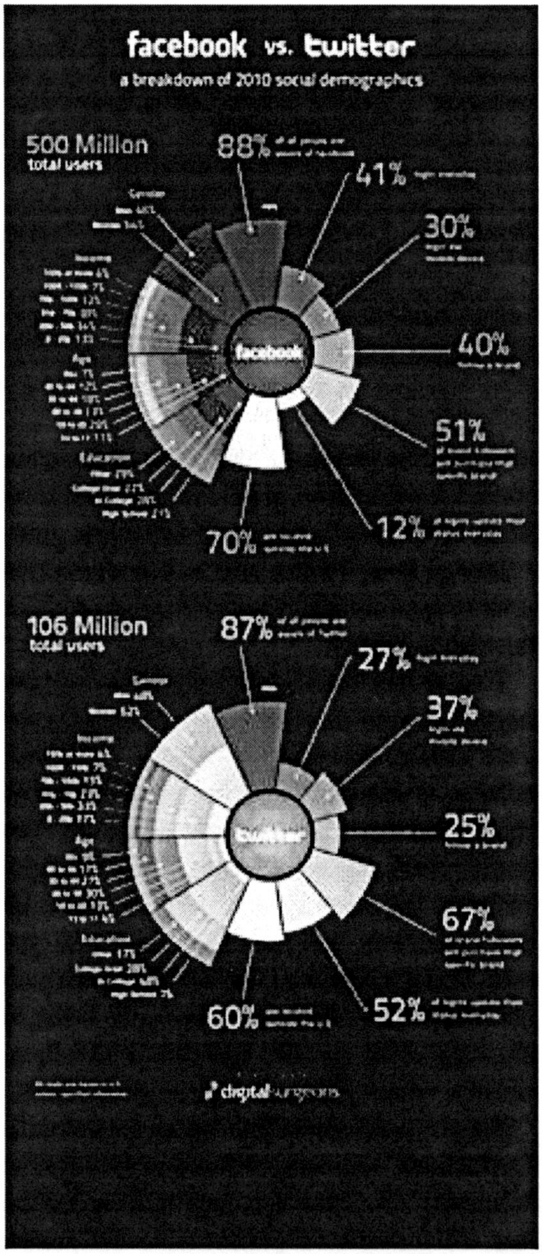

Based on a study of 2,253 adults age 18 and older, conducted by *Pew Research Center's Internet and American Life Project, Winter 2012* (Smith & Brenner, 2012), a significant number of USA twitter users are young adults, 18-29 years old (26%) and 25-34 years of age (20%). The majority of twitter users are white (51%), but African Americans are a close second (24% of the users). In this social medium, female Twitter users outnumber their male counterparts on the average (see Table 3).

YouTube

In today's information age, one only has to create and post a podcast or video, on YouTube and then sit back and watch to see if the material goes "viral"—meaning in social network vernacular, that the news of the posting spreads as a virus. YouTube has become a mechanism for instant sharing of information across continents. YouTube is:

a video-sharing service that lets users upload files to the YouTube servers .... Videos can be animations, footage of public events, personal recordings of friend .... Videos can be informational, entertaining, persuasive, or purely personal ... (EDUCAUSE, 2006, p. 1).

Individual users can post and tag videos, watch materials posted by others, engage in threaded discussions with like-minded groups, or engage in blogging or Web logs. The YouTube can also allow individuals, groups, and organizations to use the medium as a means to go viral with marketing videos or scholarly works created by a large numbers of authors, or to engage in think tanks or interest groups across similar institutions. YouTube provides a vehicle for individuals to enhance technical and visual skills in an international arena. YouTube, if properly used, can enhance creation of informative and visually appealing content in a peer review format. This format can also enhance visual literacy for the viewer and enhance the critical reviewing skills if the individual is giving the tools of assessment (see Table 4).

So does this information and use of technology address power, peril, or promise?

Table 3. Who uses Twitter?

Summary of Facts Related to Twitter Usage	
As of February 2012, 15% of online adults use Twitter, and 8% in a typical day.	Since May 2011, the proportion of online adults who use Twitter *on a typical day* has doubled and has quadrupled since late 2010, possibly due to rise in smartphone use. **As of February 2012, *46% of American adults are smartphone users*** (Smith, 2012).
More than one quarter of online **African-Americans** (28%) use Twitter, with 13% doing so on a typical day.	One quarter (26%) of Internet users are **young adults** (ages 18-29) that use Twitter, nearly double the rate for those ages 30-49. The youngest Internet users (those ages 18-24), fully 31% are Twitter users.
Residents of **urban and suburban areas are significantly more likely** to use Twitter than their rural counterparts.	22% of 18-24 year old cell owners **use Twitter on their phones**, and 15% do so on a typical day. **African Americans and Latinos** are heavy mobile Twitter users on their smartphones.
Source: *Pew Research Center's Internet and American Life Project, Winter 2012, Tracking Survey*, January 20-February 19, 2012. N=2,253 adults age 18 and older, including 901 cell phone interviews. Interviews conducted in English and Spanish. The margin of error is +/-2.7 percentage points for Internet users.	
Report by Smith and Brenner (2012). Retrieved from http://pewinternet.org/~/media//Files/Reports/2012/PIP_Twitter_Use_2012.pdf	

POWER OF INFORMATION TECHNOLOGY IN OUR COMMUNITIES

New and Creative Jobs

The US Department of Labor predicts that today's learner will have 10-14 jobs in their lifetime by the time they are 38 years of age. For many those jobs do not even exist today because the jobs have not been created. In essence learners in our classrooms today are being prepared for careers we do not have names for and will have jobs that may use tools or techniques that have not been imagined.

Developers' Roles

For example, in the past few years we have seen a proliferation of positions posted for "app developers" (application developers)—a term that did not exist until the recent past. For those individuals with either an android or an iPhone, these "apps" have become part of your daily vocabulary in an extremely short period of time.

These apps are being created by a new workforce with advanced digital skills. These same individuals may be playing in other arenas as well, such as Second Life or virtual reality, designing media that can be fun, informational and possibly can help to lead to breakthroughs in strategic leadership, community involvement, medical research, or military advancement.

Positions that have gained great momentum include: a) a "gamer" or a person that creates digital gaming devices for both educational and leisure activities; b) digital media creator can be someone that creates electronic books or video avatar-like character. The need for content creators and computer and software engineers for game learning and social media is only expected to expand. These are just a couple examples of the proliferation of a job market that did not exist 10 years ago. The shift in information will drive more unique and challenging opportunities for those individuals in school now and for those needing training to maintain employment.

Table 4. Impact of YouTube

Brief View of Summary Statistics on YouTube
4th largest site on Internet
3.5M visitors daily
#1 Video site on the Web
24 hours of video is loaded every minute
More video is uploaded to YouTube in 60 days than is loaded to 3 major networks in 60 years
People are watching 2 billion videos a day on YouTube
Clean Cut Media (2009), YouTube (2012).

Ten years ago, none of us were working in "the cloud" to do our daily work. Global connectivity, smart machines, and new media are determining how we work, redefining what work is, and are requiring us all to modify the skill base we have—not just to be employed, but to be able to function in our daily lives as active citizens (e.g., making a deposit at the bank, applying for position, checking out our groceries at Wal-Mart, voting, or staying connected to our families).

Virtual Consultants for Business and Industry

Due to the globalization of the workplace, it is also anticipated that we will need more individuals that can work across cultures and countries in a host of industries and organizations using the various smart technologies.

Educational institutions are often mired in the past and are not reticent to change quickly. In order for the current institutions to be prepared for this new shift to accommodate the change that is anticipated to come, it is essential that the institutions adhere to the 1969 words of Alvin Toffler when he was quoted saying: "The illiterate of the 21st century will not be those who cannot read and write but those who cannot learn, unlearn, and relearn" (Toffler, 1969).

To support these words, the Institute for the Future for the University of Phoenix Research Institute's Future Work Skills 2020 (Davies, Fidler, & Gorbis, 2011) suggests that educational institutions should emphasis the development of the following skills:

1. "critical thinking, insight, and analysis capabilities";
2. "integrating new-media literacy into education programs";
3. "including experiential learning that gives prominence to soft skills—such as the ability to collaborate, work in groups, read social cues, and respond adaptively";
4. "broadening the learning constituency beyond teens and young adults through to adulthood";
5. "integrating interdisciplinary training that allows students to develop skills and knowledge in a range of subjects" (Davies, Fidler, & Gorbis, 2011, p. 13).

PERILS OF INFORMATION TECHNOLOGY IN OUR COMMUNITIES

Information Overload

Many individuals are concerned that all the digital information that technology affords may change our communities and the individuals within those communities. Questions are being raised if we are:

losing our abilities to pay sustained attention, reflect deeply, or remember what we've learner . . . concern that humanity is experiencing an unprecedented change-that modern technology is creating a problem that our culture and even our brains are ill equipped to handle. We stand on the brink of a future that no one can eve have experienced before (Blair, 2010, p. 1).

This exponential information overload may cause processing of the information difficult for select individuals, particularly when the information from one source conflicts with information received from other sources or with material already learned. If the learner has not been given the tools to gauge the value of the new material, distress may occur.

Another issue may arise if the new information is contrary to the individual's perceptions or current knowledge level and the individual does not have the necessary scaffolding to deal with this new and possible expansive amount of data or new information. For some individuals all the deluge of information coming may cause the individual to retreat from the new information sources and return to venues that do not challenge them to prevent stress.

Sweller and others developed the *Cognitive Load Theory* (Sweller, 1988, 1989, 1999; Sweller & Chandler, 1991, 1994; Sweller & Cooper, 1985) as a way to address some of these concerns. The *cognitive Load Theory* deals with making information processing efficient without taxing the working memory of the individual. *Cognitive Load Theory* also deals with developing methods to help those that are the information overload may tax their ability to learn or to respond to the various working situations they find themselves in. *Cognitive Load Theory* has been empirically identified in numerous studies to affect working memory. It has also been noted to have an impact on how long the information once received can be retained. The retention of information is specifically important in technical fields that required vast storage of information in working memory. New studies are currently underway regarding the impact of cognitive overload for unique populations such as the aging and why cognitive overload is eustress for some individuals and distress for others (Sweller, 1988; Sweller, van Merrienboer, & Paas, 1988; Paas, 1992; Pass, Renkl, & Sweller, 2003; Paas, Tuovinen, Tabbers, & Van Gerven, 2003; Pass & Van Gog, 2006).

Critical Consumers of the Information

As our communities grow and attempt to manage the information age, it is important that our citizenry be given the tools to make them better consumers of the information and more technologically literate in this information age. As community leaders we need to find ways to help our citizenry recognize, as Erasmus suggested in the early 16th century, that the flood of information has to managed and critically analyze for its quality, accuracy, and subversive levels or "even things that might have done good lose all their goodness" (Blair, 2010, p. 2).

Loss of Privacy

Some individuals within our society are concerned that the proliferation of information and access to private information also enhances the George Orwell's *Nineteen Eighty-Four* concept of "Big Brother is watching you," loss of privacy, abuse of government power and more and more mass surveillance. Though this area of discourse remains an interesting topic for community educators, the discourse on this topic will be left to future exposés.

Change in Our Language

Others feel that the proliferation of information and how we are currently communicating with one another will ultimately destroy formal language. Texting, email, the use of idioms, emoticons, Twitter, are all considered by many to be too informal for research and scholarly language. David Crystal, Professor of Linguistics at the University of Wales, Bangor, expressed the following positive view in contrast to those views of peril for our language resulting from the technologies:

All that has happened, in fact, is that the language's resources for the expression of informality in writing have hugely increased—something which has not been seen in English since the Middle Ages, and which was largely lost when Standard English came to be established in the 18th century . . . . Rather than condemning it, therefore, we should be exulting in the fact that the Internet is allowing us to once more explore the power of the written language in a creative way (Crystal, 2012, p. 1).

It is up to community educators to find a way to assist individuals to know when formal language and the informal language are appropriate. Community educators can serve as trainers to help learners discover what language formats are best suited for the workplace, or to use for technical language in the science and math fields, or for scholarly writings, or marketing, and the list goes on and on. Community educators can serve as the bridge between the formal, the informal, and the non-formal learning communities.

Those in our community need to know how to avoid placing themselves in harm's way by posting vulgar or offensive language in blogs, emails, Web-posts, Facebook pages, Wikis, that can potentially go viral and affect entry to universities, loss of job offers or loss of jobs, and failed relationships. Community educators can play a role in getting the news out in creative and informative means to all ages of citizenry.

Technology and/or Internet-Related Crimes

Many of the ills of society today spring from the ability to more easily access the very information we are creating at such exponential rates and often with little safeguards. There are numerous technology assisted abuse and Internet crimes that have evolved as a result of the proliferation of information and ease of access: Identify theft; cyber-enhanced crimes verses individuals such as stalking victimization, cyber-bullying, cyber-pornography/trafficking, sexting and other issues with tweens and teens.

Identify Theft and Financial Fraud

Identify theft involves "all types of crime in which someone wrongfully obtains and uses another person's personal data in some way that involves fraud or deception, typically for economic gain" (USDOJ, 2012, p. 1). The identify theft is generally to secure some sort of financial advantage for the individual conducting the crime.

Community agencies have a responsibility to their citizenry to offer information and training on how identify theft and financial fraud can occur, what a person can do about it, and how individuals can guard their privacy to avoid these crimes. To reduce or minimize the risk of becoming a victim of identity theft or fraud, community education programs can be developed that emphasize simple techniques of password protection and SCAM:

1. Being Stingy (S) about giving out your personal information;
2. Checking (C) financial information regularly to what should be there and what should not be there;
3. Asking (A) periodically for a copy of your credit report.
4. Maintaining (M) careful records of your banking and financial accounts (USDOJ, 2012).

Identity theft and Internet related crimes (e.g., credit cards, telemarketing, etc.) that bring about financial fraud are particularly targeted against senior adults (Johnson, 2012). For these individuals financial fraud may also pose psychological harm. For many elderly individuals the identity theft or financial fraud event is equivalent to rape. Victims experience self-doubt, self-imposed isolation or societal condemnation, anger, resentment, betrayal, frustration, shame, guilt, and the fear of financial security. Many of these psychological harms can have physiological and long-term emotional effects on these victims. For many the tangible cost of the financial fraud may be more evident: Lost of financial security, home, business, savings, and even credibility.

Victims are often re-victimized because they are often too embarrassed, or guilty, to report they have been victimized. Estimates vary, but experts relate that only 15% of the nation's financial fraud victims report their crimes to law enforcement. So the role of researchers in working with victims and re-victims becomes even more critical in the arena of financial fraud.

Other Cyber-Enhanced Crimes vs. Individuals

With the proliferation of Web-enhanced devices with Internet access, digital cameras capabilities, and voice and audio capabilities, other crimes are also appearing that need vigilance at the community level. Cyber-bullying, sexting, and other issues with tweens and teens using the information technologies and the various devices is significantly related to both in school and after school behavior for today's youth. Crimes such as stalking victimization, cyber-pornography, and trafficking are also more readily available because of the same tools that offer such promise and affect both the youth and the adults within the communities community educators serve.

Cyber Bullying is a crime that causes approximately 160,000 children to miss school a day in the USA. In recent years, the crime has evolved through the use of social media tools to what is now termed cyber bullying both during and after school particularly among teens and children. Over half of adolescents and teens have been bullied online, and about the same number have engaged in cyber bullying. Reports indicate that more than one in three young people have experienced some form of cyber bullying. Often the individual retaliates in like manner to being bullied and becomes a cyber bully as well.

Social networking using cell phones, the preferred means, and Internet access has provided an entirely new environment for bullying to take place. In many cited cases, the victim of these crimes become anxious, depressed, or can move to suicide to escape the cyber bullying. In surveys, half of the bullied youth indicate that they have not reported the incident to their parents. In many cases, the cyber bullying may resurface during adulthood due to the nature of the Internet and the proliferation of files that can be retrieved.

Cyber bullying can take many forms:

- Sending mean messages or threats to a person's email account or cell phone.
- Spreading rumors online or through texts.
- Posting hurtful or threatening messages on social networking sites or Web pages.
- Stealing a person's account information to break into their account and send damaging messages.
- Pretending to be someone else online to hurt another person.
- Taking unflattering pictures of a person and spreading them through cell phones or the Internet.
- Sexting, or circulating sexually suggestive pictures or messages about a person. (Bullying Statistics, 2012, p. 1).

It is estimated by i-SAFE, Inc., that one in five teens have posted or sent sexually suggestive or nude pictures of themselves to others. Sexting puts the youth at even greater risk due to the number of sexual predators that lurk on websites posing as adolescents themselves.

Cyber bullying may resurface after the initial incident to hurt both the person being bullied and the person doing the bullying. If convicted of being a "bully," the individual may face legal issues and have difficulty in applying for schools or jobs, particularly if the bullying falls under the category of sexting (see Table 5).

Communities need to develop joint teams to address the issue and create a cyber-safe community. The youth, parents, local organizations and child-serving agencies (i.e., police department and other law enforcement agencies, schools, recreation agencies, team sports groups, local citizen groups, etc.) are need to be educated as to the severity of this problem in today's environment.

Sexting is the electronic sending and or receiving of sexually suggestive text, email, or instant messages during the courtship rituals. A new frontier has been created for teen dating abuse using digital technologies that generally accompanies harassment or some other form of cyber bullying as well. Studies vary, but generally the estimates suggest:

- Between 13 and 31 percent of teens have received sexting messages or materials and
- Between 4 and 19% of teens have sent sexting messages (see Table 6).

In Hinduja and Patchin's (2010) study with 4,400 students between the ages of 11 and 18 boys and girls were involved in sexting but boys more likely than girls reported receiving sexting.

Table 5. Cyber bullying statistics

Prevalence of Cyber Bullying Reported by i-SAFE.org: The Leader in e-Safety Education
• 42% of kids have been bullied while online. 1 in 4 have had it happen more than once.
• 35% of kids have been threatened online. Nearly 1 in 5 has had it happen more than once.
• 21% of kids have received mean or threatening e-mail or other messages.
• 58% of kids admit someone has said mean or hurtful things to them online. More than 4 out of 10 say it has happened more than once.
• 53% of kids admit having said something mean or hurtful to another person online. More than 1 in 3 has done it more than once.
• 58% have not told their parents or an adult about something mean or hurtful that happened to them online. (iSAFE.org, 2012, p. 1)
Retrieved from http://www.isafe.org/outreach/media/media_cyber_bullying

Table 6. Sexting by the numbers

	% Who Sent Message	% Who Received Message
National Campaign to Prevent Teen and Unplanned Pregnancy (2008)	19%	31%
Cox Communications (2009)	9%	17%
MTV/AP (2009)	10%	15%
Pew (2009)	4%	15%
Hinduja and Patchin (2010)	8%	13%
Based on: Hinduja and Patchin (2010). Sexting: a brief guide for educators and parents. *Cyberbullying Research Center, 2010.* Retrieved from http://www.cyberbullying.us/Sexting_Fact_Sheet.pdf		

In recent studies, it has become evident that our youth, parents, schools, law enforcement agencies, and communities do not have the tools to address these problems alone. Experts in this research area suggest that a collaborative approach is needed. The following represents some of the possible actions that need to be taken:

in-school assemblies for youth, professional development for staff, and evening workshops for parents and other community members. Additionally, information and resources can be shared through take-home memorandums, student handbooks, newsletters/correspondence to the community, letters to the editor in local newspapers, town hall meetings, and automated phone calls to the families of students. Finally, the Web can be exploited through the construction and maintenance of a Facebook Fan Page, a Twitter feed, or a page on the school website that covers sexting identification, prevention, and response while detailing legal and policy issues relevant to students and parents—and which reminds them of the appropriate, ethical, and lawful use of technology (Hinduja & Patchin, 2010, p. 4).

Teen Texting While Driving is following the pattern of their adult parents' texting and placing a large number of our youth exposed to possible criminal charges, property damage, or even loss of life situations (Halsey, 2012) (see Figure 2).

The statistics are alarming, but are the phones the evil that is putting the teens and the adults in peril? Laws are being put into place to legislate the problem. Cars are being redesigned to accommodate the phones. Apps are being developed to use voice developed capabilities that convert audio to text. Are there other methods that need to be explored to address this peril?

PROMISE OF INFORMATION TECHNOLOGY IN OUR COMMUNITIES

The social impact of the various technologies has helped to reunite friends, relatives and other acquaintances across the globe regardless of distance as long as the individuals have Internet access. The same promise is also extended to a host of other entities within the local, state, national, and international communities that wish to establish a connected existence for a host of purposes

Common Areas of Interests

People with common interest regarding music, art, literature, drama, fashion, cooking, carpentry, photography, etc., frequently use information technologies to further their areas of interests. Internet directories are currently available for the various like-minded individuals to share their interests in a host of hobby areas (see http://www.discoverahobby.com/).

Professional organizations may use the Internet in like fashion to energize their members and create Online Communities of Practice (OCoPs) with websites such as Community Education (www.VisionCommunityEd.org), AAACE (http://www.aaace.org/), AERA (http://www.aera.net/), Charles Stewart Mott Foundation (http://www.mott.org), National Council for Community and Education Partnerships (http://www.edpartner-

Figure 2. Teens at risk due to texting and distracted driving (Madden & Lenhart, 2009, p. 2). Retrieved from http://pewinternet.org/~/media//Files/Reports/2009/PIP_Teens_and_Distracted_Driving.pdf

Overview

- **75% of all American teens ages 12-17 own a cell phone, and 66% use their phones to send or receive text messages.**
- **Older teens are more likely than younger teens to have cell phones and use text messaging; 82% of teens ages 16-17 have a cell phone and 76% of that cohort are cell texters.**
- **One in three (34%) texting teens ages 16-17 say they have texted while driving. That translates into 26% of all American teens ages 16-17.**
- **Half (52%) of cell-owning teens ages 16-17 say they have talked on a cell phone while driving. That translates into 43% of all American teens ages 16-17.**
- **48% of all teens ages 12-17 say they have been in a car when the driver was texting.**
- **40% say they have been in a car when the driver used a cell phone in a way that put themselves or others in danger.**

ships.org/), and other like organizations. Some organizations produce podcasts via YouTube; or organizational Facebook accounts (for example, http://www.facebook.com/FAUAdultComEd); and or shared work spaces via various Listservs, GoogleDocs, DropBox, ZumoCasts, and other like spaces, many of which are available on mobile devices with Web-enabled cell phones.

Universities have created online communities and shared work spaces by creating their own "apps" for mail sharing, calendar sharing, document sharing. Using Google sites faculty and students are able to create their own Web sites or wikis as well for public or private sharing of information (see Figure 3).

Political Change

Individuals who are actively involved in political change or beliefs or which to support particular political agendas are using the various social network tools and the Internet to connect to others of like affiliation and to influence others. Based on the research conducted in 2010 by the *Pew Internet and American Life Project* with 2,257 USA adults ages 18 and older (see Table 7):

> *more than half of all American adults were online political users in 2010 . . . . Fully 73% of adult Internet users (representing 54% of all US adults) went online to get news or information about the 2010 midterm elections, or to get involved in the campaign in one way or another (Smith, 2011, p. 1).*

As noted in Figure 4, the Internet is gaining as a means to stay involved with the political process and offers opportunities for community educators to harness the power of the Internet to shape public opinion using information technologies and social media.

The Internet is growing as the place of choice for political news for our digital users. Individuals 18-29 years old represented 36% of those getting their news from the Internet and 30-49 years old represented 29% of those getting their news from the Internet.

Career and Employment Opportunities

In today's job market, finding employment that matches one's skill base is often challenging. The Internet and social media offers a means to conduct research of employment opportunities or career ladders of interest. Individuals seeking careers or companies seeking talented employees can use a variety of sites to achieve their purposes: Linkedin (http://www.linkedin.com), *indeed* (http://www.indeed.com/), *Careerbuilder* (http://www.careerbuilder.com/), *SimplyHired* (http://www.simplyhired.com/), and *Monster* (http://www.monster.com/) are examples of an Internet-based professional networks created to help individuals find employment, reconnect with co-workers or experts in their related fields, and find answers to career-related questions in a collegial manner.

Community educators' charge in the community has included: a) the development of a strong and sustained community via economic, social and environmental means; b) mobilization and preparation of people for workplaces that strengthen their communities; and c) creating linkages within and outside to sustain the communities overtime. All of those roles require a competitive workforce comprised of individuals who are trained not to just meet the careers of today, but the careers of the futures to come. As community educators, we have to use all the tools available to maximize the potential of our workforce—for the future, that requires the use of the information technologies. We must also assist our community learners in knowing how to use the tools.

Fundraising and Grant Writing

Organizations are actively establishing gift recruitment platforms for special needs groups. The power of fundraising and grant writing is enhanced to electronic connections to the funding agencies. With the click of a button, you can access thousands of potential funding streams, but so can thousands or even millions of other individuals needing funding for their cause or concern. The person seeking to help his or her community is now not only in competition with others seeking those funds within his or her state or country, but may also be in competition with others from around the world.

Health Treatments and Medical Research

More and more individuals are using the Internet to seek health information, view treatment options as addressed in the literature or even to discuss treatment with others with similar medical conditions. For many individuals, the online connections help to supplement their medical knowledge and

Figure 3. Sample of shared applications at a university

Figure 4. Internet impact for political information

Main sources of campaign news, 2002-2010

Based on all adults

	2002	2006	2010
Television	66%	69%	67%
Newspapers	33	34	27
Internet	7	15	24
Radio	13	17	14
Magazines	1	2	2

Source: The Pew Research Center's Internet & American Life Project, November 3-24, 2010 Post-Election Tracking Survey. n=2,257 national adults ages 18 and older, including 755 cell phone interviews. Interviews were conducted in English and Spanish. Note: totals may exceed 100% due to multiple responses.

aid them in becoming more proactive in their own disease management.

The role of the information technologies to current individuals with health issues is significant.

- 8 in 10 Internet users have looked online for health information.
- Many e-patients say the Internet has had a significant impact on the way they care for themselves or for others.
- "1 in 5 Internet users have gone online to find others like them."
- "1 in 4 Internet users living with high blood pressure, diabetes, heart conditions, lung conditions, cancer, or some other chronic ailment (23%) say they have gone online to find others with similar health concerns" (Fox, 2011, p. 2).

The Internet provides information for self-care and self-management, but it also provides an OCoP so the individuals or patients and their caregivers can connect to others for support and advice. There are numerous reported cases where people with family with high medical needs have located either treatment options or support groups for rare medical conditions. For many the value of the Internet provides a sense of control when they are feeling most vulnerable. The Internet helps people to help themselves.

Social media can also impact health in other ways by allowing medical teams to share research and treatment evolution to not only impact lifespans, but possibly to expand lifespans. Medical teams are working across continents to identify ways and means to isolate and treat diseases. Visuals, podcasts, electronic imagery, virtual surgeries are all changing the practice of 21st century medicine. Shared online workspaces are being used conduct studies, to create instruments as part of the research design, to collect the data, and to analyze the data (Fox & Purcell, 2010).

Social media also helps those with chronic disease to make decisions and compare options, to create health related content that may help others inflicted with their disease, and to support others through open source forums such as the Lupus site, www.Lupis.org. These online communities of practices are created by adult learners with common interests and experiences and represent a recent phenomenon of patients taking a more self-directed approach to the management of their own health care.

Table 7. Internet's impact on political debate in USA, 2010

Pro Comments of Online Adults	Con Comments of Online Adults
54% of online adults: *Internet makes it easier to connect with others who share their view politically*	55% of all online adults: *Internet increases the influence of those with extreme political views*
61% of online adults: *Internet exposes people to a wider range of political views they can get in the traditional news media*	56% of online adults: *usually difficult for them to tell what is true from what is not true when it comes to the political information they find online*
35% of online adults: *checked on candidate's voting records*	
28% of online adults: *research or fact check claims*	
Source: The Pew Research Center's Internet and American Life Project, November 3-24, 2010 Post Election Tracking Survey. N=2,257 national adults ages 18 and older, including 755 cell phone interviews. Interviews were conducted in English and Spanish. Note: totals may exceed 100% due to multiple responses.	
Smith (2011). Retrieved from http://pewinternet.org/Reports/2011/The-Internet-and-Campaign-2010.aspx	

The medical community refers to the development of online collaboration as "social capital." Social capital encourages social connectedness that helps to improve health outcomes and also improves self-management thus improving health outcomes. Enhancing social capital between the health care providers, the patient, and the patient's caregivers can improve the quality of the healthcare of the individual (Jain, Goyal, Fox, & Shrank, 2012).

Lifelong Learning

Lifelong learning for the masses regardless of location or disenfranchised levels is also possible using technology. A major change is occurring in our libraries and our use of information through e-books. Our libraries are evolving. More than ¾'s of nation's public libraries are now lending e-books. Many schools, colleges, and universities are moving to e-book platforms as well as other digital materials.

The e-books are transforming our libraries, but not all people know about the revolution (see Table 8).

Avid library users overall are going to the physical libraries less. The avid library users are visiting the library website more. More libraries are using their funds to purchase e-books. The libraries have opportunities to market to a new public and engage people that are not traditional library patrons (in the USA, specifically African-Americans, Hispanics, lower-income households). Some libraries are recognizing the opportunities and are trying to reach their audiences using Webpages, Twitter accounts, and media openings.

Better marketing of the e-books to all library patrons may increase readership levels and increase the number of return visits by the non e-book borrowers. In the studies conducted, e-book borrowers did report there were issues with using the e-books such as lack of knowledge on how to download to the handheld devices or the library did not carry the books they were interested in or the device or book was on a waiting list.

Table 8. Comparison of e-book borrowers and non e-book borrowers

e-book Borrowers	Non e-book Borrowers
Read 29 books per year on average (median levels were 20 books)	Read 23 books per year on average (median levels were 12 books)
Say that libraries are important to them	
Are heavy readers in all formats	
(Zickuhr, Raine, Purcell, Madden, & Brenner, 2012)	

FUTURE TRENDS

Charles Stewart Mott affirmed that a civil society should provide access to information and education to all of its citizens in an equitable fashion regardless of their diversity. In the Mott Foundation Archives in Flint, Michigan, there are numerous reports that support Mr. Mott's beliefs that an educated citizenry should be empowered; have access to the tools for economic self-sufficiency; have skills to protect the individual and his family from perilous situations. Mr. Mott viewed community education as a means to expand knowledge and to engage the community in addressing its own ills, as is supported in the following quote:

As we all recognize knowledge is a dynamic, living thing and there currently is an exponential proliferation of information in today's society. In our current world, having access to information and knowing how to use that information has become an integral part of being an educated citizen. Everything from the way we work or play to the way we manage the ebb and flow of our daily lives is being changed drastically and at warp speed by technology. Individuals possessing the skills necessary for employment, to be self-sufficient, and to maintain a quality of life, are essential if our communities to remain vibrant (Bryan, 2006, p. 10).

Due to the nature of the changing technologies, more and more individuals will be accessing information on Web-enabled devices (particularly our cell phones), engaging in collaborative networks, sharing information across continents, and finding solutions to their daily work or life needs on their phones or other digital devices. Smith's (2012) findings suggest that community educators have an opportunity to reach even greater audiences by developing content for phone platforms for just-in-time learning and "on demand" instruction and information sharing for all learners (see Table 9).

Several individuals have hypothesized that all the information technologies are bringing about more social isolation. However, contrary to these reports, the use of cell phones with Internet access are encouraging more participation in discussion networks and with individuals that may be outside the individuals normal social circles suggesting more social engagement and not less. Normally the individual with no Internet access, due to economics or other socio-demographic elements, can reach Internet created materials.

Accessing the Internet via the cell phone also allows people to be engaged in a greater variety of public places and offer the accidental opportunity to engage with other like-minded individuals. As community educators, we need to harness the potential of learning packets for cell phone usage, geo-caching (http://www.geocaching.com/) with mobile phone to cultural or historical sites, more online discussions regarding local issues of concern or helpful tips.

Table 9. Key findings on cell phone use and the Internet

Tracking survey of N=2,254 adults, ages 18 and older (including 903 interviews conducted on respondent's cell phone)
38% of cell-mostly users cite convenience of cell phones as the main reason or browsing on the phone
88% of US adults own a cell phone; 55% of these use phone to go online
31% of current Internet users go online mostly on cell phone
45% of 18-29 year olds use Internet on their cell phones
51% of African American cell Internet users browse on cell phone compared to 42% Latino and 24% of whites
Individuals who have not graduated from college or make less than $50,000 a year use cell phone more for Internet access
Only 16% of senior adults with a cell phone use it for Internet access
Based on Pew Research Center's Internet & American Life Project, March 15-April 3, 2012 Margin of error is +/-3.7 percentage points based on those who use the Internet or email on their cell phone (n=929).

Research and Development Opportunities

Research ideas are throughout this document. Research studies need to be developed that compares content delivered through various social networks and for various devices and populations types. Studies need to address how to reduce the perils and enhance the promise and empower individuals of all walks of life. More research needs to address the skills that will be needed to move us forward as individuals and as communities. Research is also needed as to how to make our learners more powerful reviewers of the information that is being produced.

CONCLUSION

The information age has altered our exchanges often from learning to doing. We now crave instant information twenty-four hours a day, seven days a week on every imaginable device we can utilize. Our gadgets bring the information to us, but it is up to us to determine the value of the information to ourselves and the communities we serve and to develop the knowledge and skill sets to use the information.

For our communities to remain vibrant, we must learn how to leverage our intellectual capital and use the various tools of the information age to create communities of practice, both face-to-face and online, that use social networks to not only share collective knowledge but also create it. We need to develop processes and products that can help us to help others learn in our communities to (see Figure 5):

1. Make sense of all the knowledge that is being created (sense-making);
2. Find ways to develop employees with high emotional quotients for the workplaces of tomorrow that have high level of social intelligences (social intelligence);
3. Help our learners to develop novel and adaptive thinking that encourages collaboration, relationships-building, and *situational adaptability* for this complex, high-skilled and competitive market place (novel and adaptive thinking);

Figure 5. The skills for the future workforce. Retrieved from http://cdn.theatlantic.com/static/front/docs/sponsored/phoenix/future_work_skills_2020.pdf

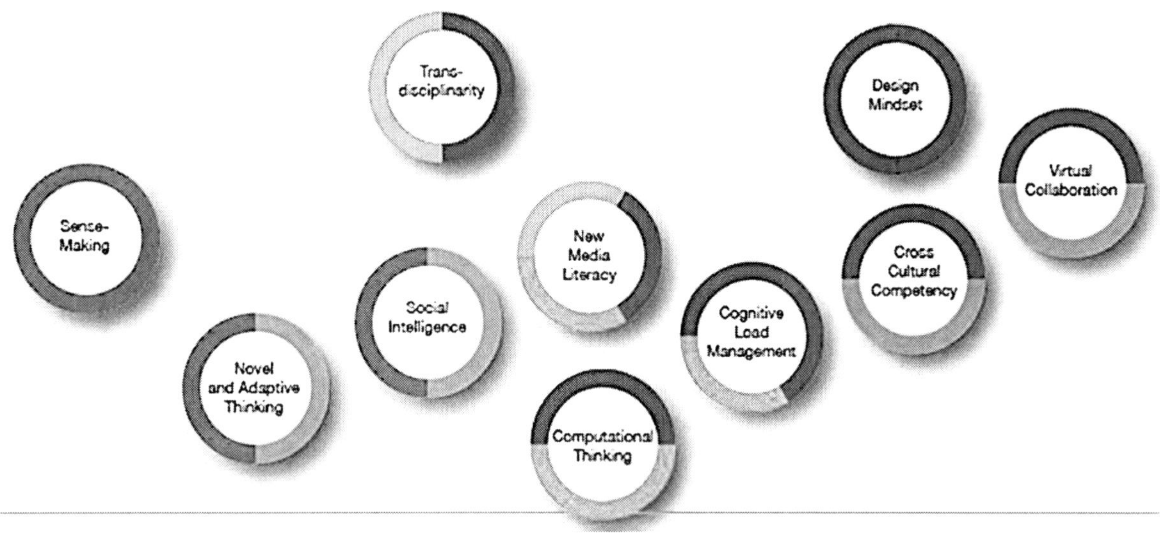

4. Create and train more individuals who are "able to operate in different cultural settings" (cross cultural competency) (Davies, Fidler, & Gorbis, 2011, p. 9);
5. Engage in computational thinking to "translate vast amount of data into abstract concepts" (computational thinking) (Davies, Fidler, & Gorbis, 2011, p. 10);
6. Become creators and users of media and content created by new media (new-media literacy);
7. Create knowledge workers in our communities to are able to cross disciplines ("transdisciplinarity") and have a:

deep understanding of at least one field, but the capacity to converse in the language of a broader range of disciplines. This requires a sense of curiosity and a willingness to go on learning beyond the years of formal education. As extended lifespans promote multiple careers and exposure to more industries and discipline, it will be particularly important for workers . . . . (Davies, Fidler, & Gorbis, 2011, p. 11);

8. Emphasize the value of adult learning; the value of new mindsets that encourage relational thinking, connections and free recall of facts; and the ability to select the thinking needed for certain tasks (design mindset) (Davies, Fidler, & Gorbis, 2011);
9. Stress the importance of cognitive load management using various tools and techniques (cognitive load management);
10. Help citizenry develop skill sets to work in virtual teams (virtual collaboration).

Educators, businesses, foundations, and policymakers need to work in collaboration to develop the skill sets for our future communities. We look forward to everyone's commitment in this endeavor.

REFERENCES

Blair, A. (2010). Information overload: The early years. *Boston Globe Newspaper Company*. Retrieved from http://www.boston.com/bostonglobe/ideas/articles/2010/11/28/information_overload_the_early_years/

Bryan, V. C. (2006). Impact of technology in community education: Its applications and effects. *Community Education Journal*, *20*(2/3), 10–13.

Bullying Statistics. (2012). *Cyber bullying*. Retrieved from http://www.bullyingstatistics.org/content/cyber-bullying-statistics.html

Charles Stewart Mott Foundation. (1973). 1973 annual report. In K. McDonald (Ed.), *Charles Stewart Mott Foundation: From Community Service to Community Organizing, Foundation Watch*. Retrieved from https://www.capitalresearch.org/2012/03/10910/

Charles Stewart Mott Foundation. (2010). 2010 annual report. In *Striking a Balance: Supporting Innovative Ideas versus Sustaining Basic Needs*. Davison, MI: The Riegel Press.

Charles Stewart Mott Foundation. (2012). *Our values*. Retrieved from http://www.mott.org/about/values/ourvalues

Cheng, J. (2009). *Study: Twitter users are mobile, urban, and engaged online*. Washington, DC: *Pew* Research Center's Internet & American Life Project. Retrieved from http://arstechnica.com/business/2009/02/study-twitter-users-are-mobile-urban-and-engaged-online/

Clairborne, L., & TRU. (2007). *Tech abuse in teen relationships study*. Retrieved from http://www.loveisnotabuse.com/pdf/06-208Tech RelationshipAbuseTPL.pdf

Clean Cut Media. (2009). *YouTube statistics: Where did my time go?* Retrieved from http://www.cleancutmedia.com/video/youtube-statistics-the-ultimate-time-suck

Crystal, D. (2012). The evolution of language on the web. *Webcopyplus*. Retrieved from http://blog.webcopyplus.com/2010/08/30/the-evolution-of-language-on-the-web/

Dachus Group/XPLANE. The Economist, McLeod, S., Fishch, K., & Berstler, L. (2009). *Did you know 4.0?* Retrieved from http://www.youtube.com/watch?v=6ILQrEWe8

Davies, A., Fidler, D., & Gorbis, M. (2011). *Future work skills 2020*. Palo Alto, CA: Institute for the Future for University of Phoenix Research Institute. Retrieved from http://cdn.theatlantic.com/static/front/docs/sponsored/phoenix/future_work_skills_2020.pdf

Digitalsurgeons. (2010). *Facebook vs. twitter: A breakdown of 2010 social demographics*. Retrieved from http://www.digitalsurgeons.com/Facebook-vs-twitter-infographic/

Duxbury, P. (2012). How to use twitter. *Squidoo*. Retrieved from http://www.squidoo.com/how-to-use-twitter

EDUCAUSE. (2006). 7 things you should know about... YouTube. *EDUCAUSE Learning Initiative*. Retrieved from http://net.educause.edu/ir/library/pdf/ELI7018.pdf

El-Ghareeb, H., & Riad, A. (2011). Empowering adaptive lectures through activation of intelligent and web 2.0 technologies. *International Journal on E-Learning*, *10*(4), 365–391.

Fisch, K., McLeod, S., & Bestler, L. (2009) *Did you know?* Retrieved from http://www.youtube.com/watch?v=6ILQrUrEWe8

Fisch, K., McLeod, S., & Bestler, L. (2011). *Shifthappens*. Retrieved from http://shifthappens.wikispaces.com/

Fox, S. (2011). *Peer-to-peer healthcare*. Washington, DC: Pew Research Center's Internet & American Life Project. Retrieved from http://www.pewinternet.org/Reports/2011/P2PHealthcare.aspx

Fox, S., & Purcell, K. (2010). *Chronic disease and the internet*. Washington DC: Pew Research Center's Internet & American Life Project. Retrieved from http://www.pewinternet.org/Reports/2010/Chronic-Disease/Part-3.aspx?view=all

Grosseck, G. (2009). To use or not to use web 2.0 in higher education? In *Proceedings of the World Conference on Educational Sciences, New Trends and Issues in Educational Sciences*. Nicosia, Cyprus: Elsevier.

Halsey, A. (2012). Teen drivers are texting just like their parents. *Washington Post Local*. Retrieved from http://www.washingtonpost.com/local/trafficandcommuting/teen-drivers-are-texting-just-like-their-parents/2012/05/13/gIQA8raQNU_story.html

Halsey, M. (2011). *Who really uses Facebook and Twitter*. Retrieved from http://www.ghacks.net/2011/02/15/who-really-uses-Facebook-twitter/

Harasim, L. (2012). *Learning theories and online technologies*. New York, NY: Routledge Taylor & Francis Group.

Hinduja, S., & Patchin, J. W. (2010). Sexting: A brief guide for educators and parents. *2010 Cyberbullying Research Group*. Retrieved from http://www.cyberbullying.us/Sexting_Fact_Sheet.pdf

i-SAFE, Inc. (2012). *Cyber bullying: Statistics and tips*. Retrieved from http://www.isafe.org/outreach/media/media_cyber_bullying

Jain, S. H., Goyal, R., Fox, S., & Shrank, W. H. (2012). Bowling alone, healing together: The role of social capital in delivery reform. *The American Journal of Managed Care*. Retrieved from http://www.ajmc.com/articles/Bowling-Alone-Healing-Together-The-Role-of-Social-Capital-in-Delivery-Reform?utm_source=Mailing+List&utm_campaign=d1c4c7686c-Newsletter_06282012&utm_medium=email

Johnson, K. D. (2012). *Financial crimes against the elderly: Problem-oriented guides for police specific guide series*. Washington, DC: U.S. Department of Justice Office of Community-Oriented Policing Services. Retrieved from http://www.popcenter.org/problems/pdfs/crimes_against_elderly.pdf

Lenhart, A., & Fox, S. (2009). *11% of online adults use Twitter or update their status online*. Washington DC: Pew Research Center's Internet & American Life Project. Retrieved from http://www.pewinternet.org/Reports/2009/Twitter-and-status-updating/Part-1/Section-2.as

Lenhart, M. M., Macgill, A. R., & Smith, A. (2007). *Teens and social media*. Washington, DC: Pew Research Center's Internet & American Life Project. Retrieved from http://www.pewinternet.org/PPF/r/230/report_display.asp

Lomas, C., Burke, M., & Page, D. L. (2008). Collaboration tools. *EDUCAUSE Learning Initiative*. Retrieved from http://net.educause.edu/ir/library/pdf/ELI3020.pdf

Madden, M., & Lenhart, A. (2009). *Teens and distracted driving*. Washington DC: Pew Research Center's Internet & American Life Project. Retrieved from http://pewinternet.org/~/media//Files/Reports/2009/PIP_Teens_and_Distracted_Driving.pdf

Mohawk College Library. (2012). How to evaluate websites. *The Brain*. Retrieved from http://brain.mohawkcollege.ca/FindInformation/websites/HowToEvaluateWebsitesForResearch.html

Paas, F. (1992). Training strategies for attaining transfer of problem-solving skill in statistics: A cognitive load approach. *Journal of Educational Psychology*, *84*, 429–434. doi:10.1037/0022-0663.84.4.429

Paas, F., Renkl, A., & Sweller, J. (2003). Cognitive load theory and instructional design: Recent developments. *Educational Psychologist*, *38*, 1–4. doi:10.1207/S15326985EP3801_1

Paas, F., Tuovinen, J., van Merriënboer, J. J. G., & Darabi, A. (2005). A motivational perspective on the relation between mental effort and performance: Optimizing learner involvement in instruction. *Educational Technology Research and Development*, *53*, 25–34. doi:10.1007/BF02504795

Paas, F., Tuovinen, J. E., Tabbers, H., & Van Gerven, P. (2003). Cognitive load measurement as a means to advance cognitive load theory. *Educational Psychologist*, *38*(1), 63–71. doi:10.1207/S15326985EP3801_8

Paas, F., & Van Gog, T. (2006). Optimising worked example instruction: Different ways to increase germane cognitive load. *Learning and Instruction*, *16*, 87–91. doi:10.1016/j.learninstruc.2006.02.004

Rainie, L. (2011). *The social side of the internet*. Washington, DC: Pew Internet & Life Project. Retrieved from http://www.pewinternet.org/Press-Releases/2011/Social-Side-of-the-Internet.aspx

Rose, D. S., & Brenman, J. XPLANE, Sony/BMG, the Economist, McLeod, S., Bestler, L., & Fisch, K. (2012). *Shifthappens, 6.0: Did you know?* Retrieved from http://www.youtube.com/watch?v=XVQ1ULfQawk

Smith, A. (2011). *The internet and campaign 2010*. Washington, DC: Pew Research Center's Internet & American Life Project. Retrieved from http://pewinternet.org/Reports/2011/The-Internet-and-Campaign-2010.aspx

Smith, A. (2012a). *17% of cell phone owners do most of their online browsing on their phone, rather than a computer or other device*. Washington DC: Pew Research Center's Internet & American Life Project. Retrieved from http://pewinternet.org/Reports/2012/Cell-Internet-Use-2012.aspx

Smith, A. (2012b). *46% of American adults are smartphone owners*. Washington DC: Pew Research Center's Internet & American Life Project. Retrieved from http://pewinternet.org/~/media//Files/Reports/2012/Smartphone%20ownership%202012.pdf

Smith, A. (2012c). *17% of cell phone owners do most of their online browsing on their phone rather than a computer or other device*. Washington, DC: Pew Research Center's Internet & American Life Project. Retrieved from http://www.pewinternet.org/~/media//Files/Reports/2012/PIP_Cell_Phone_Internet_Access.pdf

Smith, A., & Brenner, J. (2012). *Twitter use 2012*. Washington DC: Pew Research Center's Internet & American Life Project. Retrieved from http://pewinternet.org/~/media//Files/Reports/2012/PIP_Twitter_Use_2012.pdf

Smith, C. (2010). Twitter stats reveal few Americans use Twitter, although most know it (STUDY). *Huffington Post*. Retrieved from http://www.huffingtonpost.com/2010/04/30/twitter-stats-reveal-few_n_557587.html

Stibel, J. (2009). Introduction. In *Wired for Thought*. Boston, MA: Harvard Business Press.

Sweller, J. (1988). Cognitive load during problem solving: Effects on learning. *Cognitive Science*, *12*(2), 257–285. doi:10.1207/s15516709cog1202_4

Sweller, J. (1989). Cognitive technology: some procedures for facilitation learning and problem solving in mathematics and science. *Journal of Educational Psychology*, *81*, 457–466. doi:10.1037/0022-0663.81.4.457

Sweller, J. (1999). *Instructional design in technical areas*. Camberwell, Australia: ACER Press.

Sweller, J., & Chandler, P. (1991). Evidence for cognitive load theory. *Cognition and Instruction*, *8*(4), 351–362. doi:10.1207/s1532690xci0804_5

Sweller, J., & Chandler, P. (1994). Why some material is difficult to learn. *Cognition and Instruction*, *12*(3), 185–233. doi:10.1207/s1532690xci1203_1

Sweller, J., Chandler, P., Tierney, P., & Cooper, M. (1990). Cognitive load and selective attention as factors in the structuring of technical material. *Journal of Experimental Psychology. General*, *119*, 176–192. doi:10.1037/0096-3445.119.2.176

Sweller, J., & Cooper, G. A. (1985). The use of worked examples as a substitute for problem solving in learning algebra. *Cognition and Instruction*, *2*(1), 59–89. doi:10.1207/s1532690xci0201_3

Sweller, J., van Merrienboer, J., & Paas, F. W. (1998). Cognitive architecture and instructional design. *Educational Psychology Review*, *10*(3), 251–296. doi:10.1023/A:1022193728205

Toffler, A. (1969). Toffler quotes. *Alvin + Heidi Toffler Futurists*. Retrieved from http://www.alvintoffler.net/?fa=galleryquotes

United States Department of Justice. (2012). *Identify theft and identity fraud*. Retrieved from http://www.justice.gov/criminal/fraud/websites/idtheft.html

YouTube. (2012). *Animated infographic of Facebook statistics*. Retrieved from http://www.youtube.com/watch?v=XKTfCjMsUNc

YouTube.com. (2010). *YouTube fact sheet*. Retrieved from http://frameconcepts.com/youtube-fact-sheet

Zickuhr, K., Raine, L., Purcell, K., Madden, M., & Brenner, J. (2012). *Libraries, patrons and e-books*. Washington DC: Pew Research Center's Internet & American Life Project. Retrieved from http://libraries.pewinternet.org/files/legacy-pdf/PIP_Libraries_and_Ebook_Patrons%206.22.12.pdf

Chapter 2
Use of Information Technology in Organizational Learning:
Effective Practices of Award-Winning Organizations

Lila Holt
University of Tennessee, USA

Jeffrey Beard
University of Tennessee, USA

Debra S. Lee
Vanderbilt University, USA

ABSTRACT

Education and development in the workplace that promotes continual improvement is vital for sustainability and performance excellence for 21st century organizations. Likewise, organizational learning has become a focal point for organizations to quickly adapt to global markets and dynamic economies. Using two theoretical frameworks, the 2010 and 2011 National Baldrige Award Winners' applications and websites are examined to better understand how technology can support organizational learning. Information technologies are classified through the use of Huber's (1991) constructs, while Argyris and Schön's (1978) double-loop learning theory becomes a foundation for examining continuous improvement within organizations. Results indicate technology is an integral part of the Baldrige Award Winners' day-to-day processes and the improvement thereof is a focal point for these organizations. While technology itself does not create a winning organization, appropriate use of technology enables an organization to track the processes that lead to customer satisfaction, thus enabling the organization to be both innovative and agile in the global workplace.

DOI: 10.4018/978-1-4666-2955-4.ch002

INTRODUCTION

Knowledge and learning are at the core of performance excellence for 21st century organizations. Within the United States, a partnership of the public and private sectors to promote organizational excellence, the Baldrige Performance Excellence Program, was founded as an award program by Congress in 1987. The purpose of the Baldrige program is threefold—to "identify and recognize role-model businesses," "establish criteria for evaluating improvement efforts," and "disseminate and share best practices." These points support the Baldrige program's primary goal of enhancing US business competitiveness in a global economy. Included within the award criteria is a focus on organizational learning (US Department of Commerce, 2012). This chapter examines recent Baldrige Award winners' applications and public websites to investigate technologies as used for learning within the organizations. An overview of how the Baldrige program focuses on learning opens this chapter and is then followed by the theoretical frameworks for organizational learning in relationship to the Baldrige criteria. The program criteria and theoretical frameworks reviewed become the foundation for exploring technologies currently available for use in organizational learning. The technologies used by the Baldrige Award winning organizations to promote learning for performance excellence follow in a subsequent section. The conclusion of the chapter summarizes important takeaways for organizations and looks at the impact of technology use on education and professional development.

BALDRIGE AWARD CRITERIA AND LEARNING

The Baldrige criteria examine organizations via a systems approach. The application for the award includes an organizational profile in which important factors key to the organization performance are described. Following the profile, seven categories that comprise the model are addressed by the applicants. The first six categories (1. Leadership, 2. Strategic Planning, 3. Customer Focus, 4. Measurement, Analysis, and Knowledge Management, 5. Workforce Focus, and 6. Operation Focus) concentrate on processes, or the integration of people, tools, and techniques used to create the resulting product or services. Category 7, Results, concentrates on the organizational performance outcomes.

Within the process categories, award applicants describe, and Baldrige examiners evaluate, the processes based on four factors: approach, deployment, learning, and integration. While approach, deployment, and integration may have clearer definitions, a look at how Baldrige defines learning is needed. Learning encompasses "refining your approach through cycles of evaluation and improvement," " encouraging breakthrough change to your approach through innovation," and "sharing refinements and innovations with other relevant work units and processes in your organization" (US Department of Commerce, 2011, p. 66). The criteria guide further notes that:

[a]chieving the highest levels of organizational performance requires a well-executed approach to organizational and personal learning that includes sharing knowledge via systematic processes. Organizational learning includes both continuous improvement of existing approaches and significant change or innovation, leading to new goals and approaches (US Department of Commerce, 2011, p. 51).

By embedding learning into the daily operations at the organizational level, results can include improved products and value to customers, new business models and opportunities, reduction in errors and cycle times, as well as increasing effective use of resources (US Department of Commerce, 2011).

THEORETICAL FRAMEWORKS OF ORGANIZATIONAL LEARNING

Within theoretical frameworks for organizational learning, a definition of organizational learning is provided below, as well as the concepts of single and double loop learning (Argyris & Schön, 1978) and Huber's (1991) constructs through the lens of the Baldrige criteria.

Organizational Learning

To fully understand organizational learning, the term organization must first be defined. An organization is "a structured, coordinated, and goal-oriented social entity which is brought into existence and sustained in an ongoing way by humans" (Sun, 2003, p. 155). Thus organizational learning is a "learning process of an organization and by the organization in a collective (organizational) way" (Sun, 2003, p. 156). In organizational learning, knowledge is retained in an organizational memory; thus, when members leave the organization the knowledge is not lost. The learning influences both immediate members as well as the future members via the retained experiences and history (Balasubramanian, 2012).

Although many definitions of organizational learning can be found in current research, Sun (2003) defines learning as an active and constructive process. "Learners are not passive recipients of information. They are sense makers who actively construct their knowledge and skills through integration with the environment and through reorganization of their own mental structures" (pp. 154-155). As with the Baldrige criteria, Sun theorizes that the learner turns information into knowledge and creates change based on that knowledge. Thus, in organizational learning, organizations are not passive recipients of improvement. Rather the organization plans for, and incorporates cycles of improvements to not only keep the day-to-day information current, but also to keep processes current and innovative. The organization also plans and incorporates receptacles for memory. In the case of the Baldrige criteria, this may be done through the documentation of processes or retained through defined plans for employee succession.

Single and Double-Loop Learning

Within the Baldrige criteria, the process of organizational learning not only leads to reduction of errors and cycle times, but also to new goals and processes. Argyris and Schön (1978) describe this process as single-loop and double-loop learning. In single-loop learning, organizational learning occurs when errors are detected and corrected and organizations carry on with their present policies and goals. Double-loop learning occurs when, in addition to detection and correction of errors, the organization is involved in the questioning and modification of existing norms, procedures, policies, and objectives. Critical reflection is part of double- loop learning (Walsh, Hegarty, & Kelly, 2011). The Baldrige process itself can be used for double-loop learning as, along with criteria requesting information about learning processes, by writing the Baldrige application, the organization must reflect on and review their key factors, processes, and results.

Constructs of Organizational Learning

Huber (1991) provides four constructs, which contribute to organizational learning. The four constructs encompass the processes that lead to organizational memory and include: a) knowledge acquisition, b) information distribution, c) information interpretation, and d) organizational memory. More specifically, the constructs can be defined as follows:

- **Information Distribution:** A process where information is shared among teams and team members. The process promotes learning to create new knowledge and understanding.

- **Information Interpretation:** A process where distributed information takes on understood meanings by the teams and team members. Shared information is interpreted by individuals and teams and given meaning for the organization.
- **Knowledge Acquisition:** From the interpretations of the data, the outcome is the acquisition of knowledge that is used to advance and change the organization.
- **Organizational Memory:** After acquiring knowledge, the knowledge must be retained for future use. Organizational memory is the repository of the acquired knowledge. The methods of retention vary by organization.

While the Baldrige criteria account for active, planned organizational learning, according to Huber, learning need not be conscious or intentional. In applying for the Baldrige award, however, companies reflect on their processes, which effectively enables a company to take into account unconscious or unintentional organizational learning of the type Huber includes in his theoretical framework.

Within the Baldrige criteria, Huber's same constructs can be identified within the different process categories. Organizations answer questions, which encompass reflection on processes of distribution and interpretation to create acquisition of knowledge when applying for the Baldrige Award, so not only is reflection on processes a method of double-loop learning, but the resulting document also creates memory within an organization. The results section then requires an assessment of the accumulation of the knowledge acquisition over time (thus creating a memory) to reflect and analyze the effectiveness of the process outcomes.

For example, the customer focus category of the Baldrige criteria (US Department of Commerce, 2011) asks: "How do you listen to customers to obtain actionable information?" (p. 13). The use of *obtain* in the question may be equated to a distribution of information from the customer to the organization, Huber's first construct. A further question asks, "How do you determine customer satisfaction and engagement?" (p.13). Thus, the determining satisfaction and engagement calls for a look at Huber's second construct, knowledge interpretation, through an interpretation of previously obtained customer satisfaction data. Subsequently the Baldrige applicant is then asked, "How do your measurements capture actionable information ...?" (p. 13). The capturing of actionable information requires that interpretation of the information be made to determine future actions thus acquiring knowledge and further more storing it (memory) in measurements, Huber's third construct. The results section then draws on the organizational memory of measurements to create histories of trends (p. 24), Huber's fourth construct of organizational memory. While the above examples are taken from Category 3, Customer Focus, similar comparisons from the other Baldrige process categories and results can be drawn from these constructs.

ORGANIZATIONAL LEARNING FRAMEWORKS AND TECHNOLOGY

When considering Huber's constructs of information distribution, interpretation, knowledge acquisition, and organizational memory, a natural consequence of the constructs consists of the technologies that may be used to support the constructs. The section following describes technologies that support each construct and lay the foundation for the examination of technologies the 2010 Baldrige winners used for organizational learning.

Information Distribution

Many technologies are available for information distribution, including technologies available for dissemination, collaboration, training, and business applications. While it would be impossible to cover each package available, a summary of some of the most commonly used, as well as some of the emerging technologies, are presented here. Information distribution technologies can create double-loop learning; however, most are single-loop with an emphasis on correcting errors within the given policies and norms.

Dissemination Technologies

Dissemination technologies are used to distribute information, much as hard-copy memos are used in an office. Information can be posted on a bulletin board for organization members to read or distributed via email. While dissemination technologies may be used for training and other purposes, they most commonly transmit up-to-date, general information. A sample of technologies available for information dissemination is presented in Table 1.

Collaboration Technologies

With the popularity of the Internet, many collaboration technologies have been created and are now used by organizations for collaboration. While several of these technologies have emerged as social communication tools, they can also be used for collaboration in an organization. Technologies for real-time interactive collaboration as well as asynchronous interactions are available. Note the overlap between technologies useable for both dissemination and collaboration. The technology is less important than how the organization chooses to use the technology. Table 2 provides examples.

Table 1. Information distribution (dissemination) technologies

Technology	Description
Email	Electronic mail has replaced paper memos and telephone calls to become the most used form of communication in business. Thoughts can be effectively communicated between two people or shared between groups of people. The communication is documented and archived for future reference.
Websites	Websites can be on the Internet (World Wide Web) or on an intranet (a private server for only company access). Websites can be used for the dissemination of corporate information or for sharing information with select personnel for training purposes. The Websites can be designed for use with computers (e.g., desktop, laptop, or tablets) or mobile applications (e.g., cell phones).
Social Media	Through Web media, social networking is available for distributing information.
Blogs	Weblogs, more commonly called blogs, are websites containing dated entries posted in reverse chronological order, which are continuously updated by the author. The entries are the personal thoughts and opinions of the author, which is usually one person but can be more. The author(s) may allow comments from readers, but has control over the information posted.
Electronic Newsletters	Electronic newspapers have replaced the paper newsletters of the past, but are formatted much the same. The electronic newsletters allow for immediate distribution to large populations through email. There is also the added benefit of providing concise information in articles and having hyperlinks to more information on the Internet. This allows for creatively developed newsletters that are content rich with pleasing aesthetics minus the publication and distribution costs of print-based newsletters.
Schedules/ Calendars	Online calendars allow for organizing tasks and planning of events and meetings. They can be accessed from various locations by computer or cell phone. Email clients (e.g., Microsoft Outlook) have this feature built in and can alert users of meeting times and tasks due.

Table 2. Information distribution (collaboration)

Technology	Description
Instant Messaging	Instant Messaging (IM) allows for synchronous (real time) text communication between one or more people. This can be used through the Internet, intranet, or cell phone networks. It is faster than email for short communication and allows the participants to stay on task while communicating in business settings. The conversation is archived and can be used for further reference.
Email	When more information needs to be shared or participants are not available for synchronous communication, email is more effective than IM. Two or more participants can share multiple forms of data (e.g., text, images, charts, etc.) and are able to work together asynchronously as they are able.
Websites	Websites are becoming more and more interactive. Many sites allow visitors to create accounts to allow for customized and personal interaction with the site. These accounts also serve to provide feedback to organizations as to visitor demographics.
Social media	Additional collaboration can occur via the social media sites. These sites allow for posting messages by both the organization and others who choose to respond. Reading posts made by customers on social sites also support learning and needed change within an organization.
Threaded Discussions	Threaded discussions are posted on a Website and can be open for comments from all parties or the thread owner can control access. Threaded discussions allow participants to see each other's posts in a hierarchical form. The dialogues and discussions are recorded and participants can see comments and replies posted in a conversational flow. The threads are normally organized by specific content so that participants can remain on topic.
Web Conferencing	Web conferencing has replaced the need for costly travel. Participants are able to join people in other locations via Internet connections. Tools include online whiteboards where participants can communicate writing on the board with their mouse, keyboard, or touch pads or by sharing computer screens. Other possibilities include talking to each other while viewing a presentation or using live video enabling participants to see one another on screen. Conversations can be with everyone participating, in small groups, or between two people.
Wikis	The word "wiki" is Hawaiian for quick or fast and was chosen to describe a website that is quick or fast to develop and edit. Basic wikis are free with pay options available for more features. The wiki websites are hosted online and can have multiple authors with editing rights making it a great tool for collaborating. No Web design skills are needed as only basic word processing skills are needed. The basic concept is "edit, write, save" meaning select "edit mode," then write (type or insert) desired content and select "save." Photos, videos, and other forms of media are easily added. Wikis are an effective and affordable means to an Internet presence. These sites differ from standard websites in that they are usually created by participation and collaboration as opposed to websites, which are made by Webmasters.

Training Technologies

Training technologies provide focused information distribution, focusing on training materials identified as needed for on the job performance. While training technologies can be similar to dissemination and collaboration technologies, they differ in the focus on training of employees, rather than information dissemination or collaborative work teams. Instead of employees traveling to attend a course on negotiation strategies, organizations can save travel costs by using online training. The reduced travel costs for face-to-face training means that organizations can, and do, integrate eLearning within their training structures. Table 3 describes example technologies for training.

Business Application Technologies

Business application technologies are more commonly used when considering information distribution. They include information processing programs, such as spreadsheets, that guide the flow of business. Order processing, inventory, and accounting software, as well as other custom applications create avenues for information distribution. These technologies can be used to create single loop learning. To discover the business rules and process flow of an organization, one can examine these programs. These same programs can be a stumbling block to double-loop learning. Organizations incorporating continuous single-loop learning may become blinded and fail to see the need for double-loop learning. For example,

Table 3. Information distribution (training)

Technology	Description
eLearning	eLearning can take many forms, but is simply learning that is delivered through a stand-alone computer, Internet, or intranet (electronic learning). Examples include courses learners complete autonomously or instructor facilitated courses that utilize email, threaded discussions, and instant messaging. Webinars and Web conferencing are also eLearning options. Online distance learning has become a viable method for degree programs. Web-based training is now popular in industry as numerous employees can be trained simultaneously without having to leave their work environment for a classroom environment.
Simulations	A variety of simulation technologies exist with virtual simulations as a newer form of online learning environment. Initially developed for gaming, participants can interact as if they are in real world environments. Participants establish a profile and in some environments even create a personal avatar and then can log in to various virtual classrooms or learning scenarios. These simulations are used by universities and corporations as an approach to situations difficult to replicate in traditional educational settings.
eLearning Portals	Portals are usually intranet access points where tools and documents used by learners can be organized. Items consist of such things as class rosters, grade books, email exchange, places to post course materials as well as some collaboration tools. These types of training technologies are utilized by educational facilities, as well as larger organizations.

a company may go to great lengths to make sure a particular document they have produced for years is correct. However, without double-loop learning, they may fail to realize the document is actually no longer used or needed. Some of these business applications are time consuming and costly to develop (i.e. a customized business analysis package), so changing the policies and underlying rules to eliminate these technologies can become the stumbling blocks of organizational change (see Table 4).

Information Interpretation

The second of Huber's (1991) constructs is interpreting the information. (Levine & Monarch, 1998) note that "[o]rganizations are dependent on their members in that it is the free flow of ideas and interaction of individuals that form the creative source for organization learning" (p. 444). In his article Balasubramanian states:

Very often, the decision-making process is not fully captured in organizations but only the endpoint or outcomes of the process (except in the meeting minutes noted by one individual which may or may not be easily accessible at a later date). When information is required about the rationale behind certain decisions made earlier, such information may not be fully available at a later date. The ability to review and question the rationale behind decisions made earlier is the basis behind double-loop learning (Balasubramanian, 2012).

Creating meaning from previous and current information is the focus of this construct. So what technologies exist that can aid an individual in information interpretation? Several technologies,

Table 4. Information distribution (business applications)

Technology	Description
Business Applications	Extremely varied and more traditional information technologies, these applications create the reports and financial records for an organization. Examples include accounts payable, receivables, and payroll applications.
Project Management	The day-to-day applications, which are designed to manage the organization's personnel and resources, such as calendars and job tracking systems.
Groupware	These newer technologies are a confluence of collaboration software and project management software, as well as customizable ways to distribute information. These packages are usually proprietary.

used for different purposes for dissemination, collaboration, training, and business applications could also be useful for interpretation (see Table 5).

Knowledge Acquisition

The third of Huber's constructs is that of knowledge acquisition.

Organizational learning occurs when we create an organizational knowledge base, firm-specific competencies, and routines. Knowledge-bases are created by acquiring, storing, interpreting, and manipulating information both from within and outside the organization (Balasubramanian, 2012).

Identifying successful information technologies that are available for knowledge acquisition usually stems from the other constructs. Tom Butler (2003) notes "[r]esearchers in the field of information systems view IT-enabled knowledge management solutions as novel approaches to the stimulation of creativity and the innovation in post-industrial organizations." Thus, these knowledge management systems can be used to innovate. Innovation, under the Baldrige criteria, is a factor in performance excellence. While information technology has sought to develop entire knowledge-based systems, today's systems have become a collection of searchable distributed databases. Butler (2003) notes, however, that recent research indicates that many knowledge management systems are unsuccessful. Malhotra (1996) in his article Tools@work states that "in the last 20 years, U.S. industry has invested more than $1 trillion in technology but has realized little improvement in the efficiency or effectiveness of its knowledge works." (Malhotra, 1996) (see Table 6).

Organizational Memory

The fourth construct incorporates the underlying memory for the other three constructs of distribution, interpretation, and acquisition. While some organizations are dependent on individuals for organizational learning, information technologies are also available to organizations and individuals to create more permanent and residual histories. A few of these technologies are listed in Table 7.

Table 5. Information interpretation technologies

Technology	Description
Statistical Analysis	These technologies aid in the interpretation of information. Spreadsheets as well as other tools are used to create summaries for organizational members to interpret.
Collaboration Technologies	These are the same technologies used to collaborate and distribute information above. The communication now changes focus from distribution of information to team collaboration for interpretation.
Simulations	Again, this is the same technology as above, but now put to a different use. The focus turns from training to collaborative interpretation of different scenarios to test various interpretations of information. Some of the newer virtual reality simulation technologies can create diverse and interesting test case scenarios.

Table 6. Knowledge acquisition technology

Technology	Description
Knowledge Based Systems/ Databases	Also referred to as expert systems. The current expert systems have taken on the form of question/answer databases, which are structured information systems that provide the underlying components of business applications. The information is searchable by keywords and contains organizational transaction history.

Table 7. Organization memory technology

Technology	Description
Databases	These are structured information systems, which provide the underlying components of business applications. As information is processed and stored in the databases, the databases become a foundation for an organization's memory.
Operational Systems and Collaboration Documentation	The written documentation from business applications as well as from the collaboration interactions holds the history of the interpretations and knowledge from previous decisions and interactions. These records create the memories that will be available after the individuals creating them have moved on.
Libraries	These are online catalogs of information similar to the databases. Libraries traditionally contain the documents of the organization. Examples would be by-laws and meeting notes.
Courses	The actual training courses contain the history of organization training information. They are the basis for organizational business and functional (learning necessary for physical job function) learning.
Cases	The history of various problems and solutions of the organization can be stored online for recall.
Records	Business and transactions that have occurred are recorded. They usually consist of information that needs summarization and interpretation.
Intranet and Websites	Marketing and information as presented on the Internet and internally for organizational use.
Wikis	As discussed previously, these specialty websites can be created for collaboration. The sites resulting from this collaboration contain the information and discussions that are searchable for later recall.

A visual representation of the four Huber constructs of information distribution, information interpretation, knowledge acquisition, and organizational memory demonstrates that the constructs should not be seen as linear. Constant information exchange and redistribution are essential for award-winning organizations (see Figure 1).

BALDRIGE AWARD WINNERS: TECHNOLOGY AND ORGANIZATIONAL LEARNING

To determine how award-winning organizations are using technology to support organizational learning, an analysis of the application summaries of the 2010 and 2011 Baldrige Award winners was conducted. The completed application summaries are available publically on the national Baldrige site—http://www.baldrige.nist.gov/Contacts_Profiles.htm. Eleven organizations were recognized as award winners during those two years. The winners are identified as one of the following classifications: non-profit, health care, manufacturing, small business, and education. While some of the applications might fit in more than one classification, (e.g., health care and non-profit) only one application was dually classified as non-profit with a business focus of manufacturing/distribution. For this analysis, the properties of the one specific non-profit were aligned with manufacturing and no major differences were noted.

The applications include an organizational profile, an overview of the processes used for business, and results in the classification categories previously mentioned. By Baldrige program requirements, these application summaries contain the most important facts and characteristics of the organization. While there is no expectation that all uses of technologies within the organization are present in the application, the information the organization provides is important for day-to-day organizational functioning. In addition to analyzing the applications, each company's website was investigated to provide an overview of company public Internet presence and usage.

Overall results of the analysis are presented in relationship to Huber's constructs. This is fol-

Figure 1. Huber's constructs and technology

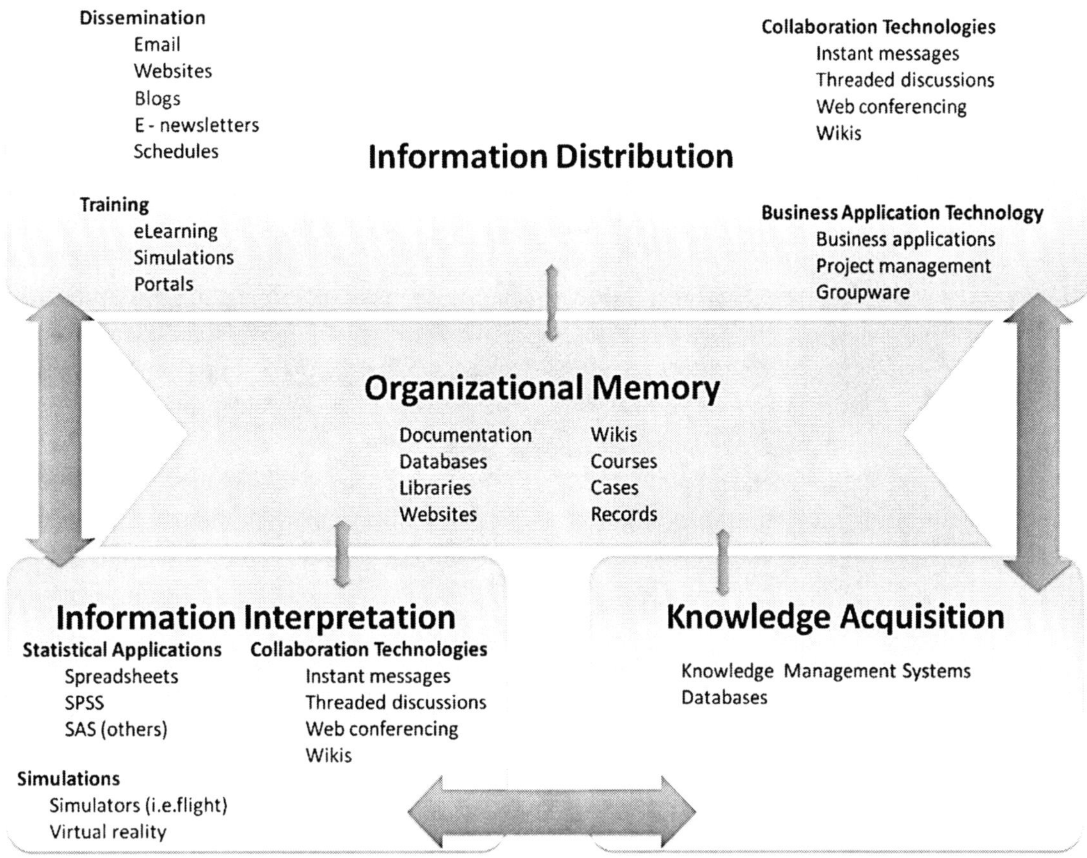

lowed by a focus on how the technologies vary by the classifications of the organizations. Instances of single-loop and double-loop learning as found in the application summaries are also discussed.

Baldrige Award Winners and Technology

In Baldrige Award winning organizations, use of technology does not just "happen." A concerted effort to promote innovation and improve business processes is at the very heart of the winning organizations. Teams and workgroups are designated to evaluate and promote innovation, and Baldrige winners support employees who initiate innovation with personal and workgroup awards. Of the 11 Award Winners, 10 applications specifically mentioned teams that met regularly to promote technical excellence. For example, one applicant stated, "teams meet six to eight times a year to improve their processes and review trends in methodologies, technologies, and regulations related to their discipline." While not all innovation is technology related, technology teams play a central role in the innovation teams. During the analysis, it was noted early on that technology itself was not a central focus. As demonstrated in the example above, technologies were used when to do so achieved a goal that the organization deemed appropriate when reviewing and improving processes. When taking a closer look at the technologies used within the processes, all four of Huber's constructs could be identified and are presented.

Huber Construct One: Information Distribution

Websites are tools focused on disseminating information and create an avenue for both one-way communication and collaboration. Together public Internet sites as well as company intranet networks support the business processes. Every Baldrige winner has a public presence on the Internet. While not all sites allowed for customer login, every site had contact information which allowed a visitor to contact the organization or for customers to pay their bills online. The organizations varied by the public and private information available. The amount of information for the general public varies by organizational categories of the award winners, although all websites were easy to navigate and understand. Additionally, the information on the sites appeared to be up-to-date.

Table 8 contains a summary of the website contents.

Within the organizational networks, each Award winner had supporting intranets and networking. Although only three of the organizations had employee logins on the public Internet sites, all applications summaries mentioned company intranets, which contained supporting information. For example, all winning organizations provided employee information about health insurance and benefits as well as employee handbooks. Additionally, two organizations mentioned providing special discounts for area attractions and/or various businesses. Additionally four of the organizations mentioned using the network technologies for recognition of employees' excellence in performance. In addition, within the organizations online surveys and anonymous suggestion forms are offered for employees to submit ideas and thoughts to the organization to create the avenue for two-way communication or collaboration. Although all organizations have employee surveys, ten specifically noted networked technologies.

Other technologies also support the information distribution capabilities within the winning organizations. All organizations use email for sending information, including electronic newsletters, interactive discussions, and collaboration technologies.

All but two organizations mentioned eLearning courses for conveying information to employees. Web and video conferencing were utilized to allow for communication and collaboration when a physical presence was not possible. All but four organizations receiving the Baldrige award have multiple locations either throughout the United States or internationally. Other examples of how the Web is used for information distribution by the award winners include:

- Project-based information systems are used to collect and disseminate data. Access to this data is available via portals that grant access by the necessary groups or organizational division.

Table 8. Baldrige winner website content

Content	# of sites (N=11)
Mission, Vision, and Values	10
Login for general public	3
Login for employees	3
Login for customers	6
Supporting information and outbound links	11
Ease of navigation	11
Up-To-Date	11
Contact information	11
Two-Way communication	11
Privacy information	4
Online bill pay	3
Apply for online account	5
Social Media – Facebook	6
Social Media –Twitter	7
Public press (newsletters)	10
YouTube video link	4
Video/not YouTube	2
LinkedIn	2
RSS feed	1
Mobile Application	1

- Client-specific portals containing all data about the client for ease of interaction with the client by the customer representative or project manager. Being able to provide top quality service to clients and customers was a high priority for all award winners.
- Ten of the 11 Award winners specifically mentioned technologies to track complaints and errors. These data are gathered and disseminated to support single-loop learning; that is, correcting the problems quickly and efficiently in a time effective manner. Additionally, the Baldrige Award winners monitored and improved the processes for listening to customers because the customers' voice is a focus for the winners.
- Five organizations specifically mentioned technologies to support marketing information portals for their sales systems and tracking of prospective clients/customers.

Huber Construct Two: Information Interpretation

Supported by a variety of technologies, information interpretation was critical in all of these award-winning organizations. Both packaged and custom business systems gathered data throughout the organizations. Statistical analysis with data comparisons and benchmarking were at the heart of interpreting information. Performance data as activities occurred within the organization were captured and through the use of the statistical tools were analyzed and then made available on the company intranets (or if intended for the general public on the Internet) for distribution. Due to confidentiality of some business processes and the removal of the information from the public versions of the application summaries available on the Baldrige website, this area of the analysis is limited. Additionally, while much data are presented about organizational functioning and results, the technologies used to interpret the data are not identified within the application summary. Due to this lack of technology identification of how information is incorporated within the Baldrige award winning organizations, to further identify specific technologies would require an in-depth exploration in person. However, such analysis was beyond the scope of this report.

Huber Construct Three: Knowledge Acquisition

Malhotra (1996) found that large repositories designed for knowledge acquisition did not appear to be economically positive and suggested question and answer databases as the emerging method for data acquisition. The analysis of the Baldrige winners revealed that this was indeed a primary method of knowledge acquisition. Baldrige organizations all used a variety of real-time searchable databases, which in effect created the knowledge base system through normal day-to-day business functions. Even though the database specifics were not identified in the application summaries, certain information was included in all databases, such as information on customers, employees, suppliers, and stakeholders as well as meeting notes and minutes detailing previous collaborations. Ease of use and effectiveness of searches were important to the organizations. For security and privacy reasons, access to the database systems vary by job function. Being able to restrict certain data was a requirement of the data systems used within the organizations.

Huber Construct Four: Organizational Memory

The technologies that process and retain data during the day-to-day activities of information distribution, information interpretation, and knowledge acquisition then become the foundation for organizational memory. Although each Baldrige winner approached technology use differently, the following examples of technologies that were used to retain data and information to create organizational memory that were highlighted in the winners' applications:

- **A wiki:** Created to contain general and historical information about products, customers, products.
- **Internal databases:** All award-winners use internal databases that support organizational processes and functions. For example, due to the nature of the focus on continuous improvement by the Baldrige award-winners, databases of information on best practices, process improvement, results, were readily available.
- **Learning Management Systems (LMS):** Four organizations tracked training and learning endeavors using LMS systems.
- **Electronic calendars:** Two organizations created organizational memory using electronic calendars. These calendars provided a historical timeline, as well as notes on people and places integrated in day-to-day processes.

Accurate and uniform data and accessibility of organizational memory were found in six of the Award winners. Examples from the applications include:

- **Screening and approval of entries:** Entries were vetted prior to placement in the databases to ensure historical data was correct.
- **Uniformity of communication standards:** One organization specifically mentioned uniformity among communication standards throughout the organization to simplify the support of hardware and software.

Technology by Award Classification

As might be expected, technology use and the focus of it in an organization differ by classification area and/or organization size. While the technologies were prevalent across all application summaries, differences noted by classification and size follow here. As a note about the external websites, the larger the organization, the more likely the external website is to allow visitors to create an account and track various their personal accounts. For example, a large health care Award winner allows a community member to create an account and login to search for specific information. The account created may keep history of areas visited (such as symptom look up) that would be readily available to the user the next time they log in. This was true also of the larger manufacturing and education organizations, but was not noted within the small businesses. However, even the smaller businesses allowed logins for the customers to either pay a bill or purchase an item if appropriate.

Healthcare

Three of the four 2011 and one 2010 Baldrige award winners were healthcare organizations. As with all of the organizations evaluated here, the Internet and intranets played an important role in Huber's four constructs. Within the healthcare industry, however, notable differences occurred with training, customer feedback, interaction with suppliers (e.g., physicians) and system security.

Rapid advances in medicine create the need for continual learning for healthcare providers. Technology used to provide online training and simulations were at the forefront for healthcare organizations. For example, special technology enabled mannequins are used for building medical skills. The larger healthcare organizations, in particular, used technology to keep employee skills current.

Along with the training, the healthcare organizations focus was on customer (patient) satisfaction and feedback. In the largest of the winning healthcare organizations, electronic devices that interfaced with in-room televisions allowed patient input and this patient input was integrated into the healthcare management plan for the patient. Likewise, wireless technologies were specifically noted within the healthcare applications. For example, the use of wireless laptops to record patient information during examinations interfaced with patient databases to keep records accurate and up-to-date.

Another aspect of the winning organizations' information for most of the healthcare application summaries was the integration of suppliers' (e.g., physicians, home health care, nursing homes) data retrieval systems with the main healthcare system. These technologies allowed patient records to be readily available both at the hospital and when seeing doctors in their offices. While the integration with suppliers may also be found in other business type classifications, the use was not as prevalent as in the healthcare industry.

As might be expected, system technology security is a focal point in the healthcare application summaries. Both in the form of information duplication and privacy, attention was given in the application as to how these organizations plan and act to keep medical information secure and private.

Lastly, within the winning healthcare applications, the focus on current technologies and staying up-to-date was presented more strongly than in the other industry-type classifications. Organizational and double-loop learning was emphasized. This may be in part because not only do errors and out-of-date information affect business excellence, but in the healthcare field, not staying current may affect someone's health.

Manufacturing and Non-Profit

As with healthcare organizations, manufacturing organizations rely heavily on the Internet and intranet for information distribution. These networks allow for interaction with employees, suppliers, stakeholders, and the general public. The public websites provide not only information about the particular product being manufactured, but additional information supporting products and items of interest are also readily available for consumers. For example, a pet supply site contained information on breeds of animals, contact with veterinarians and/or question and answer discussions concerning pets that go beyond the supplies being offered. The public website also included press articles about the company and the achievements and awards received. Thus, within the large manufacturing companies, technology provides support in all aspects of the organization.

Education

Not only do the Baldrige award winning educational institutions utilize the Internet and intranet, there are also unique technology issues for them. Computer systems support educational business functions, as well as entire educational learning environments. For the educational award winner, excellence in communication with educators, parents, and students was provided via the Web technologies. Creating an integrated environment for learning for all stakeholders by providing login accounts to access assignments and other learning information as well as personal messages supported the communication endeavor.

Small Business

The websites of the small businesses focused more on their products and less on outside supporting functions than was found on large manufacturing websites. However, the small business/consulting companies helped support clients' technology needs. For example, one small business created subject matter Web pages for customers' websites.

Single-Loop and Double-Loop Learning of Award-Winners

Both single-loop and double loop learning can be identified within the Baldrige Award winning organizations. Data is captured in the business systems and then analyzed for errors in single-loop learning. Statistical and error managing software as well as management by exception support single-loop learning. Single-loop learning and continuous improvement is built into the processes of the award winners. As problems arise, there are integral procedures to make corrections and improvement quickly.

Double-loop learning can be identified via continued cycles of analysis and improvements of the business processes themselves. Baldrige award winners integrate workgroups or teams that review processes and reflect on business practices on a regular basis. Databases of the best practices are created as well as used during the improvement processes. It should be noted that in these award winners, time was a critical consideration for not only correcting errors in the single-loop learning but also for process and over all company improvements in double-loop learning. Technology was used to aid the organization in becoming more agile to meet the rapid change and adjustments faced in this global economy.

IMPACT ON EDUCATION AND PROFESSIONAL DEVELOPMENT

Drawing from the technologies and theoretical frameworks presented, the following suggestions are provided for organizations seeking to implement award-winning technology standards in their businesses.

Information Distribution

Baldrige award winners used technology to disseminate information. Within the award winners, the focus on regular cycles of business improvement was designed to incorporate regular technology updates to support innovation. Therefore, education and professional development should include facilitation to support learning of current and upcoming technologies. While it might be argued that the next generation of workers will naturally have skills to remain current with technology, the skills of the worker today may or may not have working knowledge of Web conferencing and similar technologies.

Information Interpretation

General basic skills of retrieving the proper data (database retrieval skills) as well as skills to use spreadsheets and other analysis tools are needed to support the benchmarking and other process performance indicators in business. These benchmarks and performance indicators are seen from senior management to the front line workers in the Baldrige award winners. Thus, workers should be able to use technologies and be able to understand and interpret benchmarks applicable to their job function.

Knowledge Acquisition

With knowledge acquisition reliant on database information retrieval, being able to properly search for answers to questions becomes critically important. Information is gathered in the systems; however, that information is worthless unless obtainable. Thus, techniques to provide for better searching are warranted. For example, simple logic functions of AND, OR, and NOT, the basis of information retrieval, might be included in professional development classes.

Organizational Memory

Technology facilitates the creation of organizational memory. While some workers may not be comfortable using technologies such as electronic calendars or even email, using them helps create the continuing organizational memory as opposed to handwritten notes jotted on scrap paper which are then thrown away. Professional development should focus on helping workers use such technology to create organizational memory and then subsequently use the technology to retrieve and interpret raw data.

CONCLUSION

Technology is an integral part of the Baldrige award winners' day-to-day processes and the improvement thereof is a focal point for these organizations. While technology itself does not create a winning organization, appropriate use of technology enables an organization to track the processes that lead to customer satisfaction, thereby enabling the organization to become respected for its innovation and business agility. This overview of how technologies are interwoven into the award-winning processes through information distribution, interpretation, knowledge acquisition, and organizational memory has demonstrated how these technologies impact organizational excellence. Learning was accomplished through single-loop learning of outcome improvement, as well as double-loop learning of process improvement for these Baldrige Award winners.

Using databases for knowledge acquisition and organizational memory, education and professional development should focus on information processes to store, retrieve, and interpret the captured data. The education and development of the workplace promoting continual improvement is vital for sustainability and performance excellence for 21st century organizations.

REFERENCES

Argyris, C., & Schön, D. (1978). *Organizational learning: A theory of action perspective*. Reading, MA: Addision Wesley. doi:10.2307/40183951

Balasubramanian, V. (2012). *Organizational learning and information systems*. Retrieved from http://www.e-papyrus.com/personal/orglrn.html

Butler, T. (2003). From data to knowledge and back again: Understanding the limitations of KMS. *Knowledge and Process Management, 10*, 144–155. doi:10.1002/kpm.180

Huber, G. P. (1991). Organizational learning: The contributing processes and the literatures. *Organization Science*, *2*(1), 88–115. doi:10.1287/orsc.2.1.88

Levine, L., & Monarch, I. (1998). *Collaborative technology in the learning organization: Integrating process with information flow, access and interpretation*. Paper presented at the Annual Hawaii International Conference on System Sciences (HICSS). Kohala Coast, HI.

Malhotra, Y. (1996). Organizational learning and learning organizations: An overview. *Knowledge Management Book*. Retrieved from http://www.kmbook.com/orglmg.htm

US Department of Commerce. NIST. (2011). *2011-2012 criteria for performance excellence*. Retrieved from http://www.nist.gov/baldrige/publications/criteria.cfm

US Department of Commerce. NIST. (2012). *Baldrige performance excellence program, 2012*. Retrieved from http://www.nist.gov/baldrige/

Walsh, A., Hegarty, M. P., & Kelly, H. (2011). Reflection in a workplace qualification: Challenges and benefits. *Journal of Workplace Learning*, *23*(8), 4.

Chapter 3
The Impact of New Technologies on Professional Development

Sarah T. Meltzer
Western Carolina University, USA

ABSTRACT

Professional development in schools is not a new concept; however, the impact of new technologies in the past two decades has shown it is important to incorporate research-based strategies in order to be effective. While strategies for curriculum-focused trainings may have been effective in the past, technology-focused training must take a different approach in the 21st century. Effective professional development will positively impact student achievement and is critical for sustainable school reform. This chapter addresses the importance of developing a new learning environment conducive to supporting professional development in technology. Key strategies necessary to support students' needs in the 21st century are explained. Without an emphasis on specific activities and opportunities throughout the phases of planning and implementation, professional development will not be sustainable and student achievement will not be impacted.

INTRODUCTION

The challenge to improve and sustain a quality educational experience for our children is a top priority for today's educators. While the past can provide insight and many good lessons, we cannot continue to do business as usual. Not only has society changed in many ways, but the tools we use and are expected to use have also evolved.

DOI: 10.4018/978-1-4666-2955-4.ch003

For centuries teachers successfully taught students to read and write using only paper, pencils, and chalkboards. With the influx of technologies in the late 20th century, teachers began to experience overhead projectors in their classrooms and access to the Internet somewhere in the school. These were introduced into schools as necessary new technologies. Within a very short period of time, we have seen teachers provided with classroom access to a variety of new technologies such as classroom computers with projectors, digital cameras, interactive whiteboards, and an assortment of technology-based instructional tools and software. The expectations for teachers to use these new technologies have been met with a variety of responses from teachers ranging from excitement and anticipation to fear and frustration of the unknown. Unfortunately, the knowledge to appropriately use these often unfamiliar devices to support instruction has not evolved in conjunction with their arrival.

Regardless of the focus of the training, effective professional development has been defined as "that which results in improvements in teachers' knowledge and instructional practice, as well as improved student learning outcomes" (Darling-Hammond, Jaquity, Midich, & Wei, 2010, p. 2). This impact of new technologies in schools has had a direct impact on the need for additional professional development. Unfortunately, this influx of hardware and software into schools has translated to additional demonstrations, vendor presentations, and one-shot workshops rather than effective and sustainable trainings or workshops for teachers. School administrators often blame the technology for being ineffective when this is not necessarily the case. It is important to consider and implement the key elements of effective professional development for sustainable, technology-based professional development.

The need for teachers to receive on-going professional development or in-service training throughout their teaching career is well supported by national, state, and local school organizations. Teachers attend trainings to learn new behavioral or instructional strategies as well as to learn the most effective ways to utilize new curriculum materials. However, when professional development becomes technology-focused rather than curriculum-based, the training is often inadequate and not effective. In many cases, teachers have had difficulty integrating technology into classroom instruction; although, they have had attended what was considered sufficient professional development. Traditionally, when professional development for new curriculum materials or a behavioral strategy is introduced into a school, a single workshop is provided to explain or demonstrate the expected outcome. While it may be effective to demonstrate how a new math textbook is organized and how a new manipulative may be used in math instruction, this is not an effective way to provide training for new math software. In the past, this has often been sufficient because the workshop participants were familiar with the curriculum content area and/or the goal and purpose of the new behavioral strategy. However, teachers rarely have experience in integrating technology into their classroom instruction. Generally, curriculum-focused workshops do not consist primarily of new information that is not based on the existing foundation knowledge of most teachers. This, however, is not the case with technology-focused workshops. Teachers often do not possess strong background knowledge of the hardware or software use when they come to the workshop. Consequently, the skills learned are not transferred to the classroom. Teachers may learn how to navigate through the software; however, they rarely learn how to actually implement the software effectively within the classroom setting. Essentially, teachers are often being expected to change how they teach. Without effective professional development, teachers will lack the skills to transfer this knowledge from the workshop setting to the classroom. This disconnection between curriculum-based professional development and technology-based professional development can substantially impact student achievement over time.

This chapter addresses the support and need for effective professional development and the necessity to include research-based strategies. Recommendations by national, state, and professional organizations support the integration of technology skills into classroom instruction. The term 'professional development' will be used interchangeably with 'training' and 'workshops' as these are used for similar activities in different school systems. Specific strategies and approaches will be discussed in relation to the areas of planning, implementation, and support of effective technology-based professional development in schools.

BACKGROUND/THEORETICAL FRAMEWORK

Effective teaching requires meeting the learning needs of children and positively impacting student academics as well as their emotional and behavioral well-being. According to Killion and Hirsh (2011), effective professional development "is the single most powerful pathway to promote continuous improvement in teaching." If the professional development is not aligned to the needs of the students, there will be minimal impact on student achievement. Consider children entering classrooms in the 21st century. They have very different interests and experiences from those of our parents and grandparents. In addition, these experiences are often very different from even today's experienced classroom teachers. For example, the Kaiser Family Foundation Study (Rideout, Foehr, & Roberts, 2010) reported that children ages 8-18 have greatly increased their media use over the last five years—they spend more than 7 hours per day multi-tasking with computers, TV, and music/audio forms of media. Moreover, 98% of all public schools have Internet access with a ratio of 3.1 students to instructional computers with Internet access (Snyder & Dillow, 2011). While many schools lack the variety of technologies such as interactive whiteboards or classroom response systems, they do have the basic foundation of technology such as computers and Internet access to support integration of instruction. Many schools also have digital cameras, projectors, and a variety of software available for students. However, without effective training, teachers will not (1) develop the comfort level to implement these strategies or (2) request additional new technologies. Having the technology does not necessarily mean teachers are using it effectively to meet the needs of the students.

Recognized national and professional organizations have responded to the change in students' needs and interests impacted by technology. Indeed, the International Society for Technology in Education (ISTE) established the National Educational Technology Standards (NETS) for teachers in 2008. These standards address the skills necessary for learning, teaching, and leading in the digital age and include specific behavioral objectives not only for students but also for teachers and administrations. According to ISTE, 49 of the 50 U.S. states have adopted, adapted, or referenced ISTE's NETS in state education documents (ISTE, 2008), indicating that schools are accepting and adopting the belief that technology integration into classrooms is important. However, very few states are holding teachers accountable for using the technology effectively.

Clearly, teachers need to be competent in the skills students need today to succeed in work and life. In order to identify appropriate expectations for teachers and students, states have developed their standards, assessments, and professional development programs to ensure that the 21st century skills are being met (Johnson, 2009). For example, the Partnership for 21st Century Skills developed their *21st Century Skills, Education & Competitiveness: A Resource and Policy Guide* (2008) to assist the process. This framework, developed from discussions with educators, community groups, and business leaders, identifies four components addressing necessary skills and knowledge for success in the 21st century: (1) core subjects and 21st century themes, (2) learning and innovation skills, (3) information, media, and technology skills, and (4) life and career skills. The Partnership encourages educators to advocate for these skills and infuse them into classroom instruction. In other words, these are not isolated topics but rather skills that should be considered regardless of the content being taught. Technology should be integrated as a tool and a resource to support student achievement. When computers were first introduced in to schools, they were often looked at as something added to the curriculum. Teachers would take time away from classroom instruction to "teach computers" or use a computer lab for "free" time. The identification of technology skills by ISTE and the Partnership have helped teachers better understand how the integration of technology into classroom instruction can have an impact on student achievement. Using technology as a tool or as a resource should not require extra time on the part of teachers. Once teachers learn how to use these tools effectively and integrate them into the classroom, students will be provided with more learning opportunities.

Effective professional development is defined as "that which results in improvements in teachers' knowledge and instructional practice, as well as improved student learning outcomes" (Wei, Darling-Hammond, Andree, Richardson, & Orphanos, 2009, p. 3). Learning Forward (formerly the National Staff Development Council) developed *Standards for Professional Learning* (2011) that further define professional development as a comprehensive, sustained, and intensive approach to improving teachers' and principals' effectiveness in raising student achievement. This widely recognized organization includes technology throughout its standards. The key element within these standards is the emphasis on educators taking an active role in their continuous development and their own learning. This is a very different approach from the old-school trainings, which were primarily stand-and-deliver. Too often, professional development in schools consist of a single one- to two-hour explanation or demonstration of a new program or curriculum material needing to be implemented in the classroom. Teachers who have some background in the topic are likely to be able to build on their foundation knowledge with this new information and implement the desired expectation with adequate results. However, when a new piece of technology or new strategy to use technology in the classroom is introduced, it is a very different story. Teachers do not necessarily have the background or confidence to be active learners and be successful with developing and supporting their own learning. While teachers know they should be transferring their new-learned skills to their classroom instruction, they have not necessarily internalized and processed the new skills enough to use them competently or comfortably in a classroom. Teachers are often reluctant to try new approaches with their students they have not practiced. It requires more than telling and demonstrating for teachers to learn these often alien new approaches to instruction.

While national, state, and local school organizations strongly recommend and endorse the inclusion of technology in classrooms, it is just not happening at the fast pace that students are using technology outside the classroom. Indeed, although the National Center for Educational Statistics (NCES) reported that 97% of teachers have one or more computers in their classroom, only 40% of students use these computers often during instructional time and 29% use them sometimes during instructional time (Gray & Lewis, 2010). Moreover, whereas 23% to 72% of teachers report they have easy access to various instructional technology devices such as digital/liquid projectors (48%), interactive whiteboards (28%), and digital cameras (64%), only 72%, 57%, and 49% of those teachers report using these devices, respectively. Therefore, the availability of technology in schools for teachers and students is not as significant an issue as some might believe. Rather, the issue is more often teachers' lack of motivation, knowledge, and comfort level.

With the increased availability of hardware and software in schools, teachers have been encouraged to incorporate these resources into their instructional methods. However, without effective professional development, many teachers use technology for personal use or only as mandated. Learning Forward (2009) reported that teachers were using school computers for five major tasks:

(1) administrative process (76%), (2) monitoring student progress (41%), (3) research and information (37%), (4) instructing students (32%), and (5) planning instruction (29%). Of these activities, tasks directly influencing student achievement are implemented the least while tasks directly influencing administration are implemented the most. One reason for this may be that tasks such as recording attendance and grades are more easily mandated and quantified than the integration of technology into classroom instruction. Teachers are more likely to respond positively to being held accountable for administrative tasks than they are for changing their methods of teaching. Indeed, the U.S. Department of Education supported this finding and released a National Education Technology Plan (2010) to encourage schools to support the use of technology in the classroom. With the understanding that education is the responsibility of state and local governments, the plan implores all educators that if we are "to transform education in America, we must turn ideas into actions" (2010, p. 14). However, states have been slow implementing strategies to encourage these practices or hold schools accountable for technology-based integration. Effective professional development practices as well as the impact of these practices on student achievement have been very inconsistent from state to state (Wei, Darling-Hammond, & Adamson, 2010).

The concept that effective professional development is directly correlated with an increase in student achievement has been well established over the past two decades by researchers such as Joyce and Showers (2002). It is important to note that the National Staff Development Council (Learning Forward, 2009) included student achievement as a product of effective professional development. They reported "professional development that is longer in_duration and more sustained over time is_more effective in improving teaching practice and student achievement" (Wei, Hammond, & Adamson, 2010, p. 17). However, as noted previously, an important concept is that any training or professional development must be implemented effectively in order to impact student achievement. Merely the fact that trainings are scheduled and completed will not be reflected in the classroom. School reform in this area is imperative and business cannot be done as usual if educators expect to meet the needs of 21st century students.

National and professional organizations all support and recommend that effective professional development in technology be a part of any effective school reform plan. However, in review of these recommendations and guidelines (Meltzer, 2009), it is evident that few provide all the key elements necessary to help ensure an effective and sustainable implementation. This has made the task of providing effective training for faculty a difficult and frustrating experience for school administrators. The impact of new technologies on staff trainings has shown that providers of professional development need to support and include key elements necessary for effective professional development in technology. General recommendations are provided by organizations such as ISTE and Learning Forward. More specific elements are provided by case studies (Carroll, Fulton, & Doerr, 2010) and by authors (Meltzer, 2012). Schools need to include research-based effective strategies when implementing technology-focused professional development. This will help ensure increased sustainability of the new skills. Teachers will be more likely to transfer their new skills to the classroom which will provide an impact on student achievement.

THE NEW LEARNING ENVIRONMENT

New technologies in schools have changed both the learning environment and the expectations for professional development. Historically, when a new textbook is adopted or a new teaching strategy has been endorsed by a school district, teachers are required to attend a workshop to learn how to implement it. These workshops generally consist of teachers with a common curricular interest, reviewing the materials, and possibly discussing strategies for using the new text or implementing the new strategies. Teachers have been comfortable with receiving a few hours of information before developing their own plan for teaching their students effectively. Many schools have followed this same procedure when new technologies, such as interactive whiteboards or computer software program, have been added to the school resources. Unfortunately, this process does not work and administrators wonder why the expensive acquisitions are not being used or believe they are not effective tools. It seems logical to those planning and implementing the workshops that teachers will be comfortable with the learning environment they have experienced in the past. However, when technology is involved, the environment is very different. Technology-based professional development often requires teachers to change their teaching methods. Expectations of change can arouse feelings of apprehension or anxiety from teachers. The key elements and strategies necessary for effective professional development and sustainment must be included in the planning and implementation.

The missing link in the process is that often those who are organizing and providing the professional development activities have not taken the audience into consideration. In the past, teachers may have been comfortable with limited activities and experiences with the new material because they have previous knowledge and experiences with similar materials. However, when workshops are focused on technology, teachers do not necessarily have previous experience as a foundation. They often feel intimidated and uncomfortable with something that is entirely new and unfamiliar. This is especially common with teachers who did not grow up with technology and have had little or no previous training or experience that includes technology. Consequently, they are not able to use their basic knowledge and experiences to transfer the skill to their classrooms effectively after a short demonstration or explanation of a new technology as they would with a new textbook or behavior management strategy. More emphasis should be placed on including the researched strategies for effective professional development in order for it to be effective and sustainable.

Teachers must be involved in the process of planning and goal setting as much as possible. With this in mind, it is important to remember that teachers are adult learners and must be recognized as such. As supported by many well-known theorists and researchers (Merriam & Caffarella, 1999; Maurer & Davidson, 1998; Knowles, 1984), adult learners require critical reflection and self-examination and are motivated by intrinsic rather than extrinsic rewards. If participants believe an activity will provide valuable personal knowledge and will be directly related to their own interests, they will be more motivated to be involved. All professional development should be goal oriented with clear expectations and participants should be encouraged to provide feedback and information through a reflective-based discussion activity and/or a needs assessment survey. It is important to take the time to determine if teachers need additional technology-based training in order to have the necessary skills to meet the expectations of the training. In other words, if interactive whiteboards are purchased for classrooms, teachers will need more than a demonstration on how to use them. Needs assessments of prior skills and knowledge will help determine what training is required. The administration needs to make the expectations as to how the new whiteboards will be used in the classroom clear. At this point, the teachers can help determine what they will need in the way of content training and how much time will be required. "The public and educators alike have realized that just having the technology in place does not immediately result in it being used to further educational attainment . . . Educators have additional needs in this learning process as they are urged to immediately and proficiently bring the new learning to significant educational application in their classrooms" (King, 2002, p. 284). Without establishing a strong goal-oriented plan, time will be wasted and expectations will not be met. The involvement of all participants in developing a long-term plan and providing a comprehensive schedule for implementation and support are key elements for establishing effective professional development. This is critical to establish a comfortable learning environment.

The way in which a technology-based professional development initiative is introduced in a school can have an impact on how it is received by faculty. Clear communication between administration and faculty regarding the general goals, expectations, and limitations of the project outcomes are important. Providing this information will motivate faculty to not only complete a needs assessment survey, but it will also encourage them to participate in the implementation and feel as if they are an integral part of the process rather than the targets of top-down management mandates. Additionally, valuable information can be determined from the surveys. Teachers may be given the opportunity to respond to questions regarding preferred training times and locations which can be instrumental in developing creative schedules to accommodate the majority of participants. In addition, information can be collected to determine the technology skills of teachers and what accommodations may need to be made for teachers. A technology-focused training that assumes a high level of knowledge can frustrate teachers causing ineffective training which may be difficult to rectify. When a workshop is only curriculum-focused and not technology-focused, it may be acceptable to avoid this process and provide information that adds to existing knowledge. Meeting the needs of participants is as important as meeting the needs of any student in the classroom.

The learning environment is an important piece of any professional development activity. Prior to the introduction of new technologies, introducing a new skill to teachers or providing information was much less complex. Many of the new technologies even as simple as video recording an activity or using student response recorders can be very frightening, confusing, and even intimidating to some very experienced teachers. While teachers may be the masters of teaching in a traditional classroom setting, they may not have any experience with computers or new technologies. In addition, there are many teachers who have used computers for personal uses such as grade book records or Internet research; however, they have little knowledge of how to integrate technology into classroom instruction. It is important to develop a learning environment in which participants are not threatened and are comfortable asking questions. This is expressed well in Henschke's *Building Blocks for Adult Learners* when he said, "teaching becomes the vehicle and road map for helping the learner internalize, develop, practice and refine proficiency in the application and use of that knowledge" (1987, pp. 416-417).

Those who are reticent to embrace technology are usually those who are most resistant to taking part in hands-on or active-based learning. Opportunities for sharing or for faculty involvement are often omitted during the professional development planning process (Meltzer, 2006; Wei, Darling-Hammond, & Adamson, 2010). In order for teachers to develop a comfort level with what might be considered a vastly new approach to instruction, it is imperative to include as many hands-on interactive professional development activities as possible are included (Meltzer, 2012). Teachers who are provided time and opportunity will be more apt to implement their new skills in their classrooms. Successful implementation of new skills requires "following our inner sense, honing our skills, and practice, practice, practice" (Henschke, 1987, p. 420). Teachers do not change their teaching methods over a short period of time.

Traditionally, teachers tend to work in isolation and are not provided opportunities to work together. Fortunately, this is beginning to change across the country as the isolation of teachers in a classroom and the fragmentation of professional development for teachers has been a deterrent to retaining teachers. The MetLife Survey of the American Teacher (2009) reported that teachers are eager to team up in new roles and teachers who were more satisfied with their careers were more likely to work in schools with higher rates of collaboration. Over the past decade, there has been a focus in books, articles, and conference presentations supporting the development of professional learning communities in schools. It has become accepted that teachers who are part of a Professional Learning Community (PLC) are more likely to stay in their profession, are more motivated to be effective teachers, and have a greater impact on student achievement (Wei, Darling-Hammond, & Adamson, 2010). Indeed, 94% of teachers in the MetLife Survey (2009) reported they believed that greater collaboration of teachers and administrators would have an impact on student achievement. Establishing PLCs within the school and across the district can help the effectiveness of the professional development and increase its sustainability. Ideally, the planning process should include members of established PLCs and provide opportunities to develop new technology-focused learning communities. Being a member of a PLC will help teachers to share and support their peers as they learn new strategies. For those teachers who have no technology-based foundation knowledge, an active PLC can be the key element in reinforcing the professional development objectives. This key element should be encouraged and maintained throughout the implementation to support and enhance the expected outcomes of the professional development.

While a strong PLC can be an invaluable element for effective professional development, there are additional factors necessary to sustain and support a positive learning environment. Specifically, teachers need to have a clear understanding of exactly what expectations are being placed upon them. For example, if all teachers are required to attend professional development activities involving the use of interactive whiteboards in their classrooms, they need to know how administrators and parents will expect these to be used in the classroom. Merely learning how to operative technology does not necessarily transfer in to using it effectively in the classroom. Teachers need to be provided opportunities to observe the expected behaviors and to personally experience or practice their new skills in the classroom. These opportunities need to be incorporated within the implementation and follow-up steps in order to help teachers build a strong level of comfort with the technology. Opportunities to practice the skill in a nonthreatening environment such as a computer lab, after-school informal workshops, or allotted instructional time with an experienced peer need to be provided to teachers. Additionally, it is important for teachers to be able to observe the expected behavior by watching a colleague model the strategy or technology in a regular classroom environment. By providing opportunities for teachers to observe and practice the new skill, teachers will not only be more likely to implement the new strategies, but they will also be willing to move forward and take their skills to the next level. This success will be translated into student achievement. As Wei, Darling-Hammond, Andree, and Orphanos (2009) reported, "student achievement improved most when teachers were engaged in sustained, collaborative professional development that specifically focused on deepening teachers' content knowledge and instructional practices" (p. 13).

When teachers feel comfortable and successful using the technology, they will be more likely to use it in more creative ways. Providing opportunities for teachers to share their successes through such activities as faculty meetings, PLC meetings, on-line blogs, or parent-teacher meetings can help sustain the professional development. Throughout this on-going support, it is also important to monitor progress through additional needs assessment surveys. This will help to determine additional support and training needs as well as accountability for professional development dollars spent. "Effective teaching is possible in every classroom by ensuring every educator experiences substantive professional learning within a culture of collaboration and shared accountability" (Killion & Hirsh, 2011, p. 12). Without these key elements, there will be little instructional impact resulting from professional development. School reform and student achievement will be hindered.

FUTURE TRENDS

Most educators who have received technology-based professional development would agree with the multitude of research suggesting learning activities that are short, episodic, and non-goal oriented will provide little impact on teaching practice and student achievement. The implication of this research has been more evident with the impact of technology in the 21st century. While schools may have been able to get by with mediocre support and training of new teaching materials, this is not acceptable when it comes to technology. The higher price tag for funding technology-based resources and for providing effective training has forced schools to be more accountable. Consequently, the impact of technology has required schools to think about what effective professional development looks like and what realistic expectations can be established for classrooms. As pointed out previously in this chapter, national and professional organizations have clearly established the need for more focus on the integration of technology into classroom instruction. Successful school reform and student achievement are reflective of effective professional development in technology. States have been slowly adopting these recommendations and including them in their state standards for teachers as well as students. Many states are beginning to include these expectations as an integral part of their teacher evaluations. This trend will likely continue as school districts reform and change to meet the needs of the students in the 21st century.

With any new initiative, educators are often quick to point out why they are unable to meet the expectations. The NEA/AFT (2008) recently reported in their *Access, Adequacy, and Equity in Education Technology* and was reported by Roekel (2008) that in addition to a lack of training and technical support, teachers in urban schools report insufficient and outdated equipment and software. While it is true that not all schools have adequate hardware or software, this lack of technology is not necessarily due to a lack of funding. The report also points out that many schools do not make full use of the technology they do have available. The pace of this implementation can be slow for a variety of reasons. One reason may be that it is not a priority among the faculty and administration. It also may be due to a lack of availability of expertise, experience, or information on how to plan or implement effective professional development in technology. Without a sense of urgency to meet these expectations, schools will lag behind. As we see more accountability for teachers and administrator to integrate technology into classroom instruction, we will see more motivation and support for effective training on how to use technology.

Funding for technology in schools became more accessible with the development of the first National Technology Plan in 1996. Following this trend, more grants became available and were directed to schools to be used for technology as they saw fit. Many states were able to use grant dollars to invest in statewide computer networks to support education. When the second National Technology Plan was revealed in 2001, it was quickly overshadowed by the enactment of the No Child Left Behind Act in 2002. As a result of this trend, many districts have now shifted their technology funds toward improving their data-analysis capabilities and purchasing computer software to help measure student skills (Trotter, 2007). This practice has made it difficult in some cases for teachers to shift from using technology in an isolated fashion to integrating it into classroom instruction as a tool. In essence, many teachers need to completely change their teaching methods in the classroom. Without effective professional development activities that include opportunities to experience and model this skill, teachers will not gravitate to the integration of technology and reform their teaching methods. Many schools can attest to this fact as they inventory their computers that sit idle in classrooms. Consequently, the need for effective professional development is increasing rapidly.

The implementation of the new Common Core Standards across the nation has opened up opportunities for schools to develop collaborative groups and active PLCs. There are many strategies for initiating and encouraging collaborative groups within schools and across districts. For example, Welborn (2012) clarifies the need for commitment, time, and communication for successful implementation. Successful new school reform initiatives will be imbedded with strong collaboration opportunities. Teachers are the key players in reform and they know what works and what does not work. It is important to understand the past, but it is also important to share what is happening and can happen in our current classrooms.

The influences of Learning Forward, ISTE, and Partnership 21st Century have encouraged states to adopt more national standards as their own, or at the least, to use these as foundations for building their own. Consequently, the trend to align technology-focused professional development to teacher competencies is more evident across the nation. As administrators begin to include these expectations when they observe their teachers and prioritize the expectation of technology integration into classroom instruction, we will see more implementation of technology-focused professional development. The impact of this over time will be evident in school reform and student achievement.

School reform can be challenging when teachers do not want to change their pedagogy. Many believe what has been successful in the past will continue to be successful in the future. However, the evidence is clear that students of the 21st century are different from past generations. While they live active technology-enriched lives outside the classroom, schools are not preparing them for a technological-focused business world. When schools mandate that classrooms be void of cell phones, personal computers, and any personal electronic devices rather than promote educational uses for these, they are alienating students and reinforcing the belief that today's classrooms are not meeting their needs. Taking advantage of available research such as Meltzer's (2012) *Model of Effective Professional Development* will assist providers of professional development as they plan, implement, and support professional development in technology. As the nation moves forward to meet the challenges of the newest generations, school reform will need to account for this needed change in pedagogy.

CONCLUSION

The impact of new technologies has raised the bar on the expectations for effective professional development. According to well-accepted researchers, the definition of effective and sustainable professional development includes not only an increase in teacher knowledge but also an increase in student achievement. Traditionally, teacher training has been a single workshop or short series of workshops for teachers. These have consisted of demonstrating or providing information on how teachers can use a new curriculum-based material to enhance or support their classroom instruction. The recent introduction of technologies such as computers, digital cameras, student response recorders, and interactive whiteboards has created difficulties for many who plan and implement these workshops. Notably, previous practices of technology-focused professional development have shown to be ineffective. Technologies in schools are not being used to their best advantage, if at all. This need for a new research-based approach to professional development is needed to assist teachers as they build their foundation knowledge and comfort level with these new and different expectations. Following traditional procedures will continue to maintain a disconnection between curriculum-based and technology-base professional development.

Both federal and national organizations (ISTE, 2008; Learning Forward, 2011; Partnership for 21st Century Skills, 2008) have recognized the need to align classroom instruction with the needs and experiences of 21st century students. They have developed recommendations, standards, and skills they believe are necessary for both teachers and students to be successful in the world today. Most states are quickly adopting these suggestions in the form of Common Core Standards as well as teacher evaluation criteria. However, the professional development in most cases has not been able to keep pace with change in expected pedagogy.

Providing effective professional development in technology requires including research-based strategies and opportunities (Meltzer, 2012). The foundation for these opportunities should be a strong collaborative learning environment. Teachers who are involved and feel new professional development activities will help support their own needs will be more motivated to be involved and take part in the available opportunities. These PLCs should not only be an integral part of planning and implementing training, but also of follow-up and support.

The speed of evolving technology can be very overwhelming for schools systems with limited budgets and large numbers of faculty to support. Consequently, providing adequate hardware and software can be as much of a challenge as developing and implementing the necessary professional development. Schools are purchasing and providing teachers with more technology-based resources and tools for their classrooms than ever before. However, the training opportunities required for teachers to integrate these into their classroom instruction have not matched the same pace. Prioritization, knowledge, and motivation have kept many schools from supporting the expected change in pedagogy. The integration of technology into the classroom is not moving as quickly as the technology is appearing on the shelves. This has led to frustrations on the part of parents, teachers, and administrators as they struggle to reform education. The impact of new technology on education has not only effected professional development but also student achievement and the progress of school reform.

REFERENCES

Carroll, T. G., Fulton, K., & Doerr, H. (2010). *Team up for 21st century teaching and learning: What research and practice reveal about professional learning*. Washington, DC: National Commission on Teaching & America's Future.

Darling-Hammond, L., Jaquith, A., Mindich, D., & Wei, R. C. (2010). *Teacher professional learning in the United States: Case studies of state policies and strategies*. Oxford, OH: Learning Forward.

Gray, L., Thomas, N., & Lewis, L. (2010). *Teachers' use of educational technology in U.S. public schools: 2009*. Washington, DC: National Center for Education Statistics, Institute of Education Sciences, U.S. Department of Education.

Henschke, J. (1987). Training teachers of adults. In Klevins, C. (Ed.), *Materials and Methods of Adult and Continuing Education* (4th ed., pp. 414–422). Los Angeles, CA: Klevens Publications in Adult and Continuing Education.

ISTE. (2008). *The standards for learning, leading, and teaching in the digital age*. Retrieved from http://www.iste.org/standards.aspx

Johnson, P. (2009). The 21st century skills movement. *Teaching for the 21st Century, 67*(1), 11.

Joyce, B., & Showers, B. (2002). *Student achievement through staff development* (3rd ed.). Alexandria, VA: Association for Supervision and Curriculum Development.

Killion, J., & Hirsh, S. (2011). The elements of effective teaching. *Journal of Staff Development, 32*(6), 10–16.

King, K. P. (2002). Educational technology professional development as transformative learning opportunities. *Computers & Education, 39*(3), 283–297. doi:10.1016/S0360-1315(02)00073-8

Knowles, M. (1984). *Andragogy in action: Applying modern principles of adult learning*. San Francisco, CA: Jossey-Bass Publishers.

Learning Forward. (2011). *Standards for professional learning*. Retrieved from http://www.learningforward.org/standards/index.cfm

Maurer, M., & Davidson, G. (1998). *Leadership in instructional technology*. Upper Saddle River, NJ: Prentice Hall.

Meltzer, S. (2006). An analysis of professional development in technology for elementary school teachers. *Dissertation Abstracts International, 67*(6).

Meltzer, S. T. (2009). *Professional development in technology: An analysis of effective practices*. Paper presented at the Meeting of the Society for Information Technology & Teacher Education International Conference. Charleston, SC.

Meltzer, S. T. (2012). *Step-by-step professional development in technology*. Larchmont, NY: Eye on Education.

Merriam, S., & Caffarella, R. (1999). *Learning in adulthood*. San Francisco, CA: Jossey-Bass Publishers.

MetLife. (2009). *The MetLife survey of the American teacher: Collaborating for student success*. New York, NY: Metropolitan Life Insurance Company.

National Education Association. (2008). *Access, adequacy and equity in education technology: Results of a survey of America's teachers and support professionals on technology in public schools and classrooms*. Washington, DC: National Education Association. Retrieved from www.nea.org/research/images/08gainsandgapsedtech.pdf

Partnership for 21st Century Skills. (2008). *21st century skills, education & competitiveness: A resource and policy guide*. Tucson, AZ: Partnership for 21st Century Skills. Retrieved from http://www.p21.org/storage/documents/21st_century_skills_education_and_competitiveness_guide.pdf

Rideout, V., Foehr, U., & Roberts, D. (2010). *Generation M2: Media in the lives of 8- to 18-year olds*. Washington, DC: Kaiser Family Foundation.

Roekel, D. V. (2008). *Technology in schools: The ongoing challenge of access, adequacy, and equity. An NEA Policy Brief*. Washington, DC: National Education Association Education Policy and Practice Department.

Snyder, T. D., & Dillow, S. A. (2011). *Digest of education statistics 2010*. Washington, DC: National Center for Education Statistics, Institute of Education Sciences, U.S. Department of Education.

Trotter, A. (2007). Getting up to speed. *Education Week*, *26*, 10–16.

U.S. Department of Education. (2010). *National education technology plan 2010*. Retrieved from http://www.ed.gov/technology/netp-2010

Wei, R. C., Darling-Hammond, L., & Adamson, F. (2010). *Professional development in the United States: Trends and challenges*. Dallas, TX: National Staff Development Council.

Wei, R. C., Darling-Hammond, L., Andree, A., Richardson, N., & Orphanos, S. (2009). *Professional learning in the learning profession: A status report on teacher development in the United States and abroad*. Dallas, TX: National Staff Development Council.

Welborn, B. (2012). Six keys to successful collaboration. *Education Week Teacher*. Retrieved from http://www.edweek.org/tm/articles/2012/03/13/tln_collaboration.html

Chapter 4
Examining Adult Learning Assumptions and Theories in Technology-Infused Communities and Professions

Judith E. Parker
Columbia University, USA

ABSTRACT

Adult learning in today's society is primarily focused on the needs of adults as they function in their communities and professions. Adult learning principles and theories have been the foundation of adult education practice for over a century. However, a review of the historical context reveals that this new technology-infused learning landscape is dramatically different from its predecessor. This makes a reexamination of these ideas important for their future application. This chapter will reexamine the adult-learning principles of transformative learning, andragogy, and critical reflection in this technology-infused world and propose a new paradigm and corresponding practices for the new learning landscape in communities and professions.

INTRODUCTION

Adults in today's society are largely members of two groups: their community and their profession. Community education brings images of non-profit and social service organizations while professional development suggests more formal classroom settings. However, the effective and successful participation of adults within these groups requires continuous learning in diverse venues.

DOI: 10.4018/978-1-4666-2955-4.ch004

Technology's influence is pervasive in what they do, how they do it, and how they continually learn in order to accomplish their personal and professional goals. While technology is often treated as a piece of equipment or a methodology, in fact it has become infused into everyone's actions and thoughts. It is not technology in the world but technology as a part of the world. As people stare at personal handheld devices or new LED displays in public places, it is easy to take for granted the access to up to the minute information about where friends and family are and when the next train will arrive. Technology changes the approach to communication and reshapes the thinking process. The adaptation to this new environment provides a new idea of space and society. Consistent with this thinking, Loader (1998) notes that numerous social scientists share the idea that "society is being transformed by a revolution in information technology which is creating an entirely new social structure" (p. 4). Hakken (1999) continues on this theme by suggesting that the @ symbol used to indicate an electronic domain in an email address, is also an indication of the social space to which one is connected.

The objective of this chapter is to examine several traditional assumptions and theories that have shaped adult learning practice for over a century. However, they will be examined through the technology infused lives of today's adult learners. Technology is not just a tool or a lens. Because infusion implies that technology has permeated the very essence of the theories, they may appear different and offer new challenges and opportunities to both the theorist and the practitioner.

BACKGROUND/THEORETICAL FRAMEWORK

Historically, adult education has been practiced before its theories were developed. Now technology enhanced learning has been practiced for several decades. It seems time to examine the basic principles of adult learning in this practice. This chapter will reexamine three ideas that are key elements in the theory and practice of adult learning in community education and professional development: Mezirow's transformative learning; Knowles' self-directedness and Brookfield's critical reflection.

Mezirow's Transformative Learning

Dr. Jack Mezirow, Emeritus Professor at Teachers College/Columbia University first proposed his theory of transformative learning in the 1980s. The theory's hallmark of a disorienting dilemma as the source for reevaluating one's assumptions and progressing to leaning has been a much debated issue over the decades. Was it a singular event or a series of events that caused the dilemma? Mezirow defines transformative learning as a process by which our taken-for-granted frames of references are transformed by making them more "inclusive, discriminating, open, emotionally capable of change, and reflective" (Merriam, Caffarella, & Baumgartner, 2007, p. 255). Whether in communities or professions, transformative learning became a desirable goal of adult learning.

Knowles's Andragogy and Self-Directedness

Many theories of adult learning are grounded in the work of Malcolm Knowles. By the 1980s, he had delineated several assumptions about adult learners. He formulated them into six core andragogical principles: "the learner's need to know, self-directed learning, prior experience of the learner, readiness to learn, orientation to learning and problem solving, and motivation to learn" (Knowles, Holton, & Swanson, 2005, p. 183). Several of Knowles' principles of adult learning suggest a connection between experience and learning. Knowles indicated that adult learners had experience that could be a resource for their learning, needed to feel ready to learn, and saw an immediate application for their new knowledge. Discussion around these principles continues in the field of adult learning today.

Brookfield's Critical Reflection

A major contributor to those discussions was Stephen Brookfield. Brookfield (1986) particularly questioned Knowles ideas of self-directedness, his assumption of relating learning to particular social roles and his focus on adults' need for immediate application of learning. Brookfield (2005) moved the focus of adult learning to critical reflection. Critical thinking or critical reflection is "reflecting on the assumptions underlying our and others' ideas and actions, and contemplating alternative ways of thinking and living" (Brookfield, 1986, p. x). Brookfield (1987) described 9 key concepts of the critical thinking process but then synthesized them into two key activities: "identifying and challenging assumptions" and "exploring and imagining alternatives" (p. 15).

A NEW PARADIGM FOR ADULT LEARNING IN TECHNOLOGY INFUSED COMMUNITIES AND PROFESSIONS

The three theories and assumptions that were examined in the previous section were selected because they have been core tenants of adult learning throughout its development and evolution. They provide the foundation for much of the practice of education and training in communities and professional settings for adult learners. As technology has become more of an integral part of those communities and professions—how have these theories about learning and practice been impacted? The original premise of this author is that technology is not just a device that is utilized as a tool. Rather, technology has infused every aspect of society to essentially change the thought process in learning.

Consider the following example. The author has lived in a Victorian home in St. Paul, Minnesota built in 1900 that had a unique chandelier in the foyer. The central portion illuminated at the flip of the switch on the wall. However, the arms that extended on the edges appeared to be missing bulbs. Further examination revealed sleeves over gas jets. Typical of light fixtures of the time, the chandelier could function on gas or electricity, just in case the newly invented electric lights failed. Today, the stability of electricity is assumed. The backup gas jets are not needed. Just as it is inconceivable to consider building a new house without electricity, it is just as inconceivable to consider functioning in a world without technology and the connectedness of the Internet.

Compare this analogy to today's information technology. Many can remember the days of balancing a weighty laptop in one hand and a briefcase full of backup sheets of paper in the other—just in case the technology failed. This period of transition is over. Connectivity through handheld devices is assumed to be the norm. Today's communities include wifi everywhere from coffee shops to parks. Smart phones blur the line between phones and computers and make connectivity even more accessible. In addition, this connectivity serves to even broaden the very sense of community. Online social networks connect the planet.

There is also a blurring between community and professional lives. One's physical presence in one venue does not preclude the availability to the other. The community and profession are no longer two silos of one's life. Yermish (2000) labels this a "passing of remoteness" and describes it as a "phenomenon of the rise of the Internet and other distance-shrinking technologies" (p. 208).

Some authors refer to less dramatic changes in areas of society. For example, Gobillot (2009) refers to a "leadershift" in organizations and Welch and Welch (2012) note that a "'values drift' is pervasive in companies of every ilk" (p. 56). The history of adult teaching and learning has numerous examples of shifts and drifts in its focus. But teaching and learning has not just "shifted" or "drifted" in response to the introduction of technology. Because of technology, the essence of how theorists examine their basic foundational assumptions and how practitioners put them to use has been inextricably altered.

Historical Context for the New Paradigm of Adult Learning

Examining the history of adult education reveals only a few other events that have had as dramatic an effect as modern technology. Knowles (1989) traces the roots of adult education to the great teachers of ancient China, Rome, and Greece. He notes that it was because of their experience with adults that these educators "perceived learning to be a process of active inquiry, not passive reception of transmitted content" and therefore "invented techniques for engaging learners in active inquiry" (p. 61). He specifically credits the Chinese and Hebrews with the "case method or critical incident," the Greeks with the "Socratic dialogue" in which a dilemma was posed to the group who would pool their knowledge and experience to develop a solution and the Romans with the methodology that involved forcing the students to state positions and to defend them.

Adult learning as an academic field has its roots in the early 1900s. The Association of Adult and Continuing Education, began to sponsor studies in the Field and in 1934 and later published the first *Handbook of Adult and Continuing Education*. The 1960 edition of this Handbook was the first to include individual essays by adult educators in order to provide an overview of the current nature and trends in the field of adult education. Cyril Houle's (1961) *The Inquiring Mind* and (1972) *Design of Education* laid the foundation for Tough's (1967) *Learning Without a Teacher* and (1979) *The Adult's Learning Projects* which introduced the concept of self-directed learning and later influenced Knowles. Yermish (2000) reminds that "ever since the advent of television, educators have wrestled with the viability of using this technology to reach wider audiences. Educational television facilitated the distribution of high-quality program content in a one-directional fashion" (p. 208).

Merriam (2008) identified two recent changes in the focus of adult learning. One is from the individual learner to the learner within the various contexts in which learning takes place. This new perspective considers "learning as part of the system's cultural and historical norms...(and) how physical space and spatiality encourages or inhibits learning" (p. 94). The second shift is from learning as a purely cognitive activity to one that is multidimensional in nature. In this more holistic approach, "learning is construed as a much broader activity involving the body, the emotions, and the spirit as well as the mind" (p. 95). Illeris' (2004) three dimensions of learning (cognitive, emotional, social) offer a similar approach to the discussion of learning. Mazarr's (1999) earlier work echoes this picture by explaining that "knowledge-era learning" must become more "holistic" and "high-tech"; it must "emphasize creativity and participation" and be "characterized by more choice and competition" (p. 285).

However, between the ancient civilizations and the development of the field of adult learning, a major event impacted teaching and learning; Guttenberg invented the printing press. Lesgold (2000) notes that before the printing press, "direct discussion with a wise person was the primary way of gaining knowledge" (p. 399). Knowles (1989) credits the invention of the printing press with having a great "impact on the advancement of adult education" (p. 62). This changed every aspect of people's community and professional lives. However, even with the advent of the early printing presses, books were expensive and rare and only certain key books were reproduced widely. The industrial revolution enhanced this process by making it faster and more efficient but essentially it was the same process.

The second major event does not surface until the late 1900s. Between the printing press of the mid-1400s and today, history is filled with technological innovations. Parker (2009) notes that "Whether it was the printing press, telephone, copying machine, or computer, educators have always been challenged to use new technology for effective teaching and learning" (p. 223). However, none created the quantum leap effect of information technology. The new "information society" had arrived. Loader (1998) provides a sense of just how dramatic this impact was by announcing that "the emergence of the new information and communications technologies such as the Internet are said to herald the coming of the 'information society': a new social and economic paradigm restructuring the traditional dimensions of time and space within which we live, work, and interact" (p. 3). Jarvis (1985) attempted to quantify this information explosion by noting that each year 30 billion original documents are created, 100 billion pages come off photocopiers and 630 billion pages of print go through the postal system. Mazarr (1999) notes that "the knowledge era is an interdisciplinary time" (p. 11) and that the "new sciences of complexity remind us that boundaries between problems and disciplines are less important than the threads that connect them" (p. 12). All these suggest that Loader's earlier statement should be expanded to include a new educational paradigm which restructures the traditional dimensions of time and space within which we live, work, interact and learn.

However, as early as 1985, Jarvis (1985) suggested that this "information society" was being replaced by the "information technology society. Alheit (2009) suggested that the "communication and interaction networks of the IT age" will create the "future form of knowledge" which is "*doing knowledge*, a kind of lifestyle that determines the structures of society far beyond the purely occupational domain" (p. 119). Jarvis (1985) noted that as society moves toward this new information technology society, "it is quite essential that the designs of the adult learning be such that they encourage critical awareness about all forms of information they receive, whether their teacher is in the classroom, the purveyor of information through the media, or the billions of pages of circulars, or even the programmer of a computer learning package" (p. 14). Fenwick (2008) lists 4 emerging trends in adult learning: areas of definitions, an increased emphasis on practice-based learning, the importance of identity and literacy and power and politics. He defines learning not as an outcome but as a process that is "understood to involve not just human change but interconnections of humans and their actions with rules, tools and texts, cultural, and material environments" (p. 19).

These authors have suggested new views of knowledge, society, and learning in the communities in which we live. However, Gobillot (2009) quantifies the expansiveness of new online communities. He notes that Facebook has more than 150 million active users. To put this in perspective, if Facebook were a country, it would be the eighth largest country and the largest in the European Union. The virtual world of Second Life has over 14 million residents. In terms of numbers, this means that the 65th largest country is a land that only exists on laboratory servers and is inhabited by avatars. New paradigms of communities are also emerging.

Examining this new paradigm makes it obvious that inquiry, problem solving, and communication skills are not just catchwords in today's K-12 curriculum guides. They must be essential elements of adult education as well. They are essential to everyone's survival in communities and professions. The three issues outlined earlier in this chapter have changed. Frames of reference are expanded, self-directedness feels very different and reflection seems too time-consuming.

Transformative Learning

Does transformative learning look different today than it did as originally proposed by Mezirow? Is there a Transformative Learning 2.0? From its beginning, Transformational learning has had a longstanding impact on adult education. Sharan Merriam (2008) notes that as she reviewed three successive updates of *New Directions for Adult and Continuing Education* she observed that a chapter on transformational learning was the only constant across these updates. However, she did note differences in emphasis in how transformative learning was discussed. The 1993 edition was mostly descriptive. The 2001 chapter focused on empirical research. While empirical research continued to be an emphasis in the 2008 update, that latest edition included diverse theoretical perspectives about transformative learning. The continued global interest in Transformative learning is evident in numerous publications on the topic and the 9th Annual Transformative Learning Conference held in Athens, Greece in the spring of 2011. Various aspects continue to be discussed and argued.

The disorienting dilemma has been a much discussed component of transformative learning theory. The theory originally suggested a dilemma limited to personal interactions and experiences. In today's connected world, the source of that dilemma could be the local community, the online community, or the global community. Or the source could be the physical workplace, the virtual workplace or colleagues/competitors around the globe. All of these sources of disorienting dilemmas have the potential for severely impact lives and possibly be the source of transformative learning.

The framework of globalization is important not just as it reflects economic and environmental issues but as it frames the individual knowledge base which could be the source of a dilemma. With the plethora of information available, it might even be difficult to isolate "the dilemma." The almost immediate influx of data about one's community and profession on a local to a global level could be overwhelming. The disorienting dilemma at a distance could produce its own set of dilemmas. It could be difficult for the learner to get enough information to assess its accuracy and to have little if any control over the circumstances. Earlier learners might have a sense of control over the transformation process. However, this whirlwind of mostly opinionated information could in itself pose a dilemma.

Another view of the influence of technology could however put a positive spin on the similar issues. The following example illustrates some of these ideas. When the author teaches on campus courses in staff development and adult learning and leadership, there is always an online assignment to provide students with the experience of learning online. Using technology in an education course offers a unique advantage. In most courses, technology is utilized as a course delivery system. In an education course, the course objectives facilitate the inclusion of an analysis of the effectiveness of the use of technology. While the presence of technology in a learning mode is often new to the students, that in itself poses a dilemma. However, students are continually required to reflect on and discuss the learning advantages and disadvantages of technology as they experience it in their own learning. Their taken-for-granted assumption about the online assignment often changes as a result of the experience and the course assignments that utilize technology enhance this learning.

Since the process itself assumes a reevaluating of one's assumptions and changing one's taken-for-granted frames of reference, the continued connectedness of today's adult learner cannot help but impact this process. With a constant influx of information, one's assumptions might be continually changing, making it nearly impossible to reevaluate. How one moves from dilemma to transformative learning becomes a very different process. While the transformative nature of learning is especially important, it might be more difficult to achieve in today's communities and professions.

Andragogy and Self-Directedness

Knowles et al. (2005) see technology as providing learning opportunities in the "andragogical tradition" (p. 237) and as consistent with the adult learning idea of self-directedness. The ideas of Andragogy and particularly the self-directedness of adult learners created a power shift in the classroom. Technology has changed the very paradigm of thinking about power and brought the idea of self-directedness to a new level. If knowledge is truly power, then the speed at which information can be obtained and the bulk of information available online today certainly alters the power structure of learning.

The first power shift came with the printing press when as Lesgold noted earlier in this chapter, it was now no longer necessary to find a knowledgeable person to answer a question or solve a problem. The self-directed learner now only needed a book and could control how and when it was read. The availability of today's ubiquitous hand held devices signal the expectation that knowledge is always instantly available. Whether in the communities in which they live or in the professions in which they work, everyone is expected to be self-directed in accessing information and gaining knowledge.

The assumption is that this self-directed adult will be motivated to use technology to gain status in the community or as a competitive tool in a profession. However, motivation and learning are more complex. Several authors support the idea that learners are most successful when other learners are involved whether they are neighbors in a community or colleagues at work. As Palloff and Pratt (1999) suggest, "key to the learning process are the interactions among students themselves, the interactions between faculty and students, and the collaboration in learning that results from these interactions" (p. 5). Nilson (2003) confirms the idea that students learn best when they are actively engaged, when learning evokes emotional not just intellectual involvement. This is consistent with Illeris's three dimensions of learning. Cranton (2006) emphasizes the importance of empowering the student by interactions in the learning environment and being aware of power relationships. "The creation of a learning community supports and encourages knowledge acquisition. It creates a sense of excitement about learning together and renews the passion involved with exploring new realms in education" (Palloff & Pratt, 1999, p. 163). However, introducing technology includes an added dimension.

One example that technology introduces is the possibility of asynchronous interactions among students. An assignment requires students to post their reflection on the week's readings in a discussion board. They must then select another person's posting and respond to it. In a classroom, the student is required to listen to every students comment. The online discussion board requires the students to be self-directed in selecting an entry of interest to respond to and fosters critical thinking by allowing the students time to develop their thoughts. It fosters more engagement by each student. Blogs on community and professional issues provide similar opportunities in these venues.

A quote from a student in the author's online class provides some details. She comments on a discussion that was held in an asynchronous discussion board as part of a class assignment. "The discussion conducted here is very involving; everybody could get a chance to express his own ideas. Moreover, the discussion board online gives us a further opportunity to share ideas with all of the class. It has been developed into a real learning forum. Everybody chose their favorite articles about learning and training in their fields, and then shared their own ideas on the "blackboard," thus evokes a real open discussion. This learning style makes me feel that I can learn anytime anywhere from so many people of diverse fields. By posting, reading, and replying online, our learning location has burst out of the limited classroom and lecture time boundary, thus it has given us an authentic flexibility and motivation to learn."

It seems especially interesting to see words like real open discussion, learning forum, motivation, and authentic flexibility as part of the student reflections on the online experience. In the chapter, "The Passion of Pluralism," Maxine Greene (1995) comments about community: "We are in search of what John Dewey called 'the Great Community" but at the same time, we are challenged as never before to confront plurality and multiplicity" (p. 155). "To open up our experience to existential possibilities of multiple kinds is to extend and deepen what each of us thinks of when he or she speaks of a community" (p. 161). Elements of adult learning theory in action are evidenced in the comments and actions of participants in technology-enhanced learning cited above.

At the same time that the positive aspects of technology are applauded, there are serious questions to be addressed. Is there a dichotomy developing of not just have and have not access to technology but a dichotomy in thinking patterns with ethical and social justice implications? Communities provide tools such as computers and primarily instruction on the mechanics of their use for simple tasks. However, little attention is paid to the thinking process or decision-making process involved in their effective use.

Critical Reflection

What does critical reflection look like in a 2.0 world? Is it qualitatively different than originally proposed? Is reflection-in-action rather than reflection-on-action becoming the norm. What is the role of critical reflection? Previously, researchers meticulously plotted data points on an x-y axis and as time allowed, analyzed the resulting trends. Now the ubiquitous graphing calculator and excel software effortlessly plot the data points and offer the options for plotting trend-lines or cycles releasing time for more in-depth analysis and reflection on the results. Lesgold (2000) suggests that just as the book "removed some of the need for memorization as a force for knowledge distribution, so the computer removes some of the need for overlearning of routine information processing procedures, since these can be accomplished by computers" (p. 401). He cites the example of whether or not students need to know how to perform complex algebraic calculations if they can be done by computer or calculator. Real world problems do not have simple answers that can be searched on Google. Jarvis (1985) noted that "learners must be aware of the processes of the manufacture of information and be confident that they can process it adequately in order to make it their own personal knowledge in which they may have the certainty that the phenomena are real and have the characteristics attributed to them. In order to achieve this, adult educators must design learning experiences that encourage the creation of a critical awareness, necessary to ensure the continuation of democracy in an information society" (p. 14).

An example of an activity that facilitates critical reflection is an assignment that the author uses in her online course. She uses the asynchronous Discussion Board where students post their own ideas and comments about a reading assignment and then reply to other students' ideas. One assignment requires students to read a journal article of their choosing related to staff development. They are then to summarize their article and post their reflection on it. Following are a few representative student comments on this assignment.

One student comments on the advantages of the computer technology in eliminating communication barriers and fostering reflection. "It is a medium that does promote student engagement in discourse without the normal bias of face-to-face communication (because our appearance is reduced to letters in a computer screen). In addition, although we have the opportunity to influence and suggest tone, etc. by the use of color, sizes, etc. the initial barriers to traditional communication are somehow diminished. The use of discussion boards allows for a lot of reflection prior to committing to opinions. The student has the time and the resources to build a message that will convey every idea that s/he wants to communicate."

Other students note the importance of the well constructed questions and the depth of the reflection and conversations. "The process of responding to skilled questions posed by co-group members allowed me to consider and deeply reflect on my actions with respect to learning and how it is applied at workplace." "The conversations were not superficial interactions but purposeful, focused, and useful. The instructions allowed all group members an equal opportunity to have their 'voices' heard." While today's technological advancement is characterized by electronics and digitization, by faster and farther it is interesting to see that it can also be used to slow down and reflect before constructing a thoughtful response in a discussion. Even though Kelly (2010) notes that "Book reading strengthened our analytical skills, encouraging us to pursue an observation all the way down to the footnote. Screen reading encourages rapid pattern making, associating this idea with another, equipping us to deal with the thousands of new thoughts expressed every day. The screen rewards and nurtures thinking in real time" (p. 125). It is possible to slow that real time.

This new social paradigm changes our entire sense of space and time. Sitting with an individual or group of colleagues in a room has been replaced by typing on a computer keyboard or on any of the numerous handheld Internet accessible devices, reading text on a screen, or listening to voices on a phone. Instead of feeling the presence of other collaborators, participants are connected by voice or text and might be easily distracted by daily tasks. While the efficiency of such a round the clock network is dramatically increased, the issues of ownership and credit can become more complicated in this collaborative global world. It seems that Web 2.0 with its podcasts, blogs, twitters, Youtube, virtual realities, and global, non-stop researching will be a part of the future of adult education. The greatest challenge as professionals in the field may be to ensure that the essential component of critical reflection finds a place in this world.

Possible Solutions and Recommendations

One view of this new learning landscape places the student behind the technology in importance. Taking a closer look at the three ideas of adult learning that are the focus of this chapter reveals that the technology can actually empower the student. Below are four issues that might be addressed with this idea in mind.

Issue 1: The learner must develop a filter in order to discern important issues and focus efforts. This is important both in focusing on the dilemma that is the source of the transformative learning or being able to make the required decisions needed by the self-directed student. Likewise, technology has made tasks and decision-making in our communities and professions easier and faster. However, as "free time" becomes available it is critical that it be channeled into reflection. This personal filter can only be developed by critical reflection and will be a useful tool in working with information about the individual's community and profession.

Issue 2: The old educational goal: get the right answer. Achieving this goal usually took work to get the answer. It often required a trip to the library or pages of numerical calculations. The focus on the process of finding the answer was isolated to a few specialized areas such as designing a research study. Now answers are everywhere. New educational goal: learn the process, evaluate the source, question. Critical thinking again seems at the heart of this issue. While technology can certainly save much of the time that might have been used to explore issues and search for answers, it is important that the conscious decision be made to use the released time for analysis and reflection and not fill it with additional tasks.

Issue 3: Information cannot be taken at face value. This is not a new problem. Students with calculators have all too frequently provided the instructor with a numerical answer. In addition, if questioned about it, they have replied "but my calculator says so." The author has an example from a nursing math class that she taught several years ago. Students punched numbers into their calculator and read back the answer—ridiculous answers. It was a medication problem and students proposed large numbers of pills that were needed by the patient to achieve the recommended dosage. Only when questioned, did they stop and think that this was an unrealistic number. That questioning of any information on any screen must be part of the process of learning.

Issue 4: Current technology may promote breadth more than depth. It is easy to search for a topic and find links to other related topics but more difficult to find the interrelationship between topics and ideas. Another way of picturing the situation comes from a film "Powers of 10." It begins with a scene of a person at a picnic and moves outward through the solar system and galaxy moving through exponential distances until the scene include the universe. Then it restarts at the picnic but moves inward through the skin and DNA of the picnicer to the level quarks within the nucleus of an atom. It is just as essential for the learner to be connected to the bigger picture of the universe but also to investigate inward the psychology of her own mind through critical reflection.

This list of issues can certainly be supplemented by additional thoughts of every reader. The overarching issue though relates to the ideas of transformative learning, self-directedness, and critical reflection within the communities and professions of the adult learner.

FUTURE TRENDS

In the rapidly changing pace of new technology, the term future has a new meaning. It does not refer to years or months from now. Time really is more of a continuum. The future starts from a second from now and moves forward. The author wrote a journal article 3 years ago about the new paradigm of adult education. Parker (2010) organized the article with adult learning as one major heading and technology as another. Only later does she comment that "despite their separate beginnings, when considering adult education and technology today, it is important to acknowledge that the two are inextricably intertwined and play a complementary role in effective adult education" (p. 14). Referring to the earlier analogy with the house, this is like saying that it is important to acknowledge that the house and electricity are intertwined and play a complementary role in providing comfortable housing today. In short 3 years, these two topics no longer require two separate headings.

Therefore starting from today might be the best way to expand the view into the future. However, what does this really mean in communities and professions. Since much has been written on professional education, it might be useful to consider three community education examples from the author's own experience in her community of antiques, landscaping, and yoga.

The author enjoys viewing and sometimes buying antiques. She still enjoys browsing through the tables of items in rows of booths at Renningers' Antique Extravaganza twice a year or the local weekend antique show. However, if she is searching for a special item, she will check out photos in upcoming online auction sites. Not only does this save time, but it allows the author to evaluate the item, reflect on its condition and how much she might be willing to spend. This self-directed learner might search for similar items, compare prices and availability. At the antique show, the author is forced into an instant decision or risk having the item purchased by someone else willing to purchase the item quickly.

In past years, spring garden planning was always a ritual of walking around the yard with my landscaper who would suggest additions to the garden. This was followed by her dragging out frayed copies of books and catalogs from the back of her truck which were filled with pictures of flowers and bushes or her promising to send an email with better photos. This spring she pulled out her new tablet and produced brilliant photos of foliage, flowers and seed pods of plants in different seasons, close ups and in the landscape. She produced a short horticulture class at her fingertips.

The final example involves the local school system that has always mailed out a paper announcement of their community education classes for the upcoming semester with registration details. Then one semester the mailing never appeared. Since that mailing served as a reminder to register for yoga class, the class registration deadline passed before the author thought to check for information online. While discontinuing the mailing was likely prompted by budget cuts, the result was that the school system had assumed that adults were all self-directed learners and would certainly have checked their school system website for class and registration details.

While today, it is easy to get lost in an online game or online adventure in second life. Since books have been printed or lettered by a scribe, people have been "lost in a good book." Some authors caution that emerging new technologies will not replace the old. Valmont (2003) reminds that "oral storytelling did not die when Gutenberg created the printing press" and "novels did not go away when films became popular. Literacies simply evolve" (p. 298). Nilson (2003) agrees and adds that she expects the low-tech instructional tools such as the black or white board or overhead projector to be around for years while the high tech tools will become obsolete very quickly. While this is true on a universal scale, as evidenced by the examples above, in isolated venues, technology does in fact replaces more traditional forms of communication.

Therefore, to succeed in the communities and professions of tomorrow, some authors offer valuable advice. Hakken (1999) suggested that "we must come to terms…with an accelerated decoupling of space from place (p. 215). Bray (2009) notes that "Career and technical education is always about the future" because its focus is on preparing "lifelong learners who are able to transition today's knowledge to the needs of tomorrow" (p. 6). The author's predictions might be a future with even more connections, more blurring of boundaries; a future that values personal philosophies but shared experiences and goals.

CONCLUSION

Theories are certainly essential in any field and examining them is essential to moving the field forward. "Elias and Merriam (2005) articulate the need for theory as a foundation of practice. "Theory without practice leads to empty idealism and action without philosophical reflection leads to a mindless activism" (p. 4). Parker (2009) noted that "much of the work of the theorists has been developed through the lens of the practitioner. As theories developed, practice changed. As practice changed, new theories developed" (pp. 224-225). Today's technology infused environment in communities and professions provide opportunities for the development of even more sophisticated and insightful theories as the foundation for more effective practice. It is a new normal with new paradigms.

The three adult learning ideas that are addressed in this chapter really focus on three key elements of community and professional education: the disorienting dilemma of transformative learning, the power issues of the self-directed learner and the decision-making skill of critical reflection. While this chapter has focused on three theorists and their contributions to adult learning, Heaney (2000) reminds that "individual practitioners do not define the field of adult education, nor do experts. A definition of a field of practice is the social product of many individuals who negotiate the values and meaning of work they come to see as serving a common purpose over time" (p. 561). The interactions between these individuals that result in that social product have been and will continue to be impacted by information communication technology. The author's predictions might be of a future with even more connections, more blurring of boundaries; a future that values personal philosophies but shared experiences and goals. It is a future that Maxine Greene (2001) suggests should be approached as an opportunity for "thinking of things as if they could be otherwise" (Greene, 2001, p. 127).

REFERENCES

Alheit, P. (2009). Biographical learning – Within the new lifelong learning. In Illeris, K. (Ed.), *Contemporary Theories of Learning: Learning Theorists...in Their Own Words* (pp. 116–128). New York, NY: Routledge.

Bray, J. (2009). Embrace the future now! *Techniques*, *84*(5), 6.

Brookfield, S. (1986). *Understanding and facilitating adult learning*. San Francisco, CA: Jossey-Bass.

Brookfield, S. (1987). *Developing critical thinkers*. San Francisco, CA: Jossey-Bass.

Brookfield, S. (2005). *The power of critical theory: Liberating adult learning and teaching*. San Francisco, CA: Jossey-Bass.

Cranton, P. (2006). *Understanding and promoting transformative learning*. San Francisco, CA: Wiley.

Elias, J. L., & Merriam, S. B. (2005). *Philosophical foundations of adult education*. Malabar, FL: Krieger Publishing Company.

Fenwick, T. (2008). Workplace learning: Emerging trends and new perspectives. In *New Directions for Adult and Continuing Education* (pp. 17–26). San Francisco, CA: Jossey-Bass. doi:10.1002/ace.302

Gobillot, E. (2009). *Leadershift: Reinventing leadership for the age of mass collaboration*. London, UK: Kogan Page.

Greene, M. (1995). *Releasing the imagination*. San Francisco, CA: Jossey-Bass.

Greene, M. (2001). *Variations on a blue guitar*. New York, NY: Teachers College Press.

Hakken, D. (1999). *Cyborgs@cyberspace*. New York, NY: Routledge.

Heaney, T. W. (2000). Adult education and society. In Wilson, A. L., & Hayes, A. R. (Eds.), *Handbook of Adult and Continuing Education* (pp. 559–572). San Francisco, CA: Jossey-Bass.

Houle, C. O. (1961). *The inquiring mind*. Madison, WI: University of Wisconsin Press.

Illeris, K. (2004). *The three dimensions of learning*. Malabar, FL: Krieger.

Jarvis, P. (1985, August 6). Thinking critically in an information society: A sociological Analysis. *Lifelong Learning*, 11-14.

Kelly, K. (2110). From print to pixel. *Smithsonian*, *41*(4), 122–128.

Knowles, M. (1989). *The making of an adult educator*. San Francisco, CA: Jossey-Bass.

Knowles, M., Holton, E., & Swanson, R. (2005). *The adult learner*. Burlington, MA: Elsevier.

Lesgold, A. (2000). What are the tools for? Revolutionary change does not follow the usual norms. In Lajoie, S. (Ed.), *Computers as Cognitive Tools* (pp. 399–408). Mahwah, NJ: Lawrence Erlbaum Associates.

Loader, B. (1998). *Cyberspace divide: Equality, agency, and policy in the information society*. New York, NY: Routledge. doi:10.4324/9780203169537

Mazarr, M. (1999). *Global trends 2005: An owner's manual for the next decade*. New York, NY: St. Martin's Press.

Merriam, S., Caffarella, R., & Baumgartner, L. (2007). *Learning in adulthood: A comprehensive guide* (3rd ed.). San Francisco, CA: John Wiley & Sons.

Merriam, S. B. (2008). Adult learning theory for the twenty-first century. In *New Directions for Adult and Continuing Education* (pp. 93–98). San Francisco, CA: Jossey-Bass. doi:10.1002/ace.309

Mezirow, J. (2000). *Learning as transformation*. San Francisco, CA: Jossey-Bass.

Nilson, L. B. (2003). *Teaching at its best*. San Francisco, CA: Anker.

Palloff, R., & Pratt, K. (1999). *Building learning communities in cyberspace*. San Francisco, CA: Jossey-Bass.

Parker, J. (2009). Adult learning and CTE: A shared history influenced by technology. In Wang, V. (Ed.), *Definitive Readings in the History, Philosophy, Practice, and Theories of Career and Technical Education* (pp. 217–236). Hershey, PA: IGI Global.

Parker, J. (2010). Technology as integral to a new paradigm of adult education. *International Journal of Adult Vocational Education and Technology*, *1*(2), 10–18. doi:10.4018/javet.2010040102

Tough, A. (1967). *Learning without a teacher*. Toronto, Canada: Institute for Studies in Education.

Tough, A. (1979). *The adult's learning project*. Toronto, Canada: Institute for Studies in Education.

Valmont, W. (2003). *Technology for literacy teaching and learning*. New York, NY: Houghton Mifflin.

Welch, J., & Welch, S. (2012). Goldman, Wall Street, and the culture killing lesson being ignored. *Fortune*, *165*, 56.

Yermish, I. (2000). A case for case studies via video-conferencing. In Lau, L. (Ed.), *Distance Learning Technologies: Issues, Trends and Opportunities* (pp. 208–217). Hershey, PA: IGI Global. doi:10.4018/978-1-878289-80-3.ch015

Chapter 5
Preferred Learning Tools in Online Mathematics Classes:
Digital College Learners

Ana M. Porro
Palm Beach State College, USA

ABSTRACT

The review of the literature on the role of instructional strategies in online mathematics learning addresses the following major areas and their related subsets: motivation and academic success; online learning and andragogy; and instructional design and learning strategies. It is noted that the hypothesis that motivational strategies promote achievement and success in online mathematics courses is supported by recent investigators who suggested the need to research the effectiveness of incorporating motivational strategies in the implementation of online instructional designs (Bellon & Oates, 2002; Kelsey & D'Souza, 2004; Patall, et al., 2008; Sanacore, 2008; Skinner, 2005). Additionally, the limited role documented on motivation in online mathematics courses by both mathematicians and educators is included. Next, discussions of online learning, andragogy and learning theories, learners' characteristics and heuristics in interpersonal and cognitive tools are addressed. Lastly, laying the foundation of theory into practice, considerations for instructional designs are included along with suggestions for design and implementation of learning strategies.

INTRODUCTION

There is a rapid growth in the use of technology in all aspects of society. Colleges have embraced technology in all operations including administration, communications, human resources, accountability, and teaching and learning. As colleges incorporated technology into teaching and learning, it was often the technology that provided the direction. This was frequently done without any evidence-based decision-making. Many organizations developed distance-learning programs without regard to their effectiveness or suitability to the learning needs of their audience. Research on the effectiveness of distance learning classes often lagged far behind their implementation. In

DOI: 10.4018/978-1-4666-2955-4.ch005

recent years, however, the focus has shifted from efforts to rapidly develop distance-learning classes to refinement. The efficiency and effectiveness of distance learning programs is now being closely examined as instructional design strategies are incorporated into online instruction (Salas, Kosarzycki, Burke, & Stone, 2002).

As more institutions develop and deliver distance-learning classes, researchers have begun to ask more sophisticated and complex questions about this instructional modality. A synthesis of recent studies on online teaching and learning noted that some of the issues researchers are beginning to investigate are: (a) what motivates students to choose distance learning classes; (b) how learning styles be matched with instructional design; and (c) how to best deliver this type of instruction (Tallent-Runnels, et al., 2006). In addition, the final question remains: what motivates students to succeed in distance learning classes?

Distance education has existed for over a century. As early as 1892, schools and universities initiated offering classes by correspondence using mail or the postal system as a vehicle to reach out those who lived far from higher education institutions, but wanted an education (Monolescu, Schifter, & Greenwood, 2004). As new technologies emerged, distance education opportunities were broadened by radio (1920s), instructional television (1950s), cable television (1970s), satellite downlinks (1970s and 1980s), and videoconferencing through interactive compressed video (1990s).

The term *distance-learning* is used to describe the interactions in any course that is delivered to students who are not physically present in the same room (Tallent-Runnels, et al., 2006). Although distance learning classes may be delivered in many different formats, this investigation will examine *Web-based or online-learning* classes, courses that are delivered completely over the Internet via a computer-mediated environment. This delivery method, a common distance learning approach, may interchangeably be referred to as *Internet*, *electronic* or *elearning*, or *virtual learning* (Bork, 2005, p. 31). In select cases the students may have the opportunity to see and chat with the instructor and other students at a distance. For the purpose of this research, online learning may or may not involve this component.

In the last decade of the twentieth century, Web-based learning grew from being almost absent to suddenly appearing everywhere (Hantula & Pawlowicz, 2004). As the trend in virtual enrollment continues in colleges and universities, the need to understand adult learners surges in an effort to compete effectively in a global community. To remain competitive, faculty and administrators must identify and understand the needs and preferences of adult learners as they relate to online learning and online instructional design (Ausburn, 2004). According to Knowles (1980), the father of *andragogy*, or the art of teaching adults, adult learners tend to be self-directed. That is, they want some control over both the content of learning and the way the knowledge or skill is presented. One of the principal premises of andragogy is that the successful facilitator acknowledges that need and creates a highly interactive learning environment for adults. Therefore, andragogy tends to be process-driven more than content-driven. That is not to say that content is irrelevant to the adult learner, but that the adult learner acquires new material (content) or a taught skill more efficiently when the facilitator individualizes the learning experience. Because adults' readiness to learn is frequently affected by their need to know or do something, they tend to have a life-, task-, or problem-centered orientation to learning as opposed to a subject-matter orientation (Knowles, 1980).

Other assumptions underlying Knowles' andragogical model differentiate adults as having a growing reservoir of experience that can serve as a resource for learning. Adults are generally motivated to learn due to internal or intrinsic factors as opposed to external or extrinsic factors. A logical outcome of these assumptions is the use of a collaborative teaching model that involves the learner and facilitator as mutual partners in the learning venture (Merriam, Caffarella, & Baumgartner, 2007).

Offering a variety of resources and fostering a supportive environment are vital factors in successful adult learning (Hantula & Pawlowicz, 2004; Knowles, 1980; Merriam, et al., 2007). An important issue to consider at the forefront of instruction is the learners' processing of information. This can be known by using *instrumented learning*. Blake and Mouton (1972) defined instrumented learning as the means to gain understanding of self and others, improve performance, and enhance the processes of metacognition and learning how to learn.

One tool currently used to assess the learner's processing of information is a self-assessment instrument termed ATLAS (Ausburn, 2004; Conti, 2009). *Assessing The Learning Strategies of Adults* (ATLAS) groups learners into one of the three preferred strategies or approaches to learning. The three strategies are named: *Navigators*, *Problem Solvers*, and *Engagers*. Navigators are viewed as result-oriented learners who favor efficiency and effectiveness via a plan. Problem solvers are critical thinkers who explore options (multiple paths) and avoid rapid closure. Engagers are learners who love to learn and approach the affective domain seeking connectedness and high involvement (Conti, 2009). The information garnered through this assessment can be valuable for the instructor to design the course in a way that it offers options to learners addressing individual differences, and also for learners to become aware of how they initiate a learning task. Munday (2002) concluded that adult learners can realize a positive impact in their academic achievement if they know their learning strategy preferences. By students having self-knowledge of preferred learning strategies as Navigators, Problem Solvers, or Engagers as prescribed in ATLAS, they will be able to choose interpersonal and cognitive tools that best match their learning journey.

On October 19, 2010, CNN reported that despite the souring economy, more and more Americans are buying high-speed Internet service. As more people get on the information highway, it is likely that distance-learning programs will continue to grow. In an effort to compete effectively in a global community, colleges, and universities need to value adult learners and understand why they choose distance-learning classes. More importantly, schools need to understand what motivates students to succeed in online classes.

While enrollment in online classes continues an uphill path, administrators and faculty are being faced with issues and challenges related to retention and success of online students. Issues concerning student retention and success involve motivation and connectedness to the information delivered in the course (Sanacore, 2008). In a South Florida state college, distance learning, also called elearning, classes have significantly higher withdrawal rates in all courses across terms. This low retention rate affects the success rate in the courses as measured by the grade (or number of A/B/C/P issued) in the classes (PBCC Academic Affairs, 2006).

The student success rate in traditional college mathematics courses lags behind other courses. Particularly in online mathematics classes, student retention and success are a serious concern. Online Precalculus classes have a 32% withdrawal rate and a 47% success rate, while traditional face-to-face Precalculus classes have an 18% withdrawal rate and a 70% success rate (PBCC Institutional Research & Effectiveness, 2008). These results do not differ significantly from other online courses nationwide regardless of subject content (Wadsworth, Husman, Duggan, & Pennington, 2007; PBCC, 2006). Courses with more than 30% withdrawal rate are considered high-risk and deserve special attention (Bambara, Harbour, Davies, & Athey, 2009). Other researchers (Wadsworth, et al., 2007) also noted that although online learning enrollment is growing, very little research has been conducted that examines the use of cognitive strategies and their effects on student learning and achievement in online courses. Present research on motivating online mathematics students appears to have a narrow focus and is still in the developmental stage. Little research appears to address the issue that learners in online mathematics courses must deal with two major tasks: (a) learning the course mathematics content and (b) learning how to maneuver in an elearning environment.

In an effort to improve retention and success rates in online mathematics classes, there is a need to conduct research and develop evidence-based recommendations for instructional design (Li & Edmonds, 2005; van Merriënboer & Ayres, 2005). It is essential to recognize that one size does not fit all and to understand learning styles and learning theory in the context of motivation. Employing a multifaceted approach may lead to greater opportunities for success. There is a need to investigate the application of motivational strategies, such as preferred learning strategies, to the design of online instruction and learning, specifically by integrating aspects that promote self-knowledge, choices, and the interaction of instructional conditions (Wadsworth, et al., 2007).

As research is growing to improve retention in online classes, the exploration of a multifaceted approach to enhance student achievement is viable and needed research that should provide successful strategies for learners. The hypothesis that motivational strategies promote achievement in online mathematics classes is supported by recent investigators (Bellon & Oates, 2002; Kelsey & D'Souza, 2004; Patall, Cooper, & Robinson, 2008; Sanacore, 2008; Skinner, 2005). These researchers suggested the need to investigate the effectiveness of incorporating motivational strategies in the implementation of online instructional designs. The purpose of this study was to investigate the effect of using learner self-assessment and multifaceted instructional strategies on student achievement and retention in online mathematics classes.

The virtual world is here to stay. The Internet opened doors to a global community without physical barriers. This is clearly visible in the enrollment growth of online education (Bambara, et al., 2009; Wadsworth, et al., 2007). For example, in the last ten years at a South Florida state college, elearning enrollment had an increase from barely existent to almost five thousand students per year (PBCC Academic Affairs, 2006). This rapid growth has given rise to issues and concerns regarding student achievement. There is a vital need to increase retention and success in online education, particularly in online mathematics classes (Wadsworth, et al., 2007). Motivation has been shown to be an important attribute for success and, therefore, warrants further investigation as an integral component of instructional design.

BACKGROUND/THEORETICAL FRAMEWORK

The role of instructional strategies in online mathematics learning develops from the following major areas and their related subsets: motivation and academic success; online learning and andragogy; and instructional design and learning strategies. It is noted that the hypothesis that motivational strategies promote achievement and success in online mathematics courses is supported by recent investigators who suggested the need to research the effectiveness of incorporating motivational strategies in the implementation of online instructional designs (Bellon & Oates, 2002; Kelsey & D'Souza, 2004; Patall, et al., 2008; Sanacore, 2008; Skinner, 2005).

Motivation and Academic Success

Motivation in an elearning environment is the major factor that determines success (Bellon & Oates, 2002; Chang, 2005; Paas, Tuovinen, van Merriënboer, & Darabi, 2005; Patall, et al., 2008; Sanacore, 2008). Student motivation is perceived as the basis for student learning and success. The role of motivation needs to be recognized as the facilitator of meaningful learning. When instructors focus on learners' strengths and provide them with well-matched and structured resources across the curriculum, they increase opportunities for motivation and for successful learning (Bellon & Oates, 2002; Ozcelik & Yildirim, 2005; Sanacore, 2008; Wadsworth, et al., 2007). Easy access to quality resources is not enough to promote competency and lifetime learning, but the balance of instructional materials with effective teaching sets the stage for success (Sanacore, 2008).

As significant research dealing with increasing performance in business and industry continues to grow, the field of education is not to be left behind. Most primary grade teachers make extensive use of extrinsic rewards to motivate their students to better performance. These extrinsic rewards included *happy faces*, grades, and treats. This approach was consistent with the early research of Skinner (2005). Although the use of extrinsic rewards works for younger children, Sanacore (2008) emphasized that adult learners are primarily emotional and secondarily intellectual. He stated that intrinsic rewards are the internal psychic or spiritual satisfactions one receives from one's work, such as a personal sense of accomplishment or enjoyment of the work itself. He concurred with Knowles (1980) that connecting the students' experiences, preferences, and talent to the required content is important in motivating students to become inspired learners. That is, when instructors incorporate learners' interests into the curriculum, learners are more apt to be motivated and engaged, and their achievement is more likely to improve.

Sanacore (2008) supported that promoting student interests in the content resulted in greater student engagement, higher levels of intrinsic motivation as well as student productivity, greater self-autonomy, and higher achievement and sense of self-competence. Moreover, Patall et al. (2008) endorsed the same beliefs in a meta-analysis of 41 studies that examined the effects of choice on intrinsic motivation and related outcomes. Their results indicated that providing choice did in fact enhance intrinsic motivation, performance, and persistence. When students are afforded the opportunity to make choices (Patall, et al., 2008), students affirm their sense of autonomy.

Ausburn's (2004) study results, although limited to 67 working adults studying for teacher certification or advanced degrees in education, and a combination of online learning plus a limited number of face-to-face experiences, also showed that students place a high value on options and the ability to control their own learning environment. This finding warrants the question for this present study: Does providing choices of learning tools increase achievement and retention in online mathematics classes? It is clear that just providing choices or options is not enough. The learner must process a self-determinate approach in order to make the choices. Further studies (Patall, et al., 2008; Sanacore, 2008; Vansteenkiste, Soenens, Timmermans, Lens, & Van den Broeck, 2008) dealing with intrinsic and extrinsic motivation focused on self-determination theory and its resulting implications for learning. These studies provided an examination of whether an intrinsic goal prior to engagement in a learning activity affected differentially learning and performance among students.

In a series of experimental field studies in Belgium that focused on learning and performance outcomes, it was found that framing a learning activity in terms of the attainment of an intrinsic goal enhanced conceptual learning, performance, and persistence (Vansteenkiste, et al., 2008). The authors indicated that the relationship between an individual's life goals, achievement, and adjustment depends on the match or fit between the individual's personal goal orientations and the goals that are emphasized and encouraged in the direct environment (Vansteenkiste, et al., 2008). In the context of the classroom, Patall et al. (2008) stated that several studies have positively linked the student's level of intrinsic motivation for schoolwork to academic achievement. Significant correlations have also been found among elementary school students between intrinsic motivation and achievement as measured by standardized achievement tests in specific subjects such as mathematics (Patall, et al., 2008).

Moreover, Hughes, McLeod, Brown, Maeda, and Choi (2007) found that "online courses can provide successful, alternative learning opportunities for algebra students while maintaining similar academic standards and achievement levels, even for students who are on less rigorous academic paths" (p. 208). In addition, "students who were exposed to online discussion embedded with metacognitive guidance (Online+Meta) outperformed their counterparts (Online) on standard tasks and on the solution of real-life tasks" (Kramarski & Mizrachi, 2006, p. 228).

Recent studies on motivation and academic achievement have broadened the research to include cognitive load. Paas et al. (2005) identified motivation as an important dimension that determines learning success as well as retention rates (van Merriënboer & Ayres, 2005). They provided a motivational perspective to Cognitive Load Theory (CLT). Cognitive load refers to the total amount of mental activity imposed on short-term or working memory at one point in time. CLT is concerned with techniques for reducing working memory load in order to facilitate the changes in long-term memory associated with schema acquisition. The major factor that contributes to cognitive load is the number of elements to be attended. These include intrinsic, extrinsic or extraneous, and germane cognitive loads. Intrinsic cognitive load relates to the difficulty of the content itself. Extraneous cognitive load deals with the cognitive activities that are introduced by the information or learning materials. Germane load is information processing and varies inversely to extraneous load (Sweller, van Morriënboer, & Paas, 1998).

According to Morrinson and Anglin (2005), more recent research in CLT has switched concerns from reducing extraneous load to raising germane and intrinsic loads given prior knowledge of learners in technology skills and content background. Increasing the variability of practice is one effective way to grow germane cognitive load (van Merriënboer & Ayres, 2005). Is the variability of practice available in an interactive course management system such as MyMathLab, an effective way to grow germane cognitive load? In an informal chat conversation in Blackboard, when a student in Trigonometry was asked if he thought that MyMathLab helped, he responded: "Yes, even if you don't understand the book's interpretation you can always fall back on the videos or the endless practice problems. It seems to help each type of learning process, visual, etc." This comment is in agreement with those from students surveyed in the studies presented by Speckler (2009).

In addition, Paas et al. (2005) asserted that until now, CLT has focused on the alignment of instruction with cognitive processes, without recognizing the role of motivation in training. Mental effort and performance play an important role in CLT in defining the efficiency of the instructional conditions. The efficiency perspective does not distinguish that significant learning can only begin if training experience is joined with motivation to achieve. When learners are motivated and devote mental effort in processing instructions, then instructional manipulations can help optimize the efficiency of cognitive load (Paas, et al., 2005).

Paas et al. (2005) pointed out that to motivate students to achieve in an online learning environment involves students' perceptions of their own self-efficacy, the usefulness of exerting mental effort, and the value of the task at hand. The amount of invested mental effort is considered as an accurate measure of motivational behavior. The authors found that motivation, mental effort, and performance are positively related. When learner involvement is higher in a particular instructional condition, more mental effort or a person's ability to learn is likely to be invested, and this increase in mental effort is likely to result in higher performance (Paas, et al., 2005). Louisiana State University mathematics faculty collected data on the use of an interactive courseware (MyMathLab) and achievement (Speckler, 2009). Their analysis further reinforced the positive correlation between effort and achievement.

Furthermore, intrinsic motivation has also been positively linked to having choices and achievement, suggesting the need to investigate the impact of motivational strategies in online learning (Patall, et al., 2008). Often, learning about the delivery technology goes on simultaneously with learning the content and accomplishment of primary content goals. Significant research regarding students in online classes must incorporate the fact that not only are students expected to learn the course content but they must also become proficient in maneuvering within the online environment (Morrison & Anglin, 2005). Allowing and/or encouraging students to select the appropriate technologies for themselves, along with the appropriate learning objectives based on their previous knowledge, may reduce the cognitive load and enhance motivation and achievement.

Online Learning and Andragogy

As virtual enrollment continues to grow in higher education, the need to understand online learners increases in an effort to compete effectively in a global community. Online learners represented 17% of all higher education students in 2005, with more than half of all online learners enrolled in community colleges (Bambara, et al., 2009). An important aspect of any online learning program is evaluation for continuous improvement. Unfortunately, there has been a lack of systematic evaluation research focusing on online courses (Tallent-Runnels, et al., 2006).

As early as the 1920s when adult education started to be organized systematically, adult educators began experiencing several problems with the pedagogical model, namely the transmittal of knowledge and skills. When these leaders found their students to be resistant to prescribed pedagogical strategies, including lectures, assigned readings, drill, examinations, and rote memorization, they began experimenting by intuition with what is known today as adult education principles. Malcolm Knowles (1980), the father of andragogy and a visionary in the field of adult education, stated:

I don't see andragogy as an ideology at all, but a system of assumptions about learners that needs to be tested out for different learners in different situations. In a sense, it is a system that encompasses the pedagogical model, since it makes legitimate the application of pedagogical strategies in those situations in which the assumptions of the pedagogical model are realistic (p. 59).

Andragogy, the art and science of helping adults learn, is premised on the assumptions that as adults mature: (a) their self-concept moves from a dependent personality to one that is self-directed; (b) their experiences become a rich resource for learning; (c) their readiness to learn depends on the developmental tasks of their social roles; and (d) their time perspective changes from one of postponed application of information to immediate application; and thus, their focus on learning shifts to performance (Knowles, 1980). This infers and supports the premise that adults increasingly become self-directing as they acquire multiple roles in life as workers, spouses, parents, and citizens, their performance in these roles being the main source of self-fulfillment.

Although adults may be completely self-directing in all other aspects of their lives, when it comes to an educational activity, their previous schooling under the pedagogical model has preconditioned them to take a dependent role for learning. Knowles (1980) further emphasized that to fulfill the psychological need of adults to be self-directing, it is important to include in the educational activity some preparatory experiences that will help adults acquire a new way of thinking about the role of the learner and some new skills in self-directed learning. Adult learners tend to be self-directed; that is, they want some control over both the content of learning and the way the knowledge or skill is presented.

One of the principal premises of andragogy is that the successful facilitator acknowledges that need and creates a learning environment that is highly interactive. Therefore, andragogy tends to be process-driven more than content-driven (Knowles, 1980). That is not to say that content is immaterial to the adult learner, but that the adult learner acquires new material or a taught skill more efficiently when the facilitator individualizes the learning experience. Hence, "the modern task of education becomes one of finding new ways to link learners with learning resources" (Knowles, 1980, p. 20).

Merriam and Caffarella (1999) acknowledged that the most used operational definition of self-directed learning was provided by Guglielmino in 1977, where she stated that self-directed learning " consists of a complex [set] of attitudes, values and abilities that create the likelihood that an individual is capable of self-directed learning" (p. 307). She identified the psychological qualities involved in readiness for self-directed learning as: initiative, independence and persistence in learning; self-discipline; enjoyment in learning; acceptance of responsibility for one's own learning; viewing problems as challenges and not as obstacles; tendency to be goal oriented; strong ability to learn independently; and high degree of curiosity. Guglielmino and Guglielmino (1994) also recommend a formalized use of self-directed learning strategies. One such strategy is the use of learning contracts or study plans for overcoming resistance to self-directed learning. The goals of self-directed learning are to enhance the ability of the learner to become self-directed, to foster transformational learning, and to promote emancipation of learning and social action (Merriam, et al., 2007). The authors further emphasized that the ultimate goal should be for people to develop as lifelong learners in society. Additional investigations dealing with self-directed learning use the term metamotivation (Boekaerts, 1995). This terminology reflects higher order motivation as incorporated into Maslow's (1943) final level of self-actualization. Boekaerts also referred to self-directed learning as metacognitively, cognitively, motivationally, and behaviorally active participation in learning.

The integration of adult education theories to online learning places the needs of the learners as the foundation for success (DuCharme-Hansen & Dupin-Bryant, 2004). Although many theories exist to explain how people learn, three schools of theories dominate the discussion of learning theory: behaviorism, cognitivism, and constructivism (Driscoll & Carliner, 2005). Behaviorism developed from a movement in psychology and philosophy that emphasizes outward observable behavior; cognitivism evolved out of the increasing dissatisfaction with a behaviorism that refused to acknowledge the processes that go on in the learner's head; and constructivism is based on the premise that learners can create their own understanding of the world by reflecting on current and past experiences (Driscoll & Carliner, 2005).

In elearning, instructor and students become mutual partners in the learning journey. For this joint venture to be effective, the learner must take the initiative for learning in order to experience transformation. Mezirow conjectured that people go through a set of phases when they experience transformative learning (Merriam, et al., 2007). These phases include: experiencing a disorienting dilemma; self-examination; critical assessment of assumptions; recognizing that others have gone through a similar process; exploring options; formulating a plan of action; and reintegration. An examination of these phases shows that key in the transformation process is *reflection*. Mezirow suggested that when individuals reflect on the content or description of a problem, on the strategies used to solve the problem rather than the content of the problem itself, and on the relevance of the problem itself, transformative learning occurs (Merriam, et al., 2007). Findings of other studies (Kramarski & Mizrachi, 2006) also suggest that encouraging reflection helps mathematics students elaborate and retain information.

Instructional Design and Learning Strategies

From motivation, cognitive load, online instruction, andragogy, and learning theories among others, one must be responsive to the wide range of concepts and theories that could be put into practice to increase students' success and retention in online mathematics courses. With so many theories, approaches and models, it is hard to know what will really be effective in an online instructional mathematics situation. The literature review so far has focused on investigating strategies that promote achievement in online mathematics classes. It is now necessary to focus on the primary objective of transforming theory into practice by addressing learning theories implications in instructional design.

The research regarding online instruction emphasizes the importance of learner-focused course design (DuCharme-Hansen & Dupin-Bryant, 2004; Knowles, 1980; Merriam, et al., 2007; Tallent-Runnels, et al., 2006). Because time is precious for adult learners, they have a need for learning options that are time efficient and flexible (DuCharme-Hansen & Dupin-Bryant, 2004). Driscoll and Carliner (2005) suggested the use of a problem-based approach to design, which provides a pragmatic framework that focuses the design effort on the learning challenge to be addressed. The approach to instructional design should be one that has the best fit with the learning challenge being faced (Driscoll & Carliner, 2005). The first step is to define the problem as thoroughly as the designer believes is necessary, then to devise a solution that addresses the key issues raised by the problem.

The andragogical model of instruction described by Knowles includes the following elements: diagnosing learning needs, formulating objectives, designing a pattern of learning experiences, and evaluating results (Merriam & Caffarella, 1999). This learner-centered instructional model "has not been used a great deal in actual practice, except in non-formal or self-directed situations. Adult learning in formal settings … remains primarily instructor designed and directed" (p. 37). Because of the nature of the virtual classroom, which is characterized by independence of time and space, the online learning environment is "a highly learner-centered and self-regulated learning environment, where learners must take responsibility for what and how to learn" (Lee, 2002, p. 101).

Behavioral and motivational strategies to help students to succeed in online learning environments are a topic of practical concern to instructional designers, and of theoretical concern to researchers (Lee, 2002; Morrison & Anglin, 2005; Paas, et al., 2005). The first challenge is to redesign the prevalent instructional presentations to emphasize pedagogies in which learners actively construct knowledge, using mediated interactions enabled by current technologies (Dede, 2005). Before applying a constructivist approach to learning, at-risk mathematics students, who are at initial stages of schema development calling for traditional instructional approaches, will benefit first from behavioral learning activities (Berge, 2005; Li & Edmonds, 2005). This approach seems to complement the findings of other researchers regarding instructional design elements of online courses. The general consensus among researchers is biased towards interactivity, communication, and connectedness as essential elements at the heart of the design (Ausburn, 2004; Bellon & Oates, 2002; Bork, 2005; Kelsey & D'Souza, 2004; Salas, et al., 2002; Sanacore, 2008; Szecsy, et al., 2005). The concept of building on a solid knowledge foundation facilitates learners' mastery of the challenges of addressing new knowledge in a new learning environment.

Morrison and Anglin (2005) noted that strategies for success in an online class must include an adequate orientation toward the use of tools. Clarke, Ayres, and Sweller's study on the impact of timing on learning technology skills when learning mathematical concepts also supports this heuristic (as cited in Morrison & Anglin, 2005). They recommend further research to confirm that a strategy requiring initial learning of technology skills, and then mathematical concepts, will enhance learning for students with low levels of technology skills. Based on a multifaceted examination of motivation and online mathematics achievement, it is now necessary to briefly address cognitive load implications in instructional design.

Cognitive load theory proposes to give greater consideration to the role and limitations of working memory in instructional design (Ozcelick & Yildrim, 2005). When presenting instruction or training, there are two types of information. One is intrinsic cognitive load, which relates to the difficulty of the content itself. Intrinsic cognitive load cannot be modified by the instruction (van Merriënboer & Ayres, 2005). Extraneous cognitive load relates to cognitive activities that are introduced by the presentation of the learning materials. One of the major roadblocks in online mathematics classes is the lack of technology skills to interact with the content (Morrison & Anglin, 2005). The instructional designer's job is to limit the amount of extraneous load and to build into their presentations activities that foster germane load or schema formation (Ozcelik & Yildirim, 2005; Sweller, 2006). When intrinsic cognitive load is low (simple content) sufficient mental resources may remain to enable a learner to learn from any type of instructional material, even that which imposes a high level of extraneous cognitive load. If the intrinsic cognitive load is high (difficult content) and the extraneous cognitive load is also high, then total cognitive load will exceed mental resources and learning may fail to occur (van Merriënboer & Ayres, 2005).

Excessively high levels of cognitive load may result directly from the instructional materials presented to students. Redesigning instructional materials to reduce the levels of extraneous cognitive load may enhance learning (Sweller, et al., 1998). Content areas that are most likely to demonstrate beneficial results from improved instructional design are those that deal with complex information where the elements of to-be-learned information interact with one another, therefore imposing a high level of intrinsic cognitive load. Modifying the instructional materials to create a lower level of extraneous cognitive load will facilitate learning if the resulting total cognitive load falls to a level that is within the bounds of mental resources (Sweller, 2006). The quality of interaction within an online class depends upon learners' knowledge of the system. Facilitating the understanding of the learning system is essential to success. Providing a well-structured orientation on the use of technical tools may decrease extraneous load.

Because students in distance learning classes have a range of learning styles, faculty must adjust their instruction to meet the varying learning styles. Instructors who place a traditional course online should consider administering a student learning style inventory to their distance-learning students (Diaz & Cartnal, 1999). Knowledge of student learning preferences can aid faculty in class preparation, designing class delivery methods, choosing appropriate technologies, and developing sensitivity to differing student learning preferences within the distance learning environment (Ausburn, 2004; Conti, 2009; Diaz & Cartnal, 1999; Knowles, 1980; Wadsworth, et al., 2007).

Providing students with opportunities to integrate their knowledge through online instruction may not be effective if they lack the skills needed to regulate their learning. Strategies to prepare students for the rigors of learning at a distance in order to increase the probability of retention and success must be put into practice (Chang, 2005). "Strategic learning ... requires students to be self-regulated in their thoughts and actions to attain personal goals" (Wadsworth, et al., p. 7). According to Chang (2005), research results revealed that students' motivation perception benefited from online instruction with self-regulated learning strategies because they became more responsible for their own learning, tended to value the learning material more, and became more confident in course understanding and class performance. Lee (2002) defined self-regulated learning as "metacognitively, cognitively, motivationally, and behaviorally active participation in learning" (p. 101). He also acknowledged that learning strategies help learners guide their own learning process and make appropriate decisions independently, as well as enhance learner motivation and self-esteem.

In creating materials, it is essential to relate them to learning strategies based on student's learning preferences (Ausburn, 2004; Chang, 2005; Conti, 2009; Knowles, 1980; Lee, 2002; Wadsworth, et al., 2007). Ausburn (2004) recognized that although learning styles have long been generally accepted as stable and deeply ingrained processes for taking in and processing information, learning strategies are less rigid and more related to personal preferences and choices made by learners in undertaking learning tasks. Conti (2009) noted that learning strategies provide a way for addressing individual differences in the learning process. They are different from learning styles in that they are techniques selected for a specific assignment (Conti, 2009). He further explained that learners use various strategies to accomplish their learning needs regardless of the type of setting, and that these strategies vary by individual and by learning objective. Learning strategies are those techniques or specialized skills that the learner has developed to use in both formal and informal learning situations.

Although definitions of learning strategies vary according to the basis of the researcher's theoretical orientation, a common conceptualization includes the areas of cognitive and metacognitive strategies. One tool currently used to assess the learner's processing of information is a self-assessment instrument called ATLAS (Ausburn, 2004; Conti, 2009). ATLAS groups learners into one of the three preferred strategies or approaches to learning. The three strategies are named: *Navigators*, *Problem Solvers*, and *Engagers*. Navigators are viewed as result-oriented learners who favor efficiency and effectiveness via a plan. Problem solvers are learners that are critical thinkers who explore options (multiple paths) and avoid rapid closure. Engagers are learners that love to learn, and approach the affective domain seeking connectedness and high involvement (Conti, 2009). The information gathered through ATLAS can help instructors in designing the course in a way that it offers options to learners. The assessment results can also help learners in recognizing what tools to use when interacting socially and cognitively in order to feel most connected within the virtual learning environment.

ATLAS is a user-friendly and accessible instrument that provides a quick and accurate group placement of the learners' preferences for initiating a learning task (Conti, 2009). The website www.conti-creations.com provides online access to ATLAS (Ausburn, 2004; Conti, 2009). Based on the same construct and theory of SKILLS (Self-Knowledge Inventory of Lifelong Learning Strategies), ATLAS is a 5-item instrument used to stimulate the user's metacognitive process of thinking about how they go about learning. SKILLS is a 180-item questionnaire that measures adult learning strategies in real-life learning situations and classifies these strategies according to constructs of metacognition, memory, metamotivation, resource management, and critical thinking. With three types of validity testing, ATLAS is a reliable instrument with a reliability coefficient of

.88 (Conti, 2009). In a descriptive case study by Munday (2002), 100% of the participants agreed that ATLAS accurately described their preferred learning strategy, whereas Massey (2001) reported 89.9% accuracy.

Researchers in the field of cognitive load are challenged today with investigating the motivational effects of instructional conditions that will maximize learning and transfer in elearning environments. Keller's motivational model (Attention, Reward/Enjoyment, and Confidence) as cited in Bellon and Oates (2002) provides a typology that, together with metacognition strategies, can help instructional designers organize their knowledge about learner motivation and motivational strategies (Bellon & Oates, 2002; Paas, et al., 2005). It can also be used to assess the presence or absence of motivational design components. Paas et al. (2005) indicated that instructional manipulations to optimize the cognitive load have little effect unless learners are motivated and actually invest mental effort in processing the instructions. Of course, this leaves teachers with a no-win situation with those students that apparently were not motivated in the research studies. However, motivation has not been an issue in cognitive load research. Most studies have focused on short laboratory experiments in which learners may be more inclined to invest mental effort than in real learning situations.

Drennan, Kennedy, and Pisarski (2005) identified two key attributes of student satisfaction: positive perceptions of technology in terms of ease of access and use of flexible online learning material, and autonomous and innovative learning styles. In addition, Bellon and Oates (2002) found that there is a relationship between student personality and the student's preferred online component. The researchers suggested several techniques to enhance motivation such as: (a) the inclusion of emails from instructor and postings to the discussion board, which were rated at the highest level of motivation on interpersonal tools by graduate level students; (b) the provision of links provided by instructor to Internet sites and content; (c) the offering of a variety of course components; (d) the provision of a clear and well-structured organization; and (e) flexible target due dates set by the instructor.

Similar findings were reported by Dynan, Cate, and Rhee (2008) in their study of 250 online business students. Their study results showed that a structured environment also provides a more suitable one for improving readiness for self-directed learning for more students. This idea supports the first assumption in andragogy that as adults mature, their self-concept moves from dependent personality to that of self-directed (Knowles, 1980).

Kelsey and D'Souza's (2004) study suggested that interaction may be a predicating factor for the success of distance education courses. They found that student-instructor interaction was very important to students and instructors; and student-technology interactions were meaningful when using course websites, emails, videotapes, CD-ROMS, and a course management system called Blackboard.com. The authors recommended discontinuing the use of interactive video conferencing and streaming video as these proved to be unsatisfying for both students and instructors.

When students are able to choose online materials according to their own needs, they regulate their own learning and engage in learning and revision processes. Livingston and Condie (2006) noticed that "the independent use of the materials by students, particularly when it was self-directed rather than prompted by their teachers, and their selection of the mode of study..., provided an opportunity to experience and develop lifelong learning strategies" (p. 153). Their study results also showed that the use of technology gave students the chance to be more active in the learning process, and consequently improved their exam scores. They concluded that using a computer-assisted program for instruction moves toward the use of a more constructivist model where learners are actively involved in constructing their own knowledge.

It seems clear that a multifaceted approach to increase student success and retention in online mathematics courses should include an understanding and use of behaviorism, cognitivism, and constructivism learning theories as they relate to students' preferred learning strategies. The instructor should provide a highly structured environment in which students practice behaviors, where the information is organized to make the processing more efficient and effective so that learners can construct knowledge by means of reflecting on their own experiences. A highly interactive, learner-focused course design may be a viable approach to promote achievement and retention in online mathematics courses. Figure 1 describes the conceptual framework for the study.

DIGITAL COLLEGE LEARNERS

Results of multiple studies reported that a widely accepted view of the distance learner is one who is older than the typical undergraduate, female, likely to have multirole and multi-life commitments, married, and have an abundance of job, family, and social responsibilities (DuCharme-Hansen & Dupin-Bryant, 2004; Thompson, 1998; Vansteenkiste, et al., 2008). This information continues to be validated in a south Florida state college (PBCC Distance Learning, 2009). Moreover, as online learning options expand, Bambara et al. (2009) reported findings on dropout rates of 15% to 50% higher in online classes than in traditional face-to-face options. The authors conducted a phenomenological study that examined the lived experience of community college students enrolled in high-risk online courses. They found that all participants experienced isolation and academic challenge in some way and to some degree (Bambara, et al., 2009).

Additional vital factors to be considered when designing an online mathematics course include that high-risk mathematics students have a weak knowledge foundation, and are in need of skills that will help them succeed in these learning environments (Wadsworth, et al., 2007). Wadsworth et al. (2007) argued that Web-based learners must become accustomed to a structured learning environment without direct instruction. This argument suggests that different methods may be needed for different levels of learners even in the same online course.

Online learning technologies offer greater flexibility and increased autonomy for students, but have the potential to result in social isolation (Bambara, et al., 2009; Hantula & Pawlowicz, 2004; Kelsey & D'Souza, 2004). One of the major criticisms of distance learning is that students are isolated from each other and the instructor. Public and direct student-instructor interactions are essential characteristics of learning (Kelsey & D'Souza, 2004). In an online class, *interpersonal tools*, also called Information and Communication Technology (ICT), refer to the components available in a Web-based courseware platform like Blackboard that are used by instructors and students to interact with each other. Interpersonal tools in BlackBoard include announcements, email, discussion board, chat room, and student pages where they can post their introductions. In the virtual classroom, these are the tools available for social interaction, one of the strongest human characteristics that serves as a principle of human motivation (Vroom, 1964).

ICT tools blur artificial boundaries and provide information in a connected environment. It has been said before that "ICT tools enable the higher education community to engage students and each other in an expansive knowledge base that knows no borders and has the capacity to change preconceptions, encourage reflection, and improve professional educational practice" (Szecsy, Danzig, & Gonzales, 2005, p. 8). Szecsy et al. (2005) conducted a qualitative multiple case study on the development and use of ICT to encourage communication, interaction, and collaboration. Their findings support discussion board and emails as highly conducive to communicating and interact-

Figure 1. A multifaceted approach to online mathematics learning

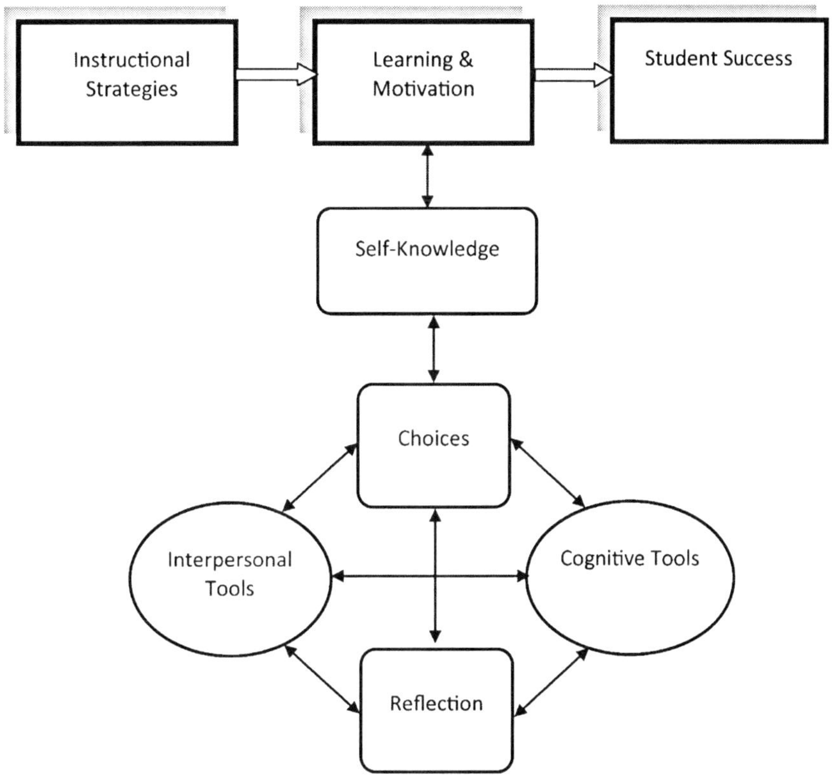

ing among students. This finding suggests the need to question if a preferred learning strategy may be significantly related to choices of interpersonal tools. Extending this concept to online mathematics learning, Kramarski and Mizrachi (2006) indicated that online discussions are not sufficient for improving mathematical literacy and self-regulated learning, unless these discussions are structured. Their findings also supported the importance of pedagogical uses with advanced technology such as metacognitive guidance.

A review of the literature shows computer-mediated instruction to be positively linked to students' perceptions and achievement (Li & Edmonds, 2005; Livingston & Condie, 2006; Morrison & Anglin, 2005; Speckler, 2009). In a study on effects of computer-assisted mathematics instruction on at-risk adult learners, Li and Edmonds (2005) found positive gains in student success as well as increased confidence and satisfaction with mathematical learning. Moreover, Ozcelik and Yildirim (2005) provided a perspective of cognitive approaches, which concluded that computer programs can help reduce memory burden for learners; and hence, facilitate schema construction and automation. Regarding *cognitive tools*, Ozcelick and Yildrim (2005) stated the following:

According to Jonassen and Reeves (1996), "cognitive tools refer to technologies, tangible or intangible, that enhance the cognitive powers of human beings during thinking, problem solving, and learning." For Kozma (1987), cognitive tools are software programs that use the computer to amplify, extend, or enhance human cognition. The authors concluded that "when computers carry out lower-level computational operations, users have more resources to engage in higher-level operations such as generating a hypothesis, thinking out casual links, and drawing conclusions" (p. 296).

Additionally, Wadsworth et al. (2007) corroborated that research examining the effectiveness of specific learning strategies for supporting online mathematics student learning is scarce. They also stated "available research has shown benefits from using metacognitive tools integrated into online software to keep students on track" (p. 12).

In examination of the findings, online learning must take place in a well-structured environment that incorporates a variety of options. Both interpersonal and cognitive tools and strategies must be integrated in the delivery of online learning instruction. The next step for educators is to translate this research along with their own assessments to the virtual classroom in order to increase student achievement. Instructional designers must realize when they attempt to do this that the teachers they support are their students who must be motivated to use the results in teaching and learning.

FUTURE TRENDS

Online classes should offer students the choice of all tools available. A general consensus among students surveyed in an online mathematics class was that all the interpersonal and cognitive tools available contributed to their learning experience. The research findings support the recommendation to use announcements in a concise manner to remind students of important deadlines listed on the calendar, always offering support and encouragement (Porro, 2011).

Efforts should continue in improving student retention. If students are not retained, then it is difficult to develop a system to reach out to them and offer support to succeed. A multifaceted model as the one presented in this review provided significant results for retention (Porro, 2011).

The effect of chat on achievement in mathematics classes warrants further research. There is a need to further test the content in the chat room. Is the discussion off topic or not? Do students reference the tutorials or PowerPoint, or any other tool? BlackBoard, the course management used, does not support mathematical equations and figures. In addition, future studies should investigate whether prior online course experience and level of computer knowledge predict achievement.

A model that includes reflection as well as ATLAS groups and online tools as predictors of achievement should be investigated further, specifically with a larger sample. Also, discussion postings should be incorporated in the class grade to help students achieve. If it is not required, there would be very little interaction in the online environment. Given the data for this study, the researcher can conclude that the choice of online tools and students' knowledge of their preferred learning strategy should continue to be investigated as part of the instructional strategies in online mathematics classes.

CONCLUSION

With the realization that student retention and success, particularly in online mathematics classes, were a serious concern at Palm Beach State College and nationwide this study was developed. Previous researchers (Wadsworth, et al., 2007) also noted that although online learning enrollment is growing, very little research had been conducted that examined the use of cognitive-strategies and their effects on student learning and achievement in online courses. The purpose of this review was to investigate the effect of using instructional strategies on student achievement and retention in online mathematics classes. Using the research of Wadsworth et al. (2007) as a foundational point and extending it to Ausburn's (2004) study, this research project applied a multi-faceted motivational perspective to the design of online instruction. By means of the ATLAS instrument for a self-diagnostic measure of preferred learning strategies, the study combined reflections on online tools with the actual hits on each of these tools.

Munday (2002) concluded that adult learners can realize a positive impact in their academic achievement if they know their learning strategy preferences. Ellington and Bryan (2010) also recommended a simple online learning-style assessment to quickly adapt to the learning style of each online student and produce the learning assignments appropriately. By students having self-knowledge of preferred learning strategies as Navigators, Problem Solvers, or Engagers as prescribed in ATLAS, they will be able to choose interpersonal and cognitive tools that best match their learning journey. In particular, the instructional model presented used a design of learning strategies to promote interpersonal and cognitive interactions. A multifaceted approach to teaching and learning may be necessary to promote achievement and retention in online mathematics classes.

REFERENCES

Ausburn, L. J. (2004). Course design elements most valued by adult learners in blended online education environments: An American perspective. *Educational Media International*, 327–337. Retrieved from http://test.scripts.psu.edu/users/k/h/khk122/woty/OnlineAdultLearners/Ausbum%20 2004.pdf doi:10.1080/0952398042000314820

Bambara, C., Harbour, C., Davies, T., & Athey, S. (2009). The lived experience of community college students enrolled in high-risk online courses. *Community College Review*, *36*(3), 219–238. doi:10.1177/0091552108327187

Bellon, T., & Oates, R. (2002). *Best practices in cyberspace: Motivating the online learner*. Paper presented at the National Education Computing Conference. Retrieved from http://www.eric.ed.gov/PDFS/ED475923.pdf

Berge, Z. L. (2005). Taking the distance out of distance education. In Kearsley, G. (Ed.), *Online Learning: Personal Reflections on the Transformation of Education* (pp. 12–25). Englewood Cliffs, NJ: Educational Technology Publications, Inc.

Blake, R. R., & Mouton, J. S. (1972). What is instrumented learning? *Training and Development Journal*, *26*(1), 12–20.

Boekaerts, M. (1995). Self-regulated learning: Bridging the gap between metacognitive and metamotivation theories. *Educational Psychologist*, *30*(4), 195–200. doi:10.1207/s15326985ep3004_4

Bork, A. (2005). Distance learning today and tomorrow. In Kearsley, G. (Ed.), *Online Learning: Personal Reflections on the Transformation of Education* (pp. 26–41). Englewood Cliffs, NJ: Educational Technology Publications, Inc.

Chang, M. (2005). Applying self-regulated learning strategies in a web-based instruction - An investigation of motivation perception. *Computer Assisted Language Learning*, *18*(3), 217–230. doi:10.1080/09588220500178939

Conti, G. J. (2009). Development of a user-friendly instrument for identifying the learning strategy preferences of adults. *Teaching and Teacher Education*, *25*, 887–896. doi:10.1016/j.tate.2009.02.024

Dede, C. (2005). An intellectual journey from distance education to distributed learning. In Kearsley, G. (Ed.), *Online Learning: Personal Reflections on the Transformation of Education* (pp. 66–72). Englewood Cliffs, NJ: Educational Technology Publications, Inc.

Diaz, D. P., & Cartnal, R. B. (1999). Students' learning styles in two classes: Online distance learning and equivalent on-campus. *College Teaching*, *47*(4), 130–135. Retrieved from http://home.earthlink.net/~davidpdiaz/LTS/html_docs/grslss.htm doi:10.1080/87567559909595802

Distance Learning, P. B. C. C. (2009). *What is distance learning?* Retrieved from http://www.pbcc.edu/x2199.xml

Drennan, J., Kennedy, J., & Pisarski, A. (2005). Factors affecting student attitudes toward flexible online learning in management education. *The Journal of Educational Research*, *98*(6), 331–338. Retrieved from http://www.heldref.org doi:10.3200/JOER.98.6.331-338

Driscoll, M., & Carliner, S. (2005). *Advanced web-based training strategies: Unlocking instructionally sound online learning*. San Francisco, CA: John Wiley & Sons, Inc.

DuCharme-Hansen, B., & Dupin-Bryant, P. (2004). *Web-based distance education for adults*. Malabar, FL: Krieger Publishing Company.

Dynan, L., Cate, T., & Rhee, K. (2008). The impact of learning structure on students' readiness for self-directed learning. *Journal of Education for Business*, *84*(2), 96–100. Retrieved from http://www.heldref.org doi:10.3200/JOEB.84.2.96-100

Ellington, L., & Bryan, V. (2010). The e-adult learner: The definitive classic in e-workplace development. In D. Guralnick (Ed.), *Proceedings of the Third International Conference on e-Learning in the Workplace,* (pp. 1-7). New York, NY: Kaleidoscope Learning, Inc.

Guglielmino, L. M., & Guglielmino, P. J. (1994). Practical experience with self-directed learning in business and industry. *New Directions for Adult and Continuing Education*, *64*, 39. Retrieved from http://www.ebscohost.com/academic/business-source-premier doi:10.1002/ace.36719946407

Hantula, D. A., & Pawlowicz, D. M. (2004). Education mirrors industry: On the not-so surprising rise of the Internet distance education. In Monolescu, D., Schifter, C., & Greenwood, L. (Eds.), *The Distance Education Evolution: Issues and Case Studies* (pp. 142–162). Hersey, PA: IGI Global. doi:10.4018/978-1-59140-120-9.ch006

Hughes, J., McLeod, S., Brown, R., Maeda, Y., & Choi, J. (2007). Academic achievement and perceptions of the learning environment in virtual and traditional secondary mathematics classrooms. *American Journal of Distance Education*, *21*(4), 199–214. doi:10.1080/08923640701595365

Kelsey, K. D., & D'Souza, A. (2004). Student motivation for learning at a distance: Does interaction matter? *Online Journal of Distance Learning Administration*, *7*(2). Retrieved from http://www.westga.edu/~distance/ojdla/summer72/kelsey72.html

Knowles, M. S. (1980). *The modern practice of adult education: From pedagogy to andragogy* (2nd ed.). Chicago, IL: Association Press/Follett.

Kramarski, B., & Mizrachi, N. (2006). Online discussion and self-regulated learning: Effects of instructional methods on mathematical literacy. *The Journal of Educational Research*, *99*(4), 218–230. Retrieved from http://search.ebscohost.com doi:10.3200/JOER.99.4.218-231

Lee, I. (2002). Gender differences in self-regulated on-line learning strategies within Korea's university context. *Educational Technology Research and Development*, *50*(1), 101–111. doi:10.1007/BF02504967

Li, Q., & Edmonds, K. A. (2005). Mathematics and at-risk adult learners: Would technology help? *Journal of Research on Technology in Education*, *38*(2), 143–166.

Livingston, K., & Condie, R. (2006). The impact of an online learning program on teaching and learning strategies. *Theory into Practice*, *45*(2), 150–158. doi:10.1207/s15430421tip4502_7

Maslow, A. (1943). A theory of human motivation. *Psychological Review*, *50*(4), 370–396. Retrieved from http://www.ebscohost.com/academic/business-source-premier doi:10.1037/h0054346

Massey, S. C. (2001). *Understanding learning styles and learning strategies of adult learners at OSU-Okmulgee*. (Unpublished Doctoral Dissertation). Oklahoma State University. Stillwater, OK.

Merriam, S. B., & Caffarella, R. S. (1999). *Learning in adulthood: A comprehensive guide* (2nd ed.). San Francisco, CA: Jossey-Bass.

Merriam, S. B., Caffarella, R. S., & Baumgartner, L. M. (2007). *Learning in adulthood: A comprehensive guide* (3rd ed.). San Francisco, CA: Jossey-Bass.

Monolescu, D., Schifter, C. C., & Greenwood, L. (Eds.). (2004). *The distance education evolution: Issues and case studies*. Hershey, PA: IGI Global.

Morrison, G. R., & Anglin, G. J. (2005). Research on cognitive load theory: Application to elearning. *Educational Technology Research and Development*, *53*(3), 94–104. doi:10.1007/BF02504801

Munday, D. R. (2002). *Effects of learning strategy awareness on learning, learners, and instructor*. (Unpublished Doctoral Dissertation). Oklahoma State University. Stillwater, OK.

Ozcelik, E., & Yildirim, S. (2005). Factors influencing the use of cognitive tools in web-based learning environments. *The Quaterly Review of Distance Education*, *6*(4), 295–308.

Paas, F., Tuovinen, J. E., van Merriënboer, J. J. G., & Darabi, A. A. (2005). A motivational perspective on the relation between mental effort and performance: Optimizing learner involvement in instruction. *Educational Technology Research and Development*, *53*(3), 25–34. doi:10.1007/BF02504795

Patall, E. A., Cooper, H., & Robinson, J. C. (2008). The effects of choice on intrinsic motivation and related outcomes: A meta-analysis of research findings. *Psychological Bulletin*, *134*(2), 270–300. doi:10.1037/0033-2909.134.2.270

PBCC Academic Affairs. (2006). *Distance learning at PBCC: A history and enrollment overview*. Retrieved from http://www.pbcc.edu/documents/academic_services/dl_history.pdf

PBCC Institutional Research & Effectiveness. (2008). *Academic history: Comparison of success/withdrawal rates for classroom, internet and telecourses*. Lake Worth, FL: PBCC.

Porro, A. M. (2011). *Investigation of instructional strategies designed to promote achievement and retentionin online mathematics classes*. (Unpublished Doctoral Dissertation). Florida Atlantic University. Boca Raton, FL.

Salas, E., Kosarzycki, M. P., Burke, S. C., & Stone, D. L. (2002). Emerging themes in distance learning research and practice: Some food for thought. *International Journal of Management Reviews*, *4*, 135–154. doi:10.1111/1468-2370.00081

Sanacore, J. (2008). Turning reluctant learners into inspired learners. *Clearing House (Menasha, Wis.)*, *82*(1), 40–44. doi:10.3200/TCHS.82.1.40-44

Skinner, B. F. (2005). *Science and human behavior*. Cambridge, MA: B. F. Skinner Foundation. Retrieved from http://www.bfskinner.macwebsitebuilder.com/f/Science_and_Human_Behavior.pdf

Speckler, M. (2009). *Making the grade, V3: A compendium of data-driven case studies on the effectiveness of MyMathLab and MathXL*. Boston, MA: Pearson Education.

Sweller, J. (2006). Discussion of emerging topics in cognitive load research: Using learner and information characteristics in the design of powerful learning environments. *Applied Cognitive Psychology*, *20*, 353–357. doi:10.1002/acp.1251

Sweller, J., van Merrienböer, J. J. G., & Paas, F. G. W. C. (1998). Cognitive architecture and instructional design. *Educational Psychology Review*, *10*(3), 251–296. doi:10.1023/A:1022193728205

Szecsy, E. M., Danzig, A. B., & Gonzales, J. M. (2005). *The use of information and communication technology (ICT) to encourage reflection, interaction and collaboration for innovation and professional growth in higher education*. Paper presented at the meeting of the Annual Conference of the Northeastern Educational Association. Kerhonkson, NY. Retrieved from http://www.eric.ed.gov/PDFS/ED490670.pdf

Tallent-Runnels, M. K., Thomas, J. A., Lan, W. Y., Cooper, S., Ahern, T. C., Shaw, S. M., & Liu, X. (2006). Teaching courses online: A review of the research. *Review of Educational Research*, *76*(1), 93–135. Retrieved from http://www.aera.net/ doi:10.3102/00346543076001093

Thompson, M. M. (1998). Distance learners in higher education. In Gibson, C. C. (Ed.), *Distance Learners in Higher Education: Institutional Responses for Quality Outcomes* (pp. 10–18). Madison, WI: Atwood Publishing.

van Merriënboer, J. J. G., & Ayres, P. (2005). Research on cognitive load theory and its design implications for elearning. *Educational Technology Research and Development*, *53*(3), 5–13. doi:10.1007/BF02504793

Vansteenkiste, M., Soenens, B., Timmermans, T., Lens, W., & Van den Broeck, A. (2008). Does extrinsic goal framing enhance extrinsic goal-oriented individuals' learning and performance? An experimental test of the match perspective versus self-determination theory? *Journal of Educational Psychology*, *100*(2), 387–397. doi:10.1037/0022-0663.100.2.387

Vroom, V. H. (1964). *Work and motivation*. New York, NY: John Wiley & Sons, Inc.

Wadsworth, L. M., Husman, J., Duggan, M. A., & Pennington, M. N. (2007). Online mathematics achievement: Effects of learning strategies and self-efficacy. *Journal of Developmental Education*, *30*(3), 6–14.

Chapter 6
Informatization and Digital Citizenship

Lesley S. J. Farmer
California State University – Long Beach, USA

ABSTRACT

This chapter examines the bases for informatization and describes the conditions for meaningful and responsible participation in the informatized society, both in the workplace and in the civic world in general. Where eighty percent of U.S. labor is concentrated in the service sector, and technology permeates workplace functions, society is becoming informatized: driven by information. Information and digital literacy are required worker skills. Additionally, workers need to use information and technology ethically. Governments and workplaces need to set the conditions for knowledgeable, responsible, and participatory citizens and workers so that institutions and society as a whole can improve. Because informatization intersects with globalization, responsible cross-cultural interaction also needs to be addressed.

INTRODUCTION

The world is changing faster than ever because of social and economic factors, which have been significantly impacted by technology. As the world seems to grow smaller, due to increased communication and population transience, the global scene reflects a more interactive mode relative to information. Economic and social activities rely on information and communication technologies. Increasingly, society has become informatized; that is, information has become a major driving force of society.

Therefore, the need for critical use of information is more important than ever. In a digital world where the amount of information doubles every two years, individuals need to evaluate resources carefully and determine how to use relevant information to solve problems and make wise decisions. It is no longer principally an issue of getting information: it is getting the right information at the right time to do things right and to do the right things.

DOI: 10.4018/978-1-4666-2955-4.ch006

This changing informational environment emphasizes the need for lifelong education to prepare today's workforce to deal with an uncertain tomorrow. Moreover, since 85 percent of twenty-first century jobs will involve technology, it makes sense to incorporate technology throughout training. Nonetheless, 22 percent of Americans lack digital literacy skills (FCC, 2010).

However, teaching about information and technology is not enough. It is imperative to teach adults how to be responsible and ethical users of them. They need to be digital citizens. This chapter examines the bases of informatization, and describes the conditions for meaningful and responsible participation in the Informatized society, both in the workplace and in the civic world in general.

BACKGROUND

Intellectual capital has replaced material capital in today's economy. Where eighty percent of U.S. labor is concentrated in the service sector, and technology permeates workplace functions, information and digital literacy are required worker skills. Additionally, they need to use information and technology ethically.

Informatization

According to Wang (1994), informatization is "a process of change that features (a) the use of information and IT (information technologies) to such an extent that they become the dominant forces in commanding economic, political, social and cultural development; and (b) unprecedented growth in the speed, quantity, and popularity of information production and distribution" (p. 5). The term was coined in 1980 in France to describe the impact of computers and other technology in society.

At the 2003 world summit on the Information Society, governments and world leaders "made a strong commitment towards building a people-centred, inclusive, and development-oriented Information Society for all, where everyone can access, utilise and share information and knowledge" (United Nations, 2006, p. 6). What constitutes an information society? Fundamentally, an information society is one in which information replaces material goods as the chief driver of socio-economics. Human intellectual capital has higher currency than material capital, or at least intellect is needed to optimize the use of material resources.

Since information and material have always been needed, what distinguishes the recent notion of an information society? New information and technology have vastly increased the speed, access, and interlinking of information worldwide. Simultaneously, information and communication have converged, such as telecommunications and broadcasting, giving rise to informational industries. The cost of technology has dropped precipitously so that the majority of people can access it, thereby reinforcing mass media and other information entities. As a result, new forms of organization and social interaction have emerged. The World Bank Institute (2008) identified four pillars of a knowledge economy:

- Economic and institutional regime that offer incentives the effective use of knowledge and innovation.
- Education and skills that enable people to create and share knowledge
- Information and communication infrastructure.
- Innovation system that can leverage knowledge.

In terms of the workplace, "technology is changing the fundamentals of economic competition" (U.S. Department of State, 2009, p. 31). The Department's report then asserted, "U.S. worker productivity and technological leadership enabled the United States to rank as the world's leading manufacturer in 2006" (p. 53), and the technology sector has been the main basis for weathering recent economic woes.

Informatization mediates and restructures work, offering more possibilities for flexible representations of knowledge, ways to manipulate that knowledge, and options for sharing it. Time and space becomes less critical factors for work, but such freedom can also impede social relations and threaten people's private sphere. Because of telecommunications, informatization meshes well with globalization, facilitating international commerce and the marketplace of ideas. However, cross-cultural interaction can also prove problematic. In any case, informatization necessitates information literacy, technology literacy, and digital citizenship in order to handle all this information effectively and responsibly.

Information Literacy within the Information Society

As early as the 1991 SCANS (Secretary's Commission on Achieving Necessary Skills) report, governmental agencies have noted the need for employees who can: locate, interpret, and organize information; communicate information; create documents; solve problems; work with a variety of technology; and know how to acquire new knowledge. International stakeholders at the World Summit on the Information Society stated their shared values of information literacy:

Information Literacy lies at the core of lifelong learning. It empowers people in all walks of life to seek, evaluate, use and create information effectively to achieve their personal, social, occupational and educational goals. It is a basic human right in a digital world and promotes social inclusion of all nations (Garner, 2005, p. 3).

UNESCO (2004) has embraced information and communication technology, and is facilitating global discussion and efforts.

Everyone should be offered the opportunity to acquire the necessary skills in order to understand, participate actively in, and benefit fully from, the Information Society and the knowledge economy. Given the wide range of ICT (Information and Communication Technology) specialists required at all levels, building the institutional capacities to collect, organize, store and share information and knowledge deserves special attention. Governments should develop comprehensive and forward-looking strategies to respond to the new human capacity needs, including the creation of an environment that supports information literacy, ICT literacy and life-long learning for the general public (p. 6).

Technology Literacy

The International Society for Technology in Education (ISTE) developed technology literacy standards that apply to young students as well as to experienced teachers (2008). Their six areas of competency include:

1. Creativity and innovation.
2. Communication and collaboration.
3. Research and information fluency.
4. Critical thinking, problem solving, and decision-making.
5. Digital citizenship.
6. Technology operations and concepts.

The International Technology Education Association (2007) also developed technology literacy standards, but these focus more on learning *about and for* technology rather than *using* technology as an intellectual tool. Their foci include:

1. The nature of technology.
2. Technology and society.
3. Design (specifically, engineering design for problem-solving).
4. Abilities for a technological world (creating technological products).

5. The designed world (i.e., agriculture, energy, medicine, transportation, manufacturing, construction, communication).

In other areas of the world, technology literacy is frequently reconfigured as Information and Communications Technology (ICT) or as Information and Technology Literacy, which recognizes the overlapping concepts. Volman and van Eck's 2001 review of research found that information and communication technology (ICT) contributes to learning by offering environments that help individuals solve real-life problems, providing tools to manipulate information, facilitating collaboration and feedback, and connecting school with the outside world.

The Education Testing Service commissioned Lowe and MacAuley (2000) to develop a framework for information and communications technology geared to adults. The elements include:

- General use of information and communication technology.
- Computer and Internet use.
- Computer use and skills in work contexts.
- Computer use in non-work contexts.
- Development of computer skills.
- Personal benefits of computer use.
- Receptivity to computer use among current non-users.

Exemplifying the need for ICT literacy, Governor Arnold Scharzenegger's Executive Order S-06-09 established a California ICT Digital Literacy initiative, asserting that it is an important goal to ensure that California residents are digitally literate, and that they recognize the importance of (1) access to information and communications technologies regardless of income, geographic location or advantage; (2) the provision of ubiquitous broadband service in a competitive marketplace at affordable cost; (3) opportunities for residents to acquire ICT digital literacy skills in order to benefit academically, economically and socially; (4) the development of a California ICT Digital Literacy Policy that declares that all residents of California should be digitally literate; and (5) a seamless continuum of digital literacy competencies with benchmarks, metrics, assessments and certifications endorsed by the State to identify the ICT digital literacy proficiencies of residents, students, and workers.

Information literacy is linked to information technology, but has a broader base and implication. Information technology skills enable an individual to use computers, software applications, databases, and other technologies to achieve a wide variety of academic, work-related, and personal goals" (ACRL, 2000, p. 3) Technology also makes information literacy more complex so that adult education needs to consider information literacy as an underlying principle of lifelong learning. While information transcends technology, as evidenced when individuals interview experts, technology certainly impacts information literacy. Thus, technology is used as a learning and productivity tool while information literacy is, in effect, an intellectual framework.

Digital Citizenship

Thus, even beyond economics, information and digital literacy is needed in order to fully realize one's self-potential and to be a responsible and participatory citizen. On a more profound level, information and digital literacy is imperative for a democratic, open society. This approach to information, particularly as it encompasses technology, leads to the notion of digital citizenship: the ability and habit of using technology safely, responsibly, critically, and proactively to contribute to society. The overarching goal is effective and responsible personal and social engagement with digital resources. While some of the motive is protection and safety, which has resulted in required filtering software and acceptable use policies, a more positive spin is the need for individuals to learn coping skills to deal with informatization, and demonstrate that they can leverage informatization to *contribute* meaningful knowledge to the digital society.

Digital citizenship assumes an even more important role as the intersection of technology and globalization has led to more intense and pluralistic interactions across societies. Because information's meaning and impact is contextualized, shared knowledge and understanding can be harder to achieve. In a world scarred with political turmoil and terrorism, digital citizenship has never been so important. Workplace decision-makers should be discussing strategies to promote the value of digital citizenship through initiatives facilitated via private and public entities.

CONDITIONS FOR DIGITAL CITIZENSHIP IN INFORMATIZED SETTINGS

In an information society, citizens need to be digitally and information literate in order to survive, let alone participate in that society. All too often people become overwhelmed with information, not knowing how to evaluate its value and relevance, let alone how to leverage information to their own advantage. In acting as a responsible digital citizen, adults need to connect their own well-being with that of the state, contributing to the greater good in order to improve life conditions that cannot be accomplished individually.

However, for people to act as responsible digital citizenship in an informatized society, several factors need to be in place: technology infrastructure and connectivity, communicative interactive technology tools, participatory techniques, participation areas, and democratic/shared decision-making processes (Columbo, et al., 2011).

Kelleher (2007) framed those conditions in terms of relational antecedents:

- Technology, including media rich communication channels that are easily accessible and affordable.
- Technology expertise and use both within organizations and in the public.
- Social structures that give context to the relationships.

It should be noted that people in power, be it in the government or other workplace, may limit digital citizenship to access, keeping people unaware or discouraging active participation and debate. Decision-makers may fear sharing power and losing control, they might lack technological expertise, and they might have difficulty crossing bureaucratic boundaries to facilitate cross-communication and collaboration. On the part of workers, digital citizenship assumes technological expertise, which some workers might lack, and responsibility, which workers might not want to assume. Workers might also sense the wariness of decision-makers to share control, and question supervisors' motives.

On the other hand, digital citizenship fosters a sense of belonging, helps make informed and effective decisions, and optimizes the potential contributions of each individual. Digital citizenship transcends information access and exchange to foster informatized relationships that improve conditions for society. For such positive outcomes to result, the workplace also needs to establish social conditions for effective participatory digital citizenship: openness, positive attitude, social assurances, social networks, and sharing of tasks (Kelleher, 2007).

Governmental Role

Governments around the world are converging operations using information technology. Some of the areas where governments are using technology follow (http://library.govtech.net):

- **Administration:** Forms, groupware, portals, e-procurement, supply-chain management, work-flow management.
- **Policy:** Telecommunications, database management, document archiving.
- **Privacy:** Employee files, privacy rights, computer crime.
- **Security:** Authentication, data encryption and security, disaster planning and recovery, Internet protocol.
- **Telecommunications:** Broadband and carrier systems, hardware, services.
- **Transportation:** Global information and positioning systems, imaging software, data visualization, data mining.
- **Workforce:** Human resource management and services, software, recruitment, staffing, training, work environment.

As governments increasingly use ICT to work more effectively, the term of e-government may be applied. In a 2011 United Nations Economic Commission for Africa report, four core areas of e-government indicators were identified:

- Government employee use of ICT.
- Availability of CIT to government entities.
- Government entity use of ICT.
- Provision of e-government services to citizens.

Realizing the need for more digitally literate government employees as well as wanted to improve employment rate and competency as a whole, the U.S. Department of Labor sponsors efforts to help train Information Technology (IT) professionals. Government technology initiatives such as e-rate help subsidize Internet connectivity costs for libraries and schools, to some degree because public information about government agencies has been digitized; otherwise people without Internet access have difficulty finding out about public services.

Yet, while many countries have embraced ICT for its speed and information capacity, and as a means to compete alongside other countries, fewer governments have leveraged ICT to foster inclusion, equity, and active participation of all its citizens.

In an effort to push opportunities for socio-economic improvement of all people, the United Nations (2005) make several recommendations for e-government:

- Develop a political commitment to provide equal opportunity for participation in the information society.
- Include equity as a prerequisite for ICT-led development.
- Harness the potential of the information society.
- Effectively use ICT in government, the marketplace, and citizenry to mutually benefit each one's role in developing the society.

Concurrently, the UN also developed a model of e-government evolution to identify the stages for inclusive capacity, as governments become more informatized, going from connectivity to access to inclusion.

1. **Emerging presence:** Website with basic, static information, such as links to agencies.
2. **Enhanced presence:** One-way communication, such as a website, with rich information on public policy and various aspects of governance.
3. **Interactive presence:** Online services to enhance convenience, and to facilitate contact with government officials.
4. **Transactional presence:** Two-way interaction between citizens and the government, including online pay.
5. **Networked presence:** Two-way open dialogue that encourages participatory deliberative decision-making.

Columbo et al. (2011) parsed public decision-making processes in terms of workflow and technical components. To get support and refine agenda topics, governments can provide social networking platforms. To create policies, virtual town meetings provide a venue for discussion and deliberation. For monitoring and evaluating policies, social networking platforms provide timely feedback. The researchers also identified practices that optimized participation: planned discussion that provides parameters for interaction, two-way feedback to improve credibility, and supportive relationships.

Workplace Literacy and Engagement

The workplace may be considered as a large and complex group, or as an open system that deals with its environment, taking in and transforming resources based on assessment and feedback process. An organization includes several goals and several groups, each of which may differ and all of which are interdependent. Choo (1996) contended that organizations use information to construct meaning (particularly of external changes and development), create knowledge through organizational learning, and make decisions. Choo further stated that organizational decision behavior is bounded by the information available and the workers' cognitive ability to deal with information, including its selection and interpretation. This need for ICT literacy seems particularly obvious for informatized workplaces, especially as they focus on competitive intelligence and other outside factors, and leverage that knowledge to solve organizational problems and improve using in-house resources.

Informatization impacts the workplace in several ways.

- Communication and actions can be recorded more easily through emails, online cart, and videoconferencing.
- Documents can be digitized for easier access, storage, and retrieval.
- Information can be easily modified and repurposed for different audiences and objectives.
- People can communicate anytime, anywhere either instantly or asynchronously, relatively free from the constraints of time and space.

The possible communication format choices are impressive: desktop publishing, databases, spreadsheets, presentation programs, telecommunications, Internet, digitized images, audio, video, and mixed media. With the advent of Web 2.0 and the concept of interactive technology, another dimension is added as messages are co-constructed and continue to evolve, thanks to technology. As a result, communication is as much a process as a product. Web 2.0 tools in particular provide leaders much needed tools to lead, inform, and engage stakeholders. "Web 2.0 is transforming the Web into a space that allows anyone to create and share information online—a space for collaboration, conversation, and interaction; a space that is highly dynamic, flexible, and adaptable" (Coombs, 2007, p. 17). In short, informatization can facilitate productivity and service; however, it requires attention and coordination at all levels of the organization for it to be effective.

Another key aspect of informatized workplaces is social interaction. In their interviews with public sector workers, Crawford and Irving (2009) found that the main source of information was gained from social interactions with people within and outside their organizations. Billett (1999) identified four sources of workplace learning: the activities of work, the workplace, other workers, and practices of listening and observing; informal learning often surpassed formal structured learning.

Social support mechanisms play an especially important role in ICT competency. Orlikowski and her research team (1995) identified groups of people associated with IT expertise: designated support staff and local experts. It was found that people who participated in a community of practice integrated technology more successfully into their work than non-participants because they learned from their peers through active exchange of information and skills.

At the same time, that technology is becoming more collaborative, leadership is becoming more participatory, which supports the notion of digital citizenship. Web 2.0 tools enable leaders to facilitate broad-based governance and organizational improvement. One of the central functions of leaders is to facilitate organizational relationships, which requires effective multi-way communication, which Web 2.0 supports. This attitude aligns with the notion of digital citizenship: leveraging technology collaboratively to contribute to the greater good.

More profoundly, digital citizenship supports the notion of a learning community. Increasingly, the workplace is adopting the concept of learning communities as a way to cope with internal and external change. A learning community is a group of individuals who learn together over time, and act on their learning to achieve a common goal. Learning communities have several benefits.

- New employees are trained more efficiently because they can get help from mentors and other experts.
- Institutional knowledge is shared so that operations can function successfully if employees are absent or leave.
- Employees can keep current in their fields by sharing their learning experiences, such as conferences and professional reading.
- Individual learning and group learning inform each other.
- Camaraderie and interdependence are facilitated through joint, meaningful actions.
- Employees can analyze and reflect on their practice with the aim of improving individual and organizational efforts.

As Laiken (2001) noted in her study of organizational learning models,

> *A focus on information organizational learning contributes to employees' collective ability to move beyond simply coping with stress to engaging in creative action, for the benefit of both the individual members and the organization as a whole* (p. 4).

A learning community, or community of practice, begins with members with common values and goals. In the workplace, that could include laborers, technical staff, managers, and even clientele. Within that arena, a specific functional group such as marketing may constitute a community of practice, reflecting various perspectives about their work. Over the years, each person learns what methods work well; this tacit knowledge can be made explicit, thus building a joint body of knowledge that can streamline communication and workplace improvement.

A good example of informatization that encompasses digital citizenship is knowledge management. This term refers to the process of systematically gathering organizational wisdom, organizing those ideas, archiving them, and providing for their easy retrieval and dissemination. The underlying concept is that people learn specialized skills and concepts on the job, which improve their own performance. Examples of such learning includes management techniques, effective communication with employees, diagnosis skills, methods for engaging groups, and tips in videotaping. This practical learning becomes internalized, but sometimes it never becomes explicit. Knowledge management codifies these insights and facilitates their use by others so the overall workplace can benefit. Additionally, it provides a mechanism to sustain learning communities because the shared documentation can outlast an individual's presence within the workplace.

In the final analysis, a learning organization provides a predictable and sustainable system of knowledge sharing, participatory management, and organizational improvement. It provides the conditions that support ICT literacy and digital citizenship, and builds on those skills to improve the workplace as whole. Senge (1990) identified five principles within this framework, which tie informatization and digital citizenship.

- Systems thinking allocates and manages resources to optimize the relationship of interdependent functions. Informatization facilitates the collection, organization, retrieval, and use of these resources. Digital citizenship enables workers to locate, analyze and use this information effectively.
- Personal mastery involves ongoing self-assessment and self-improvement, which can translate into a better workplace. Informatization can systemize such processes, and provide learning resources to help workers self-actualize. Digital citizenship becomes one way for workers to improve their practice, and channel their expertise into positive channels.
- Mental models codify the workplace's assumptions and expectations. A workplace attitude of open dialogue and positive problem solving tends to support informatization and digital citizenship.
- Shared vision anchors the workplace. Workers can determine the extent to which their efforts contribute and manifest the vision. Shared vision helps employers determine what Informatized resources and services are needed to actualize the shared vision. Shared vision can also operationalize the concept of digital citizenship, articulating what responsible and pro-active action looks like.
- Team learning acknowledges the social aspect of the workplace, and builds on each person's unique skill set. Informatization should be systematic, but its parts may be very specialized. By collaborating, workers can complement each other's expertise, which is a key sign a digital citizenship.

It must be emphasized that digital citizenship needs to be explained and taught explicitly as part of their ongoing professional development, contextualized within the vision of the workplace. To that end, workers need to:

1. Become aware of informatization and its impact on the workplace as a whole, specific task groups, and individual workers. Why is information important? How is information represented? How is it accessed? How is it used?
2. Engage with the information; access it physically and intellectually. Comprehend and assess it. What relationship does the information have with a work task? How is the information verified? How should conflicting information be addressed? What are the legal and ethical implications of the information, both in terms of its access as well as its use?
3. Manipulate the information. What should be done with it? How can the worker transform information into knowledge? How can the worker extract the information, represent it, and determine how to manipulate it? Part of this step requires that the worker know how to use available technology productivity and analytical tools.
4. Act on the information. How can the information contribute to the workplace's vision and mission? How can that information be improved? How can its access and use be improved?

Digital Citizenship for Informatized Organizations

In effect, governments and other organizations need to practice good digital citizenship themselves, both for their own good as well as the publics that they serve. They too should shoulder and model social responsibility. Hallahan (2006) identified eight ethical factors considered part of responsible public relations:

- Provide publics with opportunities for access by offering a choice of technology tools, and venues for communicating.
- Provide accurate and consistent content, both textually and visually.
- Avoid deceptive practices such as misappropriation of other people's content, misrepresenting information, unethical tracking, and manipulating search engine ratings.
- Provide reliable and timely information and service.
- Take advantage of interactivity by fostering two-way communication, and acting in response to input.
- Personalize and customize online experiences.
- Insure privacy and security.
- Supply relevant information in a format that is manageable for diverse users.

Hallan also provided a list of useful websites that address ethics and telecommunications.

- **Centre for Democracy and Technology:** http://www.cdet.org
- **Computer Ethics Institute:** http://www.computerethicsinstitute.org
- **Computer Scientists for Social Responsibility:** http://www.cpsr.org
- **Electronic Frontier Foundation:** http://www.eff.org
- **Ethics Resource Center:** http://www.ethics.org
- **Online Ethics Center for Engineering and Science:** http://onlineethics.org
- **Wired Safety:** http://www.wiredsafety.org

LEVELS OF INDIVIDUAL PARTICIPATION

Workplace and civic participation continues to be an important part of adult life so that decisions about business and governmental action can be based on factual information and be representative of all stakeholders' expectations and needs. As society becomes more pluralistic, all voices need to be heard—and all social entities need to know the realities of their communities. Kelleher (2007) identified three levels of interactivity: functional (such as RSS feeds and response forms), contingency interactivity (whereby messages are exchanged), and contingency relations (whereby actions are based on each other's behaviors). Ideally, digital citizenship encompasses all three levels.

Socio-Economic Aspects of Participation

The 2011 political uprisings in the Middle East, popularized as "Arab Spring," demonstrates how technology can empower people as social media were used extensively to empower the people. However, as long as the digital divide exists, the powerful remain most likely to take advantage of informatization. The digital divide is alive and well today. Haves and have-nots still exist in terms of access and use of technology, which then impacts their participation in an informatized society. As noted above, the first prerequisite for participation is connectivity, which remains an elusive goal in terms of reaching all citizens, particularly in inner cities and rural communities. Access to the Internet has improved, however, largely due to the rise of mobile technology. By now, almost nine in ten American adults own a cell phone. However, two in ten American adults still do not use the Internet at all, particularly senior citizens, adults with less than a high school education, and those whose household income is less than $30,000 per year (Zickuhr & Smith, 2012).

Furthermore, a second aspect of access, intellectual access, is also needed before individuals can participate. Businesses and government entities both admit that a major reason that informatization has lagged in certain areas is lack of digital skills of employees and employers. Such dearth of knowledge is due to many factors: lack of exposure (particularly for older and poorer people), lack of training (again, mainly among older and poorer people), basic literacy gaps, language barriers, physical limitations, and psychological fears about technology or education.

Burrows and Ellison (2004) examined neighborhood informatization, and found that digital citizenship practices varied by socio-economic groups, which could result in new forms of social exclusion. They posited a model with two dimensions: economic flow (live versus dead) and identity spaces (tame versus wild):

- Live/tame zones reflect post-industrial middle and upper classes with stable identities.
- Live/wide zones reflect cultural capital sector with flowing ideas but not as much money.
- Dead/tame zones reflect conservative middle and skilled laborers.
- Dead/wild zones reflect downwardly financial working class, who may be socially disorganized or disenfranchised.

The researchers asserted that the live/tame zone population has the greatest capacity to participate and drive informatization, but they might focus on privatizing and separating their networked spaces for their own good rather than for a social good. Dead/tame zones are also likely to participate inwardly, but they tend to act defensively and avoid informatization. Dead/wild zones have little capacity or stability; they are doubly disadvantaged. Live/wild zones might seem to have the greatest potential for civic engagement, although their identify instability might prevent sustainability. Nevertheless, in the social media world, they can serve as informatization catalysts, which can then be institutionalized by live/tame zoners. In other words, for civic engagement to work, each of these zones will need to cross borders, which can be ironically reinforced because the expansion of telecommunications has enabled them to focus just on information that reinforces their existing belief.

Civic Engagement

Traditionally, civic engagement aligned with income and education levels. Typically, millenials are not engaged in political action. Fewer than 20% have ever contacted a political figure. Voting among 18 year olds has declined over the past four decades. Young people prefer to support causes instead, or make their civic voices heard on local issues, where they feel they have more say. African Americans and Latinos feel that they have less impact on political issues than Anglos; they also trust the government less; both perceptions correlate with less civic engagement.

Increasingly, though, government and politics have embraced technology, and have become informatized. With the advent of the Internet in particular, a virtual political system is emerging, which can lead to active citizenship and engagement. Furthermore, the demographics for civic engagement has changed, with age being the main predictor, largely because of the level of access to, and comfort with, technology; young adults who were politically unaware have become more connected and active (Smith, et al., 2009). Instant information is now made available by a broad spectrum of interests. The Internet provides an interactive environment where individuals can receive and give timely feedback about issues they feel strongly about. The Internet offers a way to democratize ideas and give the populace a voice. Typically, people gravitate to special interest groups and social movements. In some cases, grassroots efforts can "seed" participation. An online community may develop quickly, and can be structured to leverage lobbying and advocacy actions and ultimately impact governmental policies. For those reasons, individuals at the political extremes tend to participate more actively using social media. Nevertheless, the major of U.S. adults used the Internet to get 2010 political campaign information, and about a quarter used social media (Smith, 2011).

On the down side, large corporations and lobbyist groups, such as the National Rifle Association, can crowd the Internet with their own agendas, sometimes hiding behind a beatific front. Smaller groups can get lost in the flurry, splinter, or have short-range goals. Political Internet enthusiasts tend to want freedom and control, and generally support alternative social movements on the outer edges of the political scene. For that reason, adults need to evaluate political messages critically.

Adults at the fringes of technology might not be aware of these civic issues, or realize how they can impact them. If adults' time and effort are stretched already due to immediate demands, the thought of civic responsibility may seem abstract. Adults who are politically disengaged are not likely to seek political information on the Net. Other adults may consider The Establishment to be the Enemy, and feel that they are being victimized by the powerful. Even if adults do not like those perceived oppressors, they should learn enough about civic institutions to be able to confront issues knowledgeably, offer alternative directions, and advocate for community needs and content.

On the citizen side, the UN's 2005 e-participation index measures how well e-government information and services engage citizens in public policy. The framework consists of:

1. **E-information:** Government policies and programs exist for timely access and use, including Web forums, listservs, and news groups.
2. **E-consultation:** Public policy topics are explained and posted online to encourage real-time and asynchronous discussion.
3. **E-decision-making:** Government uses citizen input in decision-making, and provides feedback on outcomes of issues.

A study from China demonstrates how digital citizenship participation levels may vary according to group characteristics and interests. In researching Chinese e-government informatization efforts relative to their citizens, Wu and Bauer applied the UN's e-government benchmarks. The researchers found that the Chinese efforts focused on the enhanced phase, providing timely one-way communication about governmental policies and services. Further investigation uncovered uneven use of that information, with Eastern provinces more engaged than Western ones. Wu and Bauer identified several significant factors for engagement: per capita GNP, urban location, overall online use, and public spending on science and technology.

CROSS-CULTURAL ISSUES

Culture may be defined as "the customary beliefs, social forms, and material traits of a racial, religious, or social group" and "the set of shared attitudes, values, goals, and practices that characterizes an institution or organization" (*Webster's Dictionary*). An individual may belong to several cultures: family, worksite, neighborhood, race, profession, social club, political party, country. Likewise, a group may belong to several cultures; technicians may be members of a site staff, a union, a system, a state organization, a national organization, and an international organization. Some of these cultures may overlap or even contradict, in which case, the individual or group must either live with the disequilibrium or resolve the conflict (i.e., reject one or the other, reject both, or incorporate parts of each). In the workplace, cultural issues apply to the customer, the staff, the workplace, and the profession.

Informatization Impact

As the global society becomes digitized, people come into contact with other cultures more frequently and deeply. In some cases, those interactions may be characterized as clashes. Misunderstandings occur because of tacit assumptions and cultural perceptions. Thus, the need for understanding different cultures is more important than ever. On the positive side, more content is being created in non-English speaking cultures, thus flattening out the language frequency distribution. Of course, such a rise in non-English materials require people to evaluate and verify the content's quality. In the process, cultural knowledge will be more prone to explicit discussion and negotiation. Thus, cultural competency will need to grow with the technology. Ideally, knowledge will become more culturally rich and varied.

In an informatized environment, technology significantly impacts workplace effectiveness, and also is subject to cultural influence. For instance, stakeholders might have different degrees of access due to cultural attitudes about technology, socially constructed gender role expectations, and socio-economic values. World experience and knowledge impacts stakeholders' ability to locate and evaluate online information. Even social attitudes about language acquisition and attitudes about English can impact technology use. These realities will probably not change over time because of the continuing advancements in technology. Local economics can still stifle access to technology at least at the upper end so that the digital divide will remain.

Kluver (2000) identified several challenges that come with informatization, especially as it interacts with globalization. People are not limited to local information, so are less dependent on their physical community, which can both enlarge opportunities as well as lesson local autonomy. As more information is disseminated widely and quickly, the trend to homogenize increases, which can threaten local cultures and practices. On the other hand, smaller cultural entities can use social media to express their ideas and gain more visibility than ever before.

Communication Skills

Kramsch and Thorne (2001) discovered that miscommunication in intercultural online discussion was caused less by linguistic differences than by the lack of understanding of "cultural genres" of discourse. For example, one of the limitations of technology is the frequent lack of context so that information by be misinterpreted; particularly in high-contextualized cultures, such "lean" communication makes it harder to express and understand ideas. When workers were trained in intercultural communication skills, they were able to analyze and interpret different cultural communication genres more accurately.

For such cross-cultural training, it is not enough for workers to comprehend the information, they also have to apply it—in most cases utilizing communication skills. Thus, part of digital citizenship training has to include how to communicate information purposefully. Trainers should design instruction so that workers can practice their communication skill with their peers, an activity that scaffolds the eventual work situation because all the participants have some knowledge of the company's products and procedures. This peer interaction—and analytical group debriefing—can also build a sense of community, and reinforce the workplace culture. In the process, instructors can reinforce the practices of sharing information, listening actively, following directions, and showing respect (Dishon & O'Leary, 1994). At the same time, though, they also need to practice communicating with representative clientele of different cultures so they can polish their cross-cultural skills.

In online communication, neither party has access to all senses. Fortunately, telecommunication channels can include video conferencing and Skype, which more approximate face-to-face interaction. Even so, they cannot duplicate informal, spontaneous interaction that can occur in the same physical space. Furthermore, asynchronous communication may be done in haste but read in leisure so that the recipient may read in unintended meanings, which can result in more misunderstanding (Holtbrügge, et al., 2011). To minimize communication barriers, online communicators need to: listen actively to others' comments, simplify language, provide feedback to ascertain understanding of what has been communicated, avoid emotionalism, avoid humor and sarcasm (Jones, 2009).

These skills of active listening, learning about cultures, showing respect, compensating for sensory-limited telecommunications all demonstrate aspects of digital citizenship in informatized settings. Effective digital citizens understand that information is contextualized, and that evaluating and interpretation of information requires open-minded critical thinking. Digital citizenship also encompasses effective communication so that understanding the audience and how technology communication channels function are required skills for today's workers.

FUTURE TRENDS

Informatization is likely to increase for several reasons: need for increased productivity, greater use of metrics, technology advances, and near ubiquity of online connectivity. However, technology competence does not suffice; just because one can do something with technology does not mean that they should do it. Digital citizenship also needs to increase. With the fears of data security, cloud computing, issues of privacy, cyberbullying, and intellectual property abuses, society has tried stopgap measures such as filtering software, encryption options, and increased surveillance. However, digital citizenship posits an educational approach: to handle information responsibly, one must become knowledgeable.

The Middle East uprisings of 2011, which the media labeled as the "Arab Spring," exemplifies the power and challenges of digital citizenship. Activists used social media to get their information into the public eye; their revolution grew in number and impact because of the eye witness images that were broadcast on YouTube. These networked people used networked information to not only engage in political action but to spearhead it. The question arises: how sustainable are such actions? Referring back to Burrows' and Ellison's model, establishment decision-makers will need to back the revolutionaries for change to transform into institutionalized reform. The political possibilities and responsibilities of social media are now just being realized.

In Citizen 2.0, Rainie (2012) raises several points about social media trends and their possible impact on digital citizenship. Civic culture is changing because of the mediasphere; more opportunities for civic engagement exist; whether that change will result in more fruitful exchanges of ideas or increased isolation from differing points of view is debatable. In any case, authority is becoming more diffused, and migrating from organizations to networks and amateur experts. Additionally, algorithmic authorities such as Google analytics and other data mining tools are informatizing authority beyond any one human. At the same time, organizations are coming under more scrutiny, and need to be more transparent; the public is practicing sousveillance, and peers are practicing coveillance). These practices are facilitated by the informatization of organizations, which enables technology to ferret out and parse information more easily than ever. In short, digital citizenship provides tools for people to become more knowledgeable in an information society, and to have more influence—and they will need to be more responsible in the process.

CONCLUSION

Information has become the principal commodity in today's society. Its strategic availability and use impacts society at all levels, from the day worker to international governmental entities. Technology and globalization have served as catalysts for this development, and now the workplace needs to deal knowledgeably and responsibly in this dynamic environment.

While most people need to be ICT literate, part of that literacy has to address safe, responsible, and critical use. It is not enough to know how to use technology and information; it must be used ethically and legally. Moreover, a moral imperative exists to contribute to this Informatized society, which is the prevue of digital citizenship.

To this end, governments and workplaces must set the conditions for digital citizenship: technology infrastructure and connectivity, easily accessible and affordable telecommunications, communicative interactive technology tools, participatory techniques, social structures and participation areas, and democratic/shared decision-making processes. Both the organizations and the public need to have technology expertise and experience. More profoundly, governments and other organizations need to practice good digital citizenship themselves, both for their own good as well as the public that they serve. They too should shoulder and model social responsibility.

Workers and other citizens also have a social obligation, deemed as digital citizenship in an informatized society. Their work and civic participation tends to reflect their social standing, although social media have changed that paradigm to some degree. Cultural differences also need to be negotiated, largely through knowledge and interaction. Nevertheless, people need to be empowered if they are to contribute positively to their community, be it their work setting, their culture, or the digital world. It is everyone's potential and responsibility, and the winner will be the world.

REFERENCES

Association of College and Research Libraries. (2000). *Information literacy competency standards for higher education*. Chicago, IL: American Library Association.

Billett, S. (1999). Guided learning in the workplace. In Boud, D., & Garrick, J. (Eds.), *Understanding learning at work* (pp. 151–163). London, UK: Routledge.

Bjørn-Andersen, N., Eason, K., & Robey, D. (Eds.). (1986). *Managing computer impact: An international study of management and organizations*. Norwood, NJ: Ablex.

Burrows, R., & Ellison, N. (2004). Sorting places out? Towards a social politics of neighbourhood informatization. *Information Communication and Society*, *7*(3), 321–336. doi:10.1080/1369118042000284588

Campion, M. (1995). The supposed demise of bureaucracy: Implications for distance education and open learning. *Distance Education*, *16*(2), 192–216. doi:10.1080/0158791950160204

Colombo, C., Kunstelj, M., Molinari, F., & Todorovski, L. (2011). Participatory policy process design: Lessons learned from three European regions. *Journal of Balkan & Near Eastern Studies*, *13*(1), 117–139. doi:10.1080/19448953.2011.550811

Coombs, W. (2007). Protecting organization reputations during a crisis. *Corporate Reputation Review*, *10*(3), 163–176. doi:10.1057/palgrave.crr.1550049

Crawford, J., & Irving, C. (2009). Information literacy in the workplace. *Journal of Librarianship and Information Science*, *41*(1), 29–38. doi:10.1177/0961000608099897

Dishon, D., & O'Leary, P. (1994). *Guidebook of cooperative learning*. Holmes Beach, FL: Learning Publications.

Federal Communications Commission. (2010). *Broadband survey*. Washington, DC: Federal Communications Commission.

Garner, S. (2005). *High-level colloquium on information literacy and lifelong learning*. Alexandria, Egypt: International Federal of Library Associations.

Hallahan, K. (2006). Responsible online communication. In Fitzpatrick, K., & Bronstein, C. (Eds.), *Ethics in public relations* (pp. 107–130). Thousand Oaks, CA: SAGE Publications.

Henderson, L. (2007). Theorizing a multiple cultures instructional design model for elearning and e-teaching. In Edmundson, A. (Ed.), *Globalized e-learning cultural challenges* (pp. 130–153). Hershey, PA: IGI Global.

Holtbrügge, D., Schillo, K., Rogers, H., & Friedmann, C. (2011). Managing and training for virtual teams in India. *Team Performance Management*, *17*(3), 206–223. doi:10.1108/13527591111143727

International Society for Technology in Education. (2008). *National educational technology standards for teachers*. Eugene, OR: International Society for Technology in Education.

International Technology Education Association. (2007). *Standards for technological literacy*. Reston, VA: International Technology Education Association.

Jones, W. O. (2009). Outsourcing: The enduring mistakes. *The Journal of Applied Business and Economics*, *10*(1), 1–14.

Kelleher, T. (2007). *Public relations online*. Thousand Oaks, CA: SAGE Publications.

Kluver, R. (2000). Globalization, informatization, and intercultural communication. *American Journal of Communication*, *3*(3), 1–4.

Kramsch, C., & Thorne, S. (2001). Foreign language learning as global communicative practice. In Block, D., & Cameron, D. (Eds.), *Language learning and teaching in the age of globalization* (pp. 83–100). London, UK: Routledge.

Laiken, M. (2001). *Models of organizational learning*. Toronto, Canada: University of Toronto.

Lowe, G., & MacAuley, J. (2000). *Information and communication technology literacy assessment framework*. Princeton, NJ: Educational Testing Service.

McWhinney, W. (1992). *Paths of change: Strategic choices for organizations and society*. Thousand Oaks, CA: Sage Publications.

Orlikowski, W., Yates, J., Okamura, K., & Fujimoto, M. (1995). Shaping electronic communication. *Organization Science*, *6*(4), 423–445. doi:10.1287/orsc.6.4.423

Rainie, L. (2012). *Citizen 2.0*. Washington, DC: Pew Research Project.

Senge, P. (1990). *The fifth discipline: The art and practice of the learning organization*. New York, NY: Doubleday. doi:10.1002/pfi.4170300510

Smith, A. (2011). *The internet and campaign 2010*. Washington, DC: Pew Research Project.

Smith, A., Schlozman, K., Verba, S., & Brady, H. (2009). *The internet and civic engagement*. Washington, DC: Pew Research Project.

Spitler, V. (2005). Learning to use IT in the workplace. *Journal of Organizational and End User Computing*, *17*(2), 1–25. doi:10.4018/joeuc.2005040101

UNESCO. (2004). Information literacy. In *Communication and information*. Bangkok, Thailand: UNESCO.

United Nations. (2005). *UN global e-government readiness report 2005 – From e-government to e-inclusion*. New York, NY: United Nations. Retrieved from http://unpan1.un.org/intradoc/groups/public/documents/un/unpan021888.pdf

United Nations Economic Commission for Africa. (2011). *Framework for a set of government core indicators*. Addis Ababa, Ethiopia: United Nations Economic Commission for Africa. Retrieved from http://www.uneca.org/aisi/scanict/Framework_eGovCoreIndicators_Final.pdf

United States Department of Labor. (1991). *Secretary's commission on achieving necessary skills (SCANS)*. Washington, DC: Government Printing Office.

United States Department of State. (2009). *Outline of the U.S. economy*. Washington, DC: Government Printing Office.

Venkatesh, V., Morris, M. G., Davis, G. B., & Davis, F. (2003). User acceptance of information technology: Toward a unified view. *Management Information Systems Quarterly*, *27*, 425–478.

Volman, M., & van Eck, E. (2001). Gender equity and information technology in education: The second decade. *Review of Educational Research*, *71*(4), 613–634. doi:10.3102/00346543071004613

Wang, G. (1994). *Treading different paths: Informatization in Asian nations*. Norwood, NJ: Ablex.

World Bank Institute. (2008). *Measuring knowledge in the world's economies*. Washington, DC: World Bank Institute.

Wu, Y., & Bauer, J. (2010). E-government in China: Deployment and driving forces of provincial government portals. *Chinese Journal of Communication*, *3*(3), 290–310. doi:10.1080/17544750.2010.499633

Zickuhr, K., & Smith, A. (2012). *Digital differences*. Washington, DC: Pew Research Project.

Chapter 7
Emergency Management Professional Development:
Linking Information Communication Technology and Social Communication Skills to Enhance a Sense of Community and Social Justice in the 21st Century

Marianne Robin Russo
Florida Atlantic University, USA

ABSTRACT

Although there is current research describing technology efforts utilized in the 21st century as it relates to emergency management, there are adult educational factors to examine regarding Information Communication Technology (ICT) and the Social Communication Skills (SCS) of emergency personnel. Technology is quickly evolving and the the population is becoming increasingly more diverse, driving the efforts of emergency personnel to harness more technological emergency advances and navigate the culture of each community to assure effective emergency measures are taken. Within the ICT and SCS framework, emergency management must concern itself with: (a) the basic tenets of emergency management; (b) the changing and new nature of global threats in the 21st century; (c) evolving emergency management technologies; (d) social considerations when interfacing with the communities served; and (e) recommendations for those who are involved in emergency management mitigation, preparation, response, and recovery emergency efforts. All of these factors revolve around the education and re-education of adults; therefore, the focus of this chapter explores subsequent educational implications for the emergency personnel workforce as well as positive results for affected communities. This chapter proposes a larger implication, one of emergency personnel professional development within technology-based response systems as well as the cultivation of social communication in an effort to build a Sense

DOI: 10.4018/978-1-4666-2955-4.ch007

of Community (SOC) with the diverse citizenry they serve. Emergency first responders, as well as other emergency personnel, must be educated in technology and social skills to better serve the community and to become a part of a holistic community. It is in this way that safety, and ultimately social justice, efforts for specific groups who may be marginalized and disenfranchised during an emergency are enhanced.

INTRODUCTION

Communities face many exigencies and effective emergency management is essential to assisting those in need. The incident of 9/11 exposed many emergency preparedness gaps, including a lack of integrated response measures. According to the 9/11 Commission Report (as cited in Khan, 2011, p. 953), "Response efforts did not have the integrated communications and unified command needed for a large-scale response, and information crucial for decision making was not shared among agencies." In addition, "…first responders were poorly trained and equipment for their roles was inadequate…" (Khan, 2011, p. 953). Several other problems were uncovered, including but not limited to: communication and coordination of efforts of emergency response teams, the fact that emergency support systems were in the Towers at the time of the attack, a lack of adequate media and emergency management communication to the public, the accuracy of public information, and the censorship of public information (Fu, 2011). Therefore, due to this lack of preparedness during 9/11, emergency management is still in the process of adjustment. Since this time, the United States has established national security structures that attempt to ameliorate potential threats, pre, during, and post occurrence.

In terms of emergency health preparedness, Congress has also created more of a funding mechanism for a safety infrastructure that concentrates efforts on local and rural communities as well as more densely populated urban environments (Khan, 2011). Health departments are also being considered as a part of the first responder system, and funding of the Center for Disease Control (CDC) has also aided national, state, local, and Web-based emergency networks (Khan, 2011).

Even though training in technology is an integral part of emergency management, training emergency professionals in social skills and community communications is also a requirement of emergency management and cannot be overlooked. This social interaction is imperative in order to coalesce, especially with a diverse community, so information can flow accurately and effectively to those in need. It is both Information Communication Technology (ICT) and Social Communication Skills (SCS) that can help to eliminate the barriers in emergency situations. It is first responders, specifically firefighters and police, who must be prepared through professional development to enhance best practices in order to optimize communities before, during, and after a crisis.

Therefore, this chapter will begin with an overview of the basics of emergency management and the natures of emergencies in the 21st century. The thrust of the chapter with concern itself with the framework of ICT and SCS, and conclude with recommendations for those who are involved in the mitigation, preparation, response, and recovery emergency efforts. A broader implication will also be developed in terms how emergency personnel can build a holistic Sense of Community (SOC), creating the ultimate construct of social justice.

BACKGROUND

The Basic Tenents of Emergency Management

In order to understand the emergency management frameworks of ICT and SCS, the basics tenents of emergency management must be explored. Emergency personnel should understand that emergency management is staged or considered to be in four phases: mitigation, preparation, response, and recovery within a crisis situation (Lindel, Prater, & Perry, 2007). In addition, rail system fire hazards are defined in slightly different ways in terms of: Threat, Vulnerability, Consequences, and Risk Assessment (TVCRA) (Meacham, Dembsey, Schebel, Johann, & Tubbs, 2012). In order to try and quantify risk assessment, risk matrices have also been designed to try and quantify the probability and magnitude of an emergency situation (Meacham, et al., 2012). Inevitably, these kinds of assessment practices and techniques must be taught to emergency personnel.

In terms of emergency management entities, the respondents to an emergency include police, firefighters, health departments and hospitals, transportation divisions, local, state, and federal governmental agencies, the latter including Federal Emergency Management Agency (FEMA) and Homeland Security (Flanigan, Blatt, Russell, Batta, & Lee, 2010). It is with this conglomeration of entities, a difficulty of communication integration exists within the four phases of emergency management; these entities must be educated to work together for the good of the community. Essentially, "When things go wrong in emergency management, the reasons are generally related to breakdowns in information, communication, and/or coordination" (Dykstra, 2003). Therefore, emergency personnel who understand these basic tenents of emergency management, new threats must be explored that maybe unique to the 21st century.

Twenty-First Century Emergencies

Emergency personnel must also be educated and updated with new emergency incidents that befall society in the 21st century, although some 21st century emergencies are not unique to this time frame.. For example, natural events that involve weather and geological interplay continue to cause public turmoil. In addition, person-made emergency threats that have emanated in the 20th century continue to plague society today. Many of these incidences, if not all of them, pose a health threat that will illicit an emergency medical response. These health responses could stem from biological, chemical, radioactive, and explosive incidences (Wilkinson, et al., 2010), or be as simple as humans living in dense urban environments within proximity of livestock (Barnett & Sorenson, 2011).

Although infectious disease and pandemics have been a part of life prior to the 21st century, like the Black Death that hit in 1347 and killed approximately a third of the European populace, the threat of pandemic or infectious disease is on the increase due to population growth. Technology has also enabled mass transit, which has led to the spreading of new outbreaks and pandemics in the populace (Barnett & Sorenson, 2011). Therefore, "Infectious disease disasters (bioterrorism, emerging infectious disease outbreak, or pandemic) have the potential to cause high morbidity and mortality" (Rebmann, 2010, p. 63).

Although the nuclear age began during WWII, nuclear fission has not retreated in usage. Nuclear reactors are now used to create power for population zones (Dauer, Zanzonico, Tuttle, Quinn, & Strauss, 2011). These reactors can cause problems should a mishap transpire, like the Chernobyl or Three Mile Island incident, or more recently, an earthquake that generated a tsunami that hit the Fukushima Daiichi nuclear power plant on the east coast of Japan. Due to this natural disaster, the Fukushima Daiichi nuclear power plant was severely damaged, leaking radiation into the environment. It is still not known to what extent the reactor is impaired and the subsequent harm to the population, food, water, and atmosphere, even after a year. In this case, approximately 200,000 people had to be evacuated and many were given potassium iodide and radioactive scans in an attempt to mitigate health problems (Dauer, et al., 2011).

Complex transportation systems have evolved over the course of time, and attacks, on these transportation hubs pose a new kind of emergency threat. For example, the subway system in Tokyo, Japan was faced with a release of sarin, which is a nerve gas. There has "...never been such a large-scale disaster caused by nerve gas in peacetime history" (Okumura, et al., 1998, p. 613).

Therefore, with new kinds of technological-driven emergencies, innovative and a reconfiguration of how to handle these new threats is necessary. It is imperative that emergency personnel be educated and trained in order to handle these kinds of unique scenarios. Professional development must be in place that allows informational updates and continuous knowledge in these areas. In order to examine these new emergencies and treat them effectively in all four stages of emergency management, ICT and SCS are two key concepts, when combined will optimize emergency preparedness.

OPTIMIZING EMERGENCY RESPONSE: TWO FRAMEWORKS

The ICT Framework

Within the framework of Information Communications Technology or ICT, all communication technology sources will be included: the Internet, all social media devices, radio, hardwired telephones, database management, integration of technological resources, and satellite. The emergency personnel who navigate ICT and are the respondents in an emergency situation include: police, firefighters, health departments and hospitals, transportation divisions, local, state, and federal governmental agencies, Federal Emergency Management Agency (FEMA) and Homeland Security (Flanigan, et al., 2010). All of these entities depend on ICT and any emerging technologies during the four phases of emergency management. These emerging technologies can include simulations and models, which can simulate meteorological events and plumes that may be the result of radiological or bio-chemical in nature (Jain & McLean, 2003). Simulations and models can also feign terrorist threats, and are used by the Departments of Defense, Energy, and the National Atmospheric Release Advisory Center (NARA) (Jain & McClean, 2003).

Various models that create a decision-generated flowchart have been developed and designed to assist those emergency personnel make better decisions. For example, a Decision Support System (DSS) developed by The Department of Environmental Engineering, the National Cheng-Kung University in Tainan, Taiwan, and the Earth and Environmental Sciences Division of the Los Alamos National Laboratory in Los Alamos, New Mexico was used for support personnel regarding chemical emergencies in urban Taiwan (Chang, Wei, Tseng, & Kao, 1997, p. 67). The DSS computer-based program fosters rapid decision-making, monitors storage and movement of chemicals, identifies community environmental hazards using a solutions-based approach (Chang, et al., 1997). DSS, incorporated with Geographical Information Systems (GIS) technologies, allows emergency networks to problem-solve, evaluate specific constraints, and develop rapid and salient operational management strategies (Chang, et al., 1997). Other computer systems, CAMEO, and SAFER, the latter created by DuPont, is also a computer decision-making computer application that evaluates toxic spills and factory chemical events, respectively (Chang, et al., 1997).

GIS, in and of itself, is coming of age and interfaces information using databases and computer-generated mapping approaches to departments involved in emergency mitigation

(Johnson, 2000). GIS is able to decipher the nature of wildfires, weapons of mass destruction, chemical and reactor releases, earthquakes, hurricanes, and storm surges. For example, GIS can establish communication linkages through Internet satellites and databases providing population densities, geography, and topography of the affected area, imagery and visual information, estimates of risk and damage, population information, as well as the monitoring of recovery management efforts (Johnson, 2000). Johnson (2000) also suggests that GIS can be used during and after terrorist actions.

ICT is also being established to assist emergency management personnel for local roadway emergencies. Motorway fatalities outnumber annual fatalities registered during earthquakes and hurricanes, and there are "Current and near-term technologies that support real-time emergency response..." (Flanigan, et al., 2010). Comprehensive transportation emergency systems or a "fully Integrated Active Transportation System (IATS)" helps responders handle car accidents and highway infrastructure problems as they arise (Flanigan, et al., 2010). IATS is technology-driven and uses "… wireless communication to provide the following connectivity" (Flanigan, et al., 2010, p. 2189). In addition, IATS uses real-time information to alert motorists and emergency services, monitor responders at the scene, and monitor the transport of victims (Flanigan, et al., 2010).

ICT has also been under development by the National Science Foundation Partnerships for Innovation Program (NSFPIP). The NSFPIP has established Wireless Grids Innovation Testbed (WiGiT) and an Advanced Situational Awareness System (ASAS) that will:

…demonstrate the delivery of situational awareness to disaster managers and response personnel through a novel wireless data dissemination backbone, or wireless grid. Information gathered by advanced airborne remote sensing and real-time data processing systems can, through the ASAS, seamlessly deliver actionable information products to a diversity of users including county emergency managers, law enforcement, first responders, and community groups (Treglia, et al., 2011, p. 2).

One very important and fairly new ICT innovation is social media. Social media has been and continues to be used through all four phases of an emergency. Social media is continuing to change, creating communication networks that use Global Positioning System (GPS) software, and location-based information like Foursqure and Loopt, so emergency personnel can assess where victims are and what is happening at the scene of an emergency (Merchant, Elmer, & Lurie, 2011). Merchant, Elmer, and Lurie (2011) report that even if Internet service is disrupted a "… new social media such as 'speak-to-tweet' (which allows brief Twitter messages to be sent through a voice connection) were being used to improve communication about health and safety within the first few days of the Egyptian uprising…"(p. 289). Social media has been used in the aftermath of the 2010 Haitian earthquake and helped those emergency workers find and treat victims within the rubble and chaos (Palen, et al., 2007). More recently, these technologies were used during the BP oil spill in the Gulf of Mexico, as well as during the H1N1 outbreak (Merchant, et al., 2011).

ICT emergency management systems become very significant for special needs populations. Sullivan and Hakkinen (2011) define vulnerable populations as those who are disabled, tourists, and immigrants who may not be familiar with their locale, those who do not speak the language of the majority population, and the aged. ICT established important messaging that needed quick routing during the tsunami of South Asia (Sullivan & Hakkinen, 2011). At a UN World Conference on Disaster Reduction (WCDR), it was suggested that emergency management communication to the disabled could be appropriated through Personal Digital Assistants (PDAs), mobile phones, and radio frequency identification (Sullivan & Hakkinen, 2011). Within the US, the National Council on Disability (NCD) suggested that for people with sight and hearing impairments, warning access was necessary, but would depend on the support of the Federal Communications Commission (FCC) (Sullivan & Hakkinen, 2011). The Digital Accessible Information System Standard (DAISY) (2005) is also available in the US and provides visual and auditory cues using computer and reading technology for the impaired (Sullivan & Hakkinen, 2011).

It has been suggested that ICT surveillance be used to monitor infectious disease and global health concerns (Barnett & Sorenson, 2011). Surveillance for health emergency initiatives include: Web-Crawling programs that can scan the Internet for information and enable authorities to censor health-related information before it the general public is apprised. Image-Cat, a California-based company has developed remote sensing geographic, Web-based, and satellite imaging of global disasters (Barnett & Sorenson, 2011). These "...new approaches potentially decenter information and thus may shift action away from governments and GPG agencies (e.g., the WHO) toward individuals or private corporations" (Barnett & Sorenson, 2011, p. 179). Surveillance used in a manner that may inadvertently hurt the public is always the caveat, however, these kinds of global communication initiatives regarding disease may be rationalized because they are for the Global Public Good (GPG) (Barnett & Sorenson, 2011).

Other ICT emergency systems that are worthy of mention include, but are not limited are: ETOILE, WIPER, IMI, MIKEBOX, Emergency-Call, and NEO: Agent Crisis Response. However, the weaknesses of these systems include problems within all four phases of emergency, may not be able to interface communication with all respondents, databases, and technology (Flanigan, et al., 2010). These aforementioned ICT examples are only some of the technology that is available to emergency management personnel, and since ICT is also evolving at such a rapid pace, adult training is also a part of the ICT package.

ICT is only one part of the framework that can assist those responsible to give aid in emergency situations. The other part of the framework that compliments and is a necessary component is SCS, which must work in tandem with ICT to create the greatest efficiency during any of the four stages of emergency management.

The SCS Framework

Social Communication Skills, or SCS, is the human behavior component that consists of interpersonal and intrapersonal skills that are necessary to have collaborative and collegial working relationships. Interpersonal skills are those behavior and communication patterns that allow an individual to relate to others, while intrapersonal skills are those behavior and communication patterns that allow an individual to be introspective. It is imperative that emergency personnel have both interpersonal and intrapersonal attributes to be able to gain a rapport with the communities they serve have a self-reflective during effective emergency mitigation, preparation, response, and recovery management. "The real challenge with any disaster preparedness or warning system lies in the human factor" (Sullivan & Hakkinen, 2010, p. 229). Therefore, emergency personnel must be educated in the skill of communication.

Interpersonal and intrapersonal skills are extremely important to public health and safety, and become even more pertinent because emergency management, and specifically first responders, operate in diverse communities. The United States is a very diverse nation, and it may be that first responders may serve a community in which ethnicities do not match their own. Many first responders, including police, may not have any kind of problem when it comes to ethnicities that are not their own, but may not be aware of cultural differences and nuances that exist when handling emergency events (Black & Kari, 2010). When life and limb are in harm's way, an understanding of a community and its culture is paramount.

"Multiculturalism is not simply an issue of race and/or ethnicity. Criminal justice professionals deal with a wide variety of cultures, including but not limited to women, religious minorities, gays and lesbians, the elderly, and the disabled" (Black & Kari, 2010, p. 3). In addition, nuances of age could make a difference in the way in which police handle individuals (Black & Kari, 2010).

And, "Despite the increasing diversity of law enforcement agencies, many minority and immigrant groups express lower levels of satisfaction with police and have less confidence in them" (Black & Kari, 2010, p. 3). "Police-minority relations have historically been strained. The racial tensions of the 1950s and 1960s led to the development of alternative policing models that would ideally reduce police-citizen tensions…" (Black & Kari, 2010, p. 3). According to Bobb, Buchner, and DeBlieck (2006), the African American populace may be more reticent to have a liaison with police because of perceived inequitable treatment.

"Individuals can, and do, make nuanced and considered judgments about the police" (Jackson & Bradford, 2012, p. 247). Therefore, trust, which is built on rapport, may be the essence of the effectiveness of emergency management in diverse communities. Trust implies the "… the right intentions…" (Hardin, 2006). Public trust and a collaborative working relationship between the police and the community will only enhance emergency response during all phases of emergency management, inclusive of public compliance (Tyler & Fagan, 2008; Bradford & Jackson, 2010).

In terms of intrapersonal or self-reflection that first responders and emergency managers forming a cognitive feedback loop with their internal dynamics is paramount. Emergency personnel must think of how their actions not only affect the communities in which they serve, but how the event affects them on a physical, psychological, emotional, and spiritual level. First responders specifically arrive at the scene, have to determine their own safety considerations, and can be traumatized due to the nature of the situation, even though they are well trained. "The traumatic symptoms of these public servants are important not only for their personal and family well-being, but also because of the potential for posttraumatic symptoms to impede firefighters from performing their work-related duties" (Farnsworth, 2010, p. 4). Therefore, firefighters suffer from Post-Traumatic Stress Disorders (PTSD) due to the very nature of the work and could create a problem for those they assist (Farnsworth, 2010). Taking this into account, in order for first responders to provide maximum service to those in dire circumstances, they must be able to psychologically and socially perform at maximum capacity when dealing with the public, and with themselves.

FUTURE RECOMMENDATIONS

The following recommendations are made within the framework of ICT and SCS, and topics discussed are the need for funding, the mitigation of existing barriers involved in ICT and SCS.

Funding for ICT and SCS

Recommendations to enhance ICT and SCS during the mitigation, preparation, response, and recovery efforts of an emergency must begin with funding. Without proper monetary allocations to develop and invest in ICT or SCS training, emergency management efforts may not be able to keep abreast of new 21st century threats. ICT funding can come from federal allocations, including Homeland Security (HLS), the private sector, and through global efforts (Khan, 2011). "Lack of financial resources and support from elected officials is a perennial problem…" but must be overcome in terms of ICT preparedness (Reddick, 2011, p. 45). In addition, ICT investment for those states that have more of a propensity of risk, need more money allocated for those potential occurrences (Reddick, 2011). Emergency response integration for cohesive operations is limited, cost may be prohibitive, and simulation is "labor intensive" (Jain & McLean, 2003, p. 5). Funding from these sources and local sources must also be allocated to ensure that emergency personnel are properly trained in terms of SCS.

Mitigating ICT Barriers

The ICT environment in emergency management, inclusive of hardware and software, is changing at an astounding rate at the federal, state, and local levels (Khan, 2011). Technology is essential for any emergency preparedness situation, and in order to mitigate ICT barriers, there are many issues that should be managed and ameliorated. These barriers include, but are not limited to communication, effectiveness of equipment, integrating communications from all aspects of those using it, and integration of systems across all emergency personnel (Khan, 2011). In addition, an analysis of where gaps in emergency efforts must be analyzed and remedied. The training that is involved to keep abreast of new technologies to assist within an emergency is also vital; ICT professional development must coincide with new technology adaptations.

ICT communication is essential for all stakeholders at all phases of an emergency. Perhaps an answer to this communication problem is integrating more social media like Twitter, Facebook, and texting. Hiltz, Diaz, and Mark (2011) state:

One of the major challenges for crisis management is integrating the information during disasters from citizens using social media, with that of official responders, disseminating messages through channels such as television, radio, SMS, and Internet Web sites. Citizen responses are bottom-up; citizens may be dispersed throughout the disaster zone, and thus are reporting on experiences 'from the trenches' (p. 5).

ICT communication must also explore "... computer science research in new directions..." and, it is the "...hope to grow a program and vision of research that focuses instead on an understudied but critical aspect of large-scale emergency response-the needs and roles of members of the public" (Palen, et al., 2010, p. 1).

Therefore, integrating ICT with stakeholders, McCabe, Barnett, Taylor, and Links (2010) created a probability model with a three-circle Venn diagram, which include the components of Ready, Willing, and Able (RWA). Where the three circles intersect is the probability of a quality response (McCabe, Barnett, Taylor, & Links, 2010). And from these components McCabe, Barnett, Taylor, and Links (2010) established a table that matches these three components to a Public Health Emergency Preparedness System (PHEPS). Agencies and entities are listed on a grid and considered to be a part of PHEPS, which include government public health infrastructure, media, Homeland Security, Public Safety, Academia, health care delivery systems, business, and communities (McCabe, et al., 2010). There is also a more in-depth assessment approach that will analyze how these PHEPS entities are ready, willing, and able to perform in case of a health care exigency. McCabe, Barnet, Taylor, and Links (2010) recommend a more specific emergency assessment approach that delineates emergency standards as well as metrics of success. In this way, these PHEPS components can provide benchmarks and access feedback from stakeholders as they operate within a dynamic environment (McCabe, et al., 2010).

However, even when communication and integration of these informational structures are in place, the data generated by ICT must be trustworthy (Hiltz, et al., 2011). In order to do this, ICT infrastructure and how emergency personnel operates ICT must be examined in terms of gaps and weaknesses. For example, in Ottawa, Canada, a workshop on Medical Preparedness for Chemical, Biological, Radiological, Nuclear, and Explosives (CBRNE) was held and a type of gap analysis, called SWOT (Strengths, Weaknesses, Opportunities, and Threats) was used to determine if any there were any "gaps in emergency mass casualty medical response" (Wilkinson, et al., 2010, p. 8). The participants were given a specific disaster scenario using radioactive cesium and used this SWOT analysis to determine recommendations for this type of scenario. In essence, SWOT could be used for any type of disaster circumstance.

More specific ICT has also been explored in emergency circumstances of infectious diseases. Inadequate emergency infectious disease preparedness has been reported by Chinese, Canadian, and American emergency entities (Rebmann, 2010). It was found that ICT assessment could not respond adequately to communications within and outside hospitals and hospitals could not manage the increased stress of large casualties in terms of equipment, medicines, and the preparedness of staffs (Rebmann, 2010). Therefore, in terms of biohazards and contamination effects, new ICT technologies, protocols, and assessments need to be employed to mitigate a biological hazard (Franco & Hansen, 2010). In essence, it is only through the analysis of emerging threats can biopreparedness fully manifest (Franco & Hansen, 2010).

In terms of a nuclear disaster, more specific ICT must also be employed to help negotiate this kind of hazard. In addition, ICT should not just be examined under the lens of short-term emergency experiences, but planned in terms of long-range engagements. "Over time, there will be a transition from the current emergency-response situation to a chronic-exposure scenario, with a committed change in management from strategies driven mainly by urgency and predominately centralized decision making to more decentralized strategies directed toward reducing exposures to as low as reasonably achievable given the circumstances" (Dauer, et al., 2011, p. 1429).

Various training methodologies using ICT are currently being explored, and include: PowerPoint modules, satellite broadcast programs, video streams, podcasts, email, fax, and telephone, and interactive online courses, which could be broadcast internationally in many languages (Waltz, et al., 2010). Inasmuch as ICT is important, training must coincide with new ICT adaptation for emergency personnel, and especially for first responders. For example, during the sarin attack, "...EMTs under Japanese law, had been allowed to maintain an airway with an endotracheal tube or use a laryngeal mask airway without physician oversight, more patients might have been saved during this chemical exposure disaster" (Okumura, et al., 1998, p. 613).

Federal, state, and local public employers of emergency personnel must take into account that emergency personnel must continue to educate the workforce in new ICT applications and communications. From an employer standpoint, ICT and training curriculum, andragogy, and assessing the learning processes emergency personnel inherently bring to the work environment is essential for optimal training.

Enhancing SCS

These advanced technologies and integrated communication systems need personnel that are trained for these new and evolving roles, but social communication training and public relations in dealing with the communities at large is equally important. According to Khan (2011), emergency personnel have to make sure citizenry is prepared for an emergency and must be trained to take into account citizens who are more at risk during an emergency. For example, "Visual, auditory, physical, speech, cognitive, neurological, and learning disabilities are all factors that can limit ready access to information" (Sullivan & Hakkinen, 2011, p. 230). Hakkinen and Sullivan (2005) as cited in Sullivan and Hakkinen (2011, p. 231) suggest the following to ensure that citizens at risk are given appropriate emergency medical treatment:

- Ensure any person will receive, understand, and be able to act upon information received in a timely manner.
- Allow an individual to make an informed decision about lifesaving measures for themselves or those they care for.
- Ensure that the preparedness/response model remains effective when parts of the technical infrastructure may fail or be under stress.
- Facilitate learning and action for people with learning and cognitive disabilities.
- Present potentially complex spatial directions to people with visual or cognitive impairments in a manner that can be understood.
- Be able to alert people who are hearing impaired or in a noisy or shielded environment.
- Anticipate that there will be linguistic differences in a community.
- Communicate effectively to people who are distracted under stress.

In terms of SCS, emergency personnel, and specifically first responders, must be educated with effective leadership skills that will help build the public trust and confidence in their ability to mitigate, prepare, respond, and recover within an emergency situation for an at-risk group or for any community, no matter its dynamics. This can be handled through optimal professional development. According to Jackson and Bradford (2012), trust and confidence are imperative to have when first responders handle an emergency situation. The police, who are first responders must develop trust and confidence with victims to "…(a) encourage active citizen participation in priority setting and the running of local services, (b) make public bodies more locally accountable and responsive, and (c) secure public cooperation with the police and compliance with the law" (Jackson & Bradford, 2012, p. 241).

SCS must begin in firefighter and police training academies, so socialization methods can be instilled early (Haarr, 2001). According to Black and Kari (2010), education correlates to more acceptance of diversity, although "…police academies cannot rely on a cadet's academic training to provide a foundation in multiculturalism. Academies may want to initiate their own multiculturalist components and include pre-training and post-training assessment to determine a new officer's perception of his or her ability to work within multicultural communities" (p. 8).

In terms of veteran police officers, firefighters, and other first responders, intrapersonal social skills must be managed and training must take place due to the high levels of post-traumatic stress (PTSD) (Cohen & Wills, 1985).. For example, "… PTSD symptoms could be assessed at the beginning of new recruits' training, and subsequently over the course of their early months and years as firefighters" (Farnsworth, 2010, p. 76). PTSD debriefing needs to be handled by each employer, because "…individuals who experience high levels of social support have less severe reactions to stressors (Cohen & Wills, 1985). First responders will continuously be in need of coping mechanisms and related healthcare services, with emergencies that are considered "traditional" and with those emergencies that are faced within the 21st century.

CONCLUSION: SOCIAL JUSTICE AND A SENSE OF COMMUNITY

There will always be threats to safety that are either natural atmospheric or geographic in nature. However, because technology is evolving so quickly in terms of weapons of war and mass destruction, ICT and SCS are two components that must be enhanced to ensure the safety of communities locally and globally. This enhancement must be done by federal, state, local, and tribal emergency response networks in the form of professional development training. If this kind of adult education does not happen in depth and breadth, the issue then becomes a community disenfranchisement issue. In addition, to compound matters, if there is not enough federal, state, and local funding for ICT or SCS training in terms of emergency management, people will be at substantial risk.

Community disenfranchisement due to lack of emergency personnel education must be explored. Emergency management needs to be especially cognizant of those who are marginalized due to lack of access, allocation, or knowledge of ICT (Baer, et al., 2009). However, "There will always be disenfranchised groups who do not get a chance to interface within this technology realm, and therefore may be less likely to be heard by government (Russo, Bryan, & Penney, 2012). Disparate ICT issues will ultimately stem from politics and leach into the design, acquisition, and allocation of technology (Baer, et al., 2009). "This means designers of ICT solutions should meet democratic political requirements should therefore keep in mind that their use may be shaped, or strongly influenced, by a history of political considerations" (Baer, et al., 2009, p. 7). In essence, political processes and how it affects the communities that are able to access ICT is directly related to the idea of social justice. With this being said, a developer of ICT, which is usually fostered by the private sector, should have a social responsibility rather than a profit in mind when it comes to the idea that all citizens require and deserve quality emergency management during any kind of incident.

According to Russo et al. (2012), technology may not help in terms in the proliferation of a democratic governance model, however, it is this last stage that will help those disenfranchised or marginalized to acquire emergency information. However, when technology becomes a basic tool for emergency management with a public interface, and not all parties are privy to equal treatment in terms of acquisition and allocation of ICT services, this technology then becomes a guidepost for who receives emergency efforts and services on their behalf.

There should be a moral obligation to provide emergency technology to all citizens, especially when it comes to a citizen's health and wellbeing. Sometimes, a moral obligation needs to be made more obvious to those who serve the public, and must be inculcated in training forums. In addition, Laurent (2011) suggests there should be an inherent "technology of democracy" that enables public participation (p. 1). Emergencies should not be politicized and apportioned out for those that may be more economically flush. Emergency management is a right and should not be for the privileged that can afford it. Essentially ICT becomes more than just an emancipating concept but a human right in the quest for safety. Therefore, ICT becomes a matter of life and death.

The ICT emergency management issue becomes more than just whether or not there is equipment, but continues to a new level of a democratic safety issue. Russo et al. (2012) state:

But, the use of ICT does not necessarily mean that one has a democratic voice in emergency situation if a type of status quo infrastructure is in place. Therefore, infrastructure, if not working for the public or the socially vulnerable, must be examined and remedied because lives are at stake (p. 7).

Hopefully this is not the case and the status quo effort is not in play when it comes to safety and the well being of human beings. In addition, a truly worthy political process should parlay into a more level playing field leaving citizens less disenfranchised, thus creating more of a democratic hub and more of a safety net (Russo, et al., 2012).

The last issue regarding the component of emergency related ICT is to address the embedded bureaucratic structure in which ICT is situated. A bureaucratic model may not guarantee democracy (Starr, 2010). ICT information must be used to communicate to the citizenry in emergency situations, and "Even though the digital divide has narrowed, any reliance of government on digital technology will put people with less income and education at an inequitable disadvantage because of persistent difference in digital skill as well as access" (Starr, 2010, p. 5). Lessig (2006) explains, "We can build, or architect, or code cyberspace to protect values that we believe are fundamental. Or we can build, or architect, or code cyberspace to allow those values to disappear. There is no middle ground" (p. 6).

In terms of SCS training during emergency situations, emergency personnel, especially first responders, but will ultimately be on the ground and the first parties responsible for the safety and wellbeing of the community. It is imperative that these first responders have the social skills to navigate the emergency, and reduce community tensions through a new bridge of understanding, especially in communities that are diverse. Firefighters, police officers, hospitals, and health care personnel need to be a part of the communities they serve, in terms of a social bonded sense. These emergency players must establish and provide a kind of oneness, or esprit de corps, with the communities they assist. When there is a collectivist effort is established in a crisis, there is a wellspring of potential benefits that accrue to all stakeholders.

Although race is a social construct and in a biologic and genetic sense, there is no such thing as race, it has been proposed that placing the same racial and/or ethnic emergency personnel in communities of the same ilk will promote a better community bond. However, this homogenous arrangement may promote more segregation and may still not bridge emergency and health gaps that still exist. It may also be that the more we keep people segregated, the more misunderstanding we continue to promulgate among racial groups. In addition, it may not be possible to ethnically match the workforce demographics with those of the community they serve. In addition, there are two schools of thought that exist regarding this homogeneity. One version suggests that "...a strong in-group identification appears to encourage in-group biases that may have deleterious effects on the value of diversity" (Townley, Kloos, Green, & Franco, 2011, p. 73), while other research suggests that "Homogenesous communities have also been linked to greater physical and emotional safety" (Townley, et al., 2011, p. 73).

Possibly more community SCS connections can be developed to create meaningful community liaisons. For example, emergency personnel can encourage community learning workshops, informal gatherings, and community outreach, which may be "One way to reconcile the tensions between sense of community and diversity is to create a common in-group identity among diverse individuals (Townley, Kloos, Green, & Franco, 2011, p. 78). To investigate this issue further, integration cannot be superficial in nature but must be sincere with a continued interactive effort (Townley, et al., 2011). When it comes to all stakeholders, a level of trust and confidence can be built with the same social norms and effective social network in which to communicate.

Therefore, within the evolving framework of ICT and SCS, can a Sense of Community (SOC) be rendered? Within the concept of SOC, stakeholders share a feeling of group identity, no matter the level of diversity. SOC is "a feeling that members have of belonging, a feeling that members matter to one another and to the group, and a shared faith that members' needs will be me through their commitment to be together (McMillan & Chavis, 1986, p. 9). SOC is not uniform and changes and adapts within different communal cultures, and SOC must be given some time to unfold. SOC is a "...positive and intentional constant (McMillan & Chavis, 1986) and "This becomes possible when practitioners adopt an attitude of working with communities, not for communities" (Townley, et al., 2011). An SOC will ultimately build a safer society, especially for first responders and victims alike.

Consequently, "...it is important to understand the ways in which environmental contexts impact all aspects of diversity, including cultural identity development in multi-cultural settings and promotion of tolerance and acceptance of diverse cultural groups" (Townley, et al., 2011, p. 71). When there is a shared emotional connection, based on a shared history and group identity, group members will be able to bridge gaps of understanding (McMillan & Chavis, 1986). When a sense of belonging happens, a sense of vision, mission, and core values will build a collective spirit and marginalized community members will be diminished (Townley, et al., 2011). This sense of community, especially during an emergency, may be the difference between life and death.

"By viewing the citizenry as a powerful, self-organizing, and collectively intelligent force, information and communication technology can play a transformational role in a crisis" (Palen, 2010, p. 1). ICT will assist the citizenry in a quest for a democratic response regarding safety and wellbeing. First responders should be trained in all realms of SCS plus be respondent and key community members within the community they serve. Therefore, within the framework of ICT and SCS a true sense of community values will lead to a true SOC. We may not be able to predict the future, or the next crisis, but if all these components are working in tandem, a sense of social justice for the entire community during any 21st century crisis will manifest.

REFERENCES

Baer, W. Borisov, Danezis, G., Dutton, Klonowski, M. W., Seda, G., . . .Zagorski, F. (2009). *Machiavelli confronts 21st century digital technology: Democracy in a network society*. Retrieved from http://ssrn.com/abstract=1521222

Barnett, T., & Sorenson, C. (2011). Infectious disease surveillance in the United States and theUnited Kingdom: From public goods to the challenges of new technologies. *Journal of Health Politics, Policy and Law*, *36*, 165–185. doi:10.1215/03616878-1191144

Black, P. J., & Kari, C. J. (2010). Policing diverse communities: Do gender and minority status make a difference? *Journal of Ethnicity in Criminal Justice*, *8*(3), 216–229. doi:10.1080/15377938.2010.502848

Chang, N.-B., Wei, L. Y., Tseng, C. C., & Kao, J. C.-Y. (1997). The design of a GIS-based decision support system for chemical emergency preparedness and response in an urban environment. *Computers, Environment and Urban Systems*, *21*(1), 67–94. doi:10.1016/S0198-9715(97)01009-0

Cohen, S., & Wills, T. (1985). Stress, social support, and the buffering hypothesis. *Psychological Bulletin*, *98*, 310–357. doi:10.1037/0033-2909.98.2.310

Dauer, T. L., Zanzonico, P., Tuttle, M. R., Quinn, M. D., & Strauss, H. W. (2011). The Japanese tsunami and resulting nuclear emergency at the Fukushima Daiichi power facility: Technical, radiologic, and response perspectives. *Journal of Nuclear Medicine*, *52*, 1423–1432. doi:10.2967/jnumed.111.091413

Dykstrak, E. (2003). Concept paper: Toward an international system model in emergency management. In *Proceedings of Toward an International System Model in Emergency Management* (pp. 1–17). Fairfax, VA: Public Entity Risk Institute.

Farnsworth, J. (2010). *Benefits and costs of social interaction among firefighters*. (Unpublished Master's Thesis). University of North Texas. Denton, TX.

Flanigan, M., Blatt, A., Russell, M., Batta, R., & Lee, K. (2010). Emergency response technology and integrated active transportation system. *Journal of the Transportation Research Board*, *21*(89), 26–36. doi:10.3141/2189-04

Franco, C., & Hansen, M. B. (2010). The state of biopreparedness: Lessons from leaders, proposals for progress. *Biosecurity and Bioterrorism: Biodefense Strategy. Practice and Science*, *8*(40), 379–383.

Fu, L. (2011). The government response to 9/11: Communications technology and the media. *Library & Archival Security*, *24*, 103–118. doi:10.1080/01960075.2011.592034

Haarr, R. (2001). The making of a community police officer: The impact of basic training and occupational socialization on police recruits. *Police Quarterly*, *4*, 402–433. doi:10.1177/109861101129197923

Hardin, R. (2006). *Trust*. Cambridge, UK: Polity Press.

Hiltz, S., Diaz, P., & Mark, G. (2011). Introduction: Social media and collaborative systems for crisis management. *ACM Transactions on Computer-Human Interaction*, *18*(4), 1–6. doi:10.1145/2063231.2063232

Jackson, J., & Bradford, B. (2010). What is trust and confidence in the police? *Policing*, *4*(3), 241–248. doi:10.1093/police/paq020

Jain, S., & Mclean, C. (2003). A framework for modeling and simulation for emergency response. In *Proceedings of the 2003 Winter Simulation Conference,* (pp. 1068-1076). Academic Press.

Johnson, R. (2000). *GIS technology for disasters and emergency management*. Redlands, CA: Environmental Systems Research Institute.

Khan, S. A. (2011). Public health preparedness response in the USA since 9/11: A national health security imperative. *Lancet*, *378*(9794), 953–956. doi:10.1016/S0140-6736(11)61263-4

Laurent, B. (2011). Technologies of democracy: Experiments and demonstrations. *Science and Engineering Ethics*, *17*(4), 649–666. doi:10.1007/s11948-011-9303-1

Lessig, L. (2006). *Code: Version 2.0*. New York, NY: Basic Books.

Lindel, M., Prater, C., & Perry, R. (2007). *Emergency management*. New York, NY: Wiley.

McCabe, O. L., Barnett, D. J., Taylor, H. G., & Links, J. M. (2010). Ready, willing and able: A framework for improving the public health emergency preparedness system. *American Medical Association, 4*(2), 161-168.

Meacham, B. J., Dembsey, N. A., Schebel, K., Johann, M. A., & Tubbs, J. S. (2012). Use of small- scale test data to enhance fire-related threat, vulnerability, consequence and risk assessment for passenger rail vehicles. *Journal of Homeland Security and Emergency Management*, *9*(1), 1–16. doi:10.1515/1547-7355.1850

Merchant, R. M., Elmer, S., & Lurie, N. (2011). Integrating social media into emergency preparedness efforts. *The New England Journal of Medicine*, *365*, 289–291. doi:10.1056/NEJMp1103591

Okumura, T., Suzuki, K., Fukuda, A., Kohama, A., Takasu, N., Ishimatsu, S., & Hinohara, S. (1998). The Tokyo subway sarin attack: Disaster management, part 1: Community emergency response. *Academic Emergency Medicine*, *5*(6), 613–617. doi:10.1111/j.1553-2712.1998.tb02470.x

Palen, L., Sanderson, K. M., Mark, G., Martin, J., Sicker, D., Palmer, M., & Grunwald, D. (2010). A vision for technology-mediated support for public participation & assistance in mass emergencies & disasters. In *Proceedings of the 2010 ACM-BCS Visions of Computer Science Conference,* (vol. 8, pp. 1-12). ACM Press.

Rebmann, T. (2010). Pandemic preparedness: Implementation of infection prevention plans. *Infection Control and Hospital Epidemiology*, *31*(1), 35–65. doi:10.1086/655993

Reddick, C. (2010). Information technology and emergency management: Preparedness and planning in US states. *Disasters*, *35*, 45–61. doi:10.1111/j.1467-7717.2010.01192.x

Russo, M., Bryan, V., & Penney, G. (2012). *Emergency preparedness: Life limb, the pursuit of safety and social justice*. Retrieved from www.igi-global.com/gateway/article/full-text-html/66092

Starr, P. (2010). The liberal state in a digital world. *Governance: An International Journal of Policy, Administration and Institutions*, *23*(1), 1–6. doi:10.1111/j.1468-0491.2009.01464.x

Sullivan, H. T., & Häkkinen, M. T. (2011). Preparedness and warning systems for populations with special needs: Ensuring everyone gets the message (and knows what to do). *Geotechnical and Geological Engineering*, *29*, 225–236. doi:10.1007/s10706-010-9363-z

Townley, G., Kloos, B., Green, E. P., & Franco, M. M. (2011). Reconcilable differences? Human diversity, cultural relativity, and sense of community. *American Journal of Community Psychology*, *47*, 69–85. doi:10.1007/s10464-010-9379-9

Treglia, J., McKnight, L. W., Venkatesh, M., & Bose, T. Volos, van Aardt, J., … Lee, M. (2001). *Social emergency response technology policy.* Paper presented at the TPRC: The 39th Research Conference on Communication, Information and Internet Policy. Arlington, VA.

Waltz, E. G., Maniccia, D. M., Bryde, R. L., Murphy, K., Harris, B. R., & Waldenmailer, M. N. (2010). Training the public health workforce from Albany to Zambia: Technology lessons learned along the way. *Public Health Reports*, *125*, 61–69.

Wilkinson, D., Waruszynski, B., Mazurik, L., Szymczak, A., Redmond, E., & Lichacz, F. (2010). Medical preparedness for chemical, biological, radiological, nuclear, and explosives (CBRNE) events: Gaps and recommendations. *Radiation Protection Dosimetry*, *142*, 8–11. doi:10.1093/rpd/ncq206

Chapter 8
Social Networking, Cyber Bullying, and the Role of Community Education

Michelle Sofo
University of Canberra, Australia

Francesco Sofo
University of Canberra, Australia

ABSTRACT

This chapter explores the link between social capital, the bullying that can occur via social networking sites, and community education. It becomes evident that social networking sites are influential sources of informal learning despite the published literature being somewhat divided on the sociological, psychological, and emotional benefits of social networking. Through the presentation of Australian statistics and case studies, the chapter demonstrates how social capital can be eroded through the misuse of social networking sites particularly in the form of cyber bullying. The Australian government has responded to the social impacts of cyber bullying by funding an extensive community education program. Through examining this program, it is possible to see how important it is to have effective and accessible community education regarding safe and responsible social networking.

INTRODUCTION

The exploration of social capital has become increasingly popular within the socioeconomic literature, but there remains some confusion about exactly what constitutes social capital (Urwin, Di Pietro, Sturgis, & Jack, 2008). The additional factor of emerging technology and its impact on individuals, groups and wider society only compound this confusion. This chapter aims to explore the link between social capital, the bullying that can occur via social networking sites and community education. What becomes apparent is that social networking sites offer a wide range of

DOI: 10.4018/978-1-4666-2955-4.ch008

informal learning opportunities that can support other learning that occurs in formal and non-formal settings. Informal learning is defined by Coombs (1985) as *"the spontaneous, unstructured learning that goes on daily in the home and...through the various mass media"* (p. 92). Within the context of this definition, Tynes (2007) effectively highlights advances in critical thinking, the taking of multiple perspectives and the acquisition of information and advice that can be informally gained through the use of social networking sites.

Given the widespread and pervasive nature of informal learning, the Organization for Economic Cooperation and Development has commenced efforts to formally recognise the learning that takes place outside of educational institutions (OECD, 2010). The OECD is actively working with member countries to acknowledge the depth of social capital that stems from informal learning. This chapter uses the concept of informal learning and the progressive work of the OECD to set the context whereby social networking can be viewed as an influential source of informal learning. By placing particular emphasis on the benefits stemming from having community members who are well connected and confident in their use of modern information and communication technology, it is possible to explore the perils, which can also arise. These perils can include occurrences of online fraud, identity theft, the presence of fake profiles and cyber bullying—all of which can actively erode social capital at both individual and community levels.

The literature is somewhat divided on the sociological, psychological and emotional benefits of social networking, particularly regarding the number and type of online 'friends' that can be made through a cyber community. Kraut et al. (1998) found that people who spend a significant amount of time on the Internet experience higher levels of loneliness and a larger number of daily stressors than people who do not spend as much time on the Internet. Through the presentation of some Australian statistics and case studies, this chapter aims to demonstrate how social capital can be eroded through the misuse of social networking sites—particularly when the misuse comes in the form of cyber bullying.

Estimates of all forms of cyber bullying incidents which target Australian school children range from 7-10% (Cross, et al., 2009) to 20% (as cited in Campbell, 2007) to even 57% (Price & Dalgleish, 2010). Occurrences of cyber bullying in particular can negatively impact upon levels of social trust, social capital and overall positive regard for online interactions. As a result, an online user's effort to become connected via social networking may in turn lead to even greater levels of social isolation as they refrain from entering the virtual environment that they perceive to be dangerous, unpredictable, difficult to control, and open to the exploitation of their conscious and unconscious vulnerabilities.

It has previously been found that an increase in chat-room activity (such as that experienced in romantic social networking sites) results in individuals being more vulnerable to identity theft and the invasion of their privacy (Milne, Rohm, & Bahl, 2004). Dating and online romance scams are particularly difficult to detect and avoid because of the involvement of emotional attachments, and the victims' perceptions that they have found companionship and happiness. Victims of dating scams are typically found through virtual environments, and romantic social networking sites provide an ideal environment for scammers, as unwitting users trust that they will meet like-minded, honest people who are in a similar situation to themselves. Through the creation of trust comes vulnerability. This is further compounded by the fact that whilst online communities facilitate social interaction, they also provide users with an "escape" from reality (Janda & Fair, 2004) that further separates them from the very real risks and dangers associated with online social networking such as incidents of cyber bullying.

As stated, the prevalence of cyber bullying within Australia ranges from 7% to 57%, and there are a number of flow-on effects to the offline environment. Given these statistics, this chapter aims to showcase how the Australian government has responded to the social impacts of cyber bullying by funding extensive community education programs. By providing an overview of these community education programs, it will be possible to see how important it is to have effective and accessible community education regarding safe and responsible social networking. It is in our interest as educators and professionals to ensure that an individual's use of social networking is safe and based on factual information and empowerment through education so that social capital can be enhanced rather than eroded.

BACKGROUND

This chapter explores the interplay between three concepts: social capital, social networking, and cyber bullying. Before exploring these issues, it is useful to set the context through some definitions. Social capital is defined as the resources which are accumulated through inter-personal relationships (Coleman, 1988) and the overall positive effects which are created through the interaction of participants in a social network (Helliwell & Putnam, 2004). According to Urwin et al. (2008), there are three types of social capital:

- *Bonding social capital* refers to the tied networks that exist between relatively homogenous individuals (such as family members or close friends). Bonding social capital is characterised by tightly-knit and emotionally-close relationships (Ellison, et al., 2007);
- *Bridging social capital* refers to ties among diverse groups of people (e.g., people in a workplace or online community) that are more distant than those of homogenous individuals (e.g., family members); and
- *Linking social capital* refers to networks that connect individuals to a group, an institution or an organisation.

Yet while social networking sites—and the accompanying increases that occur to social capital—can be viewed as the 'social glue' that keeps individuals together as a community, face-to-face relationships and in-person interactions still remain significant (Madge, Meek, Wellens, & Hooley, 2009).

Social networking is a phenomenon of the 21st century, which has opened up a world of interpersonal communication that never previously existed. Modern technology has gradually transformed the social interactions that occur among people (Katona, Zubcsek, & Sarvary, 2011), and around 80% of Australians aged over 18 report being users of the social networking site Facebook (Coopes, 2010). In recent times, Internet connections and mobile phones have become instrumental in the way that teenagers connect to, and interact with, their peers. Social networking sites have millions of registered users, with the average user has 130 friends and spends around 55 minutes per day on Facebook alone (Gil-Or, 2010). Commercially, more than 7 million applications and third party websites have been integrated with Facebook (2011), and millions of people are using social networking sites to become, and stay, connected. Facebook claims to have 845 million users (with 50% of these people being so-called 'active users' who log onto Facebook on any given day) (Facebook, 2012). Following on from these staggering statistics is the fact that social networking sites have emerged as an influential means of linking people in social, academic, and professional settings. Academically, it has been found that university students' use of Facebook is positively related to social adjustment and the students' attachment to their educational institution (Kalpidou, Costin, & Morris, 2011) while professionally, the networking site LinkedIn has around 150 million members (LinkedIn, 2012).

So what makes these networking sites—and numerous others like them—so attractive? Social networking sites enable the preservation of existing social ties and the formation of new connections (Ellison, Steinfield, & Lampe, 2007). As such, numerous benefits stem from successful social networking including the establishment of new friendships, the rediscovery of old acquaintances and the eradication of long distances that enables connections to be created across the street and across the world. In short, social networking creates ties, systems and links that can have positive effects on social capital and building knowledge. However, despite the benefits of social networking, one of the biggest downsides is the existence of cyber bullying.

Cyber bullying has been defined as a form of covert aggressive behaviour that is repeated, intended to cause harm, characterised by an imbalance of power and carried out through the use of technology (Cross, et al., 2009). With the advent of Information Communication Technologies (ICT), bullying has shifted from being "behind the scenes" to being "behind the screens" (Spears, Slee, Owens, & Johnson, 2009). This means that the more traditional, covert and subtle forms of bullying have been transformed through the introduction of ICT to be acts facilitated through electronic means and available to be witnessed by millions of people. Indeed, *"the effect of the cyber group far surpasses the schoolyard group given that the former is not bound by the school walls and the potential audience is limitless"* (Dooley, Pyżalski, & Cross, 2009, p. 187). Further, cyber bullying is said to be very 'attractive' to its perpetrators because of the apparent 'anonymity' provided by the Internet and other forms of communication technology (Price & Dalgleish, 2010; Shariff, 2005).

LINKING THE CONCEPTS OF SOCIAL CAPITAL, SOCIAL NETWORKING AND CYBER BULLYING

Social Capital

There are two distinct ways to explore the issue of social capital: from the individual viewpoint, or from the viewpoint of groups/collectives/communities (Urwin, et al., 2008). Social capital is not fixed, and social networks can change over time as relationships are created, developed or abandoned (Ellison, et al., 2007). In the past, an individual's relocation from one city to another city or country could result in a breakdown in communication, a detrimentally altered state of physical or communicative closeness and an eventual loss of social capital. The absence of social capital can have damaging effects on a community. As noted by Ellison et al. (2007) "when social capital declines, a community experiences increased social disorder, reduced participation in civic activities and potentially more distrust among community members" (p. 1145). Thankfully, through the advent of the Internet and social networking sites, these potential losses are mitigated and interpersonal contact can be maintained regardless of physical location.

Social networking sites are therefore a modern means by which social capital can be created. Kim and Lee (2011) found that Facebook friendships may be a meaningful source of social support but only to the extent that the online user can dedicate adequate time and effort to develop and maintain a close connection with their 'friends.' Urwin et al. (2008) observed that there may be an optimal level of participation in activities that create social capital. Yet while social networking sites have been found to support both the maintenance of existing social ties and the formation of new connections (Ellison, Steinfield, & Lampe, 2007), it is unclear exactly how much time must be spent each day in order to achieve the 'optimal level.'

Reports on the average daily time spent by users on social networking sites ranges from 20 (Cassidy, 2006) or 30 minutes (Ellison, et al., 2007) to 1¾ hours (Raacke & Bonds-Raacke, 2008). More recent reports put daily usage at 2 hours (Kalpidou, Costin, & Morris, 2011).

Yet while research has shown that an individual's overall Internet use has a generally positive effect on his or her level of social capital (Pasek, More, & Romer, 2009), the relatively simple act of *engaging* via the Internet does not necessarily guarantee the creation or maintenance of social capital. Indeed, Ellison et al. (2007) found that "general Internet use was not a significant predictor of bridging social capital, suggesting that only certain kinds of uses of the Internet support the generation and maintenance of bridging social capital" (p. 1157). A similar finding was made in relation to bonding social capital. With regard to the specific context of online social networking, it can therefore be useful to consider the different types of social capital and social ties that can be created.

The sociological literature explores the differences between strong and weak social ties. At the time that Granovetter wrote his seminal piece on strong and weak ties (in the 1970s), the existence of the Internet or the concept of 'social networking' had not yet been considered. Yet it seems natural and logical that the role of strong and weak social ties is now pertinent to any discussion on the link between social capital and social networking. When assessing the strength and resilience of social ties, it has been postulated that acquaintances (that is, *weak ties*) are less likely to be socially involved with one another than are close friends (*strong ties*) (Granovetter, 1983). In recent times, it has been found that online linkages are a means of establishing weak ties, which can then form the foundation for future bridging social capital (Ellison, et al., 2007). Indeed, social networking sites may be of particular benefit to individuals who would otherwise have difficulties in forming and maintaining either strong or weak ties (Ellison, et al., 2007).

The presence of a large number of online 'friends' (see for example Ellison, et al., 2007; Madge, et al., 2009) may be an example of weak ties which appear somewhat superficial, yet sociologically speaking, weak ties can be highly functional. Indeed, *"social systems lacking in weak ties will be fragmented and incoherent"* and instead of creating alienation, these weak ties are essential to an individual's integration into society (Granovetter, 1983, pp. 202-203). The existence of numerous weak ties enables individuals to be exposed to a wide variety of different viewpoints and activities, and Granovetter (1983) regards this exposure as an "essential prerequisite for the social construction of individualism" (p.203). More recently, Tynes (2007) has supported this view by acknowledging the wide range of informal learning opportunities that arise via social networking sites.

The Role of Social Networking Sites in the Creation of Social Capital

Urwin et al. (2008) observed that individuals may try to foster various types of social ties in an effort to raise their own levels of social capital and by doing so, consideration must be given as to the possible ways in which this investment could produce a tangible return. In the online environment, a tangible return would be the number of 'friends.' As noted by Kim and Lee (2011), when using social networking sites it does not take much effort to become 'friends' with another user, and the 'friendship' does not require strong attachment or close connections. Facebook in its entirety boasts more than 125 *billion* friend connections (Facebook, 2012). On an individual basis, studies have found respondents having between 5 'friends' (Pollet, et al., 2011) and 130 'friends' (Gil-Or, 2010) or up to 200 (Ellison, et al., 2007) or even 460 'friends' (Madge, et al., 2009). Much of the analytical work regarding social capital fails to actually assess the *quality* of the identified networks (Strathdee, 2001) thus it can be difficult to ascertain whether these seemingly exorbitant numbers of 'friends' are really an output of social capital, or merely a numerical representation of acquaintances and linkages between different networks. Indeed, the existence of large numbers of 'friends' may even lead one to falsely assume that they possess—or actively contribute to the creation of—social capital. On the one hand, having lots of social networking friends has been found to be positively related to social adjustment, attachment and improved social networks (Kalpidou, et al., 2011). Bridging social capital or ties weaker than bonding social capital can be highly effective as they link different groups and enable individuals who are significantly different from one another to be meaningfully connected (Granovetter, 1983). Further, Ellison et al. (2007) report that a 'robust' connection exists between reported usage of social networking sites and indicators of social capital. On the other hand, Kalpidou et al. (2011) report on findings that people spending significant amounts of time on the Internet report higher levels of loneliness and a greater number of daily stresses than people who did not report such high levels of Internet use.

It is therefore a reality that the cyber world has the potential to weaken the social capital that has been previously established in the offline world. As noted by Spears et al. (2009), "the 'parallel universe' of cyberspace, which exists alongside family and schooling contexts, presents additional challenges for 'real' world relationships" (p. 190). Indeed, it is the disruption of relationships within the real world that can then lead to cyber bullying, with the occurrence of cyber bullying then impacting upon relationships (Spears, et al., 2009).

The impact of social networking sites upon social capital can be viewed from the two complementary, yet at times seemingly opposing, viewpoints. On the one hand, social networking sites can be seen as having a negative impact on the creation and maintenance of quality social capital. For example, researchers identifying as 'cyber-pessimists' view the Internet as having a negative effect on social life, as the time spent online is viewed as the displacement of time which could be spent socialising face-to-face with family and friends (Pollet, et al., 2011). Alternatively, social networking sites can be seen as having a positive and healthy impact on the creation and maintenance of social capital. Researchers identifying as 'cyber-optimists' highlight that the Internet has a positive effect on social life by supplementing (rather than replacing) other forms of communication and by positively building and maintaining strong and satisfying social relationships (Pollet, et al., 2011). Indeed, the existence of mere acquaintances and weak social ties provides people with access to information and a wider range of resources than that which would normally be available in their own social circle (Granovetter, 1983).

Social networking sites act as a mediator between the individual and wider society (Ulusu, 2010). These links can be *known* (such as those between the individual and contacts from their past and present) or *unknown* (such as those between the individual and people they have not previously known, but who meet virtually via chat rooms, instant messages and as fellow 'friends' of a given company or interest group). Most social networking sites foster the maintenance of pre-existing social networks, yet others can help strangers connect based on particular interests, political or religious views, or specific activities (Ulusu, 2010).

In their review of other literature, Pollet et al. (2011) observe that networks tend to fall into three categories:

- *Support group* where contact is frequent and material support is provided (with the mean size of these groups being 5 people);
- *Sympathy group* where contact is also frequent and emotional support is provided (mean size 15 people), and

- *Active network* where contact is infrequent and relationships are much less emotionally intense (mean size 50-150 people).

The average user of a social networking site has between 130 (Gil-Or, 2010) and 180 (Pollet, et al., 2011) friends. Yet using the typology cited above, it is likely that many of these social networking site 'friends' would fall into the category of being part of an individual's active network, rather than being a source of frequent, material support or sympathy. Indeed, the research undertaken by Pollet et al. (2011) shows that an increasing amount of time spent on social media was associated with a larger number of *online* 'friends' but was not associated with larger *offline* networks or with people feeling emotionally closer to their offline friends.

It is therefore quite apparent why there is some criticism about the strength and ability of online 'friends' to contribute to the creation and maintenance of social capital. Frequent interaction with a lot of people does not necessarily equate to lasting, trusting, interactive reciprocity. As noted by Pollet et al. (2011), "quantity does not necessarily equal quality. Those with larger networks tend to be less emotionally close to each network member" (p. 254).

The strength of relationships in various network types may not figure in the type or strength of learning that could emanate from such diverse systems. Serendipity and paradox play a role in learning and many people attest to occasions when realisations and insights came seemingly by chance within a social setting as a result of being intent on finding solutions. That is, learning is also defined within social contexts (Jarvis, 1992, 2004). It might seem that active networks which maximise the number of human contacts could very well provide opportunities for informal learning where knowledge is created as a consequence of tacit knowledge being converted into explicit forms of knowledge. Many authors in the area of learning emphasise that an individual's thought processes within social contexts (including virtual social spaces as noted by Nonaka, Toyama, & Byoiere, 2001) transform the shared, informative but tentative knowledge into meaningful and more practical knowledge, which characterises applied knowledge used in different contexts (see for example Nonaka, Peltokorpi, & Tomae, 2005; Sessa & London, 2006). Through further individual reflection and validation, such applied knowledge gained through informal learning becomes adopted by and embedded within individuals and groups.

Informal Learning

Informal learning has been defined as the "*s*pontaneous, unstructured learning that goes on daily in the home and…through the various mass media" (Coombs, 1985, p. 92). The Internet in general, and social networking sites specifically, are rich sources of informal learning. Tynes (2007) makes a compelling argument that the education and psychosocial benefits of social networking far outweighs the potential dangers. In reviewing the educational and psychosocial benefits afforded to adolescents who engage in social networking, Tynes (2007) includes:

- Informal learning that reinforces and complements more formal types of learning;
- The development of critical thinking and argumentation skills (for example when an individual engages in online debate or posts an opinion via a chat room);
- Enhanced peer interaction;
- An opportunity to try out new ideas and enhance decision-making abilities;
- The acquisition of help, information, suggestions and advice (for example on medical issues or homework problems);
- Cross-cultural and interracial interaction occurring through peer teaching and learning that crosses racial and ethnic boundaries and fosters greater understanding and acceptance of others;

- The acquisition of skills in digital media (specifically the uploading and sharing of video clips via YouTube);
- Access to social support and advice regarding specific interests or problems; and
- Access to alternative media and political opinions, which may produce new notions of civil society.

It has been shown that weak ties serve a crucial function in their ability to link otherwise unconnected segments of a social network (Granovetter, 1983), and when put in the context of Tynes' argument, the benefits of social networking appear irrefutable. Indeed, these benefits are likely to extend beyond applying only to adolescents to hold true for most social networkers across the lifespan.

Yet while Tynes (2007) successfully argues the benefits of exposing young people to social networking, her statement that the online environment allows "young people to practice interaction with others in the safety of their homes" (p. 583) is inherently flawed. For example, by its very nature, cyber bullying is able to erode the once impermeable sanctuary of the family home. As noted by Wright, Burnham, Inman, and Ogorchock (2009), "cyber bullying has the potential to impact youth across systems (i.e. home, school and the community)" (p. 40). Despite this potential permeation into the family home, the typical modern parent feels ill equipped to respond effectively to cyber bullying (Hannah, 2010). The effect of this can be devastating, as the consequences of home-based cyber bullying has been found to be higher among families where the parents do not have the knowledge or skills to assist their child (Cross, et al., 2009). Given this, it is timely to explore some of the downsides of social networking by focusing on the occurrence and effects of cyber bullying within our communities.

Cyber Bullying

Cyber bullying is defined in Australia as "forms of bullying that use electronic means such as the Internet and mobile phones to aggressively and intentionally harm someone" (Price & Dalgleish, 2010, p. 51). The definition proffered by Smith et al. (2008) has the additional features of the perpetrator being an individual *or* group, and the reality that the victim cannot easily defend him or herself. Like more 'traditional' bullying that occurs in the schoolyard or workplace, cyber bullying usually involves repeated behaviours and the existence of a power imbalance between the aggressor and the victim (Price & Dalgleish, 2010). In helping to define the concept, Spears et al. (2009) identified two types of cyber bullying:

- *Covert cyber bullying* which features indirect, social and relational behaviours which can result in exclusion, isolation and the manipulation of friendships and relationships, and
- *Overt cyber bullying* involving the explicit, deliberate act of using technology to cause harm (such as taking an intimate photograph or video and uploading it to a public networking site and providing peers with the link).

Inherent to these two overarching categories are specific types of cyber bullying behaviours. Through their review of literature, Wright et al. (2009) devised a list of seven different types of cyber bullying that have been found to exist:

1. **Flaming**: Sending angry, vulgar messages to a person or party.
2. **Harassment**: Sending messages to a person repeatedly.
3. **Denigration**: Sending or posting harmful, untrue information.
4. **Cyber stalking**: Using threats of harm and intimidation.

5. **Impersonation**: Pretending to be another person.
6. **Outing or trickery**: Tricking a person into sending embarrassing information, and
7. **Exclusion**: Excluding someone purposefully (p. 35).

Cyber bullying is considered a relatively new form of bullying, but it is receiving increased levels of attention in the research literature (Dooley, et al., 2009). Much of the interest has been due to the role that social networking sites can play as a means of facilitating cyber bullying. In an Australian study, Price and Dalgleish (2010) found that 41% of 13-14 year olds had been cyber bullied. This figure rose to 53% amongst 15-16 year olds and 57% amongst 17-18 year olds. These findings are particularly worrying given that during these adolescent years, the process of identity formation is largely dependent upon the cues that young people receive from their social environment (Patchin & Hinduja, 2010). The types of cues (that is, cyber bullying behaviours) received by some participants of the Price and Dalgleish (2010) study included name calling, abusive comments, spreading of rumours, the threat of physical harm and the circulation of embarrassing, humiliating or defamatory images. In Patchin and Hinduja's (2010) study featuring 1,963 middle school students, 18% had received an upsetting email, 14% had something upsetting posted about them on a social networking site, 10% had been humiliated in a chat room and 9% reported being bullied online. All of these statistics related to the respondents' *past 30 days only*, suggesting a potentially alarming rate of incidence across an entire school experience or lifetime. Sadly, almost 6% of respondents subsequently felt afraid to use the computer (Patchin & Hinduja, 2010).

Despite these statistics, it would be erroneous to assume that the victims of cyber bullying are always young people. In another Australian study exploring bullying and cyber bullying in the workplace, it was found that 27% of respondents had experienced gossip or rumours being spread about them via modern technology, 18% had been technologically excluded and over 9% had been the victim of insulting or offensive remarks via some form of information communication technology (Privitera & Campbell, 2009). In total, almost half of the sample (n=103) had experienced cyber bullying on either an irregular or weekly basis.

The effects of cyber bullying have been found to include interference with real world relationships, manipulation by others, a sense of powerlessness and a sense of helplessness (Spears, et al., 2009). Further effects include reduced self-esteem and self-confidence, and a negative effect on friendships, school grades, school attendance and family relationships, with the emotional impacts reportedly being experiences of sadness, annoyance, anger, frustration, embarrassment, and of feeling afraid or even terrified (Price & Dalgleish, 2010). Importantly, higher levels of peer support have been found to reduce the odds of an individual being covertly bullied (Cross, et al., 2009), which in turn provides support for the role of social capital as a mitigating factor against the harmful effects of cyber bullying.

Australian Case Studies

While the use of social networking sites has been found to improve levels of bridging social capital for students with low satisfaction levels and poor self-esteem (Ellison, et al., 2007), it is a reality that some students' online interactions result in bullying and poor social, psychological and emotional outcomes. Indeed, a recent study by the Australian-based telephone counseling service for young people—Kids Helpline—found that young victims of cyber bullying are more likely to experience suicidal ideation than those who are victims of more 'traditional' forms of bullying. The study showed that 3% of respondents who had experienced cyber bullying had experienced suicidal ideation while 2% had engaged in some form of self-harming behaviour (Price & Dalgleish, 2010).

There are two reasons why cyber bullying may elicit much stronger emotional reactions than more 'traditional' forms of bullying:

1. When experiencing cyber bullying, it is likely that there will be a much wider audience—and thus a more devastating impact—through which the public humiliation and embarrassment occurs (Price & Dalgleish, 2010; Spears, et al., 2009). In traditional forms of bullying, humiliation may be limited to witnesses who are present in the workplace or schoolyard, while experiences of cyber bullying may go 'viral' via the Internet to witnesses throughout the world. As noted by Shariff (2005), an incidence of cyber bullying can have an infinite audience.
2. There is an increased level of invasiveness, as the cyber bullying can penetrate into the victim's home or bedroom (Price & Dalgleish, 2010) via the simple means of an Internet connection.

Given the pervasive impact of cyber bullying within the community, and the devastating effects that have been highlighted within the literature, it is useful to present two brief Australian case studies before examining the response of the Australian Government to this increasing problem (see Box 1).

These two brief yet confronting examples of cyber bulling represent only an infinitesimal proportion of the people who are cyber bullied each day. Given the relatively high rate of incidence of this type of anti-social behaviour, it is useful to consider the role that community education may play in fighting this problem. Wright et al. (2009) believe that "there is a need to raise awareness about the effects of cyber bullying and to create educational opportunities to serve multiple audiences (i.e. teachers, teacher educators, school administrators, school counsellors, mental health professionals, students, parents) in the quest to identify and hopefully prevent cyber bullying in the future" (p. 35). The Australian Government has taken this message on board, and it has implemented two community-based education programs as outlined below.

The Response of the Australian Government

The Australian Government has recently implemented a national cyber safety and cyber security community education program in an effort to stem the deleterious social effects of cyber bullying. The program titled *Cybersmart* is designed to *inform* citizens about cyber safety issues, *educate* audiences through information, resources and practical advice and ultimately *empower* children and young people to engage in online interactions that are safe. The *Cybersmart* program built on one initially launched in 1999 when AUS$189 million were allocated to the establishment of *NetAlert* which would provide the community with education and advice on Internet safety issues. The aim of the program at that time was to undertake outreach and research, and to provide the community with information on current trends and targeted awareness-raising campaigns.

The Australian Government has also been instrumental in the design and implementation of the *National Safe Schools Framework* (SLSST, 2003). The Framework provides a national approach to help schools and their communities address issues of bullying, harassment, violence, child abuse, and neglect. By extension, the Framework aims to have a positive impact in the wider community by providing educational opportunities that are free from bullying and which foster greater levels of social capital. The Framework addresses the need for sustained positive approaches that include an appreciation of the ways in which social attitudes and values impact on the behaviour of students in Australian school communities. The Framework encourages all members of the school and wider community to:

Box 1.

Australian Case Studies
In 2011, a 14-year-old Australian schoolgirl took her own life after suffering relentless online bullying. At the time of her death, the school girl was said to have in excess of 2000 Facebook friends (Devine, 2011). After becoming aware of their daughter's plight, her parents tried to assist efforts to escape the cyber bullies by relocating the family from one Australian state to another. Despite these efforts, the online bullying continued until the girl took her own life. Remarkably, the cyber bullying escalated after her passing and her memorial Facebook page was bombarded with hate messages and offensive images (Devine, 2011).
In 2012, another 14-year-old Australian schoolgirl also took her own life after suffering years of face-to-face and cyber bullying. Prior to her death, her family had become aware of the problems and had initiated steps to help their daughter (Carlyon, 2012). Following the girl's death, case study, the cyber bullying continued after her passing and abusive comments were posted on her tribute website.

- Value diversity;
- Contribute positively to the safety and wellbeing of themselves and others;
- Act independently, justly, cooperatively and responsibly in school, work, civic, and family relationships; and
- Contribute to the implementation of appropriate strategies that create and maintain safe and supportive learning environments.

FUTURE TRENDS

Both Australian government initiatives (the *Cyber Smart* program and the *National Safe Schools Framework*) have been tailored to the unique needs of the Australian environment. However, it is possible for other countries to learn from these community education programs in order to positively impact upon the levels of social capital found within a technologically-connected community. On this note, community intervention and education can occur across any of the four layers of individual, school, community, and legislation/regulation with the aim of addressing the issue of cyber bullying and strengthening the positive effects and related social capital that can be generated through the appropriate use of social networking sites.

First, communities can advocate for *individual-based strategies* such as blocking unknown or offensive 'friends' or avoiding upsetting messages (Campbell, 2005). Price and Dalgleish (2010) correctly note from other literature that the online environment provides victims with strategies that would not otherwise be available in a traditional bullying scenario, such as the ability to block their own screen name, to restrict their 'friend' lists or even to completely change their own avatar. Families can also install monitoring programs on their home-based computers which can help depersonalise or even block inappropriate Internet content (Hannah, 2010).

Second, *school-based strategies* can be implemented such as restricting and closely monitoring the use of all forms of technology (Cross, et al., 2009), embracing awareness-raising processes and ensuring the existence of transparent and enforceable school-wide policies (Campbell, 2005). The monitored use of a specially created online virtual world that enables a virtual identity to be created as a means of producing educational scenarios for school-aged children has also been recommended (Wright, et al., 2009). *Workplace strategies* are also relevant in this tier, and while research into workplace cyber bullying is in its infancy (Privitera & Campbell, 2009), there is much that can be done such as updating workplace codes of practice, implementing policies and procedures and ensuring that safe reporting mechanisms for cyber bullying victims are established and fully operational.

Third, *community strategies* can be devised and implemented such as support services and education. As noted by Merriam, Caffarella, and Baumgartner (2007), community-based learning programs have the common goal of being focused on social action and change for the betterment of society in general. Li (2006) highlights the importance of community education in the battle against cyber bullying by noting that "the education dealing with cyber bullying-related issues should be a joint endeavour of schools, families, communities, and the whole society" (p. 167). Beyond the type of community education provided by the Australian Government's *Cyber Smart* program, community-based programs might take the form of peer helper programs or buddy programs which could incorporate the direct teaching of values, empathy and the direct teaching of so-called 'netiquette' (Campbell, 2005). A number of countries around the world have undertaken work similar to the Australian government, and devised community education programs relating to cyber safety. A sample of these programs include the:

- *F@milie en ligne* (Family Online) initiative in France aimed at informing parents about the potential risks to which their children may be exposed while surfing of the Internet;
- *Make IT secure* campaign in Ireland to raise awareness of the urgent need for consumers and businesses to make their computer terminals secure from spam, identity theft, spyware and child safety risks;
- *Block Bullying Online* campaign devised by the European Commission for all member states, Iceland and Norway which aimed to empower teenagers by providing them with the information, skills and tools to deal with risks that emerge in the online environment; and the
- *Integrated National Cybersafety Programme* conducted in New Zealand which aimed to keep school students safe in an increasingly 'pervasive digital environment.'

Given the worldwide interest in designing such educational material, it is useful to provide some Australian-devised recommendations which may prove useful to other countries attempting to introduce community-based education in this area. When designing community education programs, Connolly et al. (2011) put forward a number of recommendations, which ensure that limited resources are used in an efficient and effective manner. These recommendations suggest that educational campaigns:

- Are based on a coherent education or awareness raising methodology;
- Include active, systematic and specific skill training;
- Integrate multiple program components;
- Contain interactive instructional techniques;
- Incorporate practical activities and tasks that users can undertake to enhance Cyber-Security;
- Include a 'reporting' function that allows consumers to report Cyber-Security risks and incidents; and
- Are a mix of comprehensive, long-term education and awareness raising complemented by short and specific initiatives (p. 22).

Fourth, there is opportunity for communities to consider the introduction—or strengthening—of *legislative and regulatory strategies*, including effective laws and the adequate funding for community programs. From the legislative viewpoint, the Australian Government has begun exploring the option of creating a nationally-enforceable law which specifically criminalises workplace bullying and cyber bullying (Wilkinson, 2011). If proven, bullies could face up to 10 years in jail, as cyber bullying would be added to the already existing *Crimes Act*. From a regulatory viewpoint, a review has recently been completed by the Australian Government's Law Reform Commission into the extent that existing privacy laws continue to provide an effective framework for the protection of privacy in Australia. The interplay between social networking and privacy was given particular attention, even though it was not initially an intended focus of the inquiry (ALRC, 2008). A key finding of the review was that many young people are not aware that the world of social networking can actually be quite dangerous. As a result, the review considered two main issues:

- The extent to which young people should be able to choose to disclose personal information about themselves in an online environment, and
- The ability of third parties to post, alter or remove personal information about other people in an online environment.

The future trends in this area should also be based on the potential for further research to be undertaken. Given that social relationships are prone to decay over time, and that they require effort and active maintenance to prevent this decay, it has been suggested that more research is needed to examine how effective different communication modalities (including online and offline) are at maintaining social relationships (Pollet, et al., 2011). It is also possible for existing and future community education programs to be subject to reflective evaluation whereby the aims, methods, and tangible outcomes are measured and reviewed to consider whether the strategies are indeed appropriate for the given community, and whether any improvements or alterations need to be made.

CONCLUSION

Social networking offers opportunities for creativity, knowledge creation, and insight, especially when networking is used ethically for intended purposes, which fulfill basic human needs of belonging, friendship, intimacy, respect, and self-actualisation. Although undesirable and deleterious to humanity, cyber bullying has led to the creation of opportunities to heighten awareness of the care needed with these communication processes not dissimilar to the care needed in face-to-face interactions. Progressive outcomes have included much needed additional education on social networking provided by governments and other agencies such as learning what is inappropriate content and contact, appreciating broader dimensions of respect, learning Internet/cell phone self-protective and coping behaviours and gaining know-how on being net safe and cyber savvy. Such increased community formal and informal learning opportunities themselves enhance the appeal and integrity of networking social capital and cyber learning.

This chapter has explored the link between social capital, the cyber bullying that can occur through social networking sites and community education. Through examining these links, it has become apparent that the Internet, and specific forms of social networking, are highly influential and rich sources of informal learning. However, accompanying this informal learning is the risk of anti-social behaviour, and the very real occurrence of cyber bullying. In Australia alone, cyber bullying affects anywhere between 7% and 57% of school children, with obvious flow-on effects at a personal level through to effects at a societal level which are demonstrated by reduced levels of trust and social capital. Aspects of cyber bullying can be addressed through targeted community education, and this chapter has identified four realms through which community intervention and education can occur: individual, school, community, and legislation/regulation. Many countries around the world are already designing and implementing community-based education programs addressing cyber safety and cyber bullying. Given the worldwide interest in these issues, this chapter has highlighted a number of elements considered essential for the efficient and effective use of limited community education resources. By achieving effective community education programs, we—as educators and professionals—are better placed to ensure that Internet-using individuals are educated and empowered to use social networking in a safe and genuine manner so that both online and offline social capital can be enhanced rather than eroded.

REFERENCES

ALRC. (2008). *For your information: Australian privacy law and practice (ALRC report 108).* Retrieved 10 May 2012 from http://www.alrc.gov.au/publications/report-108

Australian Institute of Criminology. (2010). Covert and cyber bullying. *Research in Practice*, *9*, 1.

Campbell, M. (2005). Cyber bullying: An old problem in a new guise? *Australian Journal of Guidance & Counselling*, *15*(1), 68–76. doi:10.1375/ajgc.15.1.68

Campbell, M. (2007). *Cyber bullying and young people: Treatment principles not simplistic advice*. Retrieved 23rd February 2007, from http://www.scientist-practitioner.com

Carlyon, P. (2012, 13 January). Tormented family and friends weep for taunted teen with secret sorrow. *Herald Sun*. Retrieved 10 May 2012 from http://www.heraldsun.com.au/news/more-news/last-words-of-a-best-friend/story-fn7x8me2-1226243026933

Cassidy, J. (2006). Me media: How hanging out on the Internet became big business. *The New Yorker*. Retrieved 10 May 2012 from http://www.newyorker.com/archive/2006/05/15/060515fa_fact_cassidy#ixzz1uQ0sneah

Coleman, J. S. (1988). Social capital in the creation of human capital. *American Journal of Sociology*, *94*(Supplement), S95–S120. doi:10.1086/228943

Commonwealth of Australia. (2012). *Cybersmart.* Accessed 8 May 2012 from http://www.cybersmart.gov.au

Connolly, C., Maurushat, A., Vaile, D., & van Dijk, P. (2011). *An overview of international cyber-security awareness raising and educational initiatives.* Retrieved 8 May 2012 from http://www.acma.gov.au/WEB/STANDARD/pc=PC_311301

Coombs, P. (1985). *The world crisis in education: A view from the eighties*. Oxford, UK: Oxford University Press.

Coopes, A. (2010, December 2). Cyber crime: Bigger than the drugs trade and growing. *Sydney Morning Herald*.

Cross, D., Shaw, T., Hearn, L., Epstein, M., Monks, H., Lester, L., & Thomas, L. (2009). *Australian covert bullying prevalence study*. Perth, Australia: Edith Cowan University.

Deery, S., & Crawford, C. (2012, January 12). Schoolgirl (name removed) takes own life after Facebook torment. *Herald Sun*. Retrieved 10 May 2012 from http://www.news.com.au/national/torment-too-much-for-teen/story-e6frfkvr-1226242267322#ixzz1uQA4j6ey

Devine, M. (2011, July 24). Parents must go online where evil lurks in many guises. *Sunday Herald Sun*. Retrieved 10 May 2012 from http://www.heraldsun.com.au/opinion/parents-must-go-online-where-evil-lurks-in-many-guises/story-e6frfhqf-1226100402166

Dooley, J., Pyżalski, J., & Cross, D. (2009). Cyberbullying versus face-to-face bullying: A theoretical and conceptual review. *The Journal of Psychology*, *217*(4), 182–188.

Ellison, N., Steinfield, C., & Lampe, C. (2007). The benefits of Facebook friends: Social capital and college students' use of online social network sites. *Journal of Computer-Mediated Communication*, *12*, 1143–1168. doi:10.1111/j.1083-6101.2007.00367.x

Facebook. (2011). *Facebook statistics*. Retrieved 12 November 2011 from http://www.facebook.com/press/info.php?statistics

Facebook. (2012a). *Statistics*. Accessed 10 May 2012 from http://newsroom.fb.com/Key-Facts/Statistics-8b.aspx

Facebook. (2012b). *Website*. Retrieved 23 March 2012 from http://newsroom.fb.com/content/default.aspx?NewsAreald=22

Gil-Or, O. (2010). Building consumer demand by using viral marketing tactics within an online social network. *Advances in Management*, *3*(7), 7–14.

Granovetter, M. (1983). The strength of weak ties: A network theory revisited. *Sociological Theory*, *1*, 201–233. doi:10.2307/202051

Hannah, M. (2010). Cyberbullying education for parents: A guide for clinicians. *Journal of the Social Sciences*, *6*(4), 530–534.

Helliwell, J. F., & Putnam, R. D. (2004). The social context of well-being. *Philosophical Transactions of the Royal Society*, *359*(1449), 1435–1446. doi:10.1098/rstb.2004.1522

Janda, S., & Fair, L. (2004). Exploring consumer concerns related to the internet. *Journal of Internet Commerce*, *3*(1), 1–21. doi:10.1300/J179v03n01_01

Jarvis, P. (1992). *Paradoxes of learning: on becoming an individual in society*. San Francisco: Jossey-Bass.

Jarvis, P. (2004). *Adult education and lifelong learning: Theory and practice*. London, UK: Routledge/Falmer.

Kalpidou, M., Costin, D., & Morris, J. (2011). The relationship between Facebook and the well-being of undergraduate college students. *CyberPsychology. Behavior & Social Networking*, *14*(4), 183–189. doi:10.1089/cyber.2010.0061

Katona, Z., Zubcsek, P., & Sarvary, M. (2011). Network effects and personal influences: The diffusion of an online social network. *JMR, Journal of Marketing Research*, *48*, 425–443. doi:10.1509/jmkr.48.3.425

Kim, J., & Lee, J.-E. (2011). The Facebook paths to happiness: Effects of the number of Facebook friends and self-presentation on subjective well-being. *CyberPsychology. Behavior & Social Networking*, *14*(6), 359–364. doi:10.1089/cyber.2010.0374

Kraut, R., Patterson, M., Lundmark, V., Kiesler, S., Mukophadhyay, T., & Scherlis, W. (1998). Internet paradox: A social technology that reduces social involvement and psychological well-being? *The American Psychologist*, *53*, 1017–1031. doi:10.1037/0003-066X.53.9.1017

Lee, G., Lee, J., & Kwon, S. (2011). Use of social-networking sites and subjective well-being: A study in South Korea. *CyberPsychology. Behavior & Social Networking*, *14*(3), 151–155. doi:10.1089/cyber.2009.0382

Li, Q. (2006). Cyberbullying in schools: A research of gender differences. *School Psychology International*, *27*, 157–170. doi:10.1177/0143034306064547

LinkedIn. (2012). *Website.* Retrieved 23 March 2012 from http://www.linkedin.com/company/linkedin

Madge, C., Meek, J., Wellens, J., & Hooley, T. (2009). Facebook, social integration and informal learning at university: It is more for socialising and talking to friends about work than for actually doing work. *Learning, Media and Technology*, *34*(2), 141–155. doi:10.1080/17439880902923606

Merriam, S., Caffarella, R., & Baumgartner, L. (2007). *Learning in adulthood: A comprehensive guide* (3rd ed.). San Francisco, CA: John Wiley & Sons.

Milne, G., Rohm, A., & Bahl, S. (2004). Consumers' protection of online privacy and identity. *The Journal of Consumer Affairs*, *38*(2), 217–232. doi:10.1111/j.1745-6606.2004.tb00865.x

Nonaka, I., Peltokorpi, V., & Tomae, H. (2005). Strategic knowledge creation: The case of Hamamatsu photonics. *International Journal of Technology Management*, *30*(3-4), 248–264. doi:10.1504/IJTM.2005.006709

Nonaka, I., Toyama, R., & Byoiere, P. (2001). A theory of organizational knowledge creation: Understanding the dynamic process of creating knowledge. In Dierkes, M., Antal, A., Child, J., & Nonaka, I. (Eds.), *Handbook of Organizational Learning and Knowledge* (pp. 491–517). Oxford, UK: Oxford University Press.

OECD. (2010). *Recognition of non-formal and informal learning: Pointers for policy development.* Retrieved 24 March 2012, from http://www.oecd.org/dataoecd/47/50/44870953.pdf

Park, N., Kee, K., & Valenzuela, S. (2009). Being immersed in social networking environment: Facebook groups, uses and gratifications and social outcomes. *CyberPsychology. Behavior & Social Networking*, *12*(6), 729–733.

Pasek, J., More, E., & Romer, D. (2009). Realizing the social internet? Online social networking meets offline civic engagement. *Journal of Information Technology & Politics*, *6*, 197–215. doi:10.1080/19331680902996403

Patchin, J. W., & Hinduja, S. (2010). Cyberbullying and self-esteem. *The Journal of School Health*, *80*(12), 614–621. doi:10.1111/j.1746-1561.2010.00548.x

Pollet, T. V., Roberts, S. B., & Dunbar, R. M. (2011). Use of social network sites and instant messaging does not lead to increased offline social network size, or to emotionally closer relationships with offline network members. *CyberPsychology. Behavior & Social Networking*, *14*(4), 253–258. doi:10.1089/cyber.2010.0161

Price, M., & Dalgleish, J. (2010). Cyberbullying experiences, impacts and coping strategies as described by Australian young people. *Youth Studies Australia*, *29*(2), 51–59.

Privitera, C., & Campbell, M. (2009). Cyberbullying: The new face of workplace bullying? *Cyberpsychology & Behavior*, *12*(4), 395–400. doi:10.1089/cpb.2009.0025

Raacke, J., & Bonds-Raacke, J. (2011). MySpace and Facebook: Applying the uses and gratifications theory to exploring friend-networking sites. *Cyberpsychology & Behavior*, *11*(2), 169–174. doi:10.1089/cpb.2007.0056

Sessa, V., & London, N. (2006). *Continuous learning in organisations: Individual, group and organisational perspectives*. Mahwah, NJ: Erlbaum.

Shariff, S. (2005). Cyber-dilemmas in the new millennium: School obligations to provide student safety in a virtual school environment. *McGill Journal of Education*, *40*, 467–487.

SLSST. (2003). *National safe schools framework*. Retrieved 11 May 2012 from www.dest.gov.au/sectors/school_education/publications_resources/profiles/national_safe_schools_framework.htm

Smith, P. K., Mahdavi, J., Carvalho, M., Fisher, S., Russell, S., & Tippett, N. (2008). Cyberbullying: Its nature and impact in secondary school pupils. *Journal of Child Psychology and Psychiatry, and Allied Disciplines*, *49*(4), 376–385. doi:10.1111/j.1469-7610.2007.01846.x

Spears, B., Slee, P., Owens, L., & Johnson, B. (2009). Behind the scenes and screens: Insights into the human dimension of covert and cyberbullying. *The Journal of Psychology*, *217*(4), 189–196.

Strathdee, R. (2001). Changes in social capital and school to work transitions. *Work, Employment and Society*, *15*(2), 311–326. doi:10.1177/09500170122118977

Taylor, L., McMinn, M., Bufford, R., & Chang, K. (2010). Psychologists' attitudes and ethical concerns regarding the use of social networking web sites. *Professional Psychology, Research and Practice*, *41*(2), 153–159. doi:10.1037/a0017996

Tynes, B. (2007). Internet safety gone wild? Sacrificing the educational and psychosocial benefits of online social environments. *Journal of Adolescent Research*, *22*, 575–584. doi:10.1177/0743558407303979

Ulusu, Y. (2010). Determinant factors of time spent on Facebook: Brand community engagement and usage types. *Journal of Yasar University*, *18*(5), 2949–2957.

Urwin, P., Di Pietro, G., Sturgis, P., & Jack, G. (2008). Measuring the returns to networking and the accumulation of social capital. *American Journal of Economics and Sociology*, *67*(5), 941–968. doi:10.1111/j.1536-7150.2008.00603.x

Wilkinson, G. (2011, April 5). Brodie's law means workplace and cyber bullies face 10 years in jail. *Herald Sun*. Retrieved 10 May 2012 from http://www.heraldsun.com.au/news/workplace-and-cyber-bullies-face-up-to-10-years-jail-under-anti-harassment-brodie-panlock-laws/story-e6frf7jo-1226033612374

Wright, V., Burnham, J., Inman, C., & Ogorchock, H. (2009). Cyberbullying: Using virtual scenarios to educate and raise awareness. *Journal of Computing In Teacher Education*, *26*(1), 35–42.

Yahoo. 7 News. (2011). *Cyber-bullied teen subject of online taunts after death*. Retrieved 10 May 2012 from http://au.news.yahoo.com/nsw/latest/a/-/newshome/9884636/cyber-bullied-teen-subject-of-online-taunts-after-death/

Young, K. (2011). Social ties, social networks and the Facebook experience. *International Journal of Emerging Technologies & Society*, *9*(1), 20–34.

Chapter 9
Technology Use and Its Changing Role in Community Education

Lesley Farmer
California State University – Long Beach, USA

ABSTRACT

Technology, particularly as it supports interactive learning communities, now plays a central role in community education. While technology affords access to information more efficiently than ever before, it also requires additional skills. For technology to play out its role effectively, community educators need to design instruction, curriculum, and programs that offer customizable learning and socially rich learning environments. Every effort needs to be made to make sure that learners have opportunities to access and learn with technology. Successful community efforts to incorporate technology tend to include these factors: local needs, local resources, local broad-based planning, partnerships among organizations, accessible and appropriate technologies, opportunities for community building and socializing, and locally meaningful content and outcomes.

INTRODUCTION

As the sense of community has expanded to encompass both physical and virtual mutual spaces and agreed-upon identities, the need for community education has also increased. Communities need to access, evaluate, and use increasing amounts of information for individual and group sustenance and improvement. Technology has served as a catalyst for such information transformation, and can also be used to educate communities. For example, government agencies increasingly include e-government initiatives that use information technology tools and systems to provide better public services that can transform relations with citizens and businesses. For technology to play its role in community, several factors need to be in place, which this chapter discusses: changes in instructional design, access issues, media literacy, technology tools, and social media.

DOI: 10.4018/978-1-4666-2955-4.ch009

COMMUNITY EDUCATION DEFINITIONS

Most simply, community education is education within the community, for the community, by the community. Community education is usually associated with community-based non-formal adult education, which forms the basis of this chapter's discussion. However, the scope of community education can vary from providing all the educational needs of the community to providing strictly informal adult education for self-development. Sometimes community education has a governmental or political agenda, be it citizenship education, "liberation" connotation, or a sense of social issues-based community development. In other circles, community education reflects moral, social, or personal development. Issues of health, environment, economics, and career development can also fall under the umbrella of community education.

The Scottish Community Education defined community education as "a process designed to enrich the lives of individuals and groups by engaging with people living within a geographical area, or sharing a common interest, to develop voluntarily a range of learning, action and reflection opportunities, determined by their personal, social, economic and political needs" (CeVe, 1990, p. 2). United States adult educators defined community education as: "the process of identification of community needs and the marshalling of resources to meet those needs so that the community and all its members can grow through social and educational programs" (Fellenz & Coker, 1979, p. 319).

In the United States, community education may relate to public education, as defined by Minzey:

Community Education is a philosophical concept, which serves the entire community by providing for all of the educational needs of all its community members. It uses the local school to serve as the catalyst for bringing community resources to bear on community problems in an effort to develop a positive sense of community, improve community living, and develop the community process toward the end of self-actualization (p. 150).

A leader in the field, Wisconsin Department of Public Instruction (2008) lists five components of community education, which serves as their philosophical foundation: citizen involvement, needs assessment and planning, extended use of public education facilities, interagency coordination and cooperation, and leadership and accountability. They also supported Decker's 1992 community education principles:

- **Self-determination:** An assessment should identify local needs and wants.
- **Self-help:** People should be encouraged to assume more responsibility for their own well-being.
- **Leadership development:** Community development should incorporate local citizen leadership.
- **Localization:** Education should be offered as close as possible to the intended community.
- **Integrated delivery of service:** Local organizations should collaborate, pooling their resources and meeting their own goals.
- **Maximum use of resources:** Local material and human resource should be integrated and maximized.
- **Inclusiveness:** Community education should involve all community constituents.
- **Responsiveness:** Public institutions should develop programs that are responsive to community needs.
- **Lifelong learning:** All ages of residents in various community settings should have access to learning.

IMPACT OF TECHNOLOGY ON LEARNING

Today's technology has substantially changed the face of learning. First, technology significantly expands and speeds up access to the world of information. Telecommunications has collapsed time and space. People potentially have more access, more quickly, to information around the world. Moreover, people can respond to each other and share group information much more easily than in the past. The convergence of communication industries such as telephony and television further expands the dissemination of information.

The nature of the information itself has been affected by digital technology. Besides the obvious combination of text, image, and sound, technology facilitates the repurposing and transformation of information to address different objectives or different audiences. More than ever, the user needs to interpret the format of information as well as its content, and their interdependence.

The interface between the information and the user comprises another element that has not been as crucial previously. That same interface also gives rise to interactive and dynamic information. For instance, hypertextuality enables the reader to go to linked information that might be further linked to other documentation; while footnotes and bibliographies serve this purpose hypothetically, they generally do not provide instant connections to the full texts/content. Furthermore, applications such as Google docs and wikis enable participants to literally change documents on the fly, thereby chipping away at the idea of a permanent recorded document (Iacono, 2010).

Thirdly, technology impacts the nature of instruction, highlighting the issue of standardization versus customization (Martinez, 2005). On one hand, technology enables instruction to be mass-produced and standardized. Course design and resources can be easily duplicated and disseminated. To a degree, grading can be done automatically once a quiz is set up. An online video conference can be scheduled for one time, with the understanding that learners anywhere in the world can meet simultaneously. On the other hand, with so many more resources available because of telecommunications and digitization, learners are more likely to find information that fits their particular needs, and educators can provide learners with more choices in what resource they use or how they can demonstrate knowledge. Technology-based instruction can be structured so that learners can self-pace their work. Instructors can develop automated needs assessment tools that direct the learner to the most appropriate resources and activities based on their responses. Likewise, instructors can store digital learning objects that can be accessed for a variety of applications across curricula, which can lead to a one-size-fits-all mentality or can support a learner's specific needs, depending on how those objects are used.

Fourthly, technology can change the relationship of teacher and learner—and the nature of learning processes themselves (Wang, Fong, & Kwan, 2010). Because more resources can be accessed independently, and learners can access and manipulate those resources at any time, learners have the opportunity to be more independent. Because access and communication can be asynchronous but still timely (as opposed to traditional correspondence courses), learners may be expected to accomplish more because they have a more flexible window of opportunity. Essentially, learners are not constrained by class time. Indeed, the wall between class time and daily life becomes more porous conversations can continue non-stop if one so wishes. Moreover, the interactivity of the Internet, particularly social media tools, enables learners to relate to one another more fully. Group projects become more feasible because students do not have to meet at one place at one time. On the other hand, when trying to assess learning progress, you have to take additional measures to decipher how each person is contributing to the end result. The instructor's status is likely to shift from sage on the stage to guide on the side, providing an educational environment in which learners can explore.

In short, the incorporation of digital technology fosters more independent, learner-centered learning. Maier and Warren (2000) listed several technology-enhanced instructional design strategies that support such a model:

- Flexible learning through ubiquitous access to resources, including the instructor.
- Resource-centered learning provided within a virtual environment, which enables learners to use tools to manipulate resources according to individual needs and interests.
- Self-paced learning, unhampered by class time or one-shot lectures.
- Collaborative learning using Web-based tools to compare learning and to generate knowledge together.
- Distance learning because course materials and structure can be accessed remote.

HISTORICAL TRENDS OF TECHNOLOGY IN COMMUNITY EDUCATION

When discussing instructional technology, educators and researchers tend to focus on the advances of the last hundred years, starting with mass media such as film, radio, and television. These non-print or audio-visual technologies extended information sensory experience to encompass sound and movement. They also enabled mass delivery of instruction such as civic education and emergency preparedness training, which could be disseminated to communities across the nation. However, the last three decades have witnessed the greatest impact on communication, largely because of three seminal developments: desktop computers (personal sized, easy-to-use hardware), productivity software (such as the spreadsheet program VisiCalc), and Ethernet for communication (including agreed upon transfer protocols.).

Technology also exists within the larger framework of society at large. In his book, *The Third Wave,* Toffler (1980) asserted that the U. S. was transitioning from an industrial society to a super- or post-industrial society. He noted the accelerated change of pace and people's sense of information overload. He thought that people saw themselves as consumers and producers, helping themselves to improve. The SCANS (Secretary's Commission on Achieving Necessary Skills) Report of the U. S. Department of Labor (1991) recommended five overarching competencies for the entire workforce: resource management, interpersonal skills, information use, systems understanding, and technology use. Specifically, workers should be able to select equipment and tools, apply technology appropriately to specific tasks, and maintain and troubleshoot equipment. By 2005, Friedman (2005) asserted that technology served as a catalyst for globalization, facilitating outsourcing and supply chaining to streamline operations. Online collaboration and sharing has become ubiquitous at all levels, from convergent corporations to individuals using personal digital devices such as cell phones and iPods.

Paradigms

Focusing on subsequent computer technologies, Koschmann (1996) identified four paradigm shifts in instructional technology, which apply to community education.

- Computer-Assisted Instruction (CAI) provided programmed instruction, and was touted for its efficacy. It was based on Skinnerian behaviorism, and its breakthrough occurred with the introduction of Coursewriter I in 1960. With its standardized interface, CAI was best suited for factual instruction such as civic education.

- Intelligent tutoring systems were introduced in 1970, and focused on interactive one-on-one tutorials. This advance focused on simulating human cognitive processes. This approach still assumed a standardized curriculum.
- Logo-as-Latin paradigm was heralded by Seymour Papert's 1980 book, *Mindstorms*. It emphasized cognitive constructivism through discover-based learning, exemplified in the simplified Logo programming software. This tool-based approach fostered deeper understanding technology structure, but did not lead itself well to adult community education.
- Computer-Supported Collaborative Learning (CSCL), introduced at a NATO workshop in 1989, emphasized collaborative learning, with instruction as an enacted practice. At that time, relevant technologies included email, threaded discussion, online chat, simulations. CSCL reflected more community-based information sharing.

Instructional Changes

In the last thirty years, technology-enhanced community education has shifted from a top-down to broad-based basis, from one-directional to two- and multi-directional communication, from static to dynamic content, from lecturer-dependent to content-dependent resources, and from administrative- to learning-oriented focus. With the advent of social media, the conditions for a true learning community involving educators, learners, and practitioners can emerge. The future will depend on each stakeholder's expertise and support.

As early as 1960, it was predicted that teachers and even the school system could be eliminated and replaced by educational technology developed alternative institutions. Such predictions have largely fallen by the wayside, but in 1979, the Association of Educational Communications and Technology did contend that educational technology affected the organizational structure of education at the curricular level such that an array of facilitated learning could exist in a variety of institutions. Instructional design, delivery, and assessment could change dramatically because of educational technology. In terms of community education, technology applications were more likely to occur in governmental initiatives that used mass media to educate their population.

In the 1980s, video entered community education. Videotapes were attractive for distance learning because presentations could be recorded, duplicated, and disseminated at relatively low cost. The size of an LP record (an even older technology), videodiscs could hold 30-60 minutes of full-motion video or other information, and supported random access. Other low-tech instructional tools included audiocassettes, overhead projectors, and lap-dissolve projection (i.e., two slide projectors). Instructors were expected to produce content that could be displayed with the appropriate equipment. Similarly, instructors developed content and used authoring languages to communicate with the student (Chambers, 1982). Community educators used technology unsystematically, largely because they usually had to learn the technology themselves; their practice largely reflected financial and administrative support.

In the 1990s, the term "learning organization" emerged, reflecting the need for organizations as a whole to develop skills and manage knowledge systematically. Instructional technology became more integrated in the 1990s, with desktop computers being able to connect peripherals such as CDs and link to the Internet. More flexibility in instructional delivery facilitated greater instructor-learner interaction, through digital forms of synchronous conferencing and asynchronous communication. Course management systems appeared, which provided for a coordinated approach to course content, communication, and management (Rossett, 2002). These systems were usually Web-based, which enabled users to communicate across computer platforms.

In the 21st century, the Internet constituted the main technology content vehicle for community education. As speed and bandwidth improved, the learning community could access information in a wide variety of formats online from around the world. Developing instructional content also became easier with "natural" programming language and templates, robust productivity applications, and lower-cost equipment such as digital cameras and camcorders. Uploading and sharing content was also facilitated by the Web's graphical interface. As a result, more applicable learning aids such as tutorials and interactive simulations were available, feeding the production and training cycle.

In general, instructional technology has become a more mature tool. Instructional design aligns outcomes with student needs, resources, learning activities, and assessment. Course and training delivery ranges from one-time workshops anywhere/anytime to permanent learning communities. Courses may incorporate technology in class or online, with hybrid delivery systems constituting the preferable stance. The underlying instructional question is: how does technology enhance community education? Community learners also make more choices as to their form and source of learning, often creating a collage of educational venues provided by a variety of content "vendors."

CONDITIONS FOR TECHNOLOGY INCORPORATION INTO COMMUNITY EDUCATION

For technology to play a significant role in community education, several conditions have to be met (Kamssu, Siekpe, & Ellzy, 2004):

- Available and affordable IT (Information Technology) equipment and telecommunications service.
- Convenient access to Internet-connected computers (or equivalent).
- Technology competence of education providers and learners.
- Basic literacy skills.
- Ideally, political and economic stability on several levels: nation, region, and community.
- Technology management policies and procedures.

At the organizational level, technology integration depends on several factors:

- Sufficient material and human resources to provide technology enhanced education.
- Organizational technology readiness.
- Top management support.
- Organizational culture that supports technology.

Learning about Technology and Learning with Technology

In the digital age, communities need to gain technological competency; the vast majority of jobs involve technology, and information largely exists and is transmitted in digital form. Even face-to-face community education involves technology at some point, most probably in accessing information. Therefore, Information and Communication Technology (ICT) literacy is a prerequisite skill for access to, and participation in, much of community education. In those cases, where people are not ICT literate, then community education should focus on teaching such ICT skills.

Learning *about* technology differs from learning *with* technology. Particularly if the concepts to be learned involve the use of technology, that added skill needs to be addressed explicitly. For instance, if learners do not know how to create a wiki, then they will need to be opportunity—and the time—to learn and practice that skill so they can participate in collective intelligence work. Educators need to figure out how that learning will occur. Do participants have access to the hardware and software? Do they have the time to access and learn the application beyond the workday or in addition to daily life demands? Does instructional design need to include resources and explicit activities to address that technical learning?

It should be noted that even before community members engage in technology learning experiences, they must be able to physically access the relevant technology. For that reason, community educators should survey learner access to technologies (hardware, software, connectivity), and frontload the conditions for learning. Additionally, ways need to be found to ensure equitable access to these technologies; for instance, educators should be sensitive to populations who may special needs such as English language learners and the physically challenged.

- **Physical access:** The educator should find out what public technology access is available: such as libraries, recreation centers, Internet cafes, universities. Instructional resources should be accessed by low-performance equipment and dial-up connectivity. Text needs to be saved in formats that can be read by open source software; .rtf files are usually an acceptable format. Unfortunately, while image-rich and multimedia documents take advantage of multiple learning styles, they also require broader bandwidth and may need plug-ins in order to play correctly. Furthermore, instructional materials should be accessible for individuals with disabilities.
- **Intellectual access:** Educators may need to provide directions on the use of technology tools such as spreadsheets or authoring programs. In some cases, even simple operations such as attaching files need to be explained. Educators can help learners be self-sufficient learners by showing them how to get technical assistance through help screens, manuals, Web FAQs, and online tutorials. While some learners are motivated to use technology, and will make the extra effort to process information, others have a negative attitude toward technology that will impede information processing.
- **Building community:** One of the main drawbacks of e-learning (i.e., electronic-based learning) can be the feeling of isolation. With the advent of social media, learners can interact with their online peers to build a community of learners. Educators need to set up the conditions for interactive learning by designing opportunities for group discussion and collaborative learning activities. Threaded discussion forums, wikis, blogs, and online conferencing are a few of the tools available. These community-based structures have to be supported through the online training of these tools.

Even with these general provisions, learning might not succeed because community members have differing pre-existing attitudes and experiences with technology, particularly if they are adult learners. Some people lack technology competence, or do not want to learn these skills. Some fear technology, thinking it might supplant valuable social or labor-intensive job skills. For some adults technology itself poses a barrier to learning; if they cannot accept the online environment, learners will not be able to have physical and intellectual access to the information itself. Yocco et al. (2011) noted several factors that led to the public's use of technology in environmental education:

- **Personal variables:** Age, learning style, prior technology use.

- **Perception of technology variables:** Perceived usefulness, perceived ease of use, its attractiveness.
- **Public behavior:** Intent to use, initial use, attrition or continued use.

At the very least, educators need to provide learners with a variety of instructional materials and learning activities to choose from. Relating to technology is affected by emotional states, so educators need to make sure that learners can feel safe in taking intellectual risks in trying technology, and are rewarded for their efforts as well as their final products (Rogers, 1962). To that end, learners should have opportunities to:

- Operate computer and other technological systems (i.e., open and close an application, save a document, print, use a mouse, use a menu and navigation bar, etc.).
- Use productivity tools.
- Navigate the Internet (i.e., use browsers and search engines, use email, etc.).
- Evaluate information critically.
- Communicate digitally.

Media Literacy

The 21st century has marked the democratization of information. Particularly with the advent of social media and low-cost Internet-connected equipment such as mobile devices, a substantial percentage of the population can not only access digital information, but can also comment on, and create, information. Generally, these new social media permit text, video, and voice input, and occur in real-time or asynchronously. Digitization speeds access and facilitates manipulation, so that both the creator can get the message out—and the receiver can turn around and repurpose, reform, and add value to the communication.

On the other hand, such ease of content generation leads to a loss of quality control; information is more readily available but might not be accurate, legitimate, or objective. The learner has to employ critical thinking, and draw upon past knowledge and experience to determine the validity, relevance, and significance of information accessed. While more information is readily available, it can take hours to ferret out and prioritize the appropriate information.

Thus, technology expertise alone does not suffice. People need to be critical users of technology, particularly as they evaluate information that they encounter. Media literacy, for example, addresses the role and impact of mass media. The Center for Media Literacy (2012) developed core concepts relative to media messages:

- All media messages are constructed.
- Media messages are constructed using a creative language with its own rules.
- Different people experience the same message differently.
- Media have embedded values and points of view.
- Media messages are constructed to gain profit and/or power.

The critical features are the purposeful means and end of the production. Even though people may comprehend the messages that mass media send, they may be unaware of the underlying agendas. People respond to the *language* that mass media use: arresting images, fast-paced scenes, clever word play. They may get so caught up in the delivery of the message that they may miss the message itself *on a conscious level,* but may fall prey to that underlying objective, be it to buy a product or support a cause. To that end, community education can teach people to examine media messages critically by considering the process by which the message is made, the message's framework and content, and the production value of the message. On a political conscious-awareness level, the Alliance of Civilizations (Douglass, 2006) contended, "Teaching viewers and listeners to recognize rhetorical and psychological techniques employed to persuade, to demonize and to incite violence or intolerance provides significant defense against violent ideologies of many types" (p. 15).

INSTRUCTIONAL DESIGNER INCORPORATION OF TECHNOLOGY

How does technology-enhanced community education reflect the community? Technology can lead to standardized, one-size-fits-all instruction that ignore local interests and resources. Fear rightly exists that technology-based community education can homogenize cultures and downplay local cultural heritages. As noted before, instructional strategies should involve both cognitive and social aspects of the local community, reflecting effective learning principles.

Instructional Design Technology Decisions

Throughout the community education instructional design process, educators need to determine which technologies will be used—and to what extent—in light of ICT competency and community interests. At the minimum, instructors need to determine whether technology will be used as a tool to deliver instruction, as a learning aid, or as the outcome itself. Even the instructional focus, whether to emphasize an information literacy task or tool, requires careful consideration. Technology-based choices apply at each step in designing instruction, as shown here.

- **Assess needs:** Online survey, video capture of behavior, analysis of website "hits."
- **Identify learners:** Online solicitations, RSS feed subscriptions, organizational lists.
- **Identify outcomes:** Technology standards, online content standards, online education syllabi.
- **Identify indicators:** Technology rubrics, technology products, electronic Delphi method (i.e., getting experts to come to consensus on key points).
- **Identify prerequisite skills:** Web-based assessment, performance observation, content analysis of sample work.
- **Identify content:** Online training documents, electronic journal articles, virtual chat.
- **Identify the instructional format:**
    - Resources (Internet, DVDs, e-books)
    - Instructor (technician, instruction designer, remote-site expert)
    - Methods (Web tutorial, hands-on manipulation, video presentation)
    - Timeframe (self-paced, real-time, just-in-time)
    - Location (computer lab, classroom, home)
    - Grouping (individual, online group, work unit)
    - Individualization (programmed instruction, choice of technology, coaching)
    - Affective domain (wiki, threaded discussion, virtual chat)
- **Contextualize instruction:** Web page within a community website, community services database, digital images of applications.
- **Implement the plan:** Project planning software program, Web page development, video conferencing.
- **Assess the plan:** Learning management system statistics, videotape, online survey.

Representative Technology Tools

Each type of technology tool lends itself to specific learning approaches. Whenever possible, the unique properties of each tool should be exploited to optimize these experiences. Each of the following approaches fosters deep engagement with curriculum because the format lends itself well to packaging and communicating content. Each approach also fosters interactivity between learner and content, and facilitates collaboration. Learners can work with each other both in real time and asynchronously, anytime and anywhere. Here are several interactive tools that work well for community education.

- **Threaded discussions:** Archive individual contributions and responses chronologically by subject.
- **Social bookmarking (public lists of recommended websites):** Helps build sources of peer-reviewed information.
- **Blogs (Web logs):** Enable individuals to write about their experiences chronologically, and others can comment on the entries.
- **Group writing:** Google Docs (http://docs.google.com), allows learners to share and edit documents using a suite of productivity tools.
- **Audio files:** Archive lectures and shorter tutorials, and learners can listen to the audio files at their convenience for as many times as they wish.
- **Video:** Captures movement and processes, and records events as they happen. Communities can document local history, and demonstrate important procedures, such as emergency measures.
- **Multimedia:** Programs such as Voicethread enable users to develop and share online group albums.
- **Image sharing:** Programs such as Flickr enable users to upload and share photos and other images; these items can be combined into albums that reflect content matter learned.
- **Online chats:** Enable individuals to discuss issues in real time. Some chat programs include features that allow documents and Web pages to be viewed in common.
- **Web-based conferencing:** Incorporate text, image, and sound to more closely approximate physical interaction.
- **Virtual environments (object-oriented online environments):** Enable individuals to interact virtually using avatars. Virtual environments usually have ways for applications to be embedded and documents to be stored.

Social Media

Probably the most influential change in teaching with technology within community education increasing acceptance of social media. Sometimes Web 2.0 is the term given to express the idea of interactivity that now marks Web-based collaborative tools such as wikis and blogs. Rather than one-way communication, Web 2.0 applications enable learners to participate in two-way (or multi-way) active communication to share and create information. In studying information management systems, JISC and SCONUL (2008) noted the impact of Web 2.0 in concentrating the aggregation of information; and diffusing the dissemination and reuse of content. The comparatively easy access of the Internet further broadens the base of participation. Another key feature of social media and networking is collective intelligence, so that it can resemble mass media channels by creating knowledge at the same time that it represents interpersonal channels that influence attitudes of peers. Especially in today's digital world, community education should consider incorporating interactivity and social networking features, such as push technology RRS feeds, comment/messaging options, incorporation of learning community repositories, enterprise mash-ups, and user-customizable subject tags.

Wikis exemplify participatory social media practice. Wikis (based on the Hawaiian term "wiki wiki," which means "fast") are Web pages that can be generated without markup language knowledge. Wikis are probably best known because of Wikipedia, a user-built Web-based encyclopedia. The underlying concept of Wikipedia is that experts around the world can contribute to the body of knowledge; the ability of individuals editing each other's works result in higher quality information. While some people may dispute Wikipedia's veracity, the concept of collaboratively edited content holds valid potential. Furthermore, most wikis have a feature that allows participants to see the page's history, so that contributions can be tracked accurately. These two features, collaborative editing and tracking, make wikis a useful learning and assessment tool for community education. The website http://www.wikimatrix.org lets users compare almost a hundred different wiki applications.

Wikis can be used to address academic and professional skills, knowledge, and dispositions: knowledge synthesis and generation, written and media communication skills, collaboration, technical skills, and organizational skills. Some of the activities that can be done using wikis follow.

- **Knowledge management:** Learner research can be organized under one wiki by incorporating frames and tags.
- **Group projects:** Each learner is responsible for one aspect of a project (e.g., a community portal containing different types of information such as education page, local agencies, health groups, upcoming programs, homework help, etc.).
- **Point of view study:** A topic such as free trade agreements can be investigated from different points of view, each student assuming the role of a different stakeholder.
- **Planning (learning activities, units, grants):** Web 2.0 tools can facilitate online development of course units and grant applications.
- **Lists/bibliographies:** Each student can suggest strategies for accommodating children with special needs; a growing list of course-related resources can be developed on a wiki.
- **Literature circles:** Each student can lead a discussion on some aspect of a book (e.g., plot, theme, character, setting).
- **Text commentary:** Students can put in comments about a text or image.
- **Case studies:** students can share their perspectives on a case study, or develop one collaboratively.

Several innovative technology-based tools have been considered for community education, particularly games, be they console or computer-based. This medium actively engages learners, provides both textual and visual cues, often requires collaboration in order to accomplish a task, often demands clear communication, facilitates problem-solving skills, provides immediate feedback, and fosters attention to detail (Gros, 2003). On the other hand, games have not yet been broadly accepted in community education because few games focus on community education content, and easy yet robust gaming authoring tools have not appeared in the educational marketplace. Nor are some educators comfortable with the underlying concept of gaming for community education purposes. Furthermore, many adults see gaming as a recreational escape rather than a useful educational pastime.

A feasible theoretical model to employ when examining the educational potential of games is Activity Theory (Engeström, 1987). It focuses on subject (i.e., learners) manipulation (that is, a learning task) of objects (e.g., concepts, artifacts) to achieve a desired outcome (i.e., meet a standard). This process is impacted by the rules, the tools used (e.g., resources), and community (including division of labor). As community educators select games for community curriculum, they need to look at the underlying concepts being addressed, the educational value of the tools, and the pedagogical "fit" of the sequence of tasks.

CURRENT PRACTICES IN TECHNOLOGY'S ROLE IN COMMUNITY EDUCATION

Communities around the world are incorporating technology into non-formal education. Successful efforts tend to include these factors: local needs, local resources, local broad-based planning, partnerships among organizations, accessible and appropriate technologies, opportunities for community building and socializing, and locally meaningful content and outcomes. As such, each example below (presently in chronological order) demonstrates unique characteristics that fit the community.

The first Pan-Canadian Forum on Community Learning Networks, held in 1998, was cosponsored by the Office of Learning Technologies and Contract North. Even then, the forum asserted that "technologies are tools helping to facilitate the creation of a lifelong learning culture—one that will support the emergence of a knowledge-based economy" (p. 1). They continued:

By its very nature, technologies have the potential to bring the world into one's home, workplace, or community learning centre with incredible speed. Today's challenge is to manage this potential effectively, and ensure that all individuals or groups of Canadians have access to these new learning opportunities using technologies (p. 1).

Several technology-based initiatives were featured at this forum. Connect NB Branche networked community access program sites across New Brunswick to provide distance training programs. Ontario's Learning Environment Foundation served as a community ISP (Internet Service Provider), and partnered with Microsoft and Bell telecommunications to train economically disadvantaged residents. Community-based radio and television provided new access to learning opportunities; In Port au Port community members help plan the programs and fostered peer facilitators. Technology leveled the skills acquisition playing field for rural women's economic development. Regularly scheduled online forums helped create a sense of community among remote Quebec residents, and helped facilitate the production of digital training tools for the region. As one result of the forum, the group developed a community education toolkit, which included guidelines for technology incorporation.

To build knowledge about early childhood education, stakeholders across Canada used a variety of technologies as a learning community. Threaded discussion were low-end technologies that enabled all participants to focus on content. Higher end technology such Webcasting was somewhat distracting for face-to-face participants, but remote participants welcomed the opportunity to engage in real time, and tolerated occasional technical difficulties. All participants became more comfortable with the technologies, and appreciated the benefits thereof. As a result of the collaboration, a strong knowledge base was developed through community building, and insights about technology experiences helped design future educational events (Zijdemans, 2005).

According to Cook and Light (2006), the United Kingdom has embraced ICT as a means to facilitate a participatory and inclusive society, while acknowledging that ICT competency has to precede e-learning. Citizens also have to understand technology's societal potential. The Adults Learning@Home project gained confidence in using ICT, using a non-threatening and convenient way to learn informally. Cook and Light also mentioned the international Digital Living Network Alliance, which posed the idea of a transparent home network based on the home entertainment center that would form the basis for informal education. However, this approach is inadequate because its focus is consumeristic but does not support citizen rights and responsibilities.

Pennsylvania State University began as a state land-grant school, with a commitment to community-based education. Now its outreach initiative focuses on knowledge-based innovative economy as it seeks to facilitate regional economic development. This new economy's technology driver is digitization as opposed to older mechanization, which impacts instructional design in that a factory-style standardized education has to be replaced by customized interactive learning experiences. Penn State has multiple campuses and an online world campus, which adult learners can navigate seamlessly in blended and online environments. Moreover, Penn State's online one-stop service center supports diverse learners' needs (Smutz & Weidemann, 2008).

Realizing the importance of a shared database of information, the American Red Cross developed the Community Disaster Information System (CDIS) in partnership with non-governmental organizations and community-based suppliers and agencies. This database includes information on national and local material, human, and informational resources, which is accessible by computer or even mobile device. Not only does the database provide current information anytime anyway, but it also increases civic collaboration and strengthen volunteer training (Troy, et al., 2008).

The European FACE IT! Project used a family learning approach to teach active citizenship. The training materials were developed by project partners in six countries and mounted as an online handbook. The workshops were delivered in a blended fashion, face-to-face and online, to socially isolated and disadvantaged families. The content matter empowered families to get more involved in their local community and contribute to it (Flanagan, 2009).

Technology is nigh ubiquitous in community environmental education (Yocco, et al., 2011). Visitors to zoos, science centers, and natural history museums routinely use RFID radio and cell phone tours, videos, and touch screen computer kiosks to learn about exhibits, increasingly in interactive ways. The incorporation of technology offers several benefits: low-cost means to update information, just-in-time information such as weather predictions, means to share information across institutions. As these institutions can increasingly rely on the public to bring mobile devices, curators can focus on content without worrying about circulating equipment for media tours; GSP (Global Positioning Systems) and RQ codes have been particularly popular ways to relay information for the convenience of the public. It should be noted that technology does need to be maintained, especially for video kiosks, because of heavy use. At the Florida Museum of Natural History, the public can: text or phone in questions about displays, download mobile apps about exhibits, and record observations of targeted animals (which provides data points for the museum's scientists). When visitors were asked about the advantages of installing technology components into exhibits, they responded that they liked having more opportunities to learn, they thought that children were attracted to technology, and they thought that technology aligned with their learning preferences.

FUTURE TRENDS IN TECHNOLOGY'S FUTURE ROLE IN COMMUNITY EDUCATION

Information Cross-Fertilization

Globalization has led to more cross-fertilization of technology integration practice. With the rapid pace of technology advancement and consequential change, communities need to constantly learn in order to maintain their societal "edge." With today's instant telecommunications, organizations and other entities have risen in number, and can significantly impact technology integration advances. Web-based communities of practice can exist anywhere, crossing national borders almost seamlessly.

A variety of communication methods facilitate collaborative community development and integration. Digitized documents can be quickly created, stored, accessed, and retrieved in remote servers. People can email, instant message, and phone one another at any time via the Internet. For group synchronous interaction, members can use chat rooms, Webcasting, and video conferencing. Web 2.0 applications enable individuals to engage in collective intelligence. The comparatively easy access of the Internet further broadens the base of participation as well as facilitates global dissemination of information. In short, a number of technology-based tools enable communities to experience learning communities and apply the latest research, even if each person is the sole expert at his or her site.

Community educators should comprise part of those organizations to optimize improved technology integration. They can design the conditions for learning by helping those organizations conduct needs assessments, define appropriate learning goals, locate or develop relevant learning resources, design activities that optimize learning and technology application, and assess efforts. Especially with the advent of social media, instructional design then would provide a coordinated framework consisting of a participatory network; members can access information and each other, as well as share their expertise and generate new ways to incorporate technology. Emphasizing the affective domain, social media tools permit social tagging for customizable access to these resources and learning activities.

Personalization

The next iteration of community education through technology is personalized learning plans. Increasingly, learning has the potential to become more customized. Already, software applications enable learners to create personal learning spaces. Google Reader represents a simple model: users identify online social networks, be they dynamic websites or blogs, that have RSS feeds. These "push" technologies push information to the end user; the consumer simply subscribes to the service. The learner then links those services on his or her Reader Web page, which is refreshed every time a digital message/feed is sent to it. Instead of getting email announcements throughout the day, the learner can go to the Reader at his convenience, picking which sources to view; the learner controls which information to access.

CONCLUSION

Technology, particularly as it supports interactive learning communities, now plays a central role in community education. While technology affords access to information more efficiently than ever before, it also requires additional skills. Successful community efforts to incorporate technology tend to include these factors: local needs, local resources, local broad-based planning, partnerships among organizations, accessible and appropriate technologies, opportunities for community building and socializing, and locally meaningful content and outcomes. As such, technology-enhanced community education demonstrates unique characteristics that fit the community.

For technology to play out its role effectively, community educators need to design instruction, curriculum, and programs that offer customizable learning and socially rich learning environments. Technology should be incorporated in meaningful and effective ways that match learning objectives and learner needs. Every effort needs to be made to make sure that learners have opportunities to access and learn with technology, and that they can choose the type of learning that best meets their needs. To that end, organizations should insure that a robust and equitable technology infrastructure is in place, and that training be appropriated supported as a right of every citizen.

Some of the current trends to foster technology integration while paying attention to the affective domain include:

- Enriching the repertoire of instructional strategies, including interactive online tutorials, personal response systems, gaming, and community-based problem-based learning.
- Developing communities of practice and peer-to-peer learning.
- Creating databases to facilitate community-supported learning.

REFERENCES

Center for Media Literacy. (2012). *Media literacy*. Malibu, CA: Center for Media Literacy.

Chambers, G. (1982). A model for the development of technical instructors. *Master Abstracts International*, *20*(4), 342.

Decker, L. (1992). *Community education: Building learning communities* (Rev. ed.). Alexandria, VA: National Community Education Association.

Douglass, S. (2006). *Research base for the high level group report: Education*. New York, NY: Alliance of Civilizations.

Engeström, Y. (1987). *Learning by expanding: An activity-theoretical approach to developmental research*. Helsinki, Finland: Orienta-Konsultit Oy.

Fellenz, R., & Coker, L. (1979). Toward a definition of adult education, community education and community development. In Cunningham, P. (Ed.), *Yearbook of adult and continuing education* (pp. 366–369). Chicago, IL: Marquis Academic Media.

Flanagan, M. (2009). Connecting family learning and active citizenship. *Adult Learner,* 92-98.

Friedman, T. (2005). *The world is flat*. New York, NY: Farrar, Straus and Giroux.

Gros, B. (2003). The impact of digital games in education. *First Monday*, *8*(7). Retrieved from http://firstmonday.org/issues/issue8_7/gros/index.htm

Iacono, A. (2010). OPAC, users, web: Future developments for online library catalogues. *Bollettino AIB*, *5*(1-2), 69–88.

JISC & SCONUL. (2008). *Library management systems study*. Sheffield, UK: Sero Consulting.

Kamssu, A., Siekpe, J., & Ellzy, J. (2004). Shortcomings to globalization: Using internet technology and electronic commerce in developing countries. *Journal of Developing Areas*, *38*(1), 151–169. doi:10.1353/jda.2005.0010

Koschmann, T. (1996). Paradigm shifts and instructional technology. In *CSCL: Theory and practice of an emerging paradigm* (pp. 1–23). Mahwah, NJ: Lawrence Erlbaum Associates.

Maier, P., & Warren, A. (2000). *Integrating technology in learning and teaching*. Sterling, VA: Kogan Page.

Martinez, M. (2005). Mass customization: Designing for successful learning. *International Journal of Educational Technology*, *2*(2). Retrieved from http://www.ed.uiuc.edu/ijet/v2n2/martinez/index.html

Minzey, J. (1972). Community education: An amalgam of many views. *Phi Delta Kappan*, *54*(3), 150–153.

Pan-Canadian Forum on Community Learning Networks. (1998). Background. In *Proceedings of the Pan-Canadian Forum on Community Learning Networks Conference,* (pp. 1-2). Ottawa, Canada: Pan-Canadian Forum on Community Learning Networks.

Rogers, E. (1962). *Diffusion of innovation*. New York, NY: Free Press.

Rossett, A. (Ed.). (2002). *ASTD e-learning handbook*. New York, NY: McGraw-Hill.

Scottish Community Education Council. (1990). *CeVe Scotland: Preservice training for community education work*. Edinburgh, UK: Scottish Community Education Council.

Senior, R. (2010). Connectivity: A framework for understanding effective language teaching in face-to-face and online learning communities. *RELC Journal: A Journal of Language Teaching and Research, 41*(2), 137-147.

Smutz, W., & Weidemann, C. (2008). Economic development in challenging times. *Continuing Higher Education Review*, *72*, 44–56.

Toffler, A. (1980). *The third wave*. New York, NY: Bantam Books.

Troy, D., Carson, A., Vanderbeek, J., & Hutton, A. (2008). Enhancing community-based disaster preparedness with information technology. *Disasters*, *32*(1), 149–165. doi:10.1111/j.1467-7717.2007.01032.x

U. S. Department of Labor. (1991). *Secretary's commission on achieving necessary skills*. Washington, DC: Government Printing Office.

Wang, F., Fong, J., & Kwan, R. R. (2010). *Handbook of research on hybrid learning models: Advanced tools, technologies, and applications*. Hershey, PA: IGI Global.

Wisconsin Department of Public Instruction. (2008). *Wisconsin's components of communication education*. Madison, WI: Wisconsin Department of Public Instruction.

Yocco, V., Danter, E., Heimlich, J., Dunckel, B., & Myers, C. (2011). Exploring use of new media in environmental education contexts: Introducing visitors' technology use in zoos model. *Environmental Education Research*, *17*(6), 801–814. doi:10.1080/13504622.2011.620700

Zijdemans, A. S. (2005). *Exploring a socio-technological design for knowledge development: The millennium dialogue on early child development.* (PhD Dissertation). University of Toronto. Toronto, Canada. Retrieved from http://search.proquest.com/docview/305360069?accountid=10351

Chapter 10
Developing an Autonomous Language Learning Framework in a Blended Learning Environment:
A Hong Kong Case Study

Helen W. M. Yeh
Hong Kong Polytechnic University (HKCC), China

ABSTRACT

Educational technologies in language learning has undergone a shift from learner's interaction with computers to interaction with other humans via the computer, and now moves towards the blended learning where traditional classroom teaching methods and computer-mediated activities are combined. However, the effectiveness of the blended learning is still inconclusive. The present chapter examines the effectiveness of autonomous language learning programmes in a blended learning environment and presents a framework that was derived from the programme. The framework describes the roles of teacher, the learning construction, and the learning process for autonomous language learning, and suggests a number of techniques that teachers can use to formulate their teaching plans for the blended learning. Findings revealed that students had favorable attitudes towards the autonomous language learning, the blended learning, and the programme, which could not only motivate them to continue autonomous learning but also improve their English competence.

INTRODUCTION

Over the past ten years, the rapid advancement of technology and the impact of globalization made Hong Kong change by leaps and bounds in every aspect of economy, education and information technology. Although Information Communication Technology (ICT) is not frequently used in teaching and learning in the classrooms, it is in fact frequently used in some specific activities and tasks in schools and institutions (Enrique Hinostroza, et al., 2011). "There is now a growing body of evidence detailing the very real impact

DOI: 10.4018/978-1-4666-2955-4.ch010

of technology on both formal and informal learning" (Underwood, 2009, p. 8), particularly about changes in behavior at learner, teacher, and school level and at academic performance. Traditional teaching methodologies and courses designed in response to the requirements of the market some years ago may turn out to be inappropriate or irrelevant upon graduation of the students. Therefore, it is necessary for institutions to review the courses according to the market needs and adopt innovative teaching and learning strategies, which are developed to support the aims to produce all round graduates with good language skills, sound disciplinary knowledge and broad generic skills for employment and life-long learning.

As Thomson (1996) describes, language learning is a life-long endeavor and Computer-Mediated Communication (CMC) seems to be the suitable tool because it frees students from the constraints of learning time and place, and students can learn at their own pace. Previous research also suggests that CMC can facilitate communication, increase oral discussion, develop the writing/thinking connection, improve writing skills, enhance student motivation and/or reduce anxiety (Cooper & Selfe, 1990; Huot, Lemonnier, & Hamers, 2008; Kern, 1995; Sullivan, 1993; Warschauer, 2003; Warschauer, Turbee, & Robers, 1996). In addition, CMC allows students/ teachers to organize grammatical, semantic and discourse into valid language learning activity. Therefore, teachers should expand their thinking about the use of computers to consider new opportunities and contexts for innovative teaching and learning, and need to look continually at the patterns of interaction that emerge. They should build bridges between the tool, the school task, the thinking skills, and the culture of institution (Schon, 1983).

However, we face two problems. Firstly, many Hong Kong Chinese students have been characterized as passive, dependent, and lacking in initiative for a long time (Pierson, 1996). A longitudinal study conducted with tertiary students in Hong Kong has indicated that students have little incentive to undertake learning outside their studies, and tend to limit their work to what is taught on the course. This kind of attitude is not beneficial to second language learning as success so much depends on the individual pursuit of opportunities for language use outside the classroom (Lee, 1998). Therefore, it is important to help students become aware of the value of autonomous language learning so that they acquire the habit of learning continuously, and maintain it after they have completed their formal studies. Classroom teachers in frequent contact with students are in an advantageous position to encourage them to do so because it is easier to establish rapport, and thus foster teacher and peer support (Lee, 1998). Secondly, many Hong Kong teachers still 'perceive their role mainly as providers of knowledge, rather than as facilitators guiding students to identify their own knowledge needs and to search for and evaluate information for themselves' (Education and Manpower Bureau, 2004a, p. ii). This is, in my opinion, mainly because they do not have the necessary knowledge and skills especially and there are few researches describing specific approaches to or frameworks of autonomous language teaching and learning with technology. Much of the L2 research has focused on the analysis of interactions generated within such ICT environments as email, chat, MOOs, or electronic bulletin boards (Parks, Huot, Lemonier, & Hamers, 2005). To solve this problem, there is a growing need for a pedagogical framework, which presents a description of the factors that were found to influence the success and to support the use of the new technologies in autonomous language teaching and learning.

The primary objective of this chapter is, therefore, to establish a framework that teachers can use for autonomous language learning in a blended learning environment. After reviewing the existing approaches, a new framework, Reflective Communication Approach (RCA), was developed to suit the needs of Hong Kong students. At the same time, a research program based on Reflective Communication Approach was designed to explore students' attitudes towards autonomous language learning in a blended learning environment. It is important and helpful to justify that the framework is effective. The findings reported in this chapter could also be used to help make decisions on the feasibility and effectiveness of the blended learning for autonomous language learning. The data collected can inform educators of future decisions about curricula changes, investment of institutional funds, and professional development. The framework is also valuable to ESL teachers because it suggests a series of Web-based and in-class activities for independent language students.

LITERATURE REVIEW

Theories of Autonomous Language Learning

According to Holec (1981), 'autonomy' is defined as the ability to take charge of one's own learning. This learning may be done with or without the help of a teacher, with or without the use of teaching aids. When we examine the importance of autonomy in relation to the theories of Second Language Acquisition, it is aligned well with constructivist theory of cognitive approaches, which views effective learning as 'active' learning. According to Burner's constructivist theory, learning is an active process in which students construct new ideas or concepts based upon their current/past knowledge and experience (Ryder, 2004). The learner selects and transforms information, constructs hypotheses, and makes decisions, relying on a cognitive structure to do so. As Candy explains, constructivism is a cluster of approaches which support that 'knowledge cannot be taught but must be constructed by the learner' (1991, p. 252). Creativity, interaction, and engagement with the target language and negotiation of meaning are all emphasized in such approaches. This exactly aligns with the ideas of autonomy. If knowledge is constructed uniquely within each individual through processes of social interaction, learning will be most effective when students are fully involved in decisions about the content and processes of learning and engaged in communicative activities (Benson, 2001).

The basic ideas of autonomy also have come into harmony with major innovations in socio-cognitive approaches to language teaching, i.e. learner-centeredness and communicative language teaching, over the last 30 years. Several prominent researchers in the field of communicative language teaching, namely Littlewood (1996, 1997), Nunan (1996, 1997), and Breen and Mann (1997), and learner-centered practice have incorporated the idea of autonomy into their work with the belief that learning is more effective when students are active in the learning process, assuming responsibility for their learning and participating in the decisions, which affect it. Therefore, we can assume that autonomous learning is equivalent to effective learning.

According to Scharle and Szabo (2000), there are five elements important for students' autonomy. They are motivation, self-confidence, learning strategies, self-evaluation, cooperation, and group cohesion. Firstly, motivation is a crucial key to all types of learning as there is no way to force students to learn if they are reluctant to do. Intrinsic motivation, which refers to the source of some inner drive or interest of the learner, helps foster students to identify their learning needs and goals, and that make them willing to take responsibility for the outcome. According to Vallerand (1997), intrinsic motivation include three subtypes: 1) to learn (to engage in an activity for the pleasure and satisfaction of understanding something new, satisfying one's curiosity and exploring the world); 2) towards achievement (to engage in an activity for the satisfaction of surpassing oneself, coping with challenges and accomplishing or creating something); 3) to experience stimulation (to engage in an activity to experience pleasant sensations). In fact, motivation and responsibility can mutually reinforce each other when social factors are adequately and appropriately utilized. As Warschauer suggests, students experience high motivation and engagement, strive for excellence and can learn to communicate more effectively in a new medium if the following conditions are met: 1) Students understand well the purpose of the activity; 2) Students find the purpose socially and culturally relevant; 3) Students find the electronic medium appropriate for fulfilling the purpose; and 4) Students are encouraged and enabled to use the range of medium-appropriate rhetorical features to fulfill the purpose (2000, p. 52).

Self-confidence, which refers to a student's belief that he or she possesses the ability to produce results, attain goals, or possesses the competence to complete tasks (Schunk, 1991), also contributes to the development of responsibility. The students have to believe that they are capable of managing their own learning and are solely responsible for their own learning. As Dickinson (1987) suggests, psychological preparation can be regarded as a process of developing self-confidence among students in their ability to work independently of the teacher. The preparation is concerned with persuading students to try self-instruction, facilitating a change of attitude away from false assumptions and prejudices, and helping to build their self-confidence in their ability to work independently of the teacher.

Moreover, students need to be made aware of learning strategies because 'strategies are the tools for active, self-directed involvement needed for developing L2 communicative ability' (Oxford, 1994, p. 1). Foreign or second language (L2) learning strategies are specific actions, behaviors, steps, or techniques students use consciously to improve their progress in apprehending, internalizing, and using the L2 (Oxford, 1990). Research has repeatedly shown that the conscious, tailored use of such strategies is related to language achievement and proficiency (Oxford, 1994). Therefore, we should show students the variety of available strategies, help them find out what works for them, and help them to discover how and when to use them. As pointed out by Wenden, 'successful' or 'expert' or 'intelligent' students have learned how to learn. They have acquired the learning strategies, the knowledge about learning, and the attitudes that enable them to use these skills, and knowledge confidently, flexibly, appropriately and independently of a teacher. Therefore, they are autonomous (1991, p. 15). In short, successful students must be well equipped with good learning strategies for their autonomous learning.

Similar to learning strategies, 'the ability to evaluate the effectiveness of one's own performance in a foreign language is an important skill in learning, and particularly important when the learning becomes autonomous' (Dickinson, 1987, p. 136). In response to the evaluation of the learning itself, 'one needs feedback and input information on learning strategies, learning techniques, etc, in other words, on the suitability and effectiveness of learning in relation to personal learning criteria and personal goals' (Henner-Stanchina & Holec, 1985, p. 18). This information can not only increase the learner's awareness of how he learns but also help him/her make decisions as to the continuation or modification of his learning activities.

Cooperative learning is influential to the development of autonomy because it affects learner's learning attitudes in several ways. Firstly, it encourages students to rely on each other and not only on the teacher. Secondly, it helps create opportunities for peer learning and evaluation. Thirdly, pair and group work can help get a higher proportion of students actively involved in completing a task (Scharle & Szabo, 2000). Through group activities, learning advantages[1] and characteristics like desired behaviors, positive interdependence and roles of group members are developed. As a result, students are motivated for each other's benefit through taking up their own responsibilities (Chafe, 1998). In other words, students learn from dependence, through independence, to interdependence, which is finally essential for social communication and interaction. As reflected in Greenfield's (2003) study on cooperative learning, the majority of Hong Kong participants enjoyed an exchange of emails because they gained general confidence in English and computer skills, and claimed that they made significant progress in writing, thinking and speaking. Ng's (2002) study also reveals that Hong Kong students were very enthusiastic about using the Web for discussions and they acknowledged that collaborative learning could enhance their understanding of the subject knowledge.

In addition to the basic principles, there are generally three phases that one must go through, though they are not strictly in linear format. They can be implemented together as they are interrelated. Raising awareness is the starting point in which students learn to identify strategy involved in the tasks and identify their own preferred learning styles; changing attitudes follows and eventually it involves transferring roles from the teacher to students (Scharle & Szabo, 2000). As Hong Kong students are dependent and have little incentive to undertake learning outside their studies, it is important to arouse their awareness of the importance of the development of autonomy. After they are made aware of the significance of autonomy, positive attitudes can be fostered and finally they can take up new roles in learning.

According to Nunan (1997), the five-level model includes Awareness, Involvement, Intervention, Creation, and Transcendence. The first phase (Raising Awareness) consists of Awareness; the second phase (Changing Attitudes) contains Involvement, Intervention and Creation, and the last phase (Transferring Roles) is Transcendence. The content and process of the model are clearly described in Table 1.

Approaches of Educational Technologies

Among different approaches to educational technologies, two approaches seem to be more suitable for Hong Kong students. Firstly, the Electronic Literacy Approach suggested by Shetzer and Warschauer (2000, p. 177) includes communication, construction and research for teaching and learning (see Table 2).

The table projects a clear direction on the type of learning elements and learning paradigm. For instance, teachers progress from teacher-directed teaching to student-directed learning; reading is integrated with critical evaluation; interactive and autonomous learning should be emphasized.

Table 1. A model to the development of autonomy

Phrase	Level	Learner action	Content	Process
Raising Awareness	One	Awareness	Students are made aware of the pedagogical goals and content of the materials they are using.	Students identify strategy implications of pedagogical tasks and identify their own preferred learning styles/strategies.
	Two	Involvement	Students are involved in selecting their own goals from a range of alternatives on offer.	Students make choices among a range of options.
Changing Attitudes	Three	Intervention	Students are involved in modifying and adapting the goals and content of the learning programme.	Students modify/adapt tasks.
	Four	Creation	Students create their own goals and objectives.	Students create their own tasks.
Transferring Roles	Five	Transcendence	Students go beyond the classroom and make links between the content of classroom learning and the world beyond.	Students become teachers and researchers.

Table 2. Earlier approaches versus electronic literacy approach (ELA)

	Earlier approaches	Electronic literacy approach
Communication	• Based on speaking and listening	• Also includes computer-mediated communication
Construction	• Based on linear texts • Excludes non-print media • Tends to focus on individual writing	• Also includes hypertexts • Combines texts and other media • Strong focus on collaboration
Reading & research	• Restricted to print sources • Focuses on linear texts • Excludes non-print media • Tends to separate reading skills from critical evaluation skills • Focuses on library search skills	• Includes on-line sources • Also includes hypertexts • Combines texts and other media • Views critical evaluation as central to reading • Includes searching and navigating on-line sources
Learning paradigm	• Often based on curricular learning paradigm	• Based on interactive learning paradigm, with emphasis on autonomous learning

However, there are limited guidelines for formulating the actual tasks and projects about autonomous and interactive learning. Clear guidelines on the application are required especially for teachers with low computer literacy because the use of technological tools and resources varies from context to context and specific methodology is necessary to bring about improvement in learning.

To fill in the gap, the Response-Based Approach (RBA) proposed by Meskill and Ranglova (2000) for the development of the literature- and technologies-based curriculum in Bulgaria can shed some light on the direction. This approach views literature as a vehicle to promote critical and creative thinking through student discourse. In addition, literature is viewed as a springboard for students to explore the worlds and feelings of provocative narrative art. Students are required to use the target language in a highly charged, extensive, and meaningful way. The EFL curriculum redesign project, whose focus changed from lecture and philology to a student-centered one, concentrated on the integration and use of technologies both as tools for teaching and learning and as a way to expand understandings of current sociocognitive theory and practice. In the project, readings were selected based on their relevance to students' interests, their degree of its authentic use of English and their potential for provoking responses with others, and tasks were designed involving audiotape, computer concordances, word processing and telecommunications. Learning, therefore, becomes 'teacher-orchestrated' and student-centered, with technology tools stimulating and supporting off-line learning and collaborative activity. The result reflected that students 'enjoyed the autonomy they experienced in undertaking activities that led them to discover aspects of English that became part of their individual developing competence. They also reported a great deal of satisfaction at being "directly involved and active in the learning and teaching process" (p. 31). Hence, this approach appears to be an effective one in the development of autonomy; however, it is only limited to those who can exert great control over the curriculum designed. In this sense, it is not applicable to Hong Kong because the Hong Kong curriculum is heavily examination oriented.

Assumptions Underlying New Approaches to Autonomy

There is a need to create a new approach to the development of autonomy because there is not one single approach, which can meet the needs of Hong Kong students. Although ELA and RBA cannot be fully used in the Hong Kong educational context, they can be combined to suit the needs of Hong Kong students. The former provides a conceptual framework for the present programme while the latter sheds lights on the application of IT into language teaching and learning. With the focus on interactive learning paradigm and autonomous learning, literature/texts are regarded as a vehicle to:

1. Arouse learner motivation through involvement and empowerment with autonomous and collaborative work,
2. Promote critical and creative thinking through learner discourse, and
3. Offer students opportunities to communicate with others through authentic use of resources.

The integrated approach, which is named as Reflective Communication Approach, is the best option to help develop autonomous language learning of the Hong Kong students.

In this approach, first priority is given to communicative activities and the contents should be created and discovered by students through observing and analyzing the authentic resources available on the Internet and the guided discovery tasks. Students are expected to learn the electronic skills and knowledge, such as searching and selecting online resources, etc. To do this, McDonough's 'self-directed' and 'interventionist approach' to strategy training are applicable. Students are allowed to choose their strategies to search for and select useful resources through practical experience and discovery learning whereas teachers can explicitly present alternative strategies to students to learn so as to accelerate their learning.

Figure 1 shows an overview of Reflective Communication Approach, which describes the role of teachers, the learning construction, and the learning process. The role of teachers is mainly to enhance students' awareness of the need and

Figure 1. Framework of the reflective communication approach (RCA) to the autonomous language learning

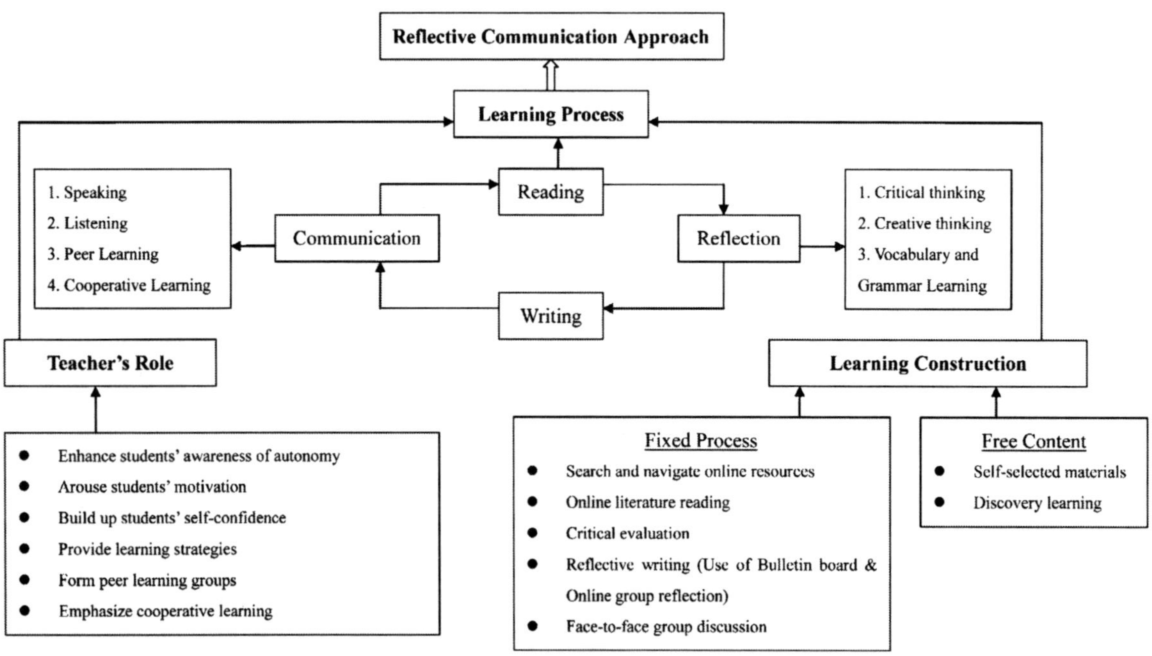

importance of autonomy, arouse their learning motivation, build up their self-confidence, provide learning strategies, help form learning groups, and emphasize cooperative learning. The learning construction consists of free content and fixed process. To arouse students' interest in the task, the freedom of choice over learning content is given to students. The fixed process refers to the pre-defined process that students must go through a cycle of reading, reflection, writing, and communication. Reading allows students to read online materials of their own choice which can help them develop critical and creative thinking, and learn vocabulary and grammar items. Reflective writing provides students with chances to express ideas and opinions and at the same time, to practise writing skills. Communication among group members takes place in the classroom discussion where they can strengthen their communication skills, discussion skills and leadership. To sum up, Reflective Communication Approach, which places emphasis on reflection and communicative activities, can provide students a blended learning environment in which the activity assisted with the computer is used as supportive tools to promote reflection, inquiry and discussion that facilitate autonomous language learning and peer learning while the activity conducted in the classroom can help enhance students' speaking and listening competence, as well as generic skills.

AUTONOMY AND BLENDED LEARNING

The Study

Thirty-five Hong Kong tertiary students were randomly chosen as the subject for the sake of convenience. They were required to attend one-hour lesson every week for three months. The project was divided into three stages, each of which lasted for one month, because it is useful to evaluate the effectiveness of the improvement measures made in the second stage and optimize the design of the program after 2-time revision. Each stage consisted of four parts: planning, implementation, observation, and reflection.

A virtual learning platform, where students took turns to submit their writing after reading an online article of their own choice and discussed about the article, was used because 'virtual environments, such as MOODLE, combine the best features of the social-constructionist paradigm with the most cutting-edge features of integrative CALL' (Shucart, Mishina, Takahashi, & Enokizono, 2008, p. 486).

The data collected through a virtual platform and classroom was analyzed qualitatively whereas those received from the questionnaires and interviews were discussed both qualitatively and quantitatively. With both qualitative and quantitative instruments, what people actually do (as in the bulletin board and group discussions) as well as what they say (as in questionnaires and interviews) could be examined. The questionnaires including both closed- and open-ended questions were used so as to elicit the degree of their attitudes and reasons for their choices. In order to diminish the neutral answer, only 4 Likert scale, in which 1 mark represents Strongly Agree and 4 stands for Strongly Disagree, was used. With an aim of diagnosing the potential problems in the programme, a focus group was also selected. In order to select the focus group, the students were divided into 3 groups according to their performance (i.e. being highly motivated, being neutral, and being less motivated) during the discussion. Four of them including one highly motivated and one less motivated were selected randomly from the groups because smaller groups (4-6 people) are preferable when the participants have a great deal to share about the topic or have had intense or lengthy experiences with the topic of discussion (Kreuger, 1988).

With reference to Reflective Communication Approach, the programme was designed and summarized in Table 3.

Table 3. Overview of the programme

Targets	• Beginners of conducting Autonomous Language Learning
Objectives	• To arouse students' awareness of autonomous language learning and life-long learning • To increase students' exposure to the use of English with content-based learning • To enhance students' abilities of four language skills (i.e. speaking, listening, reading and writing), grammar and vocabulary • To strengthen students' generic skills such as leadership skills, discussion skills and team work
Setting	• To provide a relaxing and non-threatening environment with the virtual platform • To provide face-to-face interaction with the classroom
Materials	• To supply students with a list of worksheets and reference guide o A list of suggested activities o A study plan o An awareness-raising self-evaluation form o A learner diary o A student's guided discussion form
Tasks	• Task 1: To conduct an online reading and writing task • Task 2: To conduct a follow-up in-class group discussion
Procedure	• To distribute all learning materials to students • To explain the flow of the tasks
Task 1:	• To ask students to work in groups of three and choose their own partners • To name them Student A, B and C • To instruct students to take turns to read an online article • To ask Student A to write a reflection of the chosen activity • To ask Student A to post it on the bulletin board at the virtual platform • To ask Students B & C to comment on the reflection of Student A • To ask Student A to review the comments before the next lesson
Task 2:	• To arrange the students to discuss with the group members • To give the students fifteen minutes to have in-class group discussion on the chosen topic

Results

Students' Attitudes towards Autonomous Language Learning

The result reflected from the observations, students' questionnaires, interviews with the focus group showed that the students had been developing better and favorable attitudes towards autonomous language learning. There was a significant change in the students' attitudes towards autonomous language learning after they took the programme. As the statistic showed, 84% of the students before taking the programme showed no preferences for autonomous English learning. However, 84% of them at the end of the programme expressed that they were willing to continue to conduct autonomous language learning for various reasons. The results correspond with findings of the research of Mollering and Ritter (2008) that students generally valued the authentic use of the target language and the level of autonomy with regards to choosing the topics for discussion and the emphasis given to specific aspects of the topics. The rest of the students reported that they were interested in autonomous language learning, and wanted to study and improve their English but the problem was that they did not know how to do it because they found learning English difficult. This implies that learning strategies need to be strengthened and individualized so as to help students solve their learning difficulties and problems. To conclude, the overall results reflected that the programme could help change the students' attitudes positively towards autonomous language learning and was an effective programme for the development of autonomous language learning.

At the first stage, only 16% of the students generally liked to spend time improving their English when they were not required to do so and admitted that they generally became increasingly absorbed in English as they learnt it. 87% of them would restrict their studying of English to what was specifically required by the teachers because 1) 81% of them explained that they had limited time for studying English; 2) 90% of them thought that it was not necessary to do anything extra. However, at the last stage, 84% of them showed preferences for the continuation of autonomous language learning because they acknowledged that the tasks could improve their reading, writing, speaking, listening, and vocabulary and found the tasks useful and helpful in learning English. They also enjoyed exercising their discretion over the task contents. In addition, they gained generic skills such as leadership, cooperation, communication and coordination and therefore they enjoyed working in groups. These results reflect that the tasks could generally meet the expectation/needs of students to gain improvement while they could learn what they wanted because they had full control over the contents. They acquired the knowledge rather than learnt it. This then led to personal satisfaction, self-confidence, and finally motivation. As Benson (2001) points out, learning will be most effective when students are fully involved in decisions about the content and processes of learning if knowledge is constructed uniquely within each individual through processes of social interaction. The results also correspond with conclusions of other research such as Greenfield's and Ng's study in relation to the power of cooperative learning and Huot, Lemonnier, and Hamers' (2008) longitudinal study that that the use of ICT in learning English makes an important contribution at the pedagogical, motivational, attitudinal and linguistic levels (p. 98).

In addition to the extrinsic motivation fostered by the tasks design, the students were found to have intrinsic motivation for English learning as they indicated that they would like to improve English through ILL because of various reasons (see Table 4).

As shown in Table 4, the students possessed intrinsic motivation, which Vallerand (1997) categorizes it into 'to learn,' 'towards achievement' and 'experience stimulation.' They aimed 'to learn' as reflected by items b, d, f, g and j and 'towards achievement' as indicated by items a, c, e, and h. As indicated with the open-ended questions in the questionnaire, they wanted 'to learn' because half of them realized the need of studying more and improving their weaknesses like grammar after taking the programme. They worked 'towards achievement' as they all found that their communicative competence was improved and thus it fostered their desire to surpass themselves and work harder. They also 'experienced stimulation' as they found autonomous learning entertaining because they could choose what to read and discuss such as stories or news and choose what to learn, such as vocabulary and sentence structure.

Table 4. Students' attitudes towards learning English with ILLP

Listed below are reasons that students showed for the preference of conducting the Guided Independent Language Learning to improve their English.	Mean
a. Because I have a strong desire to excel in English	2.2
b. Because learning English gives me a deep sense of satisfaction.	2.1
c. Because I want to improve my English as this will improve my chances of finding a good job when I graduate.	1.5
d. Because I want to appreciate western films, novels and culture.	2.4
e. Because I want to improve my English as this will enable me to do better in other academic subjects.	2
f. Because English can help broaden my horizon.	2.1
g. Because English can help me to make friends with people of different nationalities and cultures.	2.2
h. Because English can help me to further my studies in the future.	1.6
j. Because my teachers/employers will praise and appreciate my ability in English if my English is good.	1.9

Another important point to make is that one needs feedback on the suitability and effectiveness of learning in relation to personal learning goals as proposed by Holec (1981). One student from the focus group expressed that she found learning interesting in the beginning of the trials but lost interest gradually partly because it was difficult and time-consuming for her to search for appropriate articles and partly because she did not get any constructive feedback on her own learning. This reflects the importance of feedback for autonomous language learning. With the feedback, the learner could be made aware of how she should learn and make decisions as to the continuation or modification of her learning. To solve this problem, one possible solution is peer feedback through cooperative learning. An alternative is self-evaluation, which plays an important role in preparing students to solve their own learning difficulties or problems such as choosing appropriate level of materials for their own learning. As Dickinson (1987) points out, the ability to evaluate the effectiveness of one's own performance is also an important skill in learning and particularly important when it is autonomous learning. Therefore, it is suggested that learning strategies should include the skill of self-evaluation.

With regard to learning strategies, 14% of the students found it difficult to conduct autonomous language learning because they did not know how to do it even though they wanted to improve their English. As a result, they adopted rather pessimistic and escaping attitudes towards learning English and stated that they did not want to conduct autonomous language learning at the end of the programme. This reveals their low self-confidence. As Stevens (2003) mentioned, negative self-fulfilling prophesies lead to negative actions that they chose to give up trying to conduct autonomous language learning. According to McClelland, the most important factor for developing self-confidence is to master the needed skills. Therefore, explicit strategy training is required so as to enhance their abilities and self-confidence in learning English effectively and to manage their own learning eventually. In addition, to effectively develop autonomous language learning, students need psychological preparation to help persuade them to try self-instruction, to facilitate attitude change and to build up confidence in their ability eventually (Dickinson, 1987).

To conclude, the results correspond with the conclusion of other research that the integration of motivation, self-confidence, learning strategies, self-evaluation, and cooperative learning into the programme attributes to the success of the development of autonomous language learning for ESL students. The combination can help exert their full potential as they are interrelated and complement each other.

Students' Attitudes towards the Blended Learning: Online and In-Class Tasks

As far as the blended learning is concerned, the students showed positive attitudes towards the blended learning for English learning because it combines traditional face-to-face classroom methods with more modern computer-mediated activities. The findings showed that they liked to use the Internet and the virtual platform for online English writing, reading, listening, speaking, grammar exercises, as well as vocabulary learning. They were also in favor of Web-based projects and interactive activities and used the Internet for learning English at home. In addition, 45% of them indicated that they spent more time learning English with the Internet whereas 35% of them spent more time to learn English with the virtual platform after joining the programme. Table 5 summarizes the students' favourable preferences towards the use of CMC into English learning.

The students liked to use the Internet for English learning because they found it convenient, interesting, useful, and it was easy for them to search and use online materials for learning. Similarly, the main reasons for the students who

Table 5. Mean score of the questionnaire items

Items in the Questionnaire	Mean
I like to use the Internet for learning English.	2.2
I like to use WebCT for learning English.	2.4
I like Web-based activities.	2.4
I use the Internet for learning English at home.	2.3
I spend more time to learn English with the Internet.	2.5
I spend more time to learn English with WebCT.	2.6
I like English because there are Web-based activities.	2.5
I like Online Writing	2.4
I like Online Reading	2.2
I like Online Listening	2.2
I like Online Speaking or Chatting	2
I like Online Grammar Exercises	2.3
I like Online Vocabulary Learning	2.1
I like Web-based projects	2.4
I like Interactive activities	2.1

liked to use the virtual platform for English learning were 'convenient,' 'user-friendly,' and 'on-line materials are easy to search and use.' This directly reflected that the pace of living in Hong Kong is hectic and people want to do or get something in the shortest time. Therefore, both the Internet and the virtual platform can be the fastest channel for them to search for information for learning purposes. In addition, they found the online texts diversified, interesting and knowledgeable, which helped enhance their judgment. One student commented that it could help enhance their understanding of general knowledge and news while deepening their linguistic knowledge. They could also exchange knowledge and opinions with their group members. This corroborates with findings of Ng's (2002) study that the students' levels of involvement and incentive to learn have increased significantly with a wider and more complete understanding of the subject knowledge through collaborative learning and the Web for discussions. This also implies that the general knowledge over current news could also be an incentive for students to learn and experience stimulation. Perhaps because of the impact of globalization, students want to catch up with the knowledge-based economy and the information age. In other words, the integration of various fields of knowledge into English teaching and learning content should be encouraged.

Where the use of the virtual platform is concerned, they were also satisfied with the functions provided because it is generally easy to use and convenient. One student found it helpful to enhance her confidence in using English as she had time to express herself while writing comments in the virtual platform, which provides a non-threatening environment for them to use written English. This is found in line with the remarks of Warschauer (2000) that CMC could give students additional opportunities to plan their discourse and to notice and reflect on language use in the messages they compose and read. As a result, their learning motivation and communication can be enhanced. Furthermore, when the technical problems such as confused categorization of Bulletin Board and lack of learning resources identified in the first stage were resolved, the students could find it easier to conduct their online tasks. This may therefore facilitate their favorable attitudes towards writing English and thus the length of their entries increased two times from 50 – 100 words to 100 – 200 words. This reflected that the use of virtual learning platform requires careful administration and monitor. Otherwise, it would impair students' learning process, and eventually lead to frustration and de-motivate them to learn.

Similar to the conclusion of the students' attitudes towards the online task, the students have developed favorable attitudes towards the in-class discussion. Most of them had higher involvement and incentives for the discussion. This can be shown from the statements in Table 6.

The results correspond with the conclusions of other research such as Ng's (2002) and Greenfield's (2003) that collaborative learning is Hong Kong students' favourite activity. The reasons for their favorable attitudes, which were reflected from both the questionnaires and interviews, were summarized as follows:

- They could exchange ideas with their group members.
- They could learn from their partners.
- Discussion could improve their spoken and listening abilities as well as their communication skills.
- It could enhance their confidence in speaking in front of people.
- They could discuss in a relaxing atmosphere and share interesting topics.
- It could train their leadership skills.
- It could train their coordination and enhance their cooperation.
- It was fun and interesting to exchange ideas with others.
- Their self-confidence was greatly enhanced as they could share their experience with others, teach others as well as gain more knowledge.
- The group work could help solve all problems.
- They could obtain immediate feedback.
- They had developed a social bond and friendship with each other and thus working together to achieve the targets.

From that we can see, sharing, cooperation, group cohesion, self-confidence, generic skills and feedback could enhance students' interest in English learning. Group work and cooperative learning could motivate students to learn English.

Students' Attitudes towards the Programme

In relation to the development of autonomy with Reflective Communication Approach, the program is proved to be an effective one because the result collected from various sources showed that students have developed favorable attitudes towards the programme.

At the initial stage, the students' attitudes towards the programme were found unfavorable and that was reflected by their low involvement and motivation. With on-going modification of the programme, they started to develop favorable attitudes towards the programme. They admitted that it could help improve their English in the aspects of writing, reading, speaking, listening and vocabulary, and that they wanted to continue to conduct autonomous language learning after joining the programme. The main reason for their favourable attitudes towards the programme was satisfaction because their language skills were improved. The higher the competence of English language they have, the higher the motivation they get. However, it was not surprising! This corresponds with the finding that intrinsic motivation, 'towards achievement,' helps foster students to identify their learning needs and goals, and that make them willing to take responsibility for the outcome. Responsibility and motivation mutually reinforce each other when other factors are adequately and appropriately utilized.

Table 6. Students' attitudes towards the in-class group discussion

Items in the Questionnaire	Mean
I like the group discussion.	2.1
I like to work in groups because I can exchange ideas with my partners.	1.9
I like to work in groups because I can learn from my partner.	1.9
I like to discuss with partners because I can improve my spoken English.	1.9
I like to discuss with partners because I can improve my listening ability.	2.1

Recommendation for Teachers

As discussed earlier, most students have intrinsic motivation in learning English through this programme while a few could not find proper ways to learn English satisfactorily and effectively. In order to further enhance the effectiveness of the programme, not only intrinsic motivation but also overt extrinsic motivation, like encouragement and positive feedback should be emphasized. For instance, a competition for the most interesting reflective writing could be organized to arouse students' interest and to promote a sense of achievement.

Moreover, students need to be made aware of learning strategies not just because the strategies can serve as the tools for developing L2 communicative ability but because they help enhance the students' self-confidence in solving the possible problems or difficulties they encountered in this programme. For the less-able students, they need to be trained to analyze their needs, to recognize suitable materials, to extract the best value from them, and most importantly, understand their own contribution to the learning process. To facilitate them to master the needed skills, detailed explanation may be required, and individual or small group consultation may be needed. In response to the results, some metacognitive strategies and cognitive strategies should also be integrated into the training, such as: 1) self-evaluation – checking one's learning against one's standards is necessary; 2) selective attention – special attention on specific parts of language input; 3) resourcing – making use of language materials such as dictionary; and 4) grouping – organizing learning on the basis of 'common attributes' (O'Malley & Chamot, 1990, p. 44). To help students learn effectively, teachers should explain the strategies with them explicitly. If necessary, a task should be designed and conducted in the pre-task training so as to let students understand the application of the strategies. As Oxford (1994) suggests, 'training should be integrated into regular L2 activities over a long period of time' (p. 3).

Regarding the learning strategies, there are several aspects that need to be addressed. Firstly, since the level of students' electronic literacy differs from student to student, it is necessary to equip them with necessary strategies and skills. As students are usually the beginners of using IT for the development of autonomy, it is beneficial to give them a briefing about integrating IT for their own autonomous learning. Moreover, students should be allowed to choose how to read and write as some students commented that they did not like using computer to read and write due to health problems, and that their favorite activities include listening to radio programme, watching movies or TV programmes and reading magazines. In order to satisfy their desires, more choices for the reading part can be given. This corresponds with the result that students enjoyed selecting their learning materials and the way in which knowledge was constructed during the learning process. As Holec (1981) suggests, students should be given chances to construct and discover their own learning through communicative content, and observe and analyze the sources of information available. Effective learning is active learning in which students construct new ideas or concepts based upon their current or past knowledge.

Furthermore, many students are unaware of the practicality of online materials or tools. Therefore, it is important to awaken students to the resources in their environment such as online newspapers, reports, magazines, journals, reviews, videos, concordance, word processing, virtual learning platform, dictionary, note-taking, online tutor, etc., and to the possibilities for their use. As Ryan (1997) suggests, the following steps are useful to awaken students to the recourses in their environment:

1. Consciousness-raising discussion of available resources.

2. Presenting and practicing techniques to exploit resources.
3. Introduction to the theoretical constructs of language acquisition underlying the selection of resources and techniques (p. 218).

As far as the self-evaluation is concerned, students should be strongly advised to conduct a self-evaluation right after every task and activity to ensure the performance check and encouraged to conduct peer-evaluation with the use of a peer evaluation form so as to enforce group cohesion, positive interdependence, cooperation for group learning, and provide objective assessment. The performance-oriented self-assessment and peer-evaluation could help provide students with ways to evaluate their immediate performance of the task, make necessary changes or modification, and eventually lead to improvement for their own learning.

FUTURE TRENDS

Most of the early research was done in relation to collaborative CALL programs (e.g. simulations and games, annotation, modeling, and discovery programs) and facilitative CALL programs (e.g., word-processing and idea-processing programs with spell check and on-line thesauruses). The research was done: 1) to help course designers construct effective software, 2) to help teachers optimize content and language learning with the aid of computers, 3) to assist school administrators with purchase and effective utilization of computers in the school environment. Gradually, the trend has been toward using computers as tools and toward integrating their use into all areas of the curriculum (Trends & Status, 1987). There are self-access software, state-of-the-art facilities with electronic whiteboards, local area networks, wide bandwidth Internet connections, virtual learning classroom, Web-based projects, content CD-ROMs with video clips, tutorial applications, and so on (Hanson-Smith, 2000). Although computers and other electronic technology have often been regarded as either tools or tutors, they gradually serve as an environment in which learning can take place. In recent years, the use of IT can be elaborated in CALL Environments (Egbert & Hanson-Smith, 1999) and the interaction between humans and computers continues to evolve rapidly.

The research in this chapter has fully reflected the effective interaction between humans and computers. The framework developed in the research has also revealed the valuable change of technology use in education. With the positive results mentioned above, we can conclude that Reflective Communication Approach, depicted in Figure 2, is an effective framework for autonomous language learning in a blended learning environment. Reflective Communication Approach describes the roles of teacher, the learning construction, and the learning process for the autonomous language learning and suggests a number of techniques that teachers can use to formulate their teaching plans for the blended learning.

Technology use nowadays is not about finding ways of replacing or enhancing current activities with technology, such as replacing chalk and board by multimedia presentations/animations, but is an opportunity to re-engineer education. With reference to the Consultation Papers and Consultancy Reports (1998), the school education should be alive to the various opportunities and changing needs of the information age in which students should be able to develop an understanding of the pervasive impact of IT on the society and their daily lives, higher order thinking skills, as well as abilities to seek, evaluate, organize, and present information. In addition, they need to develop habits of life-long learning so as to adapt to the rapid changes. To meet the new requirements, the school education needs a paradigm shift - from a largely textbook-based teacher-centered approach to a more interactive and learner-centered approach. In other words, there must be changes to

Figure 2. Reflective communication approach: a modified framework for autonomous language learning in blended learning environment

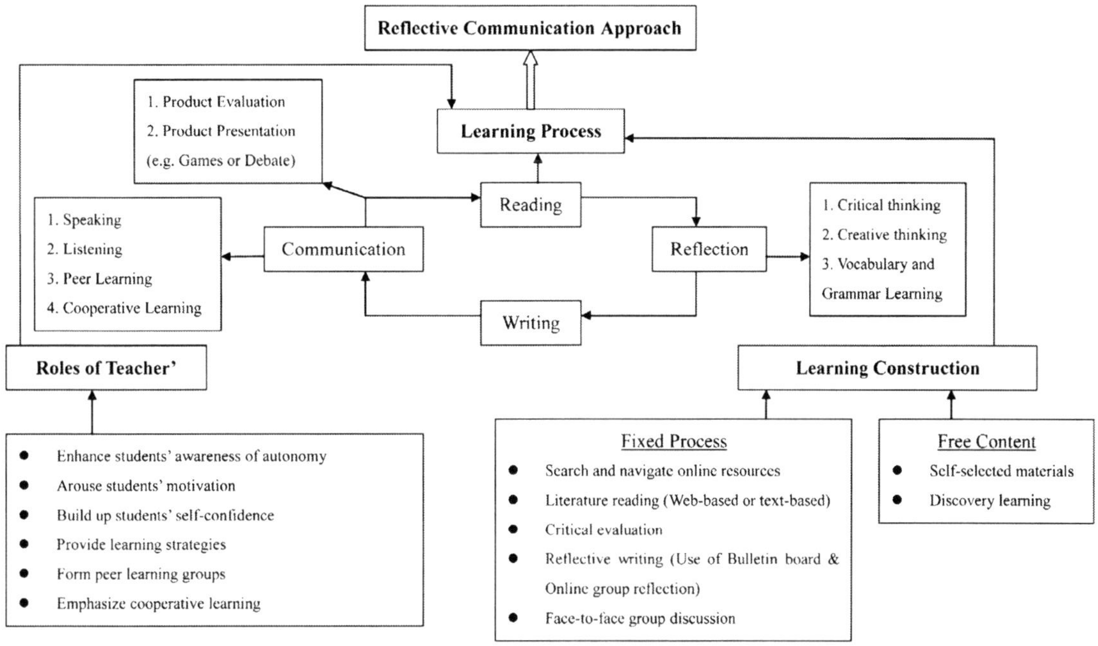

the mind set and culture among teachers, parents and students, and to the way in which the curriculum is designed and delivered and student assessment is conducted, etc. Faced with this urgent need of the paradigm shift, a community-wide culture for the proper integration of IT into teaching and learning has to be nurtured. The programme developed in this research is an exemplar. To further enhance the implementation plan of the programme, it is refined to six parts: 1) targets; 2) objectives; 3) setting; 4) materials; 5) pre-task training; and 6) tasks. The details are shown in Table 7.

To further examine the extent of the effectiveness of the framework, it can be applied and integrated to formal language teaching and learning. I presume the future research trend in teaching with educational technologies will move towards the field of blended learning such as an investigation of the effectiveness of various types of activities in blended learning, an inquiry of the use of blended learning in formal curriculum design and so on.

CONCLUSION

In response to the objectives of the research studying the students' attitudes towards the autonomous language learning, the blended learning, and the programme, the results indicate that students have favourable attitudes in all these aspects, and suggest an effective framework for the autonomous language learning in a blended learning environment. To foster autonomous language learning for less-able and -motivated students, self-confidence and strategies for both individualized learning and self-evaluation should be strengthened.

The programme was a success because it was researched in the way that it was. The key principles of the programme, which is developed in line with Reflective Communication Approach, are: 1) underlying conceptual principles including motivation, self-confidence, learning strategies, self-evaluation and cooperation & group cohesion; 2) fixed learning methodology but freedom for the selection of content; 3) emphasis on communicative content and discovery learning; 4) authentic

Table 7. Teaching plan of the refined program

Targets	• Beginners for Independent Language Learning
Objectives	• To increase students' exposure to the use of English with content-based knowledge • To provide students' chances of the use for four language skills (speaking, listening, reading and writing) • To enhance students' awareness in the self-learning of grammar and vocabulary • To arouse students' awareness of independent language learning and life-long learning • To enhance critical and analytical thinking • To strengthen students' generic skills such as leadership skills, discussion skills, communication skills and cooperation.
Setting	• To provide a relaxing atmosphere and non-threatening environment through a virtual learning platform • To provide face-to-face interaction with classroom
Materials	• To provide students a list of worksheets and reference guide o A list of suggested activities o A list of suggested websites o A study plan o An awareness-raising self-evaluation o A self-evaluation form o A peer-evaluation form o A learner diary o A student's guided discussion form o A detailed written description of the tasks
Pre-task Training	• To provide a set of strategies training for the programme o Demonstrate Searching Skills o Use of an Virtual learning platform o Give an account of the Online Assistance ▪ Online dictionary ▪ Note-taking with Note Pad ▪ Online Tutor o Give an account of Learning Strategies ▪ Individualized strategies ▪ Task-oriented strategies ▪ Metacognitive Strategies ▪ Cognitive Strategies
Tasks	• Task 1: To conduct an online reading and writing task • Task 2: To conduct an follow-up in-class group discussion

materials; 5) critical evaluation and reflective writing; and 6) face-to-face group discussion. With the teachers' ongoing plan-do-check-act approach, which is underpinned by AR, the programme is modified to suit the needs and interests of students for autonomous language learning. With the success of the programme in this study, Reflective Communication Approach can be best used as an effective tool for developing autonomous language learning programme.

The programme is not only beneficial to ESL students and in-service teachers but also school administrators. In addition to the improvement of English competence, ESL students can gain linguistic knowledge and generic skills crucial for life-long learning and employability through autonomous language learning. In-service teachers can use the framework to develop any language learning programmes for their students and should be in a better position to develop autonomous language learning with a blended learning environment. For long-term development of life-long learning, the framework can also inform school administrators of future decisions about the curricula changes, investment of institutional funds, and professional development.

REFERENCES

Beatty, K. (2002). *Describing and enhancing collaboration at the computer*. Retrieved from http://www.cjlt.ca/content/vol28.2/beatty.html

Beatty, K., & Nunan, D. (2004). Computer-mediated collaborative learning. *System*, *32*(2), 165–183. doi:10.1016/j.system.2003.11.006

Benson, P. (2001). *Teaching and researching autonomy in language learning*. New York, NY: Longman.

Breen, M. P., & Mann, S. (1997). Shooting arrows at the sun: Perspectives on a pedagogy for autonomy. In Benson, P., & Voller, P. (Eds.), *Autonomy and Independence in Language Learning* (pp. 132–149). London, UK: Longman.

Candy, P. C. (1991). *Self-direction for lifelong learning*. San Francisco, CA: Jossey-Bass.

Chafe, A. (1998). *Computer technology and co-operative learning*. Retrieved from http://www.stemnet.nf.ca/~achafe/maj_index.html

Cooper, M. M., & Selfe, C. L. (1990). Computer conferences and learning: Authority, resistance, and internally persuasive discourse. *College English*, *52*(8), 847–873. doi:10.2307/377388

Dickinson, L. (1987). *Self-instruction in language learning*. Cambridge, MA: Cambridge University Press.

Education and Manpower Bureau. (2004a). Information technology in education – Way forward. *HKSAR: Education and Manpower Bureau*. Retrieved from http://www.emb.gov.hk/consultation_ited/file/eng/wayforward.pdf

Education and Manpower Bureau. (2004b). Preliminary study on reviewing the progress and evaluating the information technology in education (ITEd) projects (December 2000 – August 2001) (final report). *HKSAR: Education and Manpower Bureau*. Retrieved from http://www.ited.emb.gov.hk/Documents/ITEd_Report/FinalReport_v3.0_web.htm

Egbert, J., & Hanson-Smith, E. (1999). *CALL environments: Research, practice and critical issues*. Alexandria, VA: Teachers of English to Speakers of Other Languages.

Enrique Hinostroza, J., Labbe, C., Brun, M., & Matamala, C. (2011). Teaching and learning activities in Chilean classrooms: Is ICT making a difference? *Computers & Education*, *57*, 1358–1367. doi:10.1016/j.compedu.2011.01.019

Greenfield, R. (2003). *Collaborative e-mail exchange for teaching secondary ESL: A case study in Hong Kong*. Retrieved from http://llt.msu.edu/vol7num1/pdf/greenfield.pdf

Hanson-Smith, E. (2000). *Technology-enhanced learning environments*. Alexandria, Va.: Teachers of English to Speakers of Other Languages.

Henner-Stanchina, C., & Holec, H. (1985). Evaluation in an autonomous learning scheme. In Riley, P. (Ed.), *Discourse and Learning* (pp. 255–263). London, UK: Longman.

Holec, H. (1981). *Autonomy and foreign language learning*. Oxford, UK: Pergamon Press.

Huot, D., Lemonnier, F. H., & Hamers, J. (2008). ICT and language learning at secondary school. In Zhang, F., & Barber, B. (Eds.), *Handbook of Research on Computer-Enhanced Language Acquisition and Learning* (pp. 84–100). Hershey, PA: IGI Global. doi:10.4018/978-1-59904-895-6.ch006

Kern, R. (1995). Restructuring classroom interaction with networked computers: Effects on quantity and characteristics of language production. *Modern Language Journal, 79*, 457–476. doi:10.1111/j.1540-4781.1995.tb05445.x

Kreuger, R. A. (1988). *Focus groups: A practical guide for applied research*. London, UK: Sage.

Lee, I. (1998). Supporting greater autonomy in language learning. *ELT Journal, 52*(4), 282–288. doi:10.1093/elt/52.4.282

Littlewood, W. (1996). Autonomy: An autonomy and a framework. *System, 24*(4), 427–435. doi:10.1016/S0346-251X(96)00039-5

Littlewood, W. (1997). Self-access: Why do want it and what can it do? In Benson, P., & Voller, P. (Eds.), *Autonomy and Independence in Language Learning* (pp. 79–92). London, UK: Longman.

Meskill, C., & Ranglova, K. (2000). Sociocollaborative language learning in Bulgaria. In Warschauer, M., & Kern, R. (Eds.), *Network-Based Language Teaching: Concepts and Practice* (pp. 20–40). Cambridge, UK: Cambridge University Press. doi:10.1017/CBO9781139524735.004

Mollering, M., & Ritter, M. (2008). CMC and intercultural learning. In Zhang, F., & Barber, B. (Eds.), *Handbook of Research on Computer-Enhanced Language Acquisition and Learning* (pp. 361–376). Hershey, PA: IGI Global. doi:10.4018/978-1-59904-895-6.ch021

Ng, E. (2002). *Enhancing collaborative learning through online discussion and peer assessment*. Retrieved from http://csdl.computer.org/comp/proceedings/icce/2002/1509/00/15090262.pdf

Nunan, D. (1996). Hidden voices: Insiders' perspectives on classroom. In Bailey, K. M., & Nunan, D. (Eds.), *Voices from the Language Classroom* (pp. 41–56). Cambridge, UK: Cambridge University Press.

Nunan, D. (1997). Designing and adapting materials to encourage learner autonomy. In Benson, P., & Voller, P. (Eds.), *Autonomy and Independence in Language Learning* (pp. 192–203). London, UK: Longman.

O'Malley, J. M., & Chamot, A. U. (1990). *Learning strategies in second language acquisition*. Cambridge, UK: Cambridge University Press. doi:10.1017/CBO9781139524490

O'Malley, J. M., & Chamot, A. U. (1990). *Learning strategies in second language acquisition*. Cambridge, UK: Cambridge University Press. doi:10.1017/CBO9781139524490

Oxford, R. (1990). *Language learning strategies: What every teacher should know*. Boston, MA: Heinle & Heinle Publishers.

Oxford, R. (1994). Language learning strategies: An update. *ERIC Digest*. Retrieved from http://www.ericfacility.net/ericdigests/ed376707.html

Parks, S., Huot, D., Hamers, J., & Lemonnier, F. H. (2005). History of theatre web sites: A brief history of the writing process in a high school ESL language arts class. *Journal of Second Language Writing, 14*(4), 233–258. doi:10.1016/j.jslw.2005.10.003

Pierson, H. D. (1996). Learner culture and learner autonomy in the Hong Kong Chinese context. In Pemberton, R. (Ed.), *Taking Control: Autonomy in Language Learning* (pp. 49–58). Hong Kong, China: Hong Kong University Press.

Ryan, S. M. (1997). Preparing learners for independence: resources beyond the classroom. In Benson, P., & Voller, P. (Eds.), *Autonomy and Independence in Language Learning* (pp. 215–224). London, UK: Longman.

Ryder, M. (2004). *Constructivism: school of education*. Retrieved from http://carbon.cudenver.edu/~mryder/itc_data/constructivism.html

Scharle, A., & Szabo, A. (2000). *Learner autonomy: A guide to developing learner responsibility*. Cambridge, UK: Cambridge University Press.

Schon, D. (1983). *The reflective practitioner*. New York, NY: Basic Books.

Schunk, D. H. (1991). Self-efficacy and academic motivation. *Educational Psychologist*, *26*(3-4), 201–231. doi:10.1080/00461520.1991.9653133

Shetzer, H., & Warschauer, M. (2000). An electronic literacy approach to network-based language teaching. In Warschauer, M., & Kern, R. (Eds.), *Network-Based Language Teaching: Concepts and Practice* (pp. 171–185). Cambridge, UK: Cambridge University Press. doi:10.1017/CBO9781139524735.010

Shucart, S. A., Mishina, T., Takahashi, M., & Enokizono, T. (2008). The CALL lab as a facilitator for autonomous learning. In Zhang, F., & Barber, B. (Eds.), *Handbook of Research on Computer-Enhanced Language Acquisition and Learning* (pp. 483–495). Hershey, PA: IGI Global. doi:10.4018/978-1-59904-895-6.ch028

Stevens, T. G. (2003). *You can choose to be happy: Self-confidence*. Retrieved from http://www.courses.csulb.edu/tstevens/h54confi.htm

Sullivan, N. (1993). Teaching writing on a computer network. *TESOL Journal*, *3*(1), 34–35.

Thomson, C. K. (1996). Self-assessment in self-directed learning: issues of learner diversity. In Pemberton, R. (Ed.), *Taking Control: Autonomy in Language Learning* (pp. 77–91). Hong Kong, China: Hong Kong University Press.

Underwood, J. (2009). *The impact of digital technology: A review of the evidence of the impact of digital technologies on formal education*. Coventry, UK: British Educational Communications and Technology Agency (Becta).

Vallerand, R. J. (1997). In Zanna, M. P. (Ed.), *Toward a hierarchical model of intrinsic and extrinsic motivation* (*Vol. 29*, pp. 271–361). Advances in Experimental Social Psychology Toronto, Canada: Academic Press. doi:10.1016/S0065-2601(08)60019-2

Wadsworth, Y. (1998). What is participatory action research? *Action Research International*. Retrieved from http://www.scu.edu.au/schools/gcm/ar/ari/p-ywadsworth98.html

Warschauer, M. (1996). Computer-assisted language learning: An introduction. In Fotos, S. (Ed.), *Multimedia Language Teaching* (pp. 3–20). Tokyo, Japan: Logos International.

Warschauer, M. (2000). On-line learning in second language classrooms: An ethnographic study. In Warschauer, M., & Kern, R. (Eds.), *Network-Based Language Teaching: Concepts and Practice* (pp. 41–58). Cambridge, UK: Cambridge University Press. doi:10.1017/CBO9781139524735.005

Warschauer, M. (2003). *Technology and social inclusion: Rethinking the digital divide*. Cambridge, MA: MIT Press.

Warschauer, M., & Healey, D. (1998). Computers and language learning: An overview. *Language Teaching*, *31*, 57–71. doi:10.1017/S0261444800012970

Warschauer, M., & Healey, D. (1998). Computers and language learning: An overview. *Language Teaching*, *31*, 57–71. doi:10.1017/S0261444800012970

Warschauer, M., Turbee, L., & Roberts, B. (1996). Computer learning networks and student empowerment. *System*, *24*(1), 1–14. doi:10.1016/0346-251X(95)00049-P

Wenden, A. (1991). *Learner strategies for learner autonomy*. New York, NY: Prentice Hall.

ENDNOTES

1 Jacobs (1998) summarizes ten potential advantages of group activities in language instruction: 1) the quantity of learner speech can increase, 2) the variety of speech acts can increase, 3) there can be more individualization of instruction, 4) anxiety can be reduced, 5) motivation can increase, 6) enjoyment can increase, 7) independence can increase, 8) social integration can increase, 9) students can learn how to work with others, and 10) learning can increase (as cited in Beatty, 2002, p. 3).

Chapter 11
Online Professional Development for Adults: Utilizing Andragogical Methods in Research and Practice

J. Bernard Bradley
American Council on Grant Writing, USA

John Rachal
The University of Southern Mississippi, USA

Lin Harper
The University of Southern Mississippi, USA

ABSTRACT

Online professional development programs for adults are increasing in frequency. Numerous scholarly articles have been written that offer polemical or anecdotal evidence supporting the effectiveness of andragogically facilitated non-formal professional development courses, including those conducted online. However, few empirical studies have been conducted to validate their usefulness, especially those offered via the Internet. Such non-formal educational programming may be most conducive to both implementing and empirically testing a more purist definition of andragogy (Pratt, 1988; Rachal, 2002; Bradley, 2011). This chapter explores the theoretical frameworks of andragogy, as well as existing experimental or quasi-experimental research studies, with a view toward creating more learner-centered non-formal educational transactions that meet the unique needs of adult learners. Lastly, suggestions for both practitioners and researchers alike are offered to help build the body of evidence-based research and extend practical advice to educators when designing and facilitating virtual learning programs for adults that emphasize professional development.

DOI: 10.4018/978-1-4666-2955-4.ch011

INTRODUCTION

Andragogy is commonly viewed as a set of assumptions about working with adults. The term was popularized in the United States by Malcolm Knowles during the late 1960s and early 1970s and has since been referred to as a unifying principle in the broad field of adult education (Merriam, 1991; Merriam & Brockett, 1997; Cercone, 2008). Although frequently described as a theory of adult learning, its efficacy has been questioned because of a dearth of conclusive quantitative evidence supporting its use.

Signifying the need for additional protocols relative to the practical application of Internet learning for adults, Isenberg (2007) suggests adult learning methods presently lag behind most other practical applications of online learning. Such theories, however, can help create more learner-centered online educational environments. Isenberg further posits, "Educators of adults lack a how-to-guide for applying adult learning principles to Internet learning" (p. 8). As a result, Cercone (2008) presents an overview for implementing key adult learning theories within both online instructional programs for adults as well as in future research studies. "The future of adult online learning research may be based on the theories discussed in this article, even though most of the theories were developed almost 20 years ago and in traditional classroom environments" (p. 151), Cercone concluded. He further describes andragogy as "the most comprehensive" theory (p. 150) of adult learning. A simple "Google" search revealed that at least 68 authors have cited Cercone's groundbreaking article since its publication in 2008, thereby further elucidating the current demand for both practitioner-focused and research-based protocols to facilitate the effective implementation of andragogy in online programs for adults.

So far as the authors were able to discover, the first online experimental study that utilized all of Rachal's (2002) criteria for conducting andragogy research for the purpose of non-formal professional development was carried out by Bradley (2011). This mixed-methods study was designed to compare the effectiveness of andragogical or student-centered instruction, and pedagogical or teacher-centered instruction, between staff members of nonprofit social service agencies who participate in or complete an online learning module on foundation grant writing using the two methods. Outcomes are presented in relation to other relevant andragogy studies to help inform future research and practice.

ANDRAGOGY'S HISTORICAL BACKGROUND AND THEORETICAL FOUNDATIONS

The Andragogy vs. Pedagogy Debate

Both historical and theoretical foundations of andragogy are discussed here to provide readers with foundational knowledge supporting future andragogy research and practice in online non-formal professional development settings.

The term "andragogy" was first developed by Alexander Kapp, a German teacher, in 1833 in an attempt to "describe the educational theory of Plato" (Davenport & Davenport, 1985a, p. 152). Davenport and Davenport (1985b) debated whether it was Malcolm Knowles or Eduard Lindeman who brought the term to the United States. Lindeman first introduced it in 1927, but Knowles brought the term to prominence with his 1967 address as the recipient of the Delbert Clark Award (Davenport & Davenport, 1985b). Knowles, as cited in Levitt, changed his conceptualization of andragogy and pedagogy, first presenting the two as dichotomous in his 1970 work, *The Modern Practice of Adult Education: Andragogy vs. Pedagogy*, but later clarifying himself in the journal critique *Andragogy Revisited – Part II*, where he wrote:

I have realized for some time now that I made a serious mistake in subtitling The Modern Practice of Adult Education: Andragogy vs. Pedagogy, and presenting their two sets of assumptions about learners as a dichotomy. The subtitle should have been From Pedagogy to Andragogy and the assumptions should have been presented on a continuum (Levitt, 1979, p. 52).

Today, andragogy is commonly viewed as a set of assumptions about working with adults. According to Knowles (1980), the assumptions of andragogy suggest that, as individuals mature:

1) Their self-concept moves from one of being a dependent personality toward being a self-directed human being; 2) they accumulate a growing reservoir of experience that becomes an increasingly rich resource for learning; 3) their readiness to learn becomes oriented increasingly to the developmental tasks of their social roles; and 4) their time perspective changes from one of postponed application of knowledge to immediacy of application, and accordingly, their orientation toward learning shifts from one of subject-centeredness to one of performance-centeredness (pp. 44-45).

The term was popularized in the United States by Malcolm Knowles during the late 1960s and early 1970s and has since been referred to as a unifying principle in the broad field of adult education (Merriam, 1991; Merriam & Brockett, 1997). Knowles' changes in belief regarding the applicability of andragogy to instructional settings for adults is clearly evident when considering the titles of two of his major works: *The Modern Practice of Adult Education: Andragogy vs. Pedagogy* (1970), and *The Modern Practice of Adult Education: From Pedagogy to Andragogy* (1980). These changes also imply the situational aspects of andragogy.

Although frequently described as a theory of adult learning, its efficacy has been questioned because of the dearth of conclusive quantitative evidence supporting its use. Rachal (1983), a former student of Knowles, described "andragogy" as "a term and concept still struggling for acceptance within the field, and virtually unknown outside of it" (p. 14). In negating the need for continuing debate surrounding whether andragogy is fully accepted as a theory versus simply a method of instruction, Davenport and Davenport (1985a) emphasized that "the method must be based on the best available educational research" (p. 158). Plecas and Sork (1986) recognized the rapidly increasing number of what they termed "explanation theory/sketches" in the field of adult education inclusive of but not limited to andragogy, that lack adequate empirical testing (p. 48). Merriam (1991) wrote that "Andragogy is an area that is weak in empirical confirmation" (p. 75). While also illustrating the need for further research, Pratt (1993) concluded, "We cannot say, with any confidence, that andragogy has been tested and found to be, as so many have hoped, either the basis for a theory of adult learning or a unifying concept for adult education" (p. 21). More recently, Henschke (2011) recommends that "Continued research will help establish andragogy as a scientific academic discipline" (p. 36).

Throughout the 1980s and 1990s, however, at least 18 empirical studies were conducted on the efficacy of andragogical and pedagogical methods of instruction. According to Rachal (2002), "Unfortunately, the studies of the 1980s and 1990s relative to andragogy's effectiveness in both achievement and satisfaction provide mixed results and often 'no significant differences' emerging from variegated methodologies, and thus reveal an unstable theoretical foundation upon which to prescribe practice" (p. 224).

Perhaps the primary issue that has perpetually challenged researchers is the use of paper-pencil tests when measuring achievement. According to Rachal (2002), "andragogy eschews paper-pencil testing, yet that is the most common and presumably easiest form of determining whether the learner has mastered content" (p. 217). Even though a large number of studies have been completed on andragogy, Rachal identified just 18 that utilized experimental or quasi-experimental methods in testing its effectiveness. Of these, only four including Clark (1991), Cross (1988) and Stevens (1986), measured achievement via performance measures as opposed to paper-pencil tests. Significantly, none of these studies was conducted via a distance education delivery system.

Even though the sheer number of empirical studies that sought to measure the efficacy of andragogy increased dramatically from the 1980s to the mid 1990s, but have since slowed, Plecas and Sork (1986) recognized that "two fundamental functions which normally characterize emerging disciplines are not apparent in the adult education literature—cumulative knowledge and theory building" (p. 48). Based on his own review of selected empirical literature surrounding the efficacy of andragogy, Rachal (2002) put forth a set of seven criteria to serve as an operational definition for future researchers and practitioners. His criteria were derived from cumulative knowledge in order to address the plethora of design problems from prior studies, including but not limited to, "mixing of adults and non-adults; absence of learner control; paper-pencil tests of achievement; and questionable volunteerism of learners" (p. 213).

Although Wilson and Hayes (2002) expressed opposition to the "implicit epistemological orientation of Rachal's research agenda" (p. 174), they do clearly support his call for future andragogy researchers to utilize more consistent hypotheses and operational definitions. These former editors of *Adult Education Quarterly* rationalized their support of Rachal's agenda by concluding "the field sorely lacks depth in even its most dominant intellectual claims" (Wilson & Hayes, 2002, p. 174). Without more consistent criteria and continuing research, the science aspect of the term that Knowles defined as "the art and science of helping adults learn" (1970, p. 38), and andragogy's status as either a key method of instruction or theory on which the field of adult education in the United States was historically based, may in terms of achievement measures forever remain unsubstantiated in the empirical literature. Continuing research may in fact determine that the "science aspect" may be a chimera, like phlogiston or cold fusion, and at some point, someone needs to say, definitively, research has tried but after decades has failed to establish the superiority of andragogy as a method of instruction.

As did Knowles (1980), however, through his book *The Modern Practice of Adult Education: From Pedagogy to Andragogy,* future andragogy researchers and adult education practitioners alike must recognize that situational variables frequently limit the purist implementation of some of andragogy's assumptions. Researchers and practitioners including online learning specialists, therefore, must design their programs and protocols accordingly. According to Rachal (2002), examples of such variables include "degree of voluntariness, learner's experience of and prior knowledge of the content, the need for quality control in assessing learner outcomes, the presence or absence of institutional and professional constraints, and general course goals" (p. 224). For example, institutional constraints within colleges and universities may not allow for the implementation of learning contracts in online courses, yet options for course assignments in line with relevant curricula may be warranted.

Rachal's Proffered Criteria for Andragogy Researchers

Future andragogy research and practice may have been obscured or even clouded by Knowles and Associates' own postulations that were put forward in his edited book, *Andragogy in Action* (1984), which essentially provided a brief overview of adult education as the art and science of helping adults learn, but focused primarily on illuminating numerous applications of andragogy from the perspectives of practitioners in divergent settings ranging from business and industry, government, colleges and universities, the professions, elementary and secondary education, and remedial education. Knowles ended this seminal work by presenting brief conclusions regarding the efficacy of andragogy in various settings.

Based on former practice, he posited that the andragogical model is a "system of elements" that may be implemented in their entirety or through individual or eclectic components thereof (Knowles, et al., 1984, p. 418). Perhaps further confusing the matter, Knowles et al. (1984) recommended: "The appropriate starting point and strategies for applying the andragogical model depend on the situation. In some situations—for instance, in new institutions or programs starting from scratch—it may be appropriate to apply the model totally and at once. In most instances, however, it would probably be more appropriate to experiment by applying the model to one course or one department in an institution or a workshop or a special project (p. 418)." Of continuing difficulty for some andragogy researchers, therefore, is the fact that Knowles never fully or clearly operationalized his assumptions of andragogy for future researchers, which may have at least partially impacted the lack of comparability of empirical research conducted on the efficacy of andragogy versus pedagogy on achievement and performance as summarized by Rachal in his article titled "Andragogy's Detectives: A Critique of the Present and a Proposal for the Future" (2002).

In light of prior research on the efficacy of andragogy, Rachal (2002) suggested his seven proffered criteria. Each of these criteria should be considered by future andragogy researchers and educators to help insure that their studies or programs utilize a true andragogical approach but within situational or institutional constraints. As a result, comparability of results across studies will also be enhanced (Bradley, 2011). Rachal's criteria are labeled: voluntary participation, adult status, collaboratively determined objectives, performance-based assessment of achievement, measuring satisfaction, appropriate adult learning environment, and technical issues.

Voluntary Participation

To better comply with the assumptions of andragogy, Rachal (2002) expressed that future studies should target only participants who are willing, and even desire, to participate. Knowles, as cited in Levitt, discovered that the reason pedagogical models were less successful when applied to adults was due to the voluntary nature of most adult education (Levitt, 1979). Rachal (2002) did not provide a strict definition of "voluntary," but mentioned that participation should not be coercive and, "Under no circumstances should externally imposed negative consequences follow for nonparticipation" (p. 219). Rachal continued, "But to restrict 'voluntary' to the idea that the only legitimate benefit of andragogy would be learning for its own sake or self-actualization seems an excessive limitation" (p. 220). The study of students in andragogical settings for future studies, therefore, would benefit from the examination of:

situations such as noncredit continuing education programs where the great majority of the learners want to be there, are motivated to learn the material because it is intrinsically interesting or useful to them, and are inclined to see the learning activity as inherently valuable and not solely valuable as a means to some end (p. 220).

Adult Status

Rachal (2002) asserted that educational environments should be comprised of only adult learners, as the inclusion of non-adult learners could jeopardize the integrity of the results of such a study and render them not as applicable to the andragogy debate. Rachal explicitly wrote, "Future andragogy studies should avoid college settings if the various groups being compared are partly comprised of traditional college students" (p. 220). When college settings comprised of traditional and adult students must be used, Rachal advised the use of four different groups (pedagogical-traditional; pedagogical-adult; andragogical-traditional; and andragogical-adult). With regard to the definition of "adult" for the purpose of such studies, Rachal wrote:

For future andragogy research, 'adult' should refer to learners who have assumed the social and culturally-defined roles characteristic of adulthood and who perceive themselves to be adults, or, if those qualities are not ascertainable, learners who have achieved an age, such as 25, which would be regarded as adult irrelevant of social circumstances (2002, p. 220).

Collaboratively-Determined Objectives

Rachal (1983) described andragogy as self-directed whereas pedagogy is often seen as teacher-directed. Rachal (2002) declared that future research should use educational settings that epitomize this notion of self-direction. According to Rachal, the learner should play "a significant or even primary role in the determination of the learning objectives" (p. 221). Suggested as potential tools to achieve this end are contracts, although Rachal advised they may not work in every setting. He wrote, "A contract with predetermined objectives prescribed by the instructor does not achieve this purpose unless the learner knows those objectives beforehand and they are what attracted the learner in the first place" (p. 221). Other situations may call for collaboration between the students and the instructors regarding course objectives, or even full determination of objectives by learners in educational settings where "satisfaction" rather than "competence" is paramount (Rachal, 2002). Rachal explained the learner's role: "Andragogy researchers should seek settings in which the learner has a substantive role in some significant aspect of planning the activity or in which there is a clear, high, and pre-existing congruence between the instructor's and the learner's objectives" (p. 221).

Performance-Based Assessment of Achievement

Traditional achievement assessment techniques, such as paper-based tests, are not proffered methods of assessment for andragogical research (Rachal, 2002). Instead, Rachal recommended that future studies evaluate achievement using performance-based techniques agreed upon by both the learner and the facilitator. With respect to the learner's role, Rachal wrote:

The desirable assessment measure is demonstration of the ability to perform the learned material through a direct means, such as actually taking and printing a photograph, rather than an indirect means, such as taking a paper-pencil test on how to take and print a photograph (p. 221).

Rachal suggested that performance tests that assess the learner's ability to either complete a task (pass) or not complete a task (fail) should be considered. Both Rachal (2002) and Knowles (1980) discussed tests created by learners themselves as appropriate for andragogy research. Self-evaluations are also noted as worthy for study (Rachal, 2002). Rachal concluded that:

performance assessments, especially where what is performed is precisely the ability the learner sought in undertaking the learning experience, or at least performance tests with learner input (such as in the use of a learning contract), are more 'real world' than paper-pencil achievement tests and would be closer to the gold standard (2002, p. 222).

Measuring Satisfaction

Participant (or learner) satisfaction should be measured in all learning environments studied by andragogy researchers (Rachal, 2002). The focus of some andragogical educational settings, however, is to achieve a level of satisfaction for its learners, regardless of achievement in acquiring learned knowledge or a skill. Of these types of educational settings, Rachal wrote:

In such settings, the measurement of satisfaction is critical to the andragogy researcher. But whereas achievement need not be measured in those settings where achievement is not the primary objective, satisfaction with the learning experience should be measured in all settings (2002, p. 222).

Appropriate Adult Learning Environment

Rachal (2002) wrote, "Future andragogy studies should make every attempt to insure that both the physical and the psychological environments are as congruent as possible with Knowlesian guidelines for adult learning settings" (pp. 222-223). These types of environments are difficult to determine, but Rachal advised against conducting studies in environments, which do not exhibit such a familiarity and level of comfort with the learners. Rachal described characteristics of the facilitator usually present in appropriate adult learning environments. These characteristics include "friendliness, confidence, content knowledge, charisma, empathy, humor, expressiveness, enthusiasm, body language, fairness, respect, kindness, and understanding" (2002, p. 223).

Technical Issues

Rachal (2002) acknowledged that "ideally, random assignment of participants should occur" (p. 223), but this practice is usually an issue of practicality and thus he considers existing groups of adult learners to be acceptable for study. He expressed a need for a single facilitator of both andragogical and pedagogical instruction which "helps assure that personality variables do not confound the outcome" (p. 223), but warned that single facilitators may also display instances of bias. When two facilitators are used, they should be as similar as possible with regard to "experience, (including experience with their assigned or selected teaching methodology), general ability, content knowledge, and teaching evaluations" (p. 223). Rachal (2002) explained that other factors to consider are "adequate numbers of participants, equal and appropriate treatment duration, informed consent, comparability of groups, and so forth" (p. 224).

Empirical Studies on Andragogy in Non-College Settings

At least 10 empirical studies, largely in the form of published doctoral dissertations, have been conducted in non-college settings that assessed the effects of andragogical instructional methods on outcomes like students' academic performance, attendance, and satisfaction. However, only four of those studies, including Rosenblum and Darkenwald (1983), Madriz (1987), Ogles (1990), and Bradley (2011), afforded learners themselves with significant input in establishing learning objectives or content. Such learner involvement in planning of their own learning is a staple of the andragogical method as espoused by Knowles.

Presented here are the results from those studies most relevant to online non-formal professional development programs for adults in relation to Rachal's (2002) seven criteria. Three of the four studies were conducted prior to the formulation of Rachal's guidelines and, in fact, were used by Rachal to help determine which criteria should be specifically proffered. These studies did not suffer from a lack of "adult status" as did the vast majority of those in college settings. However, other inconsistencies with Rachal's criteria, as informed by Knowles, are identified and evaluated below.

Rosenblum and Darkenwald (1983) examined the effects of course planning on achievement and satisfaction amongst two different samples, writing, "Adult student participation in course planning did not result in higher achievement" (p. 151). In fact, the control groups in the study had higher mean scores for achievement than did the groups that underwent the course planning, but *t*-tests indicated the difference was not statistically significant. Neither was a significant difference found regarding satisfaction. Rosenblum and Darkenwald hypothesized as to why: "Extremely high motivation may have overridden any effects of the experimental treatment. In fact, the satisfaction scores were so high that the finding of no difference may have been due to ceiling effects" (p. 52). Ogles (1990) is more optimistic, since she offers some positive outcomes of andragogical instructional methods, such as learners' attendance and persistence, as described below.

Madriz (1987) studied the effects of andragogical instruction on teachers in contrast to the effects of a traditional instructional approach. The instruction was implemented as in-service training, and thus was not voluntary, which is not in line with Rachal's (2002) criteria. However, the teachers who were recipients of andragogical instructional methods played a significant role in the determination of course objectives. Madriz (1987) clarified:

The researcher explained the purpose of the meeting, involved the teachers in the process of formulating the learning objectives, and informed them of the options available in designing the learning experience and in selecting the instructional materials, techniques, and devices (p. 78).

Paper and pencil measures, which are not ideal according to Rachal (2002), were used to determine the outcomes of the various instructional approaches. Results of this study indicated statistically significant differences in the achievement and satisfaction of teachers according to instructional method. Teachers who were instructed via the andragogical approach scored higher on achievement tests and also were more satisfied than their counterparts who were instructed by non-andragogical means.

Ogles (1990) utilized learning contracts to determine the effects of an andragogical approach on the instruction of adult beginning readers. Though dropout numbers for the contractual group were not significantly less than among the control group, the contractual group did attend "significantly more bi-weekly tutoring sessions, and the contractual group also logged "significantly more weeks in the program than did the control group" (p. iv). Ogles, therefore, found that "learning contracts had a positive impact on attendance and persistence of adult beginning readers in a one-on-one volunteer literacy program" (p. iv). The implementation of learning contracts, however, did not significantly contribute to reading gains as no significant differences were found between the contractual and control groups. Contracts were used in a truly andragogical sense by some participants in this study: "some tutor-subject pairs took the contracting seriously enough to revise it according to the newly recognized needs of the student" (p. 74). However, Ogles was quick to suggest improvements regarding the learning contract.

Although the vast majority of empirical research on andragogy in non-college settings was not affected by deviances from the "adult status" required by Rachal (2002) as the research from college settings did, this research exhibited other shortcomings. Each study except for Beder and Carrea (1988) and Cross (1988) used traditional paper and pencil tests in some fashion to evaluate the effects of andragogical methods, particularly with regard to participant achievement. Rachal and Knowles prefer assessment of achievement to be performance-based rather than via "traditional" paper and pencil tests. Only three of ten studies conducted in non-college settings, Cross (1988), Ogles (1990), and Bradley (2011), implemented learning contracts, although they may not have been appropriate for all of the studies. Some of the empirical studies of andragogy in non-college settings also suffered from involuntary participation of subjects, including Cartor (1991), Madriz (1987), and White (1989).

IMPLEMENTING ANDRAGOGY IN ONLINE PROFESSIONAL DEVELOPMENT: PROOFS AND PREMISES

Today, distance education represents an ideal delivery system for non-formal professional development programs because of three primary rationales. First, participants enjoy the convenience of time and place as afforded by online learning in an age of multi-tasking and life-balance conflicts. Second, economic considerations are causing more adults to pursue online professional development opportunities rather than in-person offerings. In other words, market demand is necessitating the growth of such programs. Third, recent technological advances now allow both for-profit and non-profit providers of professional development to create new and highly interactive programs at lower costs. For example, webinars are most suitable for sharing of late-breaking or cutting-edge content. In contrast, online learning platforms allow educators to offer in-depth courses with rich content. Both the *Moodle* online learning platform and several webinar systems may be downloaded at no charge. Notably, the assumptions of andragogy may now be implemented successfully using virtually all distance education delivery systems.

Distance education can be formally defined as, "The acquisition of knowledge and skills through mediated information and instruction, encompassing all technologies and other forms of learning at a distance" (United States Distance Learning Association, 2009). In contrast, *distance learning* and *online learning* are terms used to represent "the physical separation of teachers and learners that has become popular in recent years, particularly in the United States. While used interchangeably with *distance education*, *distance learning* puts the emphasis on the learner and is especially appropriate when students take on greater responsibility for their learning as is frequently the case when doing so from a distance (Simonson, 2008, pp. 67-68)."

According to Merriam and Brockett (1997), modern "distance education reflects many of the technological advances that allow instruction to take place between geographically separated teachers and adult students" (p. 10). Because of these advances, instructors in both formal and informal distance education classrooms may replicate in a virtual learning environment the communication transactions within traditional classrooms. Likewise, the assumptions of andragogy may also be replicated through various online delivery platforms and technologies. For example, Johncock (2011) has liberally and successfully used live webinars to implement andragogy-style teaching methods in both formal and non-formal grant education programs for adults. Similar applications of relatively low-cost webinar technologies are possible spanning a wide variety of professional development topics and providers.

Cercone (2008) presented both an overview for implementing key adult learning theories within online instructional programs for adults and strategies for creating an appropriate environment based on learner needs. "The future of adult online learning research may be based on the theories discussed in this article, even though most of the theories were developed almost 20 years ago and in traditional classroom environments" (p. 151), Cercone concluded. Suggestions for implementing andragogy, described by the author as "the most comprehensive" theory (p. 150), are outlined below using Knowles' 1980 and 1984 assumptions of andragogy as an organizational tool.

Assumption One: "As individuals mature, their self-concept moves from one of being a dependent personality toward being a self-directed human being" (Knowles, 1980, p. 43).

Instructors should engage learners by serving as a guide or facilitator and provide frameworks that will encourage adult learners to become more self-directed (Cercone, 2008).

Assumption Two: "As individuals mature, they accumulate a growing reservoir of experience that becomes an increasingly rich resource for learning" (Knowles, 1980, p. 43).

Instructors should connect new information to past experiences which must be appreciated and respected as meaningful (Cercone, 2008).

Assumption Three: "As individuals mature, their readiness to learn becomes oriented increasingly to developmental tasks of their social roles" (Knowles, 1980, p. 43).

Instructors should make the relevancy of the course obvious and present goals and objectives early in the course (Cercone, 2008).

Assumption Four: "As individuals mature, their time perspective changes from one of postponed application of knowledge to immediacy of application, and accordingly, their orientation toward learning shifts from one of subject-centeredness to one of performance-centeredness" (Knowles, 1980, p. 43).

Instructors should make clear to learners how the course activities are both problem-centered and applicable to their current lives (Cercone, 2008).

Assumption Five: "The andragogical model predicates that the more potent motivators are internal—self-esteem, recognition, better quality of life, greater self-confidence, self-actualization, and the like" (Knowles, et al., 1984, p. 12).

Instructors should encourage learner reflection as a motivator. In addition, adults react more positively to learning when the environment is non-threatening (Cercone, 2008).

Blondy (2007) offered ideas similar to Cercone for implementing the assumptions of andragogy in both formal and informal online learning environments. Both authors, however, cautioned against using an overly purist or epistemological definition of the assumptions when designing online programs for adults. Instead, Cercone (2008) wrote, "Not every recommendation can be followed, but they form the basis of the author's proposal to develop online training for adults" (p. 142). For example, Cercone (2008) realized that some adults are more self-directed than others. Consequently, some of them will need assistance to become more self-directed.

Similarly, Blondy recognized Knowles' assumptions as "an ideal starting point" from which to prescribe practice. Likewise, Blondy (2007), argued for balance when implementing andragogy in a virtual environment, positing "the type of course being taught and individual student needs can help create a learner centered approach to online education" (p. 116). Though not referring specifically to nor excluding online learning, Rachal (2002) strongly argued for "certain standards" in research designs and programs involving andragogy in general while also "recognizing that mathematics-like precision is a holy grail quest" (p. 219).

Empirical Studies on Andragogy in Online Professional Development Settings

An extensive review of the literature uncovered just one previous study comparing the relative efficacy of andragogy versus pedagogy in online non-formal adult education programs that emphasize personal or professional development. This study, the first of its kind to heed all of Rachal's suggestions as far as the author was able to discover, only begins to fill a large gap in research in this field. The Bradley (2011) study compares the effectiveness of andragogical or student-centered instruction, and pedagogical or teacher-centered instruction, between staff members of nonprofit social service agencies who participate in or complete an online learning module on foundation grant writing using the two methods.

Effectiveness was measured on the basis of adult learners' reactions to instructional modules (course evaluation ratings), program completion rates, achievement growth (level of evaluative skill), and grant-writing performance scores. Although the current study was originally conceived as purely quantitative in design, two open-ended response items were included within the course evaluation instrument to add narrative depth to the quantitative results. Details and practical implications of the Bradley (2011) study follow.

Research Hypotheses

To determine the effectiveness of the two online instructional methods, four hypotheses were formed:

H_1: There will be a statistically significant difference in self-reported reaction to learning (course evaluation ratings) between staff members of nonprofit social service agencies who participate in or complete an andragogically-facilitated or a pedagogically-conducted online learning module on foundation grant writing.

H_2: There will be a statistically significant difference in program completion rates between staff members of nonprofit social service agencies who participate in or complete an andragogically-facilitated or pedagogically-conducted online learning module on foundation grant writing.

H_3: There will be a statistically significant difference in the achievement growth (level of evaluative skill) between staff members of social service agencies who participate in or complete an andragogically-facilitated or pedagogically-conducted online learning module on foundation grant writing.

H_4: There will be a statistically significant difference in performance between grant proposal scores received by staff members of nonprofit social service agencies who participate in or complete an andragogically-facilitated or pedagogically-conducted online learning module on foundation grant writing.

The Bradley study was designed to assess the reactions to learning (course evaluation ratings), completion rates, achievement growth (level of evaluative skill), and grant writing performance scores of the participants as outcomes of andragogical and pedagogical online learning modules. The researcher satisfied Rachal's (2002) seven criteria and, as such, is the first study of its kind to do so. The participants consisted exclusively of employed adult volunteers from the identified population and thus avoided having to combine adults with traditional students. The researcher served as facilitator for both the andragogical and pedagogical modules thereby avoiding personality variations as a delimitation of the proposed study. Volunteer learners were made aware of the program objectives beforehand and thus exhibited what Rachal (2002) called "a clear, high, and preexisting congruence" with them (p. 221). Even so, a learning contract that was collaboratively determined between the learner and instructor, as well as opportunities to both develop and participate in online bulletin board discussions that encourage the sharing of knowledge through experience and best practices, afforded learners in the andragogical module with avenues to identify strategies and resources for improving their own content knowledge. The performance assessment in the form of a written proposal to a foundation appropriately measured what Rachal (2002) referred to as "the ability the learner sought in undertaking the learning experience" (p. 222). Learner satisfaction was measured by course evaluation surveys and completion rates were measured empirically. The research methods comply with each of Rachal's criteria for andragogy researchers.

In particular, the volunteers for the study were recruited from among the population of approximately 673 adults who are members of a statewide association for nonprofit professionals located in the Southeastern United States. A convenience sample of 52 potential volunteers was identified. It was anticipated that attrition would result in approximately 42 to 46 total completers, or 21 to 23 per group. Approximately 673 e-mails were disseminated to the members of community-based nonprofit organizations noted previously. The purpose of the letter was to inform these agencies of the primary module objective, format, timelines, computer requirements and registration procedures. Once confirmed via e-mail, each volunteer, who included both members and other staffers, was randomly assigned to either the andragogical or pedagogical online learning module on foundation grant writing. Rachal (2002) noted that such random assignment is ideal, preferring it to in situ groups that are most commonplace in adult education research. Each module commenced during the last week of March 2009, required an estimated 16-hour commitment of time, and ended four weeks later in order to meet with time limitations of busy professionals.

The final tally resulted in at least partial data on 33 participants and included 16 subjects who received an andragogical learning module and 17 subjects who received a pedagogical learning module. Among 33 participants, 28 were also completers and included 14 subjects who received an andragogical learning module and 14 subjects who received a pedagogical learning module.

Treatment for Andragogically Facilitated Learning Module Group

1. The adult learners in the andragogical group utilized a learning contract, mutually agreed upon between the learner and facilitator, in order to select online resources and educational strategies from which to gain additional knowledge.
2. The adult learners in the andragogical group were informed of the primary learning objectives before volunteering to participate. As a result, this research study includes what Rachal (2002) described as "a clear, high, and pre-existing congruence between the instructor's and the learner's objectives" (p. 221).
3. The adult learners in the andragogical group were asked to form groups to both develop and participate in online bulletin board discussions each week, and respond to at least two other postings from classmates. Discussions related to the primary learning objectives and readings, and emphasized the sharing of learner experiences.
4. A performance assessment post-test in the form of a written proposal to a foundation appropriately measured what Rachal (2002) referred to as "the ability the learner sought in undertaking the learning experience" (p. 222). In addition, the differences in learners' pre-post abilities to score a pre-selected grant proposal measured achievement growth. Prior to and upon conclusion of each learning module, participants scored a pre-selected mock foundation grant proposal to determine whether it meets basic threshold criteria as stated in program guidelines. Achievement was measured by comparing the group scores received to the mean scores resulting from review of the proposals by two experts to determine if there was a statistically significant difference between mean group scoring by participants and experts, respectively.

To avoid the anxiety often caused by traditional paper-and-pencil tests, however, the performance and achievement assessments were scored for group comparison purposes but participants in the andragogical group received only suggestions for improvement. Finally, each participant who completed an online module was asked to submit a course evaluation instrument consisting of Likert scale items and two open-ended questions.

Treatment for Pedagogically-Conducted Learning Module Group

1. The adult learners in the pedagogical group followed a set curriculum that was developed by the instructor.
2. The adult learners in the pedagogical group were informed of the primary learning objectives before volunteering to participate.
3. The adult learners in the pedagogical group were asked to submit responses for each assignment to the instructor.
4. A performance assessment post-test in the form of a written proposal to a foundation appropriately measured what Rachal (2002) referred to as "the ability the learner sought in undertaking the learning experience" (p. 222). In addition, the learners' pre-post abilities to score a pre-selected grant proposal measured achievement levels and achievement growth. Prior to and upon conclusion of each learning module, participants scored a pre-selected mock foundation grant proposal to determine whether it met basic threshold criteria as stated in program guidelines. Achievement was measured by comparing the group scores received to the mean scores resulting from review of the proposals by two experts to determine if there was a statistically significant difference between mean group scoring by participants and experts, respectively. Finally, each participant who completed an online module was asked to submit a course evaluation instrument, consisting of Likert scale items and two open-ended questions, to measure learners' satisfaction with the course and its instructor.

Differences in group treatments between each of two online learning modules are further delineated in Table 1.

Instrumentation

A demographic questionnaire was used to gather information about each of the participants in the study. This included obtaining information regarding the participants' (1) gender, (2) educational level, (3) experience writing, and (4) winning grants over the last five years. This information was collected prior to the start of each module to verify there were no statistically significant differences between the total means for each dependant variable, when applicable, in the study as a function of learning group.

To measure reaction to learning, a course evaluation instrument similar to the one used by Strawbridge (1994) was employed. The instrument was designed to measure a learner's satisfaction with the instructor and the course requirements and procedures (Strawbridge, 1994). For the purpose of the current study, some of the questions were modified so that they related to the current study topic. In total there were 26 Likert scale items that were used on the evaluation instrument with three subscale scores being measured: (a) the perception of the personal dimension of the teacher, (b) the instructional dimension of the teacher, and (c) the course requirements and procedures (Strawbridge, 1994). Each of the questions on the course evaluation instrument used by Strawbridge was based on a 5-point Likert scale that had a minimum score of 1 (strongly disagree) and a maximum score of 5 (strongly agree). However, for the current study, the Likert scale used within the course evaluation instrument had a minimum score of 5 (strongly disagree) and a maximum score of 1 (strongly

Table 1. Design elements for andragogical and pedagogical online learning modules on grant writing

	Andragogical Module	Pedagogical Module
Climate	Collaborative via e-mails and informal phone discussions with facilitator.	Instructor-oriented.
Planning	Mutual planning with facilitator of individualized objectives, resources, and evidence of learning.	Planning completed by instructor.
Diagnosis of Needs	Mutual diagnosis of needs with facilitator.	Needs determined by instructor.
Formulation of Objectives	Negotiation of learning contract with facilitator based on mutually identified needs.	Prescribed by instructor.
Design	Problem units.	Content units.
Activities	Experiential online bulletin board discussions based on readings and learner experiences to promote inquiry and sharing of best practices.	Readings and responses to instructor via online assignment submission box.
Evaluation	Collaborative through submission of mutually agreed upon evidence via learning contract and review of achievement and performance assessments by experts to ensure comparability.	Exclusively by experts via review of achievement and performance tests to ensure comparability of results.

agree), with a rating of 1 representing a higher or better course evaluation rating.

The mean and standard deviation of Likert scale items for reaction to learning (course evaluation ratings) among participants and completers in two learning modules are presented in Tables 2 and 3, respectively.

Evaluation of Test Reliability

The reliability of Likert scale measures on course evaluations was analyzed and the results are presented in Table 4. As can be seen, the reliability of the Likert scale course evaluation scores had a Cronbach's alpha value of .92. The high Cronbach's alpha confirmed the reliability of the course evaluation instrument as employed in this study.

Research Question One: Results

H_1 was proposed to compare the two groups' course evaluations. A one-way ANOVA revealed that the average response scales (1 = strongly agree; 5 = strongly disagree) for course evaluations among participants in the andragogical cohort (M=33.19, SD = 7.29) were lower and clearly represented *better* course evaluation scores than among the pedagogical cohort (M=36.56, SD = 10.28); however, the difference as a function of learning group failed to reach the significance level .05, with F (30, 1) = 1.15, p = .293.

A one-way ANOVA also revealed that the average response scales (1 = strongly agree; 5 = strongly disagree) for course evaluations among *completers* in the andragogical cohort (M=33.43, SD=7.22) were lower and therefore represented slightly better course evaluation scores than among the pedagogical cohort (M=34.43, SD=8.92), however the difference as a function of learning group failed to reach thesignificance level .05 with F (26, 1) = .10, p = .75.

Research Question Two: Results

H_2 was proposed to compare the two groups' program completion rates. Among 16 subjects participating in the andragogical learning module, 14 (87.5%) completed the program and 2 (12.5%) did not. Among 17 subjects participating in the pedagogical learning program, 14 (82.4%) completed the program and 3 (17.6%) did not. A chi-square test revealed that program completion

Table 2. Course evaluation for andragogical and pedagogical online learning modules among program participants

Item	Section	N	Mean	SD
Instructor prepares well for each class	Andragogical	16	1.25	.447
	Pedagogical	16	1.69	1.014
Instructor effectively communicates subject matter	Andragogical	16	1.38	.500
	Pedagogical	16	1.63	.885
Instructor stimulates interest in subject	Andragogical	16	1.44	.512
	Pedagogical	16	1.31	.602
Instructor seems enthusiastic about subject	Andragogical	16	1.31	.704
	Pedagogical	16	1.25	.447
Instructor welcomes student questions	Andragogical	16	1.00	.000
	Pedagogical	16	1.25	.577
Instructor stimulates thought/expression	Andragogical	16	1.50	.516
	Pedagogical	16	1.69	.602
Instructor is helpful outside of class, when requested	Andragogical	16	1.13	.342
	Pedagogical	16	1.38	.619
Instructor cares about students' learning	Andragogical	16	1.25	.447
	Pedagogical	16	1.50	.632
Instructor welcomes different points of view	Andragogical	16	1.56	.814
	Pedagogical	16	2.25	.856
Instructor is sympathetic/courteous	Andragogical	16	1.25	.577
	Pedagogical	16	1.31	.479
Instructor demonstrates high standards	Andragogical	16	1.81	.750
	Pedagogical	16	2.06	.854
Instructor is free from annoying mannerism	Andragogical	16	1.75	.775
	Pedagogical	16	2.06	.998
Instructor ranks among/best teacher ever	Andragogical	16	2.56	.512
	Pedagogical	16	2.56	.727
I would sign up for another course from instructor	Andragogical	16	1.56	.629
	Pedagogical	16	1.69	.946
Course seemed well planned	Andragogical	16	1.38	.500
	Pedagogical	16	1.63	.885
Course requirements are reasonable	Andragogical	16	1.56	.512
	Pedagogical	16	1.44	.512
Assignments contribute to course objectives	Andragogical	16	1.44	.512
	Pedagogical	16	1.19	.403
Textbook contributes to course	Andragogical	16	1.38	.619
	Pedagogical	16	1.31	.479
Types of measurement are reasonable	Andragogical	16	1.56	.629
	Pedagogical	16	2.13	.885

continued on following page

Table 2. Continued

Item	Section	N	Mean	SD
Instructor used a variety of teaching methods	Andragogical	16	1.88	.719
	Pedagogical	16	2.19	.911
I learned much in this course	Andragogical	16	1.75	.577
	Pedagogical	16	1.63	.619
I would recommend this course and its instructor	Andragogical	16	1.50	.516
	Pedagogical	16	1.44	.512

Range of Item Responses: 1= strongly agree; 5 = strongly disagree

rates did not differ significantly as a function of learning group, with χ^2 (1) = .17, p = .68.

Research Question Three: Results

H_3 was proposed to compare the two groups' achievement growth (level of evaluative skill) over time. A one-way ANOVA revealed that the average achievement growth of 20.93 (SD = 29.89) among participants in the andragogical cohort was slightly lower than among the pedagogical cohort (M = 22.67, SD = 27.42), however the difference as a function of learning group failed to reach the significance level .05, with F (28, 1) = .03, p =.87.

A one-way ANOVA also revealed that the average achievement growth of 22.71 (SD = 30.17) among completers in the andragogical cohort was slightly higher than among the pedagogical cohort (M = 22.28, SD = 28.41), however the difference as a function of learning group failed to reach the significance level .05, with F (26, 1) = .001, p = .97.

Research Question Four: Results

H_4 was proposed to compare the two groups' grant writing performance scores. A one-way ANOVA revealed that the average grant writing performance score of 73.0 (SD = 25.83) among participants in the andragogical cohort was slightly lower than among the pedagogical cohort (M=74.33, SD = 20.86), however the difference as a function of learning group did not reach the significance level .05 with F (28, 1) = .02, p =.88.

A one-way ANOVA also revealed that the average performance score of 72.50 (SD = 26.72) among completers in the andragogical cohort was identical to the mean score among the pedagogical cohort (M = 72.50, SD = 20.35). Therefore, there was no significant difference in average performance scores as a function of learning group, with F (26, 1) = 0.00, p = 1.00.

Qualitative Results

Within the Bradley study, two open-ended questions were included as part of the course evaluation instrument that measured reaction to learning for all participants in the andragogical and pedagogical online learning modules, as follows:

- "As an adult learner, do you enjoy learning from the experiences of fellow adults when participating in non-formal, non-credit learning opportunities? Please explain your answer briefly and provide rationale (There are no right or wrong answers)."
- "Did participation in this course encourage you to consider pursuing additional non-formal non-credit continuing education opportunities in the future? Please explain your answer briefly and provide rationale (There are no right or wrong answers)."

Table 3. Course evaluation for andragogical and pedagogical online learning modules among program completers

Item	Section	N	Mean	SD
Instructor prepares well for each class	Andragogical	14	1.29	.469
	Pedagogical	14	1.50	.855
Instructor effectively communicates subject matter	Andragogical	14	1.43	.514
	Pedagogical	14	1.43	.646
Instructor stimulates interest in subject	Andragogical	14	1.50	.519
	Pedagogical	14	1.14	.363
Instructor seems enthusiastic about subject	Andragogical	14	1.36	.745
	Pedagogical	14	1.21	.426
Instructor welcomes student questions	Andragogical	14	1.00	.000
	Pedagogical	14	1.14	.363
Instructor stimulates thought/expression	Andragogical	14	1.50	.519
	Pedagogical	14	1.64	.633
Instructor is helpful outside of class, when requested	Andragogical	14	1.14	.363
	Pedagogical	14	1.29	.611
Instructor cares about students learning	Andragogical	14	1.21	.426
	Pedagogical	14	1.43	.646
Instructor welcomes different points of view	Andragogical	14	1.57	.852
	Pedagogical	14	2.14	.864
Instructor is sympathetic/courteous	Andragogical	14	1.29	.611
	Pedagogical	14	1.21	.426
Instructor demonstrates high standards	Andragogical	14	1.86	.770
	Pedagogical	14	2.00	.877
Instructor is free from annoying mannerism	Andragogical	14	1.71	.726
	Pedagogical	14	1.93	.997
Instructor ranks among/best teacher ever	Andragogical	14	2.50	.519
	Pedagogical	14	2.50	.760
I would sign up for another course by instructor	Andragogical	14	1.57	.646
	Pedagogical	14	1.57	.938
Course seemed well planned	Andragogical	14	1.36	.497
	Pedagogical	14	1.50	.855
Course requirements are reasonable	Andragogical	14	1.57	.514
	Pedagogical	14	1.36	.497
Assignments contribute to course objectives	Andragogical	14	1.43	.514
	Pedagogical	14	1.14	.363
Textbook contributes to course	Andragogical	14	1.36	.633
	Pedagogical	14	1.36	.497
Types of measurement are reasonable	Andragogical	14	1.57	.646
	Pedagogical	14	2.00	.784

continued on following page

Table 3. Continued

Item	Section	N	Mean	SD
Instructor used a variety of teaching methods	Andragogical	14	1.93	.730
	Pedagogical	14	2.07	.829
I learned much in this course	Andragogical	14	1.79	.579
	Pedagogical	14	1.50	.519
I would recommend this course and its instructor	Andragogical	14	1.50	.519
	Pedagogical	14	1.36	.497

Range of Item Responses: 1= strongly agree; 5 = strongly disagree

Qualitative results among participants indicated that 15 of 16 (93.8%) in the andragogical module and 11 of 15 (73.3%) in the pedagogical module who responded to the first open-ended question, stated affirmatively their enjoyment of learning from the experience of others while participating in non-formal non-credit learning opportunities. In addition, 13 of 14 participants (92.9%) in the andragogical module and 14 of 16 (87.5%) in the pedagogical module who responded to the second open-ended question stated affirmatively that by participating in an online course they were more likely to pursue future educational opportunities relative to grant seeking of a similar nature.

Suggestively, nearly all responses from both participants and completers in each cohort favored andragogical teaching methods as an impetus for lifelong learning. For example, one participant from the andragogical cohort who failed to complete all program activities, and was therefore not a completer but still valued the program, expressed that she would likely pursue additional non-formal learning opportunities in the future by stating:

Yes, this was a first time for me to do a course completely online. An impediment on my computer was making my first experiences very challenging. I probably would not have persevered had the instructor not let me know that he tried my ID and password at home, and they worked. I then knew the problem of access was at this end and forged ahead. Once I got the hang of it, it was a very pleasant experience. I learned a lot about navigating around the system. I have lots of time when I can have access to the office computers because I live where I work and can stay at it in the quiet of the night as long as I please.

Similarly, regarding the collaborative or facilitative nature of goal setting and pursuit of future non-formal learning opportunities, another participant in the andragogical cohort who was also considered a completer wrote:

Yes, participation in this course did encourage me to pursue additional non-formal non-credit continuing education opportunities in the future. This is why I hope to have many opportunities to be guided by Joe in the future for continuing education opportunities. I like that the course was free, that the instructor was so helpful, and that he seemed to really care that I had a good learning experience. He was very personable, and had a great attitude about helping me reach my learning goals.

These qualitative differences, in conjunction with the clearly more favorable aggregated mean course evaluation ratings among participants in the andragogical module as compared to the pedagogical module, indicate the same trend noticed by Wilson (2005). Even though a statistically significant improvement in student performance was not gained from the andragogical model in

Table 4. Internal coefficient alphas for Likert scale course evaluations

Cronbach's Alpha	Item N
.92	22

the current study, a higher level of learner satisfaction with the course and its instructor among participants in the andragogical module was supported. Adults with such high levels of learner satisfaction frequently pursue related educational opportunities as truly lifelong learners. Though not significant, the average total response scales (1 = strongly agree; 5 = strongly disagree) for course evaluations among participants in the andragogical cohort (M = 33.19) were much lower and clearly represented better course evaluation ratings than among the pedagogical cohort (M = 36.56).

It seems plausible, therefore, to assume that better overall mean course evaluation scores on Likert scales as submitted by participants within the andragogical as compared to the pedagogical module at least partly resulted from the various experiential or knowledge sharing and collaborative planning activities that were afforded to the andragogical cohort. The validity or meaning of these better group scores, therefore, may be enhanced through triangulation of results even though the related hypotheses were not significant.

FUTURE TRENDS

Recommendations for Andragogy Researchers

Need for Further Research

An extensive review of the literature uncovered just one previous study comparing the relative efficacy of andragogy versus pedagogy in online non-formal adult education programs that emphasize personal or professional development. The Bradley study, the first of its kind to heed all of Rachal's suggestions as far as the author was able to discover, only begins to fill a large gap in research in this field. The findings call for additional studies of andragogy versus pedagogy in online non-formal professional development and continuing education programs. As Rachal posited, such settings may be most conducive to implementing a more purist definition of andragogy, while keeping in mind that programs must be designed at levels that best meet the unique needs of participants. Though both Blondy (2007) and Cercone (2008) cautioned against using an overly purist or epistemological definition of andragogy in both practice and research settings, Rachal's criteria for researchers also recognizes different levels of practice based on situational contexts yet allows for a comparison of results across studies.

Six Additional Recommendations for Researchers

1. The authors recommend that future studies in this field utilize more consistent operational definitions and comply with Rachal's (2002) seven criteria when possible based on situational contexts as previously defined.
2. The authors also recommend that future studies use higher level statistical procedures in interpreting findings and synthesizing data into conclusions. In addition to ANOVA, MANOVA, and MANCOVA specifically are recommended. Other methods, such as structural equation modeling, should also be considered.
3. A larger N might allow for additional types of non-parametric analyses such as bootstrap or jackknife.
4. Future researchers, as did Bradley, should utilize performance testing rather than paper and pencil tests. Performance testing is more suited to reflecting the results of andragogical learning and may be easier to implement

in non-formal professional development programs than in for-credit classes.

5. Future researchers should consider using both quantitative and qualitative mixed-method techniques to support results via triangulation. For example, future studies could include interviews as well as open-ended survey questions and utilize the resulting phenomenological analysis to triangulate the quantitative results. In addition, qualitative and case studies are recommended, especially when results across similar studies of andragogy in online professional development programs are compared through a meta-analysis.
6. Finally, more research on the effects of andragogy in online, non-formal professional development or continuing education settings is needed, as this study only begins to bridge the gap in literature in this particular field.

Recommendations for Adult Education Managers and Practitioners

Six Recommendations for Practitioners

1. Determine adult learners' experiences, if any, with online learning prior to enrollment. Offer learners a pre-training tutorial program in online learning as well as individualized assistance throughout the term of the professional development program when necessary.
2. Online learning offers the convenience of time and place. Even so, online learning may not be suited for all adult learners. It is, however, a viable option.
3. Offer alternative learning activities, based on individual learner input or contracts, that meet with the varying learning styles or preferences of adult learners.
4. When using learning contracts, provide instructions and work with each learner individually to maximize utility based on their own expressed gaps in knowledge or needs.
5. Recognizing the rich life experiences of adults and providing them with individualized assistance when necessary based on those experiences may impact learner satisfaction and program completion rates. This may be especially true for adults lacking computer literacy and/or experience with online education.
6. Adult learners, including those who participate in online learning for professional development, tend to prefer learning from the experiences of others. But this is not always the case.

CONCLUSION

Ultimately, it was found that compared to the number of empirical studies of andragogical methods in college settings, the effect of andragogical teaching strategies in non-college settings was understudied and poorly understood, creating a gap in research that Bradley (2011) attempted to fill, in compliance with Rachal's seven criteria. The gap is even more obvious when considering the lack of studies dealing with non-formal education or professional development, especially those utilizing online delivery systems. In the case of online learning, the Bradley (2011) study was the first that utilized all of Rachal's criteria. While the case cannot yet be made that andragogy is a superior instructional methodology, it is at least an equal to the traditional pedagogical method in many settings, as the majority of contemporary studies have found no statistically significant differences in outcomes resulting from the two contrasting methods.

Unique limitations exist in both quantitative and qualitative research. The authors feel that future andragogy researchers should utilize a combination of quantitative and qualitative research methods resulting in findings with both statistical rigor and narrative depth. The question of andragogy versus pedagogy, however, is as much a question of how adults learn as it is a question of how much.

Those online learners who are most satisfied with their educational experience, as was the case with andragogical participants in the Bradley study, are likely to participate in future non-formal professional development opportunities. Clearly, the pursuit of lifelong learning also serves to increase one's cumulative knowledge across a lifetime. Adult educators who seek to create a student-centered learning environment also serve to nurture the pursuit of lifelong learning opportunities among their adult learners. The assumptions of andragogy are an excellent starting point for creating such welcoming and nonthreatening learning environments.

REFERENCES

Beder, H., & Carrea, N. (1988). The effects of andragogical teacher training on adult students' attendance and evaluation of their teachers. *Adult Education Quarterly*, *38*, 75–87. doi:10.1177/0001848188038002002

Blondy, L. C. (2007). Evaluation and application of andragogical assumptions to the adult online learning environment. *Journal of Interactive Online Learning*, *6*(2), 116–130.

Bradley, J. B. (2011). A comparison of course completion, satisfaction, achievement, and performance among non-profit professionals who complete andragogical or pedagogical online learning modules on grant writing. *Dissertation Abstracts International*, *71*(8).

Cartor, R. A. (1991). A comparison of andragogy and pedagogy: Assessing the relationship between individual personality differences, learning styles, and training types. *Dissertation Abstracts International*, *51*(7).

Cercone, K. (2008). Characteristics of adult learners with implications for online learning design. *AACE Journal*, *16*(2), 137–159.

Clark, J. A. (1991). Self-directed learning skills and clinical performance: A comparison of traditionally taught and learning contract-taught nursing student. *Dissertation Abstracts International*, *41*(7).

Cross, D. L. (1988). The influence of self-directed learning contracts versus a passive therapy treatment in a back rehabilitation program. *Dissertation Abstracts International*, *50*(5).

Davenport, J., & Davenport, J. A. (1985a). A chronology and analysis of the andragogy debate. *Adult Education Quarterly*, *35*, 152–159. doi:10.1177/0001848185035003004

Davenport, J., & Davenport, J. A. (1985b). Knowles or Lindeman: Would the real father of American andragogy please stand up. *Lifelong Learning*, *9*(3), 4–5.

Henschke, J. (2011). Considerations regarding the future of andragogy. *Adult Learning*, *22*(1), 36.

Isenberg, S. (2007). *Applying andragogical principles to internet learning*. Amherst, NY: Cambria Press.

Johncock, P. (2011). *Issues in teaching and learning about grants. Journal of the Grant Professionals Association* (pp. 99–110). Kansas City, MO: Grant Professionals Association.

Knowles, M. S. (1970). *The modern practice of adult education: Andragogy vs. pedagogy*. Chicago, IL: Association Press/Follett.

Knowles, M. S. (1980). *The modern practice of adult education: From pedagogy to andragogy. Englewood Cliffs, NJ*. Cambridge: Prentice Hall.

Knowles, M. S. (1984). *Andragogy in action: Applying modern principles of adult learning*. San Francisco, CA: Jossey-Bass.

Levitt, L. (1979). Critique: Andragogy revisited part II. *Adult Education Quarterly*, *30*, 52–57. doi:10.1177/074171367903000104

Madriz, L. (1987). The relative effectiveness of two different approaches to in-service training of primary teachers in Venezuela. *Dissertation Abstracts International*, *56*(11).

Merriam, S. B. (1991). How to research procedures in knowledge. In Peters, J. M., & Jarvis, P. (Eds.), *Adult Education* (pp. 42–65). San Francisco, CA: Jossey-Bass.

Merriam, S. B., & Brockett, R. G. (1997). *The profession and practice of adult education*. San Francisco, CA: Jossey-Bass.

Ogles, M. T. (1990). The outcomes of using "learning contracts" with adult beginning readers in a one-on-one literacy program. *Dissertation Abstracts International*, *51*(6).

Plecas, D. D., & Sork, T. J. (1986). Adult education: Curing the ills of an undisciplined discipline. *Adult Education*, *37*, 48–62. doi:10.1177/0001848186037001005

Pratt, D. D. (1988). Andragogy as a relational construct. *Adult Education Quarterly*, *38*, 160–172. doi:10.1177/0001848188038003004

Pratt, D. D. (1993). Andragogy after 25 years. In Merriam, S. B. (Ed.), *An Update on Adult Learning Theory* (pp. 15–23). San Francisco, CA: Jossey-Bass.

Rachal, J. R. (1983). The andragogy-pedagogy debate: Another voice in the fray. *Lifelong Learning, the Adult Years*, *6*(9), 14–15.

Rachal, J. R. (2002). Andragogy's detectives: A critique of the present and a proposal for the future. *Adult Education Quarterly*, *52*, 210–227. doi:10.1177/0741713602052003004

Rosenblum, S., & Darkenwald, G. G. (1983). Effects of adult learner participation in course planning on achievement and satisfaction. *Adult Education Quarterly*, *33*, 147–153.

Simonson, M. (2008). *Distance learning: Key terms you might want to know*. Fort Lauderdale, FL: Nova Southeastern University.

Stevens, M. M. (1986). Oral hygiene instruction: Assessment of andragogical and pedagogical methods of adult patient instruction. *Dissertation Abstracts International*, *46*(9).

Strawbridge, W. G. (1994). The effectiveness of andragogical instruction as compared with traditional instruction in introductory philosophy courses. *Dissertation Abstracts International*, *55*(11).

United States Distance Learning Association. (2009). *Distance learning definition.* Retrieved from http://www.usdla.org/html/aboutUs/vmd.htm

White, B. A. (1989). Selected instructional strategies, learner outcome, and attitudes of adult learners in a mandatory education setting. *Dissertation Abstracts International*, *49*(8).

Wilson, A. L., & Hayes, E. R. (2002). From the editors: The problem of (learning in-from-to) experience. *Adult Education Quarterly, 52,* 173-175.

Wilson, L. S. (2005). A test of andragogy in a post-secondary educational setting. *Dissertation Abstracts International*, *66*(7).

Chapter 12
Technology Use and Research Approaches for Community Education and Professional Development:
Diffusion of Innovation from Medical Schools to Phlebotomy Certificate Programs

Grace L. Reynolds
California State University – Long Beach, USA

ABSTRACT

This chapter describes the use of technology in the education of health care providers. Advances in technology have led to consistent use of on-line course content such as posting of syllabi, course materials, videos, and other training materials, and deployment of on-line quizzes, tests, and certification exams that take advantage of the high availability of Internet access in most educational institutions. The diffusion of other more advanced technology, such as virtual patients, and virtual worlds, such as Second Life, is much less available across training programs for health care providers. This chapter explores differences across training programs for health care providers ranging from medical education of surgeons through the education of lower-level technicians such as phlebotomists. Consistent with the theory of diffusion of innovations, early adopters of advanced technology for student training are those with the resources who recognize the relative advantages in the technology, such as medical schools. Community education also plays a role in the diffusion of innovation in the training of lower-level technicians and clinicians as community education recognizes that processes of empowerment and social justice are important components of community capacity building. The community education philosophy is consistent with the institutions, such as community colleges, that have the largest role in training health care providers and technicians. Despite advances in the use of technology for the delivery of didactic materials, there are still challenges in the acquisition of clinical skills.

DOI: 10.4018/978-1-4666-2955-4.ch012

INTRODUCTION

Health care delivery involves a multidisciplinary approach to the strategic management of health care organizations for the delivery of health care. Ultimately, the purpose of health care is to take a patient who is experiencing compromised health and, through a process of service delivery, turn the sick patient into a well person. Key to this process is diagnosis: accurately identifying the organ system or systems involved in the disease process and taking corrective action based on the diagnosis. In most cases, making an accurate diagnosis will depend on obtaining specimens of blood, urine, other fluids and/or tissue from the patient. Traditionally, this process of obtaining specimens has been performed by several types of health care workers including nurses, phlebotomy technicians, as well as physicians. Specimens are then turned over to clinical laboratory personnel for the performance of diagnostic testing.

Training in the duties of a phlebotomy technician is usually obtained through a certificate program offered at a community college or other university setting. Requirements for certification as a phlebotomy technician vary from state to state, but usually include time spent in the classroom learning material in a didactic format, as well as "clinical" time spent under supervised conditions to obtain experience drawing blood from live human beings. An intermediate step in the process may involve the use of mannequins that are equipped with veins and upon which actual draws may be performed through an artificial device that allows for the flow of water dyed red to simulate the flow of blood through veins and arteries. Depending upon the certificate programs' requirements, and state certification regulations, candidates for the certificate in phlebotomy technician may also be required to have college credit hours in human biology, anatomy, and physiology.

Phlebotomy Technician (PBT) is an entry level position. At the lowest levels, possessing a "limited phlebotomy" certificate allows the individuals to perform skin punctures only. This generally involves the use of a lancet or other sharp device on a fingertip to obtain one to two drops of blood for rapid testing. Phlebotomy technician I requires at least 40 hours of didactic training in addition to 50-100 blood draws using venipuncture techniques under supervision. It is the first rung on a career ladder that leads from phlebotomy technician I, to phlebotomy technician II, individuals who are trained to perform skin punctures, venous blood collection, and arterial draws; to Medical Laboratory Technologist (MLT), and Clinical Laboratory Scientist (CLS). A CLS credential can eventually lead to supervisory and higher level positions in health care and laboratory settings.

Certification and licensing of phlebotomists occurs at the state level, and PBT education has changed recently due to several factors. In California in 1999, a phlebotomist admitted to reusing needles on many patients due to concerns about costs. This led to a reevaluation of public health laws governing the training and certification of phlebotomists in California. The original law dated from 1973 and allowed individuals to perform phlebotomy with only 10 hours of training by any physician who was willing to sign a certificate, accompanied by three venipunctures and three skin punctures. These minimal requirements led to complaints that programs of poor quality conducted as "weekend" programs were proliferating, complaints from patients about inept phlebotomists, and complaints from phlebotomists themselves that these minimal programs did not lead to employment in most health care settings. California changed its regulations governing phlebotomy training and certification in response to the media coverage and criticism of the California Department of Public Health after the 1999 incident. Assembly Bill (AB) 1557 required more education and training for certification as a phlebotomist, as well as passing an examination and making continuing education a requirement for recertification.

At the national level, the National Accrediting Agency for Clinical Laboratory Science (NAACLS) provides certification for phlebotomy technicians as well as clinical laboratory personnel, such as cytogenetic technicians, clinical laboratory technicians, and medical laboratory technicians (www.naacls.org). NAACLS sets accreditation standards for training programs as well as offering continuing education through on-line delivery for clinical laboratory personnel.

Training for phlebotomists is complex. Phlebotomists require knowledge of basic human anatomy; blood-borne pathogens and basic infection control techniques; professional ethics and regulatory issues; blood collection equipment; venipuncture procedures; pre-analytical complications that can cause errors in blood collection; specimen handling and processing; and special procedures for blood collection from various types of patients, including children and geriatric patients (Garza & Becan-McBride, 2010).

Medical education of general and specialist physicians and nurses can be an expensive and labor-intensive process. Like education of lower-level phlebotomy technicians, training for physicians and nurses requires a combination of didactic and clinical training, involving hands-on experience with patients. Technology has played a part in the training of these health care providers for more than a decade, and advances in both medical knowledge and the technology available has seen medical schools take the lead in the use of technology for medical education. Because technology can be expensive to acquire and integrate into teaching, academic medical centers have taken the lead largely because of the resources they are able to command. Most phlebotomy technician training takes place at the community college level and they generally have many fewer resources available to them. As technology gets adopted at the higher levels of medical education, successful innovations are much more likely to be adopted into teaching environments with fewer resources.

The objectives of this chapter are:

1. To provide an overview of the state of the art with respect to the use of technology in the area of medical education, including phlebotomy training;
2. Explore the accessibility of these technological advances to students training to be phlebotomy technicians and how the diffusion of innovations theoretical framework can guide our understanding of the use of technology for training across a wide spectrum of medical providers;
3. Demonstrate the application of social cognitive learning theory and the psychomotor domain of learning to training for phlebotomy technicians and the role of technology, including simulations, in enhancing the development of psychomotor skills;
4. Finally, examine the future trends in training for phlebotomists.

BACKGROUND AND THEORETICAL FRAMEWORKS

Diffusion of Innovation Theory

The diffusion of innovations literature notes that technological and other innovations' success is usually the result of early adopters of the innovation acting as intermediaries between the developers of the innovation and the general public. The theory states that identification of these early adopters is one way that marketers of new technologies can gain acceptance for innovations that might not otherwise enjoy broad use in the general population. These early adopters actually facilitate transmission of the new technology into mainstream use.

Rogers' provides a framework for understanding how individuals make decisions about whether to adopt a new technology or not (Garza & Becan-McBride, 2010). According to this paradigm, the new innovation is evaluated with respect to the relative advantages that it offers the user over the current technology and how difficult or complex the new innovation is to learn and use. In higher education, Smith (2012) notes that in addition to individual recognition of the merits of the new technology for accomplishing learning outcomes, other factors must be present. These other factors include support from upper management, institutional infrastructure to accommodate the use of the innovation, and recognition of the time needed for faculty and others to acquire the skills needed to use the innovative technology (Lipley, 2011). These other factors are supported by research by Surry, who applied Rogers' theory specifically to technology adoption in higher education. Surry's model consists of seven elements, including resources, infrastructure, people, policies, learning, evaluation and support (Second Life, 2008) and his model is supported by real-world application of it to higher education adoption of Web-based educational resources (Hansen, 2008).

Community education is a type of learning rooted in the process of empowerment and social justice, where each community makes decisions about its developing needs and engages members of the community in capacity building and lifelong learning (Fantini, 1980). Community education providers are represented in health care provider training by the community colleges across the national that are providing technical training to a variety of technicians, who may or may not go on for advanced academic degrees.

Because of the cost of technology, early adopters of technology within medical education were the medical schools tasked with training a wide variety of physicians. Physicians training for practice in rural areas of the United States and around the world had early exposure to telemedicine applications (Boulanger, Kearney, Ochoa, Tsuei, & Sands, 2001; Chen, Guo, Chen, Chen, & Kuo, 2001; Cullen, Hart, Whitcomb, & Rosenblatt, 1997; LeBlanc, 2000). The applications ranged from dermatology to ear-nose-throat assessments; the common factor in these early telemedicine demonstration projects was health conditions that could be visually assessed by the use of cameras by a specialist located in an urban area, and a patient residing in a rural area (Tieman, 2000). Telemedicine increased access for rural patients to health care specialists without the need for expensive travel and the associated costs of transportation and waiting time to see the specialist in person. The early use of telemedicine was quickly adopted by nonmedical providers, including social workers and behavioral health specialists in a variety of ways, including distance counseling and assessment (Jennett, Hall, Morin, & Watanabe, 1995; Kellogg, Lamb, & Lukefahr, 2000). One early initiative to fund telemedicine ventures in rural and frontier areas of the United States was funded by the National Library of Medicine (Pearce, et al., 2001). This project used store-and-forward technology in the diagnosis of ear problems in rural Alaska Native children.

These early telemedicine projects were integral to community education efforts to engage and empower these rural and distant communities in the use of technology to improve the health of individuals in these communities. Much research has made it clear that the individual health is linked to community health and community health is affected by collective beliefs and attitudes within those communities (Witmer, Seifer, Finocchio, Leslie, & O'Neil, 1995). The success of these early projects helped motivate communities to adopt telemedicine approaches.

Theories of Adult Learning and the Psychomotor Domain

The most relevant theory of learning with respect to the acquisition of the skills needed to perform phlebotomy is Bandura's theory of social cognitive theory (Boulos, Hetherington, & Wheeler, 2007). Central to Bandura's theory is the belief that human learning takes place through the imitation of behavior observed in others. Learning clinical skills, that is, skills whereby a medical paraprofessional or professional achieves rapport with a patient for the purpose of intervening to assist in the improvement in the patient's health, is usually a process of observing and then practicing these skills. Such clinical skills are a complex mix of communication and rapport-building skills involving interactions with patients as well as technical skills that allow the phlebotomist to accomplish the basic takes of phlebotomy, i.e., obtaining blood specimens. These technical skills are part of the psychomotor learning domain, initially identified by Bloom.

Bloom's taxonomy (Bloom, Englehart, Furst, & Krathwolh, 1956) is used to identify the learning outcomes associated with various learning activities. Care must be taken to ensure that the cognitive level has been identified prior to determining whether technology use is an appropriate delivery system for the materials (McGee & Kanter, 2011). It is also necessary to determine the level of affective domain engagement required of the student in developing and using technology in education. For example, many on-line learning modules may require only the lowest levels of the cognitive and affective domains, *receiving and/or responding*, where the student will passively read materials or respond to quizzes and tests deployed via the computer (Krathwolh, Bloom, & Masia, 1964).

The psychomotor domain describes the ability to manipulate tools and objectives in this learning domain usually focus on development and mastery of skills that make one proficient in the use of tools, instruments, and technology. This psychomotor domain may be particularly important in medical education, especially in the development of surgical skills for physicians, or technical skills for other types of health care providers, such as imaging technicians; clinical laboratory personnel who must operate a variety of instruments and equipment; and phlebotomists, who must learn to perform venipuncture on a variety of patients, including children, the elderly, and the obese. While the psychomotor domain was identified by Bloom and his colleagues, psychomotor taxonomies have been created by a number of others (Dave, 1970; Harrow, 1972).

The psychomotor domain includes seven domains in which the student moves through beginning to mastery levels in their ability to perform physical tasks with their applicability to phlebotomy training. These seven domains and their application to phlebotomy training are summarized in Table 1.

In medical education, clinical experience is usually the arena in which the student learns to perform increasingly complex levels of examination and intervention with the patient in the psychomotor domain. Clinical experiences are generally overseen by a more experienced practitioner who acts as a preceptor for the student. The phlebotomist or other clinician-in-training must be able to practice their skills on live patients under structured supervision before they can be licensed to intervene with patients on their own. As noted above, the process of applying technical skills to a live patient involves the learning and practice of clinical skills generally acquired through modeling the behavior of more experienced clinicians in their dealings with patients.

The importance of interactions with live patients cannot be stressed enough.

While there have been no reported deaths from phlebotomy, per se, there is liability for the phlebotomist, and risk for the patients, associated with performing and undergoing venipuncture. Minor risks include bruising at the puncture site and fainting. However, a more serious risk is that the phlebotomist will hit a nerve instead of a vein, or hit a nerve in addition to the vein. The major indication that this has occurred is pain shooting up through the patient's arm. Phlebotomists are trained to immediately remove the needle if this should occur. Unfortunately, there are instances where phlebotomists have continued with the blood draw even when the patient expresses extreme discomfort from hitting a nerve. This can cause nerve damage and litigation has occurred

Table 1. Mapping the psychomotor domain to phlebotomy skills

Levels	Description	Specific to Phlebotomy
Perception	The ability to use sensory cues to guide motor activity; key words for this level include chooses, describes, detects, identifies, selects.	Make an assessment of the patient and patient's veins, identifying correct vein for venipuncture; selects the correct equipment for venipuncture.
Set	Readiness to act. Knows and acts upon a sequence of steps in a process. Key words include begins, moves, proceeds, reacts, shows, states.	Goes through the steps of initiating venipuncture, including application of the tourniquet and preparation of the blood collection equipment; reacts to patient cues, such as nervousness.
Guided Response	This covers the early stages in learning a complex skill that includes trial and error. Adequacy of performance is achieved by practicing. Key words include copies, traces, follows, reproduces, responds.	Follows procedures for obtaining blood specimen and minimizing pre-analytical errors, achieving successful venipuncture on patients.
Mechanism	This is the intermediate stage in learning a complex skill. At this level, learned responses have become habitual and movements can be performed with confidence. Key words include assembles, calibrates, constructs, dismantles, measures, mixes.	Calibrates behavior to successfully perform venipuncture on a wide variety of patients, taking into account correct selection of needle gauge, correct type of tube, and correct blood collection device, including butterflies.
Complex Overt Response	This is the level of proficiency at which the student can now perform motor acts that involve complex movement patterns. This includes performance without hesitation and automatic performance. Keywords are the same as mechanism but include adjectives to indicate that performance is faster, better, more accurate.	Accomplishes venipuncture on a wide variety of patients using a wide variety of equipment and blood collection devices rapidly, so that accurate performance is faster than at the novice level; the number of false attempts, missed veins, will be minimized at this level of proficiency. Phlebotomist communicates confidence to patients at this high skill level.
Adaptation	Skills at this level are well developed and the individual can modify movement patterns to fit special requirements. At this level, the individual can respond to unexpected experiences. Keywords include adapts, alters, revises, changes, varies.	Phlebotomist is able to initiate and achieve venipuncture on a wide variety of patients and is called upon by co-workers to assist them with difficult blood draws. Phlebotomist manages venipuncture on patients classified as difficult including overweight and obese, injection drug users, cancer patients, elderly patients, on whom routine venipuncture can be difficult for those at the novice level. Also manages patients who faint and other unexpected or unforeseen events during venipuncture and can alter behavior to accommodate non-routine events.
Origination	At this highest level of physical performance, the individual will create new movements and patterns to fit a particular situation or specific problem. Keywords include builds, composes creates, designs, initiates.	At this level, the phlebotomist can begin to incorporate newer technologies into routine venipuncture; for example, vein finding devices, which are not part of routine phlebotomy training.

in some cases. As with most medical procedures, education to prevent hitting a nerve during venipuncture is preferred.

Problems that arise from mistakes in phlebotomy are numerous, making training in good phlebotomy technique essential to the profession. Contamination of blood specimens can occur if skin is not cleansed adequately to remove surface bacteria. Contamination of the blood specimen can be costly for the health care facility if blood specimens must be-redrawn; other problems from contaminated specimens include costs associated with misdiagnosis and treatment of patients who do not, in fact, have a bacterial infection.

If tourniquets are left on longer than one minute, hemolysis can occur; this means that the red blood cells break apart and are destroyed. The consequences of hemolysis are many and include false test results for potassium, magnesium iron, lactate dehydrogenase, phosphorus, ammonia, and total protein (Garza & Becan-McBride, 2010). Reasons for hemolysis include using the incorrect gauge of needle for the blood draw (either too small or too large); shaking tubes to mix the collected blood with the clotting factor or anticoagulant, rather than gently inverting the tubes; incorrectly obtaining a blood specimen from an IV catheter in hospitalized patients; or using outdated equipment, such as syringes (Garza & Becan-McBride, 2010). A recent study of phlebotomy performed in an emergency room setting revealed that a majority of physician residents working in that emergency department had very little training in phlebotomy, and many specimens obtained by them became haemolysed because of lack of training and poor practices (Lipley, 2011).

As noted above, nerve damage can occur if the phlebotomist hits a nerve during venipuncture and fails to immediately remove the needle, potentially causing long-term nerve damage. This is most likely to occur with patients for whom venipuncture is difficult and the phlebotomist makes the mistake of ignoring the patient's indicators of sharp pain from hitting the vein in order to obtain the blood specimen. Some of the knowledge and skills can be facilitated by technology, such as training videos, on-line continuing education modules, applications, or "apps" deployed via cellphones for preparing for certification exams, and case studies and simulations can help increase clinical decision-making skills. However, ultimately, health care providers must be able to work effectively with human patients.

The use of simulated environments and virtual patients has begun to accelerate the process of training clinicians in health care. The use of simulated clinical training environments also has the advantage that there is lower liability in these settings than in traditional clinical settings with live patients. Simulated environments will never totally replace clinical settings but can prepare students for what they will eventually encounter.

A Hierarchy of Increasingly Sophisticated Technology

The use of technology in the education of health care providers at all levels covers a broad range of applications. The levels of increasing sophistication in technology use may be conceptualized as being parallel to the levels of learning in Bloom's taxonomy. At the lowest level is the basic use of the Internet to deploy on-line resources. The next level of technology in medical provider education involves the use of software and other equipment to simulate the health care environment. The third or most sophisticated level of technology use involves virtual patients and virtual worlds, requiring both hardware and software.

Basic Internet Tools

Currently the use of basic Internet technology in academic health care training varies widely (McGee & Kanter, 2011) in scope and focus, but generally includes the use of on-line assessments of student competencies and Web-based instructional materials.

There are many examples of the use of basic Internet technology in health care education (Dror, Schmidt, & O'Connor, 2011; Gattoni & Tenzek, 2010). For example, Johns Hopkins University provided Universal Serial Bus (USB) drives to medical residents in order to facilitate their reading of important research articles in the field of medicine (Chahla, Eberlein, & Wright, 2010). This effort was successful in that all the residents who received the USB used it and most were highly satisfied with this effort to increase the residents reading of the scientific literature. This study is in contrast to others that have found that medical students seldom access peer-reviewed literature articles via university libraries and on-line database searches (Judd & Kennedy, 2011). Medical students appear to need increased instruction on the use of available on-line resources, especially for identifying and using peer-reviewed journal articles on evidence-based medical practice (Judd & Kennedy, 2011). Increasingly there is a gap between the information available to medical students and physicians and their ability and/or ability and desire to access it (Masic, et al., 2011).

This is one area where technology can assist the cognitive domain.

Continuing Medical Education (CME) is another area where technology has been employed with good results. The ability to meet medical continuing education requirements using the computer and Web-based applications has been embraced because of the ability of the physician to complete the CME units at a time that is convenient for professionals with busy schedules and for whom travel for CME units delivered in traditional formats (face-to-face) requires time away from patients and clinical practice. A study of data from the Accreditation Council for Continuing Medical Education (ACCME) provides recent information on the growth of the on-line CME market (Harris, Sklar, Amend, & Novalis-Marine, 2010). Currently, on-line CME comprises around 10 percent of all CME activities, with conferences and trainings conducted in person still constituting the bulk of these activities. However, the potential growth of this market is expected to be huge in the coming years, mainly because of convenience and low cost for participants associated with on-line CME. The quality of the on-line CMEs that will be available in the future is also expected to reflect growing trends in the delivery of on-line educational materials in general, as professional education companies expand their services in the area of on-line CMEs.

The current preference of physicians for in-person conferences and training opportunities is not unusual given that medical and other students exhibit similar preferences for in-person classes (Locatis, et al., 2006). Face-to-face instruction offers more opportunity for interaction, both with the instructor and peers; however, on-line instructional formats for courses also have advantages of flexibility for when course material can be completed.

The Center for Phlebotomy Education provides educational materials for phlebotomists in several forms. The Abbreviated Teaching Modules (ATMs) are available on-line for the use of educators and supervisors. These ATMs are files in .pdf format. Each ATM includes a short, one-page overview of a phlebotomy topic and a one-page multiple choice test and answer key. The Center for Phlebotomy Education (CPE) (www.phlebotomy.com) also has a wide range of resources available for those beginning a program in phlebotomy, looking for continuing education credits, or for supervisors of phlebotomy teams who need training resources. The CPE has a mission of providing accurate information on blood specimen collection and to improve the status of the phlebotomy profession; overall their mission is "providing education materials and resources to those who perform, teach, or supervise blood specimen collection procedures" (www.phlebotomy.com/About-us.cpe). CPE maintains the "Phlebotomy Channel" which provides phlebotomy education "on-line, on-demand, on the mark" and Abbreviated Teaching Modules (ATMs), all at some cost.

The American Society for Clinical Pathologists (ASCP) provides on-line training materials for phlebotomists and others who have passed the ASCP national certification exam. These on-line training modules are available for recertification to members who have paid the required fees. The National Accrediting Agency for Clinical Laboratory Science (NAACLS) is the largest national accrediting body for phlebotomy certificate programs. NAACLS provides many on-line tools for phlebotomists preparing for state and national licensing examinations through their website www.naacls.org as well as continuing education training for phlebotomists and other clinical laboratory personnel.

Several providers of medical waste and biohazard incineration services, such as Stericycle, Inc. also provide on-line resources for routine training issues mandated by the Occupational Safety and Health Administration (OSHA). Topics covered by these educational providers can be found in Table 2.

The website www.flashcard.com is another on-line resource for phlebotomy students. This is

Table 2. Topics covered by phlebotomy education providers

Topic	Educational Website	Type of Learning Activity
The Order of Draw	Center for Phlebotomy Education (CPE) (www.phlebotomy.com)	.pdf files of One-page scenarios with 1-10 multiple choice and true/false questions with answer key
Hematoma Prevention	CPE	.pdf files as above
Tourniquet Time	CPE	.pdf files as above
Needle stick Prevention	CPE	.pdf files as above
Hemolysis	CPE	.pdf files as above
Patient Identification	CPE	.pdf files as above
Acceptable Sites for Venipuncture	CPE	.pdf files as above
Blood Cultures Done Right	CPE	.pdf files as above
Hemoconcentration: What is it?	CPE	.pdf files as above
The Aggressive Patient	CPE	.pdf files as above
Communicating with Elderly Patients	CPE	.pdf files as above
Non-verbal Communication: What Message Are You Projecting?	CPE	.pdf files as above
Therapeutic Drug Monitoring and Peaks and Troughs	CPE	.pdf files as above
Basic Venipuncture	CPE	On-line video (30 minutes)
Preventing Pre-analytical Errors	CPE	On-line video (39 minutes)
Avoiding Phlebotomy-related Lawsuits	CPE	On-line video (36 minutes)
Skin Punctures & Newborn Screens	CPE	On-line video (32 minutes)
Arterial Blood Gas Collection	CPE	On-line video (29 minutes)
Pre-analytical Variables Affecting Laboratory Testing and the Outpatient Experience	American Society for Clinical Pathology (ASCP) https://www.ascp.org /services/research.aspx	On-line training module; Membership log-in required
Patient Identification: Risks and Consequences	ASCP	On-line training module; Membership log-in required
Improving Job Satisfaction: Harnessing the Strengths of Generations	ASCP	On-line training module; Membership log-in required
Signage in the Specimen Collection Waiting Room	ASCP	On-line training module; Membership log-in required
Laboratory Challenges for Blood Samples Collected from Central Lines	ASCP	On-line training module; Membership log-in required
Improving Quality Indicators by Replacing Emergency Department-Based Phlebotomy with Laboratory-Based Phlebotomy	ASCP	On-line training module; Membership log-in required
Managing Warfarin Treatment: Multiple Time-Dependent Reversal Options	ASCP	On-line training module; Membership log-in required
Pathology: Error Reduction in an Error-Prone Environment	ASCP	On-line training module; Membership log-in required
Blood-Borne Pathogens – OSHA training	Stericycle, Inc. www.stericycle.com/bbp	On-line training module; Log-in password required

a free, open source website where you can access flashcards on the types of questions that are relevant for phlebotomy certification. Flashcard.com is not limited to phlebotomy flashcards, but provides a forum for flashcard learning for Certified Professional Accountants (CPA), medical students, and just about any other paraprofessional or professional that requires a certification test. Any individual can create their own flashcards and deploy them at flashcard.com, creating a virtual learning community of individuals seeking to pass certification exams.

Simulations in Medical Education

Professional organizations are taking the lead in promulgating the development and deployment of technology for education in the medical field. For example, several organizations, including the American College of Obstetricians and Gynecologists (ACOG), the American Institute of Ultrasound in Medicine and the World Health Organization have offered opinions on the use of ultrasound simulators accompanied by a manikin or computer-based simulation software compared to traditional use of standardized patients in conjunction with standard ultrasound diagnostic equipment (Akins & Ho, 2009). The increased popularity of the use of computer software and simulation along with the increasing use of hand-held sonography machines in clinical practice indicates that an approach that mixes both the use of simulation as well as traditional standardized patients may result in the best student outcomes in the area of medical imaging.

Similar issues are found in the use of technology in the education of surgeons (Cristancho, Moussa, & Dubrowski, 2011). It is necessary to ensure that the training needs of the students are what drive the use of technology for surgical simulations, not the other way around. In addition, assessment of student outcomes with respect to cognitive and technical skills and an overall assessment of the effectiveness of simulation programs are needed. Simulations should focus on assisting students in acquiring "optimal mental representations that they will remember and use in practice," not simply optimizing the realism of the simulation learning tools (Dror, et al., 2011).

Simulations can also be focused on non-clinical interpersonal skills. For example, the Institute of Medicine recently recommended that medical students be trained not just in clinical competencies but also in skills needed to function as part of an interdisciplinary or "inter-professional collaboration" (Bridges, Davidson, Odegard, Maki, & Tomkowiak, 2011, p. 6035). Patient care is increasingly complex and patient care coordination across specialist team members is becoming the norm in medicine. Simulations in interdisciplinary team activities may include activities in leadership and communication. Typically, simulations of leadership and communication skills do not require technology, but rather seek to simulate the team experience within the context of the classroom. These simulations include opportunities to role-play and interact with team members in a variety of contexts.

Virtual Patients, Virtual Worlds

Virtual worlds, such as Second Life, the 3D virtual world created Linden Life and available to the general public (Second Life, 2008), is also increasingly being adapted in the education of physicians and other health care practitioners. Participants create an avatar and enter the Second Life (SL) virtual world for purposes of interacting with other participants, learning, and in many cases building parts of the virtual world as part of the learning exercises (Hansen, 2008). Many medical schools have now incorporated SL into physician and other health care professionals' training, with mixed results. Among the possible uses for SL for health care provider training include browsing information available in 3-D virtual libraries; developing social skills by socializing and interacting with other people using realistic

3-D avatars; learning clinical skills through virtual simulations of the functioning of parts of the body, designed so that the student's avatar can enter the organ or organ system and view their functioning in 3-D; attending live events, such as lectures, thus participating in learning communities; and other applications (Boulos, et al., 2007). For example, using SL, researchers at San Jose State developed the Heart Murmur Sim, which allows students to test their skills at identifying the various sounds of different types of heart murmurs. Based on sound files from a virtual stethoscope project, the Heart Murmur Sim is but one example of how SL's virtual world can be incorporated into clinical education (Boulos, et al., 2007).

Research into the use of SL and other virtual training methods has suffered from small sample sizes and methodological issues, especially the choice of outcomes to be measured by the research effort, and interpretation of the findings with respect to the outcomes studied. For example, most samples are convenience samples of students readily available to the researcher, and for surgical simulations, samples can be as small as 10 medical students (Hassinger, et al., 2010; Schlickum, et al., 2011; Schwaab, et al., 2011) though samples greater than 100 medical students have been achieved (Beermann, et al., 2010; Fritz, et al., 2011). In some instances, students have been randomized to receive testing based on a 3-D versus a 2-dimensional anatomical model, and while students receiving the 3-D variations performed better on testing, male students appeared to do better overall compared to female students. Reasons for this possible gender difference in learning outcomes are not clear.

FUTURE DIRECTIONS

The didactic portion of the training for phlebotomists consists of three major strands: 1) the basic sciences necessary to understand the purposes of blood testing, 2) the correct procedures and skills needed to ensure successful and safe venipunctures and skin punctures, 3) the acquisition of communication and clinical skills, understanding of special procedures, various environments and medico-legal issues affecting phlebotomists.

In their training programs, students are first introduced to the role of phlebotomists in health care. The basic sciences are introduced (both through material covered in the basic phlebotomy course and in other required courses such as an introduction to human biology and anatomy and physiology courses) and communication skills are practiced in both discussion and in role-playing of case studies. Basics of microbiology and immunology are a natural lead-in to infections control and safety issues in the laboratory, as well as hospital and other health care settings. Students are then ready to learn phlebotomy procedures. They practice locating veins and performing venipuncture on simulated veins in several different types of demonstration models. While acquiring skills with models, students also learn about special collection procedures, transportation, and handling procedures for specimens, quality management, and legal issues affecting phlebotomists.

Successful learning of content material and skills is generally assessed by quizzes and a final exam, written assignments and direct observation with feedback via peers and instructor checklists.

The clinical portion of training consists of: 1) phlebotomy skill development needed to insure successful and safe venipuncture and skin puncture procedures, 2) development in applying communication skills introduced in didactic section, and 3) development of appropriate attitudes and awareness of the hospital environment, which will enable the phlebotomist to perform safely within the hospital and laboratory standards.

The future of technology in the training of phlebotomists has two main trajectories: (1) improvements in the tools that phlebotomists have to assist them in obtaining specimens from patients; and (2) the technology used in the educational setting to help them improve their overall knowledge and skills for interacting with patients.

Technology is currently available to assist phlebotomists with finding veins. AccuVein Incorporated markets the AccuVein AV300; the Venoscope II Transilluminator is another device currently being marketed through medical supply vendors. These devices are based on technology that capitalizes on the fact that hemoglobin found in red blood cells absorbs infrared light. These devices are held 5 to 7 inches from the skin; they detect the difference in hemoglobin concentration between the veins and the surrounding skin, and project an image of the veins on the skin above them. With the veins easily visible to the phlebotomist, the placement of the needle is made that much easier. Due to cost (retail approximately $4500), these devices are not in general use in phlebotomy certificate programs, though videos demonstrating their ease of use can be found on manufacturers' websites (www.accuvein.com). These devices make it very easy to find veins that are hard to see or feel. They can be used as a hand-held device or attached to a phlebotomy chair or hospital bed for "hands free" use. Most of the devices run on batteries so do not need to be plugged in to electrical outlets, and they do not come into contact with patient skin, so there is no need for sterilization between patients.

The diffusion model is based on "early adopters" embracing technological innovations. New ideas and practices originate or enter communities from some external source. These external sources can be mass media and professional organizations. Adoption of the new idea or practice then flows through interpersonal contact networks. The rate of diffusion is influenced by the perceived characteristics of the innovation such as relative advantage, compatibility, observability, and complexity, radicalness, and cost. Diffusion occurs over time and individuals can be classified as early or late adopters. Individuals pass through stages during the adoption process typically classified as (1) knowledge, (2) persuasion, (3) decision, (4) implementation or trial, and (5) confirmation.

Educational institutions have clearly embraced a variety of technological innovations to bring the content typically taught in face-to-face courses to a wider audience. At the most basic level, these innovations include a variety of on-line course materials (syllabi, lectures and lecture notes, quizzes and tests) and the on-line formats include both text and video components. Over the past decade, the early adopters of these on-line teaching technologies have convinced the majority of educators to adopt them, and following Rogers's conceptual framework of the diffusion of technological innovations, their worth has been confirmed. Lifelong learning continues to be facilitated by community education efforts. Recently, Harvard University and the Massachusetts Institute of Technology began offering free on-line access to course materials. While this access does not currently lead to granting of a degree or course credit, EdX as the effort is called uses the Internet to make materials from current courses available at no cost to anyone with an Internet connection (Sherriff, 2012). Currently these materials are limited to written materials and videos produced by current faculty at these institutions (Trumbull, 2012).

However, other technological teaching aids still exist in the earlier stages of diffusion. For example, the use of virtual patients and virtual worlds (such as Second Life) as approaches to teaching has not yet been confirmed in their adoption. The costs of these technologies, in both budgets and time spent learning how to best use them for achieving education outcomes, are generally high. Individual phlebotomy instructors may incorporate these virtual worlds into their classrooms on a case-by-case basis but large-scale adoption will be rare for the foreseeable future. It is far more likely that in resource constrained environments, faculty will seek to obtain the newest tools, such as vein finders, rather than seek to expand their teaching to include virtual patients and virtual worlds, such as Second Life. They are also much more likely to find support for new equipment such as the vein finders from their administration as these items do not require the kind of technological infrastructure that maintaining virtual patients or virtual worlds require.

In summary, many technological innovations have been incorporated into training of health care providers. The teaching and learning of clinical skills comprised of both communication and rapport building skills, combined with technical skills for handling the instruments and tools of health care is complex. While many of these technological attempt to find an intermediary (such as a model or virtual patient) for students to practice on before they perform specimen collection on live patients, ultimately these devices cannot completely replace training with and on live human patients.

REFERENCES

Akins, R., & Ho, H. (2009). Clinical simulation in modern teaching and training of sonography in obstetrics and gynecology. *Donald School Journal of Ultrasound in Obstetrics and Gynecology*, *3*(4), 17–21. doi:10.5005/jp-journals-10009-1030

Beermann, J., Taetzlaff, R., Bruckner, T., Schoebinger, M., Muller-Stich, B. P., & Gutt, C. N. (2010). Three-dimensional visualization improves understanding of surgical liver anatomy. *Medical Education*, *44*(9), 936–940. doi:10.1111/j.1365-2923.2010.03742.x

Bloom, B. S., Englehart, M. D., Furst, E. J., & Krathwolh, D. R. (1956). *Taxonomy of educational objectives: The classification of educational goals: Handbook 1: Cognitive domain*. New York, NY: Lognmans Green.

Boulanger, B., Kearney, P., Ochoa, J., Tsuei, B., & Sands, F. (2001). Telemedicine: A solution to the followup of rural trauma patients? *Journal of the American College of Surgeons*, *192*(4), 447–452. doi:10.1016/S1072-7515(01)00796-7

Boulos, M. N. K., Hetherington, L., & Wheeler, S. (2007). Second life: An overview of the potential of 3-D virtual worlds in medical and health education. *Health Information and Libraries Journal*, *24*, 233–245. doi:10.1111/j.1471-1842.2007.00733.x

Bridges, D. R., Davidson, R. A., Odegard, P. S., Maki, I. V., & Tomkowiak, J. (2011). Interprofessiona collaboration: Three best practice models of interprofessional education. *Medical Education Online*, *16*, 6035–6050. doi:10.3402/meo.v16i0.6035

Chahla, M., Eberlein, M., & Wright, S. (2010). The effect of providing a USB syllabus on resident reading of landmark articles. *Medical Education Online*, *15*, 4639–4642. doi:10.3402/meo.v15i0.4639

Chen, H. S., Guo, F. R., Chen, C. Y., Chen, J. H., & Kuo, T. S. (2001). Review of telemedicine projects in Taiwan. *International Journal of Medical Informatics*, *61*(2-3), 117–129. doi:10.1016/S1386-5056(01)00134-4

Cristancho, S. M., Moussa, F., & Dubrowski, A. (2011). A framework-based approach to designing simulation-augmented surgical education and training programs. *American Journal of Surgery*, *202*, 344–351. doi:10.1016/j.amjsurg.2011.02.011

Cullen, T. J., Hart, L. G., Whitcomb, M. E., & Rosenblatt, R. A. (1997). The national health service corps: Rural physician service and retention. *The Journal of the American Board of Family Practice*, *10*(4), 272–279.

Dave, R. H. (1970). Psychomotor levels. In Armstrong, R. J. (Ed.), *Developing and Writing Educational Objectives* (pp. 73–108). Tucson, AZ: Educational Innovators' Press.

Dror, I., Schmidt, P., & O'Connor, L. (2011). A cognitive perspective on technology enhanced learning in medical training: Great opportunities, pitfalls and challenges. *Medical Teacher*, *33*, 291–296. doi:10.3109/0142159X.2011.550970

Fantini, M. D. (1980). Towards a definition of community education. *Community Education Journal*, *7*, 11–14.

Fritz, D., Hu, A., Wilson, T., Ladak, H., Haase, P., & Fung, K. (2011). Long-term retention of a 3-dimonsional educational computer model of the larynx: A follow-up study. *Archives of Otolaryngology--Head & Neck Surgery*, *137*(6), 589–603. doi:10.1001/archoto.2011.76

Garza, D., & Becan-McBride, K. (2010). *Phlebotomy handbook: Blood specimen collection from basic to advanced* (8th ed.). Upper Saddle River, NJ: Pearson Education.

Gattoni, A., & Tenzek, K. E. (2010). The practice: An analysis of the factors influencing the training of health care participants through innovative technology. *Communication Education*, *59*(3), 263–273. doi:10.1080/03634521003605808

Hansen, M. M. (2008). Versatile, immersive, creative and dynamic virtual 3D healthcare learning environments: A review of the literature. *Journal of Medical Internet Research*, *10*(3), 26. doi:10.2196/jmir.1051

Harris, J. M., Sklar, B. M., Amend, R. W., & Novalis-Marine, C. (2010). The growth, characteristics, and future of online CME. *The Journal of Continuing Education in the Health Professions*, *30*(1), 3–10. doi:10.1002/chp.20050

Harrow, A. J. (1972). *A taxonomy of the psychomotor domain*. New York, NY: D. McKay Company.

Hassinger, J. P., Dozois, E. J., Holubar, S. D., Camp, J. C., Farley, D. R., & Fidler, J. L. (2010). Virtual pelvic anatomy simulator: A pilot study of usability and perceived effectiveness. *The Journal of Surgical Research*, *161*(1), 23–27. doi:10.1016/j.jss.2009.06.016

Jennett, P. A., Hall, W. G., Morin, J. E., & Watanabe, M. (1995). Evaluation of a distance consulting service based on interactive video and integrated computerized technology. *Journal of Telemedicine and Telecare*, *1*(2), 69–78.

Judd, T., & Kennedy, G. (2011). Expediency-based practice? Medical students' reliance on Google and Wikipedia for biomedical inquiries. *British Journal of Educational Technology*, *42*(3), 351–360. doi:10.1111/j.1467-8535.2009.01019.x

Kellogg, N. D., Lamb, J. L., & Lukefahr, J. L. (2000). The use of telemedicine in child sexual abuse evaluations. *Child Abuse & Neglect*, *24*(12), 1601–1612. doi:10.1016/S0145-2134(00)00204-0

Krathwolh, D. R., Bloom, B. S., & Masia, B. B. (1964). *Taxonomy of educational objectives: The classification of educational goals: Handbook II: The affective domain*. New York, NY: Longman Green.

LeBlanc, A. (2000). Louisiana rural health access program. *The Journal of the Louisiana State Medical Society: Official Organ of the Louisiana State Medical Society*, *152*(2), 89–93.

Lipley, N. (2011). Analysis. *Emergency Nurse*, *19*(7), 9.

Locatis, C., Gaines, C., Gill, M., Carney, J., Foster, J., McCall, V., & Woods, M. (2006). A blended training approach using videoconferencing for distance education. *Journal of the Medical Library Association*, *94*(4), 464–467.

Masic, I., Pandza, H., Toromanovic, S., Masic, F., Sivic, S., Zunic, L., & Masic, Z. (2011). Information technologies (ITs) in medical education. *Acta Informatica Medica*, *19*(3), 68–78. doi:10.5455/aim.2011.19.68-79

McGee, J. B., & Kanter, S. L. (2011). How we develop and sustain innovation in medical education technology: Keys to success. *Medical Teacher, 33*, 279–285. doi:10.3109/0142159X.2011.540264

Pearce, F. W., Fisher, D. G., Fenaughty, A., Berman, M., Ferguson, S., Reynolds, G., & Statz, D. (2001). Alaska telemedicine testbed project: The evaluation of narrow bandwidth telemedicine in frontier Alaska. *Telemedicine Journal and e-Health, 7*(2), 141.

Schlickum, M., Hedman, L., Enochsson, L., Henningsohn, L., Kjellin, A., & Fellander-Tsai, L. (2011). Surgical simulation tasks challenge visual working memory and visual-spatial ability differently. *World Journal of Surgery, 35*(4), 710–715. doi:10.1007/s00268-011-0981-2

Schwaab, J., Kman, N., Nagel, R., Bahner, D., Martin, D. R., & Khandelwal, S. (2011). Using second life virtual simulation environment for mock oral emergency medicine examination. *Academic Emergency Medicine, 18*(5), 559–562. doi:10.1111/j.1553-2712.2011.01064.x

Second Life. (2008). *Second life*. Retrieved from http://webcitehttp://secondlife.com

Sherriff, L. (2012). Harvard and MIT create EdX to offer free university courses to the world. *The Huffington Post*. Retrieved from http://www.huffingtonpost.co.uk

Tieman, J. (2000). Monitoring a good opportunity: Telemedicine grows as method to reach poorly served regions. *Modern Healthcare, 30*(43), 75–78, 80.

Trumbull, M. (2012). Harvard and MIT to offer online courses: A step in lowering college costs? *Christian Science Monitor*. Retrieved from http://www.cnbc.com

Witmer, A., Seifer, S. D., Finocchio, L., Leslie, J., & O'Neil, E. H. (1995). Community health workers: Integral members of the health care work force. *American Journal of Public Health and the Nation's Health, 85*(8), 1055–1058. doi:10.2105/AJPH.85.8_Pt_1.1055

Chapter 13
Using Information and Communication Technology to Maximize Workforce Readiness

Merideth Dee
Florida Atlantic University, USA

ABSTRACT

The following chapter will provide a general discussion regarding the use of Information and Communication Technology (ICT) and how ICT can be used to help prepare students for the demands of the workforce. Additionally, the chapter will explore why ICT fluency is an important factor in preparing students for the demands of the workforce. Furthermore, the chapter will review the literature and empirical research concerned with: attitudes toward the use of ICT, the value of using ICT with regards to workforce readiness and professional development, how different learning environments, such as blended-learning, e-learning, m-learning, virtual learning communities, and social interaction impact workforce readiness, and the theories to consider when designing multimedia and why multimedia can help to prepare students for the workforce.

INTRODUCTION

Information and Communication Technology (ICT) has become an extremely popular tool used in educational learning environments. ICT can help supplement learning as well as learning activities, which can ultimately help prepare students for the time when they enter the workforce. ICT is the combination of Information Technology (IT) and communication technologies. Both IT and communication technologies include different forms of technology that allow for communication. Such examples include: the use of the computer, the Internet, cellular phones, and varied digital

DOI: 10.4018/978-1-4666-2955-4.ch013

communication and multimedia technologies. Many researchers contend that today's students are fully capable of using ICTs and are prepared to enter the workforce. Other researchers argue that today's students are not fully prepared for the demands that today's technology-rich workforce entails and reason that "the ability to use Information and Communications Technology (ICT) is now assumed by most commentators to be a prerequisite to living and working in the 'information society'" (Selwyn, 2003). As such, the use and growth of information and communication technologies have influenced the approaches in which students learn and the methods in which instructors teach. Furthermore, the growing use of ICT in our global society has increased the expectation that students will possess a high degree of ICT proficiency upon entering the workforce.

Students who are entering the workforce today are said to be skilled and proficient with the use of ICT. These students, or Digital Natives as some of the literature has named them, are said to be proficient with ICT because they have grown up using it. This, however, may not be the case. Regardless of whether or not Digital Natives truly "exist" (Brown & Czerniewicz, 2010; Junco & Mastrodicasa, 2007; Kennedy, Judd, Churchward, Gray, & Krause, 2008; Palfrey & Gasser, 2008; Prensky, 2001; Selwyn, 2008) as there is an ongoing debate regarding the generalizability of this term, for the purposes of this chapter students who were born between 1980 and the early 2000s (Palfrey & Gasser, 2008) and who have essentially not known a time when ICT was not available for their use, will be referred to as Digital Natives. Digital Natives therefore are said to be "students [who] *think and process information fundamentally differently* from their predecessors" (Prensky, 2001, p. 1). Moreover, it is argued that Digital Natives will enter higher education and the workforce with knowledge regarding ICT that previous generations of learners will not possess as these Digital Natives will have "spent their entire lives surrounded by and using computers, videogames, digital music players, video [cameras], cell phones, and all the other toys and tools of the digital age" (Prensky, 2001, p. 1). Digital Natives are said to acquire knowledge in a distinctive fashion (largely using ICT as it is argued), and therefore, it is important to consider that it may be impossible to make such a daring statement regarding how and why Digital Natives acquire information. One cannot generalize that all Digital Natives learn the same way, i.e., by using ICT, without empirical research to support such a statement. Therefore, as Digital Natives become the workforce majority, it is important for educators to focus upon the research regarding how ICT can be used to help augment learning and help prepare Digital Natives for the demands of the workforce.

Adult learners, adults who are continuing their education for professional development (or changing their career for example), also have the ability to enter today's workforce. One of the main goals of this chapter is to discuss the use of ICT in helping to prepare students for the workforce. However, one of the main factors regarding how prepared a student (Digital Native or adult learner) might be for the workforce has to do with how fluent a student is in their use of ICT. As the global use of ICT continues to mature, educators have the complicated task of keeping students up to date and competent with new technologies. Meanwhile, educators must effectively clarify why ICT is an important aspect in their education. Furthermore, educators should also aim to help students understand the importance of being fluent with ICT upon entering the workforce. Sardone agrees, stating: "organizations need individuals with higher-order IT competencies since they depend on IT as a conduit to innovation, transformation, and competition in a global society" (Sardone, 2011, p. 102).

Students, both Digital Natives and adult learners, will need to be fluent with the use of ICT in order to think critically about their work and use ICT to help solve real world problems. Knowing the "basics" of how to navigate a social networking site, like Facebook, or play a game on a cellular phone, or perform a basic Google search, is insufficient for an intense ICT work environment. ICT fluency allows students to "capture, process, store, and transfer information which in turn enables them to focus on information content, communication, analysis, information searching, and evaluation" (Madigan, Goodfellow, & Stone, 2007, p. 410). Fluency, not simply a basic understanding, is critical for success in an ICT environment. Therefore, the following chapter will discuss why using ICT, and teaching students to use ICT, is important for workforce readiness; as well as the importance of ICT fluency and workforce readiness. Specifically the chapter will provide the following: (1) a discussion regarding students' attitudes toward the use of ICT in education and the workplace, (2) a discussion addressing the value of using ICT, (3) the types of ICT learning environments that can be used to maximize workforce readiness, and (4) a brief discussion of the specific multimedia design theories that can be used in the creation of ICT training tools that may help to prepare students for the demands of the workforce.

BACKGROUND

Digital Natives are said to possess specific characteristics, and among these characteristics include the idea that Digital Natives have a cutting-edge intellect and an advanced skill level with ICT. Due to the 'advanced knowledge' regarding ICT, Digital Natives are therefore thought to have specific learning styles, which are the result of their abundant use of ICT (Bennett, Maton, & Kervin, 2008). Additionally, Digital Natives are said to "focus on social interaction and 'connectedness' with friends, family, and colleagues, and preferring group-based approaches to study and social activities" (McMahon & Pospisil, 2005, p. 421). They are also described as proficient in multitasking behavior, depend on ICT for social interaction, and are experimental learners (Bennett, et al., 2008; Judd & Kennedy, 2011; Oblinger & Oblinger, 2005). However, educators must remember that Digital Natives' use of (and fluency with) ICT is not universal. There are studies that show (see Ramanau, Hosein, & Jones, 2010) that students use ICT for different reasons. Some use ICT for learning and a moderate amount of ICT for social purposes. However, the use of ICT can vary with age, gender, and even socio-economic status (Brown & Czerniewicz, 2010; Kennedy, et al., 2008; Selwyn, 2008). Perhaps it is strategic for educators to consider that Digital Natives are not actually as digitally native as currently believed. It is possible that these Digital Natives simply do not use ICT as actively as they could (or should) to best enhance their education and to better prepare themselves for the workforce.

As stated earlier, Digital Natives are not the only learners who can enter today's workforce. Adult learners also have the ability in today's global economy to enter or return to the workforce. Therefore, it is important to understand the characteristics of adult learners and why it is important for adult learners to also be fluent in the use of ICT, and for them to understand how ICT is related to the demands of today's workforce environment. Just one of the many theories regarding adult education states that adult learners bring a considerable amount of experience to learning environments (Dee, 2011; Merriam & Caffarella, 1999). Knowles (1980) and Merriam & Caffarella, (1999) discuss the different principles regarding adult learning which include the reality that:

- Adults need to be involved in the planning and evaluation of their instruction.
- Experiences, both positive and negative, present a foundation for learning activities.
- Adult learners are concerned with learning which will ultimately have immediate importance and application to their job or personal lives.

- Adult learning is problem-centered rather than focused on content alone.

Educators should work to understand the basic principles of andragogy, the "art and science of helping adults learn" (Knowles, 1980, p. 43; Merriam & Caffarella, 1999). Moreover, educators should extend that understanding and make a bold attempt to look closer at additional influences for how adults learn and how ICT factors into their learning. Adult learners are highly motivated and want to learn; this demand for education may be intrinsic or extrinsic in nature. For instance, adult learners may rely on social relationships to meet their need for associations and friendships (Rose, 1998). They may also rely on social welfare for wanting to improve their ability to serve mankind, prepare to service the community, or improve their ability to participate in community work. Adult learners are also motivated for personal advancement in order to achieve higher status in the workplace, secure professional advancement, or stay above the competition. Furthermore, adult learners have the enthusiasm to learn simply because they want to learn and obtain knowledge for its own sake.

ICT is a fundamental driver of economic and societal change. As ICT constantly changes the nature, and requirements, of the workforce, students must continue to educate themselves in the use of ICT. Therefore, it is imperative that students are fluent with ICT in order to persist in the workforce environment and contend with such high-speed changes. Specifically, the workforce is in "need [of] professionals who combine up to date domain expertise with social and communicative skills; professionals who are well-informed, proactive learners, thoroughly familiar with actual professional practice, and capable of dealing with new situations" (Bitter-Rigpkema, Sloep, & Jansen, 2003, p. 19). As such, the workplace offers an environment that is keen on innovative practices with the intention of fulfilling the needs of the consumer. By utilizing ICTs, the workplace is able to become a frontrunner in the global economy. Additionally, the need for ICT fluency is also explained in that "in a rapidly changing society, people need to be able to learn new skills for new jobs and permanently improve their competencies" (Nechita & Timofti, 2011, p. 1510). These are just some of the factors that contribute to the need for students to be fluent with ICTs.

Reports of ICT use indicate that students (Digital Natives specifically) use ICT in a very limited manner, specifically for social activities and accessing information through the Internet. They use ICT less frequently for problem solving, creative application, or transforming information (Murray & Perez, 2010). As previously discussed, being fluent in ICT is extremely important and assessing ICT fluency is particularly vital as learners entering higher education (and eventually the workforce) may not be as fluent with the use of ICT as previously believed. The Association of College and Research Libraries (ACRL) defines information literacy as "a set of abilities requiring individuals to recognize when information is needed and have the ability to locate, evaluate, and use effectively the needed information" (Gross & Latham, 2009, pp. 337-338). Furthermore, fluency "connotes the ability to reformulate knowledge, to express oneself creatively and appropriately, and to produce and generate information (rather than simply to comprehend it)" (Lin, 2000, p. 70). Furthermore, the National Research Council (NRC) describes fluency with information technology, or FITness as something that:

requires that persons understand information technology broadly enough to be able to apply it productively at work and in their everyday lives, to recognize when information technology would assist or impede the achievement of a goal, and to continually adapt to the changes in and advancement of information technology (National Research Council, 1999, p. 15).

It is clear that the use of ICT extends beyond the basic use and knowledge of the computer or the Internet, and learners need to be able to "access, comprehend, and respond to information" (Farmer, 2012). Doing so will allow learners to operate unaided in all areas of education, work, and society in order to become successful in their academic and workforce endeavors.

Students in higher education are thought to be experienced in the fundamental use of ICT. However, educational institutions have started that students are lacking the skills needed for academic success and do not fully learn the skills needed to be successfully prepared to enter the workforce (Kaminski, Switzer, & Gloeckner, 2009; McMahon & Pospisil, 2005). For example, Hignite, Margavio, and Margavio (2009) studied levels of information literacy amongst college students. Their findings suggest that students need to learn to make expert decisions from the information they find (by using ICT) and not solely employ ICT in order to complete an assignment. Furthermore, results of a study by Sutherland-Smith (2002) indicated that many students felt discouraged when their Internet search results did not provide them with an immediate answer. Having students feel agitated for lack of instant gratification is cause for concern. If students constantly expect immediate results (i.e., the first answer being the one and only answer), critical thinking and problem solving skills will be hurt in the process (Lorenzo & Dziuban, 2006). Furthermore, educators must develop learning situations and environments that promote the opportunity to become fluent in ICT and emphasize the importance of ICT fluency. Ultimately, creating such learning environments will aid students in developing the skills they need to be successful in both their academic and working lives (Gross & Latham, 2009; Hilberg & Meiselwitz, 2008; Madigan, et al., 2007).

With the increased use of ICT, and at the rate at which ICTs change, it is important for educators to continually reexamine learning materials and environments that utilize ICT. Verifying such technologies are truly being developed and employed to properly maximize learning outcomes will ultimately help to maximize workforce readiness. The goal in creating such environments is summarized by the following statement pertaining to teacher education programs, but can be applied to all types of educational programs:

We should not teach prospective teachers about technology, but instead, we should teach them to use technology so that prospective teachers not only gain skills in working with equipment and software, but also experience how technology can be used to explore, organize, and communicate knowledge by emphasizing discovery approaches to learning in a technologically astute environment (Wang, 2009).

By understanding students' attitudes toward the use of ICT, it may be possible to determine the most favorable approach to using ICT suitably to supplement the growing needs of the technology-rich environment. Additionally, as the use of ICT offers different methods for accessing learning, such as blended or virtual learning, the opportunity exists for students to engage in learning at a time and pace that fits their needs and lifestyle (Macpherson, Elliot, Harris, & Homan, 2004). It is the objective of this chapter to provide information to help make sound decisions about educating today's student using ICT to better prepare them for the demands of the workforce.

THE USE AND DESIGN OF INFORMATION AND COMMUNICATION TECHNOLOGIES

The Use of ICT

The addition of ICT in education and the workforce has prompted researchers and educators to explore the extent to which ICT has actually impacted students; the exact results are still inconclusive. However, Verhoeven, Heerwegh, and De Wit (2012) contend that "it will be hard to imagine a job for a graduate in the future that does not involve ICT" (p. 122). Therefore, it is important to understand how students use ICT, and what their attitudes are toward the use of ICT in their education. As discussed, ICT offers students the ability to communicate, collaborate, organize, and understand knowledge. Learning how to effectively use ICT to supplement learning is an important factor to consider. Therefore, is it vital that students learn how, when, where, and why to use ICT in their learning experiences (Sam, Othman, & Nordin, 2005) in order to help prepare themselves for the workforce. As workforce requirements change, students need to have "communication skills, competencies in emerging technologies, and critical thinking skills" (Sam, et al., 2005, p. 205). In addition, students must already possess these skills as they enter the workforce. Students may only want a 'moderate' amount of ICT incorporated into their educational coursework (Salaway & Caruso, 2007) and feel that ICT is useful for its 'convenience' (Smith, Salaway, & Borreson Caruso, 2009). This student disposition is due to an increased use of handheld devices, tablets, iPods, iPads, and Internet accessible cellular phones. It is important that educators strongly consider the impact that using ICT might have on student learning and the increased possibility of better preparing students for the workforce.

Various studies regarding students' use of ICT in education have been reported. One example, a 2007 study by the EDUCASUE Center for Applied Research, reported that students like to learn through: Internet searches, playing video games and simulation games, text message and email conversations, and by making a contribution to websites, blogs, and wikis (Salaway & Caruso, 2007). Additionally, the 2009 EDUCASUE report indicated that students felt ICT was a valuable learning tool because of the convenience ICT allowed, but still valued face-to-face learning experiences (Smith, Salaway, & Borreson Caruso, 2009). Furthermore, a research study was conducted to assess nursing students' perceived level of competence and confidence in using ICT. This study extended to the students' attitudes toward the use of ICT and their perception of its relevance in clinical practice. The study indicated that nurses need to effectively use ICT in not only access diagnostic information, but also to rapidly search for the best available research to "inform their practice, and to support their clinical decisions with sound evidence" (Levett-Jones, et al., 2009, p. 612). After data collection, through an ICT survey developed by the researchers, the study resulted in the following findings: (1) students who were unfamiliar with ICT showed more anxiety toward ICT use than those who were more familiar with ICT, (2) ICT use and approaches with regards to students' education was perceived as "second rate" (Levett-Jones, et al., 2009, p. 614), (3) although initially feeling as though they lacked experience, students felt they could learn and develop the ICT skills needed for learning, and (4) many of the students did not recognize the importance or relevance of ICT to clinical practice. These findings suggest that students' confidence and competence levels in using ICT may impact their reasons for participating in educational situations that involve ICT. Although this study is specific to nursing students, educators would be remiss if they did not apply such findings to other fields of study. As educators continue to understand when and why students use ICT, it is important to build and provide students with educational ICT materials that are interactive, thought provoking, and engaging.

The Value of Using ICT

It is imperative that students have a full understanding of how they can use ICT for critical thinking, strategic planning, and problem solving upon entering the workforce. A rudimentary understanding of how to access Google, how to navigate a social networking site, play games on the computer and cellular phone, or just "surf the Web" are inadequate. However, combining effective social networking, and using ICT for critical thinking and problem-solving, would probably allow for a strong competitive advantage in today's global economy. Technological advancements have allowed for positive changes to learning in higher education. Understanding the value of using ICT is an important factor in not only preparing students for entering the workforce, but for continued professional development as well. The use of ICT "supplements and enhances learning and student engagement through access to global learning communities and rich resources, thereby creating opportunities for dialog with others, for broadening understanding and participation leading to improved social and learning outcomes" (McLoughlin, 2012, p. 2). Although ICT is clearly important with regards to learning, one must consider how educators can convince students why it is important to learn how to effectively use ICT. How do educators urge learners to "buy in" to the idea that ICT is an effective tool to supplement their learning?

There are many different reasons why the use if ICT is important, but for the purposes of this chapter the focus will reside upon meaningful and lifelong learning. What is meaningful learning exactly? It is the ability for a student to truly comprehend and understand the information and apply what has been learned already to a new situation (Jamet & Le Bohec, 2007; Tempelman-Kluit, 2006). Lifelong learning is more than just continual education (Holden, Smith, & Devins, 2003) as lifelong learning allows for self-directed learning, growth, and even social interaction in the pursuit of personal and/or professional development in a large range of situations (Fischer, 2000). For instance, "the workplace is a significant context for learning and individual employees need to be empowered to take the responsibility for developing their potential through learning" (Holden, Smith, & Devins, 2003, p. 125).

One way in which students can develop their potential is through meaningful learning, which is the result of transfer of learning. Adult learning theories contend that students must retain information in order to benefit from training which can result in transfer of learning. When designing educational opportunities and situations, the ultimate goal is to assist the student in retaining the information from that particular learning situation. To retain this information, students must see a meaning or purpose for using that information, i.e., "how does this information pertain to my current academic endeavors or workforce requirements?" Students should understand, be able to interpret, and apply the information in real life situations (Craft, Kerschenbaum, & Ware, 2007). Simply stated, if the material is not initially presented in a format that would allow for information transfer, and students are not able to fully comprehend the material, students will not be able to retain the information for later use. As such, transfer of learning is the result of training. It is the ability to use the information taught (whether it be an academic or workplace environment) in a new setting (Carey & Posavac, 1997). Furthermore, training can be explained as the "systematic acquisition of knowledge, skills, and attitudes that together lead to improved performance in a specific environment" (Grossman & Salas, 2011, p. 104).

There have been many definitions of transfer of learning over the years. However, researchers agree that transfer of learning has been deemed as a system of influences (Ford & Weissbein, 1997; Holton, Bates, & Ruona, 2000). Moreover, that "transfer of learning involves the application, generalizability, and maintenance of new knowledge and skills" (Holton, Bates, & Ruona, 2000, p. 334). In 1901 Edward Thorndike and Robert Woodworth (as cited by Schunk, 2004) explored how individuals transfer learning from one context to another when both environments share similar characteristics. Their theory implied that transfer of learning depended on the proportion to which the learning task and the transfer task were similar; otherwise known as the Identical Element Theory.

Furthermore, Baldwin and Ford (1988) established and developed a thorough review of the factors that affect transfer of learning and separated them into three distinct categories: (1) training inputs, which include trainee characteristics, training design, and work environment; (2) training outputs; which include learning and retention; and (3) conditions of transfer; which include the generalization and maintenance of training (Dee, 2011). The transfer process suggests that the amount of learning that occurs during training, and whether the information is actually retained, is extremely important. In order to promote meaningful learning, the information from training should be initially learned and retained (Baldwin & Ford, 1988).

Holton (1996) developed a conceptual evaluation model of training that focused on individual performance. Holton's model suggested that there are three important factors that contribute to transfer of learning. These three factors include: (1) motivation to transfer, (2) transfer climate, and (3) transfer design. Educators should consider Holton's model of training and Baldwin and Ford's model of the transfer process to determine if using ICT in learning environments would improve individual performance. Doing so would allow for a better understanding of how learning using ICT can result in a transfer of learning, thus leading to increased meaningful learning.

ICT Learning Environments

Quality instruction is an important factor that influences participation in learning and is not limited to just face-to-face learning. Although ICT fluency may be a factor with regards to participation, ICT may not be the complete issue, but the execution and implementation of the actual technology. Best practices of incorporating ICT into learning should focus on finding and using the most appropriate forms of ICT to best fit learning goals and objectives. Understanding how the use of ICT can support the learning process should be included in these best practices as well. Additionally, there are many different ICT-based environments that support learning and such environments include but are not limited to: blended learning environments, virtual learning communities, e-learning environments, and m-learning environments to name a few.

Blended learning combines face-to-face and ICT-mediated instruction and has the ability to transform learning when the strengths of both formats are considered. An example of blended learning would be a 'hybrid' course using the Blackboard learning management system to help deliver course content. Advantages of blended learning include cost effectiveness and easier accessibility and flexibility to learning. However, disadvantages may include limited access to ICT, limited knowledge or fluency regarding ICT, or the notion that learners may be less inclined to be as self-directed as a blended environment (McLoughlin, 2012).

Virtual Learning Communities (VLCs) on the other hand are important as blended communities providing a means by which students can collaborate with each other within and across higher education and in the workforce. VLCs also allow students the ability to access information over the Internet thereby being able to access information from home or even through their cellular phone. VLCs also allow "trainers and developers to support individual and group development across professional, organizational, temporal, and geographic boundaries" (Allen & Lewis, 2006, p. 368). VLCs offer students the opportunity to make connections, communicate, collaborate, and share ideas, experiences, and resources. Another important advantage of VLCs is that they offer students the ability to access learning at a time and place suitable to their work and personal lives. Furthermore, e-learning and m-learning (mobile learning) also offer students the opportunity to access information 'on the go.' Updated cellular phone technologies allow students to connect to a plethora of Internet resources. Many common tasks include: accessing real-time information, using email, accessing multimedia tutorials and information, as well as interacting with social networks. There are many different learning environments that utilize ICT. It is also important to know and understand which learning tools can be used to effectively help increase meaningful learning in these diverse environments. Tools that can be used in ICT learning environments include, but are not limited to: wikis, blogs, podcasts, vodcasts (video casting and sharing), virtual worlds, social networking, email, discussion boards, IM chat, Web-conferencing and Webinars (Yilmaz, 2012).

Designing ICT Learning Tools

Educational institutions are taking the steps to help promote meaningful learning and prepare students for the demands of the workforce. Finding and recognizing the tools educators can use to help showcase these institutional policies will help students understand the value of using ICT. Using multimedia technology, for example, is just one of the ways in which educators can help to increase comprehension, leading to transfer of learning, then leading to meaningful learning, and (hopefully) to lifelong learning.

Although Digital Natives may only use a moderate amount of ICT for learning, it is important that educators create learning instances that promote and encourage critical thinking, ICT fluency, and meaningful learning. By utilizing multimedia technology educators can create active learning environments which promote meaningful learning. Meaningful learning is conditional upon the students' "cognitive activity during learning rather than on the learner's behavioral activity during learning" (Mayer, 2001, p. 18). Furthermore, Mayer and Moreno (2002) state that "computer based multimedia learning environments—consisting of pictures (such as animation) and words (such as narration)—offer a potentially powerful venue for improving student understanding" (p. 108). Multimedia learning can include the use of audio, text, animations, demonstrations, and simulations. An animated demonstration is a demonstration of a procedure on a computer screen. For example, a 'ghost' user that performs the tasks on the screen for the observer and can be an extremely valuable tool in learning. Furthermore, demonstrations, or 'demos,' can also be thought of as worked examples. A "worked example is a step-by-step demonstration of how to perform a task or how to solve a problem" (Clark, Nguyen, & Sweller, 2006a, p. 190). A study of worked examples indicated that learners who participated in training and used worked examples outperformed those learners who only used problem solving during the learning and training program (Sweller & Cooper, 1985). This observation was later called the "worked example effect" (Sweller & Chandler, 1991). Furthermore, using demonstration-based learning (developed through the use of multimedia) is an important instructional feature within ICT learning environments as observation and practice is critical to learning through: (1) attention (being able to obtain information from the demonstration no matter the sensory output), (2) retention (rehearsal and creating mental representations of the information in the working memory later stored in the long-term memory, later used for recall and to direct performance), and (3) production (performance of the observed behavior shown in the demonstration) (Rosen, Salas, & Pavlas, 2010).

To better understand the use and effectiveness of multimedia in learning, a study was conducted by Palmiter and Elkerton (1991). They compared the use of animated demonstrations, written text, and narrated animations. Palmiter and Elkerton concluded that after one week of delay, the text only group was faster and just as accurate on performance tasks as the animation group who viewed the animated demonstrations. The animation group performed the task faster and enjoyed the lesson more, however. Students who viewed the animated demonstration were able to acquire skills in much less time than the other groups, but took longer and had a more difficult time with performance on the same task a week later (Palmiter & Elkerton, 1991). This effect was eventually termed as the Palmiter's animation deficit, but with continued research, researchers were unable to replicate the results (Lipps, Trafton, & Gray, 1998).

In order for multimedia to support meaningful and lifelong learning, learning experiences should be designed that employ specific theories and principles which "prime appropriate cognitive processing" (Mayer, 2001, p. 19). Multimedia can help increase critical thinking and comprehension skills, ultimately preparing students for the workforce or continued professional development. Additionally, Tempelman-Kluit (2006) maintains that multimedia technology helps to increase meaningful learning because "connections are made between information in the visual and the verbal-processing channels of working memory" (p. 365). Multimedia learning tools can include audio, narration, text, graphics, animations, demonstrations, or simulations. These elements can be used alongside each other to augment learning because information will be divided between the visual and verbal channels of the working memory, rather than simply two verbal channels or two visual channels of the working memory (Moreno & Mayer, 1999; Wickens, 1984). Furthermore, Mayer (2003) states that:

multimedia learning occurs when students build mental representations from words and pictures that are presented to them (e.g., printed text and illustrations or narration and animation). The promise of multimedia learning is that students can learn more deeply from well-designed multimedia messages consisting of words and pictures than from more traditional modes of communication involving words alone (p. 125).

Therefore, an important factor to consider when designing multimedia learning tools and resources is to identify how different multimedia design principles affect learning. Furthermore, each design principle should be taken into account in order to design an effective learning environment. Specifically this environment should facilitate learning, enhance learners' experience during training, and foster an environment conducive to transfer of learning.

Mayer (2001) developed the Cognitive Theory of Multimedia Learning (CTML). CTML is described as "a cognitive theory of how people construct knowledge from words and pictures" (Mayer, 2001, p. 42). It is based on three assumptions; (1) *dual channels* (there is a processing channel for visual stimuli and a processing channel for verbal stimuli), (2) *limited capacity* (both the visual and verbal channel each have a limited capacity through which to process information at one time), and (3) *active processing* (meaningful learning can occur when information is actively selected, organized, and integrated with previous knowledge for both the visual and verbal channels). This research led to additional multimedia design principles, which include the following:

1. **Multimedia Principle:** Words and images (pictures) should be presented concurrently because "when words alone are presented, students have an opportunity to build a verbal mental model but are less likely to build a pictorial mental model and make connections between the verbal and pictorial mental models" (Mayer, 2001, p. 63).
2. **Spatial contiguity principle:** Presenting text and pictures near each other is better for learning than farther apart so learners do not search for supplemental information and therefore can focus their attention thus holding the information in their working memory (Mayer, 2001).
3. **Temporal contiguity principle:** Words and pictures should be presented concurrently rather than sequentially, i.e., displaying audio

(narration) at the same time as the visual (text or animation) (Mayer & Johnson, 2008).

4. **Modality principle:** Words should be presented verbally as narration, rather than on screen text (Mayer & Johnson, 2008) which can be explained by the Split-Attention Principle (Mayer & Moreno, 1998).
5. **Redundancy principle:** Removing identical visual and verbal information as cognitive overload can occur (Jamet & Le Bohec, 2007; Mayer, 2001) as learners are forced to skip back and forth from one source of information to the next, i.e., learners skip from text to animation to text while listening to audio (Mayer, 2001).

By utilizing multimedia design principles. and by using both audio and visual elements when creating learning tools, students are able to process information at a faster rate, which can foster an enhanced learning environment. Using multimedia as a learning tool offers students a learning environment built upon different senses that can maximize their retention, thus leading to the increased chance for transfer of learning. For a more detailed discussion of these multimedia principles see Mayer (2005).

FUTURE TRENDS

Because the development and use of ICT is constantly changing, one cannot be certain as to a concrete direction the use of ICT in learning will take. However, it will be extremely important for educators and researchers to continue to explore the use and development of ICT in order to prepare students for the workforce. ICT is clearly changing the way in which students gain knowledge and will increase their likelihood of being prepared to enter the workforce. Therefore, it is important for educators to continue to research and develop new ICT skills and tools for the blended, online, and mobile learning environments.

Furthermore, it is important to consider that perhaps not all learning environments allow for increased engagement with ICT content. Therefore, it would be advantageous to research the influence that social communities have on learning. It is said that effective learning takes place through informal learning, or through a community of learners (Wenger, 1998). Informal learning communities can "come together informally and often spontaneously, and involve practitioners working together, collaborating and sharing their experience to solve real work-based problems" (Allen & Lewis, 2006, p. 369). Additionally, using learning management systems that incorporate social interaction is important so that formal learning is still at the crux of the learning experience. Yet informal learning takes place as well and can offer a strong opportunity for learning. It is important that educators help students understand that social interaction through social networking allows for increased collaboration, discussion, and informal learning. Social interaction should be encouraged as a productive use of time, not a waste of time. Therefore, researching the benefits of social networking, through sites like Second Life, Facebook, Google, and LinkedIn (to name a few), is extremely valuable. Social learning creates robust communities of learners who can ultimately drive change, increase productivity, and promote economic stability within organizations (de Laat, 2011).

CONCLUSION

The use of ICT is important to consider when preparing students to enter the modern technology-rich workforce, and this chapter discussed how using ICT can help prepare students for that challenge. It is important to consider how ICT can be used to enhance learning and why students must learn to not only know how to perform a simple task using ICT, but how to think critically using ICT as well. Furthermore, "it is essential that academics teaching into undergraduate programs draw explicit links between ICT used for educational purposes and that used in practice" (Levett-Jones, et al., 2009, p. 615). These links show students how ICT will impact them once they do enter the workforce. Using ICT for learning offers students the ability to use higher order critical thinking skills leading to meaningful learning. It should also lead to higher productivity, not only for the student but for the workforce as well (Wang, 2012).

Technology, specifically ICT, has reshaped the learning landscape. As learners enter the workforce, organizations are looking for those students who are active problem solvers, who can collaborate with others, who can effectively communicate values and ideas, and those who are active learners. Higher educational institutions are making continued investments in the use of ICT in learning as the use of ICT serves as a powerful tool for cognitive, behavioral, and social learning. Furthermore, utilizing ICT in learning is now cost effective. Content is easily accessible, easily updated, and can be customizable due to the learning needs of the student. Additionally, ICT offers students the luxury of accessing learning, training, and social interaction when, where, and at the time they want.

The use of ICT can increase the ability for students to transfer knowledge, leading to an increase in meaningful learning through the use of such elements as multimedia technologies and virtual learning communities. Furthermore, ICT use also has the ability to yield increased development for the workforce resulting in, for example, higher productivity, increased quality of work, increased motivation, stronger collaboration between members of the organization, therefore resulting in a strong competitive advantage in today's ICT-rich global economy.

REFERENCES

Allen, B., & Lewis, D. (2006). Virtual learning communities as a vehicle for workforce development: A case study. *Journal of Workplace Learning, 18*(6), 367–383. doi:10.1108/13665620610682099

Baldwin, T. T., & Ford, J. K. (1988). Transfer of training: A review and directions for future research. *Personnel Psychology, 41*(1), 63–105. doi:10.1111/j.1744-6570.1988.tb00632.x

Bennett, S., Maton, K., & Kervin, L. (2008). The 'digital natives' debate: A critical review of the evidence. *British Journal of Educational Technology, 39*(5), 775–786. doi:10.1111/j.1467-8535.2007.00793.x

Bitter-Rijpkema, M., Sloep, P. B., & Jansen, D. (2003). Learning to change the virtual business learning approach to professional workplace learning. *Journal of Educational Technology & Society, 6*(1), 18–25. Retrieved from http://www.ifets.info/journals/6_1/bitter.pdf

Brown, C., & Czerniewicz, L. (2010). Debunking the 'digital native': Beyond digital apartheid, towards digital democracy. *Journal of Computer Assisted Learning, 26*(5), 357–369. doi:10.1111/j.1365-2729.2010.00369.x

Carey, R., & Posavac, E. (1997). *Program evaluation methods and case studies* (5th ed.). Upper Saddle River, NJ: Prentice-Hall.

Clark, R. C., Nguyen, F., & Sweller, J. (2006a). *Efficiency in learning: Evidence-based guidelines to manage cognitive load.* San Francisco, CA: Pfeiffer. doi:10.1002/pfi.4930450920

Craft, R., Kerschenbaum, S., & Ware, J. (2007). Training tomorrow's workforce. *Training & Development, 61*(4), 58–60. Retrieved from http://vnweb.hwwilsonweb.com/hww/jumpstart.jhtml?recid=0bc05f7a67b1790e7e1f464a759977995c836d80430b76208bfbcbdbbce7221d81c490e544bcf86c&fmt=P

de Laat, M. (2011). Bridging the knowledge gap: Using social network methodology for detecting, connecting and facilitating informal networked learning in organizations. In *Proceedings of the 44th Hawaii International Conference on System Sciences*. IEEE.

Dee, M. I. (2011). *First year undergraduate students' perception of the effectiveness and transfer of multimedia training for a university course registration system*. (Doctoral Dissertation). Florida Atlantic University. Boca Raton, FL.

Farmer, L. (2012). Information competency and e-learning. In Wang, V. (Ed.), *Encyclopedia of E-Leadership, Counseling and Training* (pp. 373–390). Hershey, PA: IGI Global.

Fischer, G. (2000). Lifelong learning - More than training. *Journal of Interactive Learning Research*, *11*(3), 265–294. Retrieved from http://www.editlib.org/p/8380

Ford, J. K., & Weissbein, D. A. (1997). Transfer of training: An updated review and analysis. *Performance Improvement Quarterly*, *10*(2), 22–41. doi:10.1111/j.1937-8327.1997.tb00047.x

Gross, M., & Latham, D. (2009). Undergraduate perceptions of information literacy: Defining, attaining, and self-assessing skills. *College & Research Libraries*, *70*(4), 336–350. Retrieved from http://vnweb.hwwilsonweb.com/hww/jumpstart.jhtml?recid=0bc05a67b1790e7e1f464a759977995c836d80430b762050755a12419fe1d5c493c7fa1043b306&fmt=P

Grossman, R., & Salas, E. (2011). The transfer of training: What really matters. *International Journal of Training and Development*, *15*(2), 103–120. doi:10.1111/j.1468-2419.2011.00373.x

Hignite, M., Margavio, T. M., & Margavio, G. W. (2009). Information literacy assessment: Moving beyond computer literacy. *College Student Journal*, *43*(3), 812-821. Retrieved from http://vnweb.hwwilsonweb.com/hww/jumpstart.jhtml?recid=0bc0f7a6b1790e7e1f464a75997799f6cd7252bebc930330dbff11c838f2f0ef9aa766ec18dff7&fmt=P

Hilberg, J. S., & Meiselwitz, G. (2008). Undergraduate fluency with information and communication technology: Perceptions and reality. In J. J. Ekstrom & M. Stockman (Eds.), *Proceedings of the 9th AMC SIGITE Conference on Information Technology Education,* (pp. 5-10). New York, NY: ACM Press.

Holden, R., Smith, V., & Devins, D. (2003). Using 'employee-led development' to promote lifelong learning in SMEs: A research note. *Human Resource Development International*, *6*(1), 125–132. doi:10.1080/1367886011007142 5

Holton, E. F. (1996). The flawed four-level evaluation model. *Human Resource Development Quarterly*, *7*(1), 5–21. doi:10.1002/hrdq.3920070103

Holton, E. F. III, Bates, R. A., & Ruona, W. E. (2000). Development of a generalized learning transfer system inventory. *Human Resource Development Quarterly*, *11*(4), 333–360. doi:10.1002/1532-1096(200024)11:4<333::AID-HRDQ2>3.0.CO;2-P

Jamet, E., & Le Bohec, O. (2007). The effect of redundant text in multimedia instruction. *Contemporary Educational Psychology*, *32*, 588–598. doi:10.1016/j.cedpsych.2006.07.001

Judd, T., & Kennedy, G. (2011). Measurement and evidence of computer-based task switching and multitasking by 'net generation' students. *Computers & Education*, *56*, 625–631. doi:10.1016/j.compedu.2010.10.004

Junco, R., & Mastrodicasa, J. (2007). *Connecting to the net generation: What higher education professionals need to know about today's students*. Washington, DC: NASPA.

Kaminski, K., Switzer, J., & Gloeckner, G. (2009). Workforce readiness: A study of university students' fluency with information technology. *Computers & Education*, *53*, 228–233. doi:10.1016/j.compedu.2009.01.017

Kennedy, G. E., Judd, T. S., Churchward, A., Gray, K., & Krause, K. L. (2008). First year students' experiences with technology: Are they really digital natives? *Australasian Journal of Educational Technology, 24*(1), 108-122. Retrieved from http://www.ascilite.org.au/ajet/ajet24/kennedy.pdf

Knowles, M. S. (1980). *The modern practice of adult education: From pedagogy to andragogy. Englewood Cliffs, NJ*. Cambridge: Prentice Hall.

Levett-Jones, T., Kenny, R., Van der Riet, P., Hazelton, M., Kable, A., Bourgeois, S., & Luxford, Y. (2009). Exploring the information and communication technology competence and confidence of nursing students and their perception of its relevance to clinical practice. *Nurse Education Today*, *29*(6), 216–616. doi:10.1016/j.nedt.2009.01.007

Lin, H. (2000). Fluency with information technology. *Government Information Quarterly*, *17*(1), 69–76. doi:10.1016/S0740-624X(99)00024-6

Lipps, A., Trafton, J., & Gray, W. (1998). Animation as documentation: A replication with reinterpretation. In *Proceedings for the 45th Annual Conference of the Society for Technical Communication.* Arlington, VA: STC. Retrieved from http://www.stc.org/proceedings/ConfProceed/1998/PDFs/00006.PDF

Lorenzo, G., & Dziuban, C. (2006). *Ensuring the net generation is net savvy*. EDUCAUSE Learning Initiative Paper 2. Boulder, CO: EDUCAUSE. Retrieved from http://net.educause./ir/library/pdf/ELI3006.pdf

Macpherson, A., Elliott, M., Harris, I., & Homan, G. (2004). E-learning: Reflections and evaluation of corporate programs. *Human Resource Development International*, *7*(3), 295–313. doi:10.1080/1367886031000163063 8

Madigan, E. M., Goodfellow, M., & Stone, J. A. (2007). Gender, perception, and reality: Technological literacy among first-year students. In *Proceedings of the 38th SIGCSE Technical Symposium on Computer Science Education,* (pp. 410-414). New York, NY: ACM Press.

Mayer, R. E. (2001). *Multimedia learning*. Cambridge, UK: Cambridge University Press. doi:10.1017/CBO9781139164603

Mayer, R. E. (2003). The promise of multimedia learning: Using the same instructional design methods across different media. *Learning and Instruction*, *13*, 125–139. doi:10.1016/S0959-4752(02)00016-6

Mayer, R. E. (2005). *The Cambridge handbook of multimedia learning*. Cambridge, UK: Cambridge University Press. doi:10.1017/CBO9780511816819

Mayer, R. E., & Johnson, C. I. (2008). Revising the redundancy principle in multimedia learning. *Journal of Educational Psychology*, *100*(2), 380–386. doi:10.1037/0022-0663.100.2.380

Mayer, R. E., & Moreno, R. (1998). A split-attention effect in multimedia learning: Evidence for dual processing systems in working memory. *Journal of Educational Psychology*, *90*(2), 312–320. doi:10.1037/0022-0663.90.2.312

Mayer, R. E., & Moreno, R. (2002). Aids to computer-based multimedia learning. *Learning and Instruction*, *12*(1), 107–119. doi:10.1016/S0959-4752(01)00018-4

McLoughlin, C. (2012). Leading pedagogical change with innovative web tools and social media. In Wang, V. (Ed.), *Encyclopedia of E-Leadership, Counseling and Training* (pp. 1–11). Hershey, PA: IGI Global.

McMahon, M., & Pospisil, R. (2005). Laptops for a digital lifestyle: The role of ubiquitous mobile technology in supporting the needs of millennial students. In *Proceedings of Ascilite 2005 Conference: Balance, Fidelity, Mobility: Maintaining the Momentum?* (pp. 421-431). ASCILITE. Retrieved from http://cms.ascilite.org.au/conferences/brisbane05/blogs/proceedings/49_McMahon%20&%20Pospisil.pdf

Merriam, S., & Caffarella, R. (1999). *Learning in adulthood: A comprehensive guide* (2nd ed.). San Francisco, CA: Jossey-Bass.

Moreno, R., & Mayer, R. E. (1999). Cognitive principles of multimedia learning: The role of modality and contiguity. *Journal of Educational Psychology*, *91*(2), 358–368. doi:10.1037/0022-0663.91.2.358

Murray, M. C., & Perez, J. (2010). Generativity: The new frontier for information and communication technology literacy. *Interdisciplinary Journal of Information, Knowledge and Management*, *5*, 127-137. Retrieved from http://go.galegroup.com.ezproxy.fau.edu/ps/i.do?id=GALE%7CA247880102&v=2.1&u=gale15691&it=r&p=AONE&sw=w

National Research Council. (1999). *Being fluent with information technology*. Washington, DC: National Academy Press.

Nechita, E., & Timofti, I. (2011). Increasing independence versus increasing collaboration with ICT support. *Procedia. Social and Behavioral Sciences*, *29*, 1508–1517.

Oblinger, D., & Oblinger, J. (Eds.). (2005). *Educating the net generation*. Retrieved from http://www.educause.edu/ir/library/pdf/pub7101.pdf

Palfrey, J. G., & Gasser, U. (2008). *Born digital: Understanding the first generation of digital natives*. New York, NY: Basic Books.

Palmiter, S., & Elkerton, J. (1991). An evaluation of animated demonstrations for learning computer-based tasks. In *Proceedings of the SIGCHI Conference on Human Factors in Computing Systems: Reaching through Technology*, (pp. 257-263). ACM Press.

Prensky, M. (2001). Digital natives, digital immigrants. *Horizon*, *9*(5), 1–2. Retrieved from http://www.marcprensky.com/writing/Prensky%20-%20Digital%20Natives,%20Di gital%20Immigrants%20-%20Part1.pdf doi:10.1108/10748120110424816

Ramanau, R., Hosein, A., & Jones, C. (2010). Learning and living technologies: A longitudinal study of first-year students' expectations and experiences in the use of ICT. In *Proceedings of the 7th International Conference on Networked Learning,* (pp. 627-634). NLC. Retrieved from http://www.lancs.ac.uk/fss/organisations/netlc/past/nlc2010/abstracts/PDFs/u.pdf

Rose, A. D. (1998). Challenges in training adult educators. *Adult Learning*, *9*(3), 4–5. Retrieved from http://vnweb.hwwilsonweb.com/hww/jumpstart.jhtml?recid=0bc05f7a67b1790e7e1f464a7599779973d06fa7b4869506182501669a060a82c209472a1580a471&fmt=H

Rosen, M. A., Salas, E., & Pavlas, D. (2010). Demonstration-based training: A review of instructional features. *Human Factors*, *52*(5), 596–609. doi:10.1177/0018720810381071

Salaway, G., & Caruso, J. B. (2007). *The ECAR study of undergraduate students and information technology*. Boulder, CO: EDUCAUSE Center for Applied Research. Retrieved from http://www.edu/ecar

Sam, H. K., Othman, A. E. A., & Nordin, A. S. (2005). Computer self-efficacy, computer anxiety, and attitudes toward the internet: A study among undergraduates in unimas. *Journal of Educational Technology & Society*, *8*(4), 205–219. Retrieved from http://www.ifets.info/journals/8_4/19.pdf

Sardone, N. (2011). Developing information technology fluency in college students: An investigation of learning environments and learner characteristics. *Journal of Information Technology Education*, *10*, 101–122. Retrieved from http://www.jite.org/documents/Vol10/JITEv10p101-122Sardone846.pdf

Schunk, D. (2004). *Learning theories: An educational perspective* (4th ed.). Upper Saddle River, NJ: Pearson.

Selwyn, N. (2003). Apart from technology: Understanding people's non-use of information and communication technologies in everyday life. *Technology in Society*, *25*, 99–116. doi:10.1016/S0160-791X(02)00062-3

Selwyn, N. (2008). An investigation of differences in undergraduates' academic use of the internet. *Active Learning in Higher Education*, *9*(1), 11–22. doi:10.1177/1469787407086744

Smith, S., Salaway, G., & Borreson Caruso, J. (2009). *The ECAR study of undergraduate students and information technology*. Boulder, CO: EDUCAUSE Center for Applied Research. Retrieved from http://www.educause.edu/ecar

Sutherland-Smith, W. (2002). Weaving the literacy web: Changes in reading from page to screen. *The Reading Teacher*, *55*(7), 662–669. Retrieved from http://www.jstor.org/stable/20205116

Sweller, J., & Chandler, P. (1991). Evidence for cognitive load theory. *Cognition and Instruction*, *8*(4), 351–362. Retrieved from http://www.jstor.org/stable/3233599 doi:10.1207/s1532690xci0804_5

Sweller, J., & Cooper, G. A. (1985). The use of worked examples as a substitute for problem solving in learning algebra. *Cognition and Instruction*, *2*(1), 59–89. Retrieved from http://www.jstor.org/stable/3233555 doi:10.1207/s1532690xci0201_3

Tempelman-Kluit, N. (2006). Multimedia learning theories and online instruction. *College & Research Libraries*, *67*(4), 364–369. Retrieved from http://vnweb.hw.com/hww/jumpstart.jhtml?recid=0bc05f7a67b1790e7e1f464a7599779909c3222764db0a79b878397662eb45d7708ff0808e256904&fmt=P

Verhoeven, J. C., Heerwegh, D., & De Wit, K. (2012). First year university student' self-perception of ICT skills: Do learning styles matter? *Education and Information Technologies*, *17*(1), 109–133. doi:10.1007/s10639-010-9149-1

Wang, J. (2012). Organizational learning and technology. In Wang, V. (Ed.), *Encyclopedia of E-Leadership, Counseling and Training* (pp. 154–170). Hershey, PA: IGI Global.

Wang, T. (2009). Rethinking teaching with information and communication technologies (ICTs) in architectural education. *Teaching and Teacher Education*, *25*, 1132–1140. doi:10.1016/j.tate.2009.04.007

Wenger, E. (1998). *Communities of practice: Learning meaning and identity*. Cambridge, UK: Cambridge University Press.

Wickens, C. D. (1984). *Engineering psychology and human performance*. Columbus, OH: Merrill.

Yilmaz, H. (2012). Distance education at university settings. In Wang, V. (Ed.), *Encyclopedia of E-Leadership, Counseling and Training* (p. 587600). Hershey, PA: IGI Global.

Chapter 14
Using Educational Technology to Guide Literacy Teaching Candidates in the Delivery of Adjusted Practices for Speakers of Urban AAVE

Michelle McAnuff-Gumbs
The College of Saint Rose, USA

ABSTRACT

The chapter discusses ways in which educational technology facilitated a strengthening of literacy leadership candidates' awareness of adjusted practices suitable for application in culturally complex classrooms. It shows how the instructor in a specific course was able to infuse critical content and tasks into what would have otherwise been a generic course in literacy theories and instruction, and ensure that candidates were trained in customizing literacy practices for culturally and linguistically diverse students. Multiple online readings, lecture captures using Camtasia, WIKIs, blogs, and Elluminate virtual classroom sessions allowed for an enrichment of course content and for communication of content in powerful ways. Additionally, the tools facilitated engagement of candidates in guided reflection and case-based problem solving that facilitated a transfer of information on adjusted practices to a specific situation. Through the use of tools, the instructor was also able to monitor candidates' uptake of practices. The difference in quality and level of candidate exposure, given use of the tools, is demonstrated primarily through content analysis of their online postings. The chapter and the research it describes qualifies as what Robleyer (2005) refers to as research "address[ing] a significant educational problem" while spotlighting "a proposed technology solution" (p. 19).

DOI: 10.4018/978-1-4666-2955-4.ch014

INTRODUCTION

Technology-oriented research in education must focus on both content and medium if it is to truly demonstrate the power of technology over other delivery modes (Kadzera, 2006; Robleyer, 2005). While there has been a tendency in the educational technology research to focus on the tools of the trade, teacher educators recognize that the content of learning is at least as vital as the tool used, and that tools that prove more effective in conveying and immersing teaching candidates in critical content are more likely to be procured by higher education administration (Baylor & Ritchie, 2002; Beggs, 2000). Kozma (1991) had suggested decades ago that future research should focus on technology-enhanced instructional designs, rather than on the technologies themselves. Still, Robleyer (2005) asserts, "this kind of research has not happened to any great degree" (p. 197). Robleyer underscores the need for "more organized and persuasive body of evidence on technology's benefits to classroom practice" (p. 192). While this work does not propose to fulfill all those requirements, it does demonstrate the benefit of technology in instructional design.

This research, undertaken with the support of the Center for Citizenship, Race, and Ethnicity Studies (CREST) and the Touhey Urban Teacher Training resources, both at The College of Saint Rose, explores the training of candidates in the Old Delivery (OD) and New Delivery (ND) versions of an online graduate-level literacy course. It sought to determine candidates' level of uptake of "adjusted practices" in literacy and the extent to which tools of technology facilitated such uptake. Linking from Blackboard to vital texts and multimedia content in Ebrary and other online sources and delivery of a visually supported series of six lecture captures entitled "Lessons in Diversity," allowed the instructor (also the course designer) to integrate vital diversity content into what would have been a course in theory-supported generic literacy practices. The instructor anticipated that enhanced use of educational technology would likely allow for enhancement of candidate awareness of powerful techniques for implementing adjusted practices and would likely engage candidates in more thoughtful and reflective interchanges surrounding discussions surrounding practices. In the context of this study "adjusted practices" refer to conscious efforts on the part of teachers to amend their attitudes, work styles and values so as to facilitate greater literacy acquisition by culturally and linguistically diverse learners (See Powell & Rightmyer, 2011; Walker, 2008).

The researcher argues that technology would facilitate a more streamlined, a more user-friendly, and a far more motivating process as candidates gather and record information on theories and adjusted practices. Tools of technology would also allow for greater consistency in uptake of the various adjusted practices.

Additionally, by using tools of technology to bring together teaching candidates from diverse specializations (speech and language sciences, special education, literacy, early childhood education and curriculum and instruction)—students who would likely not have studied and problem-solved together if the course had been delivered in a face-to-face format—the instructor hoped to offset traditional "silo learning" often noted in schools of education. The course in its online format reached a variety of candidates from different fields of study. If the learning environment were designed to capitalize on this variety in specializations, the course could provide the literacy candidates, for whom the course was a key program requirement, with practice working in teams featuring practitioners from diverse fields. In addition, in a course where emphasis was on drawing from various schools of thought in flexible ways, and where open-mindedness was encouraged, allowing candidates to work in diversity-rich teams was a bonus. It would help prepare candidates for diversity complex schools in which practitioners from different field must work together to identify and address the needs of specific non-dominant groups in a targeted manner. In this case, focus was on African American students who speak African American Vernacular English (AAVE).

Thus, by placing candidates in technology-supported, cross-functional online collaborative teams and by allowing them to collectively learn and apply what they learned to practice, the instructor would increase the likelihood that a wider cross-section of techniques and approaches would be selected. Culturally-appropriate rather than generic practices would likely emerge so long as candidates were appropriately guided in accessing needed content and in applying it to problem solving. Candidates would likely gather insights from a wider variety of sources given the diverse field from they come and given the increased access to information tools. They could pool their efforts and insights in deriving a well-informed set of instructional strategies that more closely align with the various theoretical perspectives and with the specific needs of students.

Overall, it was anticipated that the course would address diversity requirements in a powerful way. Did students express awareness of the various dimensions of adjusted practice: cultural awareness and literacy practice; diverse ways of thinking, cognitive processing and assessment; diverse rhetorical norms and cognitive judgments; culture preferences and affect; diverse behavior norms, home-like environments and the classroom interactional contexts; creation of welcoming spaces; power, pedagogy and teaching style; materials, curriculum representations and expectations; literacy expression, print functions and diverse text forms; crossing borders/spaces? Did the new content and technological tools applied in the New Delivery facilitate a greater uptake of adjusted practices?

RESEARCH QUESTIONS

The following questions guide the current study:

1. At what level were candidates exposed to principles and practices for delivering "adjusted practices," in the New Delivery (ND) version of the course?
2. To what extent were specific references to adjusted practices evident in candidate products in the Old Delivery (OD) version of the course?
3. How did technology tools and added diversity content further candidates' level of attention to adjusted practices in the ND version?

BACKGROUND, CONTEXT, AND THEORETICAL FRAME

The course, *Theories of Literacy,* has been taught in the specific institution in the urban northeast for some time, and has gone through several iterations under the instructor's tenure as part of efforts t0 align course content with The National Council for Accreditation of Teacher Education (NCATE) requirements and with community demands for specific kinds of expertise of literacy leaders entering the field. The pre-research and enhanced versions of the course are presented in Table 1. The labels OD and ND are used to designate original elements in the Old Delivery (OD) and those later added in the New Delivery (ND).

The course typically runs over a 15-week period in Fall and Spring semesters, and as a 6-week intensive course of study in each of two Summer sessions. Its initial form involved exposing students to 6 modules each centered on specific school of thought (comprising as many as eight theories per school of thought), and to related instructional practices. A specific group of theories featured mostly compatible views on key components of literacy instruction and on processes proficient readers engage in as they read. Additionally, conceptualization of literacy development tends to be similar among theories within a school of thought. A specific group of theories may conflict with or complement an-

Table 1. Structure of the new delivery version of the course

Module (OD/ ND)	Topical Content and General Focus (OD/ND)	Online Readings *(Only Camtasia is ND)*	Featured Adjusted Practice (ND)	Assignments: Wikis, Blogs, and Elluminate Presentations *(Only Elluminate is ND)*
1	• Theories, Literacy and Theories of Literacy: Definitions and Major Models • Factors impacting literacy development	**• Online Readings** **• Lecture Capture: N/A** **• Videos and Web Resources**	Introspection and Reflection	**Final Reflection** done online after case analysis (Potency of Factors and Teacher Roles) – See Unit 7
2	Early Theories and Behaviorism • Social experiences, curriculum and climate • Motivation • Curriculum scope, sequence and pacing	**• Online Readings** **• Lecture Capture** – *Curriculum scaffolds, cultural preferences connections, engagement, and behavior* • Videos and Web Resources	Social Skills Curriculum in Literacy Instruction Text-To-World	**Wiki 1/Blog Reflection 1**(10%) – Using Early Theories and Behaviorism as Roots of My Practice
3	Constructivist Theories and Language Models • Prior linguistic knowledge • Meaningful learning and socially-linked proximal rewards	**• Online Readings** **• Lecture Capture** – *Language norms, texts, contexts and CLDs* **• Videos and Web Resources**	Genre Pedagogy	**Wiki 2/Blog Reflection 2** (10%) – Using Constructivist Theories as Roots of My Practice
4	Developmental Theories and Stage Models • Stages/phases of language/ literacy development • Synchrony of literacy development • The family and early literacy development	**• Online Readings** **• Lecture Capture** - *Differential progression, social contexts and CLDs* **• Videos and Web Resources**	Augmented Language Experience Approach Connections Miscue Analysis	**Wiki 3/Blog Reflection 3** (10%): Using Developmental Perspectives as Roots of My Practice
5	Social Learning Perspectives • Spheres of influence on literacy learning/ecology • Discourse, cultural scripts and literacy learning	**• Online Readings** **• Lecture Capture** – *Socio-cultural norms, cultural/social scripts and learning modalities* **• Videos and Web Resources**	Family Literacy Portfolios; Community Scripts and Community Experts; Parent-Led Dialogic Reading	**Wiki 4/Blog Reflection 4** (10%): Using Social Learning Perspectives as Roots of My Practice
6	Cognitive Perspectives • Language, literacy and cognition • Speed/nature of text processing and diverse responses - Literacy assessment	**• Online Readings** **• Lecture Capture** - *Ways of thinking, assessment, placement, and intervention* for CLDs **• Videos and Web Resources**	The Discover Assessment and Curriculum	**Wiki 5/Blog Reflection 5** (10%): Using Cognitive Perspectives as Roots of My Practice
7	**Review and Reflection**	**• Case Study:** Case of success with "hard to teach" students **• Case Study Blog**	Methodological Eclecticism	Integrating Practices in Classroom and Intervention Settings (**Elluminate Presentations**)

other group of theories and candidates learn to evaluate what theories present solid evidence for the claims made and which may no longer enjoy the research-support they once did.

In the OD version, candidates were required to read the assigned texts (available in an online format to facilitate working with the same text when necessary) and to watch related videos; to create wiki summaries of core beliefs (tenets), critical practices (for instructional and assessment in the various domains of literacy), and any adjusted practices noted in the readings; to find and insert into the wiki online resources that depicted the practices in a concrete and concise way. Candidates were then required to engage in wiki and blog reflections on how they would use or have used the highlighted practices to deliver instruction for a specific learner. The wiki reflection focused on general practices while the blog centered on a case and targeted adjusted practices. Upon exploration of blogs in one specific OD version of the course, the instructor realized that candidates, in proposing solutions for the case, cited practices that were in tune with the research and with tenets of the theories though these did not always match the needs of a learner who happened to be culturally, economically, geographically and/or linguistically different. What were selected were general practices that did not factor the uniqueness of the specific student into the equation.

The instructor was also concerned that mainstream research and theories explored in the course were not being perceived by the candidates as holding particular relevance for addressing the unique needs of diverse learners, especially African American students. Thirdly, the instructor was concerned that the course, if left unaltered, might inadvertently convey faulty assumptions that literacy theories hold no relevance for diverse learners. Such perceptions do exist. As Delpit (1995), noted researcher on the intersection between African American culture and literacy learning, provocatively asks, "Why don't these theories talk about me?" Delpit was in fact implying that on their surface, the theories are often viewed, in this manner. The instructor wanted to demonstrate to students, as Delpit did, that the theories do address the needs of diverse learners, and that tenets as well as specific practices from dominant theories could be applied in addressing the needs of diverse learners even as the needs of students in general are addressed. The content of the course needed to be augmented, and technology use facilitated this augmentation. Infusion of a series of six lecture captures on diversity and use of a general electronic rubric as well as six mini response rubrics, one for each school of thought allowed the instructor to allowed for content enhancement and to guide candidates' reflective thinking and. See sample mini-rubric (see Figure 1).

REVIEW OF THE LITERATURE

Discussions surrounding perceived failure on the part of literacy and language educators to address the needs of culturally and linguistically diverse students and to close achievement gaps have typically focused on four key issues. The first issue has its roots in school pragmatism and involves whether a specific minority population is seen as sufficiently large, its dialect/vernacular sufficiently different, and the literacy performance of its speakers so adversely impacted by 'cookie cutter' instruction as to warrant additional instructional consideration, especially given the current teaching load of instructors and the mounting expectations of administrators and state education departments. Concomitantly, there are some concerns regarding whether any one vernacular such as African American Vernacular English (AAVE) is sufficiently uniform to warrant adjusted teaching practices. A second and related issue rests with attribution of blame for perceived failure on the part of school practitioners to meet the needs of specific populations, and centers on whether schools of education, trained teachers, or the school in which teachers work should be implicated as key obstacles to the implementation of adjusted practices. A third issue centers on whether school-based practitioners must adjust what they *do* or how they *think* about diverse populations in order to improve outcomes. A fourth and final issue centers on what constitutes viable and accessible means of delivering needed insights that

Figure 1. Sample mini rubric for guided reflection

According to established research, literacy assessment (especially of fluency, comprehension and writing) can inadvertently marginalize students from non-dominant groups even before they have been exposed to school-based ways of processing and presenting texts.

Give three ways in which you would vet assessment processes (particularly screening and diagnostic measures) so these do not inadvertently marginalize diverse students.

Criteria	Points Possible	Points Earned
The student discusses concerns regarding faulty assessment of students with learning disabilities (SLDs) and students from culturally and linguistically diverse (CLDs) groups.	2	
Areas in which faulty assessment is most evident for each group are mentioned, with explicit attention to text processing at the word and meaning level.	2	
Three strategies (at least one for promoting speed of text processing and one that addresses Comprehension is mentioned. Links to theories and the student's own experiences are made. Additionally, the student engages with the reflections of at least three peers.	6	
Total	10	

would enable practitioners, especially those in urban contexts where diversity tends to be most noticeable, to appropriately adjusted practices to match the needs of diverse learners.

Powell and Rightmyer (2011) introduce the notion of "adjusted practices," seeing these as a set of instructional variations on standard teaching practices use by teachers who "recognize and grapple with the hegemonic culture of American schools" and who find means to "open up the curricula to all learners" by "connect [teaching] practices to students' lives" (p. xii). Walker (2008) weighs in on adjusted practices indicating that "Instructional adjustments are not radical changes. They are the ways teachers respond and teach diverse learners" (p. 18). The writer maintains that "teachers can easily find appropriate instructional alternatives for diverse learners" (p. 18).

In the segments below, the researcher addresses critical issues surrounding implementation of adjusted practices for speakers of AAVE, and explores the need to train teachers in adjusted practices.

Does the Presence of Speakers of AAVE in Classrooms Warrant Adjusted Practices?

Several researchers are adamant that use of specific varieties of English dialects is directly related to the quality of instructional and assessment practices to which speakers are exposed, and consequently to the quality of literacy outcomes (Christian, 1997; Labov, 1995; Renn, 2010). Arguably, AAVE is one of the most complex of English dialects, and it is estimated that about 80% of the approximately 8 million African American students in US schools speak the variety. According to the National Association for the Evaluation of Educational Progress (NAEP), in 2007 only 14% of African American students in the 4th grade performed at or above *proficient* in state reading tests. Disturbingly, 54% were below basic (National Center for Educational Statistics, 2009). Researchers implicate faulty instructional models, negative expectations, conflicts derived from cross-cultural difference in behavior and interactional styles, as well as flawed language assumptions for literacy acquisition issues facing speakers of AAVE as well as students from other non-dominant groups (Adger, Wolfram, & Christian, 2007; Dillard, 1972; Smitherman, 1997).

Concerns regarding the literacy achievement problems of students who speak AAVE, in particular, are most intense in urban centers. Wolfram (2004) maintains that large metropolitan areas are at the "center of many of the linguistic, social, and educational concerns attendant to AAVE" and that concern is spreading outward since "AAVE follows the lead of speakers in these urban areas" (p. 111). Taylor (2000) indicates that while African Americans make up 16% of the public school system, they make up "a large percentage of students in the nation's urban school districts," and that two-thirds (62.3%) of African American students predominantly attend public urban schools. Chamberlain (2005) asserts also that "children of color in urban settings are now in the majority" (p. 196). Dominance in urban contexts is not just true of student populations, but also of the African American population in general. According to Wolfram (2004), the "2000 US census indicates that approximately 60 percent of all African Americans now live in the non-South and that approximately 6 million African Americans live in the large metropolitan centers" (p. 112).

The report on The Trial National Urban District Assessment (NCES, 2007) conducted by the U.S. government in 2003 and onward in nine urban school districts exposed significant differences between student achievement in such schools and student achievement in the nation as a whole. Wolfram, Adger, and Christian (2007) support the need to focus on concerns related to literacy and language acquisition of speakers of AAVE, especially those in urban centers, since these locales are the center of African American youth culture and "many norms and models of behavior, including language, seem to radiate outward from urban cultural hubs" (p. 113) (See also Van Hofwegen & Wolfram, 2010; Renn, 2010). The writer claims that non-Southern, urban AAVE "tends to stand in stark opposition to benchmark European American varieties" in metropolitan areas, the latter variety being more in line with school-sanctioned academic English used as the basis of literacy instruction.

Invoking social variables impacting the literacy acquisition of urban AAVE speakers, Wolfram attributes widening differences between the dominant and sub-ordinate language varieties to "oppositional identity that has developed in African American youth culture" in which the young do not want to "act white," especially as they progressively view themselves as being outside the white, mainstream culture legitimized by schools (p. 130). In fact, many writers who ascribe to the divergence hypothesis of language evolution believe that contemporary AAVE is evolving in ways that widens the difference between that variety and other dialects of English (including that sanctioned by schools), and that this evolution is linked to perceptions of community and identity.

Although the debate regarding the nature and extent of innovation rages on, most researchers agree that despite complexity and variations in AAVE/AAE use, "there is a basic core in dialect features that extends across geographical regions" and which can be the target of instruction (Wolfram, 2010, p. 112) (See also Redd & Webb, 2005). Wolfram (2010) provides a detailed explication of this linguistic core and highlights the stark difference between this core and accepted varieties of English, maintaining that there is a consistent frame on which to develop targeted literacy instructional provisions.

In addition to innovations that widen the gap between AAVE and school English, researchers note a roller coaster trajectory in students' use of AAVE in the school years. This trajectory indicates that, although younger students tend to adjust their language to match the mainstream code used by teachers in the early grades, due perhaps to corrective socialization in schools and a need for membership in the school community

(Craig & Washington, 2006; Van Hofwegen & Wolfram, 2010), in the pre-teen years (at about the fourth grade) there is considerable recession in school-based English usage and intensification of AAVE use up to the end of high school (Labov, 1965, 1968; Rowe, 2005; Wolfram, 1969). In the post-high-school years, both an intensification and reduction is observed according to whether students are heading for college or not. Thus, students demonstrate purposive use of the dominant code, based on whether they feel welcomed in schools. Researchers maintain that for older students, whether they revert or not is largely influenced by powerful social forces, including group reference factors (group identity) and community language norms (See Christian, 1997, on community norm; Washington, 2004, on locality; Renn, 2010, on afro-centricity effects).

Delpit (1995) links student reversion to AAVE use to their increasing awareness of the negative light in which schools view the community to which students belong. According to Delpit, as students become increasingly aware of schools' negative attitude to their community and its culture, they invariably choose, through language display, the camp with which to identify. Nelson-Barber and Estrin (1995) and Mohatt and Erickson (1981) had found a similar pattern in a study of Native American students' use of English, suggesting also that, as students become increasingly aware of their group membership, their language shifts accordingly. In linking such reactive use to assessment outcomes, Delpit maintains that in such situations, *performance* (language use) often belies *competence* (metalinguistic awareness) (p. 52). Thus, use of language in classrooms and even displays in assessment might not accurately depict what students actually know about language and how it works.

Achievement Gaps and Failure to Adjust Practices: Who or What is to be Blamed?

Several writers maintain that faulty school practices are at the heart of low achievement profiles of AAVE speakers as compared to other populations, and that this problem is precipitated by other issues related to social forces. Linked to this palpable area of concern are issues surrounding the lenses through which speakers of substrate codes and "subordinate cultures" have been viewed and the link between such views and what teachers do. Researchers cite the following as other possible roots of achievement gaps: (a) *structural and functional conflicts*, what some refer to as reciprocal ignorance, where the teacher and student both have limited insights into and negative perceptions of each other's linguistic and cultural systems, resulting in teacher-student relational issues and misunderstandings that undermine student learning (Labov, 1995; Renn, 2010); (b)*socio-linguistic attitudes*, that is, judgments teachers make about students' intelligence, motivation, likelihood of academic success, and even their worth based in part on teacher perceptions of how students manage or "fail" to manage a particular language variety during literacy instruction and assessment (Coleman,1997; Christian, 1997); (c) *systemic issues*, that is, inequitable resource allocations and unfair allocation of expertise across schools, which lead to distrust and weakening bonds among parents, teachers, and school administrators, especially when schools are perceived to have failed in meeting the needs of specific populations (Adger, et al., 2009; Anderson & Screen, 1994; Baugh, 2000; Labov, 1995; Laing & Kahmi, 2003). The Ann Arbor and Oakland trials echo such issues.

Research support ideas regarding gaps in performance as being precipitated by cultural differences. Delpit (1995) cites differences in the narrative styles of African-American students (who tend to lean toward non-linear, episodic retellings) and their European American teachers (who look for topic-focused, linear recounts) as highly impactful on teachers' interpretation and report of students' level of competence. Cazden's (2001) experiment, which examines teacher ratings of African-American student retellings, supports this claim. Delpit links faulty interpretation of competence and resulting inappropriate instructional placement to clashes in rhetorical norms. Faulty placement occurs because a "negative valence" is assigned to the differences in language use and because a teacher might be unaware of a student's true underlying competence (p. 56). See Cummins' (1999, 2005) Iceberg Model distinguishing surface from underlying competence. Chamberlain (2005) maintains that faulty assessment practices can lead to faulty assumptions about cognitive competence, to incorrect placement for intervention, and consequently to inappropriate instruction.

Chamberlain (2005) attempted to illustrate how culture impacts actual language behavior as well as interpretation of language behaviors in classrooms. Chamberlain maintains, "Language is central to culture, defined as "the values, norms, and traditions that affect how individuals of a particular group perceive, think, interact, and make judgments about the world" (p. 196). Chamberlain maintains additionally that the majority of cultural clashes that result in inappropriate placement will be between European American teachers and children of color since students' outputs are constantly judged against "standardized procedures in the official discourse" (p. 196). The writer links perceptions of African Americans' ways of thinking and acting and others' ways of viewing the structure, content, and form of such expressions/actions to faulty assessment of the cognitive abilities of this minority population, to subsequent placement in inappropriate remediation settings, and to the over-referral and overrepresentation of African American students in special education. The writer suggests that teachers of culturally different students willingly interact with and learn from students' cultural groups and recommends the inclusion of diverse faculty, parents, and community in teacher training. Additionally, the researcher pleads for practitioners to be so conditioned that they develop the humility necessary to learn from communities and to make their practices more attuned with the community they serve.

Powell and Rightmyer (2011) blame school leadership, not teachers or teacher educators, for teacher failure to adapt practices to the needs of CLDs. Servage (2008) also implicates school leadership for schools' failure to meet the needs of those who struggle with literacy acquisition. In a critique of school literacy leadership practices, the writer cites school pragmatism, "strategic blindness," "self-perpetuating defensiveness," and neglect of higher reflective processes during needs assessment as culpable for persistent gaps in literacy achievement, citing schools' unwillingness to factor socio-cultural variables into consideration as reasons for in gaps in implementation of instructional reform efforts. Powell and Rightmyer implicate the culture of school, indicating that although "'adjusted practices' are consistently taught in teacher education programs" they are "largely unused once teachers are acculturated in the typical American school" (p. xxii). The writers called on both teachers and instructional leaders to examine the lenses through which they view students, the quality of care that characterize classroom interactions, as well as the biases and ideologies inherent in their assessment and work styles and values, maintaining that " 'best practices' is necessary but not sufficient" for literacy learning improvement (p. x). Such an assertion warrants deeper exploration. Do issues really lie with the leadership and in the culture of schools, and do teacher training programs truly guide candidates toward implementing adjusted practices?

Infusing Cultural Awareness and Adjusted Practices into Teacher Training

There have been mismatches between what is often promoted as "best practices" and what is known to work with speakers of AAVE learning to read in what is really their second language or dialect. The same is true for students from other non-dominant groups. Such recognition has existed for decades. Powell and Rightmyer (2011) maintain that excellent teachers and instructional leaders do not create learning situations that "force student to choose one or the other, academics or their own culture" but provide a culturally relevant curriculum (one that acknowledges and builds on students' lived experiences) and which, in the process, promote self-esteem, identity development and academic success (p. xii). Powell and Rightmyer refer to this kind of instruction as "adjusted practices." (See also Graham & Harris, 2007.) Teachers who practice culturally relevant teaching methods, Powell and Rightmyer claim:

1. Hone their own socio-political consciousness and perspectives in preparing to teach in diversity complex settings;
2. Make use of responsive assessment in informing what and how they teach;
3. Use knowledge of potential clashes in cultures to select instructional styles that promote positive conceptualizations and expectations;
4. Facilitate affirming discourse and instructional conversations during learning;
5. Foster parent connections and capitalize on communities' funds of knowledge in framing instruction;
6. Allow students to excel academically while retaining their culture.

Such teachers make adjustments to how they think and what they do so that they provide planned curricular experiences that are affirming, and so they employ practices linked to students' worlds. Exemplary teachers such as these also condition the learning environment so it is inclusive and fair to all.

Powell and Rightmyer (2011) provide an instructional framework—the Culturally Responsive Instruction Observation Protocol (CRIOP)—to guide teacher training and classroom observation, a framework built on "adjusted practices." They maintain that the notion *adjusting practices* is not really about instructional strategies, but more about adapting attitudes, work styles and values, since these must first change before instructional strategies will work. The writers claim that adaptations "do not have to be revolutionary to bring success to historically marginalized students" (p. xiii). They just need to be informed and thoughtful. The writers, however, did not give due attention to diverse cognitive processing by different cultural groups and the intersection of this with language/literacy acquisition, nor did they address the impact of perceptions of differential processing on assessment. Additionally, there are no gradations in the level of uptake in the CRIOP tools. Therefore, while the framework is quite useful and while it provides a means of measuring teacher uptake of practices, it must to be augmented for this study. What more should teachers learn about adjusted practices? What are they required to do in the classroom? How can we determine if teachers have learned critical practices?

Considerations for Training Teachers and Leaders in Adjusted Practices: Focusing on Competence and Affect

Three strands of research have added to our understanding of adjustments that should be made to practices geared at Culturally and Linguistically Diverse Students (CLDs). These include research describing successful teacher instructional reform efforts; research on what CLDs and their parents think students need; and research on dimensions of teacher training programs geared at integrating adjusted practices into teacher repertoire of instructional strategies.

Taylor (2000), in a study comparing teachers who had gone through the Minority/Multicultural Mentorship Project (MMP) providing them with direct intercultural experiences working with minority student and those who had not, found that the two sets of teachers differed along three main dimensions: *behavior*, *language* and *curriculum*. The teachers in the project had engaged with students and their parents in "tutoring sessions, cultural and social activities, parent education seminars, and weekly correspondence" (p. 3). At the end of the experience, the 20 teachers in the project were better able to adapt to the different *behavior and interactional styles* of the African American students—their lack of direct eye contact; other nuances in body language; group-type mentality or socio-centricity—seeing these as less offensive and more as different. Additionally, these teachers showed greater respect for students' language, seeing it not as deviant but as different and in fact used it as springboard for instruction. In terms of *language*, teachers also learned to respect students' preference for oral expression. In terms of difference between these teachers and the 20 who had not gone through the program, the MMP teachers allowed students to see themselves and black literary icons, innovators and pacesetters in the *curriculum*, showing that they embraced both the students and their culture and implicitly communicating high expectations for students.

Owens (2005) as well as Costa and Garmston (2002) maintain that change in both teacher *thinking* and *action* is needed if teacher and school transformation are to be realized (See also Lipman, 1997, on the rigidity of teacher ideology related to African American students, even in the context of massive reform efforts focused only on instruction). Taylor (2000) utters a similar sentiment to Costa and Garmston, stating that "teachers must come to grips with some of the unspoken beliefs and lowered expectations they may have about African American students" as these "internal factors may have much to do with the academic success of African American students" (p. 8). In their model of cognitive coaching, Costa and Garmston maintain that, in seeking to change teacher practices, one must assume that "invisible thought processes drive the overt skills of teaching" and that "enlightened, skilled colleagues" can [mediate] a teacher's cognitive processes" and behavior (online). The first assumption raises trainers' awareness of the crucial need, when seeking instructional change, to understanding what educators think about their practice as well as of those at which such practices are directed. Research by Green and Etheridge (2001) and by Hanley, Maringe and Ratcliffe (2008) support this notion, the latter indicating that "changing teachers' beliefs and changing their classroom practice is more of a cycle, where each reinforces and provides impetus for the other" (p. 712). The understanding that changing teacher practice must begin with ideological is supported by Christian (1997) and by Squires and Kranyik (1996). Christian maintains that literacy instructional provisions, if they are to be carried out effectively and equitably, require careful thought ranging from underlying educational philosophy to particular teaching strategies. Thus, the focus in the course on linking teacher thinking as conditioned by the theories to considerations of adjust their practices is vital. The course is an excellent arena for fostering change in both affect and practice.

Guidance in dimensions of adjusted practices also comes from two recent studies (Howard, 2002; Thompson, 2002). These two studies followed up on the seminal work of Ladson-Billings (1994), and sought the input African American students in identifying key characteristics of teachers whom they believed were effective in increasing their literacy competence in the elementary, middle school and high school years. Students in the study seemed more concerned with the *quality of instructional scaffolding* than they were with affect, the majority stating that effective teachers were those that explained things well; made learning engaging; provided extra help; were patient, fair, friendly and humorous; maintained discipline and gave them a challenge. Note that the latter two bore more on the climate and manner of instructional delivery than on the affect itself. In sharp contrast to frequent claims that teacher attitude is the primary, if not the only variable in need of change, Thompson (2002) determined that this specific group of African American high school students felt teachers liked them (85%), said teachers cared about them (75%), and felt they could graduate (86%) and become successful (86%). Delpit also notes that "cushy" treatment is not what students need since "oppression can arise out of warmth and friendliness" (p. 296). In Thompson's study, student concerns seemed focused more on the academics, especially teacher maintenance of high academic rigor in the context of appropriate levels of support. Students saw teacher *affect* as important, but really as a backdrop to academic scaffolding.

Howard (2002), in a more provocative 2-year study intended to garner urban African American elementary and high school students' perspectives on the kind of teaching and classroom climate they believed enhanced their academic achievement, found that students preferred teachers who created a *"home-like" and "community-like" environment*s in which practices (daily classroom rituals and traditions, topics, interactional styles, emotional exchanges, and phrases used in learning conversations) mirrored the styles used in the home and community. Hence, the backdrop does not constitute pampering but rather the creation of an atmosphere featuring familiarity. The writer also found that teachers who *displayed caring (about student learning) in familiar ways* (provided direct statements of affirmation; showed a range of emotions; use familiar actions as stimuli) created climates that were more facilitative of student learning. The writer admits, however, that not all interactional styles are facilitative of learning for all students (for instance, student alleged positive reaction to teacher emotional outbursts ["hollering"] once its motive is understood to be positive and link to achievement expectations). Teachers must often get to understand students as individuals in order to determine what adjusted practice works for whom. Still, the study provides confirmation of the notion that *cultural continuity in instruction* and the foundation of the teacher effect is quite critical for CLDs. That is, the closer interaction patterns, language use, and instructional styles and content are to the familiar—the less difference in cultural practices there is between home, community and school environments—the more facilitative the classroom environment tends to be of student learning (Delpit, 1995; Epstein, Sanders, Simon, Salinas, Jansorn, & Van Voorhis, 2002; González, Moll, & Amanti, 2005).

Delpit (1995) emphasizes affective factors as critical in creating enabling environments. The writer asserts that unlike learning a first language or dialect, learning a second language/dialect and learning to operate in a second culture "is heavily influenced by highly charged *affective factors*" including *"exposure, comfort level, motivation, familiarity,* and *practice*" (p. 4). Krashen's (2003) notion of *the affective filter* communicates a similar notion, that is, that "when affective conditions are not optimal, when the student is not motivated (*motivation*), does not identify with the speakers of the language being learned (*identity*), or is overanxious about his performance (*anxiety*)," this causes a "mental block" that prevents linguistic input from "reaching that part of the brain responsible for language acquisition" (p. 31). Thus, attention to both teacher and student affect is crucial if literacy achievement is to improve for CLDS, especially speakers of AAVE who often see their communities as being in opposition to the dominant culture on which school practices are framed. Teachers must receive training that hones their ability to create the right climates for learning as well as to adjust their practices. They must learn to give due consideration to factors that might cause a heightening or lowering of a child's affective filter. However, how is this done?

Delpit (1995) recommends that both leaders and teachers recognize that "the linguistic form a student brings to school is intimately connected with loved ones, community, and personal identity" and that teachers should use this recognition to provide students with a learning context in which they retain this link while "learning a new code in a nonthreatening real communicative context," one in which students are not penalized for carrying community links into the school sphere (p. 53). Ladson-Billings' (1995) research in which parents were treated as "experts" on good teachers and teaching, noted that parents viewed "good" teachers as those who show respect for parents and communities, who ignite student enthusiasm and change in attitudes toward learning, and who promoted academic success while honoring home cultures. Both competence and affect are cited as crucial and teachers must necessarily "cross borders" to meet student and parent expectations.

Other Dimensions of Teacher Training in Adjusted Practices

While we have hinted at some dimensions of training in the preceding discussion, other dimensions are evident in the literature, especially in the work of Zeichner (1992), Ladson-Bilings (1995), Gay (2002), and lately, that of Paris and Ball (2009). Ladson-Billings asserts that teachers must be trained so that they can help students: (a) *succeed academically* without becoming social isolates who must alienate themselves from their culture to be viewed as potentially successful by teachers; (b) *demonstrate social competence* by synchronizing the structure and content of school-sanctioned interaction with students' socially learned styles of speech, language interaction styles, and communication patterns; (c) *become socio-politically critical* and not be hindered by teachers who deny the existence of social inequities. Building cultural awareness in teachers of their possibly privileged existence and its contrast with student realities is critical.

Gay (2002) demands attention to existing beliefs/ideologies and practices held by teachers and which are obstacles to learning for African American student, maintaining that such orientations must change in order for teacher practice to change. Much of this claim reverberates in Chamberlain's (2002) work previously discussed. Zeichner (1992) too maintains that in general "there is a common set of dispositions, knowledge and skills which are needed to teach ethic- and language-minority students, regardless of the particular circumstances of specific groups of students" (p. 6). Two critical requirements Zeichner cites are that: (a) the teacher possesses a desire to learn about (and from) their students and the communities in which they live, and (b) the teacher is able to bring knowledge garnered to bear account on their instructional practices (p. 6). Other variables include high expectations; appropriate scaffolding; a multicultural curriculum, and culturally relevant teaching and assessment strategies in addition to the ability to use sociocultural awareness—knowledge of child/adolescent development and language acquisition, and of the intersection between language, culture socio-economics—to inform their practice. Teachers so equipped are able to enhance student performance while allowing them to retain a clear sense of their own identities.

How is Training in Adjusted Practices Typically Delivered?

Zeichner's (1992) work provides an overview of exemplary teacher training practices and approaches (both infusion-oriented and curriculum add-ons) that have targeted at least one area of diversity training for in-service teachers. Examples include:

1. PROTEACH, a program which, through *readings, discussions, and/or direct contact*, and in some cases candidate *ethnographic studies* with minority groups, allowed teachers to gain an understanding of the relationship between culture, language, and the type of learning needed to combat low expectations teachers often hold;
2. Candidate *autobiographies* which foster understanding of candidates own cultural

experiences and identities and how these may vary markedly from the lived experiences of students;

3. *Discussions in collaborative groups*, which center on teacher attitudes toward minority students;
4. *Field experience* in relevant communities;
5. *Community expert programs* in the Human Service Project which recruited community people as experts as in the National Teacher Corps Program;
6. Exposure to community *histories* as in the Teachers for Alaska program, and
7. *Viewing activities* using resources such as "Eyes on the Prize," a video about the civil rights movement.

Teacher training programs can draw on these in framing their program. In fact, *Theories of Literacy* draws on the cultural awareness and practices dimension while a follow-up course addresses embedded community practice and community activism in a serve and learn project.

Aside from work in teacher training institutions, several change efforts have sought to use the online medium to equip teacher key personnel with the linguistic and cultural awareness, instructional practices and the appropriate disposition, necessary to address the needs of Culturally and Linguistically Diverse Students (CLDs). In fact, the technology media seems to afford one of the most cost effective (often free) means of communicating needed information on diversity to the general community. Wolfram (2011) cites various attempts at conditioning the affect of both teachers and the general public toward specific language varieties. The researcher cites Geoff Nunberg' s program *Fresh Air* on National Public Radio as well as Nunberg's numerous commentaries in the *New York Times'* "Week in Review" and in other periodicals. Wolfram also cites Web-based language blogs, language-focused channels on YouTube, and special-interest groups on Facebook, Twitter, and other virtual social networks, all of which have sought to disseminate information on language and cultural diversity so as to raise public awareness of the need to adjust thinking and action in response to diversity. Wolfram highlights the "immediacy afforded" by technology, which makes it a successful medium for fostering public education. A noted and innovative trend has been to use permanent as well as limited-time museum exhibits, done in collaboration with community-based cultural preservation societies. Museums exhibits, such as the North Carolina Language and Life Project, have highlighted language diversity in specific communities, seeking to present such diversity in a positive light. Teacher educator can invite students in their courses to tune in to such programs and can organize visits to these exhibits and communities to increase their level of cultural awareness.

Several efforts have targeted teachers specifically. Projects such as *Everyone has an accent;* North Carolina University's *Dialect Awareness Curriculum* and Resources; *Talk* NC; *Do you speak American?;* and LearnNC all address dialect and linguistic awareness for teachers. Additionally, many studies available on the World Wide Web provide suggestions on isolated practices. No known online program provides a core network of training activities geared at addressing diversity issues relevant to the literacy education of African American students in particular, or focuses on training prospective literacy leaders to promote use of adjusted practices among literacy educators. Additionally, no known program links such training to exploration of theoretical perspectives on teaching.

Zeichner (1995; citing Haberman, 1991) highlight a widely held conception (or misconception) that "most typical majority teacher education students are developmentally not capable of dealing with the complexities associated with intercultural teaching" and that programs in teacher education "are not capable of producing the kind of fundamental change in values, attitudes and dispositions needed for successful teaching of ethnic- and linguistic-minority students" (p. 19). In fact, Zeichner, while arguing for such training in teacher education programs, cites evidence showing that such training often inadvertently strengthens the very beliefs and practices they wish to eradicate.

Given mandates from IRA for attention to diversity across a spectrum of competencies, the instructor wished to examine the current course for quality of attention to diversity issues and practices. The aim of the study was to determine whether a specific course geared at framing teacher orientation to literacy teaching practices and which has been re-structured to integrate adjusted practices - actually facilitated greater uptake of attitudes, work styles and values that characterize adjusted practice and which can truly result in responsive instruction for students who speak AAVE/AAE. The researcher hopes that such a scrutiny can highlight critical dimensions of adjusted practices to guide teacher training as well as the technology that can best facilitate learning of these dimensions during teacher training. The content and medium of teacher training is critical, but can one truly gauge candidates' level of uptake?

METHODOLOGY

The study relied on grounded theory, using a structure matrix to guide analysis of the data gathered from candidates' blog and wiki postings. Several frameworks previously discussed provide guidance in selecting the content of training in adjusted practices for teachers. However, only the Paris and Ball (2009) framework allows for measurement of teachers' level of engagement in and uptake of adjusted practices. The current researcher provides a modified version of that framework below, and later uses this framework as part of the matrix employed in analyzing the data. See Table 2. In this table, the levels of uptake are linked to activities in which candidates in this and a follow-up course were engaged. Activities used in the current course are underlined. Table 1 had indicated tools used but some hints of these are in the table. Levels outlined in the table later are combined with and matched to quotes from student postings and reflections in case blogs and wikis, and with codes for dimensions of adjusted practices derived from the literature. Uptake in both the OD and ND deliveries are then compared, and the degree of difference in the quality of

Table 2. Teacher uptake of adjusted practices (using levels from Paris & Ball, 2009)

Levels of Engagement	Descriptor	Candidate Activities
Generativity	The teacher begins to conceptualize his/her classroom and the classroom of others in the school as sites of change where adjusted practices can be implementing.	Student **Blog Problem-Solving, Wiki Guided Introspective Writing** and **an Action Research Project.** (The latter requirement is met in a follow-up practicum and action research project at a local refugee center over a 15-week period.)
Internalization	The teacher critiques theories and research and uses insights from research-supported practices to seek solution to classroom related problems.	Critique Of perspectives as part of wiki reflection; engagement in action research as done to some degree in the **Final Case and Wiki Reflection**.
Ideological Becoming	The teacher learns new theoretical perspectives and begins to accept, reject or question particular perspectives and practices. There is an increased sense of urgency to act.	**Wiki Guided Introspective Writing**– Mini rubrics guide teacher reflection based on prompts requiring them to think of the implications of theories for practice with CLDs.
Metacognitive Awareness	The teacher's words and deeds convey understanding of the importance of literacy acquisition for CLDs, and acknowledge societal inequities.	**Videos, Podcasts, Lecture Captures, Ebrary readings and links to other online resources.** The students are exposed to insights from theories and observe demonstrations of recommended practices in classrooms.

student output in the OD and ND version of the course explored. Data from two sets of students in two deliveries are examined. Each delivery/group featured 16 students working in teams of four.

Final Framework, Course Structure, and Outcomes

The framework used to examine candidates' blog and wiki postings for references to a broad cross-section of adjusted practices comprised the following elements:

1. Teacher cultural awareness and its link with instructional practices (CAPS);
2. Diverse ways of thinking, cognitive processing, and assessment (WAC);
3. Diverse rhetorical norms and cognitive judgments (RNC);
4. Culture preferences and affect (CPA);
5. Diverse behavior norms, home-like environments and the classroom interactional contexts (BIC);
6. Creation of welcoming and familiar spaces (CWS);
7. Power, pedagogy and teaching style (PPL);
8. Materials, curriculum representations and expectations (MCR);
9. Literacy expression, print functions and diverse text forms (LEP); crossing borders/spaces (CBS).

Below, the categories are matched to quotes from candidates' total contributions in the Old Delivery (OD) and to exemplary quotes gleaned from the New Delivery. Quotes and categories were then matched to the Ball and Paris (2009) levels of teacher uptake of adjusted practices.

Cultural Awareness and Literacy Perspectives (CAPS)

OD: "But what happens to those people who didn't have enough literacy opportunities?" "… often children today, much like Joseph, have the cards stacked against them at an early age." (*Metacognitive awareness – The candidate expresses awareness of differential opportunities in society and in schools*).

ND: "… as a teacher, notice the cultural diversity. If you have 2 or 3 "main" cultures, (for example, 5 students are from South America, and 6 students are from African or African-American cultures), and do your research into their language norms. By familiarizing yourself with their language norms, you will be more able to understand the children's thought process when reading, writing or speaking" (*Generativity: The candidate suggests to fellow teachers ways to build cultural awareness. Here the candidate adopts the role of leader and coach*).

Creating Welcoming and Familiar Spaces (CWS)

OD: "Hopefully the school has a positive environment, which could encourage this child to explore literacy for himself" *(Generativity: The candidate recognizes a need create a positive and enabling learning environment for the student).*

ND: "Teachers have a very key role in helping our society to accept and incorporate these cultures into the makeup of the larger society. They can achieve this by making small but critical efforts to include various cultures in the classroom. One way a teacher can do is by arranging field trips to different cultural events/communities" (*Generativity: The candidate the school as sites of change and teachers as key change agents in fostering acceptance of diversity).*

Rhetorical Norms and Cognitive Judgments (RNC)

OD: "… they [the child's parents] could have helped to build story knowledge with him by orally telling him stories ..." (*Ideological Becoming:*

There is an increased sense of need for action and advocacy on the candidate's part).

ND: "While math and science facts should be the same from culture to culture, text norms and writing/speaking styles can vary wildly. It is the teachers' job to acknowledge the student's 'home-based ways of thinking,' give this way of thinking merit and credit, while simultaneously teaching students how 'academic English'should look, sounds, and feel without offering it as the 'right' language, but instead, 'the appropriate language for school'" (*Metacognitive awareness – The candidate expresses awareness of differences in thinking and text forms across cultures and of a need to help students transition to school-based text forms).*

ND: "Here are 3 ways in which a teacher can try to teach literacy among culturally diverse students: Start with a lesson on "what is text structure" (create a visual, for example a mountain to demonstrate rising action, climax, and resolution). Analyze western examples of text structure as a class using short story books. Divide class into small groups and have them cooperate to analyze a different text. The next day, introduce high quality literature from different cultures. Try and represent the cultures of the students in the class (this may be a great opportunity to utilize the school librarian). In the same small groups, ask the students to analyze the text structure of the new piece of literature. Advise them to create some sort of graphic organizer or visual representation in order to make a small presentation to the class. Some students may find very similar text structures, and some literature may offer varied types of text structure. Keep the new texts in the classroom library to remind students that multicultural literature is not only used during "special" assignments, but can be a part of everyday reading, giving credit and value to the culture. To further the lesson, ask students to bring in examples of multicultural literature that they may have at home. If students bring some in, share them during read-alouds or literature circles. See if the students want to share their thoughts and feelings about the books they brought it—why they like them, and any history they have with the text. Ask to include these books in the classroom library for the remainder of the school year. Also, as a teacher, notice the cultural diversity. If you have 2 or 3 "main" cultures, (for example, 5 students are from South America, and 6 students are from African or African-American cultures), and do your research into their language norms. By familiarizing yourself with their language norms, you will be more able to understand the children's thought process when reading, writing or speaking" *(Generativity: The candidate adopts the role of coach explaining for teachers how they can change their practice).*

ND: "They enjoyed listened to other versions of the story from other cultures and then ultimately being able to write their own version. I was able to help point out some of the words pronunciations and text structures they were having difficulties with in a non-threatening way" *(Generativity – The candidate sees the classroom as a place where students can share and understand each other's culture even as they learn to be literate in the target language).*

Power, Pedagogy, and Teaching/ Learning Styles (PPL)

OD: "In a larger class teachers are not able to give as much attention as they would like to for each student and therefore it is easier for students to start falling behind without the teacher noticing" (Metacognitive awareness: The candidate expresses concern for the education of CLDs).

ND: "CLDs, Asian, African-American, Native American, and Hispanic students, may have been brought up in an environment that stresses the importance of the whole group not individuals. In the school system, most teachers focus on teaching styles where students mainly learn and earn their grades on an individual basis. CLDs' learning is negatively impacted due to this difference… students should have the option to work independently, with a partner, or in a small group which helps facilitate social collaboration among the students" *(Generativity – The candidate recognizes that teaching practices can negatively impact CLDs and suggest shifts in orientation to match student needs. The classroom then becomes a site of change").*

Literacy Expression, Print Functions, and Text Forms (LEP)

OD: "... they [the child's parents] could have helped to build story knowledge with him by orally telling him stories ..." *(Ideological Becoming: The candidate perceives an increased need for action and advocacy in the community).*

ND: "Another technique is creating Home Literacy Portfolios for each student. A Home Literacy Portfolio is a collection of materials, activities, and observations on how students learn literacy in school AND at home. Once enough information is gathered, the teacher and family member(s) sit down and have a discussion about the student's literacy development. This conversation can help students because teachers can use the literacy practices at home to differentiate instruction for students to be more successful. On the contrary, parents can use the literacy practices at school to help reinforce and promote literacy development for their child. I have no experience using this technique in my classroom experiences but I really enjoyed learning about the technique and plan to use it in my future classroom"*(Generativity – The candidate suggests strategies teachers can use to adjust their practice. The strategies here are bi-directional and promote reciprocity).*

Materials, Curriculum Representations, and Expectations (MCR)

OD: "...the teacher could have had the students make up their own stories that she could have used to teach with..." *(Generativity: There is an increased sense of need for action and advocacy on the part of the candidate).*

ND: "An example of a writing project is making a classroom recipe book. Students each write their own recipe that may reflect their cultural backgrounds and put them all together in one book. This is a great activity that helps to validate the students' cultures and it also allows for the students to learn about one another. A teacher can also extend this activity by inviting parent or family volunteers to come in and explain/show artifacts that relate to their cultural backgrounds. Teachers need to make a valiant effort to incorporate their students' funds of knowledge and their cultural backgrounds in lessons and projects so that they feel part of the learning community" *(Generativity – Teacher conceptualization of classroom as site of change and recommendation of concrete adjusted practices).*

Ways of Thinking, Cognitive Processing, and Assessment (WAC)

OD: "Limitations in text exposure as a result of limited reading ability can result in cognitive delay in the same way that cognitive delay can restrict reading development" *(Ideological becoming: Accepting new theoretical perspective, that is, Stanovich's [1986] notion of the Matthew Effect is reading).*

ND: "...tests are subject to vetting by a group of teacher and non-teacher members of a 'Bias Review Panel' ... teachers confer with each other regarding potential test bias (Propman, 2012) *(Generativity – The candidate suggests a strategy to combat test bias that may negative impact assessment judgments made about students).*

"Recognizing that even tests from reputable companies, or tests that a teacher has created themselves can often have unrecognized bias. Teachers must vet every question they ask their students to the best of their ability, often ask for a second or third opinion from diverse teachers, and continue to educate themselves and keep current on issues of test bias that can too often lead to unfair marginalization of students" *(Generativity – The candidate recognizes the potential for faulty evaluation of student competence and suggests strategies to help offset such a problem).*

Crossing or Borders Spaces (CBS)

OD: "We would like to send 'book bags' home with students so they can have some exposure at home. However, many people are resistant because of our budget and fear of books not being returned so they can circulate to everyone. I feel it is so important to find a way to bring resources into the home. ..in my school, many students had a long commute home. This made many students want to carry less, understandably. As a secondary school teacher, I expect to face difficulties trying to get students to take things home. However, it is sad to hear that there are difficulties establishing partnerships with families with young children… it is always a challenge to create effective partnerships with families. I really feel that there needs to be a push to partner with families and provided resources and support, especially for families who are resistant to being involved with their school because of their own past negative experiences. Often families with limited resources are reluctant to trust schools and teachers. In addition to lending resources and support to families, teachers have the ability to create literacy rich environments which support the culture of all different children, which unfortunately Joseph did not have access to" *(Internalization – The candidate feels a need to act and to be an advocate for students but is unsure actions will work given systemic constraints).*

ND: "I observed each student giving a presentation on any part of their culture that interested them: some students gave presentations on their religion, food, literature, language dress, or music. By offering pieces of his or her home culture, each student felt validated and included in a very diverse classroom."

"Furthermore, if teaching [social skills] through book clubs, students are able to associate time in their lives when the given "rule" has presented itself in their lives; for example, if they are learning about sharing, then can offer a personal story in which sharing plays a key role" *(Generativity – Candidates report on their own experiences with strategies and suggest additional ones).*

Dual Scaffolds and Supports (DSS)

OD: "If this was not possible, the teacher could have come to Joseph's home with the materials in the classroom and worked with him to help him read. Furthermore, instead of teaching words the teacher could have had the students make up their own stories that she could have used to teach words within the story context that [sic] way the words would become more meaningful and the students would have been able to remember them"(Internalization: Increased sense of need for action and advocacy).

ND: As I learned and researched this topic, I was reminded of a wonderful episode of NPR's radio-documentary series, *This American Life*. The theme of this particular episode was "Going Big," and this first story centered on a concept called "Baby College" presented by The Harlem Children's Zone created by Geoffery Canada. Geoffery Canada. The Harlem Children's Zone wanted to "Go Big" by giving every child living in Harlem a real chance to go to college, but it started with the parent's taking an 8-week "baby college" course, where the parents were taught how to best support their children's academic and social learning. Canada's message to parents was: it doesn't take a lot to get your child ahead, everyone can do it, and here is how… This segment of the episode is only 13 minutes long, and I would highly recommend everyone take a listen (it's free, too) (Generativity – The candidate reflects on his/her own experiences in learning about diversity and recommends a resource for teachers).

What can be observed from the quotations below is that while there was some uptake of practices in the Old Delivery, uptake in the New Delivery was at a much higher level with candidates being more capable of recommending actions and techniques for teachers. They were also able to recommend resources to further the learning of other teachers. Teachers in the New Delivery also reflected more readily on strategies they had partaken in.

Differences in levels of uptake across the deliveries are depicted in Figure 2. As can be seen, levels of uptake were limited and quite unstable in the Old Delivery with only CWS and PPL reaching the highest level of uptake (generativity) in the Old Delivery. Uptake hit generativity on all dimension of adjusted practice in the New Delivery of the course. Note in the OD that uptake of practices related to cultural awareness (CAPS) and understanding diverse behavior norms was particularly low, and is a source of concern. Uptake of practices related to rhetorical (language) norms was disturbingly low in the OD, especially given the fact that the candidates were prospective language educators. Much improvement in uptake was evident in the New Delivery.

Conclusions from the study are presented below.

FINDINGS AND CONCLUSION

At What Level Were Candidates Exposed to Principles and Practices for Delivering "Adjusted Practices" in the New Delivery (ND) Version of the Course?

Data revealed a more consistent and uniform uptake at a high level (generativity) on all dimensions of adjusted practice in the ND version of the course. Uptake in the OD version tended to be inconsistent and was at much lower levels. One will note in the graph visible fluctuation and a limited spread in uptake (one or two students demonstrating uptake of each dimension). Student postings were far more affirming of a unified focus on all dimensions of adjusted practices (though number of students demonstrating uptake was not gleaned in the ND).

A close look at the data for the OD version revealed that candidates tended to focus more on the factors impacting literacy development (discussion of causes of problems) rather than on the adjusted practices themselves, even though candidates had access to the appropriate information. In the ND version of the course, the instructor was able to direct student attention away from lengthy discus-

Figure 2. Levels of uptake of adjusted practices in the old and new delivery versions of theories of literacy

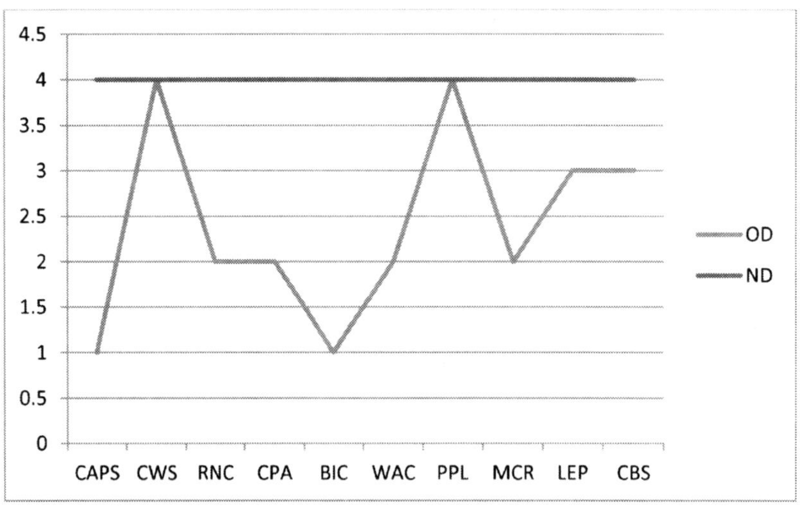

sion of causes, and toward practical solutions to address problems the student faced. The result was a higher level of uptake of practices. On average, between two and four strategies were cited by each candidate in each of the wiki guided reflections and in the blog problem solving in the ND version of the course, as opposed to the relatively few hints at practice in the OD version of the course.

To What Extent Were Specific References to Adjusted Practices Evident in Candidates' Products in the Old Delivery (OD) Version of the Course?

As indicated in Table 2, references were made to all dimensions of adjusted practice in both deliveries. What differed was *level and quality* of uptake. Comparison of OD and ND deliveries in terms of representation of Paris and Ball's (2009) dimensions revealed that levels of uptake in the ND version of the course was by far more advanced. This may have as much to do with the additional content infused into the course as with the additional tools/media used to convey this content. The two are difficult to disentangle in this preliminary exploration. Comments from students such as "I must tell you I enjoyed your course so very much, and learned so much from it. I am so glad I ended up taking it! It has been a wonderful experience" communicate students' enthusiasm and confidence in their learning having taken it.

How Did Technology Tools and Added Diversity Content Further Candidates' Level of Attention to Adjusted Practices in the ND Version?

The only difference between deliveries was the infusing of the new technology and content. While the research admits that variations in student competencies across deliveries, if such variations exist, might have accounted for variations in performance, feedback from students indicated that the means through which the content was delivered as well as the new content itself made a big difference. Motivation was much higher as seen in statements that students made which indicate that they really enjoyed the course. While the study was not meant to provide conclusive statements regarding the role of technology in student learning, it does provide anecdotal evidence to support enhanced use of technology in ensuring greater uptake of course content.

The researcher intends to follow up this study with inferential research that explores the data in much more detail.

REFERENCES

Adger, C., Christian, W., & Wolfam, D. (2007). *Dialects in schools and communities*. Mahwah, NJ: Lawrence Erlbaum Associates.

Anderson, N. B., & Screen, R. M. (1994). *Multicultural perspectives in communication disorders*. San Diego, CA: Singular Publishing Group.

Ball, A. F., & Farr, M. (2003). Dialects, culture, and teaching the English language arts. In J. Flood, J. M. Jensen, D. Lapp, & J. R. Squire (Eds.), *Handbook of Research on Teaching the English Language Arts,* (pp. 1-35). Retrieved from http://www.stanford.edu/~arnetha/pdf/BALLFARR%20w_Full%20Bibl.pdf

Baugh, J. (2000). *Beyond ebonics: Linguistic pride and racial prejudice*. Oxford, UK: Oxford University Press.

Baylor, A. L., & Ritchie, D. (2002). What factors facilitate teacher skill, teacher morale, and perceived student learning in technology using classrooms? *Computers & Education, 39*, 395–414. doi:10.1016/S0360-1315(02)00075-1

Beggs, T. A. (2000). Influences and barriers to the adoption of instructional technology. In *Proceedings of the Mid-South Instructional Technology Conference,* (pp. 1-14). Murfreesboro, TN: IEEE.

Cazden, C. B. (2001). *Classroom discourse: The language of teaching and learning*. Retrieved from http://www.wou.edu/~girodm/library/cazden.pdf

Chamberlain, S. P. (2005). Recognizing and responding to cultural diversity. *Intervention in School and Clinic*, *40*(4), 195–211. doi:10.1177/10534512050400040101

Christian, D. (1997). *Vernacular dialects in U.S. schools*. Retrieved from http://www.cal.org/resources/digest/christ01.html

Coleman, J. A. (1997). Residence abroad within language study. *Language Teaching*, *30*(1), 1–20. doi:10.1017/S0261444800012659

Costa, A. L., & Garmston, R. J. (2002). *Cognitive coaching a foundation for renaissance schools*. Norwood, MA: Christopher-Gordon Publishers, Inc.

Craig, H. K., & Washington, J. A. (2000). An assessment battery for identifying language impairments in African-American children. *Journal of Language. Speech and Hearing Research*, *43*(2), 366–379.

Cummins, J. (1999). BICS and CALP: Clarifying the distinction. *University of Toronto*. Retrieved from http://ezproxy.wou.edu:2100/hww/results/external_link_maincontentframe.jhtml?_DARGS=/hww/results/results_common.jhtml.44

Cummins, J. (2005). *Teaching for cross-language transfer in dual language education: Possibilities and pitfalls*. Paper presented at TESOL Symposium on Dual Language Education: Teaching and Learning Two Languages in the EFL Setting. Retrieved from http://74.125.155.132/scholar?q=cache:BOtf0n95sMJ:scholar.google.com/+cummins,+j+iceberg&hl=en&as_sdt=0,38

Delpit, L. D. (1988). The silenced dialogue: Power and privilege in educating other people's children. *Harvard Educational Review*, *58*(3), 280–296. Retrieved from http://faculty.washington.edu/rikitiki/tcxg464sp08/Silenced%20Dialogue%20by%20L%20Delpitpdf

Delpit, L. D. (1995). *Other people's children: Cultural conflict in the classroom: Language diversity and learning*. New York, NY: The New Press. Retrieved from http://www.d.umn.edu/~hrallis/courses/1100sp04/readings/1100pdfs/Delpit%20-Lang%20in%20Clsmr.pdf

Delpit, L. D. (2007). Skills and other dilemmas of a progressive black educator. In D. George & J. Timbur (Eds.), *Reading Culture: Contexts for Critical Reading and Writing,* (pp. 180-185). New York, NY: Pearson/Longman. Retrieved from http://eng022.files.wordpress.com/2009/01/lisa-delpit-skills-and-other-dillemmas.pdf

Dillard, J. L. (1972). *Black English: Its history and usage in the United States*. New York, NY: Random House.

Epstein, J. L., Sanders, M. G., Simon, B. S., Salinas, K. C., Jansorn, N. R., & Van Voorhis, F. L. (2002). *School, family, and community partnerships: Your handbook for action* (2nd ed.). Thousand Oaks, CA: Corwin Press.

Gay. (2002). Culturally responsive teaching in special education for ethnically diverse students: Setting the stage. *Qualitative Studies in Education, 15*(6), 613-629. Retrieved from http://www.cehd.umn.edu/ppg/Partnerships/CCresources/Gay.pdf

González, N., Moll, L., & Amanti, C. (2005). *Funds of knowledge: Theorizing practices in households, communities, and classrooms*. Mahwah, NJ: Lawrence Erlbaum Associates, Publishers.

Graham, S., & Harris, K. (2007). Best practices in teaching planning. In Graham, S., MacArthur, C. A., & Fitzgerald, J. (Eds.), *Best Practices in Writing Instruction* (p. 138). New York, NY: The Guilford Press.

Green, R. L., & Etheridge, C. P. (2001). Collaborating to establish standards and accountability: Lesson learned about systemic change. *Education, 121*(4), 821–829.

Hanley, P., Maringe, F., & Ratcliffe, M. (2008). Evaluation of professional development: Deploying a process-focused model. *International Journal of Science Education, 30*(5), 711–725. doi:10.1080/09500690701854899

Howard, T. C. (2002). Hearing footsteps in the dark: African American students' descriptions of effective teachers. *Journal of Education for Students Placed at Risk, 7*(4), 425–444. Retrieved from http://www.appstate.edu/~koppenhaverd/rcoe/5710/read/africanam/howard02.pdf doi:10.1207/S15327671ESPR0704_4

Kadzera, M. (2006). *Use of instructional technologies in teacher training colleges in Malawi*. (Doctoral Dissertation). Virginia Polytechnic Institute and State University. Blacksburg, VA.

Kozma, R. B. (1991). Learning with media. *Review of Educational Research, 61*(2), 179–212.

Krashen, S. (2003). *Explorations in language acquisition and use*. Portsmouth, NH: Heinemann.

Labov, W. (1965). Stages in the acquisition of Standard English. In Shuy, R. W. (Ed.), *Social Dialects and Language Learning* (pp. 77–103). Champaign, IL: National Council of Teachers of English.

Labov, W. (1995). Can reading failure be reversed? A linguistic approach to the question. In Gadsden, V., & Wagner, D. (Eds.), *Literacy among African American Youth* (pp. 39–68). Cresskill, NJ: Hampton Press.

Ladson-Billings, G. (1994). *The dreamkeepers: Successful teachers of African American children*. San Francisco, CA: Jossey-Bass.

Ladson-Bilings, G. (1995). Toward a theory of culturally relevant pedagogy. *American Educational Research Journal, 32*(3), 465–491. Retrieved from http://edt2.educ.msu.edu/DWong/Te150S10/CourseReader/LadsonBillingsAERJ1995_CulturallyRelevan.pdf

Laing, S. P., & Kahmi, A. (2002). Alternative assessment of language and literacy in culturally and linguistically diverse populations. *Language, Speech, and Hearing Services in Schools, 34*(4), 44–55.

Lipman, P. (1997). Restructuring in context: A case study of teacher participation and the dynamics of ideology, race, and power. *American Educational Research Journal, 20*(34), 3–37.

Mohatt, G., & Erickson, F. (1981). Cultural differences in teaching styles in an Odawa school: A sociolinguistic approach. In Trueba, H., Guthrie, G., & Au, K. (Eds.), *Culture and The bilingual Classroom* (pp. 105–119). Rowley, MA: Newbury House.

National Center for Educational Statistics. (2007). *Trial urban district assessment results at grades 4 and 8*. Retrieved from http://nces.ed.gov/nationsreportcard/pdf/dst2007/2008455.pdf

National Center for Educational Statistics. (2009). *Achievement gaps: How black and white students in public schools perform in mathematics and reading on the national assessment of educational progress*. Retrieved from http://nces.ed.gov/nationsreportcard/pdf/studies/2009455.pdf

Nelson-Barber, S., & Estrin, E. (1995). Bringing Native American perspectives to mathematics and science teaching. *Theory into Practice, 34*(3), 174–185. doi:10.1080/00405849509543677

Owen, S. (2005). The power of collegiality in school-based professional development. *Australian Journal of Teacher Education, 35*(1), 1–12. Retrieved from http://ro.ecu.edu.au/cgi/viewcontent.cgi?article=1391&context=ajte

Paris, D., & Ball, A. S. (2009). Teacher knowledge in culturally and linguistically complex classrooms: Lessons from the golden age and beyond. In Morrow, L. M., Rueda, R., & Lapp, D. (Eds.), *Handbook of Research on Literacy and Diversity* (pp. 379–395). York, NY: Guildford Press.

Pollock, K. E., & Meredith, L. H. (2007). Phonetic transcription of African American vernacular English. *Communication Disorders Quarterly, 23*(1), 47–53. doi:10.1177/152574010102300107

Powell, R., & Rightmyer, E. (2011). *Literacy for all students: An instructional framework for closing the gap*. New York, NY: Routledge.

Redd, T. M., & Webb, K. S. (2005). *A teacher's introduction to African American English: What a writing teacher should know*. Urbana, IL: National Council of Teachers of English.

Renn, J. (2010). *Acquiring style: the development of dialect shifting among African-American children*. (Doctoral Dissertation). University of North Carolina. Chapel Hill, NC. Retrieved from http://www.unc.edu/linguistics/JRenndissertation.pdf

Roblyer, M. D. (2005). Educational technology research that makes a difference: Series introduction. *Contemporary Issues in Technology & Teacher Education, 5*(2), 192–201.

Rowe, R. D. (2005). *The development of African American English in the oldest black town in America: -s absence in Princeville, North Carolina*. (MA Thesis). North Carolina State University. Raleigh, NC.

Sanacore, J. (2002). *Genuine caring and literacy learning for African American children*. Retrieved from http://www.eric.ed.gov/PDFS/ED471395.pdf

Servage, L. (2008). Critical and transformative practices in professional learning communities. *Teacher Education Quarterly*, 63–77. Retrieved from http://www.teqjournal.org/backvols/2008/35_1/10servage.pdf

Smitherman, G. (1997). The chain remain the same: Communicative practices in the hip hop nation. *Journal of Black Studies, 28*(1), 3–25.

Squires, D. A. (1996). The comer program: Changing school culture. *Educational Leadership, 53*(4), 29–32.

Taylor, V. (2000). *Perceptions of selected black female middle-level managers on advancement in higher education administration*. (PhD Thesis). Columbia University. New York, NY.

Thompson, G. (2002). *African American teens discuss their schooling experiences*. Westport, CT: Greenwood Publishers.

Van Hofwegen, J., & Wolfram, W. (2010). Coming of age in African American English: A longitudinal study. *Journal of Sociolinguistics, 14*(4), 427–455. Retrieved from http://www.ncsu.edu/linguistics/docs/pdfs/walt/Coming%20of%20Age-pdf.pdf doi:10.1111/j.1467-9841.2010.00452.x

Walker, B. (2008). Adjusting instruction to meet students' needs. *Reading Today, 25*(6), 18–19.

Willis, A. I. (2000). *Critical issue: Addressing literacy needs in culturally and linguistically diverse classrooms*. Retrieved from http://www.ncrel.org/sdrs/areas/issues/content/cntareas/reading/li400.htm

Wolfram, W. (1969). *A sociolinguistic description of Detroit Negro speech*. Washington, DC: Center for Applied Linguistics.

Wolfram, W. (2004). *The grammar of urban African American vernacular English*. Retrieved from http://www.ncsu.edu/linguistics/docs/pdfs/walt/PDF-Urban_AAE.pdf

Wolfram, W. (2010). *The grammar of rural and ethnic varieties in the southeast*. Retrieved from http://www.ncsu.edu/linguistics/docs/pdfs/walt/PDF-Rural_Southeast.pdf

Wolfram, W. (2011). *Changing misconceptions about dialect diversity: The role of public education*. Retrieved from http://www.cal.org/resources/digest/digest_pdfs/changing-misconceptions-about-dialect-diversity.pdf

Wolfram, W., Adger, C. T., & Christian, D. (2007). *Dialects in schools and communities* (2nd ed.). Mahwah, NJ: Lawrence Erlbaum Associates.

Xu, S. H. (2001, July/August). Exploring diversity issues in teacher education. *Reading Online*, *5*(1). Retrieved from http://www.readingonline.org/newliteracies/lit_index.asp?HREF=action/xu/index.html

Zeichner, K. M. (1992). Educating teachers for cultural diversity. *National Council for Research in Teaching and Learning*. Retrieved from http://education.msu.edu/NCRTL/PDFs/NCRTL/SpecialReports/sr293.pdf

Chapter 15
E-Learning Quality through Second Life:
Exploiting, Investigating, and Evaluating the Efficiency Parameters of Collaborative Activities in Higher Education

Pellas Nikolaos
University of the Aegean, Greece

Kazanidis Ioannis
Kavala Institute of Technology, Greece

ABSTRACT

The systematic utilization and dissemination of e-learning, in juxtaposition with the expansion needs for collaborative knowledge, has led to a new generation system, Virtual Worlds (VWs). The quintessence and assistance of VWs allows adult users to immerse themselves in a common 3D multimedia environment, emphasizing co-creation and co-construction of their "knowledge field." The corollary of interactivity and social form of modeling, allows the design of e-learning activities in accordance with contemporary pedagogical approaches. This chapter focuses both on how using the most advanced 3D Web-emulator of the real world, Second Life (SL), will increase users' learning ability and vehemently consecrate the common multi-user environment as an incubator of knowledge and action. The methodology is to evaluate SL with the assistance of 70 trainee users, according to four different parameters that postulate the learning progression in a virtual system. The main contribution of this research will be to highlight the suitability of SL for organizing and conducting collaborative scenarios in higher education.

DOI: 10.4018/978-1-4666-2955-4.ch015

INTRODUCTION

The expanded use of PCs and Web technologies in Higher Education with contemporary pedagogical theories that emphasize in inquiry learning, and decision-making activities, have influenced most strongly the entire range of teaching and learning process. This new "knowledge field" tend to change the traditional way of (e-) educational practice that is composed through three different dimensions: the cognitive, the emotional and the social. Inasmuch as, the need to create equal opportunities for excluded social groups, is more crucial today than ever before. Ensuring the lifelong learning and the exemption from the spatial-temporal commitments are imposed by the traditional way, worthy of Open and Distance Learning, as an equally effective training plan with a conventional.

One of the challenges of today's educational systems is to upgrade the quality of the educational process through the use of technologically advanced learning environments, with both informal and formal Education. The computer-assisted training procedure is influenced by the extension of educational software. This includes information technologies such as the Internet, virtual reality, and the newer developments of artificial intelligence. Indeed, the dynamic view of Virtual Reality (VR), which is the "consequence" of this development, due to their outstanding characteristics, attracts interest both in the researching and the practical level. Web-based technology facilitates a variety of "alternative" ways for e-learning. Important advantages of these technologies allow students to (Clark & Maher, 2006; Franceschi & Lee, 2009; Lester & King, 2009; Pellas, 2012; Youngblut, 1998):

1. Visualize innovative concepts, observe phenomena or situations in extremely small to large spatial and temporal scales,
2. Teleport and visit other environments (or worlds) and interact with specific evidence,
3. Exploit activities that include these type of characteristics, which are the basis for implementing learning scenarios based on "modern" learning theories,
4. Construct knowledge and learn acquired e-skills through individual or group activities, in specially (pre-) designed virtual spaces or places.

The arrangements that mentioned above seem to come in contrast with most two-dimensional (2D) systems that are designed exclusively for learning (LMS: Learning Management Systems), as Blackboard or Moodle, etc. On the other hand, virtual environments do not differ in regard to the final learning product, providing students, according to their experience, with:

1. Creating online communities, both for initial training, and the latter for their professional acquisition skills, i.e. for Lifelong Learning (Bull & Kajder, 2004).
2. Engaging in action-based learning activities on scientific issues, and enhancing their social behavior (Kafai, 2006).
3. Promoting and enhancing the socio-cultural development, and the transformation of social relations into mental functions (Barab, et al., 2005).
4. Providing an environment for programming and co-construction of knowledge (Read, et al., 2006).
5. Exploring new mathematical concepts, and promoting scientific research (Clarke & Maher, 2006).
6. Connecting with theoretical psycho-pedagogical frameworks that define Contemporary Learning Theories (i.e. the descendants of socio-constructivism theory, such as Situated or Distributed Learning) to better study, observe and understand users' cognition (Dieterle & Clarke, 2005).

Therefore, the added contribution for Education could:

1. Be classified under a wide range of situations where the student can proceed to remove (deductive) or generalize inductive knowledge and
2. Be verified if the "proposed" knowledge is gained in this particular case.

The guiding axes of integration in distance education are to offer assistance as educational "vas deferens" forces. In addition, the implementation of the dynamic change of ideas, taking more into account of adult users' needs and interests, helps them to form new relationships with knowledge. Given the contribution of virtual worlds in education, and aforementioned factors, Second Life (SL) emerges with fascinating educational potential. It is one of the most popular and well-known virtual worlds that depicts digital situations and roles of our everyday life. Our chapter focuses on some answers to questions, concerning the effectiveness of the educational framework for implementing e-learning applications. To find these answers, we attempted to conduct a cumulative evaluation through a survey with a random sample of trainees' users.

BACKGROUND

The varied use of the term *"collaborative learning"* by utilizing Web (2.0)-based technologies, is expressed in two different perspectives: pedagogical and psychological. The pedagogical approach is considered "restrictive," when observing two or more people who work together. We suspect that the subjects will learn more effectively in this manner. The psychological is more "descriptive," and notes the cooperation of two or more people as a "learning mechanism," i.e. "how" they learn (Graetz, 2006). Students, certainly, do not learn to cooperate because they are two or more, but because they engage in certain activities that trigger specific "learning mechanisms" (cognitive systems). These include the activities (or mechanisms), performed individually, since each cognitive function is not suppressed by group interaction. The interaction between atoms creates extra activities (explanation, disagreement, mutual regulation, etc.), which cause additional cognitive mechanisms (knowledge extraction, internalization, reducing cognitive load, etc.) (Palincsar & Brown, 1984).

Collaborative learning can be provided through any form of education by using formal or informal ICT (Information & Communication Technology), which develops horizontal interactions among users. Recent studies (Lehtinen & Hakkarainen, 2001; Johnson, Suriya, Won, Berrett, & La Fleur, 2002; Shih & Yang, 2008) have shown that the learning process becomes more effective when there is cooperation at the level of thought and action shared between the participants to achieve a common goal. This phenomenon occurs similarly in virtual worlds. Three key elements that help this process become more effective during cooperative-type e-learning activities are:

1. Diversity of innovative teaching methods or applications based on Contemporary Learning theories (see the Social-Constructivism, and Distributed Learning, Situated Cognition, etc.) (Dillenbourg, 1994),
2. The appearance of anthropomorphic avatars (digital alter egos of oneself) that develop a new dimension between physical and digital "entities." This relationship is defined as vertical interaction that can greatly enhance the presumptive personal sense of presence and awareness of the student (Meadows, 2008; Zhigeng, Zhu, Zhang, & Hu, 2005),
3. The accessibility to the learning environment for the user (i.e., the interface). Findings of previous studies showed a positive correlation between users due to the common areas of learning, and the phenomenon

> of co- presence, i.e., the "co-existence" of teammates with others (Beer, Slack, & Armitt, 2002; De Lucia, Francese, Passero, & Tortora, 2009; Slater, Sadagic, Usoh, & Schroeder, 2000). In this way, any observed inhibitions in "frightened" students can be reduced to translate through an interactive relationship, the joint action-based learning in a *"socially-constructed knowledge field."*

Collaborative e-learning in a practical framework, has been successfully applied in a variety of virtual environments (Bouras & Tsiatsos, 2008; Li, Yue, & Jauregui, 2009; Monahan, McArdle, & Bertolotto, 2008). It indicates the inquiry-based study that carried out jointly between distributed users, who are usually employed in a learning activity or a project, giving a more social dimension to their experience. The advantages of collaborative efforts are focused on conducting an effective training (Neji & Ben-Amnar, 2007), learn new social skills (McArdle, Monahan, Bertolotto, & Mangina, 2004; Roy, 2012), intercultural relations (Lee, 2009), and, finally, the increase of self-esteem. However, here it should be noticed that in any collective interaction and involvement of users' "cognitive mechanisms," and the whole "cognitive cycle" that is spent, there is always some sort of "warranty" to produce the required knowledge, and achieve the final learning outcome.

THE EVOLUTION OF E-LEARNING PROGRESSION IN SECOND LIFE

By cultivating ICT culture and digital literacy, many users (so-called "digital natives" or "digital immigrants"), have become more receptive to networking in virtual environments due to the potential "dip" and interaction (AFLF, 2007; Wood, 2009). Moreover, the rapid evolution of online social networks has transformed "cyberspace" in a rapidly growing communication system, bringing to the fore many aspects of *"networked collectivity."*

Second Life (SL) is one of the most popular virtual platforms, which have attracted the interest of both the friends of social networking and of educational institutions. The technical infrastructure, a three-dimensional networked VR system that supports communication and collaboration between geographically isolated users, is rendered on the computer screen. SL is one of the most famous three-dimensional emulators of real life (or virtual world), imaging the global reality. It is therefore considered as one of the most functional platforms for implementing collaborative e-learning scenarios and scripts (CSCL: Computer Supported Collaborative Learning) (Alvarez, 2006; Fox, Bailenson, & Binney, 2009; Pellas, 2012).

The use of SL as a "canvas" of knowledge-creation can be considered a supplement (or not), and even a traditional classroom environment that provides new opportunities for an existing curriculum. Almost daily, new educational institutions are active in SL and develop e-learning programs, exploiting the platform to deliver high quality services to a global audience at a low cost (Broaddribb & Carter, 2009).

Educational institutions can use SL to create secured geographical areas (grids) and enhance the experiential-empirical learning process. The First conception of Second Life was clearly for entertainment, not for any particular scientific research field. This issue has never prevented any universities to use it as an "educational tool" for organizing, managing, and transferring their "knowledge field" as an instrument to understand and interpret the factual teaching statements. This was one of the most important reasons that SL was chosen for our research. The present chapter tries to articulate the functional characteristics of this potential virtual environment to enhance and growth of the teaching process.

This feature may prove to be a promising and welcoming alternative approach to the traditional academic e-learning procedure. We also found with this new perspective, the term "*e-learning 2.0*." E-learning 2.0 gives more emphasis on social learning interaction and co-construction of knowledge, utilizing social media such as blogs, wikis, and virtual worlds (such as Second Life). The available multimedia-interactive applications can be regarded as a relatively new learning tool that exalts applications of modern teaching methods and strategies for e-learning collaboratively (Boulos, Hetherington, & Wheeler, 2007; Childress & Braswell, 2006; Dunn, Szapkiw, Holder, & Hodgson, 2010; Hobbs, Brown, & Gordon, 2006; Hughes & Moshell, 1997; Pellas, 2012; Vosinakis, Koutsabasis, Zaharias, & Belk, 2010).

Students usually discover new areas of interest and become "*seekers of knowledge*," not mere repositories for directives and regulations. Thence, this challenge brings problematic issues of design and implementation of e-learning programs within SL's sphere. The dilemma that appears in this case focuses, in particular, on how we can: (a) operate SL for educational support that increases learning potential and (b) transform the common multi-user environment in a "hotbed" of "team-building" knowledge and action for learners. The main concern which arises from this process lies within exploring the enhanced educational value that is offered by Second Life's environment for the organization and the conduct of distance-learning courses.

FOUNDATIONS OF THE PROBLEM

Previous studies that penned the evaluating quality of distance learning programs (Chaney, Chaney, & Eddy, 2009; Gorry, 2003; Ndahi, 2006; Report of Illinois Faculty Seminar, 1999) have not provided firm conclusions to further exploit them. Moreover, the aforementioned studies pointed out the principles in which the relevant evaluative procedures have shortcomings and gaps; both in methodology and evaluation. The main deficiencies regarding the evaluation methodology will focus on:

1. Redundantly investigating the same-known sites and teaching approaches.
2. Questioning the reliability of assessment tools for distance learning programs, particularly in terms of assessing the performance of students participating in it.
3. Relabeling the impossibility of incentives valuation of, motivation and interests in the technological innovation created for students and teachers, the key difference being from conventional teaching methods.

The evaluation is considered a very useful and effective tool for managers of education and training system designers, which can analyze and improve the quality of the educational process. As for the orientation of the evaluative process, it is focused on these weaknesses:

1. An assessment of technology and not the educational effectiveness of the program in which users identify problems, prioritizing targets, highlighting opportunities, developing research efforts, evaluating the instructional design, and redesigning the activity (Azcutia, 1999), and
2. The separation factor of technological requirements from the users' population (personal characteristics, interests, and needs), which reveals the lack of a theoretical framework of the procedure used.

Based on the above, Phipps and Merisotis (1999) led inductively to the following conclusions:

1. Technology is no substitute for the human-face communication that real life governs,
2. To ensure free access and use in various systems remains open and distance-learning is an incentive for teachers to use different

systems to pursue better learning outcomes, and
3. The effectiveness of distance-learning programs and the role of technology should identify the factors that constitute the pedagogical framework (objectives and targets, mobilizing students, etc.).

In light of these findings, it is necessary to investigate the other factors involved in the teaching and learning process, because their identification is essential for the evaluation of virtual worlds. In addition, to obtain a reliable evaluative process, students and teachers should use the environment of SL for a sufficient period of time, to better illustrate the advantages and disadvantages.

Currently exploring the pedagogical value of SL, the present chapter proposed a "holistic" evaluation model of the learning process and the result thereof. Thus, defining the purpose of this exercise, we should say that the environment has been used during the teaching process by:

1. Providing the opportunity for improvement of varied service quality of teaching and learning; when it is not possible with "traditional" way.
2. Reducing the administrative burden of organizing and distributing knowledge resources that borne participants-users. By helping to support memory/knowledge base of each student, allowing them to effectively manage time and most creative their duties.
3. Contributing through virtual three-dimensional imaging to explore scientific concepts, principles, and rules those govern the real world. By using three-dimensional simulations and the integration of pedagogical models in learning environments can be best viewed on learning processes, so that students can better understand the cognitive object.

PARAMETERS FOR EVALUATING EFFECTIVENESS

The attempt of evaluating Second Life will take place primarily through the questionnaire, which is based on 4 parameters (Michailidou & Economides, 2003; Georgiadou & Economides, 2000; Pfister, Wessner, Holmer, & Steinmetz, 1999):

A. **Psychological-Pedagogical:** Includes all mentioned criteria that affect the educational process, such as different teaching methodologies, supporting the presentation of knowledge, etc. The broader sense is used to identify all forms of presenting information and interaction with the audience. This will include the appropriate teaching and psycho-pedagogical learning methods. Then, we need to identify all processes to achieve the desired result: providing a complete and effective proposal for distance education.

Initially, it is necessary to determine the topology of education partners, the forms of communication provided by the system of SL, and a general description of the service and support needs for learners' users. Such a system must necessarily take into account the core subject of education. Determining the axis of the teaching principles of modern learning theories must account for users' features. It also helps to choose the instructional strategies that will bring the best educational outcome.

B. **Technical-Operational:** Includes criteria of the technical equipment and services that are offered, such as interaction, navigation, and a user's-environment feedback. The design and development of educational applications follows a set of general principles that should satisfy some individual circumstances related to functionality and specific characteristics. The three main categories that arise are potentially related for functionality and structure for peer-effect. The basic structure of an educational program is structured around a central axis that includes the following elements:

1. The main management task, i.e. the basic program which includes the management and control of various forms of information, flow control and navigation, ensuring the refunds to those hubs and the appeal in case of error,
2. Data set, i.e. users' concepts and users' required information, which can be presented in different forms depending on the strategy and pedagogical principles consistently applied, and
3. The dynamic interaction among the objects, making up the program in retrievable ways by users.

The control options and the evaluation obtained by proper communication among users concerning student characteristics (age, gender, etc.) are educational goals, the content, and the type of program. In this case, the specifications that must be met are:

1. The potential maintenance, renewal, enrichment, knowledge of material etc.,
2. The flexibility of the system in terms of modifications and revisions,
3. The development of the split is easier to control and maintain,
4. The scalability, which should be based on the open character.

C. **Organizational-Economical:** Include topics, such as the effectiveness of the designed system, as well as utility costs compared to traditional teaching methods, the benefits accruing primarily to the student.

D. **Social-Cultural:** Evaluate the application that is designed to be incorporated into the overall cultural and social development of individual perspectives. The globalized nature of education puts the idea of "global student body," or "e-twinning," and win over a greater interest in how to bridge the differences that conventional types of education are not able to join.

RELATED QUANTITATIVE WORKS

These investigations dealt with the introduction of new methods of teaching and learning in the virtual environment of SL. Until recently, research had not focused exclusively on a wide range of target groups of evaluation to effectively implement e-learning activities. Thus, some of the most important are presented in the following (see Table 1).

KEY FACTORS INFLUENCING THE CHOICE OF SECOND LIFE FOR RESEARCH

As discussed in detail, the three-dimensional VR features a multi-presentation virtual world, which can provide the ability to create innovative educational environments to explore and interact within an intuitive and natural way. The choice of platform was based on specific grounds, which appear to be able to meet the requirements of an educational process:

1. A wide range of various educational communities, some dating to 2006, operated a discussion forum (SLED list-SL Educators List) with more than 6,500 educators to share their experiences with colleagues from around the world.
2. SL is not considered as an on-line "game" like WoW (War of Warcraft), Lineage 2, etc.

Table 1. Important studies

Previous works	Researching areas
NMC Campus (2007)	In the spring of 2007 (1 -29 May) and 2008 (5 May - 8 June), the New Media Consortium's (NMC Campus: http://sl.nmc.org), conducted a survey of 209 teachers, about cognitive needs and elements that they want in a lesson. The purpose of the pension and two surveys gathered the necessary information for sampling activities, attitudes, and interests of teachers in the virtual environment of SL.
Vogel, Guo, Zhou, Tian, and Zhang (2008)	Vogel, Guo, Zhou, Tian, and Zhang in 2008, conducted a survey that was designed as a comparative evaluation of cooperative activities. They have been introduced in Second Life, and compared it with other media (MSN, e-mails, forums). Graduate students from Hong Kong and the Netherlands participated. After 3 weeks of research, almost half of respondents (55%) rated the SL to use with other collaborative tools, in low level.
Eduserv (2008)	The investigation of Eduserv (period July 2007 - October 2008) was designed to identify and use various virtual worlds for Higher Education in the United Kingdom (38 institutions took part). It revealed that almost half of the Higher Education colleges had the advantage of SL for education. Whereas three-quarters (3/4) of UK universities used SL in areas of Psychology and Ethnography of New Technologies education.
Mansour and Mostafa (2008)	The investigation of Mansour and Mostafa (2008) investigated the quality of social interaction of users in the virtual environment of SL. In the experiment, 20 students attended the University of Louisville in Great Britain. They learned the technique of "role playing" in a literary text and then answered questions that were common on the social interaction of users in relation to this personal contact in the classroom. Evaluation findings show that students have identified various communication channels and interact more easily in SL than a conventional method.
Slentz Project (2008)	This project includes an extensive literature review regarding the potential efforts for education. Through a case study, they assessed educational activities, in which they contributed to the effort of designing and upgrading the teaching process (aiming at asserting the educational project).
Vrellis, Papachristos, Natsis, and Mikropoulos (2010)	This paper presented some empirical data collected through an exploratory study in the virtual environment of Second Life (SL). The aim of this article was to acquire a more "experiential" knowledge for 30 sophomore students in the Department of Physics, University of Ioannina. Through this process, they investigated the sense of presence (spatial and social) and co-operation developed between them.
Vosinakis, Koutsabasis, Zaharias, and Belk (2011)	Here is an attempt to implement interactive tools by students of the Department of Product & Systems Design Engineering, creating two virtual "open source" platforms. The two systems are Open Simulator (http://opensimulator.org) and Free Switch (http://www.freeswitch.org). Upon this completion process, students chose the virtual world of SL, where they worked as a team and created a specially designed area and engaged in different types of problem-centered learning situations (problem-based). These efforts were evaluated and showed some very positive elements of both the adaptation to the environment and the convenience of having committed a lesson.

There is no beginning or end, or rules and levels of power rating of the user, nor any purpose of integration. In SL the "anthropomorphic" virtual representations (avatars) of an "open" world "society" help in a more natural and effortless interaction of participants. The result of these possibilities is the optimistic confidence to succeed that users feel that is not present in a real-life situation. This intensified confidence can be exploited in a course to facilitate student achievement.

3. In contrast to the 3D virtual platform of Fortrerra System Inc. (http://www.forterrainc.com/), anyone can enter into SL freely. Moreover, users of SL have avatar customization options and may obtain appropriate teaching tools. Users wishing to buy virtual clothes may not be of interest—however, slide-viewers, e-books, and tutorials are of keen interest for the potential educator.
4. SL, as an "open" society, provides a favorable environment for meetings with people from different parts of the world.

FORMULATION OF THE GENERAL CASE

The Greek International Society for Technology in Education (GISTE) (http://www.iste.org/about-iste.aspx) is the premier membership association for Greece's trainee users engaged in improving learning by participating in the effective use of innovative technology in Higher Education. GISTE has existed for two years and its membership from Technological Institutes from Greece, refers a powerful and meaningful way for users (instructors and students):

1. To connect them with other institutes from Greece.
2. To gather in a variety of list or forums by sharing challenges, exchange experiences and excitement of different learning progressions.
3. To let students be part of a community that leads to the transformation of e-Education.
4. To utilize common collaborative virtual spaces and tools.
5. To prepare students with life-long skills (awareness of thoughts, meta-cognitive skills for learning, self-efficacy, and self-regulation) and knowledge attained for both personal development and career advancement. It encompasses all types of facilitated learning opportunities to formal or informal learning opportunities situated in practice. It has been described as intensive and collaborative, ideally incorporating an evaluative stage, and last but not least
6. To convince a variety of approaches to professional development, including consultation, coaching, and communities of practice, mentoring, reflective supervision, and technical assistance.

According to what has already been covered in the theoretical portion of our work, we conclude that Second Life can be a beneficial environment for the educational community. We can draw some important conclusions for the evaluation of pedagogical value, by a sufficient number of trainees, who are in different time periods adjusted to the environment of SL. The exploratory evaluation is geared toward the quality of the learning process, and will not be satisfied only for measurable results.

RESEARCH QUESTIONS

Learners of distance-learning programs at the GISTE (Greek International Society for Technology and Teaching) emphasize the importance of making an exploratory evaluation. This effort is to create an educational "conceptual" project, consisting of logically connected, and empirically testable consecutive cases (Cohen & Manion, 1994). In particular, we wanted to investigate how, and to what extent, the duration of the use of Second Life ("Months of using SL"), three of the original cases and associations of the successful educational programs are related. As for the qualitative variable "Gender," it has correlated with the third hypothesis of the research: we wanted to investigate whether there is a statistically significant correlation with the questions of social-cultural characteristics of learners.

To achieve the central objective of the research were identified and separated specific objectives, which are expressed in the form of the following hypothetical-inductive exploratory questions:

1. Can the virtual world of SL provide the flexibility to implement innovative teaching methods, based on the contemporary approaches of learning?
2. Does the technology infrastructure and operational characteristics of the "window-based" environment offer: (a) the dynamic and active involvement of users in the teaching and learning process, (b) the continuous improvement of learning procedures that will serve users in the development, and the utilization of virtual spaces or places for an easier acquisition of knowledge?
3. Based on this data, does SL affect the implementation cost of e-learning courses

at a significantly lesser extent, in contrast to face-to-face settings?

4. Can SL offer incentives that give extra meaning and importance in the effort to promote access to knowledge, which is inextricably linked with socio-cultural trainee users' characteristics (e.g. differences in gender or religion)?

RESEARCH METHODOLOGY

Outline Intention and Objective

Wanting to delineate the outline intention of this work, we would say that emphasis is given in the investigation of the parameters that are deemed necessary for an effective planning and conducting training courses by distance in virtual environments. Apart from these, our objective is the students-based assessments for the final value of e-learning programs in the virtual world of Second Life ([Web] user-based investigation assessment).

Process Framework and Data Collection Tool

A quantitative questionnaire (close-structured questions) prompted the method of investigation. There was a need to penetrate the multifaceted interpretation of phenomena, such as that of involving learners in cooperative activities, but also to enunciate their personal experiences and expectations. The intention is to "formalize" ideas, opinions, and requirements, relating to the completed courses and operational characteristics of the environment that took advantage of SL. Our small study was a successful effort of setting up a probabilistic sample (random groups with representation), with 3 months duration (January-March 2012). The data obtained from the "target sample" that took part in our survey was through community non-profit GISTE.

The research sample consisted of 70 students (36 women and 34 men trained users, and also members of GISTE), who participated in educational activities of the university departments, regardless of specialty. The daily "visit" in the community of GISTE, and therefore the emerging debates that unfolded in the group, gave us the opportunity to identify and urge online users to participate in our survey. We incorporated the need for adults to be involved in both the planning, and the evaluation process of learning programs that took place (Silen & Uhlin, 2004). Foremost, we collected data in a five-grade Likert scale (1=not at all to 5=very much). Quantitative (scale) variables were the answers from the main questionnaire and the qualitative (nominal) were the demographics ("sex" and "months of using SL"). Also, for better processing and reliability of our results, we used the statistical program SPSS ver. 20, setting up the quantitative data connection, configuration, search, and creating templates.

The framework for the research data collection held around the idea of running Second Life, as an "alternative" e-learning platform, is defined as "artificial." The results that are described were mostly accomplished by electronic means (PC and Internet) in a structured and controlled environment. There are a number of elements that consist of a "natural" framework. Some are educational activities in "natural" contexts (e.g. educational seminars and traditional, lectures, etc.), while others pronounce the design and the operation of the virtual learning community, aimed at creating a (virtual) learning environment (Pasquinelli, 2010). Therefore, the conduct of research should not escape the "framework" that we set before. The appropriate place to conduct the research was the same environment of SL. The procedures of data collection were varied as the interview was taken place within the virtual spaces of GISTE (see Figure 1).

Figure 1. Efforts to collect data information

Pooled Results of the Assessment Parameters

As we know, the traditional way of learning with the personal touch (face-to-face) of teacher-pupil is a very difficult practice to circumvent. The excitement is caused by trainees' use of 3D virtual worlds, and the collection of positive results, confirming the hypothesized expectations. In our study, the evaluation of educational programs undertaken within the GISTE students, has brought some very interesting results, which are shown below:

Demographics: According to our research, the e-profile of trainees' users, 40% lived in the U.S., while in Europe all fell significantly (14.2%), except, of course, the United Kingdom, where the participation rate stood at 26.7%. 51.4% of the student population was female, while 48.6% was male, with an average age of 24-25 years ($n = 70$, $M_{age} = 24, 5$, $SD=4{,}053$). Finally, most adults use SL for 13-36 months (64.2%). Initially, even before presenting the results, we investigated the possible association between "Gender" and "Months of using SL." The findings showed a statistically significant association between two categorical variables using the x^2 test control (Pearson Chi-Square) [$x^2 = 19{,}257$, $df = 3$, $p = 0.003 < 0.05$] (see Table 2).

We observed that use of SL from 12-34 months was chosen by 44.3% (30 women) versus 20% (14 men), the ratio of women users exceeding men by double. Also, the second message of the third table [a. 0 cells (0%)], informs us about whether to satisfy the condition of the validity of the x^2 test, and we want more than 25% of the cells to have values less than 5. For this reason we trust the process of Pearson Chi-Square. Since the correlation coefficient "γ" (Gamma) of our vouchers variables ("Gender" and "Months of using SL"), is positive (γ=0.512), there seems to be a fairly 'strong' correlation and the level of statistical significance is not greater than 5% ($p<0.05$) (Approx. Sig = 0,912) (see Table 3).

A. Psychological-Pedagogical Parameters: The need of using innovative teaching methods to support distance-learning is manifested through the section of the questionnaire that refers to the characteristics of Contemporary Learning Theories. Initially, the vast majority of students agree that active participation and interaction with the system is possible, highlighting their personal strategies (quest. A1: 57.1%-much). The collaborative learning and communication between users helps them organize better in groups (team building) and understand the learning material collaboratively (team knowledge) (quest. A2: 54.3%- much) (see Figure 2).

Table 2. Chi-square test between the qualitative variables "months of using SL" and "sex"

Chi-Square Tests

	Value	df	Asymp. Sig. (2-sided)
Pearson Chi-Square	19.257[a]	3	.000
Likelihood Ratio	24.378	3	.000
Linear-by-Linear Association	7.712	1	.015
N of Valid Cases	70		

a. 0 cells (.0%) have expected count less than 5. The minimum expected count is 3.41.

Table 3. Symmetric measures for "sex" and "months of using SL"

Symmetric Measures

	Value	Asymp. Std. Error[a]	Approx. T[b]	Approx. Sig.
Ordinal by ordinal (Gamma)	.512	.181	2.621	.912
N of Valid Cases	70			

a. Not assuming the null hypothesis.
b. Using the asymptotic standard error assuming the null hypothesis.

In addition, through users' feedback, it is revealed that the system can support "constructive" learning to better understand learning phenomena (quest. A3: 57.1%-very much). Many students who were involved in activities, used for the treatment of their subjects, developed analytical skills, generalization skills, acquired e-skills and the ability to synthesize knowledge from different angles (quest. A4 [a]: 57% - much). Moreover, these students believe that all of these new skills would be "transferred" into skills applicable to real-life situations (cognitive, motor, verbal, mental) (quest. A4 [b]: 45.7% - very much). As for "adaptive" learning, it was truly given according to users' needs (the ability to explore and learn) while storing their personal activities in the database (sense of autonomy) (quest. A5: 57, 14% - very much).

The connectivity that SL offered, in contrast with other 2D e-learning platforms (e.g. Moodle), is remarkable. Users can visualize three-dimensional forms and even their work (quest. A6: 57.1%-very much). The monitoring and the "redefinition" of activities seems to be a consequence in two-way communication between teachers and students (feedback prompt). Users' responses in this case were at satisfactory levels, and they were able to redefine actions and transform the supplied knowledge (quest. A7: 31.43%-enough).

The procedures and information support learning processes have been improved significantly, with student's access to various libraries or databases to select information about courses becoming available (quest. A8: 37.1% -much). Student and teacher interaction may be enhanced by using synchronous and asynchronous communication methods. SL supports both communication channels (via bulletin boards, file sharing, and updates) (quest. A9: 57.1%-very much). SL also supports the modern form, with "channels" of communication (voice-dialing for intra-communication between team members or

Figure 2. Display statistics from the quest. A2.

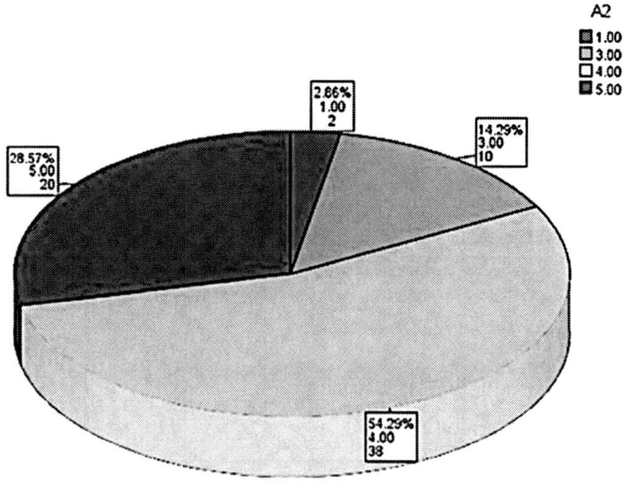

directly writing to personal contacts, instant messaging or IM) (quest. A10: 57.1%-very much), that make it quite easy to learn.

B. Technical-Operational parameters: The growth characteristics of SL, addressed by the compatibility of environmental installation on various platforms (Windows XP, Vista, 7, and Mac OS 10.7), reveal its resilience compared to other platforms (quest. B1: 97%-Yes). The use of multimedia applications (video, audio, video), enhances the transmission of information, allowing the user to learn in an interesting way, free from confusion and fatigue (quest. B2: 42.9%-much). Topics are mainly the design of a "micro world," including learning activities that are judged by the respective user-student when necessary. According to the vast majority of trainees, they did not need to know in advance any programming language (C + +, LSL), for the transformation or simulation activities (quest. B3: 57.14%-not at all) (see Figure 3).

As for the design issues in the communication environment (user interface), it seems that screens appeared to be designed with a clear and interesting way to evoke the attention of students (quest. B4: 40%-much). Even the selection or management of objects, from a "different" angle for each user, is positive and it is something that could be very useful in their work (quest. B5: 40%-much). The interaction between users-environment, and the navigation, can reinforce the concepts of space and place. In the case of SL, learning learning as a team with the system for the transfer of information was a very easy and interactive process (quest. B6: 51.4-much). The main navigation keys (such as scrolling or social emergency aid and map) are included in the virtual world, helping beginners, or advanced users (quest. B7: Yes-100%).

Nonetheless, a significant deficiency was not wearing a "smart" system behavior (e.g. an agent) (quest. B8: 94%-not at all). However, importantly, the avatar of the remote control room is moved to Help Island to learn basic movements, after the design the user's input. An important element in using such a system is that students are given "feedback." The interaction of virtual boats (agents), seemed to be achieved through non-verbal communication (visual or auditory), through body movements, or even a combination of the above (quest. B9: 57.1%-much). Indeed, the system during the design of users' activities, provide the appropriate feedback with visual or auditory states of the environment (quest. B10: 40% - enough of the 46.9% of all positive crisis),

Figure 3. Display statistics from the quest. B3.

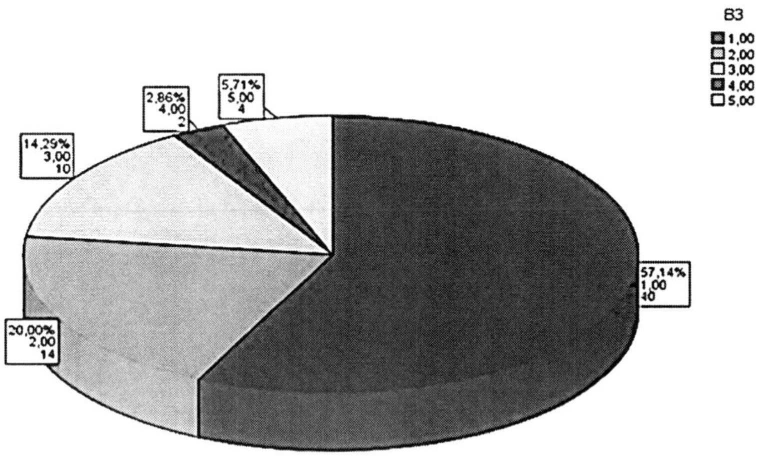

which modestly caused us great concern. Of course, in case of failure, the flow situation is repaired within a reasonable period of time, because the "stability" of a system is an important factor in the overall performance of students.

The ability of using textual authoring tools (notes, textures), is being considered to promote better management of both time and organizational design of the individual work of each student (quest. B11: 48.6%-much). SL provides functions related to file sharing or personal alarm messages via e-mail (IM), but, according to the opinion of students, is not adequately secured (quest. B12: 51.4%-very close). However, the evidence of this reluctance is present in other networked media (e.g. Facebook).

C. Organizational-Economic parameters: The support of distance learning should follow an economic policy so as to primarily benefit the trainee and service's "anthropocentric" character and not the body itself. The framework of economic policy relates both directly to the bid, and to the exploitation of "product." Therefore, in terms of a course management and workflow status of a separate server, the promoter (Linden Lab) does not offer a place specially to support the various courses (quest. C1: 86% - No).

This course can be partly justified because the primary purpose of implementation was the social networking, and not education. A positive viewpoint highlights a technical support system, free of charge that "stops" when conducting courses with other "mirror worlds" (quest. C2: 97.14% - No). There is no any particular pricing policy that restricts the number of participants (quest. C3: 86%-No). It is also remarkable that that SL could be installed and used even in laboratory facilities or islets PCs (quest. C4: 93% - Yes), with different standards and infrastructure. Second Life can be installed and running onto a laptop (e.g. netbooks), satisfying even the minimum requirements (quest. C5: 92.86%-Yes).

D. Social-cultural parameters: The practice of "transfer" principles and values in modern learning environments should be done within a framework of respect of socio-cultural development. This was reflected through the establishment of "action groups" that were not taken into account, possibly religious or cultural differences of its members, which did not affect the communication between them (quest. D1: 51.43%-very much) (see Figure 4).

Even the average age (or not) did not take into account differences among users, facilitating the completion of various activities (quest. D2: 31.4%-

Figure 4. Display statistics from the quest. D1.

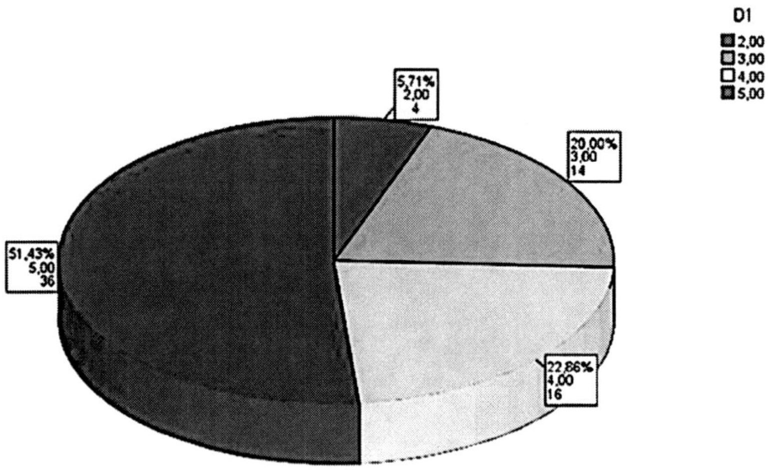

very much). Most of them seem to be familiar with the images and symbols that were encountered in the virtual environment without affecting their social group (quest. D3: 43%-much). However, the platform has stalwart conservation values / principles, and respect for different cultures (quest. D4: 42.86%-much).

Finally, it is desirable to know if SL is sufficient, for the integration issues, when applied to modern education (i.e. the provision of supplies to respond adequately to the demands of modern education). Users' answers seem to be mainly visible through interaction with the virtual environment (quest. D5: 42.9% - much).

E. Assessment of educational opportunities that are offered from SL: The majority of the student population shows that they are very satisfied with the virtual environment, at least with respect to the distance-learning programs that they attended. The possibilities from SL in the teaching processes were something that greatly enhanced the probability for reuse and the future (quest. Q1: 82.8%- very much). Students' responses highlight that they would not like to change anything in SL (quest. Q2: 97%-No). The few (3%-Yes) that responded that they would change something replied with the following: (a) the difficult programming language (LSL) for various "works" (50%), (b) no payment for "uploading" photos and documents (30%), and (c) would like to have an even greater sharing of resources and knowledge between other social media (17%).

From the last question, we realized that SL indeed was a helpful tool for learning (quest. E3: 97%-Yes). The reasons given were related to:

1. Collaboration among distributed students from around the world (35.3%), (b) effective learning activities that have occurred since the same (25%),
2. Application of technical (e-) learning (mainly "role playing"), (25.7%)
3. Whether the SL with other e-learning platforms, such as Moodle (11,4%) and (d) acquainted with other people (7.3%).

RESULTS OF THE INVESTIGATION CASES

The contribution of our research in distance learning, through an attempt to assess trainees' learning process users of Second Life, could not be separated from what comprises a "sustainable" education system. In this sense, we want to emphasize the special relationship that we believe can thrive between SL (as a "sustainable" means of education) and students respectively. We made it clear that a further advantage, from a research-educational side, is that Second Life can meet the expectations of the student community. Furthermore, SL could well be part of the whole "system" of education, which implemented the "action-plans," avoiding any problems encountered today in the academic community. To substantiate these words, we should primarily identify the connection with the initial hypotheses. Indeed, at that time we tested the reliability of the scale of responses.

Below, we describe our findings, and for the reliability analysis of each questionnaire section, we used the Chronbach alpha ("*a*"). In all tables, we have also compared Mean indicators (Mean) and Standard Deviation scores (SD) for all quantity variables, with $p<0.05$, as a statistically significant correlation factor of answers' analysis from our questions (quest.).

1st) The first question relates to posit whether *"Could the virtual world of SL provide a flexible framework for implementing innovative teaching methods, based on the modern approaches to learning?"* Through respondents' answers, this seems to be true. In our case, the delimitation of the framework was based on:

1. "Flexibility" of the scope it offers to users (see quest. A2 and A6 [$a = 0.57$]),
2. "Adaptability" of the system and feel" autonomy 'which offers the user (see quest. A5 and A8 [a=0.55]) and
3. Management of interactions and feedback received by users of the system (see quest. A7, A9, A10, B6, and B10 [a=0.65]).

Especially in the field associated with the framework flexibility, we would say that there is an "advantage" over conventional methods due to their inherent design, but also the needs of participants covered (e.g. training events, interactive applications, etc.). This was easier to understand through the adaptation of contemporary learning theories in SL's system with attributes through specific questions (see quest. A2, A5, A6, A7, A8, B6, B10 [a=0.67]), addressing the idea of "compatibility" with the Second Life.

1. To implement distance-learning programs in the environment of SL, it seemed that the system allowed users to cooperate and communicate in order to build collective knowledge (team building) and to understand it better (quest. A2 [$F(3, 66)=0.653$, $p=0.58$]). As for the learning process, the connection of the Moodle course management and the independent management of cognitive resources could become an important tool in the hands of learners. Thus, learners could better organize their work in Moodle, and then simulate their work in three-dimensional form in the SL environment (quest. A6 [$F(3, 66)=0.48$, $p= 0.744$]).
2. The initial trainees' user satisfaction, leads us to conclude that SL can be an intermediary space for collaboration and group activities under the guidance of the teacher, which helps more in the development process of teaching (quest. A8 [$F(3, 66)=1.34$, $p=2.62$]). In addition, an important point worth mentioning is the opportunity to collect and process information from the user himself. This information can feed the database with the various tools and objects ("adaptability" system) that it considers necessary for the outcome of the learning process (sense of 'autonomy') (quest. A5 [$F(3, 66)=0.63$, $p=0.596$]).
3. The effective management of interaction in distance courses, both directly relates to communication between users ("horizontal" relationship governing the users), and the feedback received from the system ("vertical" relationship). The very positive judgment gained by the students, both in intra-communication with the professor to

redesign activities and feedback on their actions (quest. A7 [$F(3,66)=0.318, p=0.813$]), as and compatibility of different ways of modern (bulletin board, file sharing) (quest. A9) and asynchronous communication (chat text, IM, voice call), appear to meet the demands and expectations (quest. A10). The effective management of the communication fabric helped to design the virtual ones, and it appeared that the Second Life users provided proper feedback with visual and acoustic means so as to facilitate the interaction between them (quest. B10). This can be described as completely positive, and so supported to a greater degree of personal problem-solving strategies of actors subjects (management of complex interactions that accepts-"intrinsic cognitive load"), which helps in addition to collaboration and personalized learning (B6 quest. [$F(3, 66)=1.130$, $p=0.156$]).

Thus, we conclude that long-term use of Second Life could rely on the flexibility of the framework within which the pedagogical principles associated with modern theories of learning, but in different forms of Web communication offered to facilitate user interaction (quest. E1).

2nd) The second question relates to whether the technological infrastructure and operational characteristics of the 3D "window" environment, offers:

1. Dynamic and active involvement of users in the trainees' teaching and learning process,
2. Continuous improvement of service that will serve users in the development and use of virtual space, or place, for easier acquisition of knowledge, and
3. In this data affected the cost of implementing distance courses.

The findings of our research reveal a number of answers (see quest. A1, A3, A4a, B9, B11 [$a=0.836$]). Active and "constructive" learning is related to the efforts undertaken by each individual, to promote personal learning strategies and, ultimately, the acquisition of knowledge. From our research, SL demonstrated that it can contribute to cognitive function both by creating shapes and automating knowledge infrastructures for users to better understand concepts (quest. A1 [$F(3, 66) = 0.539, p = 0.66$]). With the introduction to the environment of SL, the user has the possibility to choose multimedia tools and items you need, which may include a staff profile. This will result in the skillful management of "positive cognitive load" that would come from the large number of interactive elements that are shipped on the same system in SL, and can be used during the course (e.g. prims, textures, notecards), for efficient processing and organization of matter (quest. B11 [$F(3, 66)=0.437, p=0.727$]).

The creation and automation of cognitive schemas, with both the active involvement and interaction other social-practice learning, and provide more opportunities for personal exploration and experimentation (A3 quest. [$F(3, 66) = 0.19, p = 0.902$]). Through our research, we also found that the active involvement of students can be achieved: (a) at the first level of communication / interaction with their teacher (teaching process), and (b) among students (learning process) through (virtual) tools or through gestures in a visual or auditory field (B9 quest. [$F(3,66)=0.98, p=0.96$]). This in turn could act as a catalyst to shift from a teacher-centered (instructivist) model of lecturing in higher education, to a more learner-centered (active learning) model. Indeed, the use of personal skills, without an adult determination course of learning, contributes even more in depending and active involvement (A4a quest. [$F(3, 66)=0.35$, $p=0.79$]).

The continuous improvement of services relates to operating-technical parameters, which include issues related to growth characteristics, the design of the communication environment, processes and information support and management tools of SL. In particular, the growth characteristics dealing with the criteria of environmental compatibility with various software systems (Windows XP/Vista/7, Snow Leopard 10.6, Linux), for both workstations and servers is something that is permitted by this virtual environment (quest. B1).

Therefore, if the key issue was covered on software installation in various platforms, the evaluation of operating characteristics remains to be. The design of the communication environment includes criteria-like design issues and interaction, navigation and user-feedback environment and is given through the questions relating design issues in the user interface. Particularly design issues that related to the presentation screen and the ability to use multimedia elements that enhance the information (e.g. management of 3D objects and scripts), and the rights or the conditions of the virtual world are changeable. It seems that it may be a key selection criterion of SL (quest. B2). This advantage will provide an exploiting point for students who managed to combine theory with practice (e.g. conducting research, learning skills, etc.).

The answer is directly related to the use of innovative multimedia data, which could contribute to a better understanding of course content without distracting them (quest. B3). The user's interface emulates the expandable areas ("Sims") and the information, which is going to the same attractive manner (quest. B4), creating a pleasant atmosphere for learning, so as not to cause fatigue and confusion to the user. Also, the selection, management and use of objects and a "code programs" (scripts) by themselves in a "different perspective" is positive, and yet in many programs or software that was not feasible (quest. B5). Similarly for navigating and exploring the environment, the system enables the user through the keyboard to navigate and search aid to better manage the educational material and that goes in through SL (management of the "external cognitive load") (quest. B7). The navigation (or "teleportation") and search that supports SL, can be considered to reinforce the concepts of space and place.

The third sub-question is related to the continuous improvement of services offered by the virtual environment. Our research showed that SL includes some services that could help with learning, such as interactivity, realistic simulation environment, ease of use and, later in terms of user's interaction with the environment, easy account setup, communication, navigation, etc. Certainly, the provision of the technical support and the security of personal data transfer is a serious choice. However, sometimes the troubled views of users were not very encouraging (quest. B12).

In addition, users can perform important functions, such as optical virtual personification of the virtual "mask" (avatar) and provide additional means of interaction with the virtual world as movements and gestures, which is necessary for the transfer of information between users (management of the "intrinsic cognitive load") (quest. B6). These functions are related to the concepts of presence and awareness and how to integrate the environment of SL.

We eventually found the "pluralism" of multimedia data for communication between users, as they obtain information on both the actions and enrich the presence, even though gestures (digital visualization of objects and gestures of non-verbal communication) (quest. B9). The sense of "presence" and "awareness "for the ongoing activities, are serving both the communication and cooperation between users. What puzzled us most is the lack of an "agent" for further assistance to be transferred to another "places" or "spaces" (quest. B8).

3rd) Another direction that we turned our research's interest, was the need to determine the economic impact that would have the students in relation to the various forms of assistance offered.

So, a key question asked was whether it is based on this data, or affecting the cost of implementing distance-learning courses at a significantly lesser extent in contrast with that of in-person. The treatment of specific conditions, operating costs, and providing adequate resources to the organizational-economic policy of the company Linden Lab, are necessary for the conduct of educational seminars and simulation of three-dimensional objects within courses, etc. A negative which leaves us puzzled is that accepting hospitality courses are not on a separate server to avoid any unpleasant events (quest. C1).

As for the technical support framework provided, in cases of damage, it is included and does not cost any extra for the user, which proves the stability offered by the system in case of failure (quest. C2). The gain is, of course, greater if we consider the results of a large number of trainees (e.g. in seminars), without any extra charge and without even a space-time constraint (quest. C3). Furthermore, SL can support the operation of various flexible programs tailored to the needs and demands of teachers and learners, but without prejudice to further improvements, such as wider use of educational tools, online 3D multimedia objects, automatic translation, etc. (quest. E7).

It is also important to mention the cost savings over conventional training tools, and the time that an application of a large scale can require. The main feature in this case, is the installation and operation of the program on computer labs without trainees' users having to pay some amount of money to obtain a license or to compensate for the length of time spent in the environment (quest. C4). Even the choice of a laptop (e.g. netbook), is satisfactory for the minimum requirements of SL. This can bring economic benefits since market prices are not prohibitive (quest. C5).

The transformation of the educational nature and the development of innovative teaching methods by using ICT is a global phenomenon. The aim of modern education is to make all students a "social community," providing them all with necessary tools to meet the demands of modern life. There is a great deal of respect to the particular cultures and distinct cultures of the peoples on SL, and the system promotes cultural diversity through dialogue and through significant opportunities for learning. A nonprofit factor in achieving this objective is the preservation of the principles and values that the modern learning environments should develop.

4th) By our fourth hypothesis, we tried to see if SL can offer those incentives that give extra meaning and importance of the effort for easier access to knowledge, which is inextricably linked with socio-cultural characteristics of the trainee users (e.g. differences in gender or religion etc.). The survey confirmed our initial hypothesis, related to transportation practices and user rights in the environment of SL. Thus, we checked if there was any statically significant correlation between responses of socio-cultural parameters (quantitative variables) and the "months of using SL" (qualitative-categorical variable with more than two categories) with ANOVA. As we can see from Table 3 it was not be depicted a $p<0.05$.

According to the survey results, we discovered that there were phenomena of social exclusion among the "action groups":

1. Effective communications between users was present, without regard to religious and cultural differences (quest. D1 [$F(3, 66)=0.103$, $p=0.958$ / $t(68) = -0.252$, $p = 0.804$]), as in "action groups," the heterogeneity of their age seems not to affect the cooperation (quest. D2 [$F(3, 66)=0.437$, $p=0.727$ / $t(68) = -0.253$, $p=0.804$]) and
2. The symbolic representation of the environment is not hired any social group in which they belong (D3 quest. [$F(3, 66)=1.174$, $p=0.161$ / $t(68)= -0.526$, $p=0.96$]).

Furthermore, the responses suggest that the "conservation" and "transfer" values and principles of the cultural respect for diversity in the

Table 3. Socio-cultural characteristics in second life

Question	N Min Max	Mean SD	t	Sig.
1. Successful communication between teammates without mentioned cultural or religious differences.	70 3 5	1.1 3.53	-.252	.804
2. The heterogeneity of action groups.	70 3 5	3.8 2.51	-.253	.804
3. Users are familiar with symbols or icons	70 3 5	3.2 3.25	-.526	.961
4. The possibility of transferring & managing the principles or values of each user in the community.	70 2 5	2.6 4.22	-.327	.975
5. The achievement of the contemporary Education, according to formed curricula	70 2 5	3.4 3.51	-.296	1.23

real world (natural environment) within the virtual (artificial context), has permitted the collaboration and the psychology of trainees (D4 quest. [F(3, 66)=0.184, p= 0.347 / t(68) = -0.327, p=0.975]). All these point to the fact that students are available and users have increased their interest in online activities, while achieving the aims of modern education, i.e. issues related to respect for social-cultural variations of the "other" (D5 quest. [F(3, 66)=1.12, p=0.347/t (68) = -0.296, p=0.768]). It's pretty remarkable that such a development is quite positive, considering that the use of SL for educational purposes (at least for the respondents), remains on track. However, some improvements that could make it easier for users would be students, "special" for monitoring islets university courses, easier management "code objects" (scripts), etc.

CONCLUSION

As we previously reported for the sample of our research questionnaire, in relation to the educational community of people around the world, we can draw some clear conclusions regarding this research. Meanwhile, we can arrive at some conclusions from the analysis tools that are offered in the three-dimensional collaborative applications and on how they can be transported in three dimensions. User-friendly tools and an environment of simplicity improve users' performance within a three-dimensional space.

Using 3D graphics from Second Life, in general, is justified by the advantage that gives the coexistence of a "simulated cyberspace." This simulated space offers potential interaction between visual objects and users. In addition, for the same platform, users had a great variety of possibilities. One of the main exponents is the stable release of the platform, and particularly the upgrades that could help further the learning process. Beyond that, the functionality that has been implemented is quite "impressive," allowing users to surf through the Internet cooperatively to create spaces and objects and modify the LSL (Linden Scripting Language) code found in SL's virtual world. Indeed, it is important to observe the fact that the platform can support an open source language (LSL), expecting to see contributions by the communities of developers.

Summing up the aforementioned reasons shows that Second Life can be effectively integrated in the Web 2.0, as part of an online learning approach. Furthermore, based on the evaluation results that are presented above, it is understood that the Second Life platform combines a variety of features, supporting communication and cooperation, and improving performance levels that were set by previous methods of distance-learning. However, to be competitive working through Second Life with traditional approaches (e.g. face to face), current transfers, and affordances should be strengthened. Based on our study, we presented the advantages over conventional methods and identified methods to strengthen the pedagogical application through suggestions, comments, and users' requirements.

FUTURE WORK

Future studies will be conducted to use the collaborative virtual environment of Second Life for serious studies on learning models, in combination with Contemporary Learning Theories, and how to deploy them. Since it has been proven through our research of the educational value of SL and its usefulness as an educational tool, we believe that many benefits could arise. Future developments can lead to various investigations that we would like to be associated with:

1. The effort to develop integrated educational applications, data, and functions, with Moodle, along with interactive features that SL is offered (Sloodle: Simulation Linked Object Oriented Dynamic Learning Environment). Through this process, we can explore e-skills that trainees receive. This research can extend to the training of teachers of all disciplines and levels, but also in University communities.
2. Such investigations can be also carried out by students of 13-17 years in the virtual environment of Teen Grid, for religious education. The navigation in virtual "places" of Second Life, and the users' familiarity with multimedia applications, can play an important role in exploring and exploiting religious sources and, therefore, this may lead to more "interactive" teaching.

REFERENCES

Alvarez, M. (2006). *Second life and school: The use of virtual world worlds in high education*. San Antonio, TX: Trinity University. Retrieved from http://www.trinity.edu/adelwich/worlds/articles/trinity.manny.alvarez.pdf

Australian Flexible Learning Framework. (2007). *The knowledge tree: An e-journal of learning and innovation*. Retrieved from http://kt.flexiblelearning.net.au/tkt2007/wp-content/uploads/2007/10/kt_ed15-printerversion.pdf

Azcutia, J. (1999). *Educational administration and institutions for evaluation of the education system*. Retrieved from http://www.ince.mec.es/pres/pon-n8-ing.html

Barab, S., Thomas, M., Dodge, T., Carteaux, R., & Tuzun, H. (2005). Making learning fun: Quest Atlantis, a game without guns. *Educational Technology Research and Development*, *53*(1), 86–107. doi:10.1007/BF02504859

Beer, M., Slack, F., & Armitt, G. (2003). Community building and virtual teamwork in an online learning environment, hicss. In *Proceedings of the 36th Annual Hawaii International Conference on System Sciences* (HICSS 2003), (p. 66). HICSS.

Boulos, M., Hetherington, L., & Wheeler, S. (2007). Second life: An overview of the potential of 3-D virtual worlds in medical and health education. *Health Information and Libraries Journal*, *24*(4), 233–245. doi:10.1111/j.1471-1842.2007.00733.x

Bouras, C., & Tsiatsos, T. (2008). *Extending the limits of CVE's to support collaborative e-learning scenarios*. Retrieved from http://ru6.cti.gr/ru6/publications/9786892.pdf

Broaddribb, S., & Carter, C. (2009). Using second life in human resource development. *British Journal of Educational Technology*, *40*(3), 547–550. doi:10.1111/j.1467-8535.2009.00950.x

Bull, G., & Kajder, S. (2004). Digital storytelling in the language arts classroom. *Tapped in Learning & Leading with Technology*, *31*(5), 34–37.

Chaney, D., Chaney, E., & Eddy, J. (2009). *The contect of distance learngn programs in higher education: Five enabling assumptions*. Retreived from http://www.uncg.edu/oao/PDF/5%20Assumptons%20OJDLA.pdf

Childress, M. D., & Braswell, R. (2006). Using massively multiplayer online role-playing games for online learning. *Distance Education*, *27*(2), 187–197. doi:10.1080/01587910600789522

Clarke, S., & Maher, M. (2001). *The role of place in designining a learner centered virtual learning enviroment.* Retrieved from http://web.arch.usyd.edu.au/-mary/Pubs/2001pdf/CF2001.pdf

Cohen, L., & Manion, L. (1994). *Research methods in education*. London, UK: Routeledge and Kegan Paul.

De Lucia, A., Francese, R., Passero, I., & Tortora, G. (2009). Development and evaluation of a virtual campus on second life: The case of second DMI. *Journal of Computers & Education*, *52*, 220–233. doi:10.1016/j.compedu.2008.08.001

Dieterle, E., & Clark, J. (2006). *Multi-user environments for teaching and learning*. Retrieved from http://64.94.241.248/rivercityproject/documents/MUVE-for-TandL-Dieterle-Clarke.pdf

Dillenbourg, P., Baker, P., Blaye, A., & O'Malley, C. (1994). The evolution of research on collaborative learning. In Spada, E., & Reiman, P. (Eds.), *Learning in Humans and Machine: Towards an Interdisciplinary Learning Science* (pp. 189–211). Oxford, UK: Elsevier. doi:10.1007/978-1-4020-9827-7_1

Dunn, R., Szapkiw, A., Holder, D., & Hodgson, D. (2010). Of student teachers and avatars: Working towards an effective model for geographically distributed learning communities of pre-service educators using virtual worlds. In D. Gibson & B. Dodge (Eds.), *Proceedings of Society for Information Technology & Teacher Education International Conference 2010,* (pp. 423-427). Chesapeake, VA: Association for the Advancement of Computing in Education.

EDUCAUSE. (2007). *The horizon report 2007 edition*. Austin, TX: The New Media Consortium. Retrieved from http://www.nmc.org/pdf/2007_Horizon_Report.pdf

Ellis, S., Begault, R., & Wenzel, E. (1997). Virual enviroments as human-computer interfaces. In Helander, M., & Prabhu, L. (Eds.), *Handbook of Human-Computer Interaction* (2nd ed., pp. 163–203). Oxford, UK: Elsevier Sciences.

Fox, J., Bailenson, J., & Binney, J. (2009). Virtual experiences, physical behaviors: The effect of presence on imitation of an eating avatar. *Presence (Cambridge, Mass.)*, *18*(4), 294–303. doi:10.1162/pres.18.4.294

Franceschi, K., & Lee, M. (2009). Engaging group e-learning in virtual worlds. *Journal of Management Information Systems*, *26*(1), 73–100. doi:10.2753/MIS0742-1222260104

Georgiadou, E., & Economides, A. (2000). Evaluation factors of educational software. In *Proceedings of the International Workshop on Advanced Learning Technologies,* (pp. 113-116). Prague, Czech Republic: Advanced Learning Technologies.

Gorry, S. (2003). Measuring quality in online programs. *The Internet and Higher Education*, *6*(2), 159–177. doi:10.1016/S1096-7516(03)00022-8

Graetz, A. (2006). The psychology of learning environments. *EDUCAUSE Review*, *41*(6), 60–75.

Hobbs, M., Brown, E., & Gordon, M. (2006). Using a virtual world for transferable skills in gaming education. *Innovation in Teaching and Learning in Information and Computer Sciences*, *5*(3), 1–13.

Hughes, C., & Moshell, J. (1997). Shared virtual worlds for education: The explorenet experiment. *Multimedia Systems*, *5*(2), 145–154. doi:10.1007/s005300050050

Illinois Faculty Seminar. (1999). *Teaching at an internet distance: The pedagogy of online teaching and learning: The report of a 1998-1999.* Chicago, IL: University of Illinois. Retrieved from http://www.elc.uzh.ch/service/literaturtipps/tid-final-12-5.pdf

Johnson, S. D., Suriya, C., Won Yoon, S., Berrett, J. V., & La Fleur, J. (2002). Team development and group processes of virtual learning teams. *Computers & Education*, *39*, 379–393. doi:10.1016/S0360-1315(02)00074-X

Kafai, Y. B. (2006). Playing and making games for learning: Instructionist and constructionist perspectives for game studies. *Games and Culture*, *1*(1), 36–40. doi:10.1177/1555412005281767

Lee, M. (2009). How can 3D virtual worlds be used to support collaboration learning? An analysis of cases from literature. *Journal of e-Learning and Knowledge Society*, *5*(1), 149-158.

Lehtinen, E., & Hakkarainen, K. (2001). *Computer supported collaborative learning: A review*. Retrieved from http://www.comlab.hut.fi/opetus/205/etatehtava1.pdf

Lester, P. M., & King, C. M. (2009). Analog vs. digital instruction and learning: Teaching within first and second life environments. *Journal of Computer-Mediated Communication*, *14*, 457–483. doi:10.1111/j.1083-6101.2009.01449.x

Li, Z., Yue, J., & Jauregui, A. (2009). *A new virtual reality system used for e-learning*. Retrieved from http://www-public.it-sudparis.eu/~horain/GomezJauregui/gomez_fichiers/A%20New%20Virtual%20Reality%20Environment%20Used%20for%20e-Learning.pdf

Mansour, S., & Mostafa, E. S. (2008). The impact of multi-players serious games on social interaction among online students versus face-to-face students. In *Proceedings of the 7th WSEAS International Conference on Applied Computer and Applied Computational Science (ACACOS 2008)*, (pp. 772-778). Hangzhou, China: ACACOS.

McArdle, G., Monahan, T., Bertolotto, M., & Mangina, E. (2004). *A web-based multimedia virtual reality environment for e-learning*. Retrieved from http://diglib.eg.org/EG/DL/Conf/EG2004/short/short48.pdf

Meadows, M. S. (2008). *Avatar: The culture and consequences of having a second life*. Berkely, CA: New Riders Press.

Michailidou, A., & Economides, A. (2003). Elearn: Towards a collaborative educational virtual environment. *Journal of Information Technology Education*, *2*, 131–152.

Monahan, T., McArdle, G., & Bertolloto, M. (2008). Virtual reality for collaborative e-learning. *Computers & Education*, *50*, 1339–1353. doi:10.1016/j.compedu.2006.12.008

Ndahi, H. (2006). The use of innovative methods to deliver technology education laboratory courses in distant learning: A strategy to increase enrollment. *Journal of Technology Education*, *17*(2), 33–42.

Neji, M., & Ben Amnar, M. (2007). Agent-based collaborative affective e-learning framework. *The Journal of e-learning*, *5*(2), 123-134.

New Media Consortium. (2008). *Spring 2008 survey: Educators in SL*. Retrieved from http://www.nmc.org/pdf/2008-sl-survey.pdf

Palincsar, A. S., & Brown, A. L. (1984). Reciprocal teaching of comprehension-fostering and comprehension-monitoring activities. *Cognition and Instruction*, *1*(2), 117–175. doi:10.1207/s1532690xci0102_1

Pasquinelli, E. (2010). The illusion of reality: Cognitive aspects and ethical drawbacks: The case of second life. In Wankel, C., & Malleck, S. (Eds.), *Emerging Ethical Issues of Life in Virtual Worlds* (pp. 195–213). Charlotte, NC: Information Age Publishing.

Pellas, N. (2012). A conceptual "cybernetic" methodology for organizing and managing the e-learning process through [D-] CIVEs: The case of second life. In P. Renna (Ed.), *Production and Manufacturing System Management: Coordination Approaches and Multi-Site Planning*. Hersey, PA: IGI Global.

Pellas, N. (2012). Towards a beneficial formalization of cyber entities' interactions during the e-learning process in the virtual world of second life In Renna, P. (Ed.), *Production and Manufacturing System Management: Coordination Approaches and Multi-Site Planning*. Hersey, PA: IGI Global.

Pellas, N. (2012). Towards a theoretical "cybernetic" framework: Discovering the pedagogical value of the virtual world second life. In Burgga, K., & Zaman, N. (Eds.), *Software Development Techniques for Constructive Information Systems Design*. Hersey, PA: IGI Global.

Pfister, H., Wessner, M., Holmer, T., & Steinmetz, R. (1999). Evaluating distributed computer-supported cooperative learning (D-CSCL): A framework and some data. In *Proceedings of the 2nd International Conference on New Learning Technologies (NLT 1999),* (pp. 234-241). Berne, Switzerland: NLT.

Phipps, R., & Merisotis, J. (1999). *What's the difference? A review of contemporary research on the effectiveness of distance learning in higher education*. Washington, DC: The Institute for Higher Education Policy. Retrieved from http://www.ihep.com/Pubs/PDF/Difference.pdf

Read, S., Miller, L., Appleby, P., Nwosu, M., Reynaldo, S., Lauren, A., & Putcha, A. (2006). Socially optimized learning in a virtual environment: Reducing risky sexual behavior among men who have sex with men. *Journal of Human Communication Research*, *32*(1), 1–34. doi:10.1111/j.1468-2958.2006.00001.x

Roy, S. (2012). Virtual collaboration: The skills needed to collaborate in a virtual environment. *Journal of Internet Social Networking & Virtual Communities*. Retrieved from http://www.ibimapublishing.com/journals/JISNVC/jisnvc.html

Shih, Y.-C., & Yang, M.-T. (2008). A collaborative virtual environment for situated language learning using VEC3D. *Journal of Educational Technology & Society*, *11*(1), 56–68.

Silen, C., & Uhlin, L. (2004). *Self-directed learning-A learning issue for the student!* Retrieved from http://www.hu.liu.se/pedagogiskcentrum/pbl/pdf/artiklar_hu/159913/silen-uhlin2004sdl.pdf

Slater, M., Sadagic, A., Usoh, M., & Schroeder, R. (2000). Small-group behaviour in a virtual and real environment: A comparative study. *Presence (Cambridge, Mass.)*, *9*(1), 37–51. doi:10.1162/105474600566600

Vogel, D., Guo, M., Zhou, P., Tian, S., & Zhang, J. (2008). In search of second life: Nirvana. *Issues in Informing Science and Information Technology*, *5*, 11–28.

Vosinakis, S., Koutsabasis, P., Zaharias, P., & Belk, M. (2010). Problem-based learning in virtual worlds: A case study in user interface design. In *Experiential Learning in Virtual Worlds - Exploring the Complexities*. New York, NY: Interdisciplinary Press. Retrieved from http://www.inter-disciplinary.net/wp-content/uploads/2011/02/vosinakisepaper.pdf

Vrellis, I., Papachristos, N., Natsis, A., & Mikropoulos, T. (2010). Measuring presence in a collaborative physics learning activity in second life. In T. A. Jimoyiannis (Ed.), *Proceedings of the 7th Pan-Hellenic Conference with International Participation ICT in Education*, (Vol. 1, pp. 95-102). Korinthos, Greece: IEEE.

Wood, D. (2009). *Experimental learning through "real world" placements undertaken in 3D virtual world spaces*. Retrieved from http://www.ascilite.org.au/conferences/auckland09/procs/wood.pdf

Youngblut, C. (1998). VR in the schools. *Educational Uses of Virtual Reality Technology, 3*(1). Retrieved from http://www.hitl.washington.edu/scivw/youngblut-edvr/D2128.pdf

Zhigeng, P., Zhu, J., Zhang, M., & Hu, W. (2005). *Collaborative virtual learning environment using synthetic characters. Berlin, Germany*. Germany: Springer-Verlag.

Chapter 16
Technological Advancements Usage:
Demographic Variations

Sujana Adapa
University of New England, Australia

ABSTRACT

Technological advancements have provided many advantages to individuals, businesses, and communities throughout the world. However, technological advancements have also caused challenges. This chapter focuses on one particular banking service innovation that is being used by many individuals and businesses throughout the world on a day-to-day basis. This study relates to the Australian context and explores the variations in the demographic variables in determining the key factors responsible for the adoption or non-adoption of Internet banking. The data presented in this chapter relates to a part of a large survey carried out in a busy shopping mall. Results obtained are discussed and possible solutions and recommendations that are critical from the retail banking management's perspective have been provided.

INTRODUCTION

The world today is more technologically advanced than a decade or two decades ago. Individuals, businesses, and communities are receptive to these technological enhancements as the benefits associated with the use of technology are enormous. These benefits include convenience, ease of use, user friendliness, and faster access, just to name a few. Technological upgrades have provided the world with wonders, challenges, and mixed blessings so far. Technological wonders that benefit individuals and communities relate to medical advancements, upgrading of the diagnostic equipment, robotic engineering, food technology etc. The challenges associated with technology-related products or goods envisage increase in the use of nuclear weapons by coun-

DOI: 10.4018/978-1-4666-2955-4.ch016

tries, emergence of assault rifles, and rise in the usage of chemical weapons by different groups within a community. Therefore, the wonders and challenges associated with the technological advancements indicate the nature of a double-edged sword as individuals and businesses within a community are often confronted in distinguishing between what is good and what is bad for them. This gives rise to the question of problem solving and critical thinking in understanding whether technological advancements are a boon or a bane to the individuals, businesses, and communities that constitute a society.

One particular industry that has undergone major changes from its traditional mode of operations worldwide is the banking sector. This sector has undergone revolutionary changes and has embraced technology in its day-to-day operations. The banking sector is vital in influencing a country's gross domestic product and contributes significantly to the economic status of the country. Technological advancements in this sector are visible through the proliferation of distribution channels. Traditionally businesses used to differentiate their products and services on the basis of price. More recently, businesses are relying on non-price factors for differentiating their businesses from those of competitors. The banking sector is one such business entity, which has embraced differentiation of their products and services on the basis of distribution channels. As a result, modern banks throughout the world offer their services to their actual and potential consumers through physical bank branches, telephone, Internet, and mobile service delivery channels. Therefore, individuals and businesses throughout the world are also gaining awareness, knowledge, and familiarity with the use of these service innovations.

As the society consists of individuals, businesses and communities that are of heterogeneous nature, the technological advancements in general and specifically the proliferation of service delivery channels in the banking sector may not be appealing to certain categories of individuals within the society. This chapter highlights the emergence of the Internet banking service delivery channel in the Australian context. This chapter also sets out to distinguish the importance of demographic variables in the acceptance as well as the rejection of Internet banking. Important implications, which are relevant for the retail banking managers, in the effective management of their segments will be provided. The information provided in this chapter highlights the relevance of demographic characteristics for retail bank managers in designing their product and service strategies.

BACKGROUND

Demographic Characteristics

Existing studies indicate that demographic characteristics influence an individual's adoption of Internet banking services (Mattila, 2001; Jayawardhena & Foley, 2000; Daniel, 1999; Sathye, 1999). Karjaluoto, Mattila, and Pento (2002) noted that personal banking experience and demographics significantly impact the usage of Internet banking services among Finnish consumers. Similarly, extant studies highlighted that consumer' innovation characteristics and demographic characteristics influence the usage of Internet banking (Ismail & Panni, 2009; Karjaluoto, et al., 2002). In consumer behaviour studies, individual differences are often associated with the acceptance of Internet banking and Internet banking in many studies has been identified as a critical service innovation (Ismail & Panni, 2009; Assael, 1981).

Existing studies also highlighted that with regards to the demographic characteristic age of the consumer; older individuals have negative attitudes towards innovations and are often reluctant to adopt new technologies (Trocchia & Janda, 2000). Howcroft, Hamilton, and Hewer (2002) identified that older people prefer face-to-face transactions involving bank personnel and are less inclined towards Internet banking usage. Younger individuals however are more attracted to the advantages, benefits and convenience offered by Internet banking compared to branch banking (Jayawardhena & Foley, 2000). Results from previous studies also indicated that younger individuals are also more inclined to use technological advancements compared to mature-aged people (Akinci, Akoy, & Atilgan, 2004; Kolodinsky, Hogarth, & Hilgert, 2004). Existing studies also highlighted the average age range of consumers' orientation towards Internet banking or Internet shopping activities to be 25 to 44 years of age in Greece (Vrechopoulous, Siomkos, & Doukidis, 2001). Similarly, Gan, Clemes, Limsombunchai, and Weng (2006) reported that individuals above 56 years of age, who are mature age consumers,' are less likely to use electronic banking services in New Zealand.

Another key demographic variable, the marital status of consumers also affects consumers' adoption of Internet banking, with research showing that married individuals prefer electronic banking transactions (Katz & Aspden, 1997). However, in another study results obtained revealed that marital status has no impact on the adoption of electronic banking by New Zealand consumers (Gan, et al., 2006). The results obtained from the earlier studies in identifying the relationship between the variables marital status and the adoption of Internet banking has been inconclusive with conflicting outcomes.

In relation to the impact of the demographic variable occupation on the adoption of Internet banking practices by consumers' the typical Internet banking user is often identified as a member of the career-oriented upper middle class (Roemer & Buhl, 1996). Part time workers perceive electronic banking as costly and prefer not to adopt it, whereas, white collar workers exhibited a positive attitude to using electronic banking services in New Zealand (Gan, et al., 2006) and are more likely to adopt Internet banking than blue collar workers in Finland (Karjaluoto, et al., 2002). Similarly, Liu, Tsou and Hammitt (2001) reported that highly paid skilled workers are more likely to use advanced technologies than other categories of workers. Results from the existing studies indicate that Internet banking is a common practice white collar workers preferred to perform Internet banking transactions to a larger extent compared to their counterparts' blue collar workers.

According to the study by Gan et al. (2006), individuals with a high income are less likely to adopt electronic banking services and prefer to deal with bank personnel directly, particularly when dealing with complex transactions and handling large sums of money. However, other studies have reported that individuals with high levels of income are more inclined towards the adoption of Internet banking (Foucault & Scheufele, 2002; Gronau & Hamermesh, 2001; Jayawardhena & Foley, 2000). Existing studies also show that there are gender differences in technology acceptance and usage behaviour among individuals (Venkatesh, Morris, & Ackerman, 2000; Venkatesh & Morris, 2000). However, in one New Zealand study, gender has no impact on adoption of electronic banking services by individuals (Gan, et al., 2006). The impact of the variables income and gender on the adoption of Internet banking transactions by individuals produced conflicting results from the existing studies so far.

Individuals with better education respond more positively to the adoption of Internet banking (Gronau & Hamermesh, 2001). Individuals with higher levels of education may require less training in response to technological change as their general skill levels enable them to learn the new technology quicker than consumers with low levels of education (Barter & Sicherman, 1998). Internet banking users in the UK are highly educated and have a good level of knowledge of computers and the Internet (Jayawardhena & Foley, 2000). These findings contrast with those of Howcroft et al. (2002) who noted that level of education had no impact on individuals' use of telephone and Internet banking. Another aspect which significantly influences the adoption of electronic banking services is ethnic background of an individual (Katz & Aspden, 1997).

Thus in the majority of studies investigating Internet banking and information systems the role of demographic characteristics was found to be significant in predicting individuals' acceptance, intention to adopt and adoption of Internet banking. The content presented in this chapter highlights the demographic characteristics of Australian consumers' with regards to their adoption and non-adoption of Internet banking. Information obtained has been analysed and presented in the form of tables and figures after analysing the relevant data. The following information has been organised under Australian consumers' general banking behaviour, their Internet banking patterns and reasons for non-adoption of Internet banking.

The present study specifically relates to the Internet banking adoption by Australian consumers, mainly focusing on the contextual differences. This study also sets out to identify factors that favour as well as hinder individuals' adoption of Internet banking and whether difference if any, would relate to the demographic characteristics.

METHODOLOGY

The information presented in this chapter is retrieved from a large study conducted in Australia for identifying factors that influence consumer's frequent and continued use of Internet banking. A questionnaire was developed and distributed to the respondents in a busy shopping mall through a cross-sectional mall intercept survey. The questionnaire developed consisted of questions related to consumers' general banking patterns, demographic related information, consumers' orientation towards Internet banking channel and a few open-ended questions to obtain respondents own perceptions about their Internet banking practices. An assessment of the adequacy of the data obtained was made through statistical assumptions underlying the estimation methods. Thus, basic descriptive statistical analysis in SPSS helped to accomplish the initial screening criteria of the data obtained. The data screening looked for poorly completed surveys and attempted to establish accuracy in data. The overall response rate obtained from the survey was 52.5 percent. Completed surveys were received from 683 respondents of which 372 were Internet banking users (54.5%) and 311 were non-users of Internet banking (45.5%).

General Banking Behaviour

The existing literature indicates that an individual's knowledge of banking products and services, customer resources, as well as customer information reception and processing capabilities all have an impact on the individual's adoption of electronic banking channels (Polatoglu & Ekin, 2001; Karjaluoto, et al., 2002; Gerrard & Cunningham, 2003). Therefore, in order to understand the general banking patterns of the respondents, certain background questions were included in the questionnaire. Questions asked the respondents about the banking products that they were currently using and those that they were likely to use in the next six months. Both questions allowed the respondents to tick as many responses as appropriate.

The first question asked which of the following banking products are the respondents currently using. Options consisted of the following categories: (1) Savings Account, (2) Current Account, (3) Credit Card, (4) Debit Card, (5) Foreign Exchange Trading, (6) Personal Loan, (7) Mortgage, (8) Insurance, (9) Car Loan, (10) Securities Trading, (11) Overdraft, (12) Investment Fund, (13) Others (with respondents requested to specify). Second question asked, apart from the products that respondents are currently using, which other banking products are they likely to use in the next six months. Categories included were similar to those incorporated in question one: (1) Savings

Account, (2) Current Account, (3) Credit Card, (4) Debit Card, (5) Foreign Exchange Trading, (6) Personal Loan, (7) Mortgage, (8) Insurance, (9) Car Loan, (10) Securities Trading, (11) Overdraft, (12) Investment Fund, (13) Others (with respondents requested to specify). Third question asked the respondents how many different bank services they are currently using. This question consisted of five categories: (1) One, (2) Two, (3) Three, (4) Four, (5) Five, and Over.

Internet banking is an advanced technology dependent on computer networks and often individuals tend to use a new technology when the relationship between the new and previous technology is complementary (Bayus, 1987). Experience with using ATM, teletext, and prior computer experience such as use of the Internet and email, making electronic payments etc., were found to significantly influence electronic banking usage (Karjaluoto, et al., 2002; Igbaria, Guimaraes, & Davies, 1995). In addition, heavy users of banking services might adopt and further use Internet banking as a convenient option that can save time and effort (Lee & Lee, 2001). From the existing literature, it is evident that there exists a substantive relationship between the electronic connectivity and the rate of Internet banking adoption (Igbaria, et al., 1995). Therefore, later questions included in the questionnaire ask the respondents about their general Internet usage, type of Internet connectivity and place of accessing the Internet.

Fourth question asked the respondents about how long have they been using the Internet and consisted of the following categories: (1) Less than 6 months, (2) 6 months – Less than 1 year, (3) 1 year – Less than 2 years, (4) 2 years – Less than 3 years, (5) 3 years – Less than 5 years, (6) Above 5 years. Fifth question asked the respondents how many hours they spend on the Internet on an average per day and the following categories were included: (1) Less than 1 hour, (2) 1 hour – Less than 2 hours, (3) 2 hours – Less than 3 hours, (4) 3 hours – Less than 4 hours, (5) 4 hours – Less than 5 hours, (6) More than 5 hours. Sixth question asked the respondents about the type of Internet connectivity that they have: (1) Broadband, (2) Dial up, (3) Others (with respondents requested to specify). Seventh question asked the respondents where they access the Internet: (1) Office, (2) Home, (3) Public Library, (4) Internet centre/café, (5) Others (with respondents requested to specify). Information pertaining to these seven questions was collected from both the users and non-users of Internet banking, whereas, questions eight, nine, ten and eleven consisted of information relevant to Internet banking users only and asked them about their access to and frequency of using Internet banking transactions.

Eighth question asked Internet banking users where they access the Internet for performing their banking transactions: (1) Home, (2) Office, (3) Public Library, (4) Internet centre/café, (5) Others (with respondents requested to specify). Ninth question asked the respondents how frequently they use Internet banking on an average per week: (1) Fewer than once, (2) Once a week, (3) 2 times a week, (4) 3 times a week, (5) 4 times a week, (6) 5 times a week, (7) More than five times a week. Tenth question asked the respondents to rank the different banking types based on their frequency of use (1 for the most frequently used bank type) and consisted of the options bank branch, ATM, telephone banking, Internet banking, mobile banking and others (with respondents requested to specify). Eleventh question asked the respondents to indicate the range of Internet products or services they were currently using: (1) Account information, (2) Balance inquiry, (3) Electronic bill payments, (4) Funds transfer, (5) Loan application, (6) Securities trading, (7) Cheque book application/cancellation, (8) Others (with respondents requested to specify).

Demographic Characteristics

Previous research indicated inconsistent results with regard to the impact of demographic characteristics on the adoption of Internet banking by individuals. With regard to the gender, females were found to exhibit greater computer anxiety compared to males, while others found no gender differences (Teo, 2001; Igbaria & Chakrabarti, 1990; Parasuraman & Igbaria, 1990). Young, affluent, and highly educated individuals generally accepted changes more readily and favoured Internet banking acceptance (Gan, et al., 2006; Polatoglu & Ekin, 2001). Level of education was found to positively influence the adoption of Internet banking. Individuals with a higher level of education were found to readily adopt Internet banking (Hernandez & Mazzon, 2007). Employment level was found to significantly and positively influence the individual's adoption of electronic banking (Gan, et al., 2006). High income earning individuals were found to use electronic banking less while pursuing complex transactions and dealing with large sums of money and often preferred to have personal contact with the bank staff (Gan, et al., 2006). On the contrary, in another study, Internet banking was found to be attractive to those individuals in higher income brackets (Gartner, 2003; Kolodinsky, Hogarth, & Shue, 2000). Consumers' ethnic background was an influential factor in influencing their adoption rate (Katz & Aspden, 1997). The present study collected the following demographic data from the respondents.

- **Gender:** Consisted of two categories (1) Male and (2) Female.
- **Age:** Represented in seven ordinal categories: (1) 18–21, (2) 22–25, (3) 26–30, (4) 31–40, (5) 41–50, (6) 51–60, (7) 61 or over.
- **Highest level of education:** (1) Primary school, (2) Secondary (or high) school, (3) Vocational education and training (TAFE), (4) Higher education (university).
- **Personal gross annual income:** (1) \$20000 and under, (2) \$20001-\$35000, (3) \$35001–\$50000, (4) \$50001-\$65000, (5) \$65001-\$80000, (6) \$80001 and over.
- **Ethnicity:** (1) Anglo-Australian, (2) Asian, (3) English, (4) Middle Eastern, (5) New Zealand, (6) Others (with respondents requested to specify).
- **Occupation:** (1) Manager, (2) Professionals, (3) Academic, (4) Student, (5) Self-employed, (6) Executive, (7) Technician, (8) Retiree, (9) Housewife, (10) Others (with respondents requested to specify).

Non-Users of Internet Banking

In order to identify the actual reasons that inhibit consumers' Internet banking transactions as well as non-users' preferences for other service delivery channels in the Australian context, the following questions were included in the questionnaire. The first question asked the respondents whether they were current users of Internet banking or not: (1) Internet banking users (respondents whose answer would be 'Yes'), (2) Internet banking non-users (respondents whose answer would be 'No'). Second question was intended only for non-users of Internet banking, asking them which other channel they use to conduct their banking transactions if they were not Internet banking users. Four options were presented: (1) Bank branch, (2) ATM, (3) Telephone banking, (4) Mobile banking. Third question was included as an open-ended question 'Could you please tell us your reasons for not using Internet banking to perform your banking transactions?'

DESCRIPTIVE STATISTICS

The frequencies and valid percent (percent excluding any missing responses) of Internet banking users and non-users from the total respondents are presented in Table 1.

Table 1. Frequencies of the internet banking users and non-users

Item	Characteristic	Frequency	Percentage
Internet Banking	Users	372	54.5
	Non-users	311	45.5
	Total	683	100.0

Demographic Profile of Users and Non-Users of Internet Banking

The demographic profile of the participants who responded to the survey as Internet banking users and non-users of Internet banking is shown in Table 2. From the table it is evident that there were more males (53.8%) in the sample of Internet banking users than females. Among the non-users of Internet banking there were more females (65.9%) than males. Maximum numbers of the respondents identified were within the age range of 31 to 40 years as Internet banking users and non-users represented as 28.2% and 22.5% respectively. The majority of the Internet banking users had attained a higher education level, whilst for the majority of non-users of Internet banking the highest level of education was at the vocational education and training level (45.7%). Internet banking users (21.2%) were within the income range of $80 001 and over, and non-users of Internet banking (28.6%) were within the income range of $50 001 - $65 000. Most Internet banking users were of Asian ethnicity (23.7%) and most non-users were Anglo-Australians (22.8%) in the sample. Maximum numbers of the respondents as Internet banking users were derived from the managerial occupation (30.1%). The maximum number of respondents as Internet banking non-users was reported from the managerial (18.6%) and administration (18.3%) categories. The differences in the demographic profile of the users and non-users of Internet banking are elicited in Figures 1 to 6.

General Banking Patterns: Descriptive Statistics

General banking information was collected from the respondents irrespective of whether they did or did not use Internet banking. The information collated focused on the respondents' preferred banking products that they currently use and their intention to use various banking products in the next six months.

The banking products that were currently in use by Internet banking users and non-users are shown in Table 3. From this table it is inferred that saving accounts were the product held by most of the respondents irrespective of their Internet banking use. The current account was mostly preferred by the Internet banking users (53.2%), more than the non-users (13.5%). Proportionately more Internet banking users (89.8%) preferred to use their credit card compared to non-users of Internet banking (59.8%). On the other hand, a debit card was extensively used by non-users of Internet banking (88.4%) compared to Internet banking users (68.5%). Foreign exchange trading was used proportionately to a greater extent by Internet banking users (13.4%) compared to non-users of Internet banking (9.6%). A personal loan option was used to a greater extent by non-users of Internet banking (21.2%) than Internet banking users (14.2%). A larger proportion of Internet banking users had a mortgage (37.4%) loan compared to non-users of Internet banking (16.4%). Compared to the Internet banking non-users (12.5%), the option of insurance was preferred to a maximum extent by the Internet banking users (20.4%). Car loans were preferred by 14.0 percent of the Internet banking users and 9.0 percent of the Internet banking non-users. The knowledge of securities trading was minimal for Internet banking non-users (2.9%), compared to the Internet banking users (16.7%). The overdraft facility and the investment fund option were used more by the Internet banking users (15.1% and 15.1%) compared to the Internet banking non-users

Figure 1. Gender-wise percentage distribution of users and non-users of internet banking

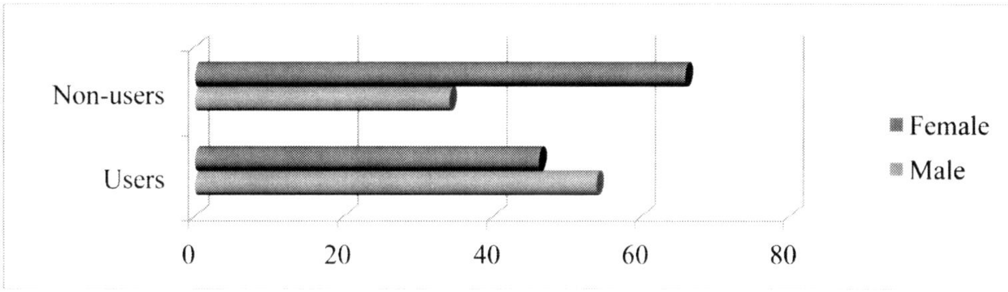

Figure 2. Age-wise percentage distribution of users and non-users of internet banking

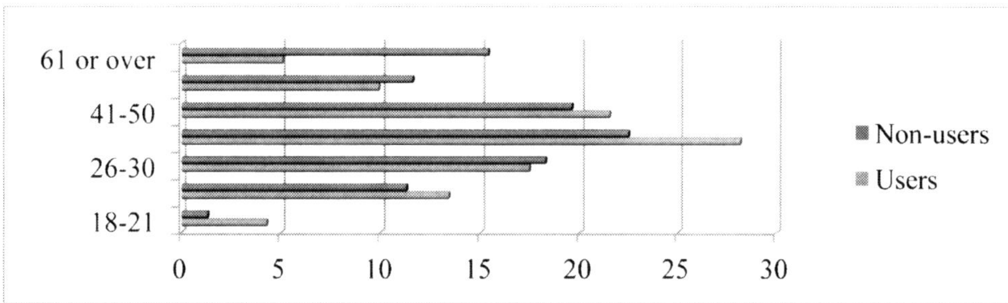

Figure 3. Education-wise percentage distribution of users and non-users of internet banking

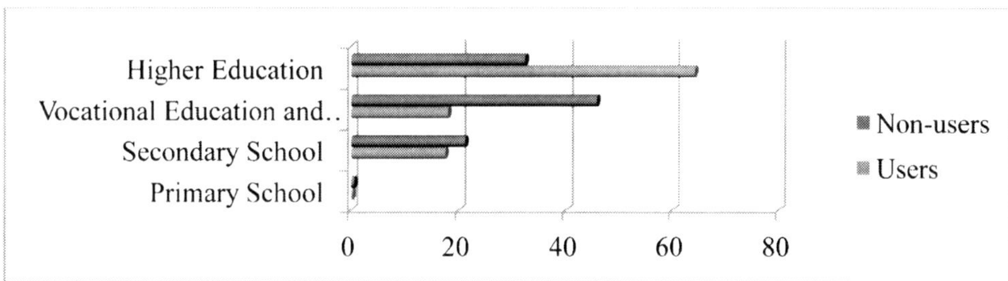

Figure 4. Income-wise percentage distribution of users and non-users of internet banking

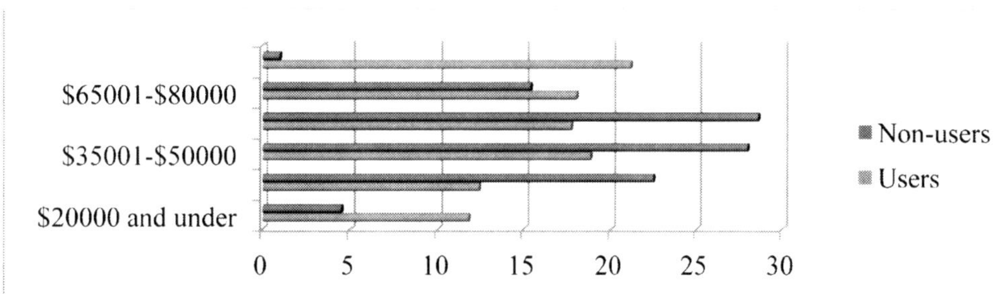

Figure 5. Ethnicity-wise percentage distribution of users and non-users of internet banking

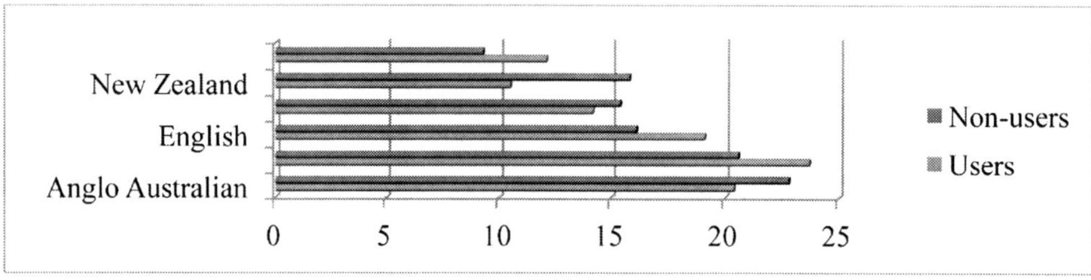

Figure 6. Occupation-wise percentage distribution of users and non-users of internet banking

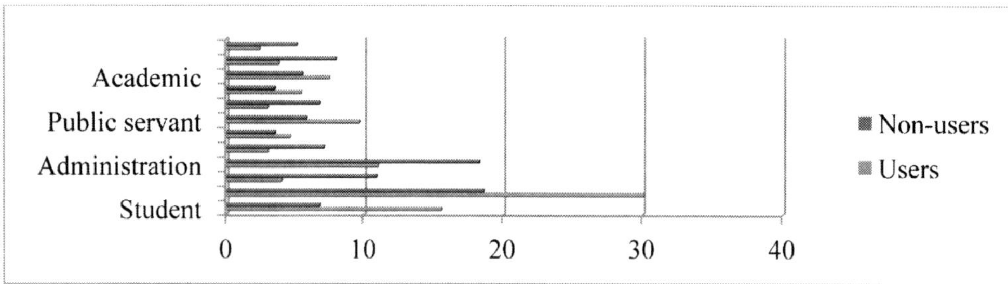

(3.9% and 2.9%). Other products were preferred to an extent of 3.8 percent by the Internet banking users.

With regard to the banking products that are likely to be used in the next six months by the Internet banking users and non-users, it is inferred that a majority of the respondents were reluctant to possess a current account in the future, irrespective of their Internet banking usage pattern. About 18.8 percent of the Internet banking users expressed their interest in possibly using foreign exchange trading in the next six months. However, 20.4 percent of the Internet banking users and 8.7% of the Internet banking non-users preferred to use the option of personal loan in the future. Whereas, 13.7 percent of the Internet banking users expressed their interest in utilising the option of a mortgage compared to only 8.7 percent of the Internet banking non-users. About 13.5 percent of the Internet banking users preferred to use the option of insurance in the next six months compared to 9.3 percent of the Internet banking non-users. Internet banking users, to a maximum extent (46.0%), indicated their preference to use a car loan in the future. The option of securities trading to be utilised in the near future was evident by the frequencies of the Internet banking users (48.1%). The option of an overdraft was also preferred to a maximum extent by the Internet banking users (59.9%), compared to the Internet banking non-users (3.9%). An investment fund was preferred to a minimal extent by both Internet banking users (0.5%) and non-users (4.2%).

It could be inferred from the Table 3 that Internet banking users are exposed to a wider range of financial products compared to the non-users of Internet banking. Internet banking customers either possessed the banking product included in the study or expressed their preference to use it in the near future, irrespective of the simplicity or complexity of the banking product. On the other hand, non-users of Internet banking were more cautious and conservative in their banking product preferences.

Table 2. Demographic characteristics of the users and non-users of internet banking

Item	Characteristic	Internet Banking Users		Non-users of Internet Banking	
		Frequency	Percentage	Frequency	Percentage
Gender	Male	200	53.8	106	34.1
	Female	172	46.2	205	65.9
Age	18-21	16	4.3	4	1.3
	22-25	50	13.4	35	11.3
	26-30	65	17.5	57	18.3
	31-40	105	28.2	70	22.5
	41-50	80	21.5	61	19.6
	51-60	37	9.9	36	11.6
	61 or over	19	5.1	48	15.4
Education	Primary School	1	0.3	2	0.6
	Secondary School	65	17.5	66	21.2
	Vocational Education and Training	67	18.0	142	45.7
	Higher Education	239	64.2	101	32.5
Income	$20 000 and under	44	11.8	14	4.5
	$20 001-$35 000	46	12.4	70	22.5
	$35 001-$50 000	70	18.8	87	28.0
	$50 001-$65 000	66	17.7	89	28.6
	$65 001-$80 000	67	18.0	48	15.4
	$80 001 and over	79	21.2	3	1.0
Ethnicity	Anglo Australian	76	20.4	71	22.8
	Asian	88	23.7	64	20.6
	English	71	19.1	50	16.1
	Middle Eastern	53	14.2	48	15.4
	New Zealand	39	10.5	49	15.8
	Others	45	12.1	29	9.3
Occupation	Student	58	15.6	21	6.8
	Manager	112	30.1	58	18.6
	Self-employed	15	4.0	34	10.9
	Administration	41	11.0	57	18.3
	Retiree	11	3.0	22	7.1
	Doctor	17	4.6	11	3.5
	Public servant	36	9.7	18	5.8
	Housewife	11	3.0	21	6.8
	Teacher	20	5.4	11	3.5
	Academic	28	7.5	17	5.5
	Community services	14	3.8	25	8.0
	Analyst	9	2.4	16	5.1

Table 3. General banking patterns of users and non-users of internet banking

Banking Product		Banking Products currently using				Banking products likely to use in the next six months			
		Users		Non-users		Users		Non-users	
		No.	%	No.	%	No.	%	No.	%
Current Account	Yes	198	53.2	42	13.5	17	4.6	0	0
	No	174	46.8	269	86.5	355	95.4	311	100
Credit Card	Yes	334	89.8	186	59.8	14	3.8	0	0
	No	38	10.2	125	40.2	358	96.2	311	100
Debit Card	Yes	255	68.5	275	88.4	18	4.8	0	0
	No	117	31.5	36	11.6	354	95.2	311	100
Foreign Exchange Trading	Yes	50	13.4	30	9.6	70	18.8	16	5.1
	No	322	86.6	281	90.4	302	81.2	295	94.9
Personal Loan	Yes	53	14.2	66	21.2	76	20.4	27	8.7
	No	319	85.8	245	78.8	296	79.6	284	91.3
Mortgage	Yes	139	37.4	51	16.4	51	13.7	27	8.7
	No	233	62.6	260	18.6	321	86.3	284	91.3
Insurance	Yes	76	20.4	39	12.5	50	13.4	29	9.3
	No	296	79.6	272	87.5	322	86.6	282	90.7
Car Loan	Yes	52	14.0	28	9.0	171	46.0	21	6.8
	No	320	86.0	283	91.0	201	54.0	290	93.2
Securities Trading	Yes	62	16.7	9	2.9	179	48.1	15	4.8
	No	310	83.3	302	97.1	193	51.9	296	95.2
Overdraft	Yes	56	15.1	12	3.9	223	59.9	12	3.9
	No	316	84.9	299	96.1	149	40.1	299	96.1
Investment Fund	Yes	56	15.1	9	2.9	2	0.5	13	4.2
	No	316	84.9	302	97.1	370	99.5	298	95.8
Others	Yes	14	3.8	0	0	2	0.5	0	0
	No	358	96.2	311	100	370	99.5	311	100

General Internet Usage Trends: Descriptive Statistics

Internet usage trends of the respondents were collected irrespective of their use of the Internet to perform banking transactions in order to find out whether significant differences existed between the two groups. Frequencies and percentages were drawn from the variables focusing on the longevity of Internet use, time spent on the Internet on an average day, type of Internet connectivity and place of Internet access. General Internet usage trends are displayed in Table 4.

More Internet banking users (52.2%) had used the Internet for more than five years. However, non-users of Internet banking (35%) reported that they had used the Internet (not for the banking purposes) for two years to less than three years. Most respondents, irrespective of their Internet banking usage or non-usage, indicated that they spent about one hour to less than two hours browsing the Internet on average per day. Broadband

Table 4. General internet usage trends of the users and non-users of internet banking

Item	Characteristic		Internet Banking Users		Non-users of Internet Banking	
			Frequency	Percent	Frequency	Percent
Experience of using Internet	Less than 6 months		5	1.3	20	6.4
	6 months – Less than 1 year		3	0.8	30	9.6
	1 year – Less than 2 years		21	5.6	65	20.9
	2 years – Less than 3 years		31	8.3	109	35.0
	3 years – Less than 5 years		118	31.7	82	26.4
	Above 5 years		194	52.2	5	1.6
Time spent on Internet on an average per day	Less than 1 hour		92	24.7	24	7.7
	1 hour – Less than 2 hours		111	29.8	154	49.5
	2 hours – Less than 3 hours		72	19.4	94	30.2
	3 hours – Less than 4 hours		25	6.7	21	6.8
	4 hours – Less than 5 hours		35	9.4	17	5.5
	More than 5 hours		37	9.9	1	0.3
Type of Internet connectivity	Broadband		342	91.9	29	9.3
	Dial up		22	5.9	282	90.7
	Others		8	2.2	0	0
Place of Internet access	Office	Yes	306	82.3	296	95.2
		No	66	17.7	15	4.8
	Home	Yes	331	89.0	295	94.9
		No	41	11.0	16	5.1
	Public Library	Yes	19	5.1	7	2.3
		No	353	94.9	304	97.7
	Internet Centre/Café	Yes	4	1.1	8	2.6
		No	368	98.9	303	97.4
	Others	Yes	4	1.1	0	0
		No	368	98.9	311	100

Internet connectivity is prominent among the users (91.9%) and dial-up Internet connectivity is prominent among the non-users (90.7%) of Internet banking. Among the Internet banking users, the majority access the Internet from home (89.0%). However, a majority of non-users of Internet banking (95.2%) access the Internet from their office.

These findings show that respondents with more Internet experience were more frequent and continuous users of Internet banking. Respondents possessing broadband type Internet connectivity were prominent users of Internet banking. Respondents accessing Internet from their home were more frequent and continuous users of Internet banking. However, time spent on the Internet on an average per day was not significantly different between the users and non-users with regard to their use of Internet banking either continuously or frequently.

Ranking the Service Delivery Channels Based on the Frequency of Usage

Information pertaining to ranking the different service delivery channels based on the respondent's frequency of use is displayed in Table 5. It is evident from the results that proportionately 58.9 percent of the Internet banking users ranked Internet banking as their most preferred service delivery channel for conducting their banking transactions. The ATM was ranked in second place by 33.9 percent of the Internet banking users. Telephone banking (5.1%) and bank branch banking (1.6%) were ranked in the third and fourth places by Internet banking users. Mobile banking was used to a minimal extent (0.3%) by Internet banking users. Non-users of Internet banking ranked ATM (41.8%) as their most preferred service channel, followed by telephone banking (31.8%) and bank branch banking (26.0%). These findings show that respondents who preferred Internet banking service delivery channel use it more frequently and continuously to perform their banking transactions. However, non-users of Internet banking preferred ATMs to a larger extent to conduct their banking transactions.

Table 5. Ranking the banking service delivery channels by internet banking users versus non-users

		Rank					
Service delivery channel	**Respondents**	**1**	**2**	**3**	**4**	**5**	**6**
Internet Banking Users							
Bank branch	Number	6	30	195	129	12	0
	Percent	1.6	8.1	52.4	34.7	3.2	0
ATM	Number	126	201	28	16	1	0
	Percent	33.9	54.0	7.5	4.3	0.3	0
Telephone banking	Number	19	28	108	206	11	0
	Percent	5.1	7.5	29.0	55.4	3.0	0
Internet banking	Number	219	110	25	9	9	0
	Percent	58.9	29.6	6.7	2.4	2.4	0
Mobile banking	Number	1	8	10	338	15	0
	Percent	0.3	2.2	2.7	90.9	4.0	0
Others	Number	8	3	1	2	1	357
	Percent	2.2	0.8	0.3	0.5	0.3	96.0
Non-users of Internet Banking							
Bank branch	Number	81	135	95			
	Percent	26.0	43.4	30.5			
ATM	Number	130	112	69			
	Percent	41.8	36.0	22.2			
Telephone banking	Number	99	65	147			
	Percent	31.8	20.9	47.3			

Services of the Different Banks Utilised by the Users and Non-Users

Data has been collected from the respondents with regard to the services of the different banks utilised by both the users and non-users of Internet banking and is presented in Table 6. The results show that, irrespective of the Internet banking usage, the majority of respondents indicated that they were clients of at least two banks. A small percentage of respondents among the Internet banking users were utilising the services of four (3.5%) or five (2.7%) banks. Among non-users of Internet banking none reported the utilisation of the services offered by more than three banks.

Information Pertaining to Internet Banking Usage from the Users

Information regarding the place they access their banking transactions, the frequency of Internet banking usage on an average per week and the Internet banking products and services that are currently used by Internet banking users is presented in Table 7. The table revealed that a majority of the Internet banking users access the Internet from home (86.8%) followed by the office (73.9%) to perform their banking transactions. Places such as the public library (1.6%) and Internet centre/café (0.3%) were used very infrequently by the users to perform their banking transactions. Internet banking users reported that they used Internet banking for account information (94.4%), funds transfer (93.3%), balance inquiry (91.1%), and electronic bill payments (90.3%) in order of importance. Facilities such as loan applications (8.9%), securities trading (7.0%) and cheque book applications/cancellation (7.0%) were utilised by Internet banking users to a lesser extent. Internet banking users mostly preferred to use Internet banking once a week (32.0%), followed by twice a week (20.2%).

The following discussion relates to the emerged themes by analysis of the open-ended question referring to the reasons for not using Internet banking from non-users of Internet banking.

Based on the actual response counts obtained from the Internet banking non-users, 'security' is identified as the macro dimension that most concerns non-users. Under the macro theme of 'security' the four micro dimensions, confidentiality, privacy, authorisation, and availability, are in descending order. Thus, 'loss of confidential information' and 'loss of personal information' prevents a major proportion of the non-users from adopting and using Internet banking. Fear of 'availability of the personal information to other parties' and fear of unauthorisation to navigate through the banks' websites when problems arise also stand as prominent micro dimensions that impede these respondents adoption of Internet banking. A closer look at the Internet banking non-users demographic data reveals that 'security' is more of a concern for females compared to males.

Table 6. Services of the different banks utilised by users versus non-users

Item		Characteristic			
		Internet banking users		Non-users of Internet banking	
		Frequency	Percentage	Frequency	Percentage
Client of how many banks	One	90	24.2	114	36.7
	Two	204	54.8	159	51.1
	Three	55	14.8	38	12.2
	Four	13	3.5	0	0
	Five and over	10	2.7	0	0

Table 7. Internet banking information from the users

Item	Characteristic	Yes/No	Frequency	Percent
Place of accessing the Internet for performing banking transactions	Office	Yes	275	73.9
		No	97	26.1
	Home	Yes	323	86.8
		No	49	13.2
	Public Library	Yes	6	1.6
		No	366	98.4
	Internet Centre/Café	Yes	1	0.3
		No	371	99.7
	Others	Yes	3	0.8
		No	369	99.2
Internet banking products or services that are in current use	Account Information	Yes	351	94.4
		No	21	5.6
	Balance Inquiry	Yes	339	91.1
		No	33	8.9
	Electronic Bill Payments	Yes	336	90.3
		No	36	9.7
	Funds Transfer	Yes	347	93.3
		No	25	6.7
	Loan Application	Yes	33	8.9
		No	339	91.1
	Securities Trading	Yes	26	7.0
		No	346	93.0
	Cheque Book Application/Cancellation	Yes	26	7.0
		No	346	93.0
	Others	Yes	6	1.6
		No	365	98.1
Frequency of using Internet banking on an average per week	Fewer than once		40	10.8
	Once a week		119	32.0
	2 times a week		75	20.2
	3 times a week		58	15.6
	4 times a week		27	7.3
	5 times a week		18	4.8
	More than 5 times a week		35	9.4

- 'Security is the major concern. Though Australia is a developed country, it does not mean that financial transactions are secure enough' (*Respondent* # 202).
- 'I am concerned with the privacy issues and I do not want more information accessible neither to the bank nor to the other parties about my monetary issues' (*Respondent* # 57).

The 'risk' associated with Internet banking also emerged as a macro theme. The associated micro themes under the macro theme of 'risk' relate to various forms of risk in descending order: financial, psychological, physical, social, and time risk. Internet banking non-users' financial risk perceptions were related to 'financial loss,' 'costly,' and 'occurrence of fraud.' A closer look at the demographic data reveals that it was female Internet banking non-users who reported physical and social risk associated with Internet banking more often than male non-users.

- 'Basically I do not want to take any risk' (*Respondent* # 17).
- 'I am concerned with the risk associated with dummy sites that procure your account and password. This happened to my friend once and he had a financial loss of $2000, which is not a small amount you know' (*Respondent* # 101).

The next macro theme identified was the 'value perceptions' non-users associate with Internet banking. The 'value' theme subsumed two micro themes of costs and lack of benefits, based on the respondents' actual response counts. Cost perceptions of the respondents were related to the auxiliary features that are essential for performing Internet banking such as 'setup costs' and 'Internet connection.' Lack of benefits referred to 'beneficial to the banks' and the value associated to Internet banking is 'too marginal' when compared to other electronic banking channels. Again, looking at the demographic data of the non-users reveals that most of the respondents whose value perceptions were related to the perceived costs fell within the low income range of $20001 to $35000.

- 'I do not have broadband connection and dial up is too slow to perform any banking transactions. I feel possessing broadband connection is really expensive in Australia' (*Respondent* # 8).
- 'I know that Internet banking do not involve any fees, but how about setup costs? Aren't they costly?' (*Respondent* # 33).

'Lack of resources' was identified as another macro theme. The most prevalent micro themes in descending order were affordability and accessibility. Affordability refers to 'lack of computer' and 'lack of Internet.' On the other hand, 'lack of Internet access at home' and 'lack of broadband connection' relate to the micro theme accessibility. In addition, a perception of the non-users towards dial-up Internet connectivity being slow encourages them to possess broadband connection, which is linked to their affordability.

- 'I have dial up connection at home and it is slow that the required site opens after a long time. I think it is of no help to perform Internet banking' (*Respondent* # 184).
- 'I do not possess a computer either at home or at work' (*Respondent* # 149).

'Social influence' was identified as another major theme that impedes adoption of Internet banking by non-users. The prevalent micro themes in connection to the social influence macro theme relates to the influence of friends, colleagues and family members on the respondents' decision-making whether to adopt Internet banking or not. Actual responses include 'friends do not use,' 'colleagues think Internet banking is of no advantage,' and 'family members has no good opinion' on performing Internet banking transactions. Data reveals that ethnicity of the respondents seems to correlate with the social influence factor. Most of the Australian respondents with Asian ethnic origin have reported that social influence is the major factor hindering them from using Internet banking service. Usually, banking transactions are considered to be performed in private and there is little scope to discuss one's banking actions with others. However, results obtained indicate that consumers with Asian ethnicity are influenced by friends and colleagues in the use of banking services.

- 'None of my friends use Internet banking and I never tried to explore that option as ATM and telephone banking is easy to use' (*Respondent* # 5).
- 'Neither my friends nor my colleagues at work use Internet banking. I am comfortable and happy with branch bank services' (*Respondent* # 33).

'Technology discomfort' was identified as the macro theme that hinders the adoption of Internet banking by non-users. Micro themes identified in order of prevalence relate to self-efficacy, safety and discomfort. Actual responses indicate that the self-efficacy theme refers to 'lack of skills' and 'lack of experience' with Internet banking, Internet, and computers. Non-users' perceptions that 'advanced technologies not safe,' 'not comfortable with technologies' and 'technological advancements are complex' relate to safety and discomfort micro themes. Technology as a factor hindering the use of Internet banking service is associated with mature consumers and is related to the age of the consumer.

- 'I never used Internet and do not possess skills or experience to work with computers' (*Respondent* # 231).
- 'I am too old to perform Internet banking. I lack the knowledge of working with computers' (*Respondent* # 152).

'Routine behaviour' was identified as another macro theme that was impeding adoption of Internet banking by non-users. Reluctance and regularity were the micro themes in descending order referring to the routine thematic area. Routinised behaviour and general inertia has been identified as one of the factors impeding consumers from using the Internet banking service. Actual responses were related to 'reluctant to switch,' 'reluctant to do myself' and 'performing transactions with the bank branch on a regular basis.' Results indicate that this factor is also related to ethnicity of some non-users. Certain non-users, irrespective of their age, income, and occupation but with certain ethnic backgrounds are reluctant to use Internet banking service just because they are used to performing in a routine manner in their home country.

- 'I have been too lazy and reluctant to set up Internet banking and have been intending to set it up but never get around to it' (*Respondent* # 4).
- 'I am used to the routine of going to the bank regularly to perform my banking transactions' (*Respondent* # 148).

The last macro theme identified was 'Internet banking performed by the spouse.' Micro themes in order of prevalence relate to tradition, usage, and knowledge. Actual responses relate to 'lack of sufficient knowledge,' 'performed by my husband,' 'performed by my partner,' 'as a tradition,' and 'usage.' The macro theme in relation to the demographic data reveals that all the non-users who attributed that Internet banking was performed by their spouse were females.

- 'My husband performs all the banking transactions as I lack sufficient knowledge' (*Respondent* # 211).
- 'Since many years it is a tradition for me to go to bank for my needs and my partner uses all recent banking methods' (*Respondent* # 74).

Thus in an Australian banking context, eight macro themes were identified to be hindering the adoption of Internet banking by the non-users.

SOLUTIONS AND RECOMMENDATIONS

Results indicated that there were more males using Internet banking, within a age range of 31-40 years, with higher levels of education, in managerial position and within an income range of $80 000 and above. On the contrary, non-users of Internet banking were represented by more number of females, within a mature age range, with vocational levels of education, mostly with Anglo-Australian background, in administrative roles and within an income range of 50 000 to 65 000. Similarly, the themes that emerged as reasons for non-adoption of Internet banking for performing their banking transactions in Australian context relate to security issues largely expressed females, a concern of physical and social components of risk and performed by spouse by females, income variable being related to lack of resources and value perceptions, ethnicity being linked with themes such as social influence and routine behaviour, and technology discomfort expressed by mature age individuals. Addressing these demographic related issues in an appropriate manner would create new segment profile for the retail banking sector.

Retail banking managers need to focus on developing strategies that can reduce technology discomfort levels of the mature age customers by organising training sessions or implementing high interactive services online. Female customers need to be comforted with the easy access of technology related banking services. Banks need to focus on communicating the safe transaction methods and further reducing the threats associated with security and risk variables. Effective communication strategies and credibility of information related to the use of technology in banking transactions would address the sensitive ethnicity issue and break the clutter of routinised behaviour and social influence related variables. Similarly, the retail-banking sector needs to partner with the service providers such as the National Broadband Network, Telstra etc., to enhance the value perceptions associated with the use of technology in everyday banking transactions. Organisation of community training centres that offer preliminary sessions on the use of the Internet, use of Internet banking and the use of searching facilities on Web would help individuals to overcome the demographic variations in the adoption and use of technology.

REFERENCES

Akinci, S., Akoy, S., & Atilgan, E. (2004). Adoption of internet banking among sophisticated consumer segments in an advanced developing country. *International Journal of Bank Marketing*, *22*(3), 212–232. doi:10.1108/02652320410530322

Assael, H. (1981). *Consumer behaviour and marketing action*. Boston, MA: Kent Publications.

Barter, A. P., & Sicherman, N. (1998). Technological change and the skill acquisition of young workers. *Journal of Labor Economics*, *16*(4), 718–755. doi:10.1086/209904

Bayus, B. L. (1987). Forecasting sales of new contingent products: An application to the compact disk market. *Journal of Product Innovation Management*, *4*, 243–255. doi:10.1016/0737-6782(87)90028-2

Daniel, E. (1999). Provision of electronic banking in the UK and the Republic of Ireland. *International Journal of Bank Marketing*, *17*(2), 72–82. doi:10.1108/02652329910258934

Foucault, B. E., & Scheufele, D. A. (2002). Web vs. campus store? Why students buy textbooks online? *Journal of Consumer Marketing*, *19*(5), 409–423. doi:10.1108/07363760210437632

Gan, C., Clemes, M., Limsombunchai, V., & Weng, A. (2006). A logit analysis of electronic banking in New Zealand. *International Journal of Bank Marketing*, *24*(6), 360–383. doi:10.1108/02652320610701717

Gartner. (2003). Online banking goes mainstream in US. In *Nua Internet Surveys*. New York, NY: Scope Communications Group.

Gerrard, P., & Cunningham, J. B. (2003). The diffusion of Internet banking among Singapore consumers. *International Journal of Bank Marketing*, *21*(1), 16–28. doi:10.1108/02652320310457776

Gronau, R., & Hamermesh, D. S. (2001). *The demand for variety: A household production perspective*. National Bureau of Economic Research Working Paper: 8509. Canberra, Australia: National Bureau of Economic Research.

Hernandez, J. M. C., & Mazzon, J. A. (2007). Adoption of internet banking: Proposition and implementation of an integrated methodology approach. *International Journal of Bank Marketing*, *25*(2), 72–88. doi:10.1108/02652320710728410

Howcroft, B., Hamilton, R., & Hewer, P. (2002). Consumer attitude and the usage and adoption of home banking in the United Kingdom. *International Journal of Bank Marketing*, *20*(3), 111–121. doi:10.1108/02652320210424205

Igbaria, M., & Chakrabarti, A. (1990). Computer anxiety and attitudes towards microcomputer use. *Behaviour & Information Technology*, *9*(3), 229–241. doi:10.1080/01449299008924239

Igbaria, M., Guimaraes, T., & Davis, G. B. (1995). Testing the determinants of microcomputer usage via a structural equation model. *Journal of Management Information Systems*, *11*(4), 87–114.

Ismail, H. B., & Panni, M. F. A. K. (2009). Factors affecting customer retention toward internet banking in Malaysia. *Journal of Information and Knowledge Management*, *8*(1), 35–43. doi:10.1142/S021964920900218X

Jayawardhena, C., & Foley, P. (2000). Changes in banking sector – A case of internet banking in UK. *Journal of Internet Research: Networking and Policy*, *10*(1), 19–30. doi:10.1108/10662240010312048

Karjaluoto, H., Mattila, M., & Pento, T. (2002). Electronic banking in Finland: Consumer beliefs and reactions to a new delivery channel. *Journal of Financial Services Marketing*, *6*(4), 346–361. doi:10.1057/palgrave.fsm.4770064

Katz, J., & Aspden, P. (1997). Motivations for and barriers to internet usage: Results of a national public opinion survey. *Internet Research: Electronic Networking Applications and Policy*, *7*(3), 170–188. doi:10.1108/10662249710171814

Kolodinsky, J., Hogarth, J. M., & Shue, J. F. (2000). Bricks or clicks? Consumer adoption of electronic banking technologies. *Consumer Interests Annual*, *46*, 180–184.

Kolodinsky, J. M., Hogarth, J. M., & Hilgert, M. A. (2004). The adoption of electronic banking technologies by US consumers. *International Journal of Bank Marketing*, *22*(4), 238–259. doi:10.1108/02652320410542536

Lee, E., & Lee, J. (2001). Consumer adoption of Internet banking: Need-based and/or skill based? *Marketing Management Journal*, *11*(1), 101–113.

Liu, J., Tsou, M., & Hammitt, J. K. (2001). The impact of advanced technology adoption in wage structures: Evidence from Taiwan manufacturing firms. *Economica*, *68*(271), 359–378. doi:10.1111/1468-0335.00251

Mattila, M. (2001). Essays on customers in the dawn of interactive banking. *Jyvaskyla Studies in Business and Economics*, *9*, 15–22.

Parasuraman, S., & Igbaria, M. (1990). An examination of gender differences in the determinants of computer anxiety and attitudes towards microcomputers among managers. *International Journal of Man-Machine Studies*, *32*, 327–340. doi:10.1016/S0020-7373(08)80006-5

Polatoglu, V. N., & Ekin, S. (2001). An empirical investigation of the Turkish consumers' acceptance of internet banking services. *International Journal of Bank Marketing*, *19*(4), 156–165. doi:10.1108/02652320110392527

Roemer, M., & Buhl, H. U. (1996). Das web also alternativ zur bankfiliale: Gestaltung innovation IKS fur das direktbanking. *Writschftsinformatic*, *6*, 565–577.

Sathye, M. (1999). Adoption of Internet banking by Australian consumers: An empirical investigation. *International Journal of Bank Marketing*, *17*(7), 324–334. doi:10.1108/02652329910305689

Teo, T. (2001). Demographic and motivation variables associated with internet usage activities. *Internet Research: Electronic Networking Applications and Policy*, *11*(2), 125–137. doi:10.1108/10662240110695089

Trocchia, P. J., & Janda, S. (2000). A phenomenological investigation of internet usage among older individual. *Journal of Consumer Marketing*, *17*(7), 605–616. doi:10.1108/07363760010357804

Venkatesh, V., & Morris, M. G. (2000). Why don't men ever stop to ask for directions? Gender, social influence, and their role in technology acceptance and change behaviour. *Management Information Systems Quarterly*, *24*, 115–139. doi:10.2307/3250981

Venkatesh, V., Morris, M. G., & Ackerman, P. L. (2000). A longitudinal field investigation of gender differences in individual technology adoption decision making processes. *Organizational Behavior and Human Decision Processes*, *83*, 33–60. doi:10.1006/obhd.2000.2896

Vrechopoulos, A. P., Siomkos, G. J., & Doukidis, G. I. (2001). Internet shopping adoption by Greek consumers. *European Journal of Innovation Management*, *4*(3), 142–152. doi:10.1108/14601060110399306

Compilation of References

Adger, C., Christian, W., & Wolfam, D. (2007). *Dialects in schools and communities*. Mahwah, NJ: Lawrence Erlbaum Associates.

Akinci, S., Akoy, S., & Atilgan, E. (2004). Adoption of internet banking among sophisticated consumer segments in an advanced developing country. *International Journal of Bank Marketing*, *22*(3), 212–232. doi:10.1108/02652320410530322

Akins, R., & Ho, H. (2009). Clinical simulation in modern teaching and training of sonography in obstetrics and gynecology. *Donald School Journal of Ultrasound in Obstetrics and Gynecology*, *3*(4), 17–21. doi:10.5005/jp-journals-10009-1030

Alheit, P. (2009). Biographical learning – Within the new lifelong learning. In Illeris, K. (Ed.), *Contemporary Theories of Learning: Learning Theorists…in Their Own Words* (pp. 116–128). New York, NY: Routledge.

Allen, B., & Lewis, D. (2006). Virtual learning communities as a vehicle for workforce development: A case study. *Journal of Workplace Learning*, *18*(6), 367–383. doi:10.1108/13665620610682099

ALRC. (2008). *For your information: Australian privacy law and practice (ALRC report 108)*. Retrieved 10 May 2012 from http://www.alrc.gov.au/publications/report-108

Alvarez, M. (2006). *Second life and school: The use of virtual world worlds in high education*. San Antonio, TX: Trinity University. Retrieved from http://www.trinity.edu/adelwich/worlds/articles/trinity.manny.alvarez.pdf

Anderson, N. B., & Screen, R. M. (1994). *Multicultural perspectives in communication disorders*. San Diego, CA: Singular Publishing Group.

Argyris, C., & Schön, D. (1978). *Organizational learning: A theory of action perspective*. Reading, MA: Addision Wesley. doi:10.2307/40183951

Assael, H. (1981). *Consumer behaviour and marketing action*. Boston, MA: Kent Publications.

Association of College and Research Libraries. (2000). *Information literacy competency standards for higher education*. Chicago, IL: American Library Association.

Ausburn, L. J. (2004). Course design elements most valued by adult learners in blended online education environments: An American perspective. *Educational Media International*, 327–337. Retrieved from http://test.scripts.psu.edu/users/k/h/khk122/woty/OnlineAdultLearners/Ausbum%202004.pdfdoi:10.1080/0952398042000314820

Australian Flexible Learning Framework. (2007). *The knowledge tree: An e-journal of learning and innovation*. Retrieved from http://kt.flexiblelearning.net.au/tkt2007/wp-content/uploads/2007/10/kt_ed15-printerversion.pdf

Australian Institute of Criminology. (2010). Covert and cyber bullying. *Research in Practice*, *9*, 1.

Azcutia, J. (1999). *Educational administration and institutions for evaluation of the education system*. Retrieved from http://www.ince.mec.es/pres/pon-n8-ing.html

Baer, W. Borisov, Danezis, G., Dutton, Klonowski, M. W., Seda, G.,...Zagorski, F. (2009). *Machiavelli confronts 21st century digital technology: Democracy in a network society*. Retrieved from http://ssrn.com/abstract=1521222

Balasubramanian, V. (2012). *Organizational learning and information systems*. Retrieved from http://www.e-papyrus.com/personal/orglrn.html

Baldwin, T. T., & Ford, J. K. (1988). Transfer of training: A review and directions for future research. *Personnel Psychology*, *41*(1), 63–105. doi:10.1111/j.1744-6570.1988.tb00632.x

Ball, A. F., & Farr, M. (2003). Dialects, culture, and teaching the English language arts. In J. Flood, J. M. Jensen, D. Lapp, & J. R. Squire (Eds.), *Handbook of Research on Teaching the English Language Arts,* (pp. 1-35). Retrieved from http://www.stanford.edu/~arnetha/pdf/BALLFARR%20w_Full%20Bibl.pdf

Bambara, C., Harbour, C., Davies, T., & Athey, S. (2009). The lived experience of community college students enrolled in high-risk online courses. *Community College Review*, *36*(3), 219–238. doi:10.1177/0091552108327187

Barab, S., Thomas, M., Dodge, T., Carteaux, R., & Tuzun, H. (2005). Making learning fun: Quest Atlantis, a game without guns. *Educational Technology Research and Development*, *53*(1), 86–107. doi:10.1007/BF02504859

Barnett, T., & Sorenson, C. (2011). Infectious disease surveillance in the United States and theUnited Kingdom: From public goods to the challenges of new technologies. *Journal of Health Politics, Policy and Law*, *36*, 165–185. doi:10.1215/03616878-1191144

Barter, A. P., & Sicherman, N. (1998). Technological change and the skill acquisition of young workers. *Journal of Labor Economics*, *16*(4), 718–755. doi:10.1086/209904

Baugh, J. (2000). *Beyond ebonics: Linguistic pride and racial prejudice*. Oxford, UK: Oxford University Press.

Baylor, A. L., & Ritchie, D. (2002). What factors facilitate teacher skill, teacher morale, and perceived student learning in technology using classrooms? *Computers & Education*, *39*, 395–414. doi:10.1016/S0360-1315(02)00075-1

Bayus, B. L. (1987). Forecasting sales of new contingent products: An application to the compact disk market. *Journal of Product Innovation Management*, *4*, 243–255. doi:10.1016/0737-6782(87)90028-2

Beatty, K. (2002). *Describing and enhancing collaboration at the computer*. Retrieved from http://www.cjlt.ca/content/vol28.2/beatty.html

Beatty, K., & Nunan, D. (2004). Computer-mediated collaborative learning. *System*, *32*(2), 165–183. doi:10.1016/j.system.2003.11.006

Beder, H., & Carrea, N. (1988). The effects of andragogical teacher training on adult students' attendance and evaluation of their teachers. *Adult Education Quarterly*, *38*, 75–87. doi:10.1177/0001848188038002002

Beer, M., Slack, F., & Armitt, G. (2003). Community building and virtual teamwork in an online learning environment, hicss. In *Proceedings of the 36th Annual Hawaii International Conference on System Sciences* (HICSS 2003), (p. 66). HICSS.

Beermann, J., Taetzlaff, R., Bruckner, T., Schoebinger, M., Muller-Stich, B. P., & Gutt, C. N. (2010). Three-dimensional visualization improves understanding of surgical liver anatomy. *Medical Education*, *44*(9), 936–940. doi:10.1111/j.1365-2923.2010.03742.x

Beggs, T. A. (2000). Influences and barriers to the adoption of instructional technology. In *Proceedings of the Mid-South Instructional Technology Conference,* (pp. 1-14). Murfreesboro, TN: IEEE.

Bellon, T., & Oates, R. (2002). *Best practices in cyberspace: Motivating the online learner*. Paper presented at the National Education Computing Conference. Retrieved from http://www.eric.ed.gov/PDFS/ED475923.pdf

Bennett, S., Maton, K., & Kervin, L. (2008). The 'digital natives' debate: A critical review of the evidence. *British Journal of Educational Technology*, *39*(5), 775–786. doi:10.1111/j.1467-8535.2007.00793.x

Benson, P. (2001). *Teaching and researching autonomy in language learning*. New York, NY: Longman.

Berge, Z. L. (2005). Taking the distance out of distance education. In Kearsley, G. (Ed.), *Online Learning: Personal Reflections on the Transformation of Education* (pp. 12–25). Englewood Cliffs, NJ: Educational Technology Publications, Inc.

Billett, S. (1999). Guided learning in the workplace. In Boud, D., & Garrick, J. (Eds.), *Understanding Learning at Work* (pp. 151–163). London, UK: Routledge.

Bitter-Rijpkema, M., Sloep, P. B., & Jansen, D. (2003). Learning to change the virtual business learning approach to professional workplace learning. *Journal of Educational Technology & Society*, *6*(1), 18–25. Retrieved from http://www.ifets.info/journals/6_1/bitter.pdf

Bjørn-Andersen, N., Eason, K., & Robey, D. (Eds.). (1986). *Managing computer impact: An international study of management and organizations*. Norwood, NJ: Ablex.

Black, P. J., & Kari, C. J. (2010). Policing diverse communities: Do gender and minority status make a difference? *Journal of Ethnicity in Criminal Justice*, *8*(3), 216–229. doi:10.1080/15377938.2010.502848

Blair, A. (2010). Information overload: The early years. *Boston Globe Newspaper Company*. Retrieved from http://www.boston.com/bostonglobe/ideas/articles/2010/11/28/information_overload_the_early_years/

Blake, R. R., & Mouton, J. S. (1972). What is instrumented learning? *Training and Development Journal*, *26*(1), 12–20.

Blondy, L. C. (2007). Evaluation and application of andragogical assumptions to the adult online learning environment. *Journal of Interactive Online Learning*, *6*(2), 116–130.

Bloom, B. S., Englehart, M. D., Furst, E. J., & Krathwolh, D. R. (1956). *Taxonomy of educational objectives: The classification of educational goals: Handbook 1: Cognitive domain*. New York, NY: Lognmans Green.

Boekaerts, M. (1995). Self-regulated learning: Bridging the gap between metacognitive and metamotivation theories. *Educational Psychologist*, *30*(4), 195–200. doi:10.1207/s15326985ep3004_4

Bork, A. (2005). Distance learning today and tomorrow. In Kearsley, G. (Ed.), *Online Learning: Personal Reflections on the Transformation of Education* (pp. 26–41). Englewood Cliffs, NJ: Educational Technology Publications, Inc.

Boulanger, B., Kearney, P., Ochoa, J., Tsuei, B., & Sands, F. (2001). Telemedicine: A solution to the followup of rural trauma patients? *Journal of the American College of Surgeons*, *192*(4), 447–452. doi:10.1016/S1072-7515(01)00796-7

Boulos, M. N. K., Hetherington, L., & Wheeler, S. (2007). Second life: An overview of the potential of 3-D virtual worlds in medical and health education. *Health Information and Libraries Journal*, *24*, 233–245. doi:10.1111/j.1471-1842.2007.00733.x

Bouras, C., & Tsiatsos, T. (2008). *Extending the limits of CVE's to support collaborative e-learning scenarios*. Retrieved from http://ru6.cti.gr/ru6/publications/9786892.pdf

Bradley, J. B. (2011). A comparison of course completion, satisfaction, achievement, and performance among non-profit professionals who complete andragogical or pedagogical online learning modules on grant writing. *Dissertation Abstracts International*, *71*(8).

Bray, J. (2009). Embrace the future now! *Techniques*, *84*(5), 6.

Breen, M. P., & Mann, S. (1997). Shooting arrows at the sun: Perspectives on a pedagogy for autonomy. In Benson, P., & Voller, P. (Eds.), *Autonomy and Independence in Language Learning* (pp. 132–149). London, UK: Longman.

Bridges, D. R., Davidson, R. A., Odegard, P. S., Maki, I. V., & Tomkowiak, J. (2011). Interprofessiona collaboration: Three best practice models of interprofessional education. *Medical Education Online*, *16*, 6035–6050. doi:10.3402/meo.v16i0.6035

Broaddribb, S., & Carter, C. (2009). Using second life in human resource development. *British Journal of Educational Technology*, *40*(3), 547–550. doi:10.1111/j.1467-8535.2009.00950.x

Brookfield, S. (1986). *Understanding and facilitating adult learning*. San Francisco, CA: Jossey-Bass.

Brookfield, S. (1987). *Developing critical thinkers*. San Francisco, CA: Jossey-Bass.

Brookfield, S. (2005). *The power of critical theory: Liberating adult learning and teaching*. San Francisco, CA: Jossey-Bass.

Brown, B. K. (2012). The impact of illiteracy. *Literacy Council of West Alabama*. Retrieved from http://literacywa.org/the-impact-of-illiteracy/

Brown, C., & Czerniewicz, L. (2010). Debunking the 'digital native': Beyond digital apartheid, towards digital democracy. *Journal of Computer Assisted Learning*, *26*(5), 357–369. doi:10.1111/j.1365-2729.2010.00369.x

Bryan, V. C. (2006). Impact of technology in community education: Its applications and effects. *Community Education Journal*, *20*(2/3), 10–13.

Bryan, V. C., & Musgrove, A. (2003). Creating virtual teams with blackboard. In *Proceedings of the Society for Information Technology & Teacher Education International Conference*. Albuquerque, NM: Society for Information Technology & Teacher Education. Retrieved from http://www.coe.fau.edu/faculty/bryan/documents/resume.pdf

Bull, G., & Kajder, S. (2004). Digital storytelling in the language arts classroom. *Tapped in Learning & Leading with Technology*, *31*(5), 34–37.

Bullying Statistics. (2012). *Cyber bullying*. Retrieved from http://www.bullyingstatistics.org/content/cyber-bullying-statistics.html

Burrows, R., & Ellison, N. (2004). Sorting places out? Towards a social politics of neighbourhood informatization. *Information Communication and Society*, *7*(3), 321–336. doi:10.1080/1369118042000284588

Butler, T. (2003). From data to knowledge and back again: Understanding the limitations of KMS. *Knowledge and Process Management*, *10*, 144–155. doi:10.1002/kpm.180

Campbell, M. (2005). Cyber bullying: An old problem in a new guise? *Australian Journal of Guidance & Counselling*, *15*(1), 68–76. doi:10.1375/ajgc.15.1.68

Campbell, M. (2007). *Cyber bullying and young people: Treatment principles not simplistic advice*. Retrieved 23rd February 2007, from http://www.scientist-practitioner.com

Campion, M. (1995). The supposed demise of bureaucracy: Implications for distance education and open learning. *Distance Education*, *16*(2), 192–216. doi:10.1080/0158791950160204

Candy, P. C. (1991). *Self-direction for lifelong learning*. San Francisco, CA: Jossey-Bass.

Carey, R., & Posavac, E. (1997). *Program evaluation methods and case studies* (5th ed.). Upper Saddle River, NJ: Prentice-Hall.

Carlyon, P. (2012, 13 January). Tormented family and friends weep for taunted teen with secret sorrow. *Herald Sun*. Retrieved 10 May 2012 from http://www.heraldsun.com.au/news/more-news/last-words-of-a-best-friend/story-fn7x8me2-1226243026933

Carroll, T. G., Fulton, K., & Doerr, H. (2010). *Team up for 21st century teaching and learning: What research and practice reveal about professional learning*. Washington, DC: National Commission on Teaching & America's Future.

Cartor, R. A. (1991). A comparison of andragogy and pedagogy: Assessing the relationship between individual personality differences, learning styles, and training types. *Dissertation Abstracts International*, *51*(7).

Cassidy, J. (2006). Me media: How hanging out on the Internet became big business. *The New Yorker*. Retrieved 10 May 2012 from http://www.newyorker.com/archive/2006/05/15/060515fa_fact_cassidy#ixzz1uQ0sneah

Cazden, C. B. (2001). *Classroom discourse: The language of teaching and learning*. Retrieved from http://www.wou.edu/~girodm/library/cazden.pdf

Center for Media Literacy. (2012). *Media literacy*. Malibu, CA: Center for Media Literacy.

Cercone, K. (2008). Characteristics of adult learners with implications for online learning design. *AACE Journal*, *16*(2), 137–159.

Chafe, A. (1998). *Computer technology and cooperative learning*. Retrieved from http://www.stemnet.nf.ca/~achafe/maj_index.html

Chahla, M., Eberlein, M., & Wright, S. (2010). The effect of providing a USB syllabus on resident reading of landmark articles. *Medical Education Online*, *15*, 4639–4642. doi:10.3402/meo.v15i0.4639

Chamberlain, S. P. (2005). Recognizing and responding to cultural diversity. *Intervention in School and Clinic*, *40*(4), 195–211. doi:10.1177/10534512050400040101

Chambers, G. (1982). A model for the development of technical instructors. *Master Abstracts International*, *20*(4), 342.

Chaney, D., Chaney, E., & Eddy, J. (2009). *The contect of distance learngn programs in higher education: Five enabling assumptions*. Retreived from http://www.uncg.edu/oao/PDF/5%20Assumptons%20OJDLA.pdf

Chang, M. (2005). Applying self-regulated learning strategies in a web-based instruction - An investigation of motivation perception. *Computer Assisted Language Learning, 18*(3), 217–230. doi:10.1080/09588220500178939

Chang, N.-B., Wei, L. Y., Tseng, C. C., & Kao, J. C.-Y. (1997). The design of a GIS-based decision support system for chemical emergency preparedness and response in an urban environment. *Computers, Environment and Urban Systems, 21*(1), 67–94. doi:10.1016/S0198-9715(97)01009-0

Charles Stewart Mott Foundation. (1973). 1973 annual report. In K. McDonald (Ed.), *Charles Stewart Mott Foundation: From Community Service to Community Organizing, Foundation Watch*. Retrieved from https://www.capitalresearch.org/2012/03/10910/

Charles Stewart Mott Foundation. (2010). 2010 annual report. In *Striking a Balance: Supporting Innovative Ideas versus Sustaining Basic Needs*. Davison, MI: The Riegel Press.

Charles Stewart Mott Foundation. (2012). *Our values*. Retrieved from http://www.mott.org/about/values/ourvalues

Chen, H. S., Guo, F. R., Chen, C. Y., Chen, J. H., & Kuo, T. S. (2001). Review of telemedicine projects in Taiwan. *International Journal of Medical Informatics, 61*(2-3), 117–129. doi:10.1016/S1386-5056(01)00134-4

Cheng, J. (2009). *Study: Twitter users are mobile, urban, and engaged online*. Washington, DC: *Pew* Research Center's Internet & American Life Project. Retrieved from http://arstechnica.com/business/2009/02/study-twitter-users-are-mobile-urban-and-engaged-online/

Childress, M. D., & Braswell, R. (2006). Using massively multiplayer online role-playing games for online learning. *Distance Education, 27*(2), 187–197. doi:10.1080/01587910600789522

Christian, D. (1997). *Vernacular dialects in U.S. schools*. Retrieved from http://www.cal.org/resources/digest/christ01.html

Clairborne, L., & TRU. (2007). *Tech abuse in teen relationships study*. Retrieved from http://www.loveisnotabuse.com/pdf/06-208Tech RelationshipAbuseTPL.pdf

Clark, J. A. (1991). Self-directed learning skills and clinical performance: A comparison of traditionally taught and learning contract-taught nursing student. *Dissertation Abstracts International, 41*(7).

Clark, R. C., Nguyen, F., & Sweller, J. (2006a). *Efficiency in learning: Evidence-based guidelines to manage cognitive load*. San Francisco, CA: Pfeiffer. doi:10.1002/pfi.4930450920

Clarke, S., & Maher, M. (2001). *The role of place in designining a learner centered virtual learning enviroment*. Retrieved from http://web.arch.usyd.edu.au/-mary/Pubs/2001pdf/CF2001.pdf

Clean Cut Media. (2009). *YouTube statistics: Where did my time go?* Retrieved from http://www.cleancutmedia.com/video/youtube-statistics-the-ultimate-time-suck

Cohen, L., & Manion, L. (1994). *Research methods in education*. London, UK: Routeledge and Kegan Paul.

Cohen, S., & Wills, T. (1985). Stress, social support, and the buffering hypothesis. *Psychological Bulletin, 98*, 310–357. doi:10.1037/0033-2909.98.2.310

Coleman, J. A. (1997). Residence abroad within language study. *Language Teaching, 30*(1), 1–20. doi:10.1017/S0261444800012659

Coleman, J. S. (1988). Social capital in the creation of human capital. *American Journal of Sociology, 94*(Supplement), S95–S120. doi:10.1086/228943

Colombo, C., Kunstelj, M., Molinari, F., & Todorovski, L. (2011). Participatory policy process design: Lessons learned from three European regions. *Journal of Balkan & Near Eastern Studies, 13*(1), 117–139. doi:10.1080/19448953.2011.550811

Commonwealth of Australia. (2012). *Cybersmart*. Accessed 8 May 2012 from http://www.cybersmart.gov.au

Connolly, C., Maurushat, A., Vaile, D., & van Dijk, P. (2011). *An overview of international cyber-security awareness raising and educational initiatives*. Retrieved 8 May 2012 from http://www.acma.gov.au/WEB/STANDARD/pc=PC_311301

Conti, G. J. (2009). Development of a user-friendly instrument for identifying the learning strategy preferences of adults. *Teaching and Teacher Education, 25*, 887–896. doi:10.1016/j.tate.2009.02.024

Coombs, P. (1985). *The world crisis in education: A view from the eighties*. Oxford, UK: Oxford University Press.

Coombs, W. (2007). Protecting organization reputations during a crisis. *Corporate Reputation Review*, *10*(3), 163–176. doi:10.1057/palgrave.crr.1550049

Cooper, M. M., & Selfe, C. L. (1990). Computer conferences and learning: Authority, resistance, and internally persuasive discourse. *College English*, *52*(8), 847–873. doi:10.2307/377388

Coopes, A. (2010, December 2). Cyber crime: Bigger than the drugs trade and growing. *Sydney Morning Herald*.

Costa, A. L., & Garmston, R. J. (2002). *Cognitive coaching a foundation for renaissance schools*. Norwood, MA: Christopher-Gordon Publishers, Inc.

Craft, R., Kerschenbaum, S., & Ware, J. (2007). Training tomorrow's workforce. *Training & Development*, *61*(4), 58–60. Retrieved from http://vnweb.hwwilsonweb.com/hww/jumpstart.jhtml?recid=0bc05f7a67b1790e7e1f464a759977995c836d80430b76208bfbcbdbbce7221d81c490e544bcf86c&fmt=P

Craig, H. K., & Washington, J. A. (2000). An assessment battery for identifying language impairments in African-American children. *Journal of Language. Speech and Hearing Research*, *43*(2), 366–379.

Cranton, P. (2006). *Understanding and promoting transformative learning*. San Francisco, CA: Wiley.

Crawford, J., & Irving, C. (2009). Information literacy in the workplace. *Journal of Librarianship and Information Science*, *41*(1), 29–38. doi:10.1177/0961000608099897

Cristancho, S. M., Moussa, F., & Dubrowski, A. (2011). A framework-based approach to designing simulation-augmented surgical education and training programs. *American Journal of Surgery*, *202*, 344–351. doi:10.1016/j.amjsurg.2011.02.011

Cross, D., Shaw, T., Hearn, L., Epstein, M., Monks, H., Lester, L., & Thomas, L. (2009). *Australian covert bullying prevalence study*. Perth, Australia: Edith Cowan University.

Cross, D. L. (1988). The influence of self-directed learning contracts versus a passive therapy treatment in a back rehabilitation program. *Dissertation Abstracts International*, *50*(5).

Crystal, D. (2012). The evolution of language on the web. *Webcopyplus*. Retrieved from http://blog.webcopyplus.com/2010/08/30/the-evolution-of-language-on-the-web/

Cullen, T. J., Hart, L. G., Whitcomb, M. E., & Rosenblatt, R. A. (1997). The national health service corps: Rural physician service and retention. *The Journal of the American Board of Family Practice*, *10*(4), 272–279.

Cummins, J. (1999). BICS and CALP: Clarifying the distinction. *University of Toronto*. Retrieved from http://ezproxy.wou.edu:2100/hww/results/external_link_maincontentframe.jhtml?_DARGS=/hww/results/results_common.jhtml.44

Cummins, J. (2005). *Teaching for cross-language transfer in dual language education: Possibilities and pitfalls*. Paper presented at TESOL Symposium on Dual Language Education: Teaching and Learning Two Languages in the EFL Setting. Retrieved from http://74.125.155.132/scholar?q=cache:BOtf0n95sMJ:scholar.google.com/+cummins,+j+iceberg&hl=en&as_sdt=0,38

Dachus Group/XPLANE. The Economist, McLeod, S., Fishch, K., & Berstler, L. (2009). *Did you know 4.0?* Retrieved from http://www.youtube.com/watch?v=6ILQrEWe8

Daniel, E. (1999). Provision of electronic banking in the UK and the Republic of Ireland. *International Journal of Bank Marketing*, *17*(2), 72–82. doi:10.1108/02652329910258934

Darling-Hammond, L., Jaquith, A., Mindich, D., & Wei, R. C. (2010). *Teacher professional learning in the United States: Case studies of state policies and strategies*. Oxford, OH: Learning Forward.

Dauer, T. L., Zanzonico, P., Tuttle, M. R., Quinn, M. D., & Strauss, H. W. (2011). The Japanese tsunami and resulting nuclear emergency at the Fukushima Daiichi power facility: Technical, radiologic, and response perspectives. *Journal of Nuclear Medicine*, *52*, 1423–1432. doi:10.2967/jnumed.111.091413

Dave, R. H. (1970). Psychomotor levels. In Armstrong, R. J. (Ed.), *Developing and Writing Educational Objectives* (pp. 73–108). Tucson, AZ: Educational Innovators' Press.

Davenport, J., & Davenport, J. A. (1985a). A chronology and analysis of the andragogy debate. *Adult Education Quarterly*, *35*, 152–159. doi:10.1177/0001848185035003004

Davenport, J., & Davenport, J. A. (1985b). Knowles or Lindeman: Would the real father of American andragogy please stand up. *Lifelong Learning*, *9*(3), 4–5.

Davies, A., Fidler, D., & Gorbis, M. (2011). *Future work skills 2020*. Palo Alto, CA: Institute for the Future for University of Phoenix Research Institute. Retrieved from http://cdn.theatlantic.com/static/front/docs/sponsored/phoenix/future_work_skills_2020.pdf

de Laat, M. (2011). Bridging the knowledge gap: Using social network methodology for detecting, connecting and facilitating informal networked learning in organizations. In *Proceedings of the 44th Hawaii International Conference on System Sciences*. IEEE.

De Lucia, A., Francese, R., Passero, I., & Tortora, G. (2009). Development and evaluation of a virtual campus on second life: The case of second DMI. *Journal of Computers & Education*, *52*, 220–233. doi:10.1016/j.compedu.2008.08.001

Decker, L. (1992). *Community education: Building learning communities* (Rev. ed.). Alexandria, VA: National Community Education Association.

Dede, C. (2005). An intellectual journey from distance education to distributed learning. In Kearsley, G. (Ed.), *Online Learning: Personal Reflections on the Transformation of Education* (pp. 66–72). Englewood Cliffs, NJ: Educational Technology Publications, Inc.

Dee, M. I. (2011). *First year undergraduate students' perception of the effectiveness and transfer of multimedia training for a university course registration system*. (Doctoral Dissertation). Florida Atlantic University. Boca Raton, FL.

Deery, S., & Crawford, C. (2012, January 12). Schoolgirl (name removed) takes own life after Facebook torment. *Herald Sun*. Retrieved 10 May 2012 from http://www.news.com.au/national/torment-too-much-for-teen/story-e6frfkvr-1226242267322#ixzz1uQA4j6ey

Delpit, L. D. (1988). The silenced dialogue: Power and privilege in educating other people's children. *Harvard Educational Review*, *58*(3), 280–296. Retrieved from http://faculty.washington.edu/rikitiki/tcxg464sp08/Silenced%20Dialogue%20by%20L%20Delpitpdf

Delpit, L. D. (1995). *Other people's children: Cultural conflict in the classroom: Language diversity and learning*. New York, NY: The New Press. Retrieved from http://www.d.umn.edu/~hrallis/courses/1100sp04/readings/1100pdfs/Delpit%20-Lang%20in%20Clsmr.pdf

Delpit, L. D. (2007). Skills and other dilemmas of a progressive black educator. In D. George & J. Timbur (Eds.), *Reading Culture: Contexts for Critical Reading and Writing*, (pp. 180-185). New York, NY: Pearson/Longman. Retrieved from http://eng022.files.wordpress.com/2009/01/lisa-delpit-skills-and-other-dillemmas.pdf

Devine, M. (2011, July 24). Parents must go online where evil lurks in many guises. *Sunday Herald Sun*. Retrieved 10 May 2012 from http://www.heraldsun.com.au/opinion/parents-must-go-online-where-evil-lurks-in-many-guises/story-e6frfhqf-1226100402166

Diaz, D. P., & Cartnal, R. B. (1999). Students' learning styles in two classes: Online distance learning and equivalent on-campus. *College Teaching*, *47*(4), 130–135. Retrieved from http://home.earthlink.net/~davidpdiaz/LTS/html_docs/grslss.htmdoi:10.1080/87567559909595802

Dickinson, L. (1987). *Self-instruction in language learning*. Cambridge, MA: Cambridge University Press.

Dieterle, E., & Clark, J. (2006). *Multi-user environments for teaching and learning*. Retrieved from http://64.94.241.248/rivercityproject/documents/MUVE-for-TandL-Dieterle-Clarke.pdf

Digitalsurgeons. (2010). *Facebook vs. twitter: A breakdown of 2010 social demographics*. Retrieved from http://www.digitalsurgeons.com/Facebook-vs-twitter-infographic/

Dillard, J. L. (1972). *Black English: Its history and usage in the United States*. New York, NY: Random House.

Dillenbourg, P., Baker, P., Blaye, A., & O'Malley, C. (1994). The evolution of research on collaborative learning. In Spada, E., & Reiman, P. (Eds.), *Learning in Humans and Machine: Towards an Interdisciplinary Learning Science* (pp. 189–211). Oxford, UK: Elsevier. doi:10.1007/978-1-4020-9827-7_1

Dishon, D., & O'Leary, P. (1994). *Guidebook of cooperative learning*. Holmes Beach, FL: Learning Publications.

Distance Learning, P. B. C. C. (2009). *What is distance learning?* Retrieved from http://www.pbcc.edu/x2199.xml

Dooley, J., Pyżalski, J., & Cross, D. (2009). Cyberbullying versus face-to-face bullying: A theoretical and conceptual review. *The Journal of Psychology, 217*(4), 182–188.

Douglass, S. (2006). *Research base for the high level group report: Education*. New York, NY: Alliance of Civilizations.

Drennan, J., Kennedy, J., & Pisarski, A. (2005). Factors affecting student attitudes toward flexible online learning in management education. *The Journal of Educational Research, 98*(6), 331–338. Retrieved from http://www.heldref.orgdoi:10.3200/JOER.98.6.331-338

Driscoll, M., & Carliner, S. (2005). *Advanced web-based training strategies: Unlocking instructionally sound online learning*. San Francisco, CA: John Wiley & Sons, Inc.

Dror, I., Schmidt, P., & O'Connor, L. (2011). A cognitive perspective on technology enhanced learning in medical training: Great opportunities, pitfalls and challenges. *Medical Teacher, 33*, 291–296. doi:10.3109/0142159X.2011.550970

DuCharme-Hansen, B., & Dupin-Bryant, P. (2004). *Web-based distance education for adults*. Malabar, FL: Krieger Publishing Company.

Dufour, R., & Eaker, R. (1998). *Professional learning communities at work: Best practices for enhancing student achievement*. Bloomington, IN: National Educational Service.

Dunn, R., Szapkiw, A., Holder, D., & Hodgson, D. (2010). Of student teachers and avatars: Working towards an effective model for geographically distributed learning communities of pre-service educators using virtual worlds. In D. Gibson & B. Dodge (Eds.), *Proceedings of Society for Information Technology & Teacher Education International Conference 2010,* (pp. 423-427). Chesapeake, VA: Association for the Advancement of Computing in Education.

Duxbury, P. (2012). How to use twitter. *Squidoo*. Retrieved from http://www.squidoo.com/how-to-use-twitter

Dykstrak, E. (2003). Concept paper: Toward an international system model in emergency management. In *Proceedings of Toward an International System Model in Emergency Management* (pp. 1–17). Fairfax, VA: Public Entity Risk Institute.

Dynan, L., Cate, T., & Rhee, K. (2008). The impact of learning structure on students' readiness for self-directed learning. *Journal of Education for Business, 84*(2), 96–100. Retrieved from http://www.heldref.orgdoi:10.3200/JOEB.84.2.96-100

Eaker, R., Dufour, R., & DuFour, R. (2002). *Getting started: Reculturing schools to become professional learning communities*. Bloomington, IN: Solution Tree.

Education and Manpower Bureau. (2004a). Information technology in education – Way forward. *HKSAR: Education and Manpower Bureau*. Retrieved from http://www.emb.gov.hk/consultation_ited/file/eng/wayforward.pdf

Education and Manpower Bureau. (2004b). Preliminary study on reviewing the progress and evaluating the information technology in education (ITEd) projects (December 2000 – August 2001) (final report). *HKSAR: Education and Manpower Bureau*. Retrieved from http://www.ited.emb.gov.hk/Documents/ITEd_Report/FinalReport_v3.0_web.htm

EDUCAUSE. (2006). 7 things you should know about... YouTube. *EDUCAUSE Learning Initiative*. Retrieved from http://net.educause.edu/ir/library/pdf/ELI7018.pdf

EDUCAUSE. (2007). *The horizon report 2007 edition*. Austin, TX: The New Media Consortium. Retrieved from http://www.nmc.org/pdf/2007_Horizon_Report.pdf

Egbert, J., & Hanson-Smith, E. (1999). *CALL environments: Research, practice and critical issues*. Alexandria, VA: Teachers of English to Speakers of Other Languages.

El-Ghareeb, H., & Riad, A. (2011). Empowering adaptive lectures through activation of intelligent and web 2.0 technologies. *International Journal on E-Learning, 10*(4), 365–391.

Elias, J. L., & Merriam, S. B. (2005). *Philosophical foundations of adult education*. Malabar, FL: Krieger Publishing Company.

Ellington, L., & Bryan, V. (2010). The e-adult learner: The definitive classic in e-workplace development. In D. Guralnick (Ed.), *Proceedings of the Third International Conference on e-Learning in the Workplace,* (pp. 1-7). New York, NY: Kaleidoscope Learning, Inc.

Ellis, S., Begault, R., & Wenzel, E. (1997). Virual enviroments as human-computer interfaces. In Helander, M., & Prabhu, L. (Eds.), *Handbook of Human-Computer Interaction* (2nd ed., pp. 163–203). Oxford, UK: Elsevier Sciences.

Ellison, N., Steinfield, C., & Lampe, C. (2007). The benefits of Facebook friends: Social capital and college students' use of online social network sites. *Journal of Computer-Mediated Communication, 12*, 1143–1168. doi:10.1111/j.1083-6101.2007.00367.x

Engeström, Y. (1987). *Learning by expanding: An activity-theoretical approach to developmental research*. Helsinki, Finland: Orienta-Konsultit Oy.

Enrique Hinostroza, J., Labbe, C., Brun, M., & Matamala, C. (2011). Teaching and learning activities in Chilean classrooms: Is ICT making a difference? *Computers & Education, 57*, 1358–1367. doi:10.1016/j.compedu.2011.01.019

Epstein, J. L., Sanders, M. G., Simon, B. S., Salinas, K. C., Jansorn, N. R., & Van Voorhis, F. L. (2002). *School, family, and community partnerships: Your handbook for action* (2nd ed.). Thousand Oaks, CA: Corwin Press.

Facebook. (2011). *Facebook statistics*. Retrieved 12 November 2011 from http://www.facebook.com/press/info.php?statistics

Facebook. (2012a). *Statistics*. Accessed 10 May 2012 from http://newsroom.fb.com/Key-Facts/Statistics-8b.aspx

Facebook. (2012b). *Website*. Retrieved 23 March 2012 from http://newsroom.fb.com/content/default.aspx?NewsAreaId=22

Fantini, M. D. (1980). Towards a definition of community education. *Community Education Journal, 7*, 11–14.

Farmer, L. (2012). Information competency and e-learning. In Wang, V. (Ed.), *Encyclopedia of E-Leadership, Counseling and Training* (pp. 373–390). Hershey, PA: IGI Global.

Farnsworth, J. (2010). *Benefits and costs of social interaction among firefighters*. (Unpublished Master's Thesis). University of North Texas. Denton, TX.

Federal Communications Commission. (2010). *Broadband survey*. Washington, DC: Federal Communications Commission.

Fellenz, R., & Coker, L. (1979). Toward a definition of adult education, community education and community development. In Cunningham, P. (Ed.), *Yearbook of Adult and Continuing Education* (pp. 366–369). Chicago, IL: Marquis Academic Media.

Fenwick, T. (2008). Workplace learning: Emerging trends and new perspectives. In *New Directions for Adult and Continuing Education* (pp. 17–26). San Francisco, CA: Jossey-Bass. doi:10.1002/ace.302

Fisch, K., McLeod, S., & Bestler, L. (2009) *Did you know?* Retrieved from http://www.youtube.com/watch?v=6ILQrUrEWe8

Fisch, K., McLeod, S., & Bestler, L. (2011). *Shifthappens*. Retrieved from http://shifthappens.wikispaces.com/

Fischer, G. (2000). Lifelong learning - More than training. *Journal of Interactive Learning Research, 11*(3), 265–294. Retrieved from http://www.editlib.org/p/8380

Flanagan, M. (2009). Connecting family learning and active citizenship. *Adult Learner,* 92-98.

Flanigan, M., Blatt, A., Russell, M., Batta, R., & Lee, K. (2010). Emergency response technology and integrated active transportation system. *Journal of the Transportation Research Board, 21*(89), 26–36. doi:10.3141/2189-04

Ford, J. K., & Weissbein, D. A. (1997). Transfer of training: An updated review and analysis. *Performance Improvement Quarterly, 10*(2), 22–41. doi:10.1111/j.1937-8327.1997.tb00047.x

Foucault, B. E., & Scheufele, D. A. (2002). Web vs. campus store? Why students buy textbooks online? *Journal of Consumer Marketing*, *19*(5), 409–423. doi:10.1108/07363760210437632

Fox, J., Bailenson, J., & Binney, J. (2009). Virtual experiences, physical behaviors: The effect of presence on imitation of an eating avatar. *Presence (Cambridge, Mass.)*, *18*(4), 294–303. doi:10.1162/pres.18.4.294

Fox, S. (2011). *Peer-to-peer healthcare*. Washington, DC: Pew Research Center's Internet & American Life Project. Retrieved from http://www.pewinternet.org/Reports/2011/P2PHealthcare.aspx

Fox, S., & Purcell, K. (2010). *Chronic disease and the internet*. Washington DC: Pew Research Center's Internet & American Life Project. Retrieved from http://www.pewinternet.org/Reports/2010/Chronic-Disease/Part-3.aspx?view=all

Franceschi, K., & Lee, M. (2009). Engaging group e-learning in virtual worlds. *Journal of Management Information Systems*, *26*(1), 73–100. doi:10.2753/MIS0742-1222260104

Franco, C., & Hansen, M. B. (2010). The state of biopre-pardness: Lessons from leaders, proposals for progress. *Biosecurity and Bioterrorism: Biodefense Strategy. Practice and Science*, *8*(40), 379–383.

Friedman, T. (2005). *The world is flat*. New York, NY: Farrar, Straus and Giroux.

Fritz, D., Hu, A., Wilson, T., Ladak, H., Haase, P., & Fung, K. (2011). Long-term retention of a 3-dimonsional educational computer model of the larynx: A follow-up study. *Archives of Otolaryngology--Head & Neck Surgery*, *137*(6), 589–603. doi:10.1001/archoto.2011.76

Fu, L. (2011). The government response to 9/11: Communications technology and the media. *Library & Archival Security*, *24*, 103–118. doi:10.1080/01960075.2011.592034

Gan, C., Clemes, M., Limsombunchai, V., & Weng, A. (2006). A logit analysis of electronic banking in New Zealand. *International Journal of Bank Marketing*, *24*(6), 360–383. doi:10.1108/02652320610701717

Garner, S. (2005). *High-level colloquium on information literacy and lifelong learning*. Alexandria, Egypt: International Federal of Library Associations.

Gartner. (2003). Online banking goes mainstream in US. In *Nua Internet Surveys*. New York, NY: Scope Communications Group.

Garza, D., & Becan-McBride, K. (2010). *Phlebotomy handbook: Blood specimen collection from basic to advanced* (8th ed.). Upper Saddle River, NJ: Pearson Education.

Gattoni, A., & Tenzek, K. E. (2010). The practice: An analysis of the factors influencing the training of health care participants through innovative technology. *Communication Education*, *59*(3), 263–273. doi:10.1080/03634521003605808

Gay. (2002). Culturally responsive teaching in special education for ethnically diverse students: Setting the stage. *Qualitative Studies in Education, 15*(6), 613-629. Retrieved from http://www.cehd.umn.edu/ppg/Partnerships/CCresources/Gay.pdf

Georgiadou, E., & Economides, A. (2000). Evaluation factors of educational software. In *Proceedings of the International Workshop on Advanced Learning Technologies,* (pp. 113-116). Prague, Czech Republic: Advanced Learning Technologies.

Gerrard, P., & Cunningham, J. B. (2003). The diffusion of Internet banking among Singapore consumers. *International Journal of Bank Marketing*, *21*(1), 16–28. doi:10.1108/02652320310457776

Gil-Or, O. (2010). Building consumer demand by using viral marketing tactics within an online social network. *Advances in Management*, *3*(7), 7–14.

Gobillot, E. (2009). *Leadershift: Reinventing leadership for the age of mass collaboration*. London, UK: Kogan Page.

González, N., Moll, L., & Amanti, C. (2005). *Funds of knowledge: Theorizing practices in households, communities, and classrooms*. Mahwah, NJ: Lawrence Erlbaum Associates, Publishers.

Gorry, S. (2003). Measuring quality in online programs. *The Internet and Higher Education*, *6*(2), 159–177. doi:10.1016/S1096-7516(03)00022-8

Graetz, A. (2006). The psychology of learning environments. *EDUCAUSE Review*, *41*(6), 60–75.

Graham, S., & Harris, K. (2007). Best practices in teaching planning. In Graham, S., MacArthur, C. A., & Fitzgerald, J. (Eds.), *Best Practices in Writing Instruction* (p. 138). New York, NY: The Guilford Press.

Granovetter, M. (1983). The strength of weak ties: A network theory revisited. *Sociological Theory*, *1*, 201–233. doi:10.2307/202051

Gray, L., Thomas, N., & Lewis, L. (2010). *Teachers' use of educational technology in U.S. public schools: 2009*. Washington, DC: National Center for Education Statistics, Institute of Education Sciences, U.S. Department of Education.

Green, R. L., & Etheridge, C. P. (2001). Collaborating to establish standards and accountability: Lesson learned about systemic change. *Education*, *121*(4), 821–829.

Greene, M. (1995). *Releasing the imagination*. San Francisco, CA: Jossey-Bass.

Greene, M. (2001). *Variations on a blue guitar*. New York, NY: Teachers College Press.

Greenfield, R. (2003). *Collaborative e-mail exchange for teaching secondary ESL: A case study in Hong Kong*. Retrieved from http://llt.msu.edu/vol7num1/pdf/greenfield.pdf

Gronau, R., & Hamermesh, D. S. (2001). *The demand for variety: A household production perspective*. National Bureau of Economic Research Working Paper: 8509. Canberra, Australia: National Bureau of Economic Research.

Gros, B. (2003). The impact of digital games in education. *First Monday*, *8*(7). Retrieved from http://firstmonday.org/issues/issue8_7/gros/index.htm

Gross, M., & Latham, D. (2009). Undergraduate perceptions of information literacy: Defining, attaining, and self-assessing skills. *College & Research Libraries*, *70*(4), 336–350. Retrieved from http://vnweb.hwwilsonweb.com/hww/jumpstart.jhtml?recid=0bc05a67b1790e7e1f464a759977995c836d80430b762050755a12419fe1d5c493c7fa1043b306&fmt=P

Grosseck, G. (2009). To use or not to use web 2.0 in higher education? In *Proceedings of the World Conference on Educational Sciences, New Trends and Issues in Educational Sciences*. Nicosia, Cyprus: Elsevier.

Grossman, R., & Salas, E. (2011). The transfer of training: What really matters. *International Journal of Training and Development*, *15*(2), 103–120. doi:10.1111/j.1468-2419.2011.00373.x

Guglielmino, L. M., & Guglielmino, P. J. (1994). Practical experience with self-directed learning in business and industry. *New Directions for Adult and Continuing Education*, *64*, 39. Retrieved from http://www.ebscohost.com/academic/business-source-premierdoi:10.1002/ace.36719946407

Haarr, R. (2001). The making of a community police officer: The impact of basic training and occupational socialization on police recruits. *Police Quarterly*, *4*, 402–433. doi:10.1177/109861101129197923

Hakken, D. (1999). *Cyborgs@cyberspace*. New York, NY: Routledge.

Hallahan, K. (2006). Responsible online communication. In Fitzpatrick, K., & Bronstein, C. (Eds.), *Ethics in Public Relations* (pp. 107–130). Thousand Oaks, CA: SAGE Publications.

Halsey, A. (2012). Teen drivers are texting just like their parents. *Washington Post Local*. Retrieved from http://www.washingtonpost.com/local/trafficandcommuting/teen-drivers-are-texting-just-like-their-parents/2012/05/13/gIQA8raQNU_story.html

Halsey, M. (2011). *Who really uses Facebook and Twitter*. Retrieved from http://www.ghacks.net/2011/02/15/who-really-uses-Facebook-twitter/

Hanley, P., Maringe, F., & Ratcliffe, M. (2008). Evaluation of professional development: Deploying a process-focused model. *International Journal of Science Education*, *30*(5), 711–725. doi:10.1080/09500690701854899

Hannah, M. (2010). Cyberbullying education for parents: A guide for clinicians. *Journal of the Social Sciences*, *6*(4), 530–534.

Hansen, M. M. (2008). Versatile, immersive, creative and dynamic virtual 3D healthcare learning environments: A review of the literature. *Journal of Medical Internet Research*, *10*(3), 26. doi:10.2196/jmir.1051

Hanson-Smith, E. (2000). *Technology-enhanced learning environments*. Alexandria, Va.: Teachers of English to Speakers of Other Languages.

Hantula, D. A., & Pawlowicz, D. M. (2004). Education mirrors industry: On the not-so surprising rise of the Internet distance education. In Monolescu, D., Schifter, C., & Greenwood, L. (Eds.), *The Distance Education Evolution: Issues and Case Studies* (pp. 142–162). Hersey, PA: IGI Global. doi:10.4018/978-1-59140-120-9.ch006

Harasim, L. (2012). *Learning theories and online technologies*. New York, NY: Routledge Taylor & Francis Group.

Hardin, R. (2006). *Trust*. Cambridge, UK: Polity Press.

Harris, J. M., Sklar, B. M., Amend, R. W., & Novalis-Marine, C. (2010). The growth, characteristics, and future of online CME. *The Journal of Continuing Education in the Health Professions*, *30*(1), 3–10. doi:10.1002/chp.20050

Harrow, A. J. (1972). *A taxonomy of the psychomotor domain*. New York, NY: D. McKay Company.

Hassinger, J. P., Dozois, E. J., Holubar, S. D., Camp, J. C., Farley, D. R., & Fidler, J. L. (2010). Virtual pelvic anatomy simulator: A pilot study of usability and perceived effectiveness. *The Journal of Surgical Research*, *161*(1), 23–27. doi:10.1016/j.jss.2009.06.016

Heaney, T. W. (2000). Adult education and society. In Wilson, A. L., & Hayes, A. R. (Eds.), *Handbook of Adult and Continuing Education* (pp. 559–572). San Francisco, CA: Jossey-Bass.

Helliwell, J. F., & Putnam, R. D. (2004). The social context of well-being. *Philosophical Transactions of the Royal Society*, *359*(1449), 1435–1446. doi:10.1098/rstb.2004.1522

Henderson, L. (2007). Theorizing a multiple cultures instructional design model for elearning and e-teaching. In Edmundson, A. (Ed.), *Globalized e-Learning Cultural Challenges* (pp. 130–153). Hershey, PA: IGI Global.

Henner-Stanchina, C., & Holec, H. (1985). Evaluation in an autonomous learning scheme. In Riley, P. (Ed.), *Discourse and Learning* (pp. 255–263). London, UK: Longman.

Henschke, J. (1987). Training teachers of adults. In Klevins, C. (Ed.), *Materials and Methods of Adult and Continuing Education* (4th ed., pp. 414–422). Los Angeles, CA: Klevens Publications in Adult and Continuing Education.

Henschke, J. (2011). Considerations regarding the future of andragogy. *Adult Learning*, *22*(1), 36.

Hernandez, J. M. C., & Mazzon, J. A. (2007). Adoption of internet banking: Proposition and implementation of an integrated methodology approach. *International Journal of Bank Marketing*, *25*(2), 72–88. doi:10.1108/02652320710728410

Hignite, M., Margavio, T. M., & Margavio, G. W. (2009). Information literacy assessment: Moving beyond computer literacy. *College Student Journal, 43*(3), 812-821. Retrieved from http://vnweb.hwwilsonweb.com/hww/jumpstart.jhtml?recid=0bc0f7a6b1790e7e1f464a7599 7799f6cd7252bebc930330dbff11c838f2f0ef9aa766ec1 8dff7&fmt=P

Hilberg, J. S., & Meiselwitz, G. (2008). Undergraduate fluency with information and communication technology: Perceptions and reality. In J. J. Ekstrom & M. Stockman (Eds.), *Proceedings of the 9th AMC SIGITE Conference on Information Technology Education,* (pp. 5-10). New York, NY: ACM Press.

Hiltz, S., Diaz, P., & Mark, G. (2011). Introduction: Social media and collaborative systems for crisis management. *ACM Transactions on Computer-Human Interaction*, *18*(4), 1–6. doi:10.1145/2063231.2063232

Hinduja, S., & Patchin, J. W. (2010). Sexting: A brief guide for educators and parents. *2010 Cyberbullying Research Group*. Retrieved from http://www.cyberbullying.us/Sexting_Fact_Sheet.pdf

Hobbs, M., Brown, E., & Gordon, M. (2006). Using a virtual world for transferable skills in gaming education. *Innovation in Teaching and Learning in Information and Computer Sciences*, *5*(3), 1–13.

Holden, R., Smith, V., & Devins, D. (2003). Using 'employee-led development' to promote lifelong learning in SMEs: A research note. *Human Resource Development International*, *6*(1), 125–132. doi:10.1080/13678860110071425

Holec, H. (1981). *Autonomy and foreign language learning*. Oxford, UK: Pergamon Press.

Holtbrügge, D., Schillo, K., Rogers, H., & Friedmann, C. (2011). Managing and training for virtual teams in India. *Team Performance Management*, *17*(3), 206–223. doi:10.1108/13527591111143727

Holton, E. F. (1996). The flawed four-level evaluation model. *Human Resource Development Quarterly*, *7*(1), 5–21. doi:10.1002/hrdq.3920070103

Holton, E. F. III, Bates, R. A., & Ruona, W. E. (2000). Development of a generalized learning transfer system inventory. *Human Resource Development Quarterly*, *11*(4), 333–360. doi:10.1002/1532-1096(200024)11:4<333::AID-HRDQ2>3.0.CO;2-P

Hornya, L., & Decker, L. (1991). *Community education principles*. Retrieved from http://dpi.wi.gov/fscp/ceprin.html

Houle, C. O. (1961). *The inquiring mind*. Madison, WI: University of Wisconsin Press.

Howard, T. C. (2002). Hearing footsteps in the dark: African American students' descriptions of effective teachers. *Journal of Education for Students Placed at Risk*, *7*(4), 425–444. Retrieved from http://www.appstate.edu/~koppenhaverd/rcoe/5710/read/africanam/howard02.pdfdoi:10.1207/S15327671ESPR0704_4

Howcroft, B., Hamilton, R., & Hewer, P. (2002). Consumer attitude and the usage and adoption of home banking in the United Kingdom. *International Journal of Bank Marketing*, *20*(3), 111–121. doi:10.1108/02652320210424205

Huber, G. P. (1991). Organizational learning: The contributing processes and the literatures. *Organization Science*, *2*(1), 88–115. doi:10.1287/orsc.2.1.88

Hughes, C., & Moshell, J. (1997). Shared virtual worlds for education: The explorenet experiment. *Multimedia Systems*, *5*(2), 145–154. doi:10.1007/s005300050050

Hughes, J., McLeod, S., Brown, R., Maeda, Y., & Choi, J. (2007). Academic achievement and perceptions of the learning environment in virtual and traditional secondary mathematics classrooms. *American Journal of Distance Education*, *21*(4), 199–214. doi:10.1080/08923640701595365

Huot, D., Lemonnier, F. H., & Hamers, J. (2008). ICT and language learning at secondary school. In Zhang, F., & Barber, B. (Eds.), *Handbook of Research on Computer-Enhanced Language Acquisition and Learning* (pp. 84–100). Hershey, PA: IGI Global. doi:10.4018/978-1-59904-895-6.ch006

Iacono, A. (2010). OPAC, users, web: Future developments for online library catalogues. *Bollettino AIB*, *5*(1-2), 69–88.

Igbaria, M., & Chakrabarti, A. (1990). Computer anxiety and attitudes towards microcomputer use. *Behaviour & Information Technology*, *9*(3), 229–241. doi:10.1080/01449299008924239

Igbaria, M., Guimaraes, T., & Davis, G. B. (1995). Testing the determinants of microcomputer usage via a structural equation model. *Journal of Management Information Systems*, *11*(4), 87–114.

Illeris, K. (2004). *The three dimensions of learning*. Malabar, FL: Krieger.

Illinois Faculty Seminar. (1999). *Teaching at an internet distance: The pedagogy of online teaching and learning: The report of a 1998-1999*. Chicago, IL: University of Illinois. Retrieved from http://www.elc.uzh.ch/service/literaturtipps/tid-final-12-5.pdf

International Society for Technology in Education. (2008). *National educational technology standards for teachers*. Eugene, OR: International Society for Technology in Education.

International Technology Education Association. (2007). *Standards for technological literacy*. Reston, VA: International Technology Education Association.

i-SAFE, Inc. (2012). *Cyber bullying: Statistics and tips*. Retrieved from http://www.isafe.org/outreach/media/media_cyber_bullying

Isenberg, S. (2007). *Applying andragogical principles to internet learning*. Amherst, NY: Cambria Press.

Ismail, H. B., & Panni, M. F. A. K. (2009). Factors affecting customer retention toward internet banking in Malaysia. *Journal of Information and Knowledge Management*, *8*(1), 35–43. doi:10.1142/S021964920900218X

ISTE. (2008). *The standards for learning, leading, and teaching in the digital age*. Retrieved from http://www.iste.org/standards.aspx

Jackson, J., & Bradford, B. (2010). What is trust and confidence in the police? *Policing*, *4*(3), 241–248. doi:10.1093/police/paq020

Jain, S., & Mclean, C. (2003). A framework for modeling and simulation for emergency response. In *Proceedings of the 2003 Winter Simulation Conference,* (pp. 1068-1076). Academic Press.

Jain, S. H., Goyal, R., Fox, S., & Shrank, W. H. (2012). Bowling alone, healing together: The role of social capital in delivery reform. *The American Journal of Managed Care*. Retrieved from http://www.ajmc.com/articles/Bowling-Alone-Healing-Together-The-Role-of-Social-Capital-in-Delivery-Reform?utm_source=Mailing+List&utm_campaign=d1c4c7686c-Newsletter_06282012&utm_medium=email

Jamet, E., & Le Bohec, O. (2007). The effect of redundant text in multimedia instruction. *Contemporary Educational Psychology*, *32*, 588–598. doi:10.1016/j.cedpsych.2006.07.001

Janda, S., & Fair, L. (2004). Exploring consumer concerns related to the internet. *Journal of Internet Commerce*, *3*(1), 1–21. doi:10.1300/J179v03n01_01

Jarvis, P. (1985, August 6). Thinking critically in an information society: A sociological Analysis. *Lifelong Learning*, 11-14.

Jarvis, P. (1992). *Paradoxes of learning: on becoming an individual in society*. San Francisco: Jossey-Bass.

Jarvis, P. (2004). *Adult education and lifelong learning: Theory and practice*. London, UK: Routledge/Falmer.

Jayawardhena, C., & Foley, P. (2000). Changes in banking sector – A case of internet banking in UK. *Journal of Internet Research: Networking and Policy*, *10*(1), 19–30. doi:10.1108/10662240010312048

Jennett, P. A., Hall, W. G., Morin, J. E., & Watanabe, M. (1995). Evaluation of a distance consulting service based on interactive video and integrated computerized technology. *Journal of Telemedicine and Telecare*, *1*(2), 69–78.

JISC & SCONUL. (2008). *Library management systems study*. Sheffield, UK: Sero Consulting.

Johncock, P. (2011). *Issues in teaching and learning about grants. Journal of the Grant Professionals Association* (pp. 99–110). Kansas City, MO: Grant Professionals Association.

Johnson, K. D. (2012). *Financial crimes against the elderly: Problem-oriented guides for police specific guide series*. Washington, DC: U.S. Department of Justice Office of Community-Oriented Policing Services. Retrieved from http://www.popcenter.org/problems/pdfs/crimes_against_elderly.pdf

Johnson, P. (2009). The 21st century skills movement. *Teaching for the 21st Century, 67*(1), 11.

Johnson, R. (2000). *GIS technology for disasters and emergency management*. Redlands, CA: Environmental Systems Research Institute.

Johnson, S. D., Suriya, C., Won Yoon, S., Berrett, J. V., & La Fleur, J. (2002). Team development and group processes of virtual learning teams. *Computers & Education*, *39*, 379–393. doi:10.1016/S0360-1315(02)00074-X

Jones, W. O. (2009). Outsourcing: The enduring mistakes. *The Journal of Applied Business and Economics*, *10*(1), 1–14.

Joyce, B., & Showers, B. (2002). *Student achievement through staff development* (3rd ed.). Alexandria, VA: Association for Supervision and Curriculum Development.

Judd, T., & Kennedy, G. (2011). Expediency-based practice? Medical students' reliance on Google and Wikipedia for biomedical inquiries. *British Journal of Educational Technology*, *42*(3), 351–360. doi:10.1111/j.1467-8535.2009.01019.x

Judd, T., & Kennedy, G. (2011). Measurement and evidence of computer-based task switching and multitasking by 'net generation' students. *Computers & Education, 56*, 625–631. doi:10.1016/j.compedu.2010.10.004

Junco, R., & Mastrodicasa, J. (2007). *Connecting to the net generation: What higher education professionals need to know about today's students*. Washington, DC: NASPA.

Kadzera, M. (2006). *Use of instructional technologies in teacher training colleges in Malawi*. (Doctoral Dissertation). Virginia Polytechnic Institute and State University. Blacksburg, VA.

Kafai, Y. B. (2006). Playing and making games for learning: Instructionist and constructionist perspectives for game studies. *Games and Culture*, *1*(1), 36–40. doi:10.1177/1555412005281767

Kalpidou, M., Costin, D., & Morris, J. (2011). The relationship between Facebook and the well-being of undergraduate college students. *CyberPsychology. Behavior & Social Networking*, *14*(4), 183–189. doi:10.1089/cyber.2010.0061

Kaminski, K., Switzer, J., & Gloeckner, G. (2009). Workforce readiness: A study of university students' fluency with information technology. *Computers & Education*, *53*, 228–233. doi:10.1016/j.compedu.2009.01.017

Kamssu, A., Siekpe, J., & Ellzy, J. (2004). Shortcomings to globalization: Using internet technology and electronic commerce in developing countries. *Journal of Developing Areas*, *38*(1), 151–169. doi:10.1353/jda.2005.0010

Karjaluoto, H., Mattila, M., & Pento, T. (2002). Electronic banking in Finland: Consumer beliefs and reactions to a new delivery channel. *Journal of Financial Services Marketing*, *6*(4), 346–361. doi:10.1057/palgrave.fsm.4770064

Kasworm, C. E., Rose, A. R., & Ross-Gordon, J. (Eds.). (2010). *Handbook of adult and continuing education*. Thousand Oaks, CA: Sage.

Katona, Z., Zubcsek, P., & Sarvary, M. (2011). Network effects and personal influences: The diffusion of an online social network. *JMR, Journal of Marketing Research*, *48*, 425–443. doi:10.1509/jmkr.48.3.425

Katz, J., & Aspden, P. (1997). Motivations for and barriers to internet usage: Results of a national public opinion survey. *Internet Research: Electronic Networking Applications and Policy*, *7*(3), 170–188. doi:10.1108/10662249710171814

Kelleher, T. (2007). *Public relations online*. Thousand Oaks, CA: SAGE Publications.

Kellogg, N. D., Lamb, J. L., & Lukefahr, J. L. (2000). The use of telemedicine in child sexual abuse evaluations. *Child Abuse & Neglect*, *24*(12), 1601–1612. doi:10.1016/S0145-2134(00)00204-0

Kelly, K. (2010). From print to pixel. *Smithsonian*, *41*(4), 122–128.

Kelsey, K. D., & D'Souza, A. (2004). Student motivation for learning at a distance: Does interaction matter? *Online Journal of Distance Learning Administration*, *7*(2). Retrieved from http://www.westga.edu/~distance/ojdla/summer72/kelsey72.html

Kennedy, G. E., Judd, T. S., Churchward, A., Gray, K., & Krause, K. L. (2008). First year students' experiences with technology: Are they really digital natives? *Australasian Journal of Educational Technology*, *24*(1), 108-122. Retrieved from http://www.ascilite.org.au/ajet/ajet24/kennedy.pdf

Kern, R. (1995). Restructuring classroom interaction with networked computers: Effects on quantity and characteristics of language production. *Modern Language Journal*, *79*, 457–476. doi:10.1111/j.1540-4781.1995.tb05445.x

Khan, S. A. (2011). Public health preparedness response in the USA since 9/11: A national health security imperative. *Lancet*, *378*(9794), 953–956. doi:10.1016/S0140-6736(11)61263-4

Killion, J., & Hirsh, S. (2011). The elements of effective teaching. *Journal of Staff Development*, *32*(6), 10–16.

Kim, J., & Lee, J.-E. (2011). The Facebook paths to happiness: Effects of the number of Facebook friends and self-presentation on subjective well-being. *CyberPsychology. Behavior & Social Networking*, *14*(6), 359–364. doi:10.1089/cyber.2010.0374

King, K. P. (2002). Educational technology professional development as transformative learning opportunities. *Computers & Education*, *39*(3), 283–297. doi:10.1016/S0360-1315(02)00073-8

Kirsch, I. S., Jungeblut, A., Jenkins, L., & Kolstad, A. (2002). *Adult literacy in America: A first look at findings of the national adult literacy survey* (3rd ed.). Washington, DC: National Center for Education Statistics Government Printing Office.

Kluver, R. (2000). Globalization, informatization, and intercultural communication. *American Journal of Communication*, *3*(3), 1–4.

Knowles, M. (1984). *Andragogy in action: Applying modern principles of adult learning*. San Francisco, CA: Jossey-Bass Publishers.

Knowles, M. (1989). *The making of an adult educator*. San Francisco, CA: Jossey-Bass.

Knowles, M. S. (1970). *The modern practice of adult education: Andragogy vs. pedagogy*. Chicago, IL: Association Press/Follett.

Knowles, M. S. (1980). *The modern practice of adult education: From pedagogy to andragogy. Englewood Cliffs, NJ*. Cambridge: Prentice Hall.

Knowles, M. S. (1984). *Andragogy in action: Applying modern principles of adult learning*. San Francisco, CA: Jossey-Bass.

Knowles, M., Holton, E., & Swanson, R. (2005). *The adult learner*. Burlington, MA: Elsevier.

Kolodinsky, J. M., Hogarth, J. M., & Hilgert, M. A. (2004). The adoption of electronic banking technologies by US consumers. *International Journal of Bank Marketing*, *22*(4), 238–259. doi:10.1108/02652320410542536

Kolodinsky, J., Hogarth, J. M., & Shue, J. F. (2000). Bricks or clicks? Consumer adoption of electronic banking technologies. *Consumer Interests Annual*, *46*, 180–184.

Koschmann, T. (1996). Paradigm shifts and instructional technology. In *CSCL: Theory and Practice of an Emerging Paradigm* (pp. 1–23). Mahwah, NJ: Lawrence Erlbaum Associates.

Kozma, R. B. (1991). Learning with media. *Review of Educational Research*, *61*(2), 179–212.

Kramarski, B., & Mizrachi, N. (2006). Online discussion and self-regulated learning: Effects of instructional methods on mathematical literacy. *The Journal of Educational Research*, *99*(4), 218–230. Retrieved from http://search.ebscohost.comdoi:10.3200/JOER.99.4.218-231

Kramsch, C., & Thorne, S. (2001). Foreign language learning as global communicative practice. In Block, D., & Cameron, D. (Eds.), *Language Learning and Teaching in the Age of Globalization* (pp. 83–100). London, UK: Routledge.

Krashen, S. (2003). *Explorations in language acquisition and use*. Portsmouth, NH: Heinemann.

Krathwolh, D. R., Bloom, B. S., & Masia, B. B. (1964). *Taxonomy of educational objectives: The classification of educational goals: Handbook II: The affective domain*. New York, NY: Longman Green.

Kraut, R., Patterson, M., Lundmark, V., Kiesler, S., Mukophadhyay, T., & Scherlis, W. (1998). Internet paradox: A social technology that reduces social involvement and psychological well-being? *The American Psychologist*, *53*, 1017–1031. doi:10.1037/0003-066X.53.9.1017

Kreuger, R. A. (1988). *Focus groups: A practical guide for applied research*. London, UK: Sage.

Labov, W. (1965). Stages in the acquisition of Standard English. In Shuy, R. W. (Ed.), *Social Dialects and Language Learning* (pp. 77–103). Champaign, IL: National Council of Teachers of English.

Labov, W. (1995). Can reading failure be reversed? A linguistic approach to the question. In Gadsden, V., & Wagner, D. (Eds.), *Literacy among African American Youth* (pp. 39–68). Cresskill, NJ: Hampton Press.

Ladson-Billings, G. (1994). *The dreamkeepers: Successful teachers of African American children*. San Francisco, CA: Jossey-Bass.

Ladson-Bilings, G. (1995). Toward a theory of culturally relevant pedagogy. *American Educational Research Journal*, *32*(3), 465–491. Retrieved from http://edt2.educ.msu.edu/DWong/Te150S10/CourseReader/LadsonBillingsAERJ1995_CulturallyRelevan.pdf

Laiken, M. (2001). *Models of organizational learning*. Toronto, Canada: University of Toronto.

Laing, S. P., & Kahmi, A. (2002). Alternative assessment of language and literacy in culturally and linguistically diverse populations. *Language, Speech, and Hearing Services in Schools*, *34*(4), 44–55.

Laurent, B. (2011). Technologies of democracy: Experiments and demonstrations. *Science and Engineering Ethics*, *17*(4), 649–666. doi:10.1007/s11948-011-9303-1

Learning Forward. (2011). *Standards for professional learning*. Retrieved from http://www.learningforward.org/standards/index.cfm

LeBlanc, A. (2000). Louisiana rural health access program. *The Journal of the Louisiana State Medical Society: Official Organ of the Louisiana State Medical Society, 152*(2), 89–93.

Lee, E., & Lee, J. (2001). Consumer adoption of Internet banking: Need-based and/or skill based? *Marketing Management Journal, 11*(1), 101–113.

Lee, G., Lee, J., & Kwon, S. (2011). Use of social-networking sites and subjective well-being: A study in South Korea. *CyberPsychology. Behavior & Social Networking, 14*(3), 151–155. doi:10.1089/cyber.2009.0382

Lee, I. (1998). Supporting greater autonomy in language learning. *ELT Journal, 52*(4), 282–288. doi:10.1093/elt/52.4.282

Lee, I. (2002). Gender differences in self-regulated online learning strategies within Korea's university context. *Educational Technology Research and Development, 50*(1), 101–111. doi:10.1007/BF02504967

Lee, M. (2009). How can 3D virtual worlds be used to support collaboration learning? An analysis of cases from literature. *Journal of e-Learning and Knowledge Society, 5*(1), 149-158.

Lehtinen, E., & Hakkarainen, K. (2001). *Computer supported collaborative learning: A review*. Retrieved from http://www.comlab.hut.fi/opetus/205/etatehtava1.pdf

Lenhart, A., & Fox, S. (2009). *11% of online adults use Twitter or update their status online*. Washington DC: Pew Research Center's Internet & American Life Project. Retrieved from http://www.pewinternet.org/Reports/2009/Twitter-and-status-updating/Part-1/Section-2.as

Lenhart, M. M., Macgill, A. R., & Smith, A. (2007). *Teens and social media*. Washington, DC: Pew Research Center's Internet & American Life Project. Retrieved from http://www.pewinternet.org/PPF/r/230/report_display.asp

Lesgold, A. (2000). What are the tools for? Revolutionary change does not follow the usual norms. In Lajoie, S. (Ed.), *Computers as Cognitive Tools* (pp. 399–408). Mahwah, NJ: Lawrence Erlbaum Associates.

Lessig, L. (2006). *Code: Version 2.0*. New York, NY: Basic Books.

Lester, P. M., & King, C. M. (2009). Analog vs. digital instruction and learning: Teaching within first and second life environments. *Journal of Computer-Mediated Communication, 14*, 457–483. doi:10.1111/j.1083-6101.2009.01449.x

Levett-Jones, T., Kenny, R., Van der Riet, P., Hazelton, M., Kable, A., Bourgeois, S., & Luxford, Y. (2009). Exploring the information and communication technology competence and confidence of nursing students and their perception of its relevance to clinical practice. *Nurse Education Today, 29*(6), 216–616. doi:10.1016/j.nedt.2009.01.007

Levine, L., & Monarch, I. (1998). *Collaborative technology in the learning organization: Integrating process with information flow, access and interpretation*. Paper presented at the Annual Hawaii International Conference on System Sciences (HICSS). Kohala Coast, HI.

Levitt, L. (1979). Critique: Andragogy revisited part II. *Adult Education Quarterly, 30*, 52–57. doi:10.1177/074171367903000104

Li, Q. (2006). Cyberbullying in schools: A research of gender differences. *School Psychology International, 27*, 157–170. doi:10.1177/0143034306064547

Li, Q., & Edmonds, K. A. (2005). Mathematics and at-risk adult learners: Would technology help? *Journal of Research on Technology in Education, 38*(2), 143–166.

Li, Z., Yue, J., & Jauregui, A. (2009). *A new virtual reality system used for e-learning*. Retrieved from http://www-public.it-sudparis.eu/~horain/GomezJauregui/gomez_fichiers/A%20New%20Virtual%20Reality%20Environment%20Used%20for%20e-Learning.pdf

Lin, H. (2000). Fluency with information technology. *Government Information Quarterly, 17*(1), 69–76. doi:10.1016/S0740-624X(99)00024-6

Lindel, M., Prater, C., & Perry, R. (2007). *Emergency management*. New York, NY: Wiley.

LinkedIn. (2012). *Website*. Retrieved 23 March 2012 from http://www.linkedin.com/company/linkedin

Lipley, N. (2011). Analysis. *Emergency Nurse, 19*(7), 9.

Lipman, P. (1997). Restructuring in context: A case study of teacher participation and the dynamics of ideology, race, and power. *American Educational Research Journal*, *20*(34), 3–37.

Lipps, A., Trafton, J., & Gray, W. (1998). Animation as documentation: A replication with reinterpretation. In *Proceedings for the 45th Annual Conference of the Society for Technical Communication.* Arlington, VA: STC. Retrieved from http://www.stc.org/proceedings/ConfProceed/1998/PDFs/00006.PDF

Littlewood, W. (1996). Autonomy: An autonomy and a framework. *System*, *24*(4), 427–435. doi:10.1016/S0346-251X(96)00039-5

Littlewood, W. (1997). Self-access: Why do want it and what can it do? In Benson, P., & Voller, P. (Eds.), *Autonomy and Independence in Language Learning* (pp. 79–92). London, UK: Longman.

Liu, J., Tsou, M., & Hammitt, J. K. (2001). The impact of advanced technology adoption in wage structures: Evidence from Taiwan manufacturing firms. *Economica*, *68*(271), 359–378. doi:10.1111/1468-0335.00251

Livingston, K., & Condie, R. (2006). The impact of an online learning program on teaching and learning strategies. *Theory into Practice*, *45*(2), 150–158. doi:10.1207/s15430421tip4502_7

Loader, B. (1998). *Cyberspace divide: Equality, agency, and policy in the information society*. New York, NY: Routledge. doi:10.4324/9780203169537

Locatis, C., Gaines, C., Gill, M., Carney, J., Foster, J., McCall, V., & Woods, M. (2006). A blended training approach using videoconferencing for distance education. *Journal of the Medical Library Association*, *94*(4), 464–467.

Lomas, C., Burke, M., & Page, D. L. (2008). Collaboration tools. *EDUCAUSE Learning Initiative.* Retrieved from http://net.educause.edu/ir/library/pdf/ELI3020.pdf

Lorenzo, G., & Dziuban, C. (2006). *Ensuring the net generation is net savvy*. EDUCAUSE Learning Initiative Paper 2. Boulder, CO: EDUCAUSE. Retrieved from http://net.educause./ir/library/pdf/ELI3006.pdf

Lowe, G., & MacAuley, J. (2000). *Information and communication technology literacy assessment framework.* Princeton, NJ: Educational Testing Service.

Macpherson, A., Elliott, M., Harris, I., & Homan, G. (2004). E-learning: Reflections and evaluation of corporate programs. *Human Resource Development International*, *7*(3), 295–313. doi:10.1080/13678860310001630638

Madden, M., & Lenhart, A. (2009). *Teens and distracted driving*. Washington DC: Pew Research Center's Internet & American Life Project. Retrieved from http://pewinternet.org/~/media//Files/Reports/2009/PIP_Teens_and_Distracted_Driving.pdf

Madge, C., Meek, J., Wellens, J., & Hooley, T. (2009). Facebook, social integration and informal learning at university: It is more for socialising and talking to friends about work than for actually doing work. *Learning, Media and Technology*, *34*(2), 141–155. doi:10.1080/17439880902923606

Madigan, E. M., Goodfellow, M., & Stone, J. A. (2007). Gender, perception, and reality: Technological literacy among first-year students. In *Proceedings of the 38th SIGCSE Technical Symposium on Computer Science Education,* (pp. 410-414). New York, NY: ACM Press.

Madriz, L. (1987). The relative effectiveness of two different approaches to in-service training of primary teachers in Venezuela. *Dissertation Abstracts International*, *56*(11).

Maier, P., & Warren, A. (2000). *Integrating technology in learning and teaching*. Sterling, VA: Kogan Page.

Malhotra, Y. (1996). Organizational learning and learning organizations: An overview. *Knowledge Management Book.* Retrieved from http://www.kmbook.com/orglmg.htm

Mancuso, D., Chlup, D. T., & McWhorter, R. R. (2010). A study of adult learning in a virtual world. *Advances in Developing Resources, 12*(6), 681-699. Retrieved from http://intl-adh.sagepub.com/content/12/6/681.full.pdf+html

Mansour, S., & Mostafa, E. S. (2008). The impact of multi-players serious games on social interaction among online students versus face-to-face students. In *Proceedings of the 7th WSEAS International Conference on Applied Computer and Applied Computational Science (ACACOS 2008),* (pp. 772-778). Hangzhou, China: ACACOS.

Martinez, M. (2005). Mass customization: Designing for successful learning. *International Journal of Educational Technology*, *2*(2). Retrieved from http://www.ed.uiuc.edu/ijet/v2n2/martinez/index.html

Martin, G. Z. (2010). *30 days to social media success*. Pompton Plains, NY: Career Press, Inc.

Masic, I., Pandza, H., Toromanovic, S., Masic, F., Sivic, S., Zunic, L., & Masic, Z. (2011). Information technologies (ITs) in medical education. *Acta Informatica Medica*, *19*(3), 68–78. doi:10.5455/aim.2011.19.68-79

Maslow, A. (1943). A theory of human motivation. *Psychological Review*, *50*(4), 370–396. Retrieved from http://www.ebscohost.com/academic/business-source-premierdoi:10.1037/h0054346

Massey, S. C. (2001). *Understanding learning styles and learning strategies of adult learners at OSU-Okmulgee*. (Unpublished Doctoral Dissertation). Oklahoma State University. Stillwater, OK.

Mattila, M. (2001). Essays on customers in the dawn of interactive banking. *Jyvaskyla Studies in Business and Economics*, *9*, 15–22.

Maurer, M., & Davidson, G. (1998). *Leadership in instructional technology*. Upper Saddle River, NJ: Prentice Hall.

Mayer, R. E. (2001). *Multimedia learning*. Cambridge, UK: Cambridge University Press. doi:10.1017/CBO9781139164603

Mayer, R. E. (2003). The promise of multimedia learning: Using the same instructional design methods across different media. *Learning and Instruction*, *13*, 125–139. doi:10.1016/S0959-4752(02)00016-6

Mayer, R. E. (2005). *The Cambridge handbook of multimedia learning*. Cambridge, UK: Cambridge University Press. doi:10.1017/CBO9780511816819

Mayer, R. E., & Johnson, C. I. (2008). Revising the redundancy principle in multimedia learning. *Journal of Educational Psychology*, *100*(2), 380–386. doi:10.1037/0022-0663.100.2.380

Mayer, R. E., & Moreno, R. (1998). A split-attention effect in multimedia learning: Evidence for dual processing systems in working memory. *Journal of Educational Psychology*, *90*(2), 312–320. doi:10.1037/0022-0663.90.2.312

Mayer, R. E., & Moreno, R. (2002). Aids to computer-based multimedia learning. *Learning and Instruction*, *12*(1), 107–119. doi:10.1016/S0959-4752(01)00018-4

Mazarr, M. (1999). *Global trends 2005: An owner's manual for the next decade*. New York, NY: St. Martin's Press.

McArdle, G., Monahan, T., Bertolotto, M., & Mangina, E. (2004). *A web-based multimedia virtual reality environment for e-learning*. Retrieved from http://diglib.eg.org/EG/DL/Conf/EG2004/short/short48.pdf

McCabe, O. L., Barnett, D. J., Taylor, H. G., & Links, J. M. (2010). Ready, willing and able: A framework for improving the public health emergency preparedness system. *American Medical Association, 4*(2), 161-168.

McGee, J. B., & Kanter, S. L. (2011). How we develop and sustain innovation in medical education technology: Keys to success. *Medical Teacher*, *33*, 279–285. doi:10.3109/0142159X.2011.540264

McLoughlin, C. (2012). Leading pedagogical change with innovative web tools and social media. In Wang, V. (Ed.), *Encyclopedia of E-Leadership, Counseling and Training* (pp. 1–11). Hershey, PA: IGI Global.

McMahon, M., & Pospisil, R. (2005). Laptops for a digital lifestyle: The role of ubiquitous mobile technology in supporting the needs of millennial students. In *Proceedings of Ascilite 2005 Conference: Balance, Fidelity, Mobility: Maintaining the Momentum?* (pp. 421-431). ASCILITE. Retrieved from http://cms.ascilite.org.au/conferences/brisbane05/blogs/proceedings/49_McMahon%20&%20Pospisil.pdf

McWhinney, W. (1992). *Paths of change: Strategic choices for organizations and society*. Thousand Oaks, CA: Sage Publications.

Meacham, B. J., Dembsey, N. A., Schebel, K., Johann, M. A., & Tubbs, J. S. (2012). Use of small- scale test data to enhance fire-related threat, vulnerability, consequence and risk assessment for passenger rail vehicles. *Journal of Homeland Security and Emergency Management*, *9*(1), 1–16. doi:10.1515/1547-7355.1850

Meadows, M. S. (2008). *Avatar: The culture and consequences of having a second life*. Berkely, CA: New Riders Press.

Meltzer, S. (2006). An analysis of professional development in technology for elementary school teachers. *Dissertation Abstracts International*, *67*(6).

Meltzer, S. T. (2009). *Professional development in technology: An analysis of effective practices*. Paper presented at the Meeting of the Society for Information Technology & Teacher Education International Conference. Charleston, SC.

Meltzer, S. T. (2012). *Step-by-step professional development in technology*. Larchmont, NY: Eye on Education.

Merchant, R. M., Elmer, S., & Lurie, N. (2011). Integrating social media into emergency preparedness efforts. *The New England Journal of Medicine*, *365*, 289–291. doi:10.1056/NEJMp1103591

Merriam, S. B. (1991). How to research procedures in knowledge. In Peters, J. M., & Jarvis, P. (Eds.), *Adult Education* (pp. 42–65). San Francisco, CA: Jossey-Bass.

Merriam, S. B. (2008). Adult learning theory for the twenty-first century. In *New Directions for Adult and Continuing Education* (pp. 93–98). San Francisco, CA: Jossey-Bass. doi:10.1002/ace.309

Merriam, S. B., & Brockett, R. G. (1997). *The profession and practice of adult education*. San Francisco, CA: Jossey-Bass.

Merriam, S. B., Caffarella, R. S., & Baumgartner, L. M. (2007). *Learning in adulthood: A comprehensive guide* (3rd ed.). San Francisco, CA: Jossey-Bass.

Meskill, C., & Ranglova, K. (2000). Sociocollaborative language learning in Bulgaria. In Warschauer, M., & Kern, R. (Eds.), *Network-Based Language Teaching: Concepts and Practice* (pp. 20–40). Cambridge, UK: Cambridge University Press. doi:10.1017/CBO9781139524735.004

MetLife. (2009). *The MetLife survey of the American teacher: Collaborating for student success*. New York, NY: Metropolitan Life Insurance Company.

Mezirow, J. (2000). *Learning as transformation*. San Francisco, CA: Jossey-Bass.

Michailidou, A., & Economides, A. (2003). Elearn: Towards a collaborative educational virtual environment. *Journal of Information Technology Education*, *2*, 131–152.

Milne, G., Rohm, A., & Bahl, S. (2004). Consumers' protection of online privacy and identity. *The Journal of Consumer Affairs*, *38*(2), 217–232. doi:10.1111/j.1745-6606.2004.tb00865.x

Minzey, J. (1972). Community education: An amalgam of many views. *Phi Delta Kappan*, *54*(3), 150–153.

Missouri Department of Elementary and Secondary Education. (2012). What is community education? *Extended Learning*. Retrieved from http://dese.mo.gov/eel/exl/eel-exl-community-ed.htm

Mohatt, G., & Erickson, F. (1981). Cultural differences in teaching styles in an Odawa school: A sociolinguistic approach. In Trueba, H., Guthrie, G., & Au, K. (Eds.), *Culture and The bilingual Classroom* (pp. 105–119). Rowley, MA: Newbury House.

Mohawk College Library. (2012). How to evaluate websites. *The Brain*. Retrieved from http://brain.mohawkcollege.ca/FindInformation/websites/HowToEvaluateWebsitesForResearch.html

Mollering, M., & Ritter, M. (2008). CMC and intercultural learning. In Zhang, F., & Barber, B. (Eds.), *Handbook of Research on Computer-Enhanced Language Acquisition and Learning* (pp. 361–376). Hershey, PA: IGI Global. doi:10.4018/978-1-59904-895-6.ch021

Monahan, T., McArdle, G., & Bertolloto, M. (2008). Virtual reality for collaborative e-learning. *Computers & Education*, *50*, 1339–1353. doi:10.1016/j.compedu.2006.12.008

Monolescu, D., Schifter, C. C., & Greenwood, L. (Eds.). (2004). *The distance education evolution: Issues and case studies*. Hershey, PA: IGI Global.

Moreno, R., & Mayer, R. E. (1999). Cognitive principles of multimedia learning: The role of modality and contiguity. *Journal of Educational Psychology, 91*(2), 358–368. doi:10.1037/0022-0663.91.2.358

Morrison, G. R., & Anglin, G. J. (2005). Research on cognitive load theory: Application to elearning. *Educational Technology Research and Development, 53*(3), 94–104. doi:10.1007/BF02504801

Munday, D. R. (2002). *Effects of learning strategy awareness on learning, learners, and instructor*. (Unpublished Doctoral Dissertation). Oklahoma State University. Stillwater, OK.

Murray, M. C., & Perez, J. (2010). Generativity: The new frontier for information and communication technology literacy. *Interdisciplinary Journal of Information, Knowledge and Management, 5*, 127-137. Retrieved from http://go.galegroup.com.ezproxy.fau.edu/ps/i.do?id=GALE%7CA247880102&v=2.1&u=gale15691&it=r&p=AONE&sw=w

National Center for Educational Statistics. (2007). *Trial urban district assessment results at grades 4 and 8*. Retrieved from http://nces.ed.gov/nationsreportcard/pdf/dst2007/2008455.pdf

National Center for Educational Statistics. (2009). *Achievement gaps: How black and white students in public schools perform in mathematics and reading on the national assessment of educational progress*. Retrieved from http://nces.ed.gov/nationsreportcard/pdf/studies/2009455.pdf

National Education Association. (2008). *Access, adequacy and equity in education technology: Results of a survey of America's teachers and support professionals on technology in public schools and classrooms*. Washington, DC: National Education Association. Retrieved from www.nea.org/research/images/08gainsandgapsedtech.pdf

National Research Council. (1999). *Being fluent with information technology*. Washington, DC: National Academy Press.

Ndahi, H. (2006). The use of innovative methods to deliver technology education laboratory courses in distant learning: A strategy to increase enrollment. *Journal of Technology Education, 17*(2), 33–42.

Nechita, E., & Timofti, I. (2011). Increasing independence versus increasing collaboration with ICT support. *Procedia. Social and Behavioral Sciences, 29*, 1508–1517.

Neji, M., & Ben Amnar, M. (2007). Agent-based collaborative affective e-learning framework. *The Journal of e-learning, 5*(2), 123-134.

Nelson-Barber, S., & Estrin, E. (1995). Bringing Native American perspectives to mathematics and science teaching. *Theory into Practice, 34*(3), 174–185. doi:10.1080/00405849509543677

New Media Consortium. (2008). *Spring 2008 survey: Educators in SL*. Retrieved from http://www.nmc.org/pdf/2008-sl-survey.pdf

Ng, E. (2002). *Enhancing collaborative learning through online discussion and peer assessment*. Retrieved from http://csdl.computer.org/comp/proceedings/icce/2002/1509/00/15090262.pdf

Nilson, L. B. (2003). *Teaching at its best*. San Francisco, CA: Anker.

Nonaka, I., Peltokorpi, V., & Tomae, H. (2005). Strategic knowledge creation: The case of Hamamatsu photonics. *International Journal of Technology Management, 30*(3-4), 248–264. doi:10.1504/IJTM.2005.006709

Nonaka, I., Toyama, R., & Byoiere, P. (2001). A theory of organizational knowledge creation: Understanding the dynamic process of creating knowledge. In Dierkes, M., Antal, A., Child, J., & Nonaka, I. (Eds.), *Handbook of Organizational Learning and Knowledge* (pp. 491–517). Oxford, UK: Oxford University Press.

Nunan, D. (1996). Hidden voices: Insiders' perspectives on classroom. In Bailey, K. M., & Nunan, D. (Eds.), *Voices from the Language Classroom* (pp. 41–56). Cambridge, UK: Cambridge University Press.

Nunan, D. (1997). Designing and adapting materials to encourage learner autonomy. In Benson, P., & Voller, P. (Eds.), *Autonomy and Independence in Language Learning* (pp. 192–203). London, UK: Longman.

Oblinger, D., & Oblinger, J. (Eds.). (2005). *Educating the net generation*. Retrieved from http://www.educause.edu/ir/library/pdf/pub7101.pdf

OECD. (2010). *Recognition of non-formal and informal learning: Pointers for policy development.* Retrieved 24 March 2012, from http://www.oecd.org/dataoecd/47/50/44870953.pdf

Ogles, M. T. (1990). The outcomes of using "learning contracts" with adult beginning readers in a one-on-one literacy program. *Dissertation Abstracts International, 51*(6).

Okumura, T., Suzuki, K., Fukuda, A., Kohama, A., Takasu, N., Ishimatsu, S., & Hinohara, S. (1998). The Tokyo subway sarin attack: Disaster management, part 1: Community emergency response. *Academic Emergency Medicine, 5*(6), 613–617. doi:10.1111/j.1553-2712.1998.tb02470.x

O'Malley, J. M., & Chamot, A. U. (1990). *Learning strategies in second language acquisition.* Cambridge, UK: Cambridge University Press. doi:10.1017/CBO9781139524490

Orlikowski, W., Yates, J., Okamura, K., & Fujimoto, M. (1995). Shaping electronic communication. *Organization Science, 6*(4), 423–445. doi:10.1287/orsc.6.4.423

Owen, S. (2005). The power of collegiality in school-based professional development. *Australian Journal of Teacher Education, 35*(1), 1–12. Retrieved from http://ro.ecu.edu.au/cgi/viewcontent.cgi?article=1391&context=ajte

Oxford, R. (1990). *Language learning strategies: What every teacher should know.* Boston, MA: Heinle & Heinle Publishers.

Oxford, R. (1994). Language learning strategies: An update. *ERIC Digest.* Retrieved from http://www.ericfacility.net/ericdigests/ed376707.html

Ozcelik, E., & Yildirim, S. (2005). Factors influencing the use of cognitive tools in web-based learning environments. *The Quaterly Review of Distance Education, 6*(4), 295–308.

Paas, F. (1992). Training strategies for attaining transfer of problem-solving skill in statistics: A cognitive load approach. *Journal of Educational Psychology, 84*, 429–434. doi:10.1037/0022-0663.84.4.429

Paas, F., Renkl, A., & Sweller, J. (2003). Cognitive load theory and instructional design: Recent developments. *Educational Psychologist, 38*, 1–4. doi:10.1207/S15326985EP3801_1

Paas, F., Tuovinen, J. E., Tabbers, H., & Van Gerven, P. (2003). Cognitive load measurement as a means to advance cognitive load theory. *Educational Psychologist, 38*(1), 63–71. doi:10.1207/S15326985EP3801_8

Paas, F., Tuovinen, J., van Merriënboer, J. J. G., & Darabi, A. (2005). A motivational perspective on the relation between mental effort and performance: Optimizing learner involvement in instruction. *Educational Technology Research and Development, 53*, 25–34. doi:10.1007/BF02504795

Paas, F., & Van Gog, T. (2006). Optimising worked example instruction: Different ways to increase germane cognitive load. *Learning and Instruction, 16*, 87–91. doi:10.1016/j.learninstruc.2006.02.004

Palen, L., Sanderson, K. M., Mark, G., Martin, J., Sicker, D., Palmer, M., & Grunwald, D. (2010). A vision for technology-mediated support for public participation & assistance in mass emergencies & disasters. In *Proceedings of the 2010 ACM-BCS Visions of Computer Science Conference,* (vol. 8, pp. 1-12). ACM Press.

Palfrey, J. G., & Gasser, U. (2008). *Born digital: Understanding the first generation of digital natives.* New York, NY: Basic Books.

Palincsar, A. S., & Brown, A. L. (1984). Reciprocal teaching of comprehension-fostering and comprehension-monitoring activities. *Cognition and Instruction, 1*(2), 117–175. doi:10.1207/s1532690xci0102_1

Palloff, R., & Pratt, K. (1999). *Building learning communities in cyberspace.* San Francisco, CA: Jossey-Bass.

Palmiter, S., & Elkerton, J. (1991). An evaluation of animated demonstrations for learning computer-based tasks. In *Proceedings of the SIGCHI Conference on Human Factors in Computing Systems: Reaching through Technology*, (pp. 257-263). ACM Press.

Pan-Canadian Forum on Community Learning Networks. (1998). Background. In *Proceedings of the Pan-Canadian Forum on Community Learning Networks Conference,* (pp. 1-2). Ottawa, Canada: Pan-Canadian Forum on Community Learning Networks.

Parasuraman, S., & Igbaria, M. (1990). An examination of gender differences in the determinants of computer anxiety and attitudes towards microcomputers among managers. *International Journal of Man-Machine Studies*, *32*, 327–340. doi:10.1016/S0020-7373(08)80006-5

Paris, D., & Ball, A. S. (2009). Teacher knowledge in culturally and linguistically complex classrooms: Lessons from the golden age and beyond. In Morrow, L. M., Rueda, R., & Lapp, D. (Eds.), *Handbook of Research on Literacy and Diversity* (pp. 379–395). York, NY: Guildford Press.

Parker, J. (2009). Adult learning and CTE: A shared history influenced by technology. In Wang, V. (Ed.), *Definitive Readings in the History, Philosophy, Practice, and Theories of Career and Technical Education* (pp. 217–236). Hershey, PA: IGI Global.

Parker, J. (2010). Technology as integral to a new paradigm of adult education. *International Journal of Adult Vocational Education and Technology*, *1*(2), 10–18. doi:10.4018/javet.2010040102

Park, N., Kee, K., & Valenzuela, S. (2009). Being immersed in social networking environment: Facebook groups, uses and gratifications and social outcomes. *CyberPsychology. Behavior & Social Networking*, *12*(6), 729–733.

Parks, S., Huot, D., Hamers, J., & Lemonnier, F. H. (2005). History of theatre web sites: A brief history of the writing process in a high school ESL language arts class. *Journal of Second Language Writing*, *14*(4), 233–258. doi:10.1016/j.jslw.2005.10.003

Partnership for 21st Century Skills. (2008). *21st century skills, education & competitiveness: A resource and policy guide*. Tucson, AZ: Partnership for 21st Century Skills. Retrieved from http://www.p21.org/storage/documents/21st_century_skills_education_and_competitiveness_guide.pdf

Pasek, J., More, E., & Romer, D. (2009). Realizing the social internet? Online social networking meets offline civic engagement. *Journal of Information Technology & Politics*, *6*, 197–215. doi:10.1080/19331680902996403

Pasquinelli, E. (2010). The illusion of reality: Cognitive aspects and ethical drawbacks: The case of second life. In Wankel, C., & Malleck, S. (Eds.), *Emerging Ethical Issues of Life in Virtual Worlds* (pp. 195–213). Charlotte, NC: Information Age Publishing.

Patall, E. A., Cooper, H., & Robinson, J. C. (2008). The effects of choice on intrinsic motivation and related outcomes: A meta-analysis of research findings. *Psychological Bulletin*, *134*(2), 270–300. doi:10.1037/0033-2909.134.2.270

Patchin, J. W., & Hinduja, S. (2010). Cyberbullying and self-esteem. *The Journal of School Health*, *80*(12), 614–621. doi:10.1111/j.1746-1561.2010.00548.x

PBCC Academic Affairs. (2006). *Distance learning at PBCC: A history and enrollment overview*. Retrieved from http://www.pbcc.edu/documents/academic_services/dl_history.pdf

PBCC Institutional Research & Effectiveness. (2008). *Academic history: Comparison of success/withdrawal rates for classroom, internet and telecourses*. Lake Worth, FL: PBCC.

Pearce, F. W., Fisher, D. G., Fenaughty, A., Berman, M., Ferguson, S., Reynolds, G., & Statz, D. (2001). Alaska telemedicine testbed project: The evaluation of narrow bandwidth telemedicine in frontier Alaska. *Telemedicine Journal and e-Health*, *7*(2), 141.

Pellas, N. (2012). A conceptual "cybernetic" methodology for organizing and managing the e-learning process through [D-] CIVEs: The case of second life. In P. Renna (Ed.), *Production and Manufacturing System Management: Coordination Approaches and Multi-Site Planning*. Hersey, PA: IGI Global.

Pellas, N. (2012). Towards a beneficial formalization of cyber entities' interactions during the e-learning process in the virtual world of second life. In Renna, P. (Ed.), *Production and Manufacturing System Management: Coordination Approaches and Multi-Site Planning*. Hersey, PA: IGI Global.

Pellas, N. (2012). Towards a theoretical "cybernetic" framework: Discovering the pedagogical value of the virtual world second life. In Burgga, K., & Zaman, N. (Eds.), *Software Development Techniques for Constructive Information Systems Design*. Hersey, PA: IGI Global.

Pfister, H., Wessner, M., Holmer, T., & Steinmetz, R. (1999). Evaluating distributed computer- supported cooperative learning (D-CSCL): A framework and some data. In *Proceedings of the 2nd International Conference on New Learning Technologies (NLT 1999)*, (pp. 234-241). Berne, Switzerland: NLT.

Phipps, R., & Merisotis, J. (1999). *What's the difference? A review of contemporary research on the effectiveness of distance learning in higher education*. Washington, DC: The Institute for Higher Education Policy. Retrieved from http://www.ihep.com/Pubs/PDF/Difference.pdf

Pierson, H. D. (1996). Learner culture and learner autonomy in the Hong Kong Chinese context. In Pemberton, R. (Ed.), *Taking Control: Autonomy in Language Learning* (pp. 49–58). Hong Kong, China: Hong Kong University Press.

Plecas, D. D., & Sork, T. J. (1986). Adult education: Curing the ills of an undisciplined discipline. *Adult Education, 37*, 48–62. doi:10.1177/0001848186037001005

Polatoglu, V. N., & Ekin, S. (2001). An empirical investigation of the Turkish consumers' acceptance of internet banking services. *International Journal of Bank Marketing, 19*(4), 156–165. doi:10.1108/02652320110392527

Pollet, T. V., Roberts, S. B., & Dunbar, R. M. (2011). Use of social network sites and instant messaging does not lead to increased offline social network size, or to emotionally closer relationships with offline network members. *CyberPsychology. Behavior & Social Networking, 14*(4), 253–258. doi:10.1089/cyber.2010.0161

Pollock, K. E., & Meredith, L. H. (2007). Phonetic transcription of African American vernacular English. *Communication Disorders Quarterly, 23*(1), 47–53. doi:10.1177/152574010102300107

Porro, A. M. (2011). *Investigation of instructional strategies designed to promote achievement and retentionin online mathematics classes*. (Unpublished Doctoral Dissertation). Florida Atlantic University. Boca Raton, FL.

Powell, R., & Rightmyer, E. (2011). *Literacy for all students: An instructional framework for closing the gap*. New York, NY: Routledge.

Pratt, D. D. (1988). Andragogy as a relational construct. *Adult Education Quarterly, 38*, 160–172. doi:10.1177/0001848188038003004

Pratt, D. D. (1993). Andragogy after 25 years. In Merriam, S. B. (Ed.), *An Update on Adult Learning Theory* (pp. 15–23). San Francisco, CA: Jossey-Bass.

Prensky, M. (2001). Digital natives, digital immigrants. *Horizon, 9*(5), 1–2. Retrieved from http://www.marcprensky.com/writing/Prensky%20-%20Digital%20 Natives,%20Di gital%20Immigrants%20-%20Part1.pdfdoi:10.1108/10748120110424816

Price, M., & Dalgleish, J. (2010). Cyberbullying experiences, impacts and coping strategies as described by Australian young people. *Youth Studies Australia, 29*(2), 51–59.

Privitera, C., & Campbell, M. (2009). Cyberbullying: The new face of workplace bullying? *Cyberpsychology & Behavior, 12*(4), 395–400. doi:10.1089/cpb.2009.0025

Raacke, J., & Bonds-Raacke, J. (2011). MySpace and Facebook: Applying the uses and gratifications theory to exploring friend-networking sites. *Cyberpsychology & Behavior, 11*(2), 169–174. doi:10.1089/cpb.2007.0056

Rachal, J. R. (1983). The andragogy-pedagogy debate: Another voice in the fray. *Lifelong Learning, the Adult Years, 6*(9), 14–15.

Rachal, J. R. (2002). Andragogy's detectives: A critique of the present and a proposal for the future. *Adult Education Quarterly, 52*, 210–227. doi:10.1177/0741713602052003004

Rainie, L. (2011). *The social side of the internet*. Washington, DC: Pew Internet & Life Project. Retrieved from http://www.pewinternet.org/Press-Releases/2011/Social-Side-of-the-Internet.aspx

Rainie, L. (2012). *Citizen 2.0*. Washington, DC: Pew Research Project.

Ramanau, R., Hosein, A., & Jones, C. (2010). Learning and living technologies: A longitudinal study of first-year students' expectations and experiences in the use of ICT. In *Proceedings of the 7th International Conference on Networked Learning*, (pp. 627-634). NLC. Retrieved from http://www.lancs.ac.uk/fss/organisations/netlc/past/nlc2010/abstracts/PDFs/u.pdf

Rawls, J. A. (2003). *Community educators' perceptions regarding the status and role of community education*. (Ph.D. Dissertation). Southern Illinois University. Carbondale, IL.

Read, S., Miller, L., Appleby, P., Nwosu, M., Reynaldo, S., Lauren, A., & Putcha, A. (2006). Socially optimized learning in a virtual environment: Reducing risky sexual behavior among men who have sex with men. *Journal of Human Communication Research*, *32*(1), 1–34. doi:10.1111/j.1468-2958.2006.00001.x

Rebmann, T. (2010). Pandemic preparedness: Implementation of infection prevention plans. *Infection Control and Hospital Epidemiology*, *31*(1), 35–65. doi:10.1086/655993

Redd, T. M., & Webb, K. S. (2005). *A teacher's introduction to African American English: What a writing teacher should know*. Urbana, IL: National Council of Teachers of English.

Reddick, C. (2010). Information technology and emergency management: Preparedness and planning in US states. *Disasters*, *35*, 45–61. doi:10.1111/j.1467-7717.2010.01192.x

Renn, J. (2010). *Acquiring style: the development of dialect shifting among African-American children*. (Doctoral Dissertation). University of North Carolina. Chapel Hill, NC. Retrieved from http://www.unc.edu/linguistics/JRenndissertation.pdf

Rideout, V., Foehr, U., & Roberts, D. (2010). *Generation M2: Media in the lives of 8- to 18- year olds*. Washington, DC: Kaiser Family Foundation.

Roblyer, M. D. (2005). Educational technology research that makes a difference: Series introduction. *Contemporary Issues in Technology & Teacher Education*, *5*(2), 192–201.

Roekel, D. V. (2008). *Technology in schools: The ongoing challenge of access, adequacy, and equity. An NEA Policy Brief*. Washington, DC: National Education Association Education Policy and Practice Department.

Roemer, M., & Buhl, H. U. (1996). Das web also alternativ zur bankfiliale: Gestaltung innovation IKS fur das direktbanking. *Writschftsinformatic*, *6*, 565–577.

Rogers, E. (1962). *Diffusion of innovation*. New York, NY: Free Press.

Rose, A. D. (1998). Challenges in training adult educators. *Adult Learning*, *9*(3), 4–5. Retrieved from http://vnweb.hwwilsonweb.com/hww/jumpstart.jhtml?recid=0bc05f7a67b1790e7e1f464a7599779973d06fa7b4869506182501669a060a82c209472a1580a471&fmt=H

Rose, D. S., & Brenman, J. XPLANE, Sony/BMG, the Economist, McLeod, S., Bestler, L., & Fisch, K. (2012). *Shifthappens, 6.0: Did you know?* Retrieved from http://www.youtube.com/watch?v=XVQ1ULfQawk

Rosen, M. A., Salas, E., & Pavlas, D. (2010). Demonstration-based training: A review of instructional features. *Human Factors*, *52*(5), 596–609. doi:10.1177/0018720810381071

Rosenblum, S., & Darkenwald, G. G. (1983). Effects of adult learner participation in course planning on achievement and satisfaction. *Adult Education Quarterly*, *33*, 147–153.

Rossett, A. (Ed.). (2002). *ASTD e-learning handbook*. New York, NY: McGraw-Hill.

Rowe, R. D. (2005). *The development of African American English in the oldest black town in America: -s absence in Princeville, North Carolina*. (MA Thesis). North Carolina State University. Raleigh, NC.

Roy, S. (2012). Virtual collaboration: The skills needed to collaborate in a virtual environment. *Journal of Internet Social Networking & Virtual Communities*. Retrieved from http://www.ibimapublishing.com/journals/JISNVC/jisnvc.html

Russo, M., Bryan, V., & Penney, G. (2012). *Emergency preparedness: Life limb, the pursuit of safety and social justice*. Retrieved from www.igi-global.com/gateway/article/full-text-html/66092

Ryan, S. M. (1997). Preparing learners for independence: resources beyond the classroom. In Benson, P., & Voller, P. (Eds.), *Autonomy and Independence in Language Learning* (pp. 215–224). London, UK: Longman.

Ryder, M. (2004). *Constructivism: school of education*. Retrieved from http://carbon.cudenver.edu/~mryder/itc_data/constructivism.html

Salas, E., Kosarzycki, M. P., Burke, S. C., & Stone, D. L. (2002). Emerging themes in distance learning research and practice: Some food for thought. *International Journal of Management Reviews*, *4*, 135–154. doi:10.1111/1468-2370.00081

Salaway, G., & Caruso, J. B. (2007). *The ECAR study of undergraduate students and information technology*. Boulder, CO: EDUCAUSE Center for Applied Research. Retrieved from http://www.edu/ecar

Sam, H. K., Othman, A. E. A., & Nordin, A. S. (2005). Computer self-efficacy, computer anxiety, and attitudes toward the internet: A study among undergraduates in unimas. *Journal of Educational Technology & Society*, *8*(4), 205–219. Retrieved from http://www.ifets.info/journals/8_4/19.pdf

Sanacore, J. (2002). *Genuine caring and literacy learning for African American children*. Retrieved from http://www.eric.ed.gov/PDFS/ED471395.pdf

Sanacore, J. (2008). Turning reluctant learners into inspired learners. *Clearing House (Menasha, Wis.)*, *82*(1), 40–44. doi:10.3200/TCHS.82.1.40-44

Sardone, N. (2011). Developing information technology fluency in college students: An investigation of learning environments and learner characteristics. *Journal of Information Technology Education*, *10*, 101–122. Retrieved from http://www.jite.org/documents/Vol10/JITEv10p101-122Sardone846.pdf

Sathye, M. (1999). Adoption of Internet banking by Australian consumers: An empirical investigation. *International Journal of Bank Marketing*, *17*(7), 324–334. doi:10.1108/02652329910305689

Scharle, A., & Szabo, A. (2000). *Learner autonomy: A guide to developing learner responsibility*. Cambridge, UK: Cambridge University Press.

Schlickum, M., Hedman, L., Enochsson, L., Henningsohn, L., Kjellin, A., & Fellander-Tsai, L. (2011). Surgical simulation tasks challenge visual working memory and visual-spatial ability differently. *World Journal of Surgery*, *35*(4), 710–715. doi:10.1007/s00268-011-0981-2

Schon, D. (1983). *The reflective practitioner*. New York, NY: Basic Books.

Schunk, D. (2004). *Learning theories: An educational perspective* (4th ed.). Upper Saddle River, NJ: Pearson.

Schunk, D. H. (1991). Self-efficacy and academic motivation. *Educational Psychologist*, *26*(3-4), 201–231. doi:10.1080/00461520.1991.9653133

Schwaab, J., Kman, N., Nagel, R., Bahner, D., Martin, D. R., & Khandelwal, S. (2011). Using second life virtual simulation environment for mock oral emergency medicine examination. *Academic Emergency Medicine*, *18*(5), 559–562. doi:10.1111/j.1553-2712.2011.01064.x

Scottish Community Education Council. (1990). *CeVe Scotland: Preservice training for community education work*. Edinburgh, UK: Scottish Community Education Council.

Second Life. (2008). *Second life*. Retrieved from http://webcitehttp://secondlife.com

Selwyn, N. (2003). Apart from technology: Understanding people's non-use of information and communication technologies in everyday life. *Technology in Society*, *25*, 99–116. doi:10.1016/S0160-791X(02)00062-3

Selwyn, N. (2008). An investigation of differences in undergraduates' academic use of the internet. *Active Learning in Higher Education*, *9*(1), 11–22. doi:10.1177/1469787407086744

Senge, P. (1990). *The fifth discipline: The art and practice of the learning organization*. New York, NY: Doubleday. doi:10.1002/pfi.4170300510

Senior, R. (2010). Connectivity: A framework for understanding effective language teaching in face-to-face and online learning communities. *RELC Journal: A Journal of Language Teaching and Research, 41*(2), 137-147.

Servage, L. (2008). Critical and transformative practices in professional learning communities. *Teacher Education Quarterly*, 63–77. Retrieved from http://www.teqjournal.org/backvols/2008/35_1/10servage.pdf

Sessa, V., & London, N. (2006). *Continuous learning in organisations: Individual, group and organisational perspectives*. Mahwah, NJ: Erlbaum.

Shariff, S. (2005). Cyber-dilemmas in the new millennium: School obligations to provide student safety in a virtual school environment. *McGill Journal of Education*, *40*, 467–487.

Sherriff, L. (2012). Harvard and MIT create EdX to offer free university courses to the world. *The Huffington Post*. Retrieved from http://www.huffingtonpost.co.uk

Shetzer, H., & Warschauer, M. (2000). An electronic literacy approach to network-based language teaching. In Warschauer, M., & Kern, R. (Eds.), *Network-Based Language Teaching: Concepts and Practice* (pp. 171–185). Cambridge, UK: Cambridge University Press. doi:10.1017/CBO9781139524735.010

Shih, Y.-C., & Yang, M.-T. (2008). A collaborative virtual environment for situated language learning using VEC3D. *Journal of Educational Technology & Society*, *11*(1), 56–68.

Shucart, S. A., Mishina, T., Takahashi, M., & Enokizono, T. (2008). The CALL lab as a facilitator for autonomous learning. In Zhang, F., & Barber, B. (Eds.), *Handbook of Research on Computer-Enhanced Language Acquisition and Learning* (pp. 483–495). Hershey, PA: IGI Global. doi:10.4018/978-1-59904-895-6.ch028

Silen, C., & Uhlin, L. (2004). *Self-directed learning-A learning issue for the student!* Retrieved from http://www.hu.liu.se/pedagogiskcentrum/pbl/pdf/artiklar_hu/159913/silen-uhlin2004sdl.pdf

Simonson, M. (2008). *Distance learning: Key terms you might want to know*. Fort Lauderdale, FL: Nova Southeastern University.

Skinner, B. F. (2005). *Science and human behavior*. Cambridge, MA: B. F. Skinner Foundation. Retrieved from http://www.bfskinner.macwebsitebuilder.com/f/Science_and_Human_Behavior.pdf

Slater, M., Sadagic, A., Usoh, M., & Schroeder, R. (2000). Small-group behaviour in a virtual and real environment: A comparative study. *Presence (Cambridge, Mass.)*, *9*(1), 37–51. doi:10.1162/105474600566600

SLSST. (2003). *National safe schools framework*. Retrieved 11 May 2012 from www.dest.gov.au/sectors/school_education/publications_resources/profiles/national_safe_schools_framework.htm

Smith, A. (2011). *The internet and campaign 2010*. Washington, DC: Pew Research Center's Internet & American Life Project. Retrieved from http://pewinternet.org/Reports/2011/The-Internet-and-Campaign-2010.aspx

Smith, A. (2012a). *17% of cell phone owners do most of their online browsing on their phone, rather than a computer or other device*. Washington DC: Pew Research Center's Internet & American Life Project. Retrieved from http://pewinternet.org/Reports/2012/Cell-Internet-Use-2012.aspx

Smith, A. (2012b). *46% of American adults are smartphone owners*. Washington DC: Pew Research Center's Internet & American Life Project. Retrieved from http://pewinternet.org/~/media//Files/Reports/2012/Smartphone%20ownership%202012.pdf

Smith, A. (2012c). *17% of cell phone owners do most of their online browsing on their phone rather than a computer or other device*. Washington, DC: Pew Research Center's Internet & American Life Project. Retrieved from http://www.pewinternet.org/~/media//Files/Reports/2012/PIP_Cell_Phone_Internet_Access.pdf

Smith, A., & Boyles, J. L. (2012, July 17). *The rise of the "connected viewer"*. Washington, DC: Pew Research Center's Internet & American Life Project. Retrieved from http://pewinternet.org/Reports/2012/Connected-vieweres.aspx

Smith, A., & Brenner, J. (2012). *Twitter use 2012*. Washington DC: Pew Research Center's Internet & American Life Project. Retrieved from http://pewinternet.org/~/media//Files/Reports/2012/PIP_Twitter_Use_2012.pdf

Smith, A., Schlozman, K., Verba, S., & Brady, H. (2009). *The internet and civic engagement*. Washington, DC: Pew Research Project.

Smith, C. (2010). Twitter stats reveal few Americans use Twitter, although most know it (STUDY). *Huffington Post*. Retrieved from http://www.huffingtonpost.com/2010/04/30/twitter-stats-reveal-few_n_557587.html

Smith, P. K., Mahdavi, J., Carvalho, M., Fisher, S., Russell, S., & Tippett, N. (2008). Cyberbullying: Its nature and impact in secondary school pupils. *Journal of Child Psychology and Psychiatry, and Allied Disciplines*, *49*(4), 376–385. doi:10.1111/j.1469-7610.2007.01846.x

Smith, S., Salaway, G., & Borreson Caruso, J. (2009). *The ECAR study of undergraduate students and information technology*. Boulder, CO: EDUCAUSE Center for Applied Research. Retrieved from http://www.educause.edu/ecar

Smitherman, G. (1997). The chain remain the same: Communicative practices in the hip hop nation. *Journal of Black Studies*, *28*(1), 3–25.

Smutz, W., & Weidemann, C. (2008). Economic development in challenging times. *Continuing Higher Education Review*, *72*, 44–56.

Snyder, T. D., & Dillow, S. A. (2011). *Digest of education statistics 2010*. Washington, DC: National Center for Education Statistics, Institute of Education Sciences, U.S. Department of Education.

Snyder, T. D., Dillow, S. A., & Hoffman, C. M. (2009). *Digest of education statistics: 2008 (NCES No. 2009-20)*. Washington, DC: National Center for Education Statistics, U.S. Department of Education.

Spears, B., Slee, P., Owens, L., & Johnson, B. (2009). Behind the scenes and screens: Insights into the human dimension of covert and cyberbullying. *The Journal of Psychology*, *217*(4), 189–196.

Speckler, M. (2009). *Making the grade, V3: A compendium of data-driven case studies on the effectiveness of MyMathLab and MathXL*. Boston, MA: Pearson Education.

Spitler, V. (2005). Learning to use IT in the workplace. *Journal of Organizational and End User Computing*, *17*(2), 1–25. doi:10.4018/joeuc.2005040101

Squires, D. A. (1996). The comer program: Changing school culture. *Educational Leadership*, *53*(4), 29–32.

Starr, P. (2010). The liberal state in a digital world. *Governance: An International Journal of Policy, Administration and Institutions*, *23*(1), 1–6. doi:10.1111/j.1468-0491.2009.01464.x

Stevens, M. M. (1986). Oral hygiene instruction: Assessment of andragogical and pedagogical methods of adult patient instruction. *Dissertation Abstracts International*, *46*(9).

Stevens, T. G. (2003). *You can choose to be happy: Self-confidence*. Retrieved from http://www.courses.csulb.edu/tstevens/h54confi.htm

Stibel, J. (2009). Introduction. In *Wired for Thought*. Boston, MA: Harvard Business Press.

Strathdee, R. (2001). Changes in social capital and school to work transitions. *Work, Employment and Society*, *15*(2), 311–326. doi:10.1177/09500170122118977

Strawbridge, W. G. (1994). The effectiveness of andragogical instruction as compared with traditional instruction in introductory philosophy courses. *Dissertation Abstracts International*, *55*(11).

Sullivan, H. T., & Häkkinen, M. T. (2011). Preparedness and warning systems for populations with special needs: Ensuring everyone gets the message (and knows what to do). *Geotechnical and Geological Engineering*, *29*, 225–236. doi:10.1007/s10706-010-9363-z

Sullivan, N. (1993). Teaching writing on a computer network. *TESOL Journal*, *3*(1), 34–35.

Sutherland-Smith, W. (2002). Weaving the literacy web: Changes in reading from page to screen. *The Reading Teacher*, *55*(7), 662–669. Retrieved from http://www.jstor.org/stable/20205116

Sweller, J. (1988). Cognitive load during problem solving: Effects on learning. *Cognitive Science*, *12*(2), 257–285. doi:10.1207/s15516709cog1202_4

Sweller, J. (1989). Cognitive technology: some procedures for facilitation learning and problem solving in mathematics and science. *Journal of Educational Psychology*, *81*, 457–466. doi:10.1037/0022-0663.81.4.457

Sweller, J. (1999). *Instructional design in technical areas*. Camberwell, Australia: ACER Press.

Sweller, J. (2006). Discussion of emerging topics in cognitive load research: Using learner and information characteristics in the design of powerful learning environments. *Applied Cognitive Psychology*, *20*, 353–357. doi:10.1002/acp.1251

Sweller, J., & Chandler, P. (1991). Evidence for cognitive load theory. *Cognition and Instruction*, *8*(4), 351–362. Retrieved from http://www.jstor.org/stable/3233599doi:10.1207/s1532690xci0804_5

Sweller, J., & Chandler, P. (1994). Why some material is difficult to learn. *Cognition and Instruction*, *12*(3), 185–233. doi:10.1207/s1532690xci1203_1

Sweller, J., Chandler, P., Tierney, P., & Cooper, M. (1990). Cognitive load and selective attention as factors in the structuring of technical material. *Journal of Experimental Psychology. General*, *119*, 176–192. doi:10.1037/0096-3445.119.2.176

Sweller, J., & Cooper, G. A. (1985). The use of worked examples as a substitute for problem solving in learning algebra. *Cognition and Instruction*, *2*(1), 59–89. Retrieved from http://www.jstor.org/stable/3233555doi:10.1207/s1532690xci0201_3

Sweller, J., van Merrienböer, J. J. G., & Paas, F. G. W. C. (1998). Cognitive architecture and instructional design. *Educational Psychology Review*, *10*(3), 251–296. doi:10.1023/A:1022193728205

Sweller, J., van Merrienboer, J., & Paas, F. W. (1998). Cognitive architecture and instructional design. *Educational Psychology Review*, *10*(3), 251–296. doi:10.1023/A:1022193728205

Szecsy, E. M., Danzig, A. B., & Gonzales, J. M. (2005). *The use of information and communication technology (ICT) to encourage reflection, interaction and collaboration for innovation and professional growth in higher education.* Paper presented at the meeting of the Annual Conference of the Northeastern Educational Association. Kerhonkson, NY. Retrieved from http://www.eric.ed.gov/PDFS/ED490670.pdf

Talking Page Literacy Organization. (2007). *The national adult illiteracy action project, 2007-2012*. Retrieved from http://www.talkingpage.org/NIAP2007.pdf

Tallent-Runnels, M. K., Thomas, J. A., Lan, W. Y., Cooper, S., Ahern, T. C., Shaw, S. M., & Liu, X. (2006). Teaching courses online: A review of the research. *Review of Educational Research*, *76*(1), 93–135. Retrieved from http://www.aera.net/doi:10.3102/00346543076001093

Taylor, L., McMinn, M., Bufford, R., & Chang, K. (2010). Psychologists' attitudes and ethical concerns regarding the use of social networking web sites. *Professional Psychology, Research and Practice*, *41*(2), 153–159. doi:10.1037/a0017996

Taylor, V. (2000). *Perceptions of selected black female middle-level managers on advancement in higher education administration*. (PhD Thesis). Columbia University. New York, NY.

Tempelman-Kluit, N. (2006). Multimedia learning theories and online instruction. *College & Research Libraries*, *67*(4), 364–369. Retrieved from http://vnweb.hw.com/hww/jumpstart.jhtml?recid=0bc05f7a67b1790e7e1f464a7599779909c3222764db0a79b878397662eb45d7708ff0808e256904&fmt=P

Teo, T. (2001). Demographic and motivation variables associated with internet usage activities. *Internet Research: Electronic Networking Applications and Policy*, *11*(2), 125–137. doi:10.1108/10662240110695089

Thompson, G. (2002). *African American teens discuss their schooling experiences*. Westport, CT: Greenwood Publishers.

Thompson, M. M. (1998). Distance learners in higher education. In Gibson, C. C. (Ed.), *Distance Learners in Higher Education: Institutional Responses for Quality Outcomes* (pp. 10–18). Madison, WI: Atwood Publishing.

Thomson, C. K. (1996). Self-assessment in self-directed learning: issues of learner diversity. In Pemberton, R. (Ed.), *Taking Control: Autonomy in Language Learning* (pp. 77–91). Hong Kong, China: Hong Kong University Press.

Tieman, J. (2000). Monitoring a good opportunity: Telemedicine grows as method to reach poorly served regions. *Modern Healthcare*, *30*(43), 75–78, 80.

Toffler, A. (1969). Toffler quotes. *Alvin + Heidi Toffler Futurists*. Retrieved from http://www.alvintoffler.net/?fa=galleryquotes

Toffler, A. (1980). *The third wave*. New York, NY: Bantam Books.

Tough, A. (1967). *Learning without a teacher*. Toronto, Canada: Institute for Studies in Education.

Tough, A. (1979). *The adult's learning project*. Toronto, Canada: Institute for Studies in Education.

Townley, G., Kloos, B., Green, E. P., & Franco, M. M. (2011). Reconcilable differences? Human diversity, cultural relativity, and sense of community. *American Journal of Community Psychology*, *47*, 69–85. doi:10.1007/s10464-010-9379-9

Treglia, J., McKnight, L. W., Venkatesh, M., & Bose, T. Volos, van Aardt, J., ... Lee, M. (2001). *Social emergency response technology policy*. Paper presented at the TPRC: The 39th Research Conference on Communication, Information and Internet Policy. Arlington, VA.

Trocchia, P. J., & Janda, S. (2000). A phenomenological investigation of internet usage among older individual. *Journal of Consumer Marketing*, *17*(7), 605–616. doi:10.1108/07363760010357804

Trotter, A. (2007). Getting up to speed. *Education Week*, *26*, 10–16.

Troy, D., Carson, A., Vanderbeek, J., & Hutton, A. (2008). Enhancing community-based disaster preparedness with information technology. *Disasters*, *32*(1), 149–165. doi:10.1111/j.1467-7717.2007.01032.x

Trumbull, M. (2012). Harvard and MIT to offer online courses: A step in lowering college costs? *Christian Science Monitor*. Retrieved from http://www.cnbc.com

Turner, T. (1991). Why community education must embrace technology now: From "community education journal". *Education Digest*, *57*(4), 60.

Tynes, B. (2007). Internet safety gone wild? Sacrificing the educational and psychosocial benefits of online social environments. *Journal of Adolescent Research*, *22*, 575–584. doi:10.1177/0743558407303979

U. S. Department of Labor. (1991). *Secretary's commission on achieving necessary skills*. Washington, DC: Government Printing Office.

U.S. Department of Education. (2010). *National education technology plan 2010*. Retrieved from http://www.ed.gov/technology/netp-2010

Ulusu, Y. (2010). Determinant factors of time spent on Facebook: Brand community engagement and usage types. *Journal of Yasar University*, *18*(5), 2949–2957.

Underwood, J. (2009). *The impact of digital technology: A review of the evidence of the impact of digital technologies on formal education*. Coventry, UK: British Educational Communications and Technology Agency (Becta).

UNESCO. (2004). Information literacy. In *Communication and Information*. Bangkok, Thailand: UNESCO.

United Nations. (2005). *UN global e-government readiness report 2005 – From e-government to e-inclusion*. New York, NY: United Nations. Retrieved from http://unpan1.un.org/intradoc/groups/public/documents/un/unpan021888.pdf

United Nations Economic Commission for Africa. (2011). *Framework for a set of government core indicators*. Addis Ababa, Ethiopia: United Nations Economic Commission for Africa. Retrieved from http://www.uneca.org/aisi/scanict/Framework_eGovCoreIndicators_Final.pdf

United States Department of Justice. (2012). *Identify theft and identity fraud*. Retrieved from http://www.justice.gov/criminal/fraud/websites/idtheft.html

United States Department of Labor. (1991). *Secretary's commission on achieving necessary skills (SCANS)*. Washington, DC: Government Printing Office.

United States Department of State. (2009). *Outline of the U.S. economy*. Washington, DC: Government Printing Office.

United States Distance Learning Association. (2009). *Distance learning definition*. Retrieved from http://www.usdla.org/html/aboutUs/vmd.htm

Urwin, P., Di Pietro, G., Sturgis, P., & Jack, G. (2008). Measuring the returns to networking and the accumulation of social capital. *American Journal of Economics and Sociology*, *67*(5), 941–968. doi:10.1111/j.1536-7150.2008.00603.x

US Bureau of Labor Statistics. (2009). *Employment projections: 2008-2018 summary*. Washington, DC: US Department of Labor. Retrieved from http://www.bls.gov/opub/mlr/2009/11/art1full.pdf

US Department of Commerce. NIST. (2011). *2011-2012 criteria for performance excellence*. Retrieved from http://www.nist.gov/baldrige/publications/criteria.cfm

US Department of Commerce. NIST. (2012). *Baldrige performance excellence program, 2012*. Retrieved from http://www.nist.gov/baldrige/

Vallerand, R. J. (1997). In Zanna, M. P. (Ed.), *Toward a hierarchical model of intrinsic and extrinsic motivation* (*Vol. 29*, pp. 271–361). Advances in Experimental Social PsychologyToronto, Canada: Academic Press. doi:10.1016/S0065-2601(08)60019-2

Valmont, W. (2003). *Technology for literacy teaching and learning*. New York, NY: Houghton Mifflin.

Van Hofwegen, J., & Wolfram, W. (2010). Coming of age in African American English: A longitudinal study. *Journal of Sociolinguistics*, *14*(4), 427–455. Retrieved from http://www.ncsu.edu/linguistics/docs/pdfs/walt/Coming%20of%20Age-pdf.pdfdoi:10.1111/j.1467-9841.2010.00452.x

van Merriënboer, J. J. G., & Ayres, P. (2005). Research on cognitive load theory and its design implications for elearning. *Educational Technology Research and Development*, *53*(3), 5–13. doi:10.1007/BF02504793

Vansteenkiste, M., Soenens, B., Timmermans, T., Lens, W., & Van den Broeck, A. (2008). Does extrinsic goal framing enhance extrinsic goal-oriented individuals' learning and performance? An experimental test of the match perspective versus self-determination theory? *Journal of Educational Psychology*, *100*(2), 387–397. doi:10.1037/0022-0663.100.2.387

Venkatesh, V., & Morris, M. G. (2000). Why don't men ever stop to ask for directions? Gender, social influence, and their role in technology acceptance and change behaviour. *Management Information Systems Quarterly*, *24*, 115–139. doi:10.2307/3250981

Venkatesh, V., Morris, M. G., & Ackerman, P. L. (2000). A longitudinal field investigation of gender differences in individual technology adoption decision making processes. *Organizational Behavior and Human Decision Processes*, *83*, 33–60. doi:10.1006/obhd.2000.2896

Venkatesh, V., Morris, M. G., Davis, G. B., & Davis, F. (2003). User acceptance of information technology: Toward a unified view. *Management Information Systems Quarterly*, *27*, 425–478.

Verhoeven, J. C., Heerwegh, D., & De Wit, K. (2012). First year university student' self-perception of ICT skills: Do learning styles matter? *Education and Information Technologies*, *17*(1), 109–133. doi:10.1007/s10639-010-9149-1

Vogel, D., Guo, M., Zhou, P., Tian, S., & Zhang, J. (2008). In search of second life: Nirvana. *Issues in Informing Science and Information Technology*, *5*, 11–28.

Volman, M., & van Eck, E. (2001). Gender equity and information technology in education: The second decade. *Review of Educational Research*, *71*(4), 613–634. doi:10.3102/00346543071004613

Vosinakis, S., Koutsabasis, P., Zaharias, P., & Belk, M. (2010). Problem-based learning in virtual worlds: A case study in user interface design. In *Experiential Learning in Virtual Worlds - Exploring the Complexities*. New York, NY: Interdisciplinary Press. Retrieved from http://www.inter-disciplinary.net/wp-content/uploads/2011/02/vosinakisepaper.pdf

Vrechopoulos, A. P., Siomkos, G. J., & Doukidis, G. I. (2001). Internet shopping adoption by Greek consumers. *European Journal of Innovation Management*, *4*(3), 142–152. doi:10.1108/14601060110399306

Vrellis, I., Papachristos, N., Natsis, A., & Mikropoulos, T. (2010). Measuring presence in a collaborative physics learning activity in second life. In T. A. Jimoyiannis (Ed.), *Proceedings of the 7th Pan-Hellenic Conference with International Participation ICT in Education*, (Vol. 1, pp. 95-102). Korinthos, Greece: IEEE.

Vroom, V. H. (1964). *Work and motivation*. New York, NY: John Wiley & Sons, Inc.

Wadsworth, L. M., Husman, J., Duggan, M. A., & Pennington, M. N. (2007). Online mathematics achievement: Effects of learning strategies and self-efficacy. *Journal of Developmental Education*, *30*(3), 6–14.

Wadsworth, Y. (1998). What is participatory action research? *Action Research International*. Retrieved from http://www.scu.edu.au/schools/gcm/ar/ari/p-ywadsworth98.html

Walker, B. (2008). Adjusting instruction to meet students' needs. *Reading Today*, *25*(6), 18–19.

Walsh, A., Hegarty, M. P., & Kelly, H. (2011). Reflection in a workplace qualification: Challenges and benefits. *Journal of Workplace Learning*, *23*(8), 4.

Waltz, E. G., Maniccia, D. M., Bryde, R. L., Murphy, K., Harris, B. R., & Waldenmailer, M. N. (2010). Training the public health workforce from Albany to Zambia: Technology lessons learned along the way. *Public Health Reports*, *125*, 61–69.

Wang, F., Fong, J., & Kwan, R. R. (2010). *Handbook of research on hybrid learning models: Advanced tools, technologies, and applications*. Hershey, PA: IGI Global.

Wang, G. (1994). *Treading different paths: Informatization in Asian nations*. Norwood, NJ: Ablex.

Wang, J. (2012). Organizational learning and technology. In Wang, V. (Ed.), *Encyclopedia of E-Leadership, Counseling and Training* (pp. 154–170). Hershey, PA: IGI Global.

Wang, T. (2009). Rethinking teaching with information and communication technologies (ICTs) in architectural education. *Teaching and Teacher Education*, *25*, 1132–1140. doi:10.1016/j.tate.2009.04.007

Warschauer, M. (1996). Computer-assisted language learning: An introduction. In Fotos, S. (Ed.), *Multimedia Language Teaching* (pp. 3–20). Tokyo, Japan: Logos International.

Warschauer, M. (2000). On-line learning in second language classrooms: An ethnographic study. In Warschauer, M., & Kern, R. (Eds.), *Network-Based Language Teaching: Concepts and Practice* (pp. 41–58). Cambridge, UK: Cambridge University Press. doi:10.1017/CBO9781139524735.005

Warschauer, M. (2003). *Technology and social inclusion: Rethinking the digital divide*. Cambridge, MA: MIT Press.

Warschauer, M., & Healey, D. (1998). Computers and language learning: An overview. *Language Teaching*, *31*, 57–71. doi:10.1017/S0261444800012970

Warschauer, M., Turbee, L., & Roberts, B. (1996). Computer learning networks and student empowerment. *System*, *24*(1), 1–14. doi:10.1016/0346-251X(95)00049-P

Wei, R. C., Darling-Hammond, L., & Adamson, F. (2010). *Professional development in the United States: Trends and challenges*. Dallas, TX: National Staff Development Council.

Wei, R. C., Darling-Hammond, L., Andree, A., Richardson, N., & Orphanos, S. (2009). *Professional learning in the learning profession: A status report on teacher development in the United States and abroad*. Dallas, TX: National Staff Development Council.

Welborn, B. (2012). Six keys to successful collaboration. *Education Week Teacher*. Retrieved from http://www.edweek.org/tm/articles/2012/03/13/tln_collaboration.html

Welch, J., & Welch, S. (2012). Goldman, Wall Street, and the culture killing lesson being ignored. *Fortune*, *165*, 56.

Wenden, A. (1991). *Learner strategies for learner autonomy*. New York, NY: Prentice Hall.

Wenger, E. (1998). *Communities of practice: Learning meaning and identity*. Cambridge, UK: Cambridge University Press.

White, B. A. (1989). Selected instructional strategies, learner outcome, and attitudes of adult learners in a mandatory education setting. *Dissertation Abstracts International*, *49*(8).

Wickens, C. D. (1984). *Engineering psychology and human performance*. Columbus, OH: Merrill.

Wilkinson, D., Waruszynski, B., Mazurik, L., Szymczak, A., Redmond, E., & Lichacz, F. (2010). Medical preparedness for chemical, biological, radiological, nuclear, and explosives (CBRNE) events: Gaps and recommendations. *Radiation Protection Dosimetry*, *142*, 8–11. doi:10.1093/rpd/ncq206

Wilkinson, G. (2011, April 5). Brodie's law means workplace and cyber bullies face 10 years in jail. *Herald Sun*. Retrieved 10 May 2012 from http://www.heraldsun.com.au/news/workplace-and-cyber-bullies-face-up-to-10-years-jail-under-anti-harassment-brodie-panlock-laws/story-e6frf7jo-1226033612374

Willis, A. I. (2000). *Critical issue: Addressing literacy needs in culturally and linguistically diverse classrooms*. Retrieved from http://www.ncrel.org/sdrs/areas/issues/content/cntareas/reading/li400.htm

Wilson, A. L., & Hayes, E. R. (2002). From the editors: The problem of (learning in-from-to) experience. *Adult Education Quarterly*, *52*, 173-175.

Wilson, L. S. (2005). A test of andragogy in a post-secondary educational setting. *Dissertation Abstracts International*, *66*(7).

Wisconsin Department of Public Instruction. (2008). *Wisconsin's components of communication education*. Madison, WI: Wisconsin Department of Public Instruction.

Witmer, A., Seifer, S. D., Finocchio, L., Leslie, J., & O'Neil, E. H. (1995). Community health workers: Integral members of the health care work force. *American Journal of Public Health and the Nation's Health*, *85*(8), 1055–1058. doi:10.2105/AJPH.85.8_Pt_1.1055

Wolfram, W. (1969). *A sociolinguistic description of Detroit Negro speech*. Washington, DC: Center for Applied Linguistics.

Wolfram, W. (2004). *The grammar of urban African American vernacular English*. Retrieved from http://www.ncsu.edu/linguistics/docs/pdfs/walt/PDF-Urban_AAE.pdf

Wolfram, W. (2010). *The grammar of rural and ethnic varieties in the southeast*. Retrieved from http://www.ncsu.edu/linguistics/docs/pdfs/walt/PDF-Rural_Southeast.pdf

Wolfram, W. (2011). *Changing misconceptions about dialect diversity: The role of public education*. Retrieved from http://www.cal.org/resources/digest/digest_pdfs/changing-misconceptions-about-dialect-diversity.pdf

Wolfram, W., Adger, C. T., & Christian, D. (2007). *Dialects in schools and communities* (2nd ed.). Mahwah, NJ: Lawrence Erlbaum Associates.

Wood, D. (2009). *Experimental learning through "real world" placements undertaken in 3D virtual world spaces*. Retrieved from http://www.ascilite.org.au/conferences/auckland09/procs/wood.pdf

World Bank Institute. (2008). *Measuring knowledge in the world's economies*. Washington, DC: World Bank Institute.

Wright, V., Burnham, J., Inman, C., & Ogorchock, H. (2009). Cyberbullying: Using virtual scenarios to educate and raise awareness. *Journal of Computing In Teacher Education*, *26*(1), 35–42.

Wu, Y., & Bauer, J. (2010). E-government in China: Deployment and driving forces of provincial government portals. *Chinese Journal of Communication*, *3*(3), 290–310. doi:10.1080/17544750.2010.499633

Xu, S. H. (2001, July/August). Exploring diversity issues in teacher education. *Reading Online*, *5*(1). Retrieved from http://www.readingonline.org/newliteracies/lit_index.asp?HREF=action/xu/index.html

Yahoo. 7 News. (2011). *Cyber-bullied teen subject of online taunts after death*. Retrieved 10 May 2012 from http://au.news.yahoo.com/nsw/latest/a/-/newshome/9884636/cyber-bullied-teen-subject-of-online-taunts-after-death/

Yermish, I. (2000). A case for case studies via video-conferencing. In Lau, L. (Ed.), *Distance Learning Technologies: Issues, Trends and Opportunities* (pp. 208–217). Hershey, PA: IGI Global. doi:10.4018/978-1-878289-80-3.ch015

Yilmaz, H. (2012). Distance education at university settings. In Wang, V. (Ed.), *Encyclopedia of E-Leadership, Counseling and Training* (p. 587600). Hershey, PA: IGI Global.

Yocco, V., Danter, E., Heimlich, J., Dunckel, B., & Myers, C. (2011). Exploring use of new media in environmental education contexts: Introducing visitors' technology use in zoos model. *Environmental Education Research*, *17*(6), 801–814. doi:10.1080/13504622.2011.620700

Young, K. (2011). Social ties, social networks and the Facebook experience. *International Journal of Emerging Technologies & Society*, *9*(1), 20–34.

Youngblut, C. (1998). VR in the schools. *Educational Uses of Virtual Reality Technology, 3*(1). Retrieved from http://www.hitl.washington.edu/scivw/youngblut-edvr/D2128.pdf

YouTube. (2012). *Animated infographic of Facebook statistics*. Retrieved from http://www.youtube.com/watch?v=XKTfCjMsUNc

YouTube.com. (2010). *YouTube fact sheet*. Retrieved from http://frameconcepts.com/youtube-fact-sheet

Zeichner, K. M. (1992). Educating teachers for cultural diversity. *National Council for Research in Teaching and Learning*. Retrieved from http://education.msu.edu/NCRTL/PDFs/NCRTL/SpecialReports/sr293.pdf

Zhigeng, P., Zhu, J., Zhang, M., & Hu, W. (2005). *Collaborative virtual learning environment using synthetic characters. Berlin, Germany*. Germany: Springer-Verlag.

Zickuhr, K., Raine, L., Purcell, K., Madden, M., & Brenner, J. (2012). *Libraries, patrons and e-books*. Washington DC: Pew Research Center's Internet & American Life Project. Retrieved from http://libraries.pewinternet.org/files/legacy-pdf/PIP_Libraries_and_Ebook_Patrons%20 6.22.12.pdf

Zickuhr, K., & Smith, A. (2012). *Digital differences*. Washington, DC: Pew Research Project.

Zijdemans, A. S. (2005). *Exploring a socio-technological design for knowledge development: The millennium dialogue on early child development*. (PhD Dissertation). University of Toronto. Toronto, Canada. Retrieved from http://search.proquest.com/docview/305360069?accountid=10351

About the Contributors

Valerie Carson Bryan is Professor in Educational Leadership in Adult Education at Florida Atlantic University. She has received a variety of awards and other recognitions: selected as Charles Stewart Mott Eminent Scholar in Community Education, 2011; recipient of FAU Graduate Mentor Award, 2011; MacAWARD Exceptional Faculty for College of Education, 2009; FAU College of Education Distinguished Teacher of the Year, 2009; recipient of FAU's President's Award, 2006-2007; FAU College of Education's Distinguished Teacher of the Year, 2006; FAU College of Education Teacher of the Year, 2005-2006; recipient of Clemson University's President's Award, 1993; North Carolina's Individual of the Year, 1984; and recognized as webmaster of One of Top Ten US Literacy Internet sites, 1998. Dr. Dee, and co-author Dr. Valerie Bryan, were awarded an Outstanding Virtual Presentation Award for their presentation at E-Learn 2011-2012 World Conference on E-Learning in Corporate, Government, Healthcare, and Higher Education, Honolulu, Hawaii. She has been recognized for several distinctions on a variety of Who's Who lists. At Florida Atlantic University, she teaches courses in Management, Adult Learning, Administration, Aging, Integration of Technology, and a host of other subjects, online, in stand-up-mode, and on several platforms. She is active in research that embraces virtual learning communities, enhanced staff productivity using a varying of technology-based tools, and the role of successful aging. Valerie is active in the integration of technology in practice, as a doctoral chair, and in her research and grant writing.

Victor C. X. Wang, an Associate Professor, joined the faculty at the prestigious Department of Educational Leadership and Research Methodology at this "High Research Activity" status university from the Carnegie Foundation for the Advancement of Teaching, Florida Atlantic University. Dr. Wang's research and writing activities have addressed workforce education, the foundations of adult education, adult teaching and learning, training, transformative learning, cultural issues in vocational and adult education, distance education, human performance technology, instructional/administrative leadership, assessment and evaluation of learning, and curriculum development. He has published more than 140 journal articles, book chapters, and books, including two encyclopedias and one handbook of research (each over 1,000 pages long) in 9 years and has been a reviewer for five national and international journals. Currently, he serves as the Editor in Chief of the *International Journal of Adult Vocational Education and Technology*. He has won many academic achievement awards from universities in China and in the United States, including the Distinguished Faculty Scholarly and Creative Achievement Award. Dr. Wang has taught extensively as a Professor in Chinese universities (1989-1997) prior to coming to study and work (Kansas, Arkansas, and California, 1997-2011) in the United States. He has taught across the curriculum for the past 21 years in university settings. He has had extensive experience in chairing and mentoring doctoral dissertations. Three of the books he has written and edited have been adopted as required textbooks by major universities in the United States and in China. In addition, numerous universities worldwide including some Ivy League Universities have cataloged his books and journal articles.

* * *

Sujana Adapa is a Lecturer in Management (Strategy and Marketing) in the UNE Business School at the University of New England (UNE), Armidale, Australia. Sujana teaches Introduction to Marketing, Marketing Strategy and Management, Services Marketing, and International Marketing units at UNE for undergraduate and postgraduate students. Her research interests relate to the adoption of technological innovations, corporate social responsibility, sales management, destination visitations, and branding. She has published research papers in reputed journals and presented her research in national and international journals.

Jeffrey L. Beard is a Ph.D. student in Educational Psychology and Research with a concentration in Adult Learning at the University of Tennessee. He completed his M.S. in Instructional Technology at the University of Tennessee and a B.A. in Business Administration at Saint Leo University. Jeff works as an instructional designer in industry and is an adjunct education technology instructor at the University of Tennessee.

J. Bernard Bradley, Ph.D., GPC, is principal/founder of the American Council on Grant Writing, a national consulting firm based in Nevada. Dr. Bradley is presently a board member of the Nevada Grant Professionals Association, Chair of the Distance Learning and Technology SIG with the American Association for Adult and Continuing Education, and a volunteer with the Rebuilding Afghanistan Summits (RAS) nonprofit organization. Bradley received the Grant Professional Certified (GPC) designation in 2009. He earned his Bachelor's and Master's degrees in Business Administration and Continuing Education from the University of West Alabama, a Ph.D. in Adult Education from the University of Southern Mississippi (USM), and a Certificate in Distance Education through the Indiana University School of Continuing Studies. Additional graduate coursework in technology was completed through Jones International University (CO) and Athabasca University (Canada). While at USM, Bradley served as a graduate research assistant and training specialist. Bradley was also the primary writer for a Continuum of Care grant that led to a national Best of the Best Practices Award in Fair Housing and Equal Opportunity from HUD. His career has spanned over 17 years of successful experience in grant administration, writing, program development, and educational administration at colleges and universities nationwide. While employed by the Grants Resource Center within a public higher education association in Washington, DC, Bradley provided technical assistance to over 30 universities in the Midwest and interviewed dozens of program officers for the online publication, *GrantWeek*. He also served as a proposal reviewer for nine federal grant programs.

Merideth Dee currently works as an Assistant Director of Academic Support Services in Freshman Academic Advising Services at Florida Atlantic University. Dr. Dee received her Ph.D. in Educational Leadership: Adult and Community Education with an emphasis on workplace learning and technology. For her dissertation, Dr. Dee created a multimedia tutorial which taught incoming freshmen students how to search and register for their classes, and the "Registration Tutorial" is still being used by Freshman Academic Advising Services today. Dr. Dee has submitted papers and virtual presentations to national and international conferences including: the American Association for Adult and Continuing Education (AAACE), the E-Learn World Conference on E-Learning in Corporate, Government, Healthcare, and Higher Education, the Global Conference on Technology, Innovation, Media and Education (Global TIME) hosted by the Association for the Advancement of Computing in Education (AACE), and the International Technology, Education, and Development Conference (INTED). Dr. Dee and co-author Dr. Valerie Bryan were awarded an Outstanding Virtual Presentation Award for their presentation "First Year Undergraduate Students' Perception of the Effectiveness and Transfer of Multimedia Training," at E-Learn 2011. Dr. Dee's academic and research interests include multimedia learning and multimedia technology, ICT literacy and fluency, workplace learning and training, and instructional design.

Lesley Farmer coordinates the Librarianship Program at California State University Long Beach. She earned her M.S.L.S. at the University of North Carolina at Chapel Hill, and her doctorate in Adult Education at Temple University. Dr. Farmer has worked in all types of libraries, and also teaches Adult Education and Educational Technology. She has written thirty professional books and over a hundred articles and book chapters. Besides presenting widely, she serves as incoming chair of Special Libraries Association Education Division and International Association of School Librarianship VP for Association Relations. She is a Fulbright Scholar, and also received the American Library Association Beta Phi Mu Award for her contributions to library education. Her research interests include school librarianship, gender issues in educational technology, digital citizenship, assessment, and information literacy.

Lin Harper, Ph.D., is an Assistant Clinical Professor of Interdisciplinary Studies at The University of Southern Mississippi, where she also serves as Interim Assistant Dean for Research and Instruction in the College of Arts and Letters. Lin has a long history of writing, procuring, and administering grants, including a 5-year Department of Education Title III-A grant to incorporate technology into teaching and learning; she has also served as peer reviewer for federal grants. Her current responsibilities include mentoring and teaching faculty and graduate students within the College of Arts and Letters those skills. Lin has previously served as Director of Distance Learning and held other positions within the university associated with the incorporation of technology into the teaching-learning interaction. She holds a Master's degree in Counseling Psychology and a Ph.D. in Adult Education, both from Southern Miss. She has worked with and served on volunteer boards for a number of nonprofit agencies within the community of Hattiesburg, MS. An area of great interest to Lin currently is the potential use of social media in the teaching-learning transaction and for maintaining contact with graduates after graduation.

Lila Holt has been working with Information Technology (IT) for over 25 years. She has managed IT and consulted with technologies in a variety of industries in both the United States and Mexico. She has served as an examiner for the Tennessee Center of Performance Excellence (A Baldrige Award Program) and also serves as an adjunct Assistant Professor at the University of Tennessee. Her research interests focus on technologies for learning and include self-directed learning, learning in the workplace, and organizational learning.

Ioannis Kazanidis is an Adjoined Assistant Professor at the Kavala Institute of Technology, Greece. He received the MSc degree in Computing from the Coventry University, and his PhD degree in Educational Technology and Adaptive Educational Systems at University of Macedonia. He has an extensive experience in lifelong learning, and helping adult groups. His main research interests lie in the area of adaptive systems, data mining methods and algorithms, virtual words in education and computer-supported collaborative learning. He has published 13 articles in international journals and book chapters, and more than 20 papers in proceedings of conferences.

Debra S. Lee has been teaching professionals for over 17 years as an English for Specific Purposes Specialist. She has conducted teacher-training workshops for the U.S. Department of State Office of English Language Programs around the world. She is co-author of *American Legal English: Using Language in Legal Contexts* (University of Michigan Press, 2nd Ed., 2007). She currently teaches legal English and advanced legal writing in face-to-face and online formats for the Vanderbilt University English Language Institute, Georgetown Law Continuing Legal Education/Lex Mercator, and IUSLaw. She is also a PhD candidate in instructional technology at the University of Tennessee, Knoxville.

Michelle McAnuff-Gumbs is an Assistant Professor at the College of Saint Rose in Albany, NY, where she develops and teaches online as well as face-to-face courses at the graduate level. Prior to working at Saint Rose, she taught at Bethlehem Moravian College in Jamaica, at the University of the West Indies, St. Augustine, Trinidad and Tobago, and through the Open Campus of the University of the West Indies (UWIOC). Her specific areas of research center on online literacy teacher training and the teaching of diverse learners.

Sarah T. Meltzer, Ed.D., is an Assistant Professor in the School of Teaching and Learning at Western Carolina University. She holds Bachelors' degrees in Biology and Elementary Education as well as a Master's degree in Educational Leadership (K-12) and a Doctorate degree in Educational Leadership (Adult Learning). She currently teaches *Computers in Education*, *Secondary Methods*, *Teachers in a Diverse Society*, and works with student teachers interning in public schools. She has taught in elementary, middle, and high school classrooms as well as an instructional support teacher at the district level for Palm Beach County Schools in Florida. Her experience as an educational consultant and project manager with Riverdeep Interactive Learning (now Houghton Mifflin Harcourt) has provided her many opportunities to work with teachers, principals, and superintendants around the country assisting them with improving their technology plans to include effective professional development. She continues to support school reform through developing effective professional development in technology when the opportunity arises.

Pellas Nikolaos is a Ph.D. Candidate at the Department of Product and Systems Design Engineering, University of the Aegean, Greece. He obtained a Master's degree in Education with ICT, in the field of e-learning through virtual worlds in 2010, at the Aristotle University of Thessaloniki. In 2011, he wrote a research book about the pedagogical value of e-learning processes in virtual environments and administration of the organizational complexity of avatars' interactions. Currently, he has begun his dissertation research that applies to the configuration and utilization of virtual worlds in education. Learning applications with the teamwork technique "Jigsaw" and the investigative independence of engagement factors, and the sense of users' presence in communities of inquiry are also in his research field. He has extensive experience in e-Education, especially teaching in adult groups. His research interests include the use of ICT in education, with an emphasis on learning progressions through "open-source" virtual worlds as "Metaverse" skins, according to contemporary instructional methodologies.

Judith Parker is an adjunct Assistant Professor in Organization and Leadership at Teachers College/Columbia University in New York teaching graduate courses on the theory and practice of adult learning that are totally on-line, totally classroom, and blended delivery formats. She has earned a doctorate, Ed.D. degree, and an M.S. degree in Adult Learning and Leadership from Teachers College/Columbia University, an M.S. degree in Physics from Purdue University in Indiana, and a B.S. degree in Physics and Mathematics from Notre Dame College in Ohio. Judith is a co-author of the book *Pedagogical and Andragogical Teaching and Learning with Information Communication Technologies* and is on the editorial review board for the *International Journal of Adult Vocational Education and Technology*. She has authored numerous chapters and articles on cross-cultural workplace training and learning, and the history, philosophy, practice, and theories of adult learning and technology integration for effective education. She has presented numerous papers at conferences globally, most recently at the International Transformative Learning Conference in Athens, Greece, but also at the Academy of Management, American Society of Training and Development, College Industry Education Conference, Quality and Productivity Management Association, Business and Multimedia Conference in Ireland, Lisbon 2000 European Conference on ODL Networking for Quality Learning, and World Open Learning for Business Conferences in the UK. Judith has over 20 years' experience in leadership positions within global business organizations. She has worked extensively with technical managers and technical employees in Asia and Europe in leadership education and training and technical employee skill development by using an action-learning model and integrating distance-learning technologies with classroom sessions. She has been elected a Fellow of the American Association for the Advancement of Science and has received the American Association of Physics Teachers Innovative Teaching Award.

Ana M. Porro, for more than twenty years, has been teaching Mathematics at Palm Beach State College. Having been an international student herself, she is mindful of the struggles that students have when learning English as an adult. Mathematics, being the language of numbers and logic, presents similar difficulties as learning another language. As an educator, she sees students struggling in mathematics every day. As chair of the college's reaffirmation for accreditation process in 2001, she gained insight in the importance of assessment and using the results of these for improvement. In addition to having a family and social responsibilities, she teaches Mathematics full-time. Her personal experience contributes to understanding the role of the adult learner with multiple obligations and potential hurdles/obstacles.

John Rachal, Ed.D., is Professor Emeritus of Adult Education at the University of Southern Mississippi. He was raised in Raleigh, NC, and received his Bachelor's from East Carolina with majors in English and Philosophy, his Master's from NC State in English, and his Doctorate from NC State in Adult and Community College Education. He came to USM in 1980. He has special interests in literacy and especially historical and philosophical aspects of adult education. He has approximately 70 publications and traveled to India on a Fulbright-Hayes grant in 1989. He won the American Association for Adult and Continuing Education's Imogene Okes Award for Outstanding Research in Adult Education in 1999 and again in 2004. The first award was for "'We'll Never Turn Back': Adult Education and the Struggle for Citizenship in Mississippi's Freedom Summer," originally published in *American Educational Research Journal*; and the second was for "A Symposium," a fictional dialogue of historical figures from Heraclitus to Nietzsche discussing the acquisition of knowledge, published in *Adult Education Quarterly*. He finds teaching rewarding, graduating over 60 doctoral students. Rachal fully retired in May 2012, but will continue his work as editorial board member of three journals.

Grace L. Reynolds is Associate Professor of Health Care Administration at the California State University, Long Beach, where she teaches graduate and undergraduate courses in quantitative methods and the health care delivery system in the United States. She received her Doctor of Public Administration degree from the University of Southern California, and she has published extensively on public health issues.

Marianne Russo is a product of the corporate sector, having been an Assistant Vice President and HR Director of a bank early in her career. She then spent 21-years as an educator with field experience at all levels of K-12, including administrative components. She has been adjunct faculty at Florida Atlantic University for approximately 16 years and is now a Visiting Assistant Professor and Associate of the Graduate Faculty who specializes in the teaching of qualitative and quantitative research, inclusive of statistical applications. She holds five college degrees: a BS in Business Management (Florida State University); an MS in English Language Education (Indiana University); an MEd in Elementary Education (Florida Atlantic University); an EdS in Educational Leadership (Florida Atlantic University); and an EdD in Educational Leadership (Florida Atlantic University). She is a member of the following honor societies: Phi Lambda Theta; Phi Kappa Phi; Kappa Delta Pi; and Phi Delta Kappa. She received the Exceptional Faculty Award at Florida Atlantic University for 2011-2012 (Northern Campuses Achievement Award). Her research is based within the framework of higher education, adult education, technology, and social justice.

Francesco Sofo (PhD) is the Director of the Centre for Research in Transnational Education Leadership and Performance in the Faculty of Education, University of Canberra Australia. His career goal is to be the best he can in assisting in the learning and development of individuals, teams, and organisations. He is a Fellow of the Australian Human Resource Institute and past winner of the Best Paper Award at the Australian and New Zealand Academy of Management Conference. His current research is in the area of educational leadership; teaching effectiveness and effectiveness of work teams; transfer of learning, team performance, and emotional intelligence; and the intellectual styles of leaders in China and Australia. He has also published in the fields of thinking styles, virtual teams, critical thinking, corporate psychopathy, and compliance.

Michelle Sofo obtained her PhD from the University of Canberra at the age of 27 after being awarded two Chancellor's Commendations, an Australian Postgraduate Award, and a nomination for the Herbert Burton University Medal. Since 2004, Michelle has been a sessional lecturer of the University of Canberra's Faculty of Education and currently holds the position of Adjunct Professional Associate within the Faculty. In the last five years, Michelle's publication output totals three book chapters, 17 refereed journal articles, and nine refereed conference papers. Michelle continues to be research active, with current interests in white-collar crime, online consumer fraud, law enforcement, critical thinking, cross-cultural comparative studies, and the transfer of learning.

Helen Yeh, over the past 10 years, has taught in secondary schools and various tertiary institutions. Since 1999, she has been providing various kinds of consultancy for language teachers to make use of Information and Communication Technology for language teaching. She has also been doing research on effective language teaching, learning methodology, and computer-mediated communication. She is currently working in the Hong Kong Polytechnic University (HKCC). She has published more than 10 books about English teaching and learning.

Index

A

active network 123
adult education 53-57, 61-65, 72-73, 82, 88, 111, 131, 135, 148, 172-175, 181-182, 189-193, 211, 222
adult learning 20, 51, 53-59, 61-65, 68, 74, 76, 172-173, 175, 177, 179, 192, 197, 211-212, 215, 223
Advanced Situational Awareness System (ASAS) 106
African American Vernacular English (AAVE) 225, 227, 229-232, 234, 236, 239
andragogical principles 54, 192
andragogy 51, 53-54, 58, 66-67, 69, 72-74, 77, 82, 110, 171-180, 182, 189-193, 212, 222
Assessing The Learning Strategies of Adults (ATLAS) 68, 76-77, 80-81
autonomous learning 150, 152-154, 156, 159-160, 163, 167, 169

B

Baldrige Performance Excellence Program 24-27, 31-39
banking product 277, 280, 282, 287
banking sector 275, 291-292
banking transaction 276, 278-279, 284, 286-287, 289-291
blended learning 150-152, 157, 160, 164-166, 209, 216
blog 10, 21, 47, 59, 61, 140, 143, 147, 214, 217, 223, 225, 229, 238-240, 245, 254
bonding social capital 119, 121-122
bridging social capital 119, 121-122, 125

C

classroom instruction 41-44, 46, 48-50
Clinical Laboratory Scientist (CLS) 195
Cognitive Load Theory (CLT) 9, 22-23, 71, 75, 83-84, 224
cognitive mechanism 252-253
cognitivism 73, 78
collaboration technology 28-29, 34
collaborative learning 50, 137-138, 140, 154, 161-162, 167-168, 252-253, 260, 271-272
communication skills 57, 97, 102-103, 107, 144, 157, 162, 203-204, 214
Communities of Practice (CoP) 4
community education 1, 3, 11, 13, 18, 20, 53-54, 62-63, 117, 119, 126-130, 134-135, 137-139, 141-148, 194, 197, 205, 207
community educator 3, 5, 10-11, 14-15, 18, 134, 138, 140, 144, 147
community learner 3, 15, 139
Computer-Assisted Instruction (CAI) 137
computer-assisted training 251
Computer-Mediated Communication (CMC) 151, 160-161, 168
Computer-Supported Collaborative Learning (CSCL) 138, 148, 253
confidentiality 35, 287
continuing education 50, 56-57, 64-65, 82, 148, 175, 188-190, 195-196, 200-201, 207
cooperative learning 100, 153-154, 157, 159-160, 162, 167, 273
critical reflection 26, 45, 53-55, 60-63
critical thinking 9, 55, 59, 61, 76, 87, 98, 118, 123, 141, 213-215, 217-218, 220, 275
cross-cultural issues 85, 87, 96
curriculum 41, 43, 51, 57, 70, 110, 134, 138, 143-144, 147, 155, 164-165, 183, 226-227, 234-235, 237-238, 240, 242, 253
cyber bullying 10-12, 20-21, 117-120, 122, 124-130
cyber-enhanced crime 10-11
cyber stalking 124

D

Decision Support System (DSS) 105, 243
democratization of information 1, 141
demographic profile 280
digital age 42, 51, 139, 210
digital citizenship 85-89, 92-99
digital immigrant 223, 253
digital literacy 85-86, 88, 253
digital media 8, 124
digital native 210-212, 217, 220, 222-223, 253
dissemination technology 28
distance-learning 65-68, 75, 78, 81-83, 137-138, 179, 192-193, 251, 254-255, 258, 260, 263-265, 268-269, 273
diversity 1-2, 18, 53, 58-59, 94, 102-103, 106-108, 111, 113-114, 116, 119, 123, 127, 146, 169, 217, 225-227, 229-230, 233-234, 237-249, 252, 268
double-loop learning 24, 26-30, 33, 37-39

E

educational institution 8-9, 37, 118-119, 194, 205, 213, 217, 220, 253
educational needs 135
educational technology 22, 42, 50-51, 81-84, 100, 138, 148, 207, 220, 222, 224-226, 248, 270, 273
eLearning 21, 29, 34, 67-69, 73, 77, 82-84, 100, 140, 145, 148, 209, 216, 221-222, 250-254, 256, 258-259, 261, 264, 270-273
emergency management 102-109, 112, 114-116
emergency preparedness 103, 105, 109, 114-116, 137
empirical study 171, 173-174, 177, 179-180, 191
engager 68, 76, 81

F

Facebook 4-6, 10, 13-14, 21, 23, 57, 109, 119-121, 131-133, 211, 219, 238, 263
face-to-face learning 214, 216

G

Geographical Information Systems (GIS) 105-106, 115
globalization 8, 58, 85, 87, 89, 97, 99-100, 137, 146, 148, 150, 161
governmental role 89
guided reflection 225, 230

H

health care provider 17, 194, 196-198, 200, 203, 206
higher education 21, 67, 72, 78, 84, 99, 149, 197, 210, 212-213, 215-216, 222, 224, 226, 248, 250-251, 258, 266, 270-271, 273, 279-280

I

ICT proficiency 210
inclusiveness 135
informal learning 76, 91, 117-118, 121, 123, 130, 132, 151, 219, 258
information broker 3
Information Communication Technology (ICT) 78, 84, 87-88, 90-91, 93, 99, 102-114, 120, 139, 142, 145, 150-151, 159, 167, 209-217, 219-220, 223-224, 252-253, 268, 273
information distribution 26-30, 32, 34-35, 37-39
information interpretation 26-27, 30-32, 35, 38
information literacy 87-88, 99-101, 142, 212-213, 221
informatization 85-87, 89, 91-101
informatized society 85-86, 89, 94, 99
inquiry learning 251
instructional design 22-23, 66-67, 69, 74-75, 83, 100, 134, 137-140, 142, 146-147, 222, 226, 254
instrumented learning 68, 81
Integrated Active Transportation System (IATS) 106
integrated delivery of service 135
International Society for Technology in Education (ISTE) 42-44, 49-51, 87
Internet banking 274-293
Internet learning 172, 192
interpersonal tool 77-79
intrinsic motivation 70-72, 83, 152, 159, 162-163

K

knowledge acquisition 26-27, 31-32, 35, 38-39, 59
knowledge field 250-251, 253

L

language learning 81, 100, 150-152, 156-160, 162, 164-169, 247, 273
leadership development 135
learning environment 37, 40, 44-47, 50, 59, 67, 70-71, 73-76, 78, 82-83, 127, 134, 145, 147, 150-152, 157, 164-167, 175, 177, 179-180, 191, 207, 209, 211, 213, 216-219, 224, 226, 234, 240, 251-252, 255, 259, 263, 268, 270-271, 273

Learning Management Systems (LMS) 36, 251
learning mechanism 252
learning process 26, 45, 59, 71, 76-77, 150, 152, 156, 161, 163-164, 216, 251-253, 255, 258, 264-266, 269
learning strategy 66, 68-69, 73-74, 76-78, 80-84, 151-153, 157-158, 160, 163, 165, 168, 266
lifelong learning 17, 64, 76-77, 87-88, 100, 131, 135, 145, 167, 191-192, 197, 205, 215, 217-218, 221, 251
linking social capital 119
localization 135

M

mainstream culture 231
maximum use of resources 135
media literacy 134, 141, 148
medical education 194, 196-198, 201, 203, 206-208
Medical Laboratory Technologist (MLT) 195
microblogging 6
m-learning 209, 216
module group 182-183

N

National Educational Technology Standards (NETS) 42
navigator 68, 76, 81
networked collectivity 253
New Delivery (ND) 226-227, 239-245
non-formal educational programs 171

O

Old Delivery (OD) 226-229, 239-245
Online Community of Practice (OCoP) 4-5
online instructional program 172, 179
online learning 66-74, 77-78, 80-82, 149, 172, 174, 179-187, 190-191, 269-271
organizational learning 24-27, 31-32, 39, 91-92, 100, 132, 224
organizational memory 26-27, 31-32, 35-36, 38-39

P

paradigm shift 1, 164-165
pedagogy 49-50, 82, 167, 172-176, 180, 189, 191-192, 222, 227, 240-241, 247, 271
Performance-Based Assessment of Achievement 175-176
Phlebotomy Technician (PBT) 195
privacy 10-11, 35, 37, 90, 94, 98, 118, 129-130, 132, 287-288
proactive learner 212
problem solver 68, 76, 81, 220
problem solving 23, 54, 57, 79, 87, 93, 212-214, 217, 224-225, 227, 245, 275
professional development 13, 25, 38-54, 93, 102-103, 105, 109, 111, 152, 166, 171-172, 177, 179-181, 189-191, 194, 209-210, 215, 218, 247-248, 258
Professional Learning Community (PLC) 47

R

Reflective Communication Approach (RCA) 151, 156
responsiveness 135

S

Second Language Acquisition 152, 168
Second Life (SL) 203-204, 250, 252-270, 272
self-confidence 125, 152-153, 157, 159-160, 162-163, 165, 169, 180
self-development 135
self-directedness 54, 57-58, 62
self-help 135
self-instruction 153, 160, 167
Sense of Community (SOC) 103, 113-114
single-loop learning 26, 29, 35, 38-39
social capital 17, 21, 117-123, 125-127, 130-131, 133
social cognitive theory 197
Social Communication Skills (SCS) 102-105, 107-114
social group 96, 251, 264, 268
social influence 289, 291, 293
social interaction 78, 86, 91, 103, 114, 118, 152, 159, 209, 211, 215, 219-220, 272
social media 3-5, 8, 11, 14-16, 22, 94-99, 105-106, 109, 115, 123, 134, 136, 138, 140-141, 143, 147, 223, 254, 264
social network 1, 4, 7, 14, 19, 55, 89, 113, 119-120, 122, 124, 131-133, 147, 217, 221, 238, 253
social networking 5-6, 11-12, 91, 117-125, 127, 129-133, 143, 211, 214-215, 217, 219, 253, 263, 273
student achievement 40-44, 47-51, 69, 80, 231, 257
student-centered instruction 172, 181
support group 16, 122
sympathy group 122

T

teacher-centered instruction 172, 181
technological advancement 60, 215, 274-276, 290
technology literacy 87-88, 100, 223
telecommunication 98
telemedicine 197, 206-208
the information age 10, 19, 161, 164
Threat, Vulnerability, Consequences, and Risk Assessment (TVCRA) 104
training materials 29, 146, 194, 201
training technology 29
transformative learning 51, 53-54, 57-58, 61-64, 73-74
Twitter 4-7, 10, 13, 17, 20-23, 106, 109, 238

U

usage trend 284-285
user-friendly 76, 81, 161, 226, 269

V

virtual learning 67, 76, 157, 161, 163-164, 171, 179, 203, 209, 213, 216, 220, 259, 271-273
virtual world 57, 69, 128, 194, 200, 203-206, 217, 250, 252-256, 258-260, 262, 265, 267, 269-273
voluntary participation 175

W

Web 2.0 4, 21, 61, 91-92, 143-144, 147, 269
workforce readiness 209, 211, 213, 222

Y

YouTube 4-8, 14, 20-23, 61, 98, 124, 238

CPSIA information can be obtained at www.ICGtesting.com
Printed in the USA
BVOW052239130113

310335BV00006B/10/P

9 781466 629554